Roots of
American Racism

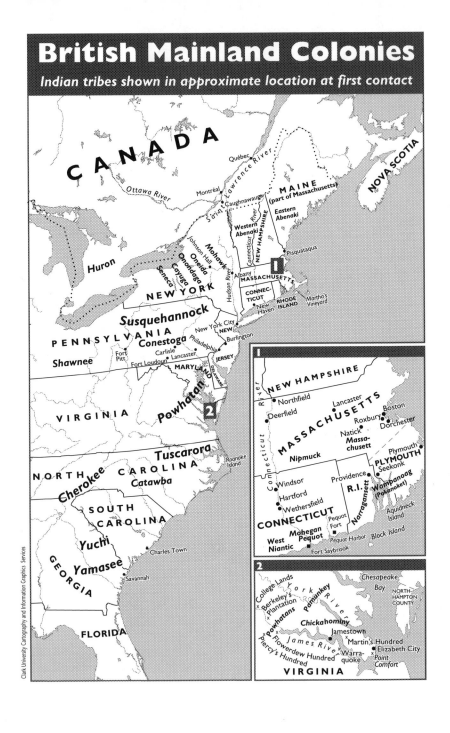

British Mainland Colonies

Indian tribes shown in approximate location at first contact

CANADA

Québec
Ottawa River
Montréal
Saint Lawrence River
NOVA SCOTIA
MAINE
(part of Massachusetts)
Caughnawauga
Eastern Abenaki
Western Abenaki
NEW HAMPSHIRE
Pisquataqua
Huron
Mohawk
Johnson Hall
Oneida
Onondaga
Cayuga
Seneca
Albany
MASSACHUSETTS
NEW YORK
CONNEC-TICUT
RHODE ISLAND
Martha's Vineyard
Susquehannock
Hudson River
New Haven
PENNSYLVANIA
New York City
NEW
Conestoga
Philadelphia
Burlington
Shawnee
Fort Pitt
Carlisle
Fort Loudoun
Lancaster
JERSEY
MARYLAND
DELAWARE
VIRGINIA
Powhatan
Tuscarora
Roanoke Island
NORTH CAROLINA
Cherokee
Catawba
SOUTH CAROLINA
Yuchi
Charles Town
GEORGIA
Yamasee
Savannah
FLORIDA

Inset 1:

NEW HAMPSHIRE
Connecticut River
Northfield
Lancaster
Deerfield
MASSACHUSETTS
Boston
Roxbury
Dorchester
Natick
Massa-chusett
Nipmuck
PLYMOUTH
Plymouth
Seekonk
Windsor
Providence
Wampanoag (Pokanoket)
Hartford
R.I.
Wethersfield
Narragansett
Aquidneck Island
CONNECTICUT
Pequot Fort
West Niantic
Mohegan
Pequot
Pequot Harbor
Block Island
Fort Saybrook

Inset 2:

Chesapeake Bay
NORTH-HAMPTON COUNTY
College Lands
York River
Berkeley's Plantation
Pamunkey River
Powhatans
Chickahominy
Jamestown
James River
Martin's Hundred
Flowerdew Hundred
Warra-quoke
Elizabeth City
Piercy's Hundred
Point Comfort
VIRGINIA

Clark University Cartography and Information Graphics Services

ROOTS
of
AMERICAN RACISM

Essays on the
Colonial Experience

ALDEN T. VAUGHAN

New York   Oxford
OXFORD UNIVERSITY PRESS
1995

Oxford University Press

Oxford   New York
Athens   Auckland   Bangkok   Bombay
Calcutta   Cape Town   Dar es Salaam   Delhi
Florence   Hong Kong   Istanbul   Karachi
Kuala Lumpur   Madras   Madrid   Melbourne
Mexico City   Nairobi   Paris   Singapore
Taipei   Tokyo   Toronto

and associated companies in
Berlin   Ibadan

Published by Oxford University Press, Inc.,
198 Madison Avenue, New York, New York 10016-4314

Oxford is a registered trademark of Oxford University Press

Library of Congress Cataloging-in-Publication Data
Vaughan, Alden T., 1929–
Roots of American racism : essays on the Colonial experience / Alden T. Vaughan.
p. cm.   Includes bibliographical references and index.
ISBN 0-19-508686-4 (c). —ISBN 0-19-508687-2 (p)
1. Racism—United States—History.   2. United States—Race relations.
3. United States—History—Colonial period, ca. 1600–1775.   I. Title.
E184.A1V35 1995
305.8'00973'09032—dc20   94-9766

3 5 7 9 8 6 4 2

Printed in the United States of America
on acid-free paper

For Ginger

Preface

Americans are vitally, if sometimes painfully, aware of our cultural variety. We used to call our polyglot nation a "melting pot"; nowadays we use less assimilationist tropes—"simmering stew" or "tossed salad." But for better or for worse (we haven't agreed on the proper cultural recipe), we are incredibly varied in geographic backgrounds and their related patterns of belief and behavior. It all began, of course, in the colonial era.

In a broader sense, it began much earlier, with the first humans who ventured across the land bridge between northeastern Asia and northwestern America. Human variety accompanied extensive immigration before the final ice age as inevitably as it would several millennia later; by the sixteenth century, when people from the "Old World" first arrived on the eastern seaboard in appreciable numbers, America already boasted a wide range of cultures—those institutions, customs, and beliefs that reflect, and shape, who we are. European immigrants from many nations soon increased and vastly complicated the cultural map, as did the forced migration of Africans with widely varying heritages. American multiculturalism and multiracialism were here to stay. But the great challenge of how to live together peacefully, productively, and equitably proved even more difficult in the colonial period than it does today.

This collection of essays explores some of the major events and issues of interaction between Europeans, Indians, and Africans in English America (and, in the first essay, the early years of the United States) in the sixteenth, seventeenth, and eighteenth centuries. Several of the essays in this collection address aspects of what, by hindsight, we call "race relations." Other essays treat interactions between Europeans and Native Americans that were not initially based on notions of race but rather on deep cultural differences—over religion, government, land, law, education, and war, to name only the most obvious arenas of early contact between peoples from opposite sides of the Atlantic Ocean. Some of those contacts were friendly and mutually beneficial; many were hostile if not lethal. British America witnessed an often bitter contest of cultures as well as an unusually blatant exploitation of "races."

Although biological and social scientists have demonstrated—convincingly, I believe—that "race" is not a valid human category,[1] a belief in race, however misguided and mischievous, often played a decisive role in early America's human interaction. The task of recognizing and assessing the role of "race" is important yet difficult, partly because the sources are less abundant than for later periods and also because certain words did not mean then what they do today. "Race" was itself applied inconsistently to a variety of social collectives that we now label nations or ethnic groups or even species. In 1619, for example, the Virginia legislature rhetorically linked human and canine categories when it prohibited the sale to Indians of any "dog or bitche whatsoever, of the English race."[2] But though the word was often used imprecisely, it sometimes had a modern ring. An early seventeenth-century English traveler to Africa insisted, with his era's typical disparagement, that the people's dark color came from God's curse on Noah's grandson Chus rather than from the climate or soil, "for neither . . . will other Races in that Soyle proove black, nor that Race in other Soyle grow to better complexion."[3] Judging, then, from English and American literary evidence and the colonists' pejorative actions, white Americans generally (and perhaps Native Americans and Afro-Americans too; much less is recorded about their perceptions of "others") sorted the Western Hemisphere's population into two, later three, broad "racial" categories.

In an earlier era, before Europe's dramatic explorations of the fifteenth and sixteenth centuries, the idea of human races—huge biologically distinct subdivisions of humankind that coincided roughly with the earth's major geographic divisions—was known but rarely affected human interaction.[4] In Europe, some theologians and laymen pondered the possible differences between the descendants of Noah's three sons, but their musings had little practical application. When contact between the world's peoples rapidly expanded in the age of reconnaissance and revealed, to many European eyes at least, striking differences in appearance, customs, and beliefs, some observers insisted that God (or nature, or circumstances) had organized humans into a few immutable categories, sometimes called "races" but often given other labels. Belief in such groupings became more widespread and more invidious as time passed, for accompanying a belief in the existence of races was usually a conviction that the differences were qualitative—that one's own branch of the human tree was innately superior in physical, mental, and moral attributes. Although "race" is now widely discredited in scientific literature as intellectually unsound and socially pernicious, the misconception profoundly shaped early Euro-American relations with Africans (from the outset) and Native Americans (from the late seventeenth century onward). In sum, race is a historical reality, though not a scientific fact, which has influenced American history from the beginnings to the present.

Along with the concept has come a substantial vocabulary of terms that both help and hinder our understanding of the social dynamics of "race relations." They help by creating some useful distinctions among various types of belief and behavior; they hinder by generating misunderstandings and inviting disputes over definitions. Some of the essays in this collection address the confusing terminology of "race," but the following brief definitions of some of the critical concepts should clarify at the outset my own preferences.

Racism: A belief that races exist and that members of one or more races are innately inferior in certain characteristics, usually in intelligence. For a classic expression of racist thought in the early twentieth century, see the entire entry for "Negro" in the magesterial eleventh edition of the *Encyclopaedia Britannica* (1911). In the sixteenth through eighteenth centuries, "racism" was less frequently articulated and less reliant than it would later become on "scientific" evidence, but, as I argue at various points in this book, its ugly head had already reared.

Racialism: Dictionaries and general usage, especially in Britain, where (unlike the United States) the term is common, use it as a synonym for racism.

Race prejudice: Prejudging a person or situation on the basis of presumed racial characteristics. "Race prejudice" has usually been interchangeable with "racism" or "racialism," but some writers draw a distinction. "Racism is to race prejudice," an English scholar proposes, "as dogma is to superstition. Race prejudice is relatively scrappy and self-contradictory. It is transmitted largely by word of mouth. Racism is relatively systematic and internally consistent. In time it acquires a pseudo-scientific veneer that glosses over its irrationalities and enables it to claim intellectual respectability. And it is transmitted largely through the printed word."[5] Although I find some merit in this distinction between ostensibly identical terms, it has not been widely adopted and is not used in this book.[6]

Race (or racial) discrimination: Unequal treatment of someone on the basis of his or her presumed racial affiliation.

Ethnocentrism: A preference for one's own ethnic or national group, sometimes to the point of hostility toward other ethnic ways and beliefs. Ethnocentrism's basis is cultural, not racial; one presumes his or her own language, literature, religion, and customs to be superior to other people's. In its mildest form ethnocentrism is almost inevitable and relatively benign, holding merely that among many admirable cultures, we have chosen—perhaps because we were born into it—a particular pattern of customs and beliefs. Early America usually witnessed the more blatant, aggressive variety.

Roots of American Racism addresses issues in Indian-white and black-white relations that seemed important and interesting to me at various times

in the three decades between the earliest essay's publication and now. I
approach some of those issues through analytic narratives that examine
how and *why* certain events occurred or ideas evolved. Other essays are
essentially historiographical, explaining *who* wrote *what* (and sometimes
why) about a controversial episode in early American cultural or racial
contact. The temporal scope of the essays varies widely too: one is confined to a single year (but with implications far beyond it); another's
span is more than three centuries; most treat a few crucial years or
decades. All of the essays focus primarily on the parts of British America that became the United States, although one chapter gives considerable attention to Barbados and another is partly about Canada. In
each case my principal concern has been to examine how the people
with the greater military and political power (almost invariably the English colonists) constructed their attitudes and shaped their actions toward the Indians and Africans in the areas of Anglo-American control.
These are not, therefore, happy stories, but they are, I submit, stories
about historical ideas and events that were important in their own time
and had formative influence on subsequent American history.

While the general concern of this book is interaction between diverse
cultures or perceived races, its more specific focus is on perceptions and
policies—that is, on the mental images that Euro-Americans fashioned
to help understand Native Americans and African Americans and the
colonial policies that evolved from those perceptions. That the perceptions sometimes rested on egregiously incorrect readings of reality is
lamentable, but the course of human history is littered with misreadings
and misperceptions, especially when the viewers have incomplete information and form their opinions against a background of false assumptions and self-serving expectations. Yet the purpose of these essays
is not to excoriate or exculpate the participants on any side of the mul-
ticultural and multiracial frontiers but rather to illuminate what the historical actors thought they saw and how and why they acted and reacted
as they did.

The three major parts of the book are organized around broad central themes or geopolitical regions. Part I looks at fundamental Anglo-
American perceptions of Native Americans and Africans and how those
perceptions evolved in significantly different patterns toward the two
non-European peoples. Chapter 1 examines three centuries of Anglo-
American perceptions of Native Americans, which evolved gradually
from assumptions of profound cultural difference to a belief in innate
racial inferiority. Because those Anglo-American perceptions and con-
sequent policies owed much to European (especially English) views of
the Indians prior to the full tide of American colonization, chapter 2
reconstructs several English paradigms that emerged before 1607 or in
the decades soon after. (Precolonization English views of Africans are
addressed, less extensively, at various points in chapter 7.) Chapter 3 examines the early articulation of a racist ideology in the British empire

as witnessed, and rebutted, by an Anglican minister in Virginia and Barbados. The final essay the first part (chapter 4) documents how perceptions and treatment of Indians in Pennsylvania had deteriorated from cultural prejudice in the seventeenth century to a lethal racial bias in the third quarter of the eighteenth century.

Part II explores cultural and racial interactions in early Virginia. Chapter 5 assesses patterns of colonial aggression and Indian resistance that culminated in bitter warfare from 1622 to 1632 and how that conflict reflected depths of hostility that had been building since 1607, despite superficial countertrends. By contrast, Virginians usually made lifelong slaves of Africans and their progeny, beginning in 1619 (a persistent modern argument for a later date notwithstanding) in accordance with a rapidly emerging racist ideology that in incipient form had come from England in the colonists' psychological baggage. Chapter 6, on Virginia's early black-white relations, examines the evidence of attitudes toward Africans in the 1620s; chapter 7 traces the long and lively scholarly debate over the origins of American slavery and American racism. A postscript to the latter essay recounts, and responds to, a recent contribution to the ongoing "origins" controversy.

Part III focuses on New England. As in part II, there is an essay (chapter 8) on the liveliest historiographical topic of the early years—in this case, the causes of the Pequot War of 1636–37. An assessment of that hardy perennial is followed in chapter 9 by a close examination of two episodes in 1638 that raised perplexing legal issues and simultaneously revealed deep fissures in colonial attitudes toward Native Americans. Chapter 10 is a wide-ranging assessment, both qualitative and quantitative, of efforts by New England colonists and Native Americans between 1620 and 1763 to win cultural converts from each other.

The goal of these exercises in historical investigation is partly to inform but also to stimulate new research and fresh interpretations. Because the essays are one historian's (in the final essay, two historians') version of the past, they are subject, as is all scholarship, to challenges from those who favor other readings of the evidence. I can only hope that I have been generally persuasive and that where readers do not accept my analyses of the historical record, they will dig as deeply in the sources to find other explanations.

On the assumption that today's readers are more interested in what an author thinks now than what he or she thought a few years or decades ago, I have revised the articles as thoroughly as each case warranted. Because a few of the older essays begged for drastic revision, I have substantially rewritten them to reflect new evidence, recent critical scholarship, and my own changing assessment of the sources. In other cases, especially recently published articles, revisions are confined to some improvements in style, correction of imprecise statements, and citation of pertinent new publications.

I have arranged these diverse essays into a quasi-sequential, though necessarily selective, exegesis of early American race relations. The blend of chronology and topicality promotes (I hope) a sense of early America's unfolding intercultural and interracial dynamics. Yet because each chapter is in fact a separate essay, telling a complete story by itself, I have retained certain contextual material, even if it paraphrases a small portion of another essay, to allow the chapters to be read in any order. On the other hand, to minimize the repetition of facts and quotations that often mar a collection of (mainly) previously published articles, I have deleted most verbatim overlaps; where a few remain, they seemed to me essential to each essay's argument. I have also adjusted quotations in some of the older essays to conform to the most recent scholarly editions of primary documents, thus imposing a consistency of citation as well as adherence to the most reliable version of each primary source. And all essays now observe a single editorial format in the texts and notes (that of the *Chicago Manual,* with some minor modifications), thereby avoiding the confusion that the diverse original formats might have encouraged. Notes to the essays, originally at the bottoms of pages in most of the published articles, are now clustered at the back of this book. Specialists in early American history or race relations will probably regret that location (as I do in many respects), but other readers will perhaps be relieved to find the text unburdened by extensive annotation.

Native American personal and place-names follow the preferred spellings in William C. Sturtevant, ed., *Handbook of North American Indians,* vol. 15, *Northeast,* ed. Bruce G. Trigger, and vol. 4, *History of Indian-White Relations,* ed. Wilcomb E. Washburn (Washington, D.C., 1978, 1988). Old Style dates (used generally in British America until 1752) are retained as they appeared in the original sources except that the new year has been adjusted to begin on January 1 instead of March 25. In quotations from early books and manuscripts, I have modernized the orthography of the original only in the case of "u" and "v" and "i" and "j," superscripts have been lowered to the line, and unfamiliar abbreviations have been expanded.

During three decades of research and writing, I have benefited immensely from wise counsel and generous institutional support. Each essay has had special intellectual and (in some cases) financial benefactors, whose names I gratefully list in the following paragraphs. But first I must acknowledge several long-term obligations, especially to three institutions that played important roles in many of these essays: Columbia University, the Folger Shakespeare Library, and the American Antiquarian Society.

At Columbia I had the good fortune to study history under the benign guidance of Richard B. Morris and then to be his colleague for many years. Dick's enthusiasm for early American history and his insistence on rigorous documentary research were infectious; he had a direct hand in none of these essays but an indirect influence on all of them. I am also grateful to Columbia for its fine library and skillful librarians; for its generous support of faculty scholarship through sabbatical leaves, research assistants, and research funds; and especially for its talented, enthusiastic faculty and students, several of whom are thanked elsewhere in this preface. All of the essays were written during my long affiliation with Columbia University's history department.

I discovered the Folger Shakespeare Library (in the sixteenth-century sense of "discover") in 1970 and ever since have been an eager, if intermittent, consumer of its incomparable collection. That collection, thanks to former director Louis B. Wright and his successors, includes rich resources in Tudor-Stuart America—part of Shakespeare's broader world. And because most of what we loosely label "early American sources" were, of course, published in England or elsewhere in Europe and are therefore firmly within the Folger's acquisitions agenda, a library dedicated principally to Shakespeareana is one of the great (and often overlooked) research libraries for early Americanists. Making the Folger even more enticing to itinerant scholars are its resplendent architecture and expert, congenial staff. During two terms of Folger fellowships and numerous other trips to Washington, I did much of the research and part of the writing on many essays in this book, especially chapters 1–3, 5, and 7.

I am comparably indebted to the American Antiquarian Society, that curiously named but incredibly important repository of early American imprints—books, newspapers, broadsides, and virtually everything else. I have been a "regular" at the AAS since 1978, sometimes for many months at a stretch (thanks to generous assistance from the society and the National Endowment for the Humanities), sometimes for only an hour or two. Cumulatively I have spent a hefty and happy portion of my professional life in Antiquarian Hall. Its staff, like the Folger's, has been superbly helpful and gracious. Chapters 1–4, 7, and 10 were written partly or wholly at the AAS. Chapters 2 and 10 were initially presented orally to annual meetings of the society and subsequently published in its *Proceedings;* both were carefully guided to press by John B. Hench, the editor of AAS publications.

Only one individual deserves to be ranked with these great institutions by dint of long-term support and intellectual stimulation. Virginia Mason Vaughan is a Shakespeare specialist rather than an early Americanist, but her commitment to scholarship, her addiction to research libraries (especially the Folger), and her sensitivity to my intellectual (and other) needs has long made her a vital part of my scholarly efforts. She is, moreover, the only person who closely critiqued the earliest incarnations of several essays and then cast a discerning eye on the entire body of this book. Her help is irreplaceable, her encouragement irrepressible.

For important help on individual essays, my debts are varied and abundant. "From White Man to Redskin" profited from prepublication readings by James Axtell, Francis Bremer, Daniel Richter, Bernard Sheehan, and members of an American history seminar at the University of Maryland, where I aired an early version. "Early English Paradigms": profited from the resources of the John Carter Brown library of Brown University as well as those of the American Antiquarian Society and the Folger Library. Since its initial publication, it has benefited from J. H. Elliott's perceptive comments. "Slaveholders' 'Hellish Principles'" has not previously been published, but preliminary drafts received helpful comments from a host of students, colleagues, and friends, especially Elaine Breslaw, Rock Brynner, Joseph Illick, Winthrop Jordan, Robert McColley, and John Recchiuti. It had essential help, too, from the libraries that hold the rare books on which the essay is based: Columbia University's Rare Book Room, the American Antiquarian Society, and, especially, the Huntington Library and the British Library. "Frontier Banditti" was improved by the late Donald Kent's comments and by Robert Grumet's bibliographic suggestions. "'Expulsion of the Salvages'" had its trial run at a Chesapeake Studies conference at the University of Maryland, where several participants made helpful suggestions, especially the late Frank Craven; much of the research and writing was done at Harvard University during a fellowship at the Charles Warren Center for Studies in American History. "Blacks in Virginia" is based on materials at the Virginia State Library, the Virginia Historical Society, and the Public Record Office, London. It was mostly written at the Huntington Library during a summer research grant. "The Origins Debate" was improved by commentaries from Carl Degler, Robert Dykstra, John Recchiuti, Michael West, and an anonymous reader for the *Virginia Magazine of History and Biography*. Marjorie Ropp gave essential computer help. "Pequots and Puritans" was written so long ago that I scarcely remember who lent helping hands, though I'm sure many did, including, most likely, David Burner and Thomas R. West. They may also have helped with "Tests of Puritan Justice," the first half of which was written at about the same time (the second half is new). "Crossing the Cultural Divide," coauthored with Daniel Richter (a graduate student then, now a distinguished ethnohistorian), had generous critiques from James Axtell, Glenn LaFantasie, and William Simmons. Ian Steele kindly suggested minor revisions to the published version.

For help in assembling illustrations for this volume, I am indebted to Georgia Barnhill and Jennifer Code of the American Antiquarian Society. The frontispiece map was prepared by the Clark University Cartographic Services.

Thanks are also long overdue to the unsung heroes of scholarly publishing—the editors and assistant editors who sharpen arguments and polish prose. Some of the editors who published my work were kind enough to leave it virtually untouched; others were equally kind to suggest improvements. At the risk of omitting some who deserve to be mentioned here (the author does not always know who wielded the blue pencil), I gratefully acknowledge the editorial skills of William Abbot, Thad Tate, and Michael McGiffert of the *William and Mary Quarterly;* Sarah Bearss of the *Virginia Magazine;* and Anne Lee Bain of the *American Historical Review.*

I'm grateful, too, for the careful attention that some of my essays received from student assistants who prevented minor errors from reaching print, especially Jacquelyn Bessell for checking "Early English Paradigms," Carlos Medina for "Slaveholders' 'Hellish Principles,'" and Mary Curtin for "Frontier Banditti." My apologies to anyone I have neglected to mention.

Worcester, Mass.   A.T.V.
July 1994

Contents

PART ONE

Changing Perceptions

From White Man to Redskin: Changing Anglo-American Perceptions of the American Indian

The use of color terminology for major social groups, especially "whites" and "blacks," is nowadays virtually universal, even though those labels are chromatically inaccurate and encourage a dangerous homogenization of human categories. Yet as shorthand labels for what most people probably perceive as significant divisions of the human species, chromatic labeling seems as deeply entrenched as is the concept of "race" on which it rests. It has not always been so: "black" and "white" were rarely applied to humans (in print, at least) until the sixteenth century; "red" and "yellow" came into frequent use two centuries later. In colonial British America and subsequently in the United States, the late emergence of "red" as a descriptive term for Native Americans is fraught with significance because, in conjunction with other trends in Indian-white relations, it tells much about changing ethnic/racial perceptions.

This essay's roots are in my immersion over the years in the documentary evidence of sixteenth- and seventeenth-century European contact with American natives. Time and again I was struck by the contrast between the virulence of the Europeans' cultural animosity toward Indians and their overwhelmingly favorable assessments of the Indians' physical characteristics. With few exceptions, the documents suggested a widely shared British and Continental perception of American natives as biologically admirable but socially abhorrent; nature had blessed them, nurture had cursed them. To ethnocentric Westerners, the obvious solution was to save the Indians from themselves by converting them to European notions—Spanish, French, English, or other, depending on the observers' own affiliation—of how to behave, to dress, to worship, to think. As the following pages relate, British Americans' perceptions and the resulting policies changed slowly but profoundly between the mid-sixteenth century and the mid-nineteenth.

The ideas presented in this essay were first aired in 1978 at a Washington, D.C., area seminar, held on the University of Maryland campus, and later, in truncated form, at other scholarly gatherings. It was published in the American His-

torical Review 86 (1982): 917–53. I have deleted a few illustrations and made mostly minor changes to the text and notes, although in the dozen years since this essay first appeared I have accumulated extensive corroborating evidence of its principal arguments.

W HEN THOMAS JEFFERSON WROTE his *Notes on the State of Virginia* (1784), he professed to draw heavily "on what I have seen of man, white, red, and black." Here, as elsewhere, Jefferson demonstrated a knack for phraseology: he was probably the first public spokesman to use the tri-color metaphor that has flourished, with minor rearrangement, ever since.[1] And now, with the historical profession's increasing attention to race and ethnicity, "red, white, and black" is enjoying a rhetorical boom. Attracted by the color trilogy's symmetry and symbolism, scholars have recently employed it in numerous book and article titles. Color terminology is as firmly fixed in writings on early America as it is in conversations about modern race relations.[2]

The tacit justification for using the chromatic metaphor in colonial and early national studies—apart from its ironic parody of "red, white, and blue"—is basically sound: Indians, Europeans, and Africans played central roles in early America, and the commonly accepted color labels are convenient and unambiguous, even though they exaggerate human complexions. Implicitly, if not explicitly, such usage further suggests that a tripartite racial division, based to an appreciable extent on perceived differences in pigmentation, underlay colonial America's social and political policies. But such an interpretation and the assumptions on which it rests are misleading: not until the middle of the eighteenth century did most Anglo-Americans view Indians as significantly different in color from themselves, and not until the nineteenth century did red become the universally accepted color label for American Indians.[3] To read later perceptions of Indian pigmentation into the first centuries of racial contact is fallacious, because, in general, it distorts the nature of early ethnic relations and, in particular, it obscures the evolution of Anglo-American attitudes toward the Indians.[4]

Color, of course, was not the only characteristic to shape British-American perceptions of non-Europeans. Also important in the formulation of attitudes toward the natives of Africa and America were cultural traits: religion, government, economy, language, technology, and social mores. Important too were physical traits other than skin color: stature, proportions, facial features, and hair texture. But from the dawn of England's intellectual awakening to the African and American continents in the mid-sixteenth century, color perceptions were fundamental to Anglo-American assessments of peoples strikingly different from themselves, because color was more than a matter of aesthetic preference. Pigmentation also symbolized a cluster of behavioral and biological characteristics. In the case of Africans—but not Indians—color prejudice combined with cultural and religious prejudice to place blacks in a tragically inferior status.[5] That eventually happened to Indians, too, though not quite to the same extent and not until two centuries of culture contact had altered Anglo-American perceptions.

To generalize baldly what this essay elaborates: English and American writers, and most likely the mass of their countrymen, believed at the outset of England's age of expansion that Africans were inherently and immutably black—a color fraught with pejorative implications—and that therefore Africans were fundamentally unassimilable even if they adopted English ways and beliefs. They were, as their color proclaimed, a separate branch of humankind. By contrast, Anglo-Americans believed that American Indians were inherently like themselves and that they were approximately as light-skinned as Europeans; they could—indeed *would*—be assimilated into colonial society as soon as they succumbed to English social norms and Christian theology. The basic beliefs about Africans held fast throughout the colonial period and beyond. The assumptions about Native Americans underwent a slow but drastic change in the late seventeenth century and throughout the eighteenth as Anglo-Americans shifted their perception of Indian character and, concomitantly, of Indian color from innately white to innately dark and eventually to red. That transformation, reflecting a confluence of European and American ideas and events, signaled important changes in white America's fundamental perception of the native population. The new perception, in turn, helped assure the Indians' continued segregation and heighten their exploitation in the nineteenth and twentieth centuries. Although the Indians' position in British America was always precarious, not until they were thought of as inherently inferior "redmen" rather than unenlightened "whites" did their separate and unequal status become firmly fixed in the American mind. Only then could the bulk of American writers hold that Indians were prevented by *nature*—rather than by education or environment—from full participation in America's democracy and prosperity.

I

Early English contact with Africa spawned a vast range of literature— plays, poems, sermons, and secular tracts, as well as accounts of travel and exploration—that reveals a profound antipathy toward African appearance and culture. As Winthrop D. Jordan's *White over Black* (1968) convincingly demonstrates, virtually all descriptions of the "dark continent" portray its inhabitants as unattractive, unChristian, and grossly uncivil. In theory at least, the Africans' cultural shortcomings, as perceived by ethnocentric Englishmen and their continental counterparts, could be ameliorated; their physical characteristics could not. And among the several aspects of African appearance—stature, facial features, and hair texture, for example—that displeased the English eye, most striking and disturbing was the darkness of African skin. Descriptions of African people invariably stressed their blackness, always disapprovingly.[6]

Europeans accepted with little debate the prevalence and permanence of the African's dark complexion. Doubts focused instead on its cause— whether from tropical heat, disease, or divine judgment—and on the reasons for the different degrees of blackness within the continent. An early example of an argument for environmental causation and its implications was André Thevet's *New Founde Worlde*, translated into English in 1568 and widely read in Britain. Extreme solar temperature, Thevet argued, drew heat from the heart and other interior parts, leaving Africans cold on the inside, scorched on the surface. Differences in prolonged exposure to the sun produced chromatic variety: "Those of *Arabia* and of *Egypt* are betweene black and white, others browne coloured whom we call white Moores, others are cleane black." Three decades later, George Abbot, master of University College, Oxford, and the future archbishop of Canterbury, summarized the prevailing English view of African color. By then, the causal explanation had largely shifted from geographical to theological, but the original color perception remained the same: "all the people in generall to the South, lying within the *Zona torrida*, are not only blackish like the Moores: but are exceedingly black . . . so at this day, they are named Negroes, as them, whome no men are blacker."[7]

As Abbot suggested, the English name for central and southern Africans came from their skin color. Throughout Europe, in fact, Africans were almost invariably labeled by color. To the English, they were "blacks," "blackamores," or "Negroes"; to the Spanish, Portuguese, and Italians, they were "negros" and "negras"; to the Dutch, they were "negers." And in each language the word for "black" carried a host of disparaging connotations. In Spanish, for example, *negro* also meant gloomy, dismal, unfit, and wretched; in French, *noir* also connoted foul, dirty, base, and wicked; in Dutch, certain compounds of *zwart* conveyed notions of anger, irascibility, and necromancy; and "black" had comparable pejorative implications in Elizabethan and Stuart England.[8] An early seventeenth-century cleric neatly tied the contempt for blackness to the standard theological explanation of African complexion, which asserted that Africans were descended from Noah's disobedient son: "the accursed seed of *Cham* . . . had for a stamp [of] their fathers sinne, the colour of hell set upon their faces."[9] Predictably, to the English eye, the lighter the skin, the less hellish its connotations. Poet Thomas Peyton incorporated the prevailing chromatic hierarchy into a verse description of Africa:

> The Libian dusky in his parched skin,
> The Moor all tawny both without and in,
> The Southern man, a black deformed Elfe,
> The Northern white like unto God himselfe.[10]

Thus, whether using an English word or borrowing an equivalent term from a Continental language, Englishmen in the sixteenth and seventeenth centuries subtly and succinctly reflected their contemptuous view of the African. Captain John Smith, who had seen far more varieties of humankind than had most of his contemporaries, articulated the assumed connection between color and character when he described Africa as "those fryed Regions of blacke brutish Negers."[11]

Not until the eighteenth century did Englishmen, either at home or in America, develop a somewhat comparable perception of Indians. Rather, Englishmen and Continental Europeans initially labeled the natives on the basis of culture, not color, and whatever pejorative connotations such terms carried were social rather than biological. No single label predominated, although since Columbian times "Indian," occasionally modified by "West" if the context did not distinguish American from Asian Indians, was the overwhelming favorite. "Natives" probably ranked second in frequency to "Indians." "Savages" (often spelled "salvages"), "barbarians," and "heathens" were also commonly used by Europeans, especially in the sixteenth century, as were, less frequently, "wild people" or "brutish people" and such neutral terms as "country people," "naturals," "inhabitants," "old inhabitants," or "old people."[12] "Americans" and "Virginians" denoted Indians until the swelling colonial population made such words ambiguous; henceforth, "Americans" usually meant European immigrants and their descendants, while the definition of "Virginians" shifted from the natives to the English settlers of the first permanent British colony. Similarly ambiguous, "natives" began as a term for Indians but was soon (though inconsistently) applied to the colonists.[13]

English and Continental writers rarely applied color terms to the original American inhabitants. Not that Europeans were unconcerned with the Indians' color. They were intrigued by it; for two centuries after 1492, most published accounts of America gave at least some attention to Indian complexion, and many examined it meticulously. During the first decades after 1492, writers took pains to deny that the Indians were black, to counteract the prevailing supposition that all people in torrid latitudes ought to be as dark as Africans. (The discovery that the Indians were not black dealt a crippling blow to the geographic explanation of human color, although that argument in modified form lingered into the nineteenth century.) Columbus, for example, reported that the natives in the Caribbean Islands were "not at all black, but the colour of the Canarians, and nothing else could be expected, since this is in one line from . . . the Canaries."[14] Voyagers to more southerly latitudes found that the inhabitants of the equatorial zone were not appreciably darker, which gave rise to more expansive descriptions of their color and to various causal explanations, especially after Europe realized that America was a separate land mass and its inhabitants were perhaps a distinct branch of humankind.

Most early chroniclers of America's natives called them olive, tawny, or brown, occasionally russet or yellow, and sometimes a combination of such colors. Sir Walter Ralegh, for example, joined two of the standard hues when he described the women of Guiana as "brown and tawnie."[15] English plays and poems of the era often resorted to more imaginative descriptions, reflecting both the variety of New World reports and the confusion they produced in the European mind. A masque of 1603 specified that *America* be represented by a woman in "a skin coate the colour of the juyce of Mulberries," and Thomas Peyton's *The Glasse of Time* (1620) described "the American" as "Olive coloured of a sad French green."[16] Presumably, Peyton's readers knew what he meant.

Surprisingly, in light of today's wide acceptance of red as the American Indians' color label, Europeans rarely associated that color with the Indians before the late eighteenth century, and the few such references are to red stains. Walter Bigges, who accompanied Sir Francis Drake to the West Indies in 1585–86, observed that the natives of Dominica had "their skin coloured with some painting of a reddish tawney." George Percy corroborated Bigges's judgment when the Virginia expedition of 1607 stopped at the island en route to the mainland: "their bodies are all painted red to keepe away the bitings of Muscetos."[17] A few years later, William Strachey described the coloring of Virginia's Indians. "Their heades and shoulders they paynt oftenest," he reported, "and those with red, with the roote of Pochone [pokeberry], brayed to poulder mixed with oyle of the walnut, or Beares grease." In the mid-1630s Father Andrew White related that the Maryland Indians painted themselves "a darke read, especially about the head."[18] But neither "redskins" nor "reds" appears in the early literature, and the few references to "red Indians" denoted East Indians. "This World's Sunne," asserted John Davies in 1599, still clinging to the climatological explanation,

> Makes the *More* black, & th' European white,
> Th' *American* tawny, and th' *East-Indian* red.[19]

Part of the confusion over the Indian's color stemmed from the differences in complexion from region to region, from tribe to tribe, and even within tribes. David Ingram, a sailor on Sir Humphrey Gilbert's expedition to North America in 1568, reported that the Indians in the southern part were olive, those in the north tawny. In 1583 Antonio de Espejo observed that in the area that later became New Mexico "the women are whiter skinned than the Mexican women." A decade later, Thomas Blundeville insisted that Indians in hot zones are "browne bay like a Chestnut, and the higher they dwell to either of the Poles Arctique or Antarctique, the whiter most commonly they be."[20] And readers of Richard Hakluyt's *Divers Voyages Touching the Discoverie of America* (1582) could find in the accounts of coastal North America a considerable chromatic range. In Florida the Indians were "of tauny colour" and in future South Carolina they were "of colour russet, . . . not much unlike the Saracens"; Virginia's Indians were "more white than those that we founde before," while the Narragansetts of southern New England had "the colour of brasse, some of them encline more to whitnes: others are of yellowe colour."[21]

Clearly the Indians were not all of the same hue. Clearly too they were—on the surface at least—appreciably darker than Englishmen and other Europeans. But the reason for the Indians' color was debatable. In the sixteenth century, both heredity and environment had their champions; by the early seventeenth century, a consensus endorsed environment. Most chroniclers who knew the Indians well insisted that they were naturally white-skinned. That judgment had to overcome an earlier contention, which circulated widely in England, that Indians were dark-skinned: Richard Eden's *Decades of the New World* (1555), a compilation of travel narratives that extensively describes America's inhabitants, includes an account "Of the Colour of the Indians" by Francisco López de Gómara, a participant in the early Spanish conquest. He argued that West Indians were "in general eyther purple, or tawny lyke unto sodde quynses, or of the colour of chestnuttes or olyves: which colour is to them natural and not by theyr goynge naked as many have thought." Gómara qualified his emphasis on heredity, however, by adding that "theyr nakednesse have sumwhat helped therunto" and by acknowledging wide variation within the Indies, "with suche diversitie as men are commonly whyte in Europe and blacke in Affricke, even with lyke variety are they tawny in these Indies, with divers degrees diversly inclynynge more or lesse to blacke or whyte." And a few pages later Gómara quoted, without comment, Jacobus Gastaldus's description of Newfoundland's inhabitants as "whyte people."[22]

Perhaps in reaction to Gómara's insistence that some West Indians were naturally dark, and to other observers' failure to account for the Indians' outward appearance, many subsequent authors stressed the innate whiteness of North American Indians. In 1578 George Best argued against climate as the cause of human complexion, partly because "under the Equinoctiall in *America* the people are not blacke, but white."[23] In 1587 René de Laudonnière, commander of an ill-fated Huguenot outpost in Florida, depicted the Indians there as olive. He added, however, that "when they are borne they be not so much of an olive colour and are far whiter. For the chief cause that maketh them to be this colour, proceedes of annointings of oyle . . . and because of the sun which shineth hotte upon their bodies." A Dutch scholar, Jan Huygen van Linschoten, echoed Laudonnière. "When they come first into the world," he wrote in 1598, they "are not so blacke but very white: the blacke yellowish colour is made upon them by a certaine oyntment. . . . Their colour likewise changeth because they goe naked, and with the burning heate of the sunne."[24] Shortly after the turn of the century, Martin Pring explained that the Indians he had seen along the northeast coast were "a swart, tawnie, or Chestnut colour, not by nature

but accidentally." William Strachey, writing of the Indians around the
Chesapeake Bay, insisted in "A True Description of . . . Their Collour"
that their tawny skin came partly from the sun and partly from a combination of "arsenickstone," ointments, and juices applied "so sone as
they ar borne" and reinforced with daily painting. That Strachey may in
some measure have been attempting to refute Gómara is suggested by
the analogy both used to describe the resulting complexion. The Indians dye themselves, Strachey noted, because they consider it "the best
beauty, to be neerest a kynd of Murrey, as a sodden Quince is."[25] Both
"murrey" (reddish blue) and "quince" (dull yellow) appeared frequently
in European descriptions of the Indians.

For English readers, the most convincing evidence of the Indians'
whiteness undoubtedly came from their compatriots, such as Strachey,
who settled temporarily or permanently in America. From Virginia, Captain John Smith described the Indians near Jamestown as "a colour
browne when they are of any age, but they are borne white." Another
participant in the Jamestown venture thought the Indians' skin to be
tawny, "not so borne but with dying and paynting them selves, in which
they delight greatly." And John Rolfe, whose marriage to Pocahontas
made him an unimpeachable authority on the natural hue of at least
one Virginia Indian, attributed "their blackness" to ointments and smoky
houses, which, he contended, had the same effect on Indian hides that
smokehouses had on English bacon.[26]

Virginia's Indians differed in customs and language from those in
many parts of British America, but not, apparently, in their innate color.
In 1666 George Alsop described the Susquehannocks of Maryland and
eastern Pennsylvania: "Their skins are naturally white, but altered from
their originals by the several dyings of Roots and Barks, that . . . meta-
morphize their hydes into a dark Cinamon brown." William Penn reported similarly on the natives of his colony. They are "of Complexion,
Black," he observed in 1683, "but by design, as the Gypsies in England."[27] And several New England writers, whose familiarity with Indians could scarcely be doubted, reached the same conclusion. William
Wood (1634), Thomas Morton (1637), and Roger Williams (1643),
among others, testified that the Indians in their vicinity were naturally
white.[28] Many of these early English colonists, including Penn, Williams,
and missionary John Eliot, believed that Indians were probably descended from the lost tribes of Israel and that Indians therefore possessed essentially the same pigmentation as Europeans.[29]

There were, of course, varying shades of pigment even among Europeans—from very light in Scandinavia to relatively dark in Spain—and
occasionally Indians were compared to "swarthy Spaniards." But several
commentators insisted that the natives of North America were scarcely,
if at all, darker than the average Englishman. "Their color is not much
unlike the Sunne burnte Countrie man, who laboureth daily in the

Sunne for his living," according to Dionyse Settle, who had accompanied Martin Frobisher to the northern coast in 1577. "Their infants," insisted Thomas Morton after several years among the Massachusetts Indians, "are of complexion white as our nation, but their mothers in their infancy make a bath of . . . such things as will staine their skinne for ever, wherein they dip and washe them to make them tawny." And the Reverend William Crashaw, a staunch supporter of the Virginia enterprise, told of "a Virginian [Indian], that was with us here in *England*, whose skinne (though hee had gone naked all his life, till our men persuaded him to bee clothed) . . . was little more blacke or tawnie, than one of ours would be if he should goe naked in the South of *England*."[30] Englishmen, then, perceived Indians as essentially white and, at most, a shade darker than themselves.

Despite this belief, and despite almost universal praise of the Indians' physique and physiognomy, Englishmen in Europe or America harbored a deep prejudice against almost all aspects of Indian culture. William Strachey is representative. Writing from Virginia in 1612, he described the Indians as "generally tall of stature, and streight, of comely proportion, and the women have handsome lymbes, slender armes, and pretty handes." Of Indian beliefs and customs, however, Strachey was mostly contemptuous: "their chief god . . . is no other indeed then the devill"; "they are a people most voluptuous"; "vindictive and jelous they be" and "very barbarous."[31] In fact, many of the same pejoratives that had been applied to Africans appear in descriptions of Indians. In 1559 William Cuningham described Africans as "blacke, Savage, Monstrous, & rude." He considered Indians not much better—in some respects "comparable to brute beasts"—but the absence of a color label for the Indians points to a crucial difference in perception.[32] Although Englishmen's descriptions of Indians often are almost as negative as their accounts of Africans, their criticisms are of customs, not bodies, of nurture, not nature. To be sure, the catalogue of imagined Indian shortcomings is long: nakedness, cannibalism, barbarism, idolatory, devil worship, brutality, lechery, indolence, and slovenliness. Some observers mitigated the New World natives' alleged vices by reciting their virtues: hospitality, integrity, eloquence, hardiness, stoicism. But the lists of negative qualities, especially those compiled by armchair explorers, are usually more extensive and more emphatic. George Best, for example, had seen Inuits (Eskimos) in the Far North and admired their intelligence, modesty, and strength; he also thought them "brutishe and uncivil people" who "live in Caves of the Earth, and hunte for their dinners . . . even as the Beare, or other wilde beastes do. They eat rawe fleshe and fishe, and refuse no meate, howsoever it be stincking. They are desparate in their fighte, sullen of nature, and ravenous in their manner of feeding." *The Historie of Travayle in the West and East Indies* (1577), the last of Richard Eden's influential translations of Continental narratives, offers a diatribe against the Mexican Indians that concludes, "God never created so corrupte a people for vice and beastliness, without any mixture of goodnesse and civilitie." And George Abbot accused the Indians of being "naked, uncivill, some of them devourers of mans flesh, ignorant of shipping, without all kinde of learning, having no rememberance of history or writing among them, . . . utterly ignorant of scripture, or Christ, or Moyses, or any God."[33] Even John Rolfe, requesting permission to marry Pocahontas, complained that her "education hath bin rude, her manners barbarous, her generation accursed, and . . . [she is] discrepant in all nurtriture from my selfe." Finally, King James I, in a statement that effectively summarized his subjects' ethnocentric perception of America's natives, called them "beastly *Indians*, slaves to the Spaniards, refuse of the world, and as yet aliens to the holy covenant of God."[34]

James's "as yet" was important. However, much he and his countrymen abhorred Indian customs and beliefs, they thought that the Indians would one day be converted into neo-Englishmen. The English themselves, many writers readily admitted, had once been barbarian and pagan; their Roman conquerors had brought the twin blessings of civility and Christianity, for which Rome deserved abundant praise.[35] Would not the Indians similarly respond? Once they saw the clear superiority of English life and faith, the American natives would embrace such advantages avidly (Fig. 1.1). Early English reports from the New World encouraged such expectations. George Best recalled that natives captured by the Frobisher expedition quickly "beganne to growe more civill"; George Peckham announced optimistically that the Indians were "thirsting after christianitie"; and the elder Richard Hakluyt drew on ex-

Fig. 1.1

Seal of the Massachusetts Bay Colony, 1629–90. Early Anglo-American expectations of Indian conversion are reflected in this woodcut, carved by John Foster, in which the Indian invites the English to "COME OVER AND HELP US." Courtesy, American Antiquarian Society.

plorers' chronicles to predict that the Indians in the area of prospective English settlement were ready "to submytte them selves to good government, and ready to imbrace the christian faythe." Accordingly, much of the promotional literature of the late sixteenth and early seventeenth centuries made conversion and the uplifting of the Indians a major goal of English colonization.[36]

In short, early English writings reflect a deep bias against Indian culture but not against Indian color, shape, or features; the American native was socially deplorable but physically admirable. The challenge to English colonists was therefore educational: the natives must be converted to Protestant Christianity, taught English language and law, and trained in the social mores of Tudor-Stuart England. They must become Englishmen in everything except geographic origin. Africans, however, largely for reasons of inherent outward appearance and what it implied about their fundamental nature, were already deemed permanently debased and actual or potential slaves. The difference in English attitudes toward Indians and Africans is underscored in Nathaniel Field's epitome of the two major parts of the world that had recently been opened to English scrutiny: "wilde *Virginia*, Black Affricke."[37] Black people would remain forever different in appearance and probably in behavior, England's imperialists believed, but wildmen could be transformed by instruction in civility and Christianity.

II

In 1634 William Wood, an early Massachusetts settler who had recently returned to England, published a detailed description of New England's flora, fauna, and native inhabitants. Wood left no doubt about the natural color of the Indians in that region. "Their swarthiness is the sun's livery," he insisted, "for they are born fair." The first American edition of Wood's book appeared in Boston in 1764. Its editor, Nathaniel Rogers, added a footnote to that observation: "this was one of the popular errors given into by our author."[38]

Rogers's editorial comment reflects a fundamental shift in color perception from the early seventeenth to the late eighteenth century: by the later date, most Anglo-Americans no longer saw the Indian as inherently white. "The number of purely white People in the World is proportionably very small," Benjamin Franklin observed in 1751. "All Africa is black or tawny. Asia is chiefly tawny. America (exclusive of the new Comers) wholly so."[39] Many of Franklin's contemporaries concurred in his basic judgment, although they did not necessarily accept his choice of colors. Jonathan Carver, who traveled through the American colonies in the 1760s, noted that "their skin is of a reddish or copper colour." And, although Carver denied that he would "enter into a particular enquiry whether the Indians are indebted to nature, art, or the temperature of the climate for the colour of their skin," he gave his opinion anyway. "It appears to me to be the tincture they received originally from the hands of their Creator; but . . . at what time the European whiteness, the jetty hue of the African, or the copper cast of the American were given them . . . I will not pretend to determine."[40] Robert Hunter, writing in the 1780s, similarly described the Indians' hue when he observed a boy "not contented with his natural copper color . . . [who] was painted red in different places." A more explicit statement of the Indians' innate darkness and their efforts to be even darker appeared in John Filson's *Kentucke* (1774): "the Indians are not born white; and take a great deal of pains to darken their complexion, by anointing themselves with grease, and lying in the sun. They also paint their faces, breasts and shoulders, of various colours, but generally red."[41]

The perceptual shift from Indians as white men to Indians as tawnies or redskins was neither sudden nor universally accepted. Throughout the eighteenth century, some authors insisted that the Indians were inherently white. After a brief residence in Pennsylvania in the 1750s, German immigrant Gottlieb Mittelberger reported—perhaps from personal observation, perhaps from reading William Penn—that the Indians "are born as white as we ourselves are."[42] More impressive dissent from the new consensus came from James Adair, a longtime supervisor of Indian affairs and an authority on Indian life. The first page of his *History of the American Indians* (1775) stated unequivocally that the "copper or red-clay colour" of the American Indians was "merely accidental, or artificial"; following most sixteenth- and seventeenth-century writers, he ascribed Indian complexion to climate and ointments. Yet at times even Adair hinted at a fundamental color distinction between Europeans and Indians. "All the Indians," he noted, "are so strongly attached to, and prejudiced in favour of, their own colour, that they think as meanly of the whites, as we possibly can doe of them."[43] Adair thus had it both ways: he considered the Indians innately white—which was necessary to his belief in their Jewish origin—yet he implicitly reinforced the image of dark-skinned natives and white-skinned Europeans viewing each other as distinct color categories.

That perception had been growing since the late seventeenth century. At first it appeared as a contention that stains and paints increased, rather than caused, the Indians' darkness. "They are of a tawny colour," reported a Virginia colonist in 1689, "and they make themselves more so, by annointing their bodies with bear's grease." Soon after the turn of the century, former South Carolina governor John Archdale attested that the "Natives are somewhat Tawney, occasioned, in a great measure, by Oyling their Skins, and by the naked Raies of the Sun." Similarly, John Lawson in 1709 described the Indians of the Carolinas as "tawny, which would not be so dark, did they not dawb themselves with Bears Oil, and a colour like burnt Cork."[44] By 1728, when William Byrd published his *History of the Dividing Line*, the Indians' color seemed indisputably darker than European-Americans', but Byrd thought it could be "blanched" by two generations of intermarriage. Other commentators, by mentioning the Indians' dark hue without attributing it to environmental or cultural influences, implied a natural darkness. "Their skins," according to Daniel Gookin, supervisor of Indians in Massachusetts, "are of a tawny colour, not unlike the tawny Moors in Africa." Reverend Samuel Lee, also of Massachusetts, described the Indians as "tawny colourd: like the Tartarians."45 Writing in the last quarter of the seventeenth century, neither Gookin nor Lee attributed the dusky hue to stains or the sun, as had most of their New England forebears.

The shift in color ascription, explicit or implicit, is not the only sign that European perceptions had changed. The terminology of ethnic identification also altered significantly between the early years of English colonization and the eve of the American Revolution. Almost without exception, sixteenth- and seventeenth-century writers referred to people of the Old World as Englishmen, Spaniards, Frenchmen, and so forth, often as Christians, seldom as whites except to distinguish them from blacks. The few exceptions suggest that the contrast between the Indians' *acquired* color and the Europeans' *natural* hue provided some observers with a handy label for Europeans of whatever nationality, but such usage remained rare in Indian-European contexts until the eighteenth century. A New Netherland document of 1652, for example, complained that "some malicious and evil disposed persons have not scrupled to inform . . . the Indians what sum and price the Dutch or Whites are giving each other for small Lots," but few if any other seventeenth-century Dutch documents use "whites" (*blancken*) in Indian contexts. The author of the anomalous statement from 1652 may have previously served on the African coast, as had many early Dutch officials, and hence have drawn on the vocabulary of black-white relations in the Dutch slave trade.46

Now and again early English writers also used "white" to designate Europeans. At Roanoke Island in the 1580s, Arthur Barlowe described the natives as "yellowish" and the Europeans as "white people"; Ralph Lane in one instance designated the latter "white men." Both cases are unusual in early English chronicles. In a somewhat different vein, Quaker leader George Fox's journal of his American travels—recorded in the 1670s but not published until the twentieth century—reported a New England Indian's account of an ancient belief that "a white people should come in a great thing of the sea." Assuming that Fox correctly transcribed the Indian's words and that Fox's editor faithfully transcribed his manuscript, Indians may have adopted color terminology as early as did Anglo-Americans, although here too the chromatic term did not necessarily imply innate rather than acquired color. It may have been a native parallel to the early European use of "tawny" and "sodden quince."47

No such ambiguity clouds a South Carolina law of 1696 "for . . . Determining all Causes and Controversies between *White Man* and *Indian*." Among Carolina legislators at least, and presumably among some of their contemporaries, "whites" was emerging as a legitimate label for Americans of European descent in lieu of "Christian" and "English." Perhaps the South's recent influx of Africans prompted an increased sensitivity to pigmentation and encouraged color classifications: the earliest surviving instances of such terminology appear in southern documents. But authors and officials in northern colonies were not far behind. Cotton Mather's *Negro Christianized* (1706) used "whites" primarily in contrast to blacks, but in one passage he differentiated both from a third division of humanity: "As if the great God went by the *Complexion* of men, in His Favours to them! As if none but *Whites* might hope to be Favoured and Accepted with God! Whereas it is well known that *Whites*, are the least part of Mankind. The biggest part of Mankind, perhaps, are Copper-Coloured; a sort of *Tawnies*." By the 1730s "whites" appeared frequently in Pennsylvania Council minutes and in Indian treaties.[48] By the second half of the eighteenth century, "white" had become a common appellation for a European of whatever nationality or whatever longevity in America. (National labels, of course, continued to be used where appropriate, especially to distinguish among several groups of European colonists.) For example, Philadelphia naturalist John Bartram usually referred to "Indian" and "English" in his published *Travels* (1751), but he occasionally used "whites" and "white men" to mean Europeans in general. Similarly, Jefferson asserted in his *Notes on the State of Virginia* that he considered "the Indian . . . to be in body and mind equal to the white man," and he clung to such terminology whenever he compared natives and European-Americans.[49]

Apparently, Indians adopted a similar vocabulary—if we can accept the surviving translations—as George Fox's journal entry implied and as several eighteenth-century sources corroborate. As early as 1687, an Onondaga sachem contended that the kings of England and France "are both of one Skinn meaning [the interpreter added] white Skinned, & not brown as they [*sic*] Indians are." This evidence of an emergent Indian sense of color categories and the implication that the differences were innate became more frequent and more explicit in the eighteenth century. In 1744 an Indian spokesman argued that the difference between Europe and America "may be known from the different Colours of our Skin." In 1751 John Bartram quoted an Indian who advocated "peace and good harmony between the *Indians* and *White People*"; a quarter century later missionary Samuel Kirkland recorded an Indian spokesman as saying, "We have no . . . inclination of interfering in the dispute between Old England and Boston; the white people may settle their own quarrels between themselves." Indian speeches even applied such words in retrospective accounts, as in an oration of 1773, which began with a brief résumé of Indian-European contact: "Brother, when we first saw the White People. . . ."[50]

Anglo-American usage of *tawny* also reflected the new emphasis on color terminology. Until the last quarter of the seventeenth century, it was almost always an adjective, modifying Indians or natives; thereafter, it increasingly became a noun. In 1680, for example, Morgan Godwyn in *The Negro's & Indians Advocate* discussed the conversion to Christianity of "Tawneys and Blacks"; in the next several decades many authors employed similar terminology.[51] No doubt the temptation was strong among Anglo-Americans and Indians to find generic words to describe themselves and each other. Europeans had applied—or, rather, misapplied—"Indians" to the natives since 1492 but had no convenient term for themselves. "Europeans" implicitly excluded Euro-Americans; "Christians" soon lost its diagnostic precision; and British America's growing ethnic diversity made "Englishmen" inappropriate. To some extent, perhaps, the coinage of color terms was inevitable as blacks became more numerous and as Indians came increasingly to be seen in racial rather than national or tribal terms. But the persistence of "Indians" and the tardy appearance of "redmen" on the linguistic scene suggest a lingering reluctance to perceive the Indians in an essentially biological rather than cultural light, a reluctance that weakened, however, as the eighteenth century wore on.

Other, more subtle, indications of a growing pejorative perception of Indian color appear in American writings of the late seventeenth and early eighteenth centuries. Some are vague, as in Cotton Mather's tale of a "bewitched" girl's encounter with the devil: "hee was not of a *Negro*, but of a *Tawney*, or an *Indian* Colour." Even if Mather meant an Indian's *acquired* hue, the assignment of "an *Indian* Colour" to the devil tells something about Mather's—or the girl's—image of Indians.[52] Also vague but at least as suggestive in its implications is Governor William Gooch's commentary on the Virginia law of 1724 for "the better government of Negroes, Mulattoes, and Indians," which deprived men in those categories of the political franchise, even if they were free and owned property. In a series of letters to Alured Popple in 1735–36, Gooch explained that the basic issue was complexion: dark-skinned inhabitants were disfranchised purely on the basis of color. Gooch admitted that the number of free blacks and mulattoes "is so inconsiderable, that 'tis scarce worth while to take any Notice of them," but a dark skin, he insisted, should not disable anyone who had attained freemanship. He said nothing about Indians. Gooch either tacitly included them among blacks and mulattoes, or else none had been accorded freemanship. That he probably subsumed Indians under the rubric of mulattoes is strongly suggested by the Virginia Assembly's declaration of 1705 that "the child of an Indian and the child, grand child, or great grand child of a negro shall be deemed, accounted, held and taken to be a mulatto." In any event, the implication of Gooch's remarks and the intention of Virginia's legislation were to include Indians among the colony's colored population.⁵³

Similar intentions appear in other colonial statutes. During the seventeenth century, specific laws rarely applied to both Indians and blacks; the two groups were usually accorded separate and distinct legislative attention. Eighteenth-century lawmakers, however, often lumped them together. New York, for example, frequently proscribed the activities of its "Negro, Indian or Mulatto" populations; southern colonies used similar language but often added a category of "mustizoes" (part Indian, part black or white). Laws against intermarriage are particularly telling. As early as 1691 Virginia passed an antimiscegenation law aimed at Indians as well as blacks. (Its 1662 law, while using color as the basis for racial separation, did not mention Indians.) To be sure, Virginia's antimiscegenation laws after 1705 ostensibly ignore Indians, but they were automatically encompassed by the new definition of mulattoes. In 1715 and again in 1741 North Carolina curbed racial intermarriage. Drawing on the intent and almost verbatim on the blatantly racist language of Virginia's act of 1691, the Carolina legislators in 1741 sought to prevent an "abominable Mixture and spurious Issue" by levying a prohibitive fine against any white person who married "an Indian, Negro Mustee, or Mulatto Man or Woman, or any Person of mixt Blood, to the Third Generation, bond or free."⁵⁴ Other colonies did not explicitly prohibit Indian-white marriages before the American Revolution, although Massachusetts almost did in 1705. Samuel Sewall, a supporter of missionary efforts among the New England tribes, claimed to have thwarted the attempt.⁵⁵ In most colonies the taint of color prejudice and the cultural gulf were sufficient deterrents to intermarriage.

Comparable clues to changing Anglo-American perceptions of the Indian are laws concerning servants and slaves. In 1705 Virginia legislated protections for white servants by bracketing together the people it considered non-Christian and nonwhite: "[N]o Negroes, Mulattoes, or *Indians*, although Christians, or *Jews, Moors, Mahametans*, or other Infidels, shall, at any Time, purchase any Christian Servant, nor any other, except of their own Complexion." South Carolina in 1712 considered "all negroes, mulatoes, mustizoes or Indians" to be slaves unless they could prove otherwise; later in the century Georgia borrowed heavily from her colonial neighbor when prescribing slavery for "all negroes, Indians, mulattoes, or mestizoes, who now are, or hereafter shall be in this province (free Indians in amity with this government, and negroes, mulattoes, or mestizoes, who now are or hereafter shall become free, excepted)."⁵⁶

Even eighteenth-century New Englanders, with their sparse black and Indian populations, were almost as ready as their southern counterparts to fuse the two groups in legislation. Cases in point are New Hampshire's "Act to Prevent Disorders in the Night" of 1714 and the regulations proposed in 1723 by Boston's selectmen to control its colored population. The New Hampshire legislation empowered local officials and "Her

Majesties good Subjects" to "Apprehend or Cause to be Apprehended any Indian, Negro, or Molatto, Servant or Slave that shall be found abroad after Nine a Clock at Night, and shall not give a good and Satisfactory Account of their business." Boston's "Articles for the Better Regulating Indians Negroes and Molattos within this Town" set appalling restrictions on non-European residents, whether slave, servant, or free. One provision, for example, required that "every free Indian Negro or Molatto Shal bind out, all their Children at or before they arrive at the age of four years to Some English master."[57] That Indians shared with blacks and mulattoes such repressive policies in colonies as diverse as New Hampshire, Massachusetts, New York, Virginia, the Carolinas, and Georgia (others could be cited) speaks volumes about shifting Anglo-American racial perceptions.

By the eve of the American Revolution, Anglo-Americans had taken the next logical step: they defined "Americans" wholly in terms of themselves. Americans, James Otis assured readers of his *Rights of the British Colonies Asserted and Proved* (1764), were not "a compound mongrel mixture of *English, Indian*, and *Negro*, but . . . freeborn *British white* subjects." Hector St. John de Crèvecoeur agreed. "The American, this new man," he explained in 1786, was a transplanted European or his descendant. A year later, John Jay expanded that notion in *The Federalist*, number 2: "Providence has been pleased to give this one connected country, to one united people, a people descended from the same ancestors, speaking the same language, professing the same religion, attached to the same government, very similar in their manners and customs."[58] By the prevailing definition, Indians (and Negroes) simply were not Americans.

Nor, in the eyes of many Anglo-Americans, did Indians merit eventual incorporation into American society. Anglo-America's fundamental contempt for Indian culture remained relatively constant throughout the history of British America and beyond. What changed under the influence of the new perception of Indians as innately dark-skinned were expectations of the Indians' civil and theological redemption. Initially the Indians had been viewed as likely prospects for anglicization; by the middle of the eighteenth century they were usually dismissed as incapable and unworthy. Accompanying that judgment was a weakening of the few protections that Indians, as individuals or as tribes, had enjoyed in the previous century.

In the sixteenth and early seventeenth centuries, English optimism had served as a real, though grossly imperfect, shield against wholesale slaughter, enslavement, or flagrant abuse of the Indians, except in periods of outright war. Although all British colonies subjected Indians to some legal discrimination—prohibitions against serving in the militia or acquiring guns, horses, and liquor, for example—and to individual acts of insult or exploitation, colonial governments often protected Indian rights and punished white transgressors.[59] Governmental concern stemmed partly from self-interest, of course: abuse of the Indians could

bring lethal retaliation and costly wars. But in most colonies some genuinely humane leaders shared the widespread contempt for Indian culture but tried to treat individual Indians justly and peacefully. Because
those leaders considered the Indians to be as truly and as perfectably
God's creatures as anyone, they counted on education and conversion
to make Indians into Englishmen. Among the most solicitous of Indian
welfare were George Thorpe in early Virginia, the second Lord Baltimore
in Maryland, William Penn in Pennsylvania, and Edward Winslow and the
elder Jonathan Mayhew in New England.[60] Most missionaries, too, sought
to protect the Indians' lives and well-being while attempting—as missionaries by definition must—to alter the Indians' basic beliefs.

The protections afforded by government and church officials gradually faded during the seventeenth century as public sentiment turned
increasingly cynical about the possibility of coexistence and ultimate conversion and as the swelling European-American population became increasingly difficult to regulate. By the mid-eighteenth century, the best
the Indian could expect was seclusion on an ever-shrinking reservation
or westward migration in the face of an advancing colonial frontier. Powerful tribes won some respect for their usefulness as allies or their danger as enemies; the rest, judging from the writings of the time, were considered by most Anglo-Americans a nuisance to be ignored, enslaved,
or eliminated. As Benjamin Franklin observed in 1764 after a major
atrocity in western Pennsylvania, "The Spirit of killing all Indians,
Friends and Foes, [has] spread amazingly thro' the whole Country." Two
years later, Sir William Johnson reported to Whitehall that in the backcountry from Virginia to New York the settlers "murder, Robb and otherwise grossly misuse all Indians they could find . . . and [are] treating
the Indians with contempt, much greater than they had ever before experienced." The settlers, Sir William lamented, "perpetrate Murders
whenever opportunity offers."[61] The stereotypical frontier view that "the
only good Indian is a dead Indian" was an American reality long before
General Sheridan coined the infamous phrase.

Even missionaries reflected the changing view of Indian color and
character. During the eighteenth century a new wave of missionary enthusiasm revived efforts in many colonies to Christianize the Indians,
now that the danger from Indian hostility had receded and as the Great
Awakening aroused Christian consciences throughout British America.
In a resurgence of attempts to indoctrinate the Indians in English ways
and beliefs, several new schools and colleges admitted native youths.
Even among educators and institutions, however, the image of the Indian was less hopeful and more susceptible to racial—as distinct from
cultural—bias than it had been in the previous century. Plans for Virginia's Indian College at Henrico in the early 1620s and the Harvard
charter of 1650 had reflected the seventeenth century's expectation of
rapid success based on the biological equality of Indians and Englishmen.[62] Eighteenth-century efforts reveal a different perception.

The early career of Dartmouth College is illustrative. Several critics of Eleazar Wheelock's missionary school in Lebanon, Connecticut, the precursor to his college in Hanover, New Hampshire, attributed its slim success to English prejudice, freely admitting that they themselves "could never respect an Indian, Christian or no Christian, so as to put him on a level with white people on any account." One of the critics insisted, on the basis of "the irresistable avertion that white people must ever have to black [sic]," that "Mr. Wheelock's attempt [is] altogether absurd and fruitless. . . . [A]s long as the Indians are despised by the English we may never expect success in Christianizing of them." And it can hardly be coincidental that Wheelock frequently referred to his Indian students as "black" or to his prize pupil, Samson Occom, as "my black son." Even some of Wheelock's students absorbed notions of abject inferiority and its related color terminology. One Mohegan called himself a "good for nothing Black Indian," and "a despicable Lump of polluted Clay . . . inclosed in this tawny skin."[63] The degradation of the Indians had, for Wheelock and his students at least, reached the point where Native Americans were rhetorically almost indistinguishable from the Africans who had suffered a century and a half of enslavement and extreme prejudice. It is not, therefore, surprising that in 1764 Thomas Hutchinson of Massachusetts complained, "We are too apt to consider the Indians as a race of beings by nature inferior to us, and born to servitude." By Hutchinson's time, thousands—perhaps tens of thousands—of Indians were, in fact, enslaved in British colonies from Massachusetts to Barbados.[64] The eighteenth century's view of Indians as innately dark and inferior thus had frightful implications for America's aboriginal inhabitants.

III

Documenting the shifts in Anglo-American perceptions of Indian color is easier than explaining them. Contemporary authors were oblivious to the changes; they were too close to the phenomena and too involved in them. To a large extent, of course, the reasons for changing attitudes can only be surmised, for they reflect a vast and complicated alteration in millions of disparate individuals whose perceptions of the Indian cannot be precisely reconstructed. Nonetheless, Anglo-American writings of the eighteenth century offer important clues to the psychological imperatives that encouraged "white" Americans to believe that Indians were significantly and irrevocably darker than themselves. At least three major interrelated and mutually reinforcing influences are apparent: the Anglo-Americans' anger at Indian hostility, their frustration over Indian rejection of Christianity and "civility," and their adoption of eighteenth-century racial theories.

First, chronologically, was the transformation of the Indian in English eyes from potential friend to inveterate enemy. That change took place gradually and unevenly, occurring at different times in different places, as military conflict increasingly characterized Indian-English contact. From the standpoint of Anglo-American attitudes, the causes of conflict were irrelevant: Englishmen at home or in America almost invariably blamed the Indians for hostilities and, hence, came to think of them as incorrigibly aggressive and ruthless.[65] It was only a short step from regarding the Indians as bloodthirsty foes to perceiving them as naturally inferior in morality and humanity, and eventually in physiology and pigmentation.

The initial Anglo-American view of the Indians was largely amiable and optimistic. Most of the "savages," imperial spokesmen contended, would be friendly. They would also be eager for commerce and the gospel, partly because it would be in their own self-interest but mainly because the English professed to come peacefully, offering voluntary acceptance of English culture and religion. (By contrast, English imperialists viewed Spanish settlement as a model of how to alienate and exterminate the natives.) The Indians would therefore welcome English outposts, willingly sell surplus land, engage in mutually profitable trade, and enthusiastically embrace Reformed Christianity. Yet, from the earliest days of English colonialism, its champions predicted—judging from a century of European experience in America—that some natives would oppose settlement no matter how fairly they were treated. And Indians who persisted in hostility or obstinately rejected free trade and proselytizing, the imperialists argued, deserved no quarter; the English never seriously questioned their own right to occupy part of America, by force if necessary. England's deeply ingrained ethnocentrism (a characteristic other European nations possessed, but apparently to a lesser degree), and England's determination to make profits and converts, which it hoped would emulate Spanish success but not Spanish methods, would brook no native opposition. Even the usually benign younger Hakluyt minced no words on this point: "To handle them gently, while gentle courses may be found to serve . . . be without comparison the best: but if gentle polishing will not serve, then we shall not want hammerours and rough masons enow, I meane our old soldiours trained up in the Netherlands, to square and prepare them to our Preachers hands." With the few recalcitrants chastised, colonization would proceed peacefully, to the benefit of settlers and Indians alike.[66]

Such expectations died early. At Roanoke Island in the 1580s, most of the Indians turned against the colonists, for justifiable reasons, and the neighboring Powhatans probably exterminated the "Lost Colony" of 1587.[67] In Virginia, settlers and natives clashed almost incessantly from 1607 to 1613, often in open warfare, sometimes in sporadic skirmishes, occasionally in bloodless but hostile negotiations. Nearly a decade of relative calm followed the captivity and conversion of Pocahontas in 1613; the brief and imperfect respite from hostilities ended suddenly with the massacre of 1622, which almost exterminated the colony. Even though responsibility for the massacre ultimately belonged with the English, as their own accounts unwittingly reveal, the Anglo-American attitude toward the Indians quickly shifted from contempt to hatred—a sentiment intensified by the ensuing decade of blatant carnage and by a similar massacre in 1644.[68]

New England's experience offers some parallels and some marked contrasts to Virginia's. Unlike Virginia, the New England colonies had generally peaceful relations with the local tribes until 1675. To a considerable extent that reflected New England's unusual population ratio: epidemics in 1616–17 and 1633–34 greatly reduced the natives while barely touching the colonists, which lessened Indian resistance and further encouraged Puritan immigrants to believe that God intended them to create a New English Zion. So did the Pequot War of 1637, which briefly threatened New England's view of the Indians as potential friends and converts, but when most of the tribes remained neutral or actively supported the colonists, and when the colonial forces emerged almost unscathed, the Puritans' confidence in their own invincibility and in the Indians' vulnerability was reinforced rather than undermined.[69] By contrast, early Virginians faced an Indian population that vastly outnumbered them and that had enough political cohesion to use its numerical strength effectively.

But numbers do not tell the whole story. Important too was the strong missionary impulse among New England's founders, an impulse that eventually enjoyed a quarter century of modest achievement. New England's missionary activity began belatedly in the 1640s, but its success from then until King Philip's War seemed to justify earlier expectations. The uprisings of 1675—once again an Indian response to colonial encroachment and abuses—dashed Puritan assumptions about the eventual transformation of the Indians into proper Englishmen. Henceforth, the British colonists in New England joined those in the Chesapeake and elsewhere in a growing conviction that Indians in general were their enemies. That conviction hardened in the late seventeenth century and throughout the eighteenth as the British colonial frontier became a vast English-Indian battleground, often exacerbated by troops or agents from other colonial powers. Even Pennsylvania, after the effective withdrawal of the Quakers from political control and after the influx of a predominantly non-Quaker population, had its share of racial conflict.[70]

Frequent and ferocious hostilities, regardless of who was at fault, inevitably corroded the earlier Anglo-American view of the Indians and reshaped its vocabulary. References to the Indians, never especially flattering, now became almost universally disparaging. In the aftermath of 1622, Anglo-American spokesmen portrayed the Virginia natives as "having little of Humanitie but shape," "more brutish than the beasts they hunt," and "naturally born slaves."[71] New Englanders reacted similarly to King Philip's War. The Indians were "Monsters shapt and fac'd like men," wrote one New England poet, and most of his compatriots undoubtedly agreed.[72] Even book titles reflect the shift in attitude. In 1655 John Eliot could write hopefully of the Indians' progress toward conversion in *A Late and Further Manifestation of the Progress of the Gospell amongst the Indians in New England: Declaring Their Constant Love and Zeal to the Truth, with a Readiness to Give Account of Their Faith and Hope, as of Their Desire to Be Partakers of the Ordinances of Christ.* Twenty years later, in the midst of New England's struggle for survival, an anonymous pamphleteer suggested a far different view of the Indians in a *Brief and True Narration of the Late Wars Risen in New-England, Occasioned by the Quarrelsome Disposition, and Perfidious Carriage of the Barbarous, Savage, and Heathenish Natives there.*[73] As warfare increasingly became the dominant mode of English-Indian contact, the image of the Indian as vicious savage made deep inroads on the Anglo-American psyche. Cotton Mather, whose rhetorical flights often exaggerated but seldom misrepresented colonial sentiments, gave revealing advice to New England's soldiers in King William's War: "Once you have but got the Track of those Ravenous howling Wolves, then pursue them vigourously; *Turn not back till* they *are consumed. . . . Beat* them small as the *Dust before the Wind. . . . Sacrifice them to the Ghosts of Christians whom they have Murdered. . . . Vengance, Dear Country-men! Vengance upon our Murderers.*" The culmination of a century and a half of military escalation came in 1776 in the Declaration of Independence's only reference to the Indians: The king "has endeavored to bring on the inhabitants of our frontiers, the merciless Indian savages, whose known rule of warfare is an undistinguished destruction of all ages, sexes and conditions." Nearly a decade of border warfare exacerbated the revolutionaries' fear and hatred of the Indians. "The white Americans," observed a British traveler in 1784, "have the most rancorous antipathy to the whole race of Indians; and nothing is more common than to hear them talk of extirpating them totally from the face of the earth, men, women, and children."[74]

War-bred animosities did not require a difference in color perception, but the unconscious temptation to tar the Indian with the brush of physical inferiority—to differentiate and denigrate the enemy—appears to have been irresistible.[75] Wartime epithets have often invoked outward appearance, however irrelevant (witness the "yellow Japs" of World War II), and British Americans frequently resorted to pejorative color labels. In the late seventeenth and early eighteenth centuries, as war raged along the northern New England frontier, Cotton Mather castigated "those Tawny Pagans, than which there are not worse Divels Incarnate upon Earth," and "a *swarthy* Generation of *Philistines* here; the *Indian* Natives, I mean, whom alone we are like to have any *Warrs withal.*" Nearly a century later, when the bulk of the Indians sided with Great Britain during the American Revolution, Henry Dwight complained of "copper Colour'd Vermine" and hoped that an American army would "Massacre those Infernal Savages to such a degree that [there] may'nt be a pair of them left, to continue the Breed upon the Earth."[76] Logically enough, "redskins" eventually emerged as the epithet for enemies who usually used red paint on the warpath. Not coincidentally, perhaps, the first reported use of that term appears in a passage about Indian assaults on frontier settlements. In a sentence that suggests the impact of war on changing English attitudes, Samuel Smith of Hadley, Massachusetts, recalled in 1699 that several decades earlier his father had endured Indian raids in the Connecticut valley. "My Father ever declardt," Smith remembered (using terminology his father probably did not), "there would not be so much to feare iff ye Red Skins was treated with suche mixture of Justice & Authority as they cld understand, but iff he was living now he must see that wee can do nought but *fight* em & that right heavily."[77]

The Indians' refusal to adopt English concepts of civility and religion poisoned Anglo-American attitudes as thoroughly as did warfare. Sixteenth- and seventeenth-century expectations of rapid and wholesale anglicization met constant rebuff; by the end of the seventeenth century it must have been clear to all but the more optimistic missionaries that most Indians would never be Christian in faith or English in allegiance and customs. Converts in the southern and middle colonies numbered only a handful; most of John Eliot's "praying towns" had been scuttled by King Philip's War and its aftermath; and even the Quakers in Pennsylvania, despite a commendable effort to treat the Indians fairly, had won few to English ways or beliefs. Occasional successes notwithstanding, the missionary movement had failed. Even less successful was the broader mission of eliminating customs that Englishmen subsumed under the heading of "savagery," such as nakedness, scarification, tribal law and government, hunting instead of herding, and, perhaps most important of all, an exclusively oral language. Some technological assimilation had occurred, as had some imaginative blending of religious ideas, but the overwhelming majority of Indians steadfastly held to their traditional ways and rejected most of the alien culture's offerings.[78]

Who was to blame? The most obvious scapegoat was the Indian himself. He stubbornly resisted spiritual and material improvement, his critics charged, and they eventually concluded that his resistance stemmed either from a deeply ingrained antipathy to "civilization" or from a natural incapacity for improvement. Benjamin Franklin explained to a correspondent in 1753 that "Little Success . . . has hitherto attended every attempt to Civilize our American Indians in their present way of living. . . . When an Indian Child has been brought up among us, taught our language and habituated to Our Customs, yet if he goes to see his relations and make one Indian Ramble with them, there is no perswading him ever to return." Franklin did not consider the Indians inherently incapable of adopting English ways; they simply and obstinately preferred their own.[79] Many of Franklin's contemporaries were less charitable. The editor of the 1764 edition of William Wood's *New England's Prospect,* for example, thought the Indians incurably barbarian and pagan. "The christianizing the Indians," he peevishly noted,

> scarcely affords a probability of success; for their immense sloth, their incapacity to consider abstract truth . . . and their perpetual wanderings, which prevent a steady worship, greatly impede the progress of Christianity, a mode of religion adapted to the most refined temper of the human mind. . . . The feroce manners of a native Indian can never be effaced, nor can the most finished politeness totally eradicate the wild lines of his education.

Almost predictably, the editor believed that Indians were not born white: with few exceptions, contempt for Indians as people, as well as for their culture, correlated highly with a belief in their innate darkness.[80]

A third major influence toward perceiving the Indians as inherently tawny or red came from eighteenth-century naturalists. Few of them had firsthand information about the American Indians—most were European scholars who never visited the New World—but in their frantic attempt to classify systematically all plant and animal life, including the principal divisions of humankind, they contributed directly to the notion of Indians as inherently red and indirectly at least to the belief in their inferiority.

Initially, the naturalists' categories had no hierarchical intent. Their taxonomies were horizontal, not vertical, and each branch of humanity enjoyed equality with all others. Before long, however, the subdivisions of *Homo sapiens* acquired descriptive judgments that suggest a relative superiority in Europeans and corresponding inferiority in other races. Such a view meshed comfortably with the eighteenth century's emphatic belief in natural order, metaphorically expressed as a "Great Chain of Being," in which all creatures from microorganisms to angels had permanent places on a hierarchical continuum. The idea of an orderly chain of life had existed for centuries; it flourished in the fifteenth century, for example, when Sir John Fortescue recorded a classic description: "In this order angel is set over angel, rank upon rank in the Kingdom of Heaven; man is set over man, beast over beast, bird over bird, and fish over fish . . . so that there is no worm that crawls upon the ground, no bird that flies on high, no fish that swims in the depths, which the chain of this order binds not in most harmonious concord."[81] Not until the eighteenth century, however, did ranks within humankind receive much attention. Then, because natural scientists almost invariably chose skin color as the principal criterion of racial identity, darkness of hue became "scientifically" linked to other undesirable qualities. As Winthrop Jordan has pointed out, for Africans the "Great Chain of Being" soon became a "Great Chain of Color" on which whites regarded blacks as divinely relegated to a lesser rank of humanity.[82] In the eighteenth century, American Indians also became victims, though not quite so pejoratively, of the color chain's invidious implications.

The second edition of Charles Linnaeus's *General System of Nature* (1740) presented the Swedish botanist's preliminary attempt at human classification. The previous edition (1735) had said almost nothing about humankind; the new and greatly enlarged version gave only a few lines to the subject, but they were enough to establish four basic groups: "Europaeus albus, Americanus rubescens, Asiaticus fuscus, Africanus niger." Seven subsequent editions, published between 1740 and 1756, repeated those color categories verbatim. In the tenth edition (1758), Linnaeus expanded his discussion of humans. To the four original categories he added two others—wild men and monsters, to whom he assigned no colors—while again ascribing white, red, yellow, and black to Europeans, Americans, Asians, and Africans. But Linnaeus no longer restricted his entries to physical description; he now attributed several character traits to each race. Europeans were, among other things, sanguine, brawny, gentle, and inventive; Americans choleric, obstinate, content, and free; Asians melancholy, rigid, haughty, and covetous; Africans phlegmatic, crafty, indolent, and negligent.[83] The Indians, to be sure, fared far better than Africans and Asians in this Linnaen glossary, and Linnaeus even hinted at the noble savage image ("content," "free") that was rapidly gaining favor among European intellectuals. But an unavoidable message in Linnaeus's highly subjective and immensely influential treatise was that American Indians were naturally red and somewhat inferior to whites.

Most of Linnaeus's scientific contemporaries concurred. In 1744, four years after Linnaeus's first description of Americans as red, Dr. John Mitchell of Virginia investigated "the proximate cause of the Colour of *Negroes*, Indians, white People, etc." Drawing on Newton's *Opticks*, Mitchell argued that the thickness of the skin determined the amount of light reflected by the epidermis and, hence, the extent of its darkness. He saw all humankind as varying only in shade—the Indians differed from Europeans in degree rather than substance—yet even Mitchell argued that the Indians of America and Asia (whom he considered of about the same color) constituted a distinct race and a distinct color category. He also contended that tawny was the original human color: Africans had become darker, Europeans lighter, "Americans retaining the primitive and original Complexion."[84] Perhaps from a desire to defend Native Americans from European charges of physical inferiority, Mitchell thus gave considerable dignity to Indian color. In that regard, Mitchell was unique.

Of the two prominent eighteenth-century authors who differed significantly with Linnaeus on the Indians' natural hue, one preceded him by almost two decades and admitted sparse knowledge of America. Richard Bradley's *A Philosophical Account of the Works of Nature* (1721) lists Indians among the world's white-skinned people. Of his five categories of humankind, which Bradley based on hair texture as well as on skin color, he included in "the *White Men*" two subcategories: "*Europeans,*

that have *Beards;* and a sort of *White Men* in *America* (as I am told) that
only differ from us in having no *Beards.*"[85] Bradley represents a waning
stage in the perception of Indian complexion. More distinguished than
Bradley, and more notorious for the counterattacks he provoked, was
Georges Louis Leclerc, Comte de Buffon. The French scientist's *Natural
History* appeared in several editions and innumerable volumes (forty-
four in the 1749 version) and was hailed as one of the great works of
the time. His disparaging remarks on America in general and on the Indians in particular, however, aroused Jefferson's ire and inspired other
critics as well. Some attacked Buffon for his contention that all humankind was naturally white, "which may be varied by climate, by food,
and by manners, to yellow, brown, and black. . . . Nature, in her most
perfect exertions, made men white." This extreme environmentalism
prodded Henry Home, Lord Kames, to issue an extensive critique.
Kames took Buffon to task on several counts, including the notion that
climate is the principal cause of color. If that were true, Kames asked,
why were "all Americans without exception . . . of a copper-colour,
though in that vast continent there is every variety of climate?"[86]

No answer was really needed, however, for Buffon—much like James
Adair at a later date—was simultaneously on both sides of the argument.
Although Buffon attributed human color variations to environmental
influence, he believed them to be almost permanent: centuries of exposure to a certain climate and to certain foods and body stains could
produce essentially different races. And, although Buffon recognized
that American Indian complexions varied considerably, he argued that
"the whole continent of American contains but one race of men, who
are all more or less tawny."[87] In sum, while Buffon disagreed sharply
with Kames and others about the fundamental cause of human colors,
he nonetheless perceived the Indians almost exactly as his critics did—
innately dark and racially distinct. That perception appeared with particular virulence on the eve of the American Revolution in Bernard Romans's *Concise Natural History of East and West Florida* (1775). "From one
end of America to the other," Romans contended, "the red people
are the same nation and draw their origin from a different source,
than . . . any other different species of the human genus. . . . [They are]
a people not only rude and uncultivated, but incapable of civilization."[88]
The overwhelming thrust of eighteenth-century naturalism thus supported the growing conviction that American Indians were inherently
deficient in color and basic characteristics. Science had joined forces
with war-bred animosities and missionary disillusionment to brand the
Indians with an ineradicable mark of inferiority.

IV

It is beyond the scope of this essay to trace in detail the evolution of
white America's attitudes and policies toward Indians in the early na-

tional and antebellum periods. The story has recently received extensive scholarly attention and undoubtedly will continue to attract analysis and debate.[89] But a brief overview will suggest the major trends and relate them to changing color perceptions.

American racial thought in the post-Revolutionary era underwent subtle but significant changes. Ever since the sixteenth century, Europeans had viewed Africans and Indians as fundamentally different from each other in postdiluvian biological development and in their prospects for absorption into British-American society. In the eighteenth century, the gap gradually closed as the Indian became, in the eyes of most white observers, inherently tawny. As earlier, most Anglo-Americans considered Africans immutably black; in the late eighteenth and early nineteenth centuries some writers further debased the Afro-American by contriving polygenic theories to explain what they believed to be the black race's irredeemable physical and behavioral inferiority. Indians, by contrast, were sometimes lauded for superior appearance, virtue, or ability, yet increasingly they too suffered the stigma that white America attached to peoples of darker skin (Fig. 1.2).[90]

That the Indian was, in fact, inherently darker than the European, and that his pigmentation was the sign of a separate branch of humanity, had become axiomatic by the outbreak of the American Revolution. What remained for the Jeffersonian generation and its early nineteenth-century successors was to determine the Indians' proper color label and to reach a rough consensus on the implications of a racial status that was clearly inferior to the white man's but also superior to the black's.

The precise reason for the gradual adoption of red, instead of tawny or some other hue, can only be surmised. Although the earliest recorded use of "redskins" dates from the very late seventeenth century, it is an isolated example and its authenticity is slightly suspect. (Samuel Smith's letter of 1699, which uses "Red Skin Men" and "Redskins," was not published until 1900, when it appeared as a purported transcription inserted in a descendant's Revolutionary-era diary; it may reflect a later editorial hand.) Not until the second half of the eighteenth century did "red" emerge as a fairly common label. By 1765 some Indians may have adopted the primary color label for themselves, either in a pan-Indian sense or perhaps in reference to a particular tribe: "We, red people," a native speaker asserted, "are a very jealous people." (That quotation, too, did not appear in print until much later.) By the 1760s the continuing association of red body paint and an almost perpetual enmity—later heightened by the War for Independence—made "redskin" the most plausible epithet. Linnaeus's use of red gave additional impetus. Although the reasons for his choice remain obscure, most likely he sought a primary color to parallel the other races' black, white, and yellow. Red was the obvious candidate because Indians used red stains so widely, because of its association with humoral medicine theories, and because it avoided the confusion that might have come from colors such

AMERICA

London, Pub.^d by C&T Stampa & C.º 62 Kirby St.^t Hatton Garden Dec.^t 1 1804.

Fig. 1.2

Emblematic print of "America," 1804. By the early nineteenth century, many
Anglo-Americans saw the Indians as neither noble savages nor symbols of the
American continent. Rather, as this English print suggests, Minerva, the god-
dess of war, now symbolizes America, while the Indian has merged with the
African into a minor motif. Courtesy, Winterthur Museum.

as brown, olive, and tawny, which were sometimes applied to racial subgroups, especially to North Africans and mulattoes and occasionally to European ethnic groups. In any event, Jefferson and some of his contemporaries used "red" as a racial category in the 1770s and 1780s, a trend that spread rapidly. "Indians," "natives," and "savages" continued to be common appelations, but the conviction sown in the third quarter of the eighteenth century that Indians were inherently red took firm root during the next half century. In the middle of the nineteenth century, James Fenimore Cooper's *The Redskins* (1846) and anthropologist Henry Rowe Schoolcraft's *The Red Race in America* (1847) symbolically marked Caucasian America's full recognition, in both fiction and science, of Indians as innately red and racially distinct.[91]

Once red became a viable designation, it seems to have satisfied everyone. To the Indians' bitterest critics, red could signify ferocity, blood, and anger; to their most avid supporters and to the Indians themselves, red could suggest bravery, health, and passion; to those who fell between the judgmental extremes, red could mean almost anything or nothing. In short, red was sufficiently flexible and ambiguous to meet the metaphysical imperatives of a society that did not wholly agree about the Indian's basic character or social and political fate.

The emerging perception of the Indians as innately different and inferior was widespread but not universal. Had it been universal, missionary activity would have languished or expired everywhere; most Indians would have been enslaved or exterminated; and the use of Indians as symbols of America would have stopped abruptly. None of these happened. Despite abundant instances of wholesale disregard for Indian rights and welfare, the late eighteenth and early nineteenth centuries witnessed a lesser but significant countertrend in attitudes toward the Indians that afforded them some protection and kept the hostile view from wholly controlling Indian policy in the new nation.

Hints of the Indian as a noble savage had appeared in the earliest decades of European contact with America, but the concept did not reach major stature until the middle of the eighteenth century in Europe and the early nineteenth century in America. Largely as a reaction against what they considered the corruptions of their own societies, European philosophes sought models of the natural simplicity and order from which "civilized" society supposedly had fallen in its insatiable quest for property and power. Two attractive foils were available: the "Golden Age" of antiquity and aboriginal America. Both were widely used, and in the process the virtues of both were exaggerated. That was perhaps inevitable when writing of the Indians because none of the philosophes had firsthand knowledge of Indian life; in striking contrast to Buffon, they idealized Indian society, although, like Buffon's, their interpretation served their political and intellectual needs. A few European-Americans, especially along the eastern seaboard, adopted similar sentiments.[92] They and others who respected Indian culture—traders and missionaries, for example, whose personal acquaintance with Indians tempered their ethnocentricity, or systematic students of Indian life, such as William Bartram and John Heckwelder—largely resisted the groundswell of racist attitudes toward the Indians. Although pro-Indian sentiment was a minority viewpoint, it had important repercussions: it encouraged the political, educational, and missionary endeavors of the Revolutionary and early national periods that Bernard Sheehan has labeled "Jeffersonian philanthropy."[93]

The noble savage countertrend in American thought insisted that certain Indian characteristics were laudable in their own right and—more important—were especially admirable when compared to contemporary European society. Because the Indians seemed to live an unfettered and unacquisitive life amid unspoiled nature, they were hailed by some Americans (following the philosophes) as the ideal to which modern man should, to some extent at least, return. Because the Indians appeared to be a "vanishing race," they were romanticized in history, art, and literature. Because the Indians were America's most truly native inhabitants, they personified the nation in statues, cartoons, and cartouches.[94]

Even among their supposed supporters, however, the Indians fared badly, as a host of examples from Jefferson through Thomas McKenney and Lewis Cass amply illustrate. Such "friends" of the Indians contended that in the long run the Indian must be thoroughly incorporated into the American mainstream, but increasingly in the nineteenth century the number of such advocates declined and the duration of the Indians' expected tutelage expanded. The Indians, assimilationists argued, must become farmers, landowners, and citizens; they must adopt "white" America's language, laws, and customs. They must cease to be Indians[95]—even if it took centuries to reach that end. Along the way, Indian desires were rarely considered. Although the overwhelming majority wanted to retain their land and their culture, the Eastern tribes had little choice. In the first half of the nineteenth century, the basic options were assimilation or extermination, with removal to the West as a temporary stage in either case.

Some assimilationists advocated miscegenation as the surest path to de-Indianization. Ironically, the biological solution emerged almost simultaneously with laws in many states against Indian-white intermarriage.[96] Such laws hint at hypocrisy and racial intransigence among the majority of Americans and reveal the implausibility of intermarriage as a solution to race relations in nineteenth-century America. But whatever the solution—miscegenation, allotment of farmlands in the East, removal to the West, or education in white-controlled boarding schools—the Indian was marked for gradual extinction by the uneasy coalition of his friends and foes. For both groups, as well as for the bulk of Americans who were neither friend nor foe but merely indifferent, the conviction that the Indians were innately and ineradicably "redmen" underlay their concern, or lack of it, for the Indians' fate. And to most white observers—certainly to the Indians' foes and almost certainly to the millions who scarcely cared—the stereotypical color carried a host of unfavorable associations that prevented the Indians' full assimilation into the Anglo-American community and simultaneously precluded their acceptance as a separate and equal people. Although a few dissenters resisted the prevailing color taxonomy and its correlative racial policies, the surviving literature, both factual and fictional, shows that the Indian was no longer considered a member of the same race; he remained forever distinct in color and character. Even relatively sympathetic spokesmen now believed the Indians to be permanently different. "No Christianizing," declares Natty Bumppo in Cooper's *Pathfinder* (1840), "will ever make even a Delaware [Indian] a white man, nor any whooping and yelling convert a paleface into a red-skin." Bumppo earlier—in *The Prairie* (1827)—puts the same idea more succinctly: "Red natur' is red natur'."[97]

By the middle of the nineteenth century, the dominant (though never universal) shift in Anglo-American perception had reached its logical conclusion: Indian culture was merely a reflection of primordial racial shortcomings and impervious to education or missionization. The Indian was inherently deficient in *character*, which his color proclaimed for all to see. In 1850 the influential *United States Magazine and Democratic Review* could assert as indisputable the "fact that the dark races are utterly incapable of attaining to that intellectual superiority which marks the white race." Four years later, *DeBow's Review* epitomized the antebellum South's attempt to blend racism, ethnography, and polygenesis into a bulwark of white supremacy. "The doctrine of the Unity of the Race, so long believed by the world," one writer insisted, "is ascertained to be false. We are not all descended from one pair of human beings. . . . The negro till the end of time will still be a negro, and the Indian still an Indian." Nor should the white race meddle with a situation beyond its control. Another essayist in *DeBow's* drew the obvious lesson from nearly a century of racist thought: The Indian's "race is run, and probably he has performed his earthly mission. He is gradually disappearing, to give place to a higher order of beings. The order of nature must have its course."[98] A popular pseudoscientific study, *Types of Mankind* (1854), was less philosophical: "[I]t is in vain to talk of civilizing [the Indians]. You might as well attempt to change the nature of the buffalo." Given such nineteenth-century sentiments, based on a pervasive perception of Indians as inherently dark, incurably savage, and intrinsically non-American, the Indians' subsequent plight comes as no surprise.

CHAPTER TWO

Early English Paradigms
for New World Natives

Perceptions of people unlike ourselves are not made in a cultural vacuum. Each observer brings to his or her contact with an "other" certain assumptions or expectations that determine to a large extent our initial attitudes toward people outside our own group. Some of the shaping preconceptions are individual, that is, based on the observer's particular experiences; others are collective—national or regional or even continental—for they draw on an extended society's, rather than an individual's, prior contact with similar beings or prior assumptions about people of other cultural groups. This essay is about the rise and fall of several fundamental perceptions that a large portion of the English people and their compatriots who moved to British America held in the sixteenth and early seventeenth centuries as they contemplated the New World's natives.

The evidence for such paradigmatic perceptions comes almost exclusively from fragmentary literary and pictorial remains. We can only glimpse how the English and English Americans several centuries ago perceived the Indians by reading what they wrote, seeing what they drew, and reconstructing how they acted. This essay focuses especially on the first two kinds of evidence for clues to the reasoning behind British colonial policies that are explored elsewhere in this book.

I delivered a condensed version of this essay to a meeting of the American Antiquarian Society, held at the John Carter Brown Library of Brown University, in April 1992. A longer version was published in the Proceedings of the American Antiquarian Society *102 (October 1992): 33–67, and is reprinted here with the editor's permission. I have made only a few minor adjustments to the text and notes except in section III, where the changes are somewhat more substantial. Some of the original version's illustrations are omitted.*

ᕙ

Even before christopher columbus returned from his revolutionary voyage of 1492–93, he began to describe for European readers the people he had encountered on the other side of the world. At times

34

he portrayed the Indians in some detail, generalizing, to be sure, but avoiding stereotypical images. At other times he resorted to descriptive shorthand, saving time and space by comparing the unknown inhabitants of America and their customs with images familiar to Europeans. The Indians' skin, for example, he likened to "the colour of the Canary Islanders"; their hair was coarse "like that of a horse's tail"; their paddles were shaped "like a baker's shovel"—images that were essentially neutral and probably helpful to readers back home.[1] But after Columbus, European observers increasingly described the Indians in more emblematic terms, casting them as representative human or quasi-human figures. Such identifying metaphors were usually freighted with moral or political judgments and functioned more as prescriptions than as descriptions, as paradigms for how Europeans should perceive American natives and, implicitly at least, how Europeans should treat them.[2] Almost invariably, perhaps inevitably, the proposed paradigms abetted European misunderstanding of American natives and often encouraged catastrophic colonial policies toward the Indians, in which Europeans treated New World natives as if they really were the types to which they were rhetorically compared.

This essay explores some of the paradigms on which English commentators drew in the era from Columbus's first voyage until the late seventeenth century.[3] Space precludes a consideration of all the paradigms invoked in Tudor-Stuart England; instead, the focus here is on five models that flourished at various times during those two centuries and that embodied England's groping efforts to comprehend the peoples of the New World: (1) the mythical wild men of medieval and Renaissance lore; (2) the imaginary monsters of antiquity and after; (3) the Irish of the sixteenth and seventeenth centuries; (4) the "old Britons" of fourth-century A.D. England; and (5) the Lost Tribes of ancient Israel. The first two models were handy initial images, universally recognized in late medieval Europe and easily, though inaccurately, applied to the newly encountered peoples. The latter three paradigms were English inventions—late sixteenth- and early seventeenth-century models contrived by imperial spokesmen when New World natives suddenly assumed a significant role in England's public discourse. Until then, the wild man and monster served the English much as they served all of Europe.

I

No generic figure, real or imaginary, had more "name recognition" in Renaissance Europe than the wild man. His national name varied from place to place: *wildeman* in Germany, *l'homme sauvage* in France, *uomo selvaggio* in Italy, wild man, woodwose, and green man in England. By whatever label, he was a ubiquitous figure in European folklore, pageantry, prose, poetry, drama, song, painting, sculpture, tapestry, and book illustration.⁴ Probably everyone in Europe, regardless of rank, location, or age, acknowledged wild men to be integral parts of his or her world. Few people claimed to have seen wild men, but they were too notorious and too frequent in the era's texts, iconography, and folklore to be doubted for a moment.

A minor strand in wild-man lore painted him in benign hues, uncivilized but gentle, often accompanied by a comparably naked and hirsute wife and child. More often the wild man was portrayed as a savage—a crude, rude, forest creature, untamed and untrustworthy. He was easily recognized by his nakedness, for he was clad only in abundant body hair and shaggy beard. He lived in a cave or crude hut; he bludgeoned his prey with a sturdy club; he lived on raw meat, wild fruit, and other forest fare, though in his most bestial manifestations he devoured human flesh. He assaulted anyone who intruded on his secluded world and ravished women who came within his grasp. He was godless, lacked right reason, and was inclined to evil rather than good (Fig. 2.1). Late in the sixteenth century, Edmund Spenser's *Faerie Queene* captured the essence of the "wilde and saluage man . . . all ouergrowne with hair" so familiar to Renaissance readers,

> With huge great teeth, like to a tusked Bore:
> For he liv'd all on ravin and on rape
> Of men and beasts; and fed on fleshly gore,
> The signe whereof yet stain'd his bloudy lips afore.⁵

Those bloody lips usually were unintelligible too, able to utter only a few guttural sounds. But if the wild man lacked social and linguistic refinements, he had extraordinary sexual prowess, physical strength, and knowledge of nature's secrets. The wild man was Europe's "other," the symbol of incivility, of near bestiality, of untamed nature against which the presumably civilized citizens of the sixteenth and seventeenth centuries measured and congratulated themselves.

Superficial connections between the wild man and the American Indian sprang readily to European minds. Most obvious was the Indians' habitation in a distant, unknown region. As Hayden White has observed in a different context, wild men were always "associated with . . . the wilderness—the desert, forest, jungle, and mountains—those parts of the physical world that had not yet been domesticated."⁶ To Europeans, America seemed to be just that: the distant jungle and forest ("desert" and "wilderness" were the era's common terms) that Europeans had not yet subdued. The natives of that strange, distant, and uncivilized land *must* be wild men and hence must share with the European branch of the family tree the usual list of wild-man traits. From Columbus on, European narratives of America emphasized Indian characteristics that mirrored the wild men's deplored qualities: nakedness and cannibalism especially, but also an unintelligible language (to European ears), a lack

Fig. 2.1
The wild man as cannibal or werewolf. Woodcut, c. 1510–15 by Lucas Cranach
the Elder. The Metropolitan Museum of Art, Harris Brisbane Dick Fund, 1942
(42.45.1).

of religion (by European definitions), and a reputed sexual libertinism
(by European standards).[7] This was a mangled image, of course; it homogenized disparate Indian cultures; it stressed their worst features, distorted other features, and overlooked the Indians' many virtues. But the
wild-man image of Indians spread rapidly through Europe, partly because the explorers so often arrived with wild-man expectations and

partly because European listeners' and readers' preconceived notions
of the wild man encouraged them to add wild-man characteristics to
their mental picture of the Indian as soon as a few truly similar characteristics—nakedness, most obviously—were put before them.

The assumption that Indians were American wild men emerged early
and lasted long, despite abundant evidence to the contrary. Indian hairi-
ness is a case in point. Columbus reported that the natives had remarkably little hair, which other early firsthand accounts confirmed, yet
for decades, European engravings of Indians frequently portrayed them
with profuse beards or considerable body hair. A flagrant example is the
illustration in a 1505 edition of Amerigo Vespucci's *De Novo Mundo*,
which vividly contradicts the author's earlier insistence that the Indians
"have no hair whatever on their bodies."[8]

European accounts of the Indians sometimes used the term "wild,"
but more often they substituted other labels that had been applied to
the mythical forest dweller. In any case, the paradigm was unmistakable.
Indians, like wild men, were perceived as "uncivil," "barbarian,"
"brutish," and "savage." Similarly, European commentators' numerous
lists of qualities the Indians supposedly lacked implicitly employed the
paradigm: they had no laws, no morals, no personal property, no government, no reasonableness, and so on and on.[9] In sum, American natives shared enough presumed characteristics with Europe's mythical
"other" to make European observers of Native Americans imagine the
conventional wild-man traits even where they emphatically did not exist. Europeans back home, getting information mainly through word of
mouth over vast distances, were even more prone to plug the few reported facts into a preconceived model. Eventually, as the reports from
America accumulated and became more accurate, and as Indians in Europe became more commonplace—as slaves or curiosities or emissaries
to European governments—a truer picture of the Indians emerged on
the Continent and in England. But the process was slow and uneven. In
English pageantry, Indians often resembled wild men far into the seventeenth century.

II

Wild men, of course, were imaginary in that none really existed. Still,
they were perceived as primarily human in appearance and in salvage-
ability: given the right encouragement and a change in environment,
they could become good citizens. Many wild men, in fact, were reputed
to be fallen men—backsliders, who escaped to the forest for some traumatic reason and who could be reclaimed by the love of a maiden or a
forgiving society.[10] Not so the true monsters of ancient and medieval
lore. Whereas wild men were essentially human despite some beastly
characteristics, monsters were essentially bestial, with some human attributes of body or mind. And if wild men inhabited the nearby forests,
monsters lived in more remote places—the ocean deep, for example,

or far, far into the land, in what John Donne called "the round earth's imagined corners."[11]

Few people doubted the monsters' existence, even though such creatures, like wild men, rarely showed their faces but were always over the next ridge or in the next river valley. Sightings at sea, on the other hand, were not unusual, probably prompted by dolphins, whales, floating debris, or moonbeams on the water. Such evidence only corroborated Greek and Roman authorities, especially Pliny the Elder's *Natural History*, and medieval authorities, especially Saint Augustine's *City of God*. Several English editions of Pliny's works appeared in the sixteenth and seventeenth centuries and must have been widely read by educated men and women; surely Renaissance enthusiasm for classical writers reinforced existing notions of creatures without heads or with several heads, with scales and fins, or with a single foot that served as an umbrella.[12] In the early seventeenth century, Edward Topsell's heavily illustrated books on the world's quadrupeds and serpents, although skeptical of most undocumented sightings, included some imaginary species.[13] And for the less educated reader, cheap and sensational pamphlets pandered to the age's fascination with monsters of every kind and purpose.[14]

Columbus's voyage opened a new hemisphere for monster lairs, and new sightings came quickly. Some were of giants, some of mermen, some of human bodies with dog-shaped heads.[15] Not that any well-informed European (many, of course, were not well informed) believed that all Indians were monsters, at least of the grotesque types. Columbus had squelched that rumor on his return from America in 1493. He had not, he assured anxious readers, "found the human monsters which many people expected." Yet Columbus planted the seeds for the very supposition he denied. His Indian informants told him that on one island the people had tails and that on another island they ate their captives, stories that Columbus passed along without denying—because he could not—their veracity.[16] It was a short step from believing in such inhuman humans to assuming that the headless Blemmyae of classical lore prospered in America.[17] Predictably, the Blemmyae and other bizarre monsters appear frequently and graphically on maps, in book illustrations, and in other American iconography. Several English narratives of the sixteenth and early seventeenth centuries lent credence to the legends. The redoubtable Walter Ralegh, as late as 1596, told of monsters in Guiana with "eyes in their shoulders, and their mouths in the middle of their breasts." No, he hadn't actually seen any, he admitted, but after repeated confirmation of their existence by his native friends, "I am resolved it is true."[18]

As the probability faded that America harbored grotesque monsters—except, perhaps, the headless anthropophagi—the suspicion grew that Indians might be outwardly human but inwardly monstrous. Pope Paul's bull of 1537 and the pleadings of Bishop las Casas in the 1550s had tried to establish definitively that Indians were true humans, but doubts persisted.[19] A frequent refrain in European writings admitted that Indians looked like humans but lacked essential human qualities. An English tribute to explorer Martin Frobisher, for example, lauded his expeditions of the 1570s to lands

> Where dreadfull daungers are not scarce,
>   where pleasures few are found,
> Where savage beastes devoyde of sense,
>   doe runne like men on ground.[20]

Three decades later, the Reverend Robert Gray articulated the same persistent sentiment: the Indians in Virginia, he advised his readers, are "worse than those beasts which are of most wild and savage nature."[21]

Such notions of Indian monstrosity in character and habits rather than in form were spurred by frequent and exaggerated accounts of New World cannibalism. To Europeans, cannibalism was ipso facto monstrous; if Indians were cannibals, Indians were monsters. This logic, combined with the suspicion that Indians were too cruel to be human (while turning a blind eye to their own forms of cruelty), encouraged Europeans to resort almost instinctively to the monster paradigm during peaks of animosity against American natives. Samuel Purchas, clergyman and the younger Hakluyt's successor as England's principal literary propagandist, proclaimed in the aftermath of the Powhatan uprising of 1622 that the Indians of Virginia had "little of Humanitie but shape [and were] . . . more brutish then the beasts they hunt"; in the throes of New England's worst Indian war, a colonial poet dubbed the enemy "bruitish wolves," crueler than "Bears & panthers"; the Reverend Cotton Mather variously decried the same natives as "*Indian Dragons*," "horrid *Cannibals*," "*Devils Incarnate*," and "the most beastly and bloody things that ever wore the Shape of *Men*."[22]

Despite some superficial similarities, the monster paradigm functioned differently than its wild-man counterpart. The latter had initially been Europe's image of all Indians; and if it was fundamentally pejorative, it nonetheless was flexible enough to acknowledge benign characteristics and even to evolve in the eighteenth century into the noble savage image.[23] The monster paradigm, by contrast, was not a description of the norm but instead a wholly pejorative metaphor, a verbal excess, an excoriation of Indians at their imagined worst. The perception of Indians-as-monsters existed alongside Indians-as-wild-men throughout the sixteenth century and faded rapidly thereafter, although in America the paradigm enjoyed a long and inglorious career as a sporadic militant metaphor.[24]

III

By the final quarter of the sixteenth century, English interest in America had begun to catch up to the Continent's. Prodded by the two Richard Hakluyts and a handful of other literary imperialists, English officials and especially English investors began to appreciate America's usefulness. The available territory between Spanish Florida and French Canada did not contain precious metals to be mined (though the hope persisted), or Indian cities to be plundered, or a vast native population to be exploited for labor and tribute, but as a place to settle England's surplus population, to produce mundane raw materials, to attack Spanish fleets or ports, and to promulgate the gospel to the heathen, the middle latitudes of North America had impressive potential. To achieve the desired goals, however, the natives must be addressed as integral to empire building and confronted as realities rather than abstractions. The English now had compelling reasons to contrive their own, largely self-serving, paradigms for understanding New World natives.

Historians have recently argued that in the second half of the sixteenth century and well into the seventeenth, Ireland was England's principal paradigm for the conquest of America. "The colonization of Ireland," writes Bernard Bailyn, ". . . provided England with its model for permanent overseas settlement," a model that many scholars find especially pertinent to English perceptions and treatment of the Indians.[25] The gist of the interpretation is that when English efforts to reconquer Ireland in the 1560s met with formidable resistance, the ethnocentric English deepened still further their contempt for Irish ways and beliefs, labeling them barbarian, savage, bestial. A few decades later, when the English first encountered American Indians on a substantial scale, colonists and commentators saw them as overseas Irishmen: "English treatment of the American Indians . . . has its origins in their attitudes toward tribal Irishmen."[26] The Irish, in short, served the English in a similar but more specific way than wild men had earlier served all of Europe—a readily recognizable pejorative paradigm.

The attributes the English thought they saw in both the Irish and Indians included nakedness, animal-skin clothing (where necessary), ferociousness, licentiousness, and drunkenness.[27] Facilitating the projection of these assumed Irish shortcomings onto the Indians, according to modern champions of the Irish paradigm, was involvement in both Irish and American colonization schemes by a sizable set of promoters, explorers, and settlers: Walter Ralegh, Humphrey Gilbert, Ralph Lane, Lord De La Warr, and others. They initially served English imperialism in Ireland, where they abhorred the natives for not instantly adopting English theology and customs and for resisting English rule. Later, in America, English officers saw uncooperative Indians in the same unflattering light, applied to them the same disparaging epithets, and accorded them the same brutal treatment. Howard Mumford Jones summed up the Irish-American connection: "[T]he doctrine that the only good Indian is a dead Indian first took shape . . . in the doctrine that the only good wild Irishman is a dead wild Irishman. . . . Used to savagery in the one place, [the English] looked for it, they provoked it, in the other."[28]

The argument, I suggest, has some validity but is often exaggerated. That some observers of Britain's imperial ventures drew parallels between the relatively familiar Irish and the relatively unknown Indian worlds is indisputable and unsurprising. There may have been, too, a formative experience for Ralph Lane and a few other Englishmen who toiled for an appreciable time in Ireland and then in America, but the lists of parallels invoked and men involved are short. Perhaps American colonists acquired vicariously the lessons that a few Englishmen had learned firsthand, but if so it seems to have made little dent in the colonial consciousness.[29] Rather, the evidence points to a handful of Irish-Indian similarities, most of them incidental, but rarely to a formative model. Historians who argue for a shaping Irish precedent are barking in the wrong bog.

Early English analogies between the Irish and Indians focused principally on clothing and shelter. Writers on both sides of the Atlantic sometimes likened Indian houses to Irish hovels and described Indian clothing as "Irish-like mantles." Critics of the Indians also occasionally castigated Indians for doing—or not doing—various things that Englishmen considered typical of the Irish: for living like nomads and practicing sorcery, for example, or for not manuring their fields or fencing their lands. Indian character, in English eyes, also suggested some highly pejorative parallels: treachery, lechery, superstition. In 1646 the Reverend Hugh Peter, who had spent six years in New England, proposed a military parallel, but his advice was for the Old World rather than the New. Explaining how Cromwell's army could conquer Ireland, Peter opined that "The wild *Irish* and the *Indian* doe not much differ, and therefore should be handled alike"—to wit, "burne up the Enemies provisions every where." Peter probably had in mind the scorched-earth tactics used successfully in Virginia (1622–32) and Connecticut (1636–37).[30]

In sum, from an English perspective, the Irish and Indians were comparably uncivilized and un-Christian and in certain situations should be viewed, and treated, accordingly (see Fig. 2.2). But a similar judgment applied, in English eyes, to much of the world's population. As an English schoolmaster lamented in 1622, ignorance of true religion and sound learning promoted "inhumanitie" in "the Irish, the Virgineans, and all other barbarous nations."[31] The Irish happened to be the nearest "barbarians" of significance to the English; Native Americans were the most distant.

If colonial Ireland had been colonial America's principal model, and if the Irish had been a paradigm for the Indians, the surviving literature would not, presumably, be so silent on both subjects. England's leading imperialists—the two Hakluyts, George Peckham, John Smith, Samuel Purchas, and their contemporaries—wrote much about colonization but extremely little about Ireland's relevance to America. They rarely devoted a whole sentence, never a whole treatise, to the subject.[32]

The labels within the illustration read:
The Gentleman of Ireland · The Gentlewoman of Ireland
The Civill Irish Woman · The Civill Irish man
The Wilde Irish man · The Wilde Irish Woman

Fig. 2.2
Irish men and women of the early seventeenth century. Border illustrations to map of Ireland in John Speed, *The Theatre of the Empire of Great Britain* (London, 1611). The "Gentleman" and "Gentlewoman" were probably intended by the artist to be Anglo-Irish rather than native Irish. Reproduced by permission of the Huntington Library, San Marino, California.

43

The reason, I submit, is that the men concerned with England's overseas expansion were too aware of the profound differences between the
Irish and American peoples, and between the Irish and American colonial contexts, to expend much ink on minor parallels. Judging from the
literary and pictorial evidence, the Irish experience played a far lesser
role in shaping English thinking about colonization and native inhabitants than did the Spanish experience in America (a large topic in its
own right), which served some English observers as a positive model
and—just as important—served others as a negative paradigm.[33] That
said, it is nonetheless true that in the early decades of English America,
occasional Irish parallels helped English readers to form handy, if often
distorted, images of the newly encountered natives and their customs.[34]

IV

Another idea spawned by England's expansion into America had a more
tangible influence on English images of the Indians. Like the other paradigms considered here—indeed like extended metaphors at any time
and place—this new model surfaced, spread, then disappeared in keeping with its users' conscious or subconscious needs. The wild man and
the monster served Europeans effectively as long as Indians were considered largely in the abstract and as long as the basic questions about
them remained elementary: What do they look like? Are they human?
Are they incorrigible cannibals? When answers to the fundamental questions gained general acceptance, those paradigms lost their interpretive
power, except—as noted earlier—for rhetorical or theatrical flourishes.

By the time England joined the race for New World colonies, its imperialists and prospective colonists needed paradigms that addressed
more subtle and more specifically English concerns about the Indians,
especially about their character and malleability. Were they amenable
to English control? Would they barter gladly and, from the English standpoint, profitably? Did they crave the English variety of Christianity? (The
English were sure that the Indians had overwhelmingly rejected Spanish Catholicism, but Protestantism—Anglican or Puritan—might be another matter.) Would the Indians adopt English customs of agriculture,
education, family structure, dress, and speech?

If English colonization of North America were to be successful and
peaceful, England needed Indians who could be gently subdued, gradually converted to English ways, and eventually absorbed into Anglo-
American society. In 1587, the younger Hakluyt expressed a widespread
late-sixteenth-century English assumption that "no greater glory can be
handed down [to posterity] than to conquer the barbarian, to recall the
savage and the pagan to civility, to draw the ignorant within the orbit of
reason, and to fill with reverence for divinity the godless and the un-
godly."[35] Hakluyt and many of his contemporaries had no doubt that

they could do just that to the Indians. Accordingly, a new notion of Indian pliability emerged in the 1580s, initially in reports on England's efforts at colonization on Roanoke Island off the Carolina coast and later in the promotional literature of early Virginia.[36] The principal symbolic players in this new paradigm were the Englishman's own ancestors—the Picts and Britons who inhabited the island when Julius Caesar and the Roman legions imposed their brand of civility in the early centuries after Christ.[37]

The first significant application of this paradigm to the Indians appeared in the second edition (1590) of Thomas Hariot's *Briefe and True Report* on the Roanoke colony.[38] Hariot had accompanied the expedition of 1585–86 as resident scientist, cartographer, ethnologist, and interpreter, having learned a smattering of the Algonquian language from two Indians carried to England a year before.[39] Hariot's pamphlet, first published in quarto in 1588, had no illustrations; two years later, it was reissued in folio by the Flemish Protestant publisher Theodor de Bry, lavishly illustrated with his engravings of watercolor paintings by John White. The latter had also been on the Roanoke expedition and would return as governor of the 1587 colonial effort; in 1585–86 and possibly in 1584, White sketched almost everything he saw—flora, fauna, and especially Indians. Scholars now praise White's Roanoke paintings as accurate and significant contributions to anthropology, art history, botany, literature, and zoology.[40]

Rarely mentioned by modern writers, except as a curiosity, is the de Bry edition's appendix: five large pictures—three of Picts and two of their neighbors. According to the *Briefe and True Report*, White found illustrations of these early Britons "*in a oolld English cronicle*" and rendered copies in watercolor for de Bry, who then made engravings—somewhat mannered and embellished—for the new edition of Hariot's book.[41] The purpose of the pictures, according to Hariot (or perhaps the younger Hakluyt, who may have written the captions) was "*to showe how that the Inhabitants of the great Bretannie have bin in times past as sauvage as those of Virginia.*"[42] To emphasize the point, White and de Bry made the ancient English appear more barbarous and ferocious than the Indians portrayed in the main section of Hariot's book: one Pictish man is wholly naked (not even a loincloth), hideously tattooed from head to foot; his right hand holds a dripping head, and another severed head lies on the ground. The women appear less militant than the men but are almost as bare-skinned and ostensibly uncouth (Figs. 2.3 and 2.4). The implication is clear: henceforth the reader should think of the Indians of North America in terms of his or her own ancestors—those barbarous, heathen primitives who might have remained in idolatry and ignorance had not Roman soldiers introduced them to Christianity and European civility. A new paradigmatic trend was under way.

Evidence of the Indian-as-old-Briton echoed repeatedly in England's early-seventeenth-century imperialist literature. In 1610, for example,

Fig. 2.3

"Picte" man, engraved by Theodor de Bry from a watercolor by John White, as an illustration in Thomas Hariot, *A Briefe and True Report of the Newfound Land of Virginia* (Frankfort, 1590). Courtesy, American Antiquarian Society.

Fig. 2.4
"A Women nig[b]hour to the Pictes" in the same book. Courtesy, American Antiquarian Society.

the Reverend William Crashaw preached to the Virginia Company of London that

> the time was when wee were as savage and uncivill, and worshipped the divill, as now they do, then God sent some to make us civill, and others to make us christians. If such had not been sent us we had yet continued wild and uncivill, and worshippers of the divell: . . . [S]hall we not be sensible of those that are still as we were then?[43]

A broadside ballad, issued in London in 1612 to raise money for the Virginia colony through an English lottery, expressed a similar sentiment (to be sung "To the tune of Lusty Gallant"):

> Who knowes not *England* once was like
> a Wildernesse and savage place,
> Till government and use of men,
> that wildnesse did deface:
> And so *Virginia* may in time,
> be made like England now;
> Where long-lovd peace and plenty both,
> sits smiling on her brow.[44]

Use of the old Britons paradigm reached its apogee in the 1620s, with Samuel Purchas its most prominent proponent. He incorporated the image in his monumental anthology of travel narratives, *Purchas His Pilgrimes*, by asking in an editorial marginal note: "Were not wee our selves made and not borne civill in our Progenitors dayes? and were not *Caesars Britaines* as brutish as *Virginians?*" (By Virginians, Purchas meant Indians of the Chesapeake region, though critics of the English settlement at Jamestown thought the colonists were brutish as well.) Almost simultaneous with Purchas's pronouncement, a promotional tract for English colonization asserted that "the old *Brittons* . . . were as rude and barbarous" as the Indians; rather than despise them because of their present condition, the English should pity them and hope "within short time, [to] win them to our owne will, and frame them as we list."[45]

Spokesmen on the American side of England's fledgling empire drew on the same paradigm. After several years in Virginia, William Strachey believed that

> Had not this violence, and this Injury, bene offred unto us by the Romanis, . . . even by *Julius Caesar* himself . . . we might yet have lyved [like] overgrowne Satyrs, rude, and untutred, wandring in the woodes, dwelling in Caves, and hunting for our dynners, (as the wyld beasts in the forrests for their prey,) prostetuting our daughters to straungers, sacrificing our Children to our Idolls, nay eating our owne Children, as did the Scots in those dayes. . . .[46]

These frequent invocations of the ancient Britons (many more could be cited) carried a dual message: first, and most obvious, was the paradigm that has been explicated here—that Indians should be thought of as fundamentally like the British themselves except for their backwardness in religious beliefs and behavior; both shortcomings could be rectified if the colonists converted and educated the Indians for their own good. The other message, equally significant for the future of Anglo-Indian relations, was that armed force, such as Caesar had used, might well be necessary. Purchas put the case bluntly in another editorial aside: "The *Romane* swords were [the] best teachers of civilitie."[47] No wonder the record of English colonization contains so much bloodshed. No wonder either that the paradigm's gentler side eroded rapidly when Indian resistance, both military and cultural, convinced English imperialists that American natives were not as malleable as the Britons (by hindsight) had been. Especially in the Chesapeake Bay area, where the paradigm was born and where it received most of its endorsements, the image of the Indians soured quickly after the Powhatan uprising of 1622.[48] The paradigm's hopeful message had proved illusory, and with its principal point no longer viable, the old Britons model of the American Indian slowly faded from use.[49]

V

The final rhetorical model to be considered here had a more benign origin and outcome. Although it emerged in England and America soon after the old Britons model had run its course, the notion that the American Indians were lineal descendants of one or more of the ten Lost Tribes of Israel was less a successor to the previous paradigm than it was a New England–focused counterpart. It was optimistic in that, like the old Britons model, it assumed the Indians to be ripe for conversion; it was benign in that it encouraged the colonists to "uplift" rather than enslave or exterminate them.

The authority for the Lost Tribes paradigm was not an "*oolld English cronicle*" or national memory but the far more compelling authority of Holy Writ—at least Holy Writ as some Christians interpreted certain Old Testament passages and some Jews interpreted several sacred texts. To Christian theorists, the conversion of the Jews was a necessary first step toward the final millennium; many Jews believed that the regathering of the dispersed Jews in Israel would herald the arrival of the Messiah. These millennial and messianic strands of eschatology came into brief and cordial conjunction in the 1640s and helped to shape English beliefs about the Indians for nearly two decades. Thereafter, the Lost Tribes paradigm faded rapidly from the limelight but resurfaced from time to time in the remainder of the colonial era and still survives.[50]

Until Ferdinand Magellan's expedition circumnavigated the globe in 1521–22, the issue of Indian origins was moot: the Americans were, presumably, Asians. Doubts nonetheless proliferated, and once the Western Hemisphere's remoteness from the Asian continent was established, Eu-

ropean theorists began to debate the vexing question of where the Indians had come from.[51] It was now axiomatic that the Indians were the
New World's earliest immigrants, for Genesis established definitively that
all humans were descended from Adam and Eve and subsequently from
Noah's sons. Japhet's heirs were popularly believed to have settled in
Europe, Shem's in Asia, and Cham's in Africa. From which of these
strands did the Indians descend and by what route(s) did they reach the
New World? The answer, some argued, was that after the Assyrians forced
the Ten Tribes from Israel in the eighth century B.C., one or more of
them, or parts of them, pushed slowly eastward into Tartaria and eventually, perhaps after many centuries, crossed onto the North American
continent and dispersed throughout the New World. Some advocates of
this theory claimed that *only* the Lost Tribes came to America; others
accepted the Indians' Hebrew lineage but not their Lost Tribes origin;
still others said that the Jews, whatever their tribal affiliation, shared
American settlement with other Old World peoples. In any case, during
the long migration across Asia and America, the Jews' religious and cultural traditions gradually eroded, hence the uncertainty in recognizing
the Indians' true origins.

In the sixteenth century, several Spanish missionaries, including the
great Dominican, Bartolomé de Las Casas and the near-great Francis-
can Bernardino de Sahagún, speculated on the possibility that the Indians might be Jews, but the prospect stirred little enthusiasm in Spain
and elsewhere; the Spanish court, unsympathetic to Jews in any guise,
found the theory intolerable and tried to suppress it.[52] As a paradigm
for understanding or manipulating Indians, the Lost Tribes explanation
apparently served no useful purpose.

Nearly a century later, it appealed strongly to many Englishmen, especially to Puritans, who emphasized the preeminence of biblical authority and, in many cases, the imminence of the millennium.[53] In the
1640s, when several strands of millennialism flourished in England,
some clergymen and their followers concluded that if the Indians were
Jews a golden opportunity was at hand to convert them quickly to Christianity and thereby hasten the Judgment Day; God would hardly have
put the Jews in so convenient a location if He had not intended His people to see the message and seize the opportunity. So thought the Reverend Thomas Thorowgood, a Presbyterian minister in Norfolk, England, who in about 1646 began to write *Iewes in America; or Probabilities
that the Americans Are of That Race,* published in 1650.[54] Almost simultaneously, Rabbi Menasseh ben Israel of Amsterdam reached a similar conclusion, though for different theological reasons, and the two men—
brought together by a mutual friend and fellow Lost Tribes advocate,
John Durie—began to correspond.[55] Soon an important third party
joined the international network: the Reverend John Eliot of Roxbury,
Massachusetts. He had learned about the Thorowgood/ben Israel position from a fellow New Englander, Plymouth's Edward Winslow, who

in the late 1640s was raising funds in England for Eliot's missionary program.[56] Menasseh ben Israel shared with Thorowgood and Eliot the basic contention that the Indians were descended from the Lost Tribes;
the English edition of his *Hope of Israel* endorsed emphatically the theory "*that the first inhabitants of America, were the ten Tribes of the* Israelites."[57]
The rabbi differed, of course, from his Christian correspondents in the
desired outcome of English colonization. They wanted to make the Indians into neo-English Protestants; he hoped for their return to the Jewish fold.

For both camps, the linchpin of the Lost Tribes paradigm was the
long catalogue of Indian "rites, fashions, ceremonies, and opinions" that
presumably disclosed their Jewish origins. Cases in point were the Indians' use of parables, their sequestration of women during menstruation,
certain words that sounded to credible ears much like Hebrew words,
and especially the practice of circumcision. The latter custom was,
Thorowgood insisted, "the mainest point of Jewish Religion." But evidence of the Indians' Jewish practices would be persuasive in England
and elsewhere in Europe only if corroborated by Englishmen in America who knew native customs well; hence Thorowgood incorporated a
letter from Roger Williams in the first edition of his book, one from
John Eliot in the second.[58]

Eliot had not initially subscribed to the Lost Tribes theory—perhaps
had never seriously considered it—until informed by Winslow of
Thorowgood's ruminations. In any event, Eliot quickly took up the cause
and in the early 1650s wrote a long open letter of support that Thorowgood published in 1660 as an appendix to the second edition of his *Jews
in America*. Eliot's letter was an exhaustive exegesis of certain biblical
passages; they persuaded him that some of the Indians were descended
from the Lost Tribes, the rest from a tribe that had never been "lost"
but had, over the centuries, migrated eastward through Asia to America. Eliot provided no list of parallel Indian/Jewish words or customs,
for Scripture itself demonstrated that "these naked *Americans* are *He-
brewes*."[59]

Leaving aside the complicated theological issues that so absorbed Eliot
and Menasseh ben Israel, the new paradigm was important to both men
because, for the former, it encouraged English philanthropists to contribute heavily toward the missionization of the New England Indians
since it would hasten the millennium as well as promote Puritan notions
of civility; for the latter, it furthered the movement to readmit the Jews
to England because (among many reasons) Protestant millennialists
could thereby gain access to additional potential converts.[60] (In 1290,
more than two hundred years before Spain's expulsion of Jews in the
year Columbus reached America, King Edward I ousted them from England.) In the end, Menasseh's hope was only partly fulfilled: Jews were
not officially readmitted, though unofficially they returned in appreciable numbers in the 1650s and thereafter. At the same time, in old

and New England, the Lost Tribes paradigm invigorated long-delayed missionary efforts. With financial help from English believers, Eliot created more than a dozen "praying towns"—communities of Indian converts who left their tribal homes and traditionalist relatives to join in Christian fellowship and who gradually adopted English ways of dress, housing, and farming. But fittingly for descendants of the ancient Jews, Eliot organized their government along Old Testament guidelines, appointing rulers of tens and hundreds.[61]

The Lost Tribes paradigm enjoyed a relatively short boom. About two decades after it first appeared in England, the theory of Jewish origins had few active advocates, partly because the paradigm's greatest champions passed from the scene: in 1655 Winslow succumbed to disease in the English campaign against Jamaica, and in 1657 Menasseh ben Israel died, brokenhearted, en route to Holland after pleading the Jews' case to Oliver Cromwell.[62] Thorowgood lived to 1669 but was silent (at least in print) after 1660. Eliot lived until 1690, but as early as the mid-1650s his enthusiasm seems to have waned. Although his missionary work continued with undiminished vigor, he ceased to give public support to the Lost Tribes explanation of Indian origins.[63] Not that he discarded it altogether; as his fellow Puritan clergyman Cotton Mather wrote in a biographical sketch of Eliot, the apostle to the Indians "was willing a little to indulge himself" in the "wish" that the Indians were dispersed Israelites and continued to find cultural parallels for which, Mather quipped, Eliot believed there were "*thorowgood* Reasons." Until the end of his life, Mather implies, Eliot's attachment to the Lost Tribes theory wavered but did not break.[64]

Eliot's enthusiasm for the theory may have eroded in light of his own experience and counterattacks by skeptics. Chief among the latter was Hamon L'Estrange, whose book of 1652, *Americans no Jewes, or Improbabilities that the Americans Are of that Race*, argued that the supposed Jewish customs exhibited by the Indians were figments of wishful thinking that withered under close scrutiny. L'Estrange insisted, for example, that instances of cannibalism among the ancient Jews (cited by Thorowgood) were rare and from necessity, whereas "the barbarous custome of the Americans is a nationall helluonisme innatured by fierce malice and fewde, . . . an habituall practise and delight in eating mans flesh."[65] Probably Eliot also lost confidence in the Indians' Jewish origin as he increasingly understood the natives of eastern New England and their languages. He lived too close to the Indians—especially at the praying town of Natick—not to see that their customs bore only superficial resemblance to Jewish practices; he was too good a linguist of both Hebrew and Algonquian to be misled by false verbal similarities; and he was too keen an observer not to notice, sooner or later, that most of the proposed parallels were simply not true. Circumcision, for example, was not a custom among New England Indians, despite a report to the contrary that for a time Eliot had taken to be accurate.[66]

With the list of supposed Jewish customs among the Indians sharply reduced, Eliot could no longer endorse the Lost Tribes theory with his earlier sureness, and without Eliot's enthusiastic support, the Jewish paradigm in England was severely damaged unless new experts on Indian culture offered new evidence. None did. Advocates of the paradigm appeared later in the century—William Penn, for example, and, in the eighteenth century, the Indian trader and administrator James Adair—but they expressed faith more than facts.[67] As a significant paradigm for English perceptions of the Indians, the end had come in the 1660s. Millennial-minded New Englanders continued to wonder about the fate of the Lost Tribes and about the origin of the Indians, but they were not persuaded that the two questions had the same answer. About the time of Eliot's conversion to the Lost Tribes paradigm, the New England poet Anne Bradstreet had expressed a more skeptical view:

> Where now those ten Tribes are, can no man tell,
> Or how they fare, rich, poor, or ill or well;
> Whether the *Indians* of the East, or West,
> Or wild *Tartarians*, as yet ne're blest,
> Or else those *Chinoes* rare, whose wealth & arts
> Hath bred more wonder then belief in hearts:
> But what, or where they are; yet know we this,
> They shall return, and *Zion* see with bliss.[68]

Half a century later, Cotton Mather would conclude less gracefully but more concisely that "we know not *When* or *How* those *Indians* first became Inhabitants of this mighty Continent." That seemed to be the prevailing view.[69]

VI

Indians-as-Jews would not be the last paradigm applied widely by Europeans to the American Indians, but it was the last predominantly English model and very nearly the last effort by Europeans to try to cram the Indians into preconceived notions of how they looked, how they would behave, and how they should be treated. Henceforth, with the important exception of the eighteenth century's noble savage image (another large topic in itself), the English and other Europeans sought to understand America's natives more particularly and realistically. To be sure, Old World perceptions were often clouded by prejudice and stereotypes and increasingly by racism, but the application of paradigms from the English experience had largely run its course.

England's two centuries of reliance on paradigms that reflected its own perception of strangers and that served its own political interests was, of course, neither unique nor surprising. As Edward Said observes, "all cultures impose corrections upon raw reality, changing it from free-floating objects into units of knowledge," because "[i]t is perfectly nat-

ural for the human mind to resist the assault on it of untreated strangeness. . . ."[70] Unfortunately for the colonial experience in general and
the Indians in particular, the initial Old World reaction to the "untreated
strangeness" of the New World was to demonize it by applying pejorative paradigms—wild men or monsters—to its inhabitants. (The countertrend that saw America as a Garden of Eden and the natives as un-
defiled primitives would largely lie fallow until resurrected by the
eighteenth-century philosophes.) And demonizing too often led to de-
stroying. "Once perceived as beasts," Keith Thomas concludes about the
sixteenth-century English tendency to dehumanize some categories of
humankind, "people were liable to be treated accordingly." When lines
began to be drawn more clearly between animals and humans, the new
perception "legitimized the ill treatment of those humans who were in
a supposedly animal condition."[71] The wild-man and monster paradigms
thus help to explain, though not of course to justify, the early colonial
policies of the Spanish and Portuguese, and later of the French, Dutch,
and English. To the limited extent that the English also employed a pejorative Irish paradigm in America, it was largely old wine in new bot-
tles: the wild man transmogrified into the wild Irishman.

The other two English paradigms were far less pejorative; old Britons
and Lost Tribes reflected a significantly different sociological syndrome.
Again, Edward Said's generalization is apt: "[C]ultures have always been
inclined to impose complete transformations on other cultures, receiving these other cultures not as they are but as, for the benefit of the re-
ceiver, they ought to be."[72] Because the English desperately hoped that
the Indians in their sphere of control could be won to Protestantism
and English ways, they saw them as they wanted to see them—rude pagans like their own ancestors or displaced Jews whom God had placed
where his people would fulfill his mission. In both cases, so long as the
paradigms remained vital, they wielded an ameliorative influence on
colonial policy: away from warfare and enslavement, toward education
and acculturation. But even then, the effect was not fundamentally, only
relatively, benign, for the projectors of the paradigms gave the Indians
limited choices in the matter. Although ostensibly fashioned to help Europeans understand American natives and their cultures, the paradigms
more often reinforced the Europeans' own expectations and intentions
and validated, in their eyes, conquest and conversion.

CHAPTER THREE

Slaveholders' "Hellish Principles": A Seventeenth-Century Critique

Although British colonists generally interacted with the native population in each North American colony many decades before they began to import African labor, in England's island colonies African slavery usually preceded Indian-white contact and was always more prominent. That was especially true of Barbados, where the natives had succumbed to disease and warfare before the English launched a major colonizing effort in the late 1620s. A few Indians were subsequently brought to the island as workers, but the principal labor force consisted (initially) of white indentured servants and then (very quickly) of African slaves. Dominating the political, economic, and religious life of the island were the plantation owners, who resented any suggestion that their way of life was contrary to the sound principles of God and England. Not surprisingly, a few bold critics challenged that position, most notably an Anglican clergyman who spent about a decade on Barbados and who wrote several highly condemnatory tracts after his return to England.

Because the author of those tracts had lived in Virginia as well, he was in a rare position to comment on the two areas of British America that by the 1680s had turned with a vengeance to the exploitation of Africans for agricultural labor, had passed numerous laws to perpetuate the system, and had undergirded their policies with an ideology of white superiority. That ideology, I contend, was left largely undocumented because it had so few challengers within the white community. The writings of the Reverend Morgan Godwyn and a few of his contemporaries are important not only because they condemn emphatically the slaveholder's inhumane practices but especially because they give a rare insight into the racial mindset of the planter class. This essay examines what Godwyn observed of plantation slavery in the colonies and what he heard the owners say in defense of their brutal treatment of the Africans in their midst.

The genesis of this essay was a research trip to the Huntington Library in the summer of 1989, where I serendipitously came upon some of Godwyn's rarely cited publications. I was instantly intrigued by the passion and extent of God-wyn's critique of slavery and fascinated by his insights into a dialogue over the nature of Africans that historians have widely assumed did not occur until the middle of the eighteenth century. The essay is here published for the first time.

ONE DAY IN THE EARLY 1670s, a Quaker missionary in Barbados thrust a pamphlet by George Fox into the hands of a newly arrived Anglican clergyman. Although the cleric considered Fox's pamphlet a "*tedious Harangue*," it contained a rhetorical question that changed his life: "*Who made you Ministers of the Gospel to the White People only, and not to the Tawneys and Blacks also?*" That query, in less confrontational terms, had been gnawing at the minister's mind for several years—first, probably, during his service in Virginia in the 1660s and more poignantly since his arrival in Barbados around 1670—but he had done little about it. After reading Fox's words, he later remembered, "I could have no pretense to be silent" and "ought not *to lay my* (tho slender) *Talent up in a* Napkin." Henceforth the Reverend Morgan Godwyn bent his life and writings to bringing Christianity—the Anglican, not the Quaker, variety—to Indians and especially to Africans in the British empire. Simultaneously, and more important from today's perspective, he revealed the intellectual shabbiness of the racial prejudice that permitted his fellow countrymen, at home and abroad, to enslave, maltreat, and denigrate people of African ancestry.[1]

Godwyn's publications, most of them issued between 1680 and 1685 but based on his experiences in the 1660s and 1670s, candidly criticized the Church of England's sparse attempts to proselytize the heathen; he hoped thereby to jolt his coreligionists into an effective missionary campaign. But he gave more attention, and wrote more bitterly, against the slave owners' obstinate refusal to permit the conversion of their black bondsmen and against the plantocracy's incredible cruelty to slaves in general and Christianized slaves in particular. Godwyn's several pamphlets thus provide a rare, extensive insight into seventeenth-century bound-labor practices in England, Virginia, and Barbados, and, by implication, in the rest of British America as well.

Godwyn's writings also undermine the long-standing assumption that clues to the early English colonists' fundamental beliefs about their African-American neighbors, slave or free, must be gleaned from such tangential sources as laws, court cases, inventories, censuses, and wills; extended commentaries on Anglo-American slavery and explanations of racial prejudice during the first century of colonization, according to conventional wisdom, do not exist.[2] There is an "absence from the American record of any clear argument for the innate inferiority of blacks before 1776," one historian of American race relations insists; another contends that in the seventeenth century "there was little or no overt sense that biological race or skin color played a determinative role in making some human beings absolute masters over others."3 This assumed dearth of evidence on the early colonists' racial perceptions has in turn fostered deep differences of interpretation and, especially in recent decades, heated debate over the relationship between seventeenth-century "white" America's assessment of Africans and its burgeoning system of human bondage.4 Godwyn's writings, however polemical and (at times) parochial, shed vital light on the basic issues of that ongoing debate. To convince his readers of the slave owners' moral and practical errors, Godwyn reiterated the principal arguments they spouted to justify abusive policies toward enslaved Africans and forcefully rebutted each point by appeals to Scripture, common sense, and common decency, thereby articulating both sides of the English empire's usually tacit controversy over the nature of "the negro" and the legitimacy of slavery.

That Godwyn was exceptional among early Anglo-American social commentators is sometimes acknowledged. His tracts are occasionally cited and even quoted, but usually in passing and more often for his harsh critique of Virginia's ecclesiastical structure than for his observations on Anglo-American racial dynamics, although it is to the latter subject that he addressed the overwhelming bulk of his writings. And when historians do invoke Godwyn's views on race and slavery, they almost invariably cite only his first publication—*The Negro's & Indians Advocate* (1680).5 Usually overlooked are Godwyn's several subsequent publications and their additional insights into the lives of Africans in the British empire—slave and free, in England and America—and the underlying assumptions that shaped English racial practices. Godwyn's criticism of slave owners' abuse of slaves and refusal to let them become Christians was the most forceful and persistent of his era; his explanation of racism's insidious emphasis on pigmentation preceded by almost a century the insights of several Revolutionary era reformers; and his verbal jousting with the slave owners' racist ideology presaged in many ways the antebellum debate over the African American's innate qualities and potentialities.6 Godwyn's publications are uniquely revealing at a time when the British empire's racial policies were embryonic and largely unwritten.

I

The first thirty years of Morgan Godwyn's life gave little hint of his eventual role as a vociferous social critic, although his clerical profession was almost predictable at birth. His father, Dr. Morgan Godwyn, was rector at Bricknor, Gloucestershire, and later canon of Hereford; his paternal grandfather, Dr. Francis Godwyn, was bishop of Hereford; his paternal great-grandfather, Dr. Thomas Godwyn, served as a chaplain to Queen Elizabeth and was later bishop of Bath and Wells.7 Grandfather Godwyn was something of a paragon: "a good Man, a grave Divine, a skilful Mathematician, excellent Philosopher, pure Latinist, and incomparable Historian";[8] his son, Morgan Godwyn senior, translated Francis Godwyn's principal historical writings from Latin to English in 1638.[9] Thus the younger Morgan Godwyn, born in 1640, appears to have gravitated by family example to preaching and publication.

In his early years Godwyn strayed from the family pattern only in the relative brevity of his formal education. His paternal uncle, grandfather, and great-grandfather held doctorates from Oxford; his father earned a doctorate in civil law at the University of Dublin. The younger Morgan Godwyn received a bachelor of arts degree at Christ Church, Oxford, in the spring of 1665; that, the Oxford antiquarian Anthony Wood reported, "was the highest degree he took in this University."[10] Soon after, Godwyn received holy orders in the Anglican Church and served for a year or two as vicar of Wendover, Bucks. Then he veered sharply from ancestral precedent by relinquishing his pastorship and sailing to America.[11]

The records are silent on Godwyn's reasons for migration. He may have had a contentious streak (judging from later events) that disenchanted his Wendover parishioners and encouraged a parental push to the colonies for maturity and stability. There is a possibility, too, that Godwyn saw America as a missionary frontier, spurred by the Venerable Bede's *Ecclesiastical History of the English Nation* or, more likely, by his grandfather's book on English bishops. The second edition (1615) of Francis Godwyn's treatise included a "discourse concerning the first *conversion of our Britaine unto Chr*istian Religion"; it drew no explicit parallel between ancient Britons and the natives of British America (the author's agenda was more antipapal than promissionary), but it did convey the basic urgency of spreading Protestant Christianity to the four corners of the world.[12] Or perhaps young Godwyn responded to appeals from the Virginia Assembly, beginning in the early 1660s, for Oxford and Cambridge graduates to take clerical positions in the colony.[13]

Whatever the motive, Godwyn arrived in Virginia in 1666 or soon after. For a year or so he served in Marston Parish, near Middletown (later Williamsburg) and then, for perhaps a year or two, in Stafford County.[14] That stint seems to have ended acrimoniously, for reasons that remain unclear. Judging from his later publications, he very likely incurred the wrath of leading men in his community, especially vestrymen, by condemning the quality of his fellow clerics and the vestrymen's penchant for hiring pliable pastors.[15] Very likely too—and more germane to his later career—he criticized his parishioners for not baptizing their slaves and for ignoring the Indians' souls. "[S]oon after my arrival into this new World," Godwyn recalled, he encouraged piety in a Carolina Negro who had been baptized in England; later Godwyn baptized two Africans in Virginia. Such acts set badly with his neighbors, who heaped abuse on the fledgling missionary. The plantocracy acted similarly when another Virginia preacher sought conversions among slaves: "[H]e was laughed to Scorn" Godwyn remembered.[16] Although Godwyn's major commitment to the Africans' cause was still in the future, he already had a glimpse of its obstacles and its contentiousness.

It is barely possible that Godwyn's insistence on baptizing blacks spurred the Virginia legislature to clarify the heretofore uncertain relationship between slavery and Christianity. In 1667 (he had been in the colony only a year or two), the assembly announced that

> WHEREAS some doubts have risen whether children that are slaves by birth, and by the charity and piety of their owners made pertakers of the blessed sacrament of baptisme, should by vertue of their baptisme be made ffree; *It is enacted* . . . that the conferring of baptisme doth not alter the condition of the person as to his bondage or ffreedome; that divers masters, ffreed from this doubt, may more carefully endeavour the propagation of christianity by permitting children, though slaves, or those of greater growth if capable to be admitted to that sacrament.[17]

Godwyn's publications do not mention this enactment, but its final point must have pleased him. Henceforth he had a legal as well as a moral call to baptize slaves. If he took advantage of it, he may well have fomented the squabble that erupted in late 1667 or early 1668 and lasted until his departure from the colony.

The superficial facts of the case are clear. Godwyn borrowed a horse from Colonel John Dodman, probably a member of his parish and probably a vestryman too, since high rank in community and church customarily overlapped. For unspecified reasons, the horse disappeared and could not be found, despite Godwyn's professed efforts. Dodman showed little compassion: he sued the minister, and on January 29, 1668, the county court (composed, almost certainly, of the colonel's friends) awarded the plaintiff one thousand pounds of casked tobacco. Godwyn could not pay; the sheriff, on orders from the court, seized Godwyn's books and other possessions. Two years later, Godwyn's countersuit before the Virginia Council—sitting as the colony's supreme court—reversed the earlier decision, ruling that Godwyn had not had lawful notice of the charges against him and that he had genuinely tried to find the missing horse. Dodman was ordered to return the seized goods to Godwyn and pay court costs. The case ended when Dodman announced in open court "that he was sorry for the words he Spake ag[ains]t the s[ai]d *Godwyn*," and Godwyn, in a separate suit, was ordered to pay 160 pounds of tobacco to a witness subpoenaded on his behalf.[18] There is nothing in the trial record about Negroes or Indians or baptism, or about criticism of the vestries; the case may have simply concerned the missing horse. Yet the hostility that Godwyn witnessed against all clergymen who advocated the incorporation of dark-complexioned inhabitants into the Christian community and his insistence on trying to accomplish that goal, however modestly, hints strongly at a connection between Colonel Dodman's lawsuit and "the words he Spake agt the sd *Godwyn*" on the one hand, and the incipient social-theological issue on the other hand. In any event, in 1670 or thereabouts, Morgan Godwyn quit North America but not the English empire. He soon appeared in Barbados, Britain's most southern and most slave-based American colony.

On Barbados, Godwyn quickly secured a clerical post. He complained a few years later that there were only five Anglican clergymen on the island, whereas a comparable area of England, with a smaller population, would have had one hundred; a minister of Godwyn's credentials must have been in high demand.[19] But given the island's unsavory reputation, it was not a promising assignment. When English settlement began in the 1620s, the geography of Barbados held promise of its being a "little England," and in the 1630s migrants flocked there in numbers far exceeding the contemporaneous and more heralded "great migration" to New England. By midcentury, the island's reputation was badly tarnished. Although it was still "one of the Riches Spotes of ground in the wordell and fully inhabited," according to a visitor in 1655, it was also "the Dunghill wharone England doth cast forth its rubidg: Rodgs and hors and such like peopel are those which are gennerally Broght heare." Control of the island was in the hands of its large-scale planters, men who had arrived in the early free-for-all years and garnished—through varying combinations of intelligence, hard work, luck, and unscrupulous tactics—the largest and best estates. They now lived comfortably on sugar profits ("The genterey heare live far better then ours doue in England"); the hard work was done by slaves ("whou they command as they pleas" and whose children they "sele . . . from one to the other as we doue shepe").[20] The vast majority of those slaves had been imported from Africa and were augmented by a constant flow of new imports; a few were Indians from the American mainland.[21] Because of the colony's scarce land, the planter population was almost static, and the total white population had declined since midcentury. The number of slaves, by contrast, had increased dramatically as the booming sugar industry demanded ever more workers. By the time Godwyn stepped ashore, blacks outnumbered whites by about three to two; a decade later the ratio would be three to one, and the predominance of Africans would increase through most of the colonial era (Fig. 3.1).[22]

Godwyn's ostensible responsibility, like that of the island's other clergymen (and like Virginia's), was to serve his white male parishioners—plantation owners, overseers, shopkeepers, indentured servants—and their families. Little thought was given to the religious lives of African and Indian slaves, Godwyn discovered, except by a few Quakers, who had limited success among either the white or black populations because the planters mistrusted the Quakers' egalitarian intentions and hobbled their access to slaves.[23] Despite his own strong antipathy to Quakerism—then in its aggressive stage and outspokenly critical of the established clergy—Godwyn responded to its call for action. As he later recounted, he already knew and rejected the plantocracy's justifications for denying baptism and Christian instruction to slaves: the impossibil-

Fig. 3.1

A foldout map of Barbados from Richard Ligon, *A True & Exact History of the Island of Barbados* (London, 1657). Several apparent Africans are shown in the vignettes; the only Indian (right center, holding a bow) has been decapitated in this slightly (but significantly?) vandalized copy of the book. Courtesy, American Antiquarian Society.

ity, the owners argued, of converting a people so deficient in language and mind; the pointlessness of sharing refined religion with human property; and the dangerousness of putting into slaves' minds a theology that might encourage disobedience or even rebellion. "Now whilst in my thoughts I reflected upon these wild *Fancies* and absurd *Positions*," Godwyn recalled, "which I had often heard . . . [and] saw *universally practised*," he encountered the "*officious* FRIEND" and read Fox's "petty *Reformado* Pamphlet." Godwyn was offended by its "malitious (but crafty) *Invective*, levelled against the *Ministers*," but he nonetheless took its basic message to heart.[24] Thereafter Godwyn openly and forcefully championed the instruction, baptism, and better treatment of slaves.

Godwyn gives no dates for his encounter with the Quaker missionary or of his own eventual departure from Barbados. The former event probably occurred in 1672 or 1673, the latter in 1679 or 1680. In between were years of frustration over his inability to gather African adherents to Christ because of the planters' mounting opposition: the harder he tried to promote the gospel among slaves, the more barriers their masters erected in his path. Finally, overwhelmed by the slave owners'·intransigence, he returned to England. Not, however, before he penned two tracts that eventually appeared as a single volume and brought him temporary prominence in his homeland and, no doubt, substantial notoriety in his former colonial communities.

The first tract, in order of composition, was an open letter to Governor Sir William Berkeley of Virginia on "The State of Religion" in that colony, which Godwyn wrote (or at least expanded) in about 1674.[25] In 1675 Francis Moryson, Virginia's agent to England, complained of "a virulent libel against all the plantations, and Virginia in particular" that had been sent to every bishop in England by Godwyn, an "inconsiderable wretch."[26] If the document in question was a draft of the one he later published, Godwyn should not have been surprised at the hostile reaction; it impugned the Virginia clergy's competence and the quality and integrity of the vestrymen who controlled the parishes. Vestries, he charged, were "made up for the most part of sordid Plebians, the very Dregs of the *English Nation*." The final version of Godwyn's letter appeared in London in 1680 as an appendix to his second (in sequence of authorship) and even more provocative tract, *The Negro's & Indians Advocate, Suing for Their Admission into the Church*.[27] Godwyn's controversial literary career was doubly launched.

That career, as well as his clerical duties, continued for the next five years. In 1681 he published a twelve-page *Supplement to the Negro's & Indian's Advocate*; in 1682 he issued a broadside advertisement for a huge public sculpture that would call visual attention to the Negroes' and Indians' plight; and in 1685 his last major work, *Trade Preferr'd before Religion and Christ Made to Give Place to Mammon*, reached print, also in London. Sometime between 1680 and 1685, probably, Godwyn also wrote "A *Brief Account* of *Religion*, in the *Plantations*, with the *Causes* of the *Neglect* and *Decay* thereof in those *Parts*," which appeared in 1708 as the introduction to a missionary tract by Francis Brokesby, a clergyman and reformer, which noted that Godwyn's piece had been given to one Mr. Dodwell—presumably Henry Dodwell, an Oxford historian—"above Twenty Years ago" and by Dodwell at some unspecified date to his friend Brokesby.[28]

This final and probably posthumous publication, like *Trade Preferr'd before Religion*, may not initially have been intended for the press. The former is a brief epistolary summation of his thoughts on British America's clerical shortcomings and "the Indispensable Necessity" of Christianizing Negroes and Indians; it seems unlikely that he expected it to be printed. *Trade Preferr'd*, by contrast, was initially a sermon, first preached at Westminster Abbey and (according to the title page) subsequently delivered "in divers Churches in London"—a sign that Godwyn's stature, in 1685 at least, was appreciable. He was probably vicar of Bulkington, Warwick, at the time, after brief service upon his return from Barbados as rector of Woldham, Kent.[29] Surprisingly, for a man so eminent in family connections, so prominent in the pulpit, and so widely published, Godwyn suddenly dropped from sight. His date and place of death are not recorded in the standard biographical directories. The unpopularity of his views apparently earned Morgan Godwyn a singular anonymity in his later years.[30]

II

Godwyn's ostensible goal was, he announced in his first tract, "*the Christianizing of our* Negro's *and other Heathen in those* Plantations, *and . . . settling (or rather reviving) of* Religion *amongst our own People there.*"[31] In reality, only the first of those objectives—Christianizing the Negroes—engaged his time and passion. Indians figured prominently in the titles of two of his publications (*The Negro's & Indians Advocate* and *A Supplement to the Negro's & Indian's Advocate*) but received scant attention in the texts.[32] Similarly, the design for a great sculpture to vivify English efforts to proseletyze "Infidels in America, and elsewhere" was to include a figure of a New Englander preaching to the Indians, but most of the proposed sculpture's figures and iconography concerned blacks and their sufferings.[33] At the conclusion of his *Supplement*, Godwyn promised to address in subsequent writings the conversion of "the free Tributary *Indians* and the *English* (each of them a Task of the like *difficulty* with the former)," but there is no record of such publications.[34] Godwyn's last-written tract, *Trade Preferr'd before Religion*, occasionally mentioned "Tawnies" and "Indians," but the overwhelming focus remained on blacks—slave and free—in England and especially in English America.[35]

England itself, of course, had few black residents, and accordingly Godwyn devoted little space in his publications to their (mal)treatment. Yet, Godwyn reminded his audience at Westminster Abbey in 1685, England held some blacks in bondage, and, as in the colonies, their souls were seriously jeopardized by the owners' hostility to Christianization.

That "superlative Wickedness," Godwyn charged, had "spread amain, even from Sea to Sea; infected both the *East* and *West,* and gotten at the very heart of this Kingdom." He offered four cases in point from the many he had heard of. In three instances—a "Negro wench" owned by a gentlewoman in an unspecified part of England, "a poor Wretch of the like sort" seventy miles from London, and a black male a few miles outside London—the owners or malignant neighbors thwarted efforts to instruct or baptize the slaves. In the fourth case, near Bristol, the owner protested that he would as soon have the clergyman baptize a horse. To shield his slave from the minister's message, the owner chained his bondsman beneath a table and finally shipped him "to *America*: Where 'tis to be presumed, that according to the *general custom* there, he shall never more hear of *Christianity.*"[36]

Drawing on his extensive knowledge of the colonies—Virginia and Barbados from firsthand experience, others by hearsay—Godwyn vented most of his wrath against the officials and especially the slave owners who shielded British America's growing slave population from the consolations of the gospel. The slaves and the few free blacks were in no position to read or react to Godwyn's message, of course, nor was there any point in addressing his tracts to the handful of clergymen who shared his concerns. Rather, Godwyn's intended audiences were, on the one hand, the slave owners themselves and the colonial officers who could remedy the deplorable situation and, on the other hand, English public opinion, especially leaders of church and state, who might shame or force the first group into eventual reform.

Godwyn employed two principal types of argument. The first and more thorough was a rational, though occasionally heated, refutation of all the arguments he had heard against the Christianization of blacks—their mental unsuitability for receiving the gospel, for example, or the impracticality of converting a slave population. Godwyn's second form of argument was to excoriate everyone who thwarted missionary efforts, calling them hypocritical and more truly heathen than the benighted blacks. Both rhetorical tactics, especially the latter, ran the risk of further alienating the very people Godwyn sought to persuade, but he apparently preferred a frontal assault on a calamitous situation that, given the current economic, demographic, and ideological trends, would otherwise grow worse.

Godwyn insisted that his opponents, not the slaves, were the principal obstacle to Christianization. His dedication to the king of England in *Trade Preferr'd* predicted that the propagation of the gospel abroad had good prospects for success because most of the heathens "hunger and thirst after it"; if only *"their Desires [were] seconded by suitable Inclinations in their Owners."*[37] But, Godwyn lamented, the missionaries had little chance when their best efforts were *"(I cannot express it without shame and horror!) even scofft at and opposed by"* those very owners, even staunch members of the Anglican Church.[38] One ostensibly pious woman, Godwyn related, "told me with no small *Passion* and Vehemency . . . that I might as well Baptize a Puppy, as a certain young *Negro*" of hers; another woman rebuked Godwyn for baptizing one of her adult male slaves because, she contended, the sacrament "*was to one of those [people] no more beneficial than to her black Bitch.*"39

Slave owners, Godwyn charged, used a host of brutal tactics to thwart the Christianization of slaves. One was to give the slaves no time for Christian instruction by working them almost continuously; another was to deride the few blacks who showed any interest in conversion. More effective no doubt, and more shocking to Godwyn and his readers, were the vicious punishments imposed on the very few blacks who somehow achieved baptism. Godwyn recounted the fate of a Barbadian slave who was baptized on a Sunday morning at the parish church; that afternoon his "*brutish* Overseer," objecting to baptism "*for those of his Complexion,*" flogged the slave relentlessly. The slave complained to the minister, who in turn complained to the governor, but that only brought greater abuse from the overseer. Eventually the slave escaped into the woods and died. Godwyn was appalled by the events and predicted divine revenge, including an ironic baptism for the overseer "*in the Lake that Burns with Fire and Brimstone.*"40 The episode was also irresistible grist for Godwyn's propaganda mill. He first related the atrocities in *Negro's & Indians Advocate*; he recalled them in *Trade Preferr'd*; and he sought to immortalize them in stone. His *Directions for a Sculpture* included a figure representing an American overseer "whipping and most unmercifully tormenting a poor Negro-Slave," with the overseer's words carved for all to see: "Ye Dog, as you were baptized in the Morning with Water, so in the Afternoon ye shall be baptized in Blood."41

Slave owners did not stop at discouraging their human property from receiving Christianity but interfered as well with the clergy by "*muzzling Their Mouths*" and "rendring the Work very unsafe." Some ministers, Godwyn reported, suffered only verbal abuse; others were threatened with financial ruin; and one clergyman's proposed missionary plan "was so maliciously represented amongst the *Rabble*, that . . . *he was endangered thereby.*" Still other ministers shirked proselytizing, despite their approval of it in principle, for fear that they would be persecuted the rest of their lives.42 Godwyn had himself felt the slave owners' wrath. They had thwarted his modest missionary efforts in Virginia and may have harassed him from the colony, and they treated him no better in Barbados. "I cannot easily forget," he wrote, "the *supercilious* Checks and *Frowns* (to say no worse)" that greeted his arguments for the Christianization of blacks and "the hard Words, and evil Language I have upon this account received."43 He also lamented the difficulty of spreading in England the truth about the Negroes' plight because his opponents falsely reported that all was well in the colonies and assumed that no one dared to challenge them. With a touch of self-appointed martyrdom, Godwyn announced in *Negro's & Indians Advocate* his determination "*to break through this Opposition; . . . without any regard to those Gentlemens displeasure, which I must expect even to the utmost degree.*" Five years later, Godwyn's preface to *Trade Preferr'd* predicted stiff resistance to his latest pronouncements, as his earlier efforts had received, from "mammonists" who put profit before principle.[44] Godwyn waged a lonely and losing battle against the philistines.

Although condemnation of his opponents—those who abused converts or thwarted ministers or slandered his own efforts—was the most contentious part of Godwyn's literary campaign, he devoted more space and more intellectual rigor to refuting his opponents' arguments against slave conversions. Godwyn's summaries of their manifold "*Fig-leafe* Reasons and Objections against our *Negro's Christianity*" varied somewhat in his several works, but they fall into four general propositions: (1) The Negro is not fully human and is therefore incapable of conversion; (2) the Negro is cursed by God to eternal inferiority and subservience and is therefore unworthy of conversion; (3) the Negro, if Christianized, might harm the lives and property of the whites and is therefore too dangerous for conversion; and (4) the Negro's unfamiliarity with the English language, his barbarian faith, and his general uncouthness make conversion impossible.[45]

Godwyn considered his opponents' denial of the African's humanity to be their most deplorable but vulnerable position. Even in England, he lamented, he had heard the opinion "privately (*and as it were in the dark*) handed to and again . . . That the *Negro's*, though in their Figure they carry some resemblances of Manhood, yet are indeed *no Men.*" Godwyn considered that a "disingenuous and unmanly *Position*," and he accordingly devoted more than thirty pages in *Negro's & Indians Advocate* to refuting it.[46] Again in his brief publication of 1708, written much earlier, Godwyn mentioned the "Hellish Principles, viz. that *Negroes* are Creatures destitute of Souls, to be ranked among Brute Beasts, and Treated accordingly. . . ."[47] In 1680, when his first tract went to press, Godwyn gave top priority to proving that dark-complexioned people were—contrary to the view that he believed was widely held—full members of the human community.

Godwyn's specific proofs were largely commonsensical. Africans, he pointed out, obviously have human shape and appearance; and although they are of a darker complexion than the English and most other Europeans, so are five-sixths of the world's people. Even if one were to grant (as he did not) that blackness was a deformity, Godwyn insisted that it was no more a sign of bestiality than was any mental or physical human abnormality; people with dark pigmentation can reproduce themselves, in fact they often reproduce with *whites*—a sure sign of their humanity. Godwyn's position on color preference was also refreshingly evenhanded for a seventeenth-century Englishman. There is no universal standard of beauty, Godwyn reminded his readers: blacks favor their own color just as whites do, and if a subjective objection to skin colors were allowed to consign some people to the category of brutes, fair-skinned Europeans might someday find themselves so labeled. Moreover, after a few generations in hot climates, Godwyn argued (endorsing the climatological explanation of human pigmentation), even the English "become quite *Black*, at least very *Duskie* and *Brown*." Are they to be considered brutes rather than men?[48]

Some slaveholders asserted that Africans were descended from a separate and prior creation to Adam and Eve. Such "a *Pre-Adamites* whimsey," Godwyn warned, was blasphemous and nonsensical, and he countered its proponents' arguments with lengthy appeals to Old Testament authority. His contempt for heterodox theories is palpable and predictable.[49] He also objected at great length to the blatant "*Falsehoods*, or (at best) *Uncertainties*" that seventeenth-century Africans were the accursed descendants of Noah's disobedient son Cham, "who, they say, was together with his whole *Family* and Race, *cursed* by his *Father*." In the eyes of many Christians, the penalty imposed on Cham's posterity, through his son Canaan, not only darkened their skin but demoted all Africans—by divine wrath than pre-Adamite creation—to a quasi-human category. "Thus it is usually discoursed," Godwyn complained, that "Because they are *Black*, therefore they are *Cham*'s Seed; and for this [reason] under the *Curse*, and therefore no longer *Men*, but a kind of *Brutes*."[50]

Godwyn vehemently denied that Genesis 9:25–26 meant that all dark-complexioned people were destined by divine wrath to eternal inferiority and subservience. Scripture, he insisted, did not specify the line of Cham's descent beyond a few generations, nor the geographic boundaries of his progeny's settlement, nor the relationship, if any, between Canaan's descendants and seventeenth-century Africans. If the curse did fall on Cham's son in the distant past, there was no reason to believe that it still obtained; history, geography, logic, and equity joined with Scripture to suggest otherwise. In any event, Godwyn argued, nothing in the Bible implied that Cham's descendants—whoever they might be and whatever the nature of God's curse on them—should be denied the consolations of Christianity. Even "granting it true," which Godwyn emphatically did not, that "this whole People of *Blacks* . . . were thus devoted to Misery, and become the objects of God's Wrath; yet will not this justifie our barring them of the Knowledg and Exercise of *Religion*."[51]

What biology and the Bible demonstrated beyond a shadow of doubt, at least to Godwyn, sociology reinforced. Some blacks, he reminded skeptics of black competence, could read and write, whereas many whites could not. With suitable training, blacks could conduct business skillfully; some were already entrusted by their owners with substantial authority over their fellow slaves. "It would certainly be a pretty kind of *Comical* Frenzie," Godwyn twitted his critics, "to imploy Cattel about Business, and to constitute them *Lieutenants*, *Overseers*, and *Governours*, like as *Domitian* is said to have made his Horse a *Consul*." And why did owners beat slaves for alleged wrongdoings if they were unreasonable brutes rather than intelligent beings? Indeed they must be human, Godwyn chided; otherwise the owners who satisfied their lusts on slave women were guilty of bestiality and thereby merited both human and divine punishment.[52] In sum, all evidence, including his opponents' own actions, attested that black people, slave or free, were "the most genuine and perfect characters of Homoniety."[53]

Because dark-skinned people were fully human, Godwyn insisted, they had every right to hear the gospel. Surely enslavement did not preclude "the *Negro*'s Right to Religion," as many owners contended; to link access to religion with social status was, in Godwyn's view, "a kind of *Spiritual Gentility*" whereby anyone in bondage, regardless of complexion or nationality, was unworthy of Christ's message. In the case of Negroes, Godwyn lamented, the combination of color and condition made them doubly unacceptable as converts in the eyes of the ignorant: "*What, those black Dogs be made Christians? What, shall they be like us?*" In a lengthy rebuttal to this line of impiety, Godwyn invoked both Testaments and numerous classical authors to demonstrate the theological and historical right of all people, of whatever social condition, to worship the Creator. "[T]he *Soul* of the Slave," he reminded his readers, "is no part of the *Master*'s purchase."[54]

III

With the theoretical objections to the Christianization of blacks refuted to his satisfaction, Godwyn turned in his first tract (and returned in later writings) to his opponents' practical objections. Heading the list was their paranoid fear of violence, "It being their common *Affirmation,* That the *Baptizing* of their *Negro's, is the ready way to have all their Throats cut.*" Visions of mutiny and murder swirled through slave owners' heads; they insisted, despite all evidence to the contrary, that Christianity would make slaves more vicious than they were already perceived to be. At the very least, the opponents of conversion insisted, Christianity would make slaves less governable and less productive. In the end, Godwyn's Barbadian opponents predicted, "*If the* Negro's *get to be Baptized,* they *must then e'ne take the* Island *to themselves.*"[55]

Godwyn rebutted such arguments with a proslavery interpretation of Scripture that foreshadowed nineteenth-century rationalizations. Its now familiar essence was Christianity's compatibility with human bondage: "It establisheth the *Authority of Masters,* over their Servants and Slaves"—Christian slaves would be dutiful, forbearing, and loyal. Godwyn did not invent this argument, of course; it reflected a long line of Christian apologetics. But he revitalized it for British America by applying it to immediate colonial concerns. He illustrated the potential loyalty of converts, for example, with evidence from the recently concluded Indian war in New England, where the "*Christian-Indians Fidelity* was tried to the uttermost" by their heathen Indian friends and by uncharitable colonists, "Yet *in despite of all,* they remained *firm to the Eng-*

lish." The bonds of religion, Godwyn theorized, encourage "Men to *forget their own People, and their Fathers House,* and joyning them in affection to the most *distant Strangers.*" A case in point, Godwyn proposed, should have been the aborted slave uprising on Barbados in 1675, which had traumatized white Barbadians. Although no whites were injured, the authorities executed at least thirty-five blacks, and five hanged themselves. Godwyn surmised that the conspiracy would have been less threatening had the slaves been Christians.[56]

Even if Christian slaves eschewed rebellion or insolence, Godwyn's opponents argued, they would seek legal remedies for real or imagined grievances. Worse still, from the owners' viewpoint, their slaves might sue for freedom. That complaint was common but unfounded. Although a supposition lingered throughout British America that baptism conferred freedom on its recipient, both law and custom argued the contrary. By the late 1670s, when Godwyn wrote *Negro's & Indians Advocate,* Virginia, Maryland, and Barbados had statues denying liberation through Christianization, as Godwyn noted emphatically; and he reminded slave owners that they need merely point to the continuing slavery of the few Christianized slaves to convince other slaves that conversion was no path to freedom.[57] The Bible, he contended, was clear too. Both Testaments tell of bond servants whose status persisted despite conversion to the faith. "Christ's *Kingdom* being not of this World," Godwyn concluded, "his *Religion* was never designed to deprive any Man [read "master"] of his *civil Rights. . . . Bondage* is not *inconsistent* with *Christianity.*"[58]

Legally and scripturally, no, but doubts remained. In several of his publications Godwyn tried to convince the remaining skeptics. One solution, he suggested, was to adopt the Bermuda scheme of ninety-nine-year indentures for blacks, which sidestepped the legal issue while entrenching slavery; another solution was to revoke as soon as possible any English or colonial legislation that cast doubt on the compatibility of slavery and Christianity; still another strategy would be to pass laws in every jurisdiction specifically denying that baptism was incompatible with slavery, as several colonial legislatures already had. Godwyn was himself sure that English law was wholly on the slave owners' side, and for authority he cited Sir Robert Southwell, a prominent diplomatic and political figure; he had told Godwyn that the late Lord Chancellor, Heneage Finch, denied that English law allowed a slave to sue for freedom on the grounds of baptism. If any moral prescriptions based on Christian principles implied that slaves should be freed, Godwyn assured his readers, they were "*meerly voluntary . . .* to which a Christian (as such) is no more bound, than to *sell all his Goods, and give them to the Poor.* Which yet may be a good work, and very commendable, in those that shall aspire after such perfection."[59]

Although Godwyn devoted most of his efforts to refuting notions that blacks were brutes or cursed by God or, if Christianized, that they would become free or ungovernable, he also gave appreciable attention to the argument that slaves simply could not comprehend Christianity. One reason his opponents tendered was the language barrier. Godwyn admitted that ignorance of English among newly arrived Africans was at first "a real *Impediment*" to Christianization, but they learned the language quickly, he pointed out, and their American-born progeny spoke it as a matter of course; by his estimate, in 1680 more than half of the blacks in the colonies spoke English quite well. He also insisted on the mutability of their traditional customs and beliefs. Civil behavior among newly arrived Africans, Godwyn observed with more sarcasm, perhaps, than hubris, can hardly "be so Gentile and Modish as our *Europeans*, who perchance must be acknowledged as not to be parallel'd by any other." Shortcomings comparable to the Africans' could be found among the ancient Greeks, Godwyn believed, or the ancient Britons or the current Irish, especially those in Barbados: none matched the modern Europeans' gentility. But education, he argued, could remedy any barbarousness, and Christianity could supplant any false worship. Godwyn assured his readers that blacks craved the consolations of Christianity; given opportunities for instruction and baptism, they would quickly embrace true religion. They would then become better slaves and—far more important in Godwyn's eyes—be more likely to achieve eternal life, "the Slave's Soul being as precious, and his danger and hopes equal with his Master's."[60]

To prod Anglican consciences into active support of Christianity for blacks, Godwyn offered a comparative assessment of missionary achievements that reflected poorly on his own denomination. However much he deplored Roman Catholicism, he admitted that its missionaries had been quite successful in Africa, Asia, and America to "*The Reproach of Protestants*."[61] Godwyn lauded at even greater length New England's Puritans for their proselytizing of blacks and especially Indians. This praise reflected no puritanical leanings on Godwyn's part; he frequently chided Puritans at home and abroad for what he considered the theological and political shortcomings of "the late *pretended* Saints" and the "*seditious Reformers*."[62] But mainly, no doubt, to spur his fellow Anglicans by shaming them with odious comparisons, and partly because he could boast of few Anglican achievements, Godwyn praised New Englanders unstintingly. "[I]f we look into *New-England*," he wrote in his first tract, "they scruple not to admit either *Negro's* or *Indians*, when capacitated and fit for it, to their very *Sacraments*, which very many of the *English* cannot obtain. The Infants also of such are allowed *Baptism*."[63] Elsewhere Godwyn credited New Englanders with being the only British Americans to comply with the requirement of colonial charters that the settlers propagate the gospel.[64] Except for a handful of Quakers, he complained, the Puritans were "the *only* Witnesses of this Truth in those Parts."[65]

In his effort to prick Anglican consciences, Godwyn continued to be unrealistically effusive about New England's Indian policies. Despite the Puritans' sparse and declining missionary efforts in the years after King Philip's War, Godwyn proposed in 1682 that his grand sculpture include figures of "one or more of the Preachers of *New-England*, in their customary and usual Habit, preaching to the Natives there. Over this, write their known motto, *Come over and help us, Act 16.9.* Underneath it put, *The Shame of Others.*" Similarly, Godwyn's sermon at Westminster Abbey in 1685 contrasted, on the one hand, "the great Industry of our People in *New-England*[,] . . . their converting of *Nations,* turning the *whole Bible into the Indian tongue*; their *Colledg built* and *endowed,* for the *Education of Indian* Youth: Their *Missioners* sent forth," with, on the other hand, the Anglicans who "have not produced the *least Grain of Harvest* to God's Glory in those Parts." Outside of New England, Godwyn asserted, the very mention of converting the heathen "is Esteemed as most Ridiculous, and as the effect of Madness."[66] Godwyn's Church of England listeners must have squirmed. As a staunch Anglican and chauvinistic Englishman, Godwyn probably winced at the necessity of praising other faiths and other nations for more vigorously and successfully propagating the gospel.

To readers who were inspired or shamed into supporting his cause, Godwyn offered guidelines for political action. One method was to recruit better clergymen for colonial service and enhance their missionary role. Throughout his tracts, especially in the open letter to Governor Berkeley on the church in Virginia, Godwyn lamented the colonial clergy's poor quality and sparse quantity.[67] Among the reforms he proposed were greater governmental support, protection of the clergy in the colonies, and guaranteed preferment in England after five to seven years of overseas service; the clergy, in sum, were to be transient rather than permanent, and honored agents of the church and state rather than pawns of the plantocracy. The absence of church and state support had already, he claimed, seriously undermined the ministers' morale and efficiency; they could hardly be expected "to adventure the *getting of broken Heads in the Churches service, afterwards at their return* [*home*] *to be rewarded with that which shall break their Hearts too.*"[68]

But better clergymen would only be successful, Godwyn believed, if the power of the vestries were curbed. In Virginia, ministers "are most miserably handled by their *Plebeian Junto's,* the *Vesteries,*" which have the authority to hire and fire preachers (or to do without them) and to coerce them by threats and manipulation of their salaries. To be effective messengers of the gospel, clergymen who remain in the colonies must have life benefices, Godwyn proposed, "otherwise they shall pass their time in perpetual *fear* of *offending,* and to be afterwards Checkt and Starved for *consciensiously discharging their Duty.*" Not surprisingly, Godwyn also favored the extension to America of the Church of England's hierarchy. But even before such reforms might be introduced, the colonial ministers must themselves take the lead in propagation of the faith among African Americans. They should catechize and baptize their own slaves, if any; they should preach monthly on masters' Christian obligations to slaves; and they should themselves proseletyze slaves in their parishes whenever possible.[69]

That last requirement depended, of course, on at least tacit cooperation from the slave owners, whose resistive powers Godwyn knew only too well. He suggested several strategies to force or shame the planters into line. One was to advertise their impiety in England (as Godwyn's writings repeatedly did), especially in London, where they "have an extraordinary *Ambition* to be *thought well of.*" Frequent sermons at court, in the cities, and in the seaports where slave traders and merchants congregate might also convince planters "that their *impiety* was so *decryed* and *odious* here" that they would end their opposition to missionary efforts abroad. A general fast to implore God's blessing on missionary work might also help.[70] Godwyn, ever the cleric, thus put all his emphasis on moral suasion, none on economic controls. His reformist program was accordingly on shaky ground, judging from his own belief that colonial slave owners "*know no other* God *but* Money, *nor* Religion *but* Profit." In 1680 Godwyn leveled that charge not only against the planters of Barbados, England's most notoriously profit-centered colony, but "indeed of the whole *Plantations.*" Five years later Godwyn made greed the central theme of his sermon at Westminster Abbey. The schemes he had proposed earlier to jostle the plantocracy's conscience had accomplished nothing.[71]

Time and again, Godwyn berated slave owners not only for failing to bring, or even allow anyone else to bring, the gospel to their slaves but for treating them with such un-Christian cruelty that the masters were more heathenish than their bondsmen. The slaves he described were often pitifully underfed, inadequately clothed, and ruthlessly overworked (Fig. 3.2). Especially among "the *Mightier*" Barbadian planters, Godwyn charged, the slaves' very lives were less important than profits; replacement was cheaper than preservation—"the death of a good *Horse*, and of a *Negro*, is of equal moment." Even the slaves' progeny were doomed to short lives, Godwyn lamented, because their mothers were forced to work constantly in the fields. Occasionally his writings foreshadowed nineteenth-century abolitionist exposés of sadistic owners. The Barbadian planters' cruelty to slaves included "their Emasculating and Beheading them, their *croping off their Ears* (which they usually cause the Wretches to broyl, and then compel to eat them themselves); their *Amputations of Legs*, and even Dissecting them alive."[72] Perhaps Godwyn's revelations spurred the Crown to complain in 1684 to the Barbados legislature that in its laws "concerning Negroes there is no sufficient punishment provided for those that shall willfully and wantonly kill a Negroe."[73]

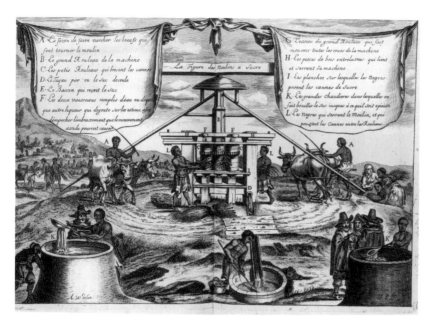

Fig. 3.2

Diagram of a sugar mill in the French Caribbean. This engraving suggests, rather benignly, some of the tasks that slaves performed on Barbados in the decade when Morgan Godwyn observed and criticized their treatment. From Charles de Rochefort, *Histoire Naturelle et Morale des Îles Antilles de l'Amerique*, 2d ed. (Rotterdam, 1665). Courtesy of the John Carter Brown Library at Brown University.

So vehement was Godwyn's condemnation of slave owner brutality that had he not insisted repeatedly on the compatibility of Christianity and human bondage, he might be labeled an early abolitionist. Perhaps Godwyn saw no point in opposing outright a system of social control and economic exploitation that was already firmly entrenched in the colonies and that brought immense profit to the mother country. The best he could do under such circumstances, he may have thought, was to ameliorate the slaves' lives while bending most of his energies to the clergyman's principal task of saving souls. But that he harbored a revulsion toward the whole slave institution is suggested by clues (often oblique) scattered through his writings. His adjectives, for example, are telling, as in "this *Soul-murthering and Brutifying-state of Bondage*." He argued, moreover, that it is worse to consign slaves to eternal damnation by keeping them from the gospel than to enslave them in the first place, which implied that both were sins against humankind. He also advocated emancipation for slaves whose owners refused to permit their conversion. Godwyn's intent in such situations may have been primarily to punish the impious master, but his advocacy of the "present and absolute release of the *Slave* for ever" was surely meant as a consolation to

the slave; otherwise Godwyn would have proposed a transfer of ownership to a master more amenable to missionaries. And near the end of
his final tract, Godwyn came close to condemning slavery outright: the
English, he admitted, "have exceeded the *worst* of Infidels, by our first
enslaving, and then *murthering* of Men's *Souls*."[74] Godwyn may have considered the second crime the more onerous, but his disapproval of slavery, however muted, is nonetheless unmistakable.

IV

Godwyn's inability to jostle his compatriots' consciences owes much to
other reformers' failure to endorse or emulate him—which in itself tells
volumes about the racial attitudes of seventeenth-century England and
America. Aside from a few Quaker pamphleteers (for whom Godwyn
had little regard) the only significant English authors of the time who
might be considered ideological allies were Richard Baxter, the prominent dissenting clergyman, and Thomas Tryon, a quixotic social reformer and theological gadfly. Both are notable for the bluntness of
their sentiments against human bondage, but neither unequivocally opposed slavery and neither made the plight of slaves' bodies or souls his
major concern. Yet Baxter, writing a few years before Godwyn, and
Tryon, whose relevant works roughly coincide with Godwyn's, reflect a
strand in English reformist thought that the Anglican preacher, however unsuccessfully, sought to marshal against what he perceived to be
the major social evil of his time.

Readers of Baxter's mammoth *Christian Directory* (more than one thousand folio pages) encountered, about halfway through, five pages of "*Directions to those Masters in foraign Plantations who have* Negro's *and other
Slaves*." Enslaved people, Baxter reminded their owners, "are reasonable
Creatures, as well as you; and born to as much natural liberty"; masters
were obligated to treat slaves humanely and to encourage them to hear
and obey God's word. On this matter, Baxter and Godwyn saw eye to
eye, as they did on New England's missionary efforts, which Baxter
touted in glowing terms and perhaps thereby inspired Godwyn's later
praise of the Puritans. Baxter and Godwyn differed, however, in that the
latter went to vastly greater lengths to refute the ideology of Negro inferiority that he had encountered (especially) in the colonies, while Baxter was more outspoken against the initial enslavement of free people—
"one of the worst kinds of Thievery in the world"—and urged anyone
who bought a victim of unjustified slavery to "do your best to free him."
Still, Baxter and Godwyn were in the long run less concerned with the
slaves' status than with their salvation. "Make it your chief end in buying and using slaves," Baxter admonished, "to win them to Christ and
save their souls." And Baxter virtually dropped the issue of slavery with
the publication of *Christian Directory* in 1673.[75]

Thomas Tryon's extensive writings, dating from 1682 to 1700, addressed, among other topics, religion, metaphysics, temperance, fru-
gality, education, and the art of brewing beer.[76] Tryon now and then
castigated slavery, but he tucked his criticisms into the interstices of
other concerns. In 1684, for instance, he published *Friendly Advice to the
Gentlemen-Planters of the East and West Indies,* a pamphlet of 222 pages.
The first third of *Friendly Advice* is a meticulous description of Barbadian
flora; it gives no hint of the theme of the second section. Readers who
got that far encountered an essay of about 75 pages that tells poignantly
and sympathetically "The Negro's Complaint of their *Hard Servitude,* and
the CRUELTIES Practised upon them By divers of their Masters." Like Godwyn, Tryon damned as hypocrites the nominal Christians who abuse
their slaves ("though your Tongues may be Christian, your Hands are
Heathen"), and like Godwyn he refuted the apparently prevalent notion that darkness of skin validates cruel treatment of its possessors. Unlike Godwyn, Tryon challenged the right of anyone to enslave people
on the basis of skin color. Should a man, he asked, using a fictional slave
as narrator, "be made a *Slave* forever, meerly because his Beard is *Red,*
or his Eyebrows *Black?* In a word, if our *Hue* be the only difference, since
White is as contrary to *Black,* as *Black* is to *White,* there is as much reason
that you should be our *Slaves,* as we yours." But whatever blows Tryon
landed against slavery in the second part of *Friendly Advice* he may have
vitiated in the third part, a long satirical dialogue between a Barbadian
slave and his master. The former pleads not for freedom but for better
treatment; in return, he promises, "I shall on all occasions press them
[my fellow slaves] to be obedient, humble, just and respective to all their
Masters." The owner finally agrees and bids good night to "honest
Sambo," who replies "Good Night, my good dear Master."[77] That came
close to Godwyn's public position on slavery.

Tryon also implicitly corroborated Godwyn's view of Anglo-American
racial attitudes, but again he buried his evidence under a mountain of
other concerns. Godwyn's tracts, especially *Negro's & Indians Advocate,*
demonstrated—as none had before or would for another half century—
the pervasiveness of Anglo-American racism by repeatedly revealing the
pejorative beliefs that applied only to people of "black" complexion. Not
everyone in the colonies, he observed, believed that Negroes were not
true humans, but the dissenters from that opinion he estimated to be
"very *few.*" Tryon put a comparable quasi-human argument into the
mouth of his fictive slave owner: "Does not your very *Hue,* that *sooty Skin*
of yours, serve for an Emblem of the darkness of your Minds? . . . [I]n
a word, you are in most particulars the very next Door to *Beasts.*"[78] Similarly, Godwyn lauded ancient Africans for their accomplishments in arts
and warfare but complained that Africans in his day were "suspected for
Brutes, as we here [in Barbados] find and see"; Tryon praised the
African's intelligence and aptitude but testified too that the white owner

considered his slave "a dark ignorant Heathen, scarce capable of *common Sense*."[79] In sum, Godwyn and Tryon saw, as few of their contemporaries apparently did, that the fundamental barrier to missionary efforts in America or even in England was a widely held belief that Africans and their descendants in the British empire were innately inferior creatures. Tryon, and especially Godwyn, railed against that notion and its invidious corollaries: that the Negroes' presumed inferiority justified harsh treatment, and that efforts to Christianize them were either irrelevant or downright dangerous. Even Baxter, though less prolific on this issue, insisted on a fundamental "difference between *Men* and *Bruits*"; slaves must not be thrust into the latter category, as their owners invariably did.[80] People of dark pigmentation, all three reformers recognized, must be acknowledged by English authorities—indeed by all true Christians—to be fully human and therefore entitled to full rights of body and soul.

Tryon's emphasis on the centrality of the Africans' pigmentation to the prejudice against them echoed Godwyn's repeated implications that color was the symbol and perhaps partly the substance of English and colonial racial bias. But Godwyn, unlike Baxter or Tryon or anyone else in the seventeenth century, at least in print, offered an explanation of the warped psychology by which blacks were singled out by whites for contempt and exploitation. The outward sign of the Africans' brutality and consequently their slavery, Godwyn hypothesized, was "their *Complexion*, which being most obvious to the sight, by which the *Notion* of things doth seem to be most certainly conveyed to the Understanding, is apt to make no *slight* impressions upon rude Minds." This visual perception of blacks as brutes and therefore suitable for enslavement led in turn to a set of crucial linguistic equations: "These two words, *Negro* and *Slave*, being by custom grown Homogeneous and Convertible; even as *Negro* and *Christian, Englishman* and *Heathen*, are by the like corrupt Custom and Partiality made *Opposites*; thereby as it were implying, that the one could not be *Christians*, nor the other *Infidels*."[81] If that syllogism was as prevalent in England and its colonies as Godwyn's evidence suggests it was, his failure to convince his compatriots of the Negroes' right to Christianity and decent treatment should not have surprised him.

V

When Godwyn returned to England from Barbados in about 1680, he was determined to further the missionary cause "*notwithstanding . . . the greatest discouragements whatsoever, until arrived within a prospect of its accomplishment*."[82] If he died near the end of the century, as seems likely, Godwyn never saw an appreciable increase in Christianized Negroes or Indians nor a decline in the institution of slavery. Instead, slavery's growth on the mainland as well as the islands was spectacular compared with the early years of British America. In Virginia the number of blacks, almost all of them enslaved, jumped from fewer than 2000 when Godwyn arrived in the mid-1660s to perhaps 15,000 by the end of the century; in Barbados, the comparable figures are approximately 30,000 and 50,000; for all of British America they are 40,000 and nearly 150,000.[83] Simultaneously, the slave laws in most colonies expanded substantially, sometimes with wording that embodied the very attitudes Godwyn deplored. The Virginia House of Burgesses, for example, declared in 1699 that American-born Negroes were generally baptized (the evidence suggests otherwise) but not the Africans (the greater portion of the black population): "for Negroes Imported hither the Gros Barbarity and rudeness of their manners, the variety and Strangeness of their Languages and the weakness and Shallowness of their minds renders it in a manner impossible to attain to any Progress in their Conversion."[84] If Godwyn was still alive, his heart must have faltered at such a stark repudiation of his life's work.

He might have taken some comfort, however, from having written the most poignant description of Anglo-American slavery of his era, even though it was neither complete nor impartial. He never intended it to be the latter. As a polemicist arguing a cause and berating those who stood in its way, Godwyn painted a skewed portrait of the white people who profited from the importation and exploitation of African labor and of the black people who endured privations and punishments in a system that was not of their making. He says nothing, for example, about the routine—as distinct from the aberrant—tasks of plantation slavery and nothing about the efforts of blacks to thwart the system and to preserve their native cultures. Godwyn's account tells much about slavery nonetheless. Especially in *Negro's & Indians Advocate*, he exposed the brutality that slavery so often engendered on the sugar islands; his emphasis on the extreme cruelty of some masters and on the indifference of some owners to their slaves' very survival reveals that the harshness usually attributed to later decades of the seventeenth century, and especially to the eighteenth century, was prevalent by the 1670s, at least in Barbados. Similarly, his descriptions of virulent opposition to the Christianization of slaves and even of free blacks show the plantocracy's early and adamant hostility to missionary efforts in both the mainland and the island colonies.

More important, Godwyn exposed the reasons for the planters' opposition—reasons that he considered "either *false*, or *frivolous*, or both" but which slave owners staunchly maintained.[85] Among the practical reasons, whether justified or not, fears of insurrections, murders, and intransigence were ostensibly paramount; important, too, though less vital, were predictions that Christian slaves would be entitled to better treatment, including shorter hours and better clothing, which in turn would diminish the owners' profits. And the frequency with which Godwyn encountered the notion that conversion to Christianity was tantamount to freedom, and his repeated denials that either law or doctrine endorsed such a conclusion, reveal the persistence of an idea supported more by folk tradition than by church or state. Although few slaves, if any, secured their freedom solely or even primarily on the grounds of Christian baptism, suspicions that it *might* entail emancipation convinced many owners to keep Godwyn and his ilk at arm's length.

Significant, too, are Godwyn's observations on slavery's vitality in the three parts of the British empire he knew at firsthand. He wrote mostly of Barbados, of course, where slavery was more deeply entrenched than anywhere in the empire, where he first became deeply committed to the conversion of blacks, and where he wrote his longest and best-known tract. Yet Godwyn makes clear that in some respects his comments applied to Virginia and England as well. His few specific references to Virginian slavery suggest a similarity of attitudes in the mainland and island colonies, especially in the reluctance of owners to baptize blacks or even to consider them fully human.[86] There was less similarity in the *practice* of slavery, however, for Virginia's much smaller black population was spared the rigors of sugar production and generally escaped the worst sorts of brutality.

In England, opposition to the Christianization of blacks and to the idea that they were truly human seems to have been far less virulent than in the colonies—partly, no doubt, because their number in England was extremely small and because Englishmen at home were less dependent upon a slave economy; also, perhaps, because Englishmen at home suffered less from the psychological insecurities that seem to have fostered exploitation and cruelty among their overseas cousins.[87] Although baptism was sometimes opposed in England, it was apparently often performed.[88] And if Godwyn heard "divers even in *England*" defend the "*monstrous opinion*" that blacks were brutes rather than humans, at least it was a less common judgment in the mother country than in the colonies. Yet Godwyn, writing in Barbados about attitudes toward blacks in England, lamented that while "the respect there to them is *notorious*, and even become the Scoff of this place," a change was apparently under way in the mother country: "their *Zeal* [in favor of fairness to Africans] is said of late to be much abated." Godwyn attributed the slump in English enthusiasm for the Africans' welfare to "mammonists."[89] Had he wished to further indict his countrymen at home, Godwyn could have cited the English custom, prevalent by the 1680s, of riveting a metal collar around a slave's neck, inscribed with the owner's name or coat of arms.[90]

A similar conclusion about regional differences applies to the freedom of advocacy: Barbados was the most repressive, Virginia less so, and England the most liberal. In Barbados the minister who baptized the Negro who was subsequently whipped almost to death was himself subjected to "*Calumnies* and *spiteful* Reproaches," and, as Godwyn repeatedly protested in his pamphlets, the island's planters and government officials conspired to keep the black population in brutal bondage while preventing the few reformist clergymen from ameliorating the slaves' spiritual or physical conditions.[91] In Virginia, Godwyn was not the only missionary to be thwarted; the few other advocates of Christianity for blacks faced similar resistance, yet they had managed some conversions and by 1667 had enacted a law that encouraged missionary efforts, even though it simultaneously tightened the slave system.[92] In neither Virginia nor Barbados, however, were Godwyn's critiques of slavery's abuses and his advocacy of missionary work made available to the public. Neither colony had a press at the time, and the likelihood that copies were imported is almost nil.[93] His ideas were anathema to the ruling oligarchies and probably to the overwhelming majority of the white populations. Thus his opponents had no need to publish attacks on Godwyn or to articulate their own racial ideology. Godwyn was a minor thorn in the slaveholders' sides while he remained in America; once gone, he could safely be forgotten.

In England, by contrast, Godwyn was heard and presumably read. He proclaimed his message in Westminster Abbey and elsewhere, and his appeals were printed and distributed. He may even have influenced the Crown's instructions of 1680 to the governor and assembly of Barbados "to find out the best means to facilitate and encourage the conversion of Negroes and Indians to the Christian religion." That admonition was sent subsequently to the other royal governors, although initially it also urged the governments of Barbados, Jamaica, and Virginia (but not the other colonies) "to have a due caution and regard to the property of the inhabitants and safety of the colony"——a major loophole for legislators unsympathetic to the conversion of slaves.[94] By and large, Godwyn's ideas made as little headway in England as in the colonies against the tides of hostility and indifference toward Africans.

One sign of that hostility may have been Godwyn's difficulty in securing established publishers for his pamphlets. *Negro's & Indians Advocate* was not issued by an established bookseller but instead was "Printed for the Author," probably at Godwyn's expense. His *Supplement* and *Directions for a Sculpture* were printed by John Darby, who, according to the standard biographical guide to printers of that era, was "constantly in trouble with the authorities for printing satires, lampoons, and other unauthorized literature. . . ."[95] *Trade Preferr'd*, by contrast, was printed for Benjamin Took, one of the most substantial publishers of the time, which suggests that Godwyn had finally found a sponsor. Perhaps a Westminster Abbey sermon automatically attracted some customers and therefore appealed to Took's business acumen, or perhaps Took, the son of a clergyman, sympathized with Godwyn's cause regardless of its profitability. In any event, none of Godwyn's publications enjoyed a second edition or even a second printing, despite their ongoing topicality; the demand for his polemics was conspicuously slim.[96] And there is the curious absence of information about his life after 1685: no subsequent publications (except the probably posthumous snippet), no new parish assignments, not even, as mentioned before, a death date. England was not as hostile to Godwyn's cause as were Virginia and Barbados, but it was scarcely supportive. Godwyn accused his colonial opponents of a conspiracy of lies; his crusade in England encountered a less formal but almost as damaging conspiracy of silence.[97]

Eventually, long after Godwyn's day, the racist ideology he exposed and challenged would be attacked by more numerous and effective voices, and the Church of England would take a more aggressive stance. Early in the eighteenth century the Society for the Propagation of the Gospel in Foreign Parts, joined later by the Associates of Dr. Bray, would institutionalize Anglican missionary efforts, though their success with slaves would be curbed substantially—as Godwyn's had been—by suspicions that Christianity was incompatible with slavery. As the author of the 1708 pamphlet that incorporated Godwyn's "*Brief Account of Religion, in the Plantations*" complained, the planters put up "a stiff Opposition," partly because they feared—despite all the experience and laws to the contrary—that baptism would bring freedom to their bondsmen.[98] And even though the brand of Christianity offered to the slaves still followed the line that Godwyn had implicitly proposed—an emphasis on Christian obedience to masters, on the duty of servants to work diligently at their divinely appointed tasks, and on the slave's obligation to wait for faith's rewards in heaven rather than seizing them on earth—few slaves in British America had been baptized or instructed.[99] Midway through the eighteenth century, a new generation of reformers in England and America began to articulate a different sort of Christian obligation that challenged not only the ideology but the institution of slavery itself. These reformers, too, encountered bitter opposition, and their successes came slowly and modestly, yet increasingly they were heard and read, and their critiques of racism and slavery began to reach receptive minds.[100]

That Morgan Godwyn, almost a century earlier, had addressed overwhelmingly hostile or indifferent audiences and had therefore made little dent in the ideological underpinnings of British American slavery and the other forms of racial discrimination should not obscure his importance to the uneven but ongoing eighteenth-century critique of the Anglo-American empire's racial policies and beliefs. At least his writings were available for the reformers to cull for insights into the slave owners' ideology and for arguments to undermine it. And Godwyn's writings remain useful today, partly because they recount so extensively and vividly the abuses heaped on Africans in England and America that might otherwise go unnoticed in the historical record, but especially because—in conjunction with the more fragmentary sources that have long been used—they reveal the prevalence and virulence of a racial ideology in seventeenth-century Anglo-America that sanctioned perpetual bondage only for people of dark skin and African heritage. The ideology's early appearance in America and its tenacity, as Godwyn so poignantly discovered, made it impossible to eradicate in his day, or, as subsequent reformers have also discovered, in their days either.

CHAPTER FOUR

Frontier Banditti and the Indians: The Paxton Boys' Legacy, 1763–75

This essay is less about changing colonial perceptions of Indians from 1763 to 1775 than about how drastically perceptions had disintegrated in one British province between the late seventeenth century and the third quarter of the eighteenth. From the outset of William Penn's colonial venture in the 1680s, the Quaker leader sought respect and equity for native inhabitants; "lett them have Justice," he urged, "& you win them." Penn established policies to implement that goal and repeatedly admonished Pennsylvania's officials and the growing flow of European immigrants to practice Quaker ideals of kindness and nonviolence. Eighty years later, his colony—no longer dominated by Quakers either in the government or among the Euro-American population—set a sorry standard in its treatment of Indians. This essay documents the record of atrocities from the Paxton Boys' assassinations of Conestoga Indians in late 1763 until the eve of the American War of Independence.

Emphasized here is the pervasiveness of an anti-Indian sentiment that surely qualifies as racism. Prevalent among the Pennsylvania frontiersmen was an assumption that Indians were innately inferior people who, many Euro-Americans insisted, were unworthy even to exist. This essay also emphasizes the role of legal institutions—laws, courts, juries, prisons—and how they, almost as much as racial perceptions, had changed. A fair administration of justice on the Pennsylvania frontier had become the exception rather than the rule—a change that the Indians deplored and acted upon in the ensuing decades.

Neither perception nor law was universally hostile to the Indians. As the essay reveals both explicitly and implicitly, many Pennsylvanians deplored the words and actions of the lawless multitude and strove vigorously to bring offenders to "condign punishment." And the law itself was not always deficient, as Governor William Franklin demonstrated in the neighboring colony of New Jersey. Yet the abundance of evidence (much of it presented here; far more could be added) shows beyond reasonable doubt that whatever benign view of the Indians may have prevailed in the 1680s, and whatever equality of justice may have been meted to Indians in the colony's first half century, they had given way to racial disharmony and inequity by the 1760s.

A preliminary version of this essay was presented to a seminar at the American Antiquarian Society in the spring of 1983; it was subsequently revised and expanded for publication in Pennsylvania History 51 (1984): 1–29, and is reprinted here by permission of that journal. I have made several minor modifications to the text and added a few recent publications to the notes.

On SEPTEMBER 13, 1766, secretary of state for the Southern Department, Lord Shelburne, addressed a circular letter to the governors of Britain's North American colonies. "His Majesty's Superintendents for Indian Affairs," he wrote with evident consternation, report "that the most unprovoked violences and Murthers have lately been committed on the Indians . . . whose Tribes are at present in Peace and Amity with His Majesty's Provinces, and that the offenders have not yet been discovered and brought to Justice." The danger was imminent and immense. In conjunction with frequent encroachments on Indian lands and sharp practices by colonists engaged in the Indian trade, recent crimes against friendly Indians threatened to embroil British America in a massive frontier war. Through Shelburne's letter, King George commanded his governors "to remedy and prevent those Evils, which are as contrary to the Rules of good Policy as of Justice and Equity."[1]

Pennsylvania was one of the most culpable colonies.[2] Until the 1750s, William Penn's province had enjoyed unparalleled peace with its Native American inhabitants; when abuses of Indians occasionally occurred, colonial authorities had generally administered impartial justice.[3] That idyllic picture changed dramatically in the mid-1750s. The French and Indian War brought several years of frontier carnage that returned, after a brief lapse, during Pontiac's uprising of 1763. Although peace was soon restored, interracial harmony was not. Frontier frustrations and racial antagonism reached a symbolic climax in December 1763 when a band of Lancaster County ruffians slaughtered twenty friendly Indians and attempted, several weeks later, to wreak the same vigilante violence on 140 Christian Indians sheltered in Philadelphia. The Pennsylvania government's inability to apprehend, let alone punish, any of the perpetrators inaugurated a new stage in American frontier justice that King George and Lord Shelburne so rightly deplored. The alternative was clear enough—equity for Indians and "condign Punishment" for colonial offenders—but from the moment of the Paxton Boys' first depredation until the outbreak of the American War of Independence a dozen years later, that alternative remained elusive. During that period, all parties to the events suffered severely: Indians from repeated casualties, frontiersmen and their families from Indian retaliations, and colonial officials (both provincial and imperial) from the frustrations of an ungovernable frontier. Indian respect for Anglo-American concepts of justice and its administration suffered too. Heretofore Indians had accorded Anglo-American justice grudging respect; by the eve of the American Revolution they viewed it with widespread contempt. The dis-integration of colonial justice on the frontier thereby contributed to the growing breach between American colonists and their Indian neighbors.

Pennsylvania's frontier assassins of 1763, quickly dubbed "the Paxton Boys," have not been ignored by subsequent generations. Their exploits have been castigated, and occasionally defended, in countless chapters, articles, and dissertations that have searched the events in Lancaster County and Philadelphia for political, social, or literary lessons.[4] Such quests are fruitful: the Paxton Boys' massacre of the Indians and their march on Philadelphia had important ramifications for Pennsylvania's political alignments and were important reflections of class and religious tensions; they also spawned a vigorous though transient array of broad-sides and pamphlets. But far more lasting and profound for colonial Pennsylvania and the other mainland colonies was the Paxton Boys' detriment to frontier justice in particular and Indian-white relations in general. From 1763 until 1775, imperial officials lamented the failure of colonial authorities to curb the "lawless Banditti" of the colonial fron-tier, especially in Pennsylvania, and predicted dire consequences.[5] Of-ten these officials, along with other observers of Indian affairs, insisted that the flood of unpunished crimes against Indians had been initiated and invigorated by the Paxton Boys' brazen disregard for law and au-thority. Their legacy was more than political factionalism, more than de-nominational and social bickering, more than polemical banter. The Paxton Boys' principal legacy was "open season" on the Indians, friend or foe, a circumstance the Indians surely remembered when they chose sides in the American Revolution.

I

Between 1754 and 1763, thousands of men, women, and children on the western frontier of Pennsylvania and the adjacent colonies were killed, wounded, or captured by the several Indian tribes at war with Britain's mainland colonies.[6] The Pennsylvania Assembly, dominated by Quaker pacifists, did little to relieve the frontiersmen's plight. As one dis-gusted Pennsylvanian observed early in the French and Indian War, "In the midst of all this misery, the citizens [in the East] are doing their Busi-ness as usual, without much seeming Concern; they neither muster, nor arm, nor fortify, nor make one Effort for the Relief of the Back Inhabi-tants. . . ." Even after the Quakers largely withdrew from provincial poli-tics in 1756, a series of commanders-in-chief of British forces in Amer-ica found Pennsylvania's representatives unwilling to contribute their share to offensive operations against the French and their Indian allies or against hostile tribes during Pontiac's uprising in 1763–64. Settlers on Pennsylvania's frontier—mostly Scotch-Irish Presbyterians with little love for their English Quaker compatriots—still suffered from marauding Indians. And because the five frontier counties had only ten seats in the assembly to twenty-six for Philadelphia and the three eastern counties, westerners had little hope of political redress. Their petitions fell on deaf ears. People in the "back country" increasingly considered their enemies to be most easterners and Quakers as well as all Indians.[7]

In Pennsylvania, as elsewhere, frontiersmen rarely distinguished between friendly and enemy Indians, especially when wartime tensions gave way to hysteria. So it was at daybreak on December 14, 1763, when fifty or more armed men from the Lancaster County town of Paxton and its vicinity rode into a tiny community of Christian Indians at Conestoga Manor, eight miles west of Lancaster, killed and scalped the six inhabitants—two men, three women, and a child—and burned their houses. County officials quickly rounded up the remaining fourteen Conestogas who had been away at the time of the massacre and put them for protective custody (willingly, according to some accounts, reluctantly according to others) in the workhouse adjacent to the Lancaster jail. Two weeks later another gang rode into Lancaster, pushed aside token resistance from the sheriff and coroner, and slaughtered every Indian man, woman, and child in the workhouse. Once again the murderers rode off unmolested and unidentified. Even a proffered reward of six hundred pounds for information leading to the arrest of the ringleaders went unclaimed as the frontier community closed ranks.[8]

The destruction of the Conestogas failed to quench the Paxton Boys' thirst for human destruction. With their number now swelled to hundreds, they marched in early February toward Philadelphia with the rumored intention of killing the 140 Indians who, with a few Moravian missionaries, had sought asylum in the city's military barracks.[9] The Paxton Boys never got that far; an advanced force of perhaps 250 stopped at Germantown on learning that between them and the barracks were more than five hundred citizen-volunteers and nearly two hundred royal troops, all well-armed, with cannon primed, ready to repell any attempt to harm the Indians. The Paxton Boys wisely disbanded on promise from Benjamin Franklin and other government spokesmen of amnesty for their threat to public order and an opportunity to present their grievances to the governor and legislature. Their major grievances—paucity of frontier defenses, underrepresentation, and Quaker favoritism to Indians—received scant attention from the legislature. But the immediate crisis was over. The Moravian Indians were unscathed, and eventually they returned to their frontier homes.[10]

A few days before the Paxton Boys reached Germantown, Benjamin Franklin published a scathing attack on "The Rioters" that ignited a year-long literary conflagration. Throughout 1764, critics and defenders of the Paxton Boys traded accusations and insults, many of them aimed at religious affiliations (Quakers versus Presbyterians) or geographic location (easterners versus westerners) as Pennsylvanians vented their frus-

trations in verbal battle. Several pamphleteers reflected the prevalence
of an attitude toward Indians that partly explains the Lancaster County
massacres, the government's inability to make arrests, and the Pennsylvania frontier's imperviousness to equity for Indians.[11] At their mildest,
the pro-Paxton writers dismissed the Conestogas as "a *drunken, debauch'd,
insolent, quarrelsome* Crew." More virulent was the contention that *all* Indians were "Perfidious." Extremists wanted to "extirpate from earth this
Savage Race."[12]

Although hostility toward the Indians was strongest on the frontier,
the Paxton Boys had substantial support in the east too, even in Philadelphia, especially among the Germans and Scotch-Irish. On the eve of the
Paxton Boys' arrival at Germantown, many government leaders feared
that frontier hostility had "Spread like a Contagion into the Interior
parts of ye province & Even ye City it self." Franklin attested that the approaching insurgents were "encourag'd by the general Approbation of
the Populace," and after they disbanded at Germantown he concluded
that "The Spirit of killing all Indians, Friends and Foes, spread amazingly thro' the whole Country: The Action [against the Conestogas] was
almost universally approved by the common People. . . ." Even allowing
for some exaggeration on Franklin's part—he boasted that his condemnation of the Paxton Boys had turned the tide in the government's
favor—there is no doubt that anti-Indian sentiment was widespread in
the East as well as the West and that racial stereotypes were beginning
to pervade Pennsylvania's mental landscape.[13]

In keeping with incipient racism, some of the pamphleteers in 1764
insisted that the Indians were inherently inferior to European-Americans. An anti-Paxton pamphleteer parodied the frontier view by having
its fictional spokesman assert, "[I]f I tho't that any of their Colour was
to be admitted into the Heavenly World, I would not desire to go there
myself." That exaggerated the anti-Indian position, perhaps, but not by
much. A writer generally sympathetic to frontier grievances put the matter starkly: "the White People most in General, hates any Thing that
Savours of the Name of an Indian." Franklin had already tried to counter
such racist nonsense, with little apparent success. In his *Narrative of the
Late Massacres, in Lancaster County*, he had argued poignantly against cat-
egorical prejudice:

> If an *Indian* injures me, does it follow that I may revenge that Injury on all
> *Indians?* It is well known that *Indians* are of different Tribes, Nations and
> Languages, as well as the White People. In *Europe*, if the *French*, who are
> White People, should injure the *Dutch*, are they to revenge it on the *Eng-
> lish*, because they too are White People? The only Crime of these poor
> Wretches seems to have been, that they had a reddish brown Skin, and black
> Hair; and some People of that Sort, it seems, had murdered some of our
> Relations. If it be right to kill Men for such a Reason, then, should any Man,
> with a freckled Face and red Hair, kill a Wife or Child of mine, it would be
> right for me to revenge it, by killing all the freckled red-haired Men, Women
> and Children, I could afterwards any where meet with.

There was, of course, no logical answer to Franklin's rhetorical question except the one he wanted, but neither Pennsylvania's frontiersmen nor, probably, the bulk of its citizens throughout the colony were ready to grant his point.[14]

II

The Paxton Boys' vigilante tactics and their successful flouting of Anglo-American law set a pernicious example along the Pennsylvania frontier. To the dismay of the Indians in amity with the colony and to the chagrin of government officials responsible for maintaining a peaceful frontier, the Paxton Boys continued to violate laws and to vent with impunity their hostility toward Indians.

Not all frontier crimes involved murder, for there were less drastic ways to maltreat Indians and defy colonial laws. A year after the Paxton Boys returned home from their march on Philadelphia, an observer charged that "The Paxton Boys still continue to interrupt the Laws of Community, and are daily doing Acts in defiance of government."[15] Later in 1765, a crowd of frontiersmen with blackened faces, called "Black Boys" by some and by others "Paxton Boys" (the latter term by then encompassed a wide range of Pennsylvania frontiersmen) destroyed several wagon-loads of goods in Cumberland County en route to Pittsburgh for distribution to the Indians. When soldiers from Fort Loudoun confiscated some of the remaining goods and took a few frontier leaders into custody, the Paxton Boys laid siege to the fort and eventually took its commander hostage. "The Outrages committed by the Frontier People are really amazing," Benjamin Franklin gasped from London. "Impunity for former Riots has emboldened them. Rising in Arms to destroy Property publick and private, and insulting the King's Troops and Forts, is going great Lengths indeed!" For none of these actions was anyone punished. A few were charged, but the grand jury at Carlisle, entirely sympathetic to the frontiersmen, returned no indictments.[16]

Although the Fort Loudoun incident had its roots in frontier hostility to Indians, few if any Indians were involved in the fracas itself, perhaps because they feared the consequences of close proximity to the settlers. "The lawless Inhabitants of Cumberland County," a Philadelphian predicted, "will massacre all Indians, who enter the interior part of it . . ." Indians could expect little better in neighboring Lancaster County. Tuscaroras migrating from North Carolina to Iroquois country in 1766 were "well used, by the Inhabitants during their whole Journey 'till they came to *Paxton*"; there they were abused by the inhabitants and robbed of their horses. Once again no arrests were made, no courts were convened, no frontiersmen were punished for abusing peaceful Indians. Colonial officials could only grumble at the frontiersmen's perversity. Sir William Johnson, Superintendent of Indian Affairs in the northern colonies, complained of the "ill timed resentment of ye Country People, who think they do good Service when they Knock an Indn in the Head, and I am well informed they intend to do so with all they meet in small partys. . . ." In March 1766 General Thomas Gage informed Penn that he was "sorry to find that the lawless Banditti on your Frontiers continue giving you fresh troubles. The Robberies and disturbance they have been guilty of with Impunity, emboldens them to every Act of Violence, whilst they flatter themselves that they are secure from Punishment." A few months later, Benjamin Franklin added his voice to the sorrowful chorus. "It grieves me," he wrote from London, "to hear that our Frontier People are yet greater Barbarians than the Indians, and continue to murder them in time of Peace. I hope . . . the several Governments will find some Method of preventing such horrid Outrages. . . ."[17]

General Gage, as the principal imperial official in British America and the only one with professional troops at his command, tried hard to quell frontier violence and oust illegal squatters—prime instigators of interracial friction—through military might. He ordered all royal forces to assist governors in the maintenance of law and order, and he threatened offenders with "Military Execution." However, Anglo-American law allowed few opportunities for royal troops to control civilians or to hail them before courts-martial. On the eve of the Paxton Boys' arrival at Germantown in 1764, Governor Penn warned the assembly that he could not request assistance from the Royal Americans in the Philadelphia barracks until all efforts by civil authorities had failed—hence the sudden mobilization of Philadelphia's manpower. A year later, the commander of royal forces at Fort Loudoun discovered the impotence of his troops against hostile mobs and their sympathetic magistrates. "The several Governments" were stymied.[18]

Worse still for the prospect of curbing frontier crimes against Indians was the reluctance of colonial assemblies to grant changes of venue to permit murderers of Indians to be tried before (presumably) impartial juries. Frontiersmen accused of crimes against Indians often protested that they were about to be sent east for trial where they would be denied fair hearings—a charge too often believed by historians. The law, however, was clear on this point, and it wholly favored the frontiersmen. The few attempts to change the law in specific cases were fruitless; criminals would be tried where the crimes were committed or not at all.[19] Only three exceptions applied: (1) a Pennsylvania law of 1744 required that *Indians* accused of capital crimes in distant areas be tried in Philadelphia County; (2) Parliament's Mutiny Act of 1765 authorized the removal of civilian offenders from "places within his Majesty's dominions in *America*, which are not within the limits or jurisdiction of any civil government" to "the next adjoining province"; and (3) a Pennsylvania act of 1770, aimed specifically at the "Black Boys," authorized change of venue if the accused wore a disguise. Of the three laws, only the Mutiny

Act was likely to be used against abusers of Indians, and it was distressingly ambiguous because the jurisdictional boundaries of Pennsylvania and its neighbors were often difficult to determine and because it was not always clear which of several bordering colonies was "next adjoining." In effect, the Mutiny Act allowed military authorities to send suspected criminals from west of the Proclamation Line of 1763 (and its subsequent readjustments) to any nearby provincial capital for trial. Rarely did such circumstances arise.[20] Crimes committed on the far western frontier were as likely, in fact more likely, to go unpunished as were those perpetrated in Lancaster or Cumberland Counties.

With culprits almost assured of immunity, atrocities against Indians continued apace. In 1765 two hunters—one from Virginia, the other from Maryland—boasted of killing two Indians near Pittsburgh and "shew[ing] the Scalps publickly"; the same year an Iroquois chief was murdered on the road between Fort Cumberland and Fort Bedford, and nine Shawnees were killed in nearby Augusta County, Virginia, by "a number of the Country People."[21] In 1766 a principal Delaware warrior was killed between Redstone Creek and Cheat River and three Delaware chiefs near Fort Pitt; a Mohawk was killed and scalped about twelve miles from Fort Cumberland. The suspect in the latter case was Samuel Jacobs, who reportedly fled to some other part of the frontier. Governor Penn asked his counterparts in Maryland and Virginia to help find Jacobs, but to no avail. Governor Francis Fauquier of Virginia could get no information about Jacobs and was not surprised. "I have found by experience," he told Penn, "it is impossible to bring anybody to Justice for the Murder of an Indian, who takes shelter among our back Inhabitants. It is among those People, looked on as a meritorious action, and they are sure of being Protected."[22]

Fauquier's assessment was prophetic of the next major crisis on the Pennsylvania frontier. In January 1768, John Penn furnished Sir William Johnson with "the disagreeable and Melancholy Intelligence of a very Barbarous and unprovoked Murder" of ten Indians in Cumberland County. The situation was especially serious because Indian affairs were precarious and because the murderer, like so many others before him, scalped his victims. In Indian protocol, that was tantamount to a declaration of war. According to agent Alexander McKee, "the Scalping those Indians is worse than murdering. . . ."[23] Rumors of imminent war swept across the frontier.

Penn, Johnson, and General Gage were all determined to bring the culprit, Frederick Stump—a German settler at Penn's Creek—to justice. The governor offered a £200 reward, but Johnson, for one, was skeptical that Stump could be captured (Fig. 4.1). Although Sir William considered the murders "one of the most dangerous Accidents that could have happened at this Period," he knew the likely sequel: "I much fear that the Lawless Gentry on the Frontiers will render it worse by screening the Murderer or contributing to his Escape." Pennsylvania's Indian

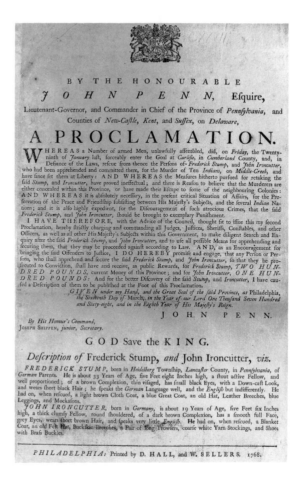

Fig. 4.1

Proclamation of 16 March 1768 for the apprehension of two white men for the murder of ten Indians. Stump and Ironcutter had been in the Carlisle jail awaiting trial when an anti-Indian mob freed them by force. The Historical Society of Pennsylvania.

agent George Croghan was equally pessimistic. "I Raly begin to fear the Consequences," he told Johnson. The Delawares and Shawnees were deeply upset, "and thire is No prospect of this Government being able to give them thet Satisfaction w[hic]h Might Convince them that this Murder was Nott Commited with Desine[,] fer the perbetraters of itt is Nott Likely to be brought to Justus. . . ."[24]

Johnson and Croghan predicted accurately. Despite the certainty of his guilt and the enormity of his crime, Stump remained at large. He admitted to William Blyth, a Cumberland farmer, that on January 10, 1768, he killed in his own house six Indians—four men and two women—and stuffed their bodies through a hole in an ice-covered river;

the next day he tried to prevent news of the murders from spreading among the Indians by killing an Indian woman, two girls, and an infant (apparently they knew of the crime) and burning their cabins. Perhaps in response to Penn's promise of a reward, Stump was eventually arrested by Captain William Patterson, "A Smart young Felow," aided by nineteen men, and delivered to the sheriff at Carlisle; the prisoner and his servant, John Ironcutter, were ordered to Philadelphia for questioning. Cumberland's magistrates, however, refused to release the prisoners until the government gave assurances that the trial would be held in the county, and local magistrate John Armstrong discharged the prisoners' guard.[25] Six days later Stump and Ironcutter were rescued "by A Number of pople from the Fronteers in ye Middle of ye Day." Armstrong gave Penn the details of the rescue by which, he admitted, "we are deceived and disgraced at once": about ten o'clock on January 29, seventy to eighty armed men surrounded the jail, some jostled the magistrates while others took the jailer's keys at gunpoint, opened the dungeon, and whisked away Stump and Ironcutter "in open Triumph." As at Lancaster, no one admitted to recognizing a single member of the mob, although Penn bluntly charged Armstrong that "many of [them], it is more than probable, you and those other Magistrates who were present with you and were Witnesses of the whole Transaction personally knew." Stump and Ironcutter were never recaptured; some of their rescuers were indicted but none convicted. "I have not Words to Convey fully to thee," a discouraged Quaker complained to Benjamin Franklin in early February 1768, "the Prevalence of a Disposition in the Inhabitants of Cumberland County, to support All persons who kill Indians. . . ."[26]

Pennsylvania's friendly Indians remained understandably suspicious of colonial intentions and integrity; they could see plainly enough that despite the efforts of some administrators and legislators, the bulk of the white population—at least on the frontier and perhaps throughout the colony—would allow Indians to be murdered with impunity. Several months before the Stump episode, General Gage saw little hope of doing justice to the Indians. "[I]t is a Fact," he told Lord Shelburne, "that all the People of the Frontiers from Pennsylvania to Virginia inclusive, openly avow, that they will never find a Man guilty of Murther, for killing an Indian." After the massacre by Stump and Ironcutter and their rescue from jail, George Croghan warned:

> The many Murders committed on Indians in and on the Frontiers of Pennsylvania and Virginia and no one being Ever punished for them, cannot fail of exciting in the Minds of the Natives, the most unfavorable opinion of the Justice and Strength of the Government and its Effects must be extremely prejudicial to the King's general Interest in America.[27]

The Paxton Boys' legacy was very much alive.

The Pennsylvania Assembly put much of the blame on the proprietary government. With a mixture of genuine concern and partisan bias, the legislators assailed Governor Penn for encouraging a lawless climate by his earlier failure to prosecute anyone for the crimes at Conestoga and Lancaster. "There is a manifest failure of Justice somewhere," the Assembly charged, and accused the executive branch of letting murderers think they were immune from legal accountability. "[T]he Authors of Crimes of so black a dye," it admonished Penn, "should be strictly punished. It is in all Probability owing to the Encouragement arising from the Impunity with which these Criminals [at Conestoga and Lancaster] have been permitted to escape, that the subsequent Murders in this Province have been committed." Penn protested that he had taken "every Measure . . . on that Melancholy occasion which the Law would Warrant," but the Assembly insisted that he at least should have held the local officials—sheriffs, coroners, magistrates—to strict accountability and removed them from office if they could not justify their "unparalleled Inactivity." He should also, the assembly argued, promise a reward of at least five hundred pounds and protection from retaliation for information about the murderers. Penn took offense at such criticism. He called the assembly's suggestions "indecent and unbecoming" and defended his handling of both the Paxton and Stump affairs. But the assembly had the last word. "The proper Time for punishing Offenders," it reminded the governor, "is as soon as possible after the offense is committed; every neglect or delay does but encourage them and others to the Perpetration of the like or other Crimes." In the relative privacy of a letter to Benjamin Franklin, Speaker of the Assembly Joseph Galloway was blunter. "The Government Truckles to the Lawless Banditti," he charged. "The Impunity with which Offenders escape is a perpetual Encouragement to the Licentious and Wicked to commit new Offences."[28]

With unpunished murders came greatly increased danger of retaliation by the Indians, which likely would lead to counterretaliation and eventually to full-scale war. Such a possibility no doubt underlay King George's response to the Stump murders. He learned of the episode from Lord Hillsborough, his new secretary of state for the American colonies, who reported to Penn "His Maty's pleasure that every Method shou'd be used to bring the Perpetrators of this shocking Butchery to the most exemplary Punishment, in the manner most satisfactory to the Indians. . . ." Royal wishes, however, were meaningless in such matters. No perpetrators were punished and the Indians remained unappeased. Predictions of a devastating Indian war now emanated from almost every provincial capital and every Indian agent, as racial tensions in western Pennsylvania reached their most volatile point since Pontiac's Rebellion. In this crisis, the colony's hopes for peace rested on condolence gifts and the Indian agents' arts of persuasion. As George Croghan observed shortly after the massacre by Stump, "the Repated Murders on those Fronteers and ye Want of power in ye Government to bring ye Murdrers to punishment Must bring on hostilitys unless Some Attonment Can be Made the Indians by Condoleing & presents Very Early this Spring." Pennsylvania took Croghan's advice. In February 1768 the assembly voted £3000 for resolution of the crisis: £500 for rearresting Stump and Ironcutter, £2500 for presents to the Indians.[29] Of that amount, Sir William Johnson distributed £1300 in grievance gifts at his conference with the Iroquois in March; Croghan dispersed the rest at Fort Pitt the following month.

Johnson called his Indian congress "the most troublesome I ever held." The problem was not the number of Indian delegates (more than eight hundred) but the Indians' growing suspicion that the English couldn't be trusted. "To remove their discontent totally," he explained, "when we consider the Nature and Number of their Grievances, was more than could possibly be done; nor can it be expected, till they experience the Change in us." The French, an Iroquois spokesman told Johnson, had warned his people not to trust the English, and they seem to have been right. "[I]nstead of the English protecting us . . . they employed their superior Cunning to wrong us; they Murdered our People in Pensilvania, Virginia, and all over the Country. . . . [W]ho is to help us? we can't ramble over the Country for Justice, and if we did, we begin now to grow Old and Wise, and We see that your Wise Men in the Towns will always be against us." If the English governments couldn't manage their own people, the Indian insisted, "surely it is but right that we should punish those who have done this Mischief." After several days of formal and informal meetings, Johnson convinced the Iroquois to keep the peace (Fig. 4.2).[30]

In April and May, Croghan was similarly successful with more than one thousand Indians representing several Ohio valley tribes and the western Iroquois.[31] In some respects Croghan's job was easier than Johnson's because western Indians had killed twelve Europeans the previous year on the Ohio River, and none of Stump's victims were from the western tribes. Thus the English could claim to be the aggrieved party. In any event, the almost simultaneous conferences at Johnson Hall and Fort Pitt prevented the Stump murders and the still-rankling Paxton Boys' atrocities from bringing on the greatly feared and frequently predicted general Indian war.

Hard as it was to pacify the Indians, at least it could be done for awhile. Provincial and imperial officials had no parallel success with Pennsylvania's frontiersmen. In July 1769 a Seneca Indian was killed, apparently by a German yeoman, Peter Reed, near the Susquehanna River. Reed was apprehended and jailed at Lancaster, and a grand jury investigated the facts. A letter describing the murder to William Johnson expressed fear of a rescue and the probability that the testimony of the Indian witnesses would not in any event be allowed. On the latter point the prediction was accurate: Reed was soon "discharged by Proclamation." The next year, servant John Ingman killed "Indian Stephen" in Pennsylvania; Ingman was arrested in Virginia and extradicted after he confessed.

Fig. 4.2

Johnson Hall, home of Sir William Johnson and site of several major Indian-white conferences. This conjectural view was painted by Edward Lamson Henry in 1903. From the Collection of the Albany Institute of History and Art.

Governor Botetourt of Virginia advised Penn that "never was an Act of Villany more unprovoked or more deliberately undertaken," yet again there is no evidence of a trial or the "rigid punishment" urged by Lord Botetourt.[32] In 1771 Mathew Haley, a runaway indentured servant, admitted that he had murdered two Senecas near Fort Pitt and described the deed in gruesome detail. There is no record of a trial and no reference in the surviving documents to the disposition of the case. Presumably it went unpunished.[33] In May 1774 a Delaware Indian, Joseph Wipey (or Weepy), was murdered, apparently by John Hinkson and James Cooper of Westmoreland County. Arthur St. Clair, the Penns' agent on the frontier, had been informed in advance that the murder was likely to be committed but was unable to prevent it, and the sudden disappearance of the body thwarted attempts to hold an inquest. Pennsylvania's representatives voted a hundred-pound reward for Hinkson's and Cooper's arrest and condemned the ongoing crime wave. "The House, with horror, look upon the frequent Murders that have been of late committed on some of the Western Indians in and to the Westward of this Province," the legislators wrote, and Governor Penn assured the Delawares that he would try to punish the offenders. Apparently they were never caught. Nor were the two parties of colonists, "said to be Virginians," who killed eleven Delawares and Shawnees ninety miles south of Pittsburgh at about the same time Joseph Wipey was meeting his fate near Ligonier.[34] Despite a decade of lamentations, proclamations, admonitions, and rewards, Indians received scant justice on the Pennsylvania frontier.

III

To a large extent the situation was incorrigible. Widespread frontier hatred of Indians encouraged abuses and the sheltering of culprits; settlements scattered over a vast area weakened government attempts to gather information; a paucity of provincial and imperial officials—distinct from town and county officials who usually shared the frontier prejudices—thwarted judicial administration at every stage. Yet neighboring New Jersey set an example of what could be done with luck and an aggressive chief executive.

New Jersey, to be sure, did not have Pennsylvania's unbounded western domain, nor did it have Pennsylvania's substantial Indian population; its frontier problems were accordingly more manageable. On the other hand, New Jersey's self-interest in obtaining justice for the Indians may have been weaker. As Governor William Franklin informed Lord Shelburne in 1766, New Jersey was "less interested in keeping up a good Understanding with the Indians than almost any other Colony in N. America, as they do not pretend any Claim to Lands within our Limits, and as we have no Trade or Intercourse with them except now & then a Hunter of the Six Nations straggles down among our Frontier Settlements."[35]

Whatever the peculiarities of New Jersey's situation, like other colonies it had a frontier and like other colonies it had interracial murders. But under Governor Franklin murderers paid a heavy price, for he refused to let popular antipathy to Indians frustrate the administration of justice. In response to Shelburne's circular letter of 1766 to colonial governors that complained of recent "violences and Murthers," Franklin insisted that "whatever may be the Case in the other Colonies, nothing of the kind has been suffered to pass with Impunity in this Province. This I believe, His Majesty's Commander in Chief [Thomas Gage], & the Superintendant for Indian Affairs [William Johnson] will do me the Justice to acknowledge."[36] And indeed they would, based on Franklin's recent efforts to arrest, prosecute, convict, and execute two murderers of Indians and to apprehend another murderer who sought protection among his frontier neighbors. A close look at the two cases reveals some parallels between New Jersey's frontier crimes and Pennsylvania's and highlights Governor Franklin's persistent efforts for interracial equity.

June 26, 1766: two Delaware women, Hannah and Catherine, residents of an Indian reservation in Burlington County, New Jersey, were "robb'd and murdered . . . in a most barbarious Manner." When their bodies were found three days later, county authorities made a hasty search for James Anen and James McKenzy, who had recently arrived from the Pennsylvania and Virginia frontiers and were reportedly en route to New York. Apparently they did not expect to be arrested: their identities were easily secured, they had publicly abused the two women shortly before the murder, they sold the victims' belongings a few hours after the crime, and they made little or no attempt to escape. Anen was soon seized in New Jersey; McKenzy was arrested a few days later in Philadelphia on the basis of a description in the *Pennsylvania Gazette* that urged readers to apprehend "a Scotchman, about 18 or 20 Years of Age, [who] wears his own Hair, light coloured, has no Beard, but a white Down on his Chin; one Leg sore, and thereby is lame, a Pair of whitish Stockings, one of which was stained with the Blood of the Indians. . . ." Anen and McKenzy were incarcerated in the Burlington jail until July 30 when they went before a court of oyer and terminer. If the culprits expected a mock trial, they badly misjudged Governor Franklin, who later boasted to Lord Shelburne that "I omitted nothing in my Power to have the Villains apprehended, & was so lucky as to have them taken in a few Days after, and brought to Justice."[37]

Franklin's justice was rigorous but apparently fair. The prisoners were examined separately; each admitted that he had intended to ravish the squaws and that he had witnessed the murders, but each blamed the other for the lethal blows. The guilt of both men seems beyond doubt (one later confessed), and their brazen brutality must have offended all but the most vehement Indian-haters. "The youngest of the Squaws was near the Time of Delivery," the *Pennsylvania Journal* reported, "and had Marks of shocking Treatment, which the most savage Nations on Earth could not have surpassed." Such brutality apparently stemmed from the same frontier attitudes that inspired the Paxton Boys: Anen, fifty-four years old and a former resident of the Pennsylvania frontier, declared on the gallows that "he thought it a duty to extirpate the Heathen." Among his audience were "a few of the principal Indians of Jersey," whom Governor Franklin invited to bear witness to his colony's impartial justice. On August 1, 1766, Anen and McKenzy were hanged.[38]

Franklin was also responsible for the only other case in the Pennsylvania or New Jersey records of the 1760s and 1770s in which murderers of Indians were brought to "condign Punishment." In April 1766, Robert Seymour (Seamor, Seamon, Simmons, Simonds) and David (some accounts say Robert) Ray were suspected of murdering an Oneida Indian who was trading in Minisink, New Jersey. Franklin was, he asserted to Shelburne, "indefatigable in my Endeavors" to have them arrested and tried. That proved more difficult than in the Anen and McKenzy case. Seymour, "a base Vagabond fellow" who had deserted from the British army, was soon apprehended, but not for long. His neighbors rescued him from Sussex County jail, hid him from the authorities, and "threatened Destruction" to anyone who tried to rearrest him. When Seymour eventually came out of hiding and "appeared as publickly about his Business as any other Farmer in the Neighbourhood," Franklin induced the sheriff of Morris County to seize him. And when the sheriff of Sussex County, where the trial would have to be held, insisted that no local jury would find Seymour guilty, Franklin urged the assembly to legislate a change of venue. It refused (as had the Pennsylvania legislature when Benjamin Franklin sought a similar law in the Paxton case), and the county's magistrate showed no inclination to call a special court to try Seymour; they were content to wait five months or more for the circuit court to reach Sussex. Franklin would not wait. He again appointed a court of oyer and terminer to conduct a trial in the county where the crime occurred, and again he sought Indian observers. In this instance he preferred Indians who lived on the frontier near the English, "as their Connections & Acquaintance may make their Report to the Oneidas, & particularly to the Relations of the Murdered Indian the more readily Credited, & thereby induce them to continue their Confidence in the British Government."39

On December 18, 1766, a grand jury indicted Seymour for murder and Ray for manslaughter. At the trial the next day, Ray pleaded guilty and asked benefit of clergy; he was branded on the hand and released. Seymour, despite abundant evidence against him—including witnesses who swore that he admitted the crime "and declared he would destroy any Indian that came in his way"—seemed so confident of eventual release that he "behaved with great Boldness." It did him no good. After a fair trial, judging from contemporary accounts, the jury found Seymour guilty. Even then he expected to be rescued. Franklin, however, had taken precautions: twenty-five militiamen guarded the prisoner day and night. Their presence cooled the ardor of the large crowd that attended the trial, and for good measure the presiding judge, Charles Read, "seemed to calculate his Discourse pretty much to the Audience, by painting the Heinousness of the Crime, the terrible Effect it might have had on the Frontiers, if the Indians had been possessed by the same Spirit of Revenge with the Prisoner [and] the ingratitude of it, as it was well known that the Oneida Nation, to which the murdered Indian belonged, had during the whole Course of the last War, cooperated with his Majesty's Troops." Although the prisoner continued to expect a rescue until he went to the gallows under heavy guard, an eyewitness reported that there was "not . . . a Murmur among the People, and the most Sensible were fully convinced of the Justice of his Sentence." Shortly before his execution, Seymour confessed his guilt. Abraham, an Oneida, attended the trial and execution and "appeared highly satisfied with the Justice of the Proceeding, which he said he should represent to his Brethren."40

Governor Franklin's efforts were widely praised in the segment of the colonial population that favored order and equity. A few days after the execution, a Philadelphia businessman wrote to Superintendent Johnson that "The Government of New Jersey, certainly deserve great Credit for the Laudable Spirit, They have evinced, in punishing Indian Murderers. And to do Governor Franklin Justice It must be admitted, That

He has been very industrious, To have, the last Fellow, in particular, convicted, As his Crime was aggravated, by a most atrocious Robbery." Franklin also won praise from both houses of the New Jersey Legislature. "We and every Inhabitant of this Colony," the Upper House declared "have Reason to rejoice that Justice has been executed on such abandon'd Villains." The Pennsylvania legislature lauded Franklin's success too and called upon Governor Penn to emulate it. The Paxton murders and the government's failure to avenge them, the assembly told Penn, have engendered a special Indian animosity toward Pennsylvania, but "like Offences, in the King's Neighbouring Government of New Jersey, have been brought to condign Punishment, and thereby a satisfactory Attonement made to the Indians for the Loss of their Brethren." Only such a vigorous administration of justice could restore "the Government [of Pennsylvania] to its former Power and Dignity, lately so insolently trampled on," and convince "those Offenders, that altho' Justice may sometimes *Sleep*, it can never *Die*."[41]

IV

New Jersey's handling of the two murder cases in 1766 demonstrated that not every colonist wanted to exterminate the Indians and that colonial courts on rare occasions administered impartial justice; the baneful shadow of the Paxton Boys did not reach every corner of British America. But New Jersey's record was atypical. While Sir William Johnson and his subordinates made good use of the New Jersey cases in their attempts to convince friendly tribes of the colonists' good intentions and commitment to interracial equity, the successes of a single colony in a single year could hardly offset Pennsylvania's sorry record or similar cases in other colonies. More representative was an instance of wholesale murder just across Pennsylvania's northern border. In 1772, David Ramsay, a frontier trader living in the vicinity of Fort Niagra, murdered and scalped eight Indian men, women, and children. Despite abundant evidence against him, including a confession which pleaded self-defense under improbable circumstances, William Johnson saw little chance of a conviction, even if Ramsay were taken to Canada (under the Mutiny Act) where the prospect of a fair trial was greater than in New York. "He is a fellow of a bad Character," Johnson told Croghan, "and was banished from the [trading] Posts before, for his Villainy. However I don't think he will Suffer, had he killed a Hundred." And so it was. Ramsay was tried in Montreal but released for lack of evidence.[42]

As early as the summer of 1766 General Gage summed up the pattern that would exist with alarming consistency from 1763 to 1775: "The Murthers which have been too frequently committed and gone unpunished, and the people settling themselves upon Lands belonging to the Indians, It's greatly to be feared, unless some speedy and vigorous measures are taken to prevent both, will too soon involve us again in all the misery of an Indian war." Imperial agents such as George Croghan, who knew the Indians well, corroborated the general's fears. In May 1766 Croghan reported that representatives of the Shawnees, Delawares, Iroquois, and Hurons who visited him at Fort Pitt were "very discontented in their Minds on account of having several of their people killed by the English, some on the Frontiers of Virginia, Pennsylvania, and the Jerseys, besides three Shawanese murdered & Plundered by two men who ran away from this Post down the River." To the Indians the pattern seemed more than incidental; they sensed a fundamental colonial plot to oust them altogether. "This Conduct they say of their Fathers the English," Croghan reported, "does not look as if they were disposed to live in Peace with their Children, the Indians." Several years later, Sir William warned Governor Penn that "the Ill treatment which the Indians have of late but too often received from the Frontier Inhabitants, . . . have occasioned more general discontent than is imagined, for altho' the friends of the deceased are always pleased at being condoled with, yet where so many Instances happen, and such a Spirit manifests itself amongst the Inhabitants, the Indians are induced to think that we have some general Design against them."[43] Condolence gifts, even retributive justice as in New Jersey's cases, simply could not offset the cumulative effect of frequent frontier murders that went unpunished.

Colonial Pennsylvania never solved the problem. Governor Penn acted sincerely but ineffectually after each episode; the Pennsylvania Assembly repeatedly voted funds for rewards and gifts; and the imperial agents concerned with Pennsylvania's frontier strove tirelessly to quell the Indians' unrest and to blunt their inclination toward revenge. Although no major war broke out between 1764 and 1775, for several months in 1774 Virginia was embroiled in "Lord Dunmore's War" with the Shawnees, and unresolved murders and frequent retaliatory raids remained a standard frontier feature to the embarrassment of Pennsylvania officials and the exasperation of England's Indian agents.[44] "It is the most astonishing thing in the world," Arthur St. Clair told John Penn after Joseph Wipey's murder in 1774, that "the common people of this Country, actuated by the most savage cruelty, . . . wantonly perpetrate Crimes that are a disgrace to humanity."[45]

Lawless frontiersmen plagued Sir William Johnson to the end of his life. His last letter, dated July 4, 1774, reported to General Gage that Captain Michael Cresap and others had murdered thirty or more Shawnees and Iroquois near the forks of the Ohio River. "This lawless Banditti according to Custom fled, after doing the mischeif," Johnson explained, and many innocent settlers fell to the Indians' wrath. But, Johnson assured Gage, "The Irregularities committed on the Frontiers since You went for England [Feb. 1773; Gage returned to America in May 1774] were indeed so many & encreased so fast that they alone would be sufficient to bring on a War without the recent provocation the Indians received from *Cressop*, for Numbers of these Ruffians . . . relying on the impotence of the Several Governm[en]ts are regardless of any restraint, and are daily guilty of Robberies & Murders. . . ." Johnson sadly concluded that frontier justice was beyond his control: "I have the mortification to find that my Schemes & endeavours for preserving or restoring tranquility are frequently defeated by the gross Irregularities of our worst Enemies the Frontier Banditti."[46]

V

From the earliest days of American colonization, English authorities insisted in treaties with friendly or defeated tribes that henceforth Indians who damaged English property or took English lives be tried and punished by colonial courts, not by tribal authorities; at the same time, colonial courts explicitly or implicitly retained jurisdiction over Englishmen who violated Indians or their property. Provisions to that effect appear frequently in seventeenth- and eighteenth-century treaties.[47] Pennsylvania was no exception. In 1685 William Penn summarized the judicial arrangement he had made with the tribes near Philadelphia: "[I]f any of them break our Laws, they submit to be punisht by them: and to this they have tyed themselves by an obligation under their hands." Half a century later, Governor George Thomas reminded Indian delegates to the Lancaster Treaty conference of 1744 that if whites killed or abused Indians, "You are not to take your own satisfaction, but to apply to me and I will see that Justice be done you; and should any of the Indians rob or murder any of our People, I do expect that you will deliver them up to be tryed and Punished in the same manner as White people are. That is the way to preserve Friendship between us, and will be for your benefit as well as our's." Governor Thomas thereupon demanded custody of two Indian suspects.[48]

Several assumptions underlay English insistence on judicial monopoly over crimes involving Indians and Europeans. Primarily it came from the notion that the Crown had political sovereignty over the whole continent—though not necessarily ownership of lands occupied by Indians—and all the peoples in it. The king's law must therefore prevail whenever possible.[49] (It was not possible, of course, in remote Indian villages or among powerful independent tribes.) Of almost equal importance was the assumption that a system of written laws and codified procedures was superior to "savage" customs and concepts based on oral traditions. "[T]he Indians," contended a treaty provision of 1765, "have no establish'd Laws for punishing the Guilty."[50] Third, Indian leaders were assumed to have little coercive power over their subordinates, who often went to war for individual motives rather than reasons of state. According to Croghan, Indian leaders "can't be accountable for the . . . Conduct of their Warriors, who are governed only by the persuasion of the Chiefs." Indian leaders admitted as much. "[W]e can nott be accountable fer our Warers [warriors'] Conductt," an Iroquois spokesman acknowledged in 1761, "as we have No Laws to punish them as you have to punish y[ou]r people."⁵¹ Finally, the colonists assumed that an aggrieved Indian—or in the case of murder, the victim's kin—would take revenge against the culprit or a substitute figure, usually a member of the culprit's family or clan or, if the transgressor were a colonist, against a member of his colony or his race. Conrad Weiser, a skillful eighteenth-century interpreter and negotiator, observed that "when an Indian in his own Judgment thinks him self wronged by Some Body, more Especially by the white people, he will never forgive, and he is apt to revenge himself, and urged to do it by his Country people."⁵² Despite such deep-rooted and pervasive cultural sanctions, Indians in the Pennsylvania area showed remarkable restraint in the face of overwhelming provocation. Individual acts of revenge continued, but many tribes accepted—at least outwardly—colonial insistence on exclusive jurisdiction in interracial cases. As late as 1774 the Senecas delivered two accused tribesmen to colonial authorities for trial and punishment.⁵³

Perhaps in the seventeenth century, when English settlement was relatively sparse and most colonists lived close to the centers of authority, there was some validity in the English claim to having ensured an orderly and equitable frontier. It was certainly *not* valid in the 1760s and 1770s, a fact the Indians soon recognized. They complained frequently and justifiably of traders who flouted colonial and imperial regulations, of settlers who squatted on Indian lands in violation of gubernatorial and royal proclamations, and of murderers who killed Indians without fear of reprisal by their own governments. "You that have Laws, and say you can make your People do what they are desired," an Iroquois speaker admonished in 1768, "should prevent all this, and if they won't let us alone you should shake them by the Head. We believe that you are wise, and that you can do all this, but we begin to think that you have no Mind to hinder them." The speaker was right about the proper course for colonial authorities but wrong about their ability to accomplish it. The truth was that on the frontiers of Pennsylvania and neighboring colonies the provincial and imperial authorities could not do what the Indians, or they themselves, wanted. William Johnson, increasingly disturbed by the rebelliousness of American colonists against England, blamed frontiersmen and colonial governments alike: peace was improbable in light of "the disorderly measures of the inhabitants, & the present imbecility of the American Governments, who are I fear as unable to procure, as their people are unwilling to afford[,] justice for the Indians."⁵⁴ In Indian affairs, the frontier had succumbed to anarchy. There was no effective law, no method of enforcement, and no adherence to superior authority. To a considerable extent, colonists and Indians had reversed their roles: now Indians rather than colonists needed protection from bloodthirsty enemies; now colonists rather than Indians took revenge on a perpetrator or his "kin"; now Indians rather than colonial spokesmen complained that their opponents could not control their subjects.

The reality of the reversed roles was not lost on the Indians or on a few insightful Englishmen. "You often tell us," an Iroquois speaker noted in 1768, that "we don't restrain our People, and that You do so with Yours; but, Brother, your Words differ more from your Actions than ours do." Six years later, a Seneca chief admonished Superintendent Johnson: "Brother, We are sorry to observe to you that your People are as ungovernable, or rather more so, than ours." About a month before his death, Sir William acknowledged the Indians' equal or greater adherence to law and order. "The few [hostile] Acts they have committed compared with what they suffer are nothing," he confided to General Frederick Haldimand, "especially when we consider that they are a People without Laws or Authority, & that we pretend to both, tho as they say we Manifest neither." General Gage implicitly endorsed the assessment when he reported to the earl of Dartmouth that New York had relinquished—on orders from George III—the two Senecas who had been turned over to colonial authorities as suspected murderers. "Accounts came in so fast," Gage explained, "of Murders committed by the Frontier People upon Indians, that we could give them no Satisfaction for, that it was judged adviseable to restore the two Prisoners to their Nation, as the only means to pacify them."[55] The surviving records confirm what Gage, Johnson, and the Indians perceived: by the second half of the eighteenth century, Indians in the area from New York to Virginia had the more law-abiding society.

The colonists' inability to maintain order and punish frontier miscreants proved especially dangerous after 1775 when the rift with England widened. Both parties to the imperial dispute wanted Indian allies, or at least they wanted to deny such allies to the opposition; both parties therefore courted the major tribes.[56] From the outset, however, royal spokesmen held the better cards. With some justification they could claim that they had tried to restrain the colonists by establishing a "permanent" boundary line, by punishing—when possible—frontier murderers, and by making generous condolence gifts to aggrieved tribes. If the Indians considered any Englishmen true friends, or at least lesser enemies, the honor must have gone to imperial officials such as Sir William Johnson (and his nephew/son-in-law Guy Johnson, who succeeded him in 1774 as superintendent of Indian affairs in the Northern Department), William Franklin, George Croghan, and several other agents to the Indians.[57] Surely the Indians knew that their most dangerous enemies were the American frontiersmen who seized Indian lands and committed crimes, even murder, against Indians with indifference and impunity, and because neighbors offered sanctuary to even the most vicious criminals. When the American rebellion reached the point where Indians along the Pennsylvania border had to align themselves with one side or the other, the issue was scarcely in doubt. The Paxton Boys and their legatees had left them little choice.[58]

PART TWO

Culture and Race in Early Virginia

CHAPTER FIVE

"Expulsion of the Salvages": English Policy and the Virginia Massacre of 1622

Two antithetical versions of Anglo-Indian relations have dominated the histori-cal literature on early Virginia. Both acknowledge the physical and psychologi-cal devastation of 1622, when an uprising led by the Powhatan leader Opechan-canough almost exterminated the colony and instantly persuaded imperial spokesmen that the Indians in general were a problem to be overcome rather than an opportunity to be encouraged. But one school of interpretation emphasizes the harmony—imperfect but improving—that existed before 1622; the other stresses the persistence of antagonism, in both attitudes and actions, between Indians and colonists from 1607 until the (virtually inevitable) explosion under Opechan-canough.

This essay falls somewhere between the extremes. It sees some of the colony's leaders, both in England and in America, striving for good relations and mak-ing some superficial progress toward a mutually acceptable modus vivendi; *but the essay also emphasizes underlying incompatibilities of Anglo-American inten-tions and attitudes that undercut the possibility of Indian acquiescence. The ev-idence for the Virginians' contempt for their native neighbors and its implica-tions for Indian-white relations was no doubt apparent at the time (as later testimony reveals), but imperial and colonial policymakers seem to have been largely oblivious to it until the massacre. Thereafter, scarcely a single English voice was raised in defense of Indian rights or in favor of a conciliatory policy.*

A word about massacre. *It has lately been politically incorrect to apply that word to an Indian attack on colonists, on the grounds that it is deeply pejora-tive, implying sneakiness and indiscriminate slaughter. I find the argument spe-cious. "Slaughter of a large number of people or animals" is the dictionary def-inition, and, in fact, Opechancanough's men did both, and for understandable reasons. Early Anglo-Virginians too committed massacres, as historians should and sometimes do proclaim, and there's almost universal application of the term in subsequent American history, as in Colonel Chivington's massacre of Cheyenne Indians in 1864. The word, I contend, is descriptive rather than judgmental*

and is therefore used in this essay, as is uprising, *another appropriate term for
the dramatic event of 1622.*

*This essay, like the next one in this volume, emerged from my research during the
early 1970s for a book on Captain John Smith. Given my interest in early American race relations, it was unsurprising that part of my interest in Smith was his
close involvement with the natives of Virginia; in order to understand his role,
I needed to explore the broader context of Indian-white contact in early English
colonization. A preliminary version of the article was presented in October 1974
to a conference at the University of Maryland on the Chesapeake colonies in the
seventeenth century, and a fuller account appeared in the* William and Mary
Quarterly, *3d ser. 35 (1978): 57–84. It is reprinted here with minor revisions
in the text and notes.*

F EW EVENTS IN EARLY AMERICAN history match the drama or significance of the Virginia massacre of 1622. It cost the fledgling colony the
lives of almost 350 settlers; it contributed to a subsequent famine and
epidemic that killed another five or six hundred; it hastened the collapse of the Virginia Company of London; and it brought on a ruthless
counterattack against the Indians, in which scores of settlers and hundreds of Indians perished. It also wrought a major shift in English policy.[1] For almost a decade before the massacre, a substantial number of
imperial spokesmen on each side of the Atlantic favored peaceful and
cooperative contact—albeit on their own terms—with the tribes of eastern Virginia and had begun to fashion an integrated society of Indians
and Europeans within the English settlements. After the assault, such a
scheme was no longer advocated or attempted. Instead, there emerged
a policy of unrestrained enmity toward independent neighboring tribes
and almost total separation of the English and Indians that reflected a
persistent but often repressed contempt for the American natives. Governor Francis Wyatt put the matter bluntly. "Our first worke is expulsion of the Salvages . . . ," he wrote soon after the massacre, "for it is in-
finitely better to have no heathen among us, who at best were but as
thornes in our sides, then to be at peace and league with them."[2]

Wyatt's judgment, widely shared by the London Company and by his
fellow colonists, forecast Virginia's posture for the remainder of the century. For ten years after the massacre, the colony, abetted by the company and the crown, waged merciless war against its neighboring tribes,
whether or not they had participated in the uprising. The eventual peace
agreement of 1632 established separate domains for Englishmen and
Indians. A very few natives, converts to Christianity or totally subservient
to Anglo-American culture, were thereafter permitted to live within the
colonial perimeter; for the vast majority of the Indians, however, the

events of 1622 meant permanent exclusion from the areas controlled by the intruders. All prospects of an integrated society had vanished.

I

From the beginning of their colonial movement Englishmen held ambivalent and sometimes contradictory views of the American Indian. On the one hand, they perceived him as a fit prospect for conversion to Christianity and a desirable partner in trade; accordingly, the champions of colonization advocated settlement near sizable native populations. On the other hand, Englishmen recognized the Indians as potential enemies. Even the most ardent imperialists predicted that at some point Indian resistance was inevitable. It must not, however, thwart England's other objectives. As early as 1585 the elder Richard Hakluyt candidly stated the prevailing English position: "The ends of this voyage [to America] are these: 1. To plant Christian religion. 2. To trafficke. 3. To conquer. Or, to doe all three. To plant Christian religion without conquest will bee hard. Trafficke easily followeth conquest: conquest is not easie." But the solution was clear. "If we finde the countrey populous, and desirous to expel us . . . that seeke but just and lawfull trafficke, then by reason that we are lords of navigation, and they are not so, we [can] . . . in the end bring them all in subjection and to civilitie."[3] Almost a generation later, when England was at last on the verge of planting a permanent colony, the expectation of Indian enmity remained. In its instructions to the expedition of 1606–7 to Virginia, the London Company advised its settlers not to allow the Indians to live between the English outpost and the sea, for "you Cannot Carry Your Selves so towards them but they will Grow Discontented with Your habitation and be ready to Guide and assist any Nation that Shall Come to invade You."[4]

Underlying the fear of Indian resistance was a variety of European experiences in the New World. The Spanish had met formidable hostility (Englishmen for the most part considered it well deserved), so had Portuguese and French expeditions, and so too had England's Roanoke colonists in the 1580s. The Roanoke experience intensified English ambivalence: Indian trade and assistance had been crucial to the initial success of the colony, and descriptions of the Indians by Arthur Barlowe and Thomas Hariot, as well as John White's paintings, were generally favorable, yet Indian opposition had almost certainly doomed the first English outpost.[5]

Equally important in shaping attitudes toward the Indian were preconceptions of native culture, which ethnocentric Englishmen and their European neighbors held in contempt, partly because it differed from theirs and partly because it had certain characteristics—nakedness, for example—which to English eyes seemed barbarian or savage.[6] Moreover, as a people wholly unfamiliar with Christ's message, the Indians were heathens at best, the devil's minions at worst. And so, without ever seeing an American native, English writers decried his customs and his religion. In the mid-sixteenth century William Cunningham believed the Indians to be in some ways "comparable to brute beastes"; half a century later, Robert Johnson considered them "wild and savage people, that live . . . like heards of Deare in a Forrest."⁷ King James's judgment was harsher still. His *Counter-blaste to Tobacco* (1604) did more than damn the "filthie novelitie" of smoking; it also revealed a virulent antipathy to the natives of America. Indians brought by English explorers, the king contended, had introduced "the corrupted baseness" of smoking into the British Isles. "What honour or policie," he wondered, "can moove us to imitate the barbarous and beastly manners of the wilde, godlesse, and slavish *Indians*, especially in so vile and stinking a custome? . . . Why doe we not as well imitate them in walking naked as they doe? in preferring glasses, feathers, and such toyes, to golde and precious stones, as they do? Yea why do we not denie God and adore the Devill, as they doe?" "It seemes a miracle to me," he professed, "how a custome . . . brought in by a father so generally hated, should be welcomed."⁸

Most English spokesmen were less vituperative. Many of them were clergymen who longed to convert the Indians to Christianity. Clerical opinion was accordingly more sympathetic and hopeful than its secular counterpart. The elder Hakluyt, lawyer and geographer, predicted conquest of the natives; his clerical cousin and namesake saw matters somewhat differently. "The people of America," the younger Hakluyt insisted, "crye oute unto us . . . to come and helpe them, and bringe unto them the gladd tidinges of the gospell."⁹ Hakluyt and his fellow clergymen were undoubtedly sincere. They had no desire to destroy the Indians— that would make conversion impossible—and they repeatedly insisted that the Indians were children of God whom all Christians had an obligation to help. But clerical pamphleteers nonetheless viewed Indian society as pejoratively as did their secular compatriots. In 1609 the Reverend William Crashaw offered a concise summary of the churchmen's position. "Out of our humanitie and conscience," he promised, "we will give them . . . 1. *Civilitie* for their bodies, 2. *Christianitie* for their soules: The first to make them *men:* the second *happy men.*"¹⁰

England's colonial advocates merged the elder Hakluyt's premise that the English had a natural right to trade with the Indians and Crashaw's belief that until they acquired English "civilitie" they would not be human in the fullest sense into a further assumption: England had an obligation to establish the foothold that would facilitate commerce and conversion. Perhaps the land belonged to the natives, perhaps not; Englishmen were undecided on that point. But they were certain that the Indians misused their territory. "The Lord," asserted Robert Gray in a sermon in 1609, "hath given the earth to the children of men, yet . . . is the greater part of it possessed and wrongfully usurped by wild beasts, and unreasonable creatures, or by brutish savages, which by reason of their godles ignorance, and blasphemous Idolatrie, are worse then those beasts which are of most wilde and savage nature." England, at the same time, was overcrowded and needed desperately to export "such unnecessarie multitudes as pester a commonwealth."[11] Under those circumstances, neither clerical nor lay imperialists doubted England's right to plant settlements in the American forest.

Once in the New World, Englishmen would begin the social and spiritual conversion of the natives. It would be, their spokesmen claimed, benign conversion—"by faire and loving meanes," insisted Robert Johnson, "suiting to our English natures."[12] Yet he and Robert Gray, like the elder Hakluyt, saw the possibility of bloodshed. "A wise man, but much more a Christian," Gray cautioned, "ought to trie all meanes before they undertake warre: devastation and depopulation ought to be the last thing which Christians should put in practice." But if the Indians rejected trade and the gospel, the Bible provided a rationale for action: "forasmuch as everie example in the scripture ... is a precept," Gray contended, "we are warranted by this direction of Joshua, to destroy wilfull and convicted Idolaters, rather then to let them live, if by no other meanes they can be reclaimed." Gray assured his readers that Englishmen, unlike Spaniards, would not force the Indians off the land or wage offensive war; he nonetheless quoted with approval Saint Augustine's opinion that "warre is lawfull which is undertaken ... for peace and unities sake: so that lewde and wicked men may thereby be suppressed, and good men maintained and relieved."[13]

II

Armed with this logic, Jamestown's early colonists made more use of the sword than the olive branch. During the first several years they treated the Indians as real or potential foes, seldom as prospective converts. The colony had too few clergymen to serve its own sick and unruly population, the language barrier proved more formidable than expected, and the Indians showed far more interest in English goods than in the English god. The missionary objective was therefore temporarily set aside; politics, not theology, dominated early Indian-English relations.[14] When, for example, Christopher Newport explained to suspicious Indians the meaning of a cross the settlers erected on Indian soil, he made no mention of its religious symbolism. Rather, he contended, the arms represented himself and Chief Powhatan, and the junction point symbolized their bond of unity.[15] Thus while writers back home continued to insist that conversion of the natives was the principal purpose of colonization, the men on the scene—John Smith, Thomas Dale, Thomas Gates, and the other early leaders of Virginia—acted on a different premise.[16] They were military men and saw the Indians as essentially a military problem. John Smith later summed up his experience in terms that applied, mutatis mutandis, to all of the colony's leaders—hardened veterans to a man. "The Warres in *Europe, Asia,* and *Affrica,*" he recalled, "taught me how to subdue the wilde Salvages in *Virginia.*"[17]

This is not to say that the colonists resorted at once to murder and rapine. Neither they nor the company were so witless as purposely to enrage a people who vastly outnumbered them and from whom they must obtain badly needed food and information. The London Company, in fact, ordered Captain Newport to treat the natives well. It also admonished Captain Smith when it thought he acted too brusquely.[18] But the company's primary concern was for the survival and eventual prosperity of the colony, and for the present the Indians appeared more a hindrance than a help. The company shaped its policy accordingly.

The evolution of that policy reflected the disdainful English attitudes toward native culture as well as the colony's immediate needs. Initially, the company, through its resident leaders, tried to keep the Indians from understanding the colonists' intentions and thus from resisting with full force the planting of a permanent colony. Smith, among others, tried to allay Indian apprehension by foisting a cock-and-bull story on Powhatan. The English had not come to stay, Smith told him, but had landed to escape a Spanish squadron; Newport had gone back to England for help and would soon bring an expedition to carry the survivors home. Newport returned all right, but with additional men to strengthen the garrison and with the company's latest strategem to divert potential Indian resistance. He would place a crown on Powhatan's head, symbolic of the chief's supremacy over his own people but indicative, too, of his subservience to King James. Powhatan saw through the ploy. He refused to go to Jamestown for the ceremony, and he refused to kneel to accept the crown when Newport brought it to his village. Although it was eventually placed on his head, Englishmen could take little comfort in the event.[19] The Indians remained, as they had been from the outset, skeptical of English intentions. They wanted trade; they did not want Christianity or encroachment on their lands.

Since the founding of Jamestown, the Indians had made clear their opposition to extensive English colonization. As early as August 1607 Sir Walter Cope wrote to Lord Salisbury—on the basis of information brought home by Newport—that the Indians "used our men well until they found they begann to plant and fortefye. Then they fell to skyrmishing and kylled 3 of our people." George Percy, a member of the original expedition, concurred. "The Savages murmured at our planting in the Countrie," he recalled, but he took consolation in a petty chief's assurance that all would be well if the English did the Indians no harm and took only "a little waste ground, which doth [neither] you nor any of us good." But the colony grew. A Dutch chronicler reported that within two years of the founding of Jamestown, "the Indians seeing that the English were beginning to multiply, were determined to starve them and drive them out."[20] Intermittent warfare between the colonists and Tidewater tribes dragged on for seven years. On several occasions the natives attacked English expeditions probing the interior; the capture of John Smith and his subsequent rescue by Pocahontas stemmed from one such episode. On other occasions Indian forces assaulted the English plantations. Their lack of firearms, and the settlers' use of cannon in their forts and on ships tied up nearby, prevented the Indians from annihilating the colony, though they inflicted substantial losses on English stragglers.[21] Still, throughout the early years English spokesmen insisted that relations with the Indians would soon be amicable and that conversion would readily follow. "In steed of Iron and steele," Robert Johnson, a staunch member of the company, advised the colonists, "you must have patience and humanitie to manage their crooked nature to your form of civilitie."[22]

Neither patience nor "humanitie" was plentiful in Jamestown. During most of its first two and a half years, John Smith dominated relations with the Indians; he believed the colony would do better under a firm and aggressive policy than under Newport's mollycoddling. Smith was seldom ruthless—especially compared to his successors—and he managed to avoid open clashes that would have been devastating to both the colonists and the Indians. But his handling of the natives was highhanded at best, and he often threatened force with every apparent intention of using it. An early settler summed up the situation: "To express all our quarrels, trecheries and incounters amongst those Salvages I should be too tedious: but in breefe, at all times we so incountered them, and curbed their insolencies, that they concluded with presents to purchase peace; yet we lost not a man: at our first meeting our Captaine ever observed this order[,] to demaund their bowes and arrowes, swordes, mantells and furrs, with some childe or two for hostage, whereby we could quickly perceive, when they intended any villany."[23] Smith allowed no Indian recalcitrance. On one occasion he seized Opechancanough, leader of the Pamunkey tribe and half brother of Powhatan, by the hair. "You promised to fraught my Ship [with corn] ere I departed, and so you shall, or I meane to load her with your dead carkases."[24] (Fig. 5.1) A few weeks later, Smith grappled with another chief, dragged him into a nearby river, and almost drowned him. He spared the Indian, however, when "having drawne his faucheon to cut off his head, seeing how pittifully he begged his life, he led him prisoner to *James* Towne, and put him in chaynes."[25] Such tactics prevented open warfare. They did not promote cordiality or conversion.

Smith's success was ensured by the feebleness of Powhatan's efforts to dislodge the colony. Not that the chief misunderstood the settlers' objectives. Smith recorded a revealing conversation of early 1609 (filtered, of course, through Smith's ear and pen): "Captaine *Smith*, (saith the king) some doubt I have of your comming hither . . . for many do informe me, your comming is not for trade, but to invade my people and possesse my Country." Powhatan wanted peace. "Having seene the death of all my people thrice . . . I knowe the difference of peace and

Fig. 5.1

Captain John Smith grappling with Opechancanough, 1608, as engraved by Robert Vaughan for Smith's *Generall Historie of Virginia, New-England, and the Summer Isles* (London, 1624). Courtesy, Virginia Historical Society.

warre, better then any in my Countrie." If he fought the English, Powhatan predicted, he would "be so hunted by you, that I can neither rest, eat, nor sleepe; but my tired men must watch, and if a twig but breake, everie one crie there comes Captaine *Smith*, then must I flie I knowe not whether, and thus with miserable feare end my miserable life."[26] Reluctantly the chief accepted the English presence, especially since the colony remained small and rent by dissension.

In 1609 the London Company promulgated a new plan. The trouble, it decided, lay not with the Indians at large but with their leaders; by controlling them the colony could control their followers. The company's instructions to Sir Thomas Gates, newly appointed colonial governor, conceded that Powhatan "loved not our neighbourhood and therefore you may no way trust him." The solution: "if you finde it not best to make him your prisoner yet you must make him your tributary, and all other his weroances [subordinate chiefs] about him first to acknowledge no other Lord but Kinge James." By shifting their allegiances from Powhatan to the English, the lesser chiefs would contribute much-needed provisions to the colony, for they must pay the English for releasing them from Powhatan's tyranny and for protecting them from other enemies. Such tribute in corn, dye, and skins, and in labor, would not only provide desired commodities but also "be a meanes of Clearinge much ground of wood and of reducing them to laboure and trade." Should the Indians flee into the country on the approach of the English, Gates was to capture their chiefs and all known successors. If their future leaders were trained in English manners and religion, and installed at the head of tribes, "their people will easily obey you and become in time Civill and Christian."[27]

Indian religious figures, the company thought, were as dangerous as the chiefs. Gates's instructions advised him to "remove from them their Quiocasockes or Priestes by a surprise of them all and detayninge them prisoners." This tactic seemed reasonable to ardent Christians who believed that the Indian priests so beguiled and terrified their subjects that "while they live amounge them to poyson and infecte them their mindes, you shall never make any greate progres into this glorious worke, nor have any Civill peace or concurre with them." That, in turn, justified more drastic measures. "In case of necessity, or conveniency," the company informed Gates, "we pronounce it not crueltie nor breache of Charity to deale more sharpely with them and to proceede even to dache [death] with these murtherers of Soules."[28] The Indians were probably unimpressed by the distinction between Smith's threats while taking temporary hostages and seizing food, and the company's ostensible kindness while intending to exterminate their chiefs and priests.[29]

Before Gates could implement the new policy, the Indians—abetted by famine and the settlers' ineptitude—almost exterminated the colony. During the horrendous winter of 1609–10, Powhatan, by direct assaults and withholding food, contributed appreciably to the ghastly mortality of the "starving time."[30] The chief no doubt rejoiced when the famished English remnant evacuated Jamestown in the spring of 1610. He must have been equally disappointed when Lord De La Warr arrived at the last moment to reestablish the colony. For De La Warr brought more than fresh supplies and more colonists; he brought the resources and determination to end Indian resistance once and for all.[31] His commission as captain general, as well as governor, authorized him to attack the colony's enemies. War already existed when he arrived. He prosecuted it more vigorously than his predecessors because he had the necessary men and equipment.

During the next several months English forces under George Percy, Thomas Gates, and Thomas Dale demonstrated the elder Hakluyt's dictum that control of navigation would be a major advantage in war against the Indians. Still the natives remained elusive, well aware that their own advantage lay in isolated ambushes rather than open confrontations. Harassed and frustrated, the English rapidly abandoned all regard for customary rules of war and gained much of their success by guile and merciless treatment of captives. Gates lured some Indians into the open with a music-and-dance act by his drummer, then slaughtered them. Percy routed the Paspahegh tribe, destroyed its village and fields, and allowed his men to throw the Indian queen's children into the river and shoot out their brains for sport. Lord De La Warr wanted to burn the queen; Percy convinced him to let her die by the sword instead.[32]

Hostilities lasted until 1614, when Dale used a combination of strength and cunning to extort a treaty from Powhatan. Samuel Argall provided the scheme. He would seize Pocahontas, Powhatan's favorite daughter, and hold her until the chief met the colony's demands. With the assistance of some pliable Indians, whom he bribed into reluctant cooperation. Argall enticed the princess on board his ship; he then demanded that Powhatan release all English captives (a dozen or more), return all English weapons taken by his warriors, and agree upon a lasting peace. In the meantime Pocahontas would remain a prisoner, and English forces would continue to wage offensive war.[33]

Powhatan succumbed. He did not, of course, get his daughter back. She married John Rolfe, sailed to England to meet the king and promote English colonization, and died before she could return to Virginia. But Powhatan would fight no longer. "I am now olde," he told Resident Secretary Ralph Hamor, "and would gladly end my daies in peace, so as if the English offer me injury, my country is large enough, I will remove my selfe farther from you." That satisfied the English, especially when the neighboring tribes followed Powhatan's lead and signed treaties of amity and trade.[34] The colony now had peace, abundant land (for the moment), and evidence, in Pocahontas, that Indians could be made civil and godly.

III

By April 1614—the date of the Rolfes' marriage—Virginia at last enjoyed a modicum of ethnic harmony, which in turn brought a shift in English outlook and policy. The new approach, never universal but increasingly advocated by company leaders and their agents in Virginia, employed kindness, not the sword, to win over the Indians. Earlier predictions seemed to be coming true: an initial welcome from some of the

Indians, resistance from a few leaders, a just war (by English interpretation), the inevitable victory and spoils, and finally the Indians' conversion and acceptance of English ways. The process had taken longer than expected and only one convert could be claimed, but all signs now pointed to a hopeful future. Virginia's Indian policy for almost a decade after 1614 reflected the new optimism.

If the initial Virginia policy had been personified by John Smith, who bullied the Indians but rarely attacked them, and if the more belligerent approach of 1610–14 found its symbol in Thomas Dale or Samuel Argall, Virginia's new emphasis on humanitarianism between 1614 and 1622 was best embodied in George Thorpe. "That worthy religious Gentleman . . . sometimes one of his Majesties Pensioners," had social standing, political influence, and an unusual degree of public conscience. Arriving in the colony in 1620, Thorpe quickly became identified with all phases of the new conciliatory disposition. According to Smith's *Generall Historie*, Thorpe "did so truly affect [the Indians'] conversion, that whosoever under him did them the least displeasure, were punished severely. He thought nothing too deare for them, he never denied them any thing; in so much that when they complained that our Mastives did feare [frighten] them, he to content them in all things, caused some of them to be killed in their presence, to the great displeasure of the owners, and would have had all the rest guelt to make them the milder, might he have had his will." Thorpe also built an English-style house for Opechancanough, with a lock which the bemused Indian reputedly opened and closed a hundred times a day.[35]

Thorpe's principal responsibility was management of the territory set aside by the company to support an Indian college which would eventually be affiliated with an English university, both to be built at the inland town of Henrico.[36] When completed, the college would, its backers hoped, train preachers to spread Christianity among the tribes. Financial support came from England, both from private gifts and from collections taken at the king's command in the Church of England. Early in 1616 James directed the archbishops of Canterbury and York to make semiannual solicitations for the next two years in every parish, toward "the erecting of some Churches and Schooles, for the education of the children of those Barbarians."[37] By 1619 the church had forwarded fifteen hundred pounds to the company treasurer.[38] The company spent some of the contributions in the early 1620s to send farmers to the thousand acres set aside as "college lands," where Thorpe supervised their labors. Other funds went for bricklayers and carpenters to erect a college building. And even before Thorpe arrived, the colonial government had taken the first steps toward recruiting students. "Be it enacted by this present assembly," decreed Virginia's first legislature in 1619, "that for laying a surer foundation of the conversion of the Indians to Christian Religion, eache towne, citty Borough, and particular plantation do obtaine unto themselves by just meanes a certaine number of the natives Children to be educated by them in true Religion and civile course of life. Of which children the most towardly boyes in witt and graces of nature [are] to be brought up by them in the firste Elements of litterature, so as to be fitted for the Colledge intended for them, that from thence they may be sent to that worke of conversion."[39]

While Thorpe labored to make the lands profitable, the London Company sought further financial contributions to underwrite buildings and teachers' salaries. It met with considerable success, for optimism over the eventual anglicization of the Indians had spread in England even more thoroughly than in the colony. Nicholas Ferrar, whose brother John was for a time deputy treasurer of the company, bequeathed £300 to the college, payable when it enrolled ten Indians. He had earlier contributed £24 to each of three Virginia clergymen for raising Indian youths "in Christian Religion, and some good course to live by." And under the pseudonym of "Dust and Ashes" an anonymous donor gave £550 for Indian conversion and vocational training. At the age of twenty-one, the donor stipulated, the Indians were to "enjoye like liberties and pryveledges with our native English in that place." Rather than disburse the principal, the company invested the munificent gift in a colonial ironworks (a poor choice, it turned out); profits were reserved for the education of thirty native children.[40]

Raising funds proved easier than obtaining students. Initially, Indian parents refused to part with their children, and partly for that reason the colony postponed construction of mission buildings. To overcome parental reluctance, Governor George Yeardley contrived a more ambitious plan of integration: he arranged with Opechancanough to bring whole families into the English plantations and to provide them with houses, clothes, cattle, and cornfields. The adults would acquire English ways while the children received religious and secular instruction. Yeardley expected, he reported to London, "to draw in others who shall see them live so hapily."[41] How many Indians lived among the colonists in the early 1620s is impossible to gauge—probably a few dozen at most. But the trends were hopeful. Funds continued to flow from England; bricklayers were at last beginning the first educational buildings; and thanks largely to the efforts of Yeardley and Thorpe, intercultural relations were so cordial that when Sir Francis Wyatt assumed the governorship in 1621 he found "the houses generally set open to the Savages, who were alwaies friendly entertained at the tables of the English, and commonly lodged in their bed-chambers."[42] All in all, prospects seemed bright for turning Virginia's Indians into facsimile Englishmen.

England's imperial spokesmen hailed the colony's progress toward ethnic cooperation. Samuel Purchas later recalled that "Temperance and Justice . . . kissed each other, and seemed to blesse the cohabitations of English and Indians in Virginia." And in the spring of 1622 the Reverend Patrick Copland, a London minister and rector-designate of the Indian college, made ethnic harmony a theme of his sermon to the

London Company. Among "the *Wonderful workes* of the Lord," Copland reminded his audience, was " a happie league of Peace and Amitie fondly concluded and faithfully kept, betweene the *English* and the *Natives*, that the feare of killing each other is now vanished away."[43]

IV

Copland misjudged the situation in Virginia. What appeared to be a new era of peace and cooperation masked underlying tensions that boded ill for Indian-English amity. Those tensions came partly from the settlers' pejorative attitude toward Indian culture, partly from their increasing pressure on Indian lands, and partly from changes within Powhatan's tribe.

Perhaps George Thorpe best reflected the persistence of English ethnocentricity. Thorpe's concern for the natives was undoubtedly genuine, but his fundamental aim, as Smith pointed out, was "insinuating himselfe into this [Indian] Kings favour for his religious purpose"—the temporal and ecclesiastical conversion of the Indians.[44] Thorpe's acts of kindness—whether building houses, gelding mastiffs, punishing miscreant colonists, or promoting the Indian college—were dedicated to the larger goal of transforming Indian society. That theme of English imperial thought had not changed appreciably despite the several shifts in overt policy. Even Rolfe, who had set an impressive example of cultural amalgamation, revealed in his request for permission to marry Pocahontas that he, too, held Indian society in low esteem. He wanted, he told Governor Dale, to honor God, England, and Virginia; only such motives would permit him "to be in love with one whose education hath bin rude, her manners barbarous, her generation accursed, and so discreptant in all nurtriture from my selfe." Pocahontas accepted Christianity, changed her name to Rebecca, and took on a veneer of English manners. Only then did she become acceptable to English society.[45]

The Rolfe-Pocahontas marriage did not, of course, establish a pattern of ethnic fusion. Almost a century later, historian Robert Beverley expressed regret at the early Virginians' failure to intermarry with the Indians.[46] But he and other critics of the early settlers underestimated the depth of Jacobean England's cultural myopia. Most colonists implicitly agreed—even before the massacre—with a pamphleteer of 1624 who explained why few of them took Indian wives. Indian women, he contended, were neither "handsome nor wholesome"; intermarriage would not be "profitable and conveneient (they having had no such breeding as our women have)."[47]

More serious than the Englishman's reluctance to intermarry with natives was his unwillingness to leave them as they were. During the early years the colonists had seized Indian corn, exacted tribute, and wherever possible forced Indian submission to English authority. The colonists admitted as much. The Virginia assembly of 1624 described

Sir Thomas Smythe's regime (1607–19) with remarkable candor: "We never perceaved that the natives of the Countrey did voluntarily yeeld them selves subjects to our gracyous Sovraigne, neither that they took any pride in that title, nor paide at any tyme any contributione of corne for sustentation of the Colony, nor could we at any tyme keepe them in such good respect of correspondency as we became mutually helpful each to the other but contrarily what at any [time] was done proceeded from feare and not love, and their corne procured by trade or the sworde."[48] In sum, English colonial policy had sought the subordination and transformation of native society. As William Strachey articulated the imperial goal: "we shall by degrees chaung their barbarous natures, make them ashamed . . . of their savadge nakednes, informe them of the true god, and of the waie to their salvation, and fynally teach them obedience to the kings Majestie and to his Governours in those parts."[49]

Strachey wrote in 1612. A decade later the goal remained the same, and so did the contempt for Indian culture that all too often became an excuse for maltreating individual natives. Despite the colonists' claims that they and the Indians "lived together, as if wee had beene one people,"[50] the years of relative harmony from 1614 to 1622 were tranquil only on the surface. When, for example, the assembly of 1619 passed laws to protect the Indians from abuse, its motives appear to have been similar to those of the London Company in 1607. "Noe injury or oppression [is to] be wrought by the *English* against the Indian whereby the present peace might be disturbed and ancient quarrels might be revived," the assembly insisted, but it also decreed the death penalty for selling any weapons to the Indians, set a limit of five or six Indian laborers per plantation, and warned "that good guard in the night be kept upon them, for generally (though some amongst many may proove good) they are a most trecherous people, and quickly gone when they have done a villany."[51] Two years later—only ten months before the massacre—Thorpe complained that "there is scarce any man amongest us that doth soe much as afforde them a good thought in his hart and most men with their mouthes give them nothinge but maledictions and bitter execrations. . . . [I]f there bee wronge on any side it is on ours who are not soe charitable to them as Christians ought to bee, they beinge (espetiallye the better sort of them) of a peaceable and vertuous disposition."[52] Even the clergy had lost some of its earlier hope and restraint. In 1621 a Virginia minister saw no prospects of converting the Indians "till their Priests and Ancients have their throats cut."[53]

The period of ostensible concord also saw the rise of a new and irreconcilable issue. During the first years of English settlement the territorial needs of the colony had been small. Few records survive to tell exactly how the early colonists acquired their land from the Indians, but scraps of evidence suggest that some had been freely given, some purchased with tools and beads, and some—probably the greater part—

seized as spoils of war.[54] But coinciding with the rapprochement of 1614, English appetite for land became insatiable. A rapid rise in population and the sudden profitability of tobacco triggered a land boom that threatened every neighboring tribe. Again, the records are frustratingly sparse, but Rolfe left a clue to how the colony acquired vast new stretches of the Tidewater. As early as 1615, he observed, several minor chiefs mortgaged to the colony all their lands, some nearly the size of an English shire, in exchange for wheat.[55] Less than three years later, Governor Samuel Argall reported to the company (only a summary of his letter survives), "Indians so poor cant pay their debts and tribute."[56] It is impossible to estimate how much land the Indians lost through their inability to redeem their mortgages, but the statements by Rolfe and Argall suggest that the total may have been considerable. Whatever the amount, it added another item to the swelling list of Indian grievances. As an English observer acknowledged after the massacre, the Indians had attacked largely out of "dayly feare" that the English would push them off their lands altogether, much as the Spanish had done to the natives of the West Indies.[57]

Not all the changes in policy were undertaken by the English. Powhatan, too, had shifted his strategy from time to time—from cautious friendship to warfare to reluctant acquiescence. His tribe made further alterations between 1614 and 1622. When Powhatan died in 1618 (the year after Pocahontas succumbed to disease in London), tribal leadership passed to Powhatan's younger and bolder half brothers. His immediate successor, Itopan, survived only briefly; Opechancanough followed, and although he promised that "the Skye should sooner falle" than peace with the English be broken,[58] his subsequent actions revealed a profound distrust of the English and a readiness to fight if their encroachment and effrontery became unbearable.

By the early 1620s they had. As land pressure increased and the signs of English disdain for Indian culture mounted, the Indians—especially those between the James and York Rivers—faced several unsavory alternatives. They could accede to the demands for land and for social and religious transformation; they could keep retreating inland as the English settlement expanded; or they could make a desperate attempt to rid Virginia of Englishmen. These alternatives were unequal. Acceptance of English demands meant cultural suicide, and even passive acquiescence to missionaries and land speculators offered no sure protection against tribal disintegration. Movement inland had equally serious drawbacks: it not only required desertion of tribal lands but would bring conflict with enemies in the interior who might destroy the tribe as thoroughly as the English could. And although an attack on the colonists involved frightful risks, the possibility of success in 1622 must have impressed Opechancanough and his advisers. Besides his own substantial forces, he could count on assistance from the Chickahominy tribe, which, according to later English testimony, had been alienated from its 1614 treaty with the colony by a "perfidious act" of Governor Yeardley in which thirty or forty Chickahominies were killed without provocation. Moreover, mortality among the Virginia settlers remained scandalously high; although some 3,570 Europeans arrived between 1619 and 1622 to jump the colonial total to approximately 4,370, only 1,240 were alive on the eve of the massacre.[59] Most of these survivors were inexperienced in forest combat, and they were scattered among eighty-odd plantations, some of them miles from the nearest help.[60] In 1619 the Virginia assembly had cautioned that "in these doubtful times between us and the Indians, it would behoove us not to make so lardge distances between Plantation and Plantation."[61] The warning went unheeded.

By the early 1620s Virginia had every ingredient for an explosion except the spark. That was provided in the spring of 1622 in what John Smith called "The Prologue to this Tragedy":

> *Nemattanow* otherwise called *Jack* of the *Feather*, because hee commonly was most strangely adorned with them; and for his courage and policy, was accounted amongst the Salvages their chiefe Captaine, and immortall from any hurt could bee done him by the *English*. This Captaine comming to one *Morgans* house, knowing he had many commodities that hee desired, perswaded Morgan to goe with him to *Pamau[n]ke* to truck, but the Salvage murdered him by the way; and after two or three daies returned againe to *Morgans* house, where he found two youths his Servants, who asked for their Master: *Jack* replied directly he was dead; the Boyes suspecting as it was, by seeing him weare his Cap, would have had him to Master *Thorp*: But *Jack* so moved their patience, they shot him.[62]

Jack of the Feather died soon after. When Opechancanough threatened revenge, Smith reported, "the *English* returned him such terrible answers, that he cunningly dissembled his intent, with the greatest signes he could of love and peace."[63] Two weeks later, Opechancanough struck.

V

On the morning of March 22, 1622, scores of Indians came to the settlers' homes to trade or converse, "yea in some places sat downe at breakfast." Suddenly the visitors seized their hosts' weapons, or drew knives concealed in their own clothing, and attacked every white man, woman, and child they could reach. Friendship proved no shield. The Indians slew George Thorpe along with the rest, and "with such spight and scorne abused his dead corps as is unfitting to be heard with civill eares."[64] At many of the outlying plantations everyone perished. The list of victims showed seventeen slain at the College lands, twenty-seven at Captain Berkeley's Plantation, seventy-five or more at Martin's Hundred—only seven miles from Jamestown—and scores of others throughout the colony. Among the dead were several members of the council and other prominent residents, as well as many of humbler station, some of them scarcely identified: "The Tinker," "Mary, and Elizabeth, Maidservants," "6 Men and Boyes," "Henry a Welchman," and "A French boy." A few of the communities, including Jamestown, survived because of timely warning by a Christian Indian. By the end of the day the toll reached approximately 340, or more than one-fourth of the population.[65] In the weeks that followed, the Indians picked off stragglers and small parties of settlers. "Since the massacre," Argall reported, "they have killed us in our own doores, fields, and houses."[66] (Fig. 5.2)

In mid-June *Seaflower* arrived in England with the chilling news. The initial response was military. King James donated arms and ammunition from the Tower of London, though his contribution proved to be only some old arms that were "altogether unfitt, and of no use for moderne Service."[67] The London Company also gathered weapons and supplies, and Smith offered to return to Virginia to "inforce the Salvages to leave their Country, or bring them in[to] feare and subjection."[68] The company turned a deaf ear to the captain's proposition, but it acted on the same premise that he did. The Indians must be crushed.

Fig. 5.2
The massacre of Virginians in 1622, depicted with considerable artistic license by the engraver. From Johann Theodor de Bry, *America*, part XIII (Frankfort, 1634). Courtesy of the John Carter Brown Library of Brown University.

During the next decade the colony waged total war against the tribes in tidewater Virginia. Before the massacre it had readily distinguished between friendly and unfriendly tribes; now, rhetorically at least, it viewed all natives as foes. Armies of settlers set out to destroy every vestige of Indian presence in the areas between the James and York Rivers and beyond, while courting military and economic help from still-friendly natives. In January 1623 the Virginia Council of State claimed that "by Computatione and Confessione of the Indyans themselves we have slayne more of them this yeere, then hath been slayne before since the beginning of the Colonie." Governor Wyatt saw the task starkly as the "extirpating of the Salvages."[69]

So thoroughly had the colonists been taken by surprise, and so completely did they project the responsibility onto their enemies, that Wyatt and his council dispensed with conventional methods of warfare. When Opechancanough eluded all attempts to capture him, they invited the chief to a sham peace parley, "to be concluded in a helthe or tooe in sacke which was sente of porpose in the butte with Capten Tucker to poysen them." Perhaps two hundred Indians succumbed to tainted drink; many of them were slaughtered by Tucker's men, who "brought hom parte of ther heades." Opechancanough escaped, but in the opinion of one settler the slaughter was "a great desmayinge to the blodye infidelles."[70]

Such tactics disturbed the London Company. Of course, the Indians must be defeated, the company advised Governor Wyatt in the spring of 1623, but by honorable means. The colonists, however, insisted on a free hand. "Wheras we are advised by you to observe rules of Justice with these barberous and perfidious enemys," the Virginia council retorted, "wee hold nothinge injuste, that may tend to theire ruine, (except breach of faith) [.] Stratagems were ever allowed against all enemies, but with these neither fayre Warr nor good quarter is ever to be held, nor is there other hope of theire subversione, who ever may informe you to the Contrarie."[71] The company did not agree, but in fact its own advice of a few months earlier had encouraged such a policy. In August 1622 it had called for "a perpetuall warre without peace or truce." Children only were to be spared. The company recommended that soldiers pursue the adults, "surprisinge them in their habitations, intercepting them in theire hunting, burninge theire Townes, demolishing theire Temples, destroyinge theire Canoes, plucking upp theire weares, carying away theire Corne, and depriving them of whatsoever may yeeld them succor or relief."[72] In October the company advocated "rooting them out for being longer a people uppon the face of the Earth."[73]

While colonial forces attempted the "rooting out," the company made a frantic effort to restore public enthusiasm for its Virginia venture. In the year following the massacre it issued several propaganda pamphlets, some under its own authorship, some by its friends. Partly the tracts sought to explain how the massacre happened in the first place (the Indians' treachery and God's wrath at the colonists' sinful ways were stock explanations); mainly, they tried to find a silver lining in the war clouds. In both efforts the Indians fared poorly. Gone were the occasional noble qualities that had been credited to them before 1622; gone, too, was any recognition of Indian rights to land and freedom. As Edward Waterhouse, author of the company's apologia of 1622, stated the case: "our hands which before were tied with gentlenesse and faire usage, are now set at liberty by the treacherous violence of the Savages . . . so that we, who hitherto have had possession of no more ground then their waste, and our purchase . . . may now by right of Warre, and law of Nations, invade the Country, and destroy them who sought to destroy us. . . . Now their cleared grounds in all their villages (which are situate in the fruitfullest places of the land) shall be inhabited by us." Other benefits could be expected, Waterhouse promised, in the form of bondservants, "because the *Indians*, who before were used as friends, may now most justly be compelled to servitude and drudgery, and supply the roome of men that labour." Waterhouse considered them especially suited for "inferiour workes of digging in mynes, and the like, of whom also some may be sent for the service of the Sommer Ilands [Bermuda]." His conclusions fulfilled his premise "that the Countrey is not so good, as the Natives are bad, whose barbarous Savagenesse needs more cultivation then the ground it selfe."[74]

As Waterhouse's pamphlet suggested, the massacre of 1622 had reversed the trend of English attitudes toward the Indians. The earlier view of many spokesmen that the natives were redeemable, both religiously and culturally, yielded to a belief that most of them were hopelessly debased. And with that shift in perception came a drastic reversal in policy. Plans for the Indian college were shelved, and voices such as John Donne's and Patrick Copland's that had earlier pleaded for the wholesale conversion of the American natives fell silent or were ignored. Even England's leading champion of imperial Christianity, Samuel Purchas, joined the verbal assault on the Indians. They "bee not worthy of the name of a Nation," Purchas proclaimed, "being wilde and Savage: yet as Slaves, bordering rebels, excommunicates and outlaws are lyable to the punishments of Law, and not to the priviledges." The massacre, he believed, "hath now confiscated whatsoever remainders of right the unnaturall Naturalls had, and made both them and their Countrey wholly English." Like other clergymen, Purchas still hoped to convert some of the Indians; he was no longer sanguine, however, about the prospects of "so bad a people, having little of Humanitie but shape, ignorant of Civilitie, of Arts, of Religion; more brutish then the beasts they hunt."[75]

The crown and the company took a similar stance. In a pamphlet of 1622, designed primarily to tell Virginians how to raise silkworms and other agricultural crops, John Bonoeil, a French horticulturalist employed by the company, voiced what had apparently become the official

English viewpoint on the Indian. Bonoeil's treatise carried endorsements from the king and from the earl of Southampton, the company's treasurer. Tucked away in the last part of the book, but conspicuous enough to have caught the eye of any reader, lurked an invitation to enslave the Indian remnant. "I utterly disclaime them," Bonoeil wrote, for they "know no industry, no Arts, no culture, nor no good use of this blessed Country heere, but are meere ignorance, sloth, and bruitishnesse, and [are] an unprofitable burthen. . . . [They] are naturally borne slaves. . . . There is a naturall kind of right in you, that are bred noble, learned, wise, and virtuous, to direct them aright, to governe and to command them."[76] Bonoeil's pamphlet, widely distributed in Virginia, was not publicly challenged. The subsequent record of Indian-colonial relations suggests that its message fell on receptive ears.

Despite its propaganda campaign, the company failed to revive public confidence in Virginia. It failed, too, to convince the king that it deserved to survive as England's agent of colonization. Not merely because of the massacre, for that could be blamed on the stealth of the Indians and the carelessness of the settlers. But the company had unquestionably been irresponsible in recruiting new settlers who perished in frightful numbers. During the remainder of 1622 and throughout the following year it sent hundreds of men and women to a colony that suffered from a severe shortage of food and shelter and in which disease again took a heavy toll.[77] Many of the recruits died at sea, for conditions of passage had become worse than ever (Lady Wyatt complained that on her crossing in 1623 "our Shipp was so . . . full of infection that after a while we saw little but throwing folkes over boord"). Sir Edwin Sandys's brother wrote from the colony that since the massacre a "generall sicknes" had taken almost five hundred lives, "and not manie of the rest that have not knockt at the doores of death." Letters from the colony rang with plaintive pleas for deliverance: *"I am quite out of hart to live in this land[,] god send me well out of it"; "we lyve in the fearefullest age that ever christians lyved in"; "we are all undone."* The future of the colony, recently so promising, now seemed bleaker than ever. "The last massacre killed all our Countrie," lamented one survivor; "beside them they killed, they burst the heart of all the rest."[78]

The colony's plight convinced James to disband the London Company. He had long been disappointed with its performance, and since 1619 he had been at odds with its leadership. Between 1606 and 1619 the company had been headed by Sir Thomas Smythe. In the latter year a coalition under Sir Edwin Sandys gained control.[79] Because of pressure from the king, who resented his opposition in Parliament, Sandys served as treasurer for only a year, but he managed to secure the election of the earl of Southampton, a loyal follower, for the next three years. Sandys and Southampton now had to face charges of gross mismanagement, for however incompetent the administration of Smythe, it had avoided—out of blind luck, perhaps—the tragedies of recent years. In 1623 the crown began to investigate the company. A year later the Court of King's Bench revoked the company's charter; Virginia became the first royal colony. The impact of the massacre had been far-reaching indeed.

Changes in its government in no way altered the colony's pursuit of the Powhatans. In the spring of 1623 the governor and council promised "to geve them shortly a blow, That shall neere or altogether Ruinate them." In 1624 the assembly ordered "that at the begininge of July next the Inhabitantes of every Corporatione shall falle uppon theire adjonyinge Salvages as we did the last yeere."[80] Such campaigns became so customary that the colonists were divided into four units, each to attack assigned targets every November, March, and July.[81] In 1629, seven years after the massacre, the governor and council reminded the colonists to keep Indians out of the plantations altogether and to "esteeme them utter Enemies."[82] That same year the colony gained an unexpected ally. "A certaine Indian," reported Reverend Joseph Mead, "offered himself, his wife, and four children wholly to become English both in affection and religion; and to assure them of his fidelity, he conducted their little army this harvest to the secret habitations of the Indians their enemies; upon whose corn and persons, by his guidance, they wrought more spoil and revenge than they had done since the great massacre."[83] Still the Indians resisted. In September 1632 the colonists still considered "*the neighbouringe Indians our irreconcileable enemyes,*" but that fall the major tribes finally capitulated.[84]

VI

In one sense, the shift in English policy after the massacre was slight; it reflected more openly the profound prejudice that had clouded Indian-English contact from the beginning. Many Englishmen, especially those in the colony, could at last admit a conviction briefly and incompletely suppressed: the Indians were a nuisance to be pushed aside or forced to labor. Thus, Opechancanough's assault of 1622 not only released the Indians' long-suppressed hostility but also unmasked the colonists' covert disdain. The massacre simply hastened the inevitable confrontation of incompatible positions.

In another respect, however, 1622 marked a turning point. Until then, leading English imperialists, both secular and missionary, assumed that some Indian tribes would live in friendly proximity to the colony and that many individuals and families would mix—economically, socially, and perhaps biologically—with the settlers. Those who held such a view may have been a minority in England, as they almost certainly were in Virginia, but from 1614 to 1622 they were influential enough to take the first hesitant steps toward an integrated community. London policymakers such as Robert Johnson, Edwin Sandys, and Patrick Copland, and Virginia colonists such as John Rolfe, George Thorpe, and George

Yeardley expected colonial society to consist of Europeans and Indians, all speaking the English language, adhering to English customs, abiding by English authority, and worshiping in the English church. In 1622 the Powhatans and their allies served unmistakable notice that they would not accept such terms. In frustration and anguish, even former champions of integrations—Samuel Purchas and Francis Wyatt, for example—threw the whole blame onto the Indian; they concluded that he was too treacherous to befriend, too savage to civilize, too superstitious to convert. He must be expelled from the English sphere, and as that area expanded the Indian must retreat. English Virginia and Indian Virginia were henceforth to be separate domains.

Virginia's experience helped to shape Indian-colonist relations throughout British America. "Hapie is he whom other mens harmes doth make to beware," advised the writer who informed Plymouth, the only other mainland colony at the time, of the massacre of 1622. In the next few months the Pilgrims built a sturdy fort and posted continual watch. "Since the massacre in *Virginia*, . . . wee are more wary of them [the Indians] then before; for their hands hath beene imbrued in much English bloud," noted one of the settlers; and early in 1623 Miles Standish slew several Indians suspected of conspiring against the colony.[85] And yet Plymouth's relations with most if its neighboring tribes remained generally cordial, for the Pilgrims rejected Virginia's corollary that most neighboring Indians, by definition, must be tributaries or enemies, and the Wampanoags, under Massasoit's leadership, proved faithful allies.

But New Englanders continued to invoke the massacre of 1622. In 1629, the parent company of the infant Massachusetts Bay Colony warned resident director John Endecott at Salem "not to bee too confident of the ffidellitie of the salvages. . . . Our countrymen [have suffered by] theire too much confidence in Virginea."[86] Less than a decade later, the first published account of the Puritan war against the Pequots contrasted New England's "severe execution of just revenge" with "[t]he long forbearance, and too much lenitie of the English toward the Virginian Salvages, [which] had like to have beene the destruction of the whole Plantation." And when in 1644 Opechancanough launched a second Virginia uprising almost as destructive as the first, John Winthrop saw Virginia's calamity as another explicit warning to New England, although he stopped short of laying full blame on the Indians. "This massacre," he pointedly observed, "came upon [the Virginians] soon after they had driven out the godly ministers we had sent to them," and Edward Johnson more explicitly linked Virginia's rejection of Puritanism to the assault by "barbarous, inhumane, insolent, and bloody Indians."[87]

Whatever the reasons for the latest uprising, the Puritans acted with a caution born partly of Virginia's tragedies. As the anonymous author of *New Englands First Fruits* boasted to his readers in England, "we are wont to keep [the Indians] at such a distance, (knowing they serve the Devill and are led by him) as not to imbolden them too much, or trust them too farre; though we do them what good we can." Separation, not integration or amalgamation, accordingly characterized New England's missionary efforts under John Eliot and Daniel Gookin—the latter a Puritan refugee from Virginia who had lost heavily in the massacre of 1644. Most of New England's Christian Indians were confined to "Praying Towns," and civil and military officials kept a close eye on the unconverted.[88] Indians were prohibited from buying firearms, serving in the militia, or entering English settlements without permission. Harvard College lodged its few Indian students in a separate building.[89] Despite some sincere attempts at ethnic concord, New England remained suspicious of its Indian neighbors both individually and collectively. And in 1675, King Philip's War convinced most New Englanders of what some had long suspected: the Indians, with few exceptions, were inexorably heathen, savage, and demonic—"atheisticall proud, wild, cruel, barbarous, bruitish . . . diabolicall creatures."[90]

By the beginning of the eighteenth century, in Virginia and elsewhere, the disintegration of the coastal tribes and the resurgence of missionary ardor partially revived earlier expectations of the Indians' social and religious transformation. It was too late. The cultures had lived so long apart and animosities had so long festered that the efforts of a few missionaries and educators made little dent in the larger pattern of Indian-European relations, a pattern that lasted the lifetime of British America and predisposed the Indian policy of the new nation. For in keeping with traditional English attitudes, in the mother country and the colonies, champions of the Indians' welfare still insisted that to be acceptable they forsake their native culture. Most Indians, of course, would not.

CHAPTER SIX

Blacks in Virginia: Evidence from the First Decade

The earliest evidence of Africans in mainland British America is frustratingly sparse and sometimes inconsistent. The most obvious questions are accordingly difficult to answer: When were the first Africans brought to its shores? What was their status—slave, free, indentured, or some combination of those conditions? What did the Euro-Americans in Virginia (mostly English, of course, but with scatterings of many nationalities) think about the presence of Africans and about their appropriate role in the colony? Was there a fairly clear consensus among Euro-Americans on such matters, or did they disagree, perhaps adamantly, on some points?

Surely historians do not agree. Although 1619 is generally accepted as the earliest arrival date for an African in England's mainland colonies, and Point Comfort, Virginia, as the location, none of the other questions has enjoyed much agreement. Yet the events and perceptions of those early years may have been crucial to the evolution of the institution of slavery and the formation of racial ideology. It is accordingly important to learn as much as we can about the experiences of the first Africans in Virginia.

This essay looks closely at the scraps of surviving evidence, especially the Virginia censuses of 1624 and 1625, and teases from them some tentative conclusions about the first British colony's racial perceptions and policies.

While doing archival research in the early 1970s for a book about Captain John Smith, I read most of the relevant documents in American and British repositories. I did not expect to find evidence about Africans (I assumed that there was almost none) but knew that there was substantial information about Smith's role in English colonization. To my surprise, clues about the black population emerged here and there, and they seemed, the more closely I read, to reveal an unmistakable perceptual pattern of "otherness." "Blacks in Virginia: A Note on the First Decade" appeared in the William and Mary Quarterly, *3d ser. 29 (1972): 469–78, and is here reprinted with the journal's permission. I have inserted a few additional items of evidence and slightly altered the conclusion to reflect my present convictions about the first decade's message. I have also expanded some of the notes to call the reader's attention to important recent scholarship. The title too is slightly different, reflecting more accurately my intentions.*

AMID THE HISTORIOGRAPHICAL WRANGLING that has in recent years focused on the origins of American slavery and race prejudice, at least one item of agreement has held firm: almost nothing is known about the status of blacks in America until 1630 or later.[1] Unhappily for our attempts to understand the emergence of lifetime bondage for Africans and their descendants, information on the early years remains frustratingly sparse. But on closer look, the evidence for the 1620s is not so lacking or as unrevealing as has long been supposed.

Two principal sources and a smattering of lesser items tell much about how white Virginians viewed and treated blacks during the first decade of African importation. What the sources reveal is not a solution to the slavery versus servitude puzzle; they do not make clear how many of the Africans in Virginia were being held in permanent bondage nor what effect conversion to Christianity may have had on the Negro's status. Yet the sources do shed some light on these matters. They also show with disturbing clarity that the black men and women brought to Virginia from 1619 to 1629 held from the outset a singularly debased status in the eyes of white Virginians. If not subjected to permanent and inheritable bondage during that decade—a matter that needs further evidence—black Virginians were at least well on their way to such a condition. For the Elizabethan Englishmen's deep-rooted antipathy to Africans, so well documented by Winthrop D. Jordan in *White over Black*, reveals itself in a variety of subtle ways in the records of early Virginia.

The earliest references to Africans in mainland British America leave uncertain their long-term status but suggest that most were servile laborers at first, perhaps for the remainder of their lives. John Rolfe's two letters concerning the events of August 1619 are our only surviving accounts of the arrival of the (presumably) first Afro-Americans. In a letter of January 1620 to Sir Edwin Sandys, treasurer of the Virginia Company, Rolfe described the arrival the previous year of a Dutch man-of-war at Point Comfort which "brought not any thing but 20. and odd Negroes, which the Governor and Cape Marchant bought for victualles. . . ."[2] Rolfe's other mention of the event is even less informative; in a letter reprinted in John Smith's *Generall Historie of Virginia*, Rolfe reported that "about the last of August came in a dutch man of warre that sold us twenty Negars. . . ."[3] Clearly the arrival of the first Africans meant little to Rolfe; clearly also they were considered items of merchandise. But so were white indentured servants whose labor could also be bought and sold, and they too were occasionally mentioned with a callousness that matches Rolfe's.

There is no further reference to blacks in the surviving records until 1624. On the last day of November of that year, "*John Phillip* A negro Christened in *England* 12 yeers since" testified in a suit against a white man. Phillip, it appears, was no slave and perhaps not even a servant; his conversion to Christianity had taken place before he reached the colony, and from his testimony before the General Court it seems likely that he was a member of a ship's crew.[4] About a year later the court ordered that the "negro caled by the name of *brase* shall belonge to *Sir Francis Wyatt*, Governor etc., As his servant"; this was probably the same black man that a month earlier had been assigned by the court to Lady Yeardley, wife of the former governor, who was ordered to allow Brass "monthly . . . forty pownd waight of good marchantable tobacco for his labor and service so longe as he remayneth with her."[5] (The record is not crystal clear that Brass himself is to get the monthly payments; they more likely went to Captain Nathanial Bass, who, at that time, had custody of him.) These court entries and the evidence that survives concerning Anthony Johnson, a Negro who eventually claimed headrights for Africans *he* imported into Virginia, make clear that not all of the blacks who entered Virginia in the decade after 1619 were thrust into permanent bondage. A few may have arrived as free men or women, while others perhaps served a period of service from which they were released into freedom much as were white indentured servants. From the legal standpoint the black and white servants differed only in the absence, so far as we know, of any written terms of indenture by which the servant had engaged in service. The distinction may have been important, though. Most English servants came voluntarily with contract in hand. The blacks came under duress and were sold, most likely, for as long a period of service as the purchaser desired or the law permitted. But since Virginia had no relevant laws, and since those of England were sufficiently vague as to permit almost any interpretation, the probability is that most purchasers of blacks held them for life or at least for longer than white servants.[6]

That such a construction of the evidence is likely receives strong support from two colony-wide censuses taken in the middle of the decade. On orders of the Virginia Company of London, the colonial authorities in February 1624 compiled "Lists of the Livinge and Dead in Virginia" in each of the twenty-three clusters of settlement that then constituted the colony. The original of this document survives in the Public Record Office in London, and it was printed as early as 1874 in the *Colonial Records of Virginia*.[7] The lists give evidence of twenty-two blacks among the living and of one who died since the previous April. What is most striking about the appearance of these blacks in the census is that although most of them had been in America for five years, none is accorded a last name and almost half are recorded with no name at all.

Typical entries read "One negar," "A Negors Woman," or in the case of
Flowerdew Hundred, as:

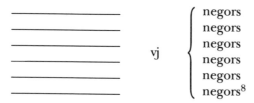

$$\text{vj} \left\{ \begin{array}{l} \text{negors} \\ \text{negors} \\ \text{negors} \\ \text{negors} \\ \text{negors} \\ \text{negors}[8] \end{array} \right.$$

By contrast, very few entries for non-Negroes have incomplete names.
Occasionally a first name is absent and the omission indicated by a dash,
and a few listings of presumably white servants appear as "A servant of
Mr. Moorewood's," or "Mary, a maid." Two Italian glassmakers are designated by their surnames only.[9] There are also a few entries for whites
in the 1624 census on a level of impersonality that approaches the listings of the Negroes: "two Frenchmen," "Symon, an Italien," and
"Thomas, an Indian."[10] One can only speculate on what such listings reveal about the attitudes of ethnocentric Englishmen toward persons of
other nationalities, but the point to be made here is that Negroes as a
group received by far the scantiest and most impersonal entries in the
census. Ten of the twenty-three are without first or last names, the rest
have first names only. By contrast, the same page that records two
Frenchmen anonymously also lists two others with full names and a third
with a surname only. Similarly, an Italian, Bernardo of the glassworks, is
followed on the list by "Mrs. Bernardo" in marked contrast to the entries for black women, none of whom is designated as married, although
it seems unlikely that some were not. In short, the census of 1624 suggests the early appearance of an attitude deeply prejudicial toward blacks
in Virginia.

More telling is the census taken a year later.[11] The "Muster of Inhabitants in Virginia," of January and February 1625, like its predecessor, is arranged by plantations, beginning in this case with the
"Colledge–Land," and running through more than a score of localities.
Again a name, or at least an identifying label, is given to each inhabitant. But in addition, for most men and women the census shows age,
date of arrival in Virginia, and ship of passage, plus for each free family its possessions in houses, armaments, munitions, food staples, and
livestock. The resulting gold mine of military, economic, and demographic data has barely been tapped by historians and thus far has received its most extensive attention from genealogists.[12] But like the census of 1624, that of 1625 tells much about the status of black men and
women in British America.

Again, twenty-three Negroes appear. Nine of them lived in James City,
seven at Percy's Hundred, three at Elizabeth City, two at Warrasquoke,
one in the "Neck of land near James City," and one at "Elizabeth Citty
beyond Hampton River"—a fairly wide geographic distribution of black

laborers. Of particular interest is the nearly even balance in sex: twelve men and eleven women, an indication that the sexual disparity of the West Indies, where a severe shortage of females had grave implications for population increases and for social adjustment, found from the outset no parallel on the mainland.[13]

Compared to the 1624 census, the 1625 report is more complete as well as more ambitious. Very few names are incomplete; age is indicated for the vast majority of inhabitants, and the remaining information—date and ship of arrival, provisions, cattle, and so forth—shows few gaps. But again most of the Negroes are relegated to anonymity or partial identification. For example, the muster of Abraham Peirsey's "servants" lists thirty-six individuals, including seven blacks. Four of them are designated as Negro men, with no names, first or family, no date or ship of arrival, no age; the others are entered as "Negro woman," and "Negro woman and a young Child of hers." All of Peirsey's twenty-nine white servants, however, are recorded with full names and ship and date of arrival; ages are given for twenty-seven of the twenty-nine.[14] Similarly, of the twenty-four servants at James City, full information is given on all except the wife of one (who presumably arrived in the same ship as her husband and is therefore deficient only in age), and the eight blacks who are shown as: "Negro Men 3 Negro Woemen 5."[15]

Continuing the practice of the 1624 census, given names do appear for some blacks, and in a few instances additional information is recorded. The muster of Captain William Peirce includes "Angelo a Negro Woman in the *Treasuror*."[16] That entry may be significant: other census entries show that *Treasurer* brought colonists to Virginia in 1613, 1614, 1615, 1617, and 1618, and from other sources it is known that the ship returned to Virginia in the fall of 1619 with a load of Negroes but was not permitted to land her human cargo for fear of arousing Spanish animosity. Perhaps the ship identification on Angelo is in error, or perhaps she alone came ashore from *Treasurer* in 1619, but barring such possibilities, Angelo's arrival in Virginia would precede by from one to six years the date usually assigned for the advent of blacks in Virginia.[17] Neither John Rolfe, it will be remembered, nor any other contemporary claimed that the Dutch ship brought the *first* Negroes to Virginia.

On five of the Negroes recorded in the 1625 census we have fuller entries, although only one received a complete listing: "John Pedro, a Neger aged 30 in the *Swan* 1623." This was probably the "John, a negro" of the 1624 report, who along with several other servants of Captain Francis West appears "At the Plantation over against James Cittie" in 1624, and in 1625 at "Elizabeth Cittie Beyond Hampton River, Beinge the Companyes land."[18] In the case of John Pedro we have not only a full listing but a full name, the only black other than the aforementioned John Phillip of the 1624 General Court records to so appear in the decade from 1619 to 1629. We know also of at least one African-

American family: listed in 1624 only as Anthony and Isabella, Negroes, in the 1625 report their entry reads "Antoney Negro: Isabell Negro: and William Theire Child Baptised." Another Anthony, surnamed Johnson after his master, subsequently became free, married Mary, who arrived in 1622, and later owned black servants himself.[19]

The remaining two blacks whose entries show more than a given name are "Antonio a Negro in the *James* 1621" and "Mary a Negro Woman in the *Margarett and John* 1622," both at Warrasquoke.[20] Significant in these listings is evidence that blacks continued to enter Virginia, perhaps at the rate of two or three per year, and on English ships that also carried free and indentured whites, thus presumably coming from England and either bringing a black or two from there, or stopping at the Caribbean islands where a few Afro-West Indians may have been purchased for importation to Virginia.

Once in Virginia the black servants probably fared worse than their white servant counterparts, at least in length of service. There are strong hints from the census of 1625 that they were already a different category of labor: witness the absence for most of the blacks of age and date of arrival—crucial data for white servants since terms of indenture usually stipulated service for a specified number of years or until a specified age. Furthermore, although most of the blacks of the 1625 census had been in Virginia for six years, none of them is shown as free; all are either specifically listed under the heading of "servants" or are included in the holdings of free white men who held white as well as black "servants." In most cases the blacks are at the end of such lists of "servants." And their anonimity, in conjunction with their status as servants or slaves, is telling too. On 4 August 1619, about three weeks before the first Africans were purchased at Point Comfort, the legislature decreed that every master must submit to the secretary of state, within one month of their arrival, "all his servants names, & for what terme, or upon what conditions they are to serve, upon penalty of paying 40s."[21] Perhaps the Africans' names—their original names or English substitutes—were duly recorded (no lists survive), yet very few Africans were named in the censuses or in other extant documents of the 1620s and after. It seems likely that many of them were not given names, at least full names, because they were considered slaves to be owned and hence not encompassed by the law that required the registration of servants. In any event, the overall impression conveyed by the census of 1625 is of a significantly separate and inferior position for the Negro in the social structure of white Virginia.

That impression gains further credence from two wills of 1627. In September, John Throgmorton's will "gave unto ye wife of *Oliver Jenkins* the service of his Negar for a yere: And further he gave unto his two servants, *William Edes & Thomas Stent* two yeares a peece of their time"; his cousin Henry, apparently indentured, was given his freedom. Assuming that Throgmorton, in keeping with the other documentary ev-

idence of the 1620s, would have indicated that Edes and Stent were
Africans had they been so, he was treating his two categories of bound
labor very differently—terminating his cousin's bondage, shortening the
terms of his other two white indentured servants, and assigning the
nameless "Negar" to someone else for a year, perhaps in payment of a
debt. There is no indication that the Negro's servitude ended after the
year with Jenkins' wife; it more likely reverted to Throgmorton's estate.
The other will of 1627 that mentions blacks was executed for Sir George
Yeardley, governor in 1619–21 and 1626–27; his heirs were to inherit
his "goods debts chattles servants negars cattle or any other thynge."
The separate category for "negars" suggests that Yeardley considered
them a distinct category of his assets, and the sequence of categories in
which Negroes come between servants and cattle implies an especially
low status for black bondservants.[22]

For the remainder of the decade, the evidence of Africans in Virginia
is again shrouded in obscurity. From papers preserved in the British
Public Record Office, we know that additional Africans entered the
colony, but the number and circumstances are unclear. In 1628 Captain Arthur Guy in the *Fortune* seized a ship from Angola "with many negroes" on board; he took them to Virginia to barter for tobacco. The
same year the *Straker* delivered an unspecified number of Africans to the
colony.[23] With these imports of the late 1620s, Virginia's black population must have increased to a figure much greater than the "20 and
odd" of 1619. Some natural increase, moreover, had probably occurred,
and because most of the blacks must have been young and fairly healthy
on arrival, having been "seasoned" to European diseases in Britain or
the West Indies, the mortality rate may have been lower than it was for
white immigrants. In March 1629, the Virginia government called for
another plantation-by-plantation census, this time "of all the inhabitants
men woemen and Children as well *Englishe* as Negroes."[24] That census
does not survive to reveal the exact number of Africans in the colony's
population or to give additional clues to their status, but it is notewor-
thy that among Virginia's wide variety of non-English inhabitants, only
Negroes merited special mention in the government's directive.

What the evidence of the decade after 1619 reveals is inconclusive
but not insignificant. It shows with alarming clarity that blacks from the
outset were objects of a prejudice that relegated most, perhaps all, of
them to the lowest rank in the colony's society, and there are strong
hints that bondage for blacks did not carry the same terms as for whites.
The latter served for limited times and then were freed; the former, apparently in most cases, were not freed, at least within the decade after
many of them arrived in Virginia. The surviving documents makes clear,
too, that a small but growing traffic in slaves had begun in which Virginia served as the final destination. Finally, there is evidence that a few
blacks, principally if not exclusively those who had been converted to
Christianity before their arrival in Virginia, may have held a higher sta-

tus than other blacks and eventually obtained their freedom. But on balance, the scattered evidence from the first decade strongly supports the contentions of Winthrop Jordan and Carl Degler that a deep and pervading racial prejudice served as a formative precursor to American Negro slavery.

CHAPTER SEVEN

The Origins Debate: Slavery and Racism in Seventeenth-Century Virginia

Historians—like lawyers, physicians, and movie critics—are often at loggerheads over interpretations of major matters. Sometimes the different viewpoints are almost predictable, stemming from the interpreters' disparate backgrounds or ideologies, especially on issues that bridge the usual boundaries between events of the past and the present. But sometimes the reasons for differences are harder to discern, being rooted in the unique definition a scholar gives to crucial terms, or the idiosyncratic significance placed on certain words, or in the very personal intellectual context into which the historian tries to fit new evidence. Whatever the explanation for scholarly disagreements, surely the debate over the origins of slavery, and especially of racism, in early Virginia has been a prime example for nearly half a century.

Part of the problem, of course, is the paucity of evidence. Little survives, and a disturbing portion of it is ambiguous. What, for example, did the author of a seventeenth-century document mean by slave? *We have a clear definition of the word today, but early colonial usage was imprecise; several meanings were simultaneously possible.* Servant *was ambiguous, too, as were a host of other terms that are essential to the dialogue, including* nation, country, race—*even* Christian. *Yet, as the previous essay illustrates, some evidence on early black-white relations does survive which, if not crystal clear, is at least suggestive and occasionally persuasive.*

The purpose of my essay on "The Origins Debate" is threefold: to review the scholarly argument of the past century, especially its evolution since 1950; to analyze the major strands of evidence that underlie the interpretive differences; and to present my own convictions about early American slavery and racism. When this essay was published in 1989, I hoped it might put the debate to rest for a few years or more, but the issue is too vital, too connected to the present, and too ambiguous in its sources to ever remain quiescent. Barely a year after "The Origins Debate" first appeared, Barbara Jeanne Fields (a friend and colleague at Columbia University) published a very different explanation of the origins of

American racism. I append to this reprinting of my essay a summary of her interpretation and a fairly long rebuttal that brings this ongoing interpretive discussion as up to date as possible.

I had pondered for many years the sources on which this chapter is based, and had often presented the essence of them to my students at Columbia University, before I put my thoughts on paper in the late 1980s. The resulting article was published in the Virginia Magazine of History and Biography *97 (1989): 311–54, and is here reprinted with that journal's permission and with numerous minor changes to the text and notes. The appended postscript was first drafted in 1990, as a personal letter to Barbara Fields, and rewritten a year later as an open letter; the current version is considerably condensed.*

ᕕᕗ

FEW HISTORIOGRAPHICAL DEBATES have generated so much scholarly attention and emphatic disagreement as the origins of black bondage in Virginia and its relation to race prejudice. Although historians discovered the issue only in the twentieth century and have argued it vociferously only since 1950, the elusive connection between British America's most lamentable institution and its most deplorable ideology make the issue important to the nation's present and future as well as to Virginia's distant past.

Colonial Virginia held no monopoly on either slavery or racism, of course. Both were endemic in Europe's American colonies from the sixteenth century on, and neither depended on Virginia's example for its vitality or longevity, even within the British empire. Virginia's primacy among Britain's mainland possessions in the introduction of black laborers and the emergence (sooner or later, depending on one's interpretation) of racial prejudice against them, however, has made the Old Dominion central to the verbal wrangling. Scores of books and articles and at least three anthologies explore the ambiguous connection between the institution and the ideology in early Virginia, and the end is not in sight.[1] In 1962 Winthrop D. Jordan referred to "the long duration and vigor of the controversy." More than a quarter century later, the vigor has not abated.[2]

I

Prior to the twentieth century, historians assumed without closely investigating the matter that slavery began in Britain's mainland colonies with the arrival in 1619 of the first blacks in Virginia.[3] William Goodell's mid-nineteenth-century history of slavery and abolition, for example, simply stated that "Soon after the settlement of the British North American Colonies, Africans were imported into them, and sold and held as slaves." A quarter century later, Richard Hildreth was more specific: "Twenty negroes, brought to Jamestown by a Dutch trading vessel, and purchased by the colonists, were held, not as indentured servants for a term of years, but as slaves for life." Historians assumed too (when they thought about it at all) that racial prejudice appeared simultaneously. As George Bancroft, late in the nineteenth century, summed it up, "The negro race, from its introduction, was regarded with disgust."[4] The consensus, in brief, was that there was no issue to debate. Arguments over the nature and mortality of antebellum slavery abounded; the colonial period, by contrast, generated little interest and less controversy.

In 1902 James C. Ballagh cracked the consensus by arguing that Virginia's early Africans were not slaves but indentured servants until the slave laws of the 1660s and 1670s decreed otherwise. Ballagh's evidence was legalistic and largely inferential. "Domestic slavery," he contended, "could find no sanction until the absolute ownership in the bodies of the negroes was vested by lawful authority in some individual." Ballagh showed convincingly that some blacks in the early decades were free and concluded that the other Africans in Virginia, about whom little was known, must have been free too because no colonial laws authorized enslavement: "Though the practice and incidents of negro and Indian slavery in the Spanish colonies were perfectly familiar to the people of Virginia, for some reason the notion of enslavement gained ground but slowly, and . . . the colonists seem to have preferred to retain him [a Negro or Indian] only as a servant."[5]

Ballagh's argument soon attracted adherents, though many of them stopped short of his wholesale revisionism. John H. Russell's study of Virginia's free blacks accepted Ballagh's reassessment only for the two decades after 1619. Russell was less convinced than Ballagh by the absence of slave laws in the early period—custom, if not legislation, could have kept blacks in bondage—yet he too was impressed by the many instances of free blacks in the decades before statutory slavery appeared.[6]

A similar partial acceptance of Ballagh's interpretation appeared in Ulrich B. Phillips's classic account of *American Negro Slavery* (1918). Phillips's brief discussion of the seventeenth century opened with a nod toward Ballagh's position:

> The first comers were slaves in the hands of their maritime sellers; but they were not fully slaves in the hands of their Virginia buyers, for there was neither law nor custom then establishing the institution of slavery in the colony. The documents of the times point clearly to a vague tenure. In the county court records prior to 1661 the negroes are called negro servants or merely negroes—never, it appears, definitely slaves.

Phillips pointed to freed blacks (by owner's action or court order) as evidence that Africans in early Virginia were servants rather than slaves, but later in the same paragraph he shifted to a stance closer to Russell's:

> As early as the sixteen-forties the holders of negroes were falling into the custom of considering them . . . as servants for life and perpetuity. The fact

that negroes not bound for a term were coming to be appraised as high as £30, while the most valuable white redemptioners were worth not above £15 shows also the tendency toward the crystallization of slavery before any statutory enactments declared its existence.[7]

During the 1620s and 1630s, Phillips seemed to be saying, all blacks were servants or free; during the 1640s and 1650s they were increasingly de facto slaves. The laws of the 1660s affirmed the custom, expanded it, and made it de jure. In *Life and Labor in the Old South* (1929), Phillips presented his analysis more generally: "No preceding statute was requisite for the buying and holding of a Negro in bondage. . . . [C]ustom preceded law and fixed its course." Elsewhere in the book, however, Phillips again exempted the earliest blacks from slavery. "A few Negroes attained freedom in early Virginia," he assured his readers (with a footnote crediting Russell), "because the first comers, imported before definitive slavery was established, were dealt with as if they had been indentured servants."[8]

The Ballagh-Russell-Phillips doctrine made mixed headway among scholars of American slavery. James M. Wright's study of Maryland's free blacks (1921) did not apply it to Virginia's neighboring colony; instead he cited favorably two earlier studies of Maryland that said slavery existed from the colony's beginnings in 1634 and hinted at a concomitant racism. Yet Wright also referred the reader to Ballagh's book for developments in Virginia, thus implying that the two colonies may have had different customs and attitudes. Helen Catterall, on the other hand, wholly accepted Ballagh's thesis in her introduction to judicial cases concerning blacks.[9] But by and large, historians ignored the debate. David Saville Muzzey epitomized the early twentieth-century diffidence toward black bondage in early America. In 1927 his *American Adventure* did not mention slavery until the narrative reached the eve of the Missouri Compromise; there Muzzey reminded his readers that "Negro slavery had been introduced into the colony of Jamestown in 1619."[10]

If Muzzey was typical of the generalists, Susie M. Ames reflected the continuing interest of colonialists in the historical origins of slavery. In 1940 her book on Virginia's Eastern Shore denied that Ballagh's argument fit the evidence and rejected his contention that indentured servitude was the earliest status for blacks. Freedom for some blacks in early Virginia, she protested, resulted not from termination of servitude but usually from manumission; other free blacks may have been the offspring of emancipated slaves or mulatto children of white fathers before the law of 1662 decreed that status depended on the mother's condition. Ames contended that by the time slavery became fixed in law, it was "a custom well established," much like the system already flourishing in England's island colonies.[11]

Ames's stance was soon endorsed and expanded in a study of wider geographic scope. Wesley Frank Craven's judicious *Southern Colonies in the Seventeenth Century* (1949) quietly pulled Virginia's early Afro-American history back to nineteenth-century conclusions by warning against "generalizing too much from the relatively few cases recorded" of freed blacks. "[T]he trend from the first was toward a sharp distinction between [the Negro] and the white servant," Craven insisted, and in a footnote he applauded Ames's "pertinent criticism" of the doctrine that servitude preceded slavery. Craven also questioned "the modern assumption that prejudice against the Negro is largely a product of slavery." Although he did not identify the proponents of that "modern assumption," Craven may well have had in mind Eric Williams's *Capitalism and Slavery*, a quasi-Marxist analysis of the New World slave system, which declared—as a necessary part of its theoretical argument—that "slavery was not born of racism; rather racism was the consequence of slavery." In any event, Craven's insistence that most blacks were probably slaves and subjected to racial prejudice from the outset foreshadowed an interpretation that would emerge emphatically a decade later.[12] Despite these occasional discussions of slavery's origin and the rare mentions of early racial prejudice, both issues and their interconnectedness remained in limbo until 1950. College textbooks—those litmus tests of scholarly dissemination—gave almost no attention to either topic.

II

In 1950 Oscar and Mary Handlins' seminal article resuscitated Ballagh's interpretation and went far beyond it.[13] The times were ripe for seeing slavery as an afterthought of colonial development rather than as a conscious design and for finding the roots of racism in economic and legal debasement rather than in the mind-set of American colonists. As Winthrop Jordan suggested in his own influential article a dozen years later, the Handlins' position reflected the optimistic liberalism of its time. "Embedded in this description of diverging status," Jordan noted, "were broad implications: Late and gradual enslavement undercut the possibility of natural, deep-seated antipathy toward Negroes. . . . [I]f whites and Negroes could share the same status of half freedom for forty years in the seventeenth century, why could they not share full freedom in the twentieth?"[14] Why not indeed, at a time when Jackie Robinson and other black athletes were erasing color lines in professional sports and when integration of the armed forces was well under way?

The Handlins made no such connections between their argument and their sociopolitical hopes. Rather, their essay was historical and evidential, a tightly knit challenge to the Ames-Craven belief that the first Africans in America were held as slaves and to the less frequently articulated assumption that blacks were subjected to racial prejudice from the outset. Seventeenth-century England, the Handlins pointed out, had no legal slavery but did have an abundance of "unfree" people—indentured servants, debtors working off obligations, criminals serving sentences, and the like—statuses that transferred automatically to British

America. According to the Handlins, the few Africans who arrived in the Chesapeake colonies were similarly unfree: "The status of Negroes was that of servants; and so they were identified and treated down to the 1660's." If Negroes were occasionally called slaves, it merely meant that they performed the most menial labor or occupied the lowest rung on society's ladder. Slavery came late in the century, racism still later.[15]

If, as the Handlins asserted, slavery—permanent, inheritable bondage—had no legal or traditional standing in England, why did it emerge in America? Not, according to the Handlins, because the settlers copied an institution already prevalent elsewhere: "American slavery was no direct imitation of Biblical or Roman or Spanish or Portuguese or West Indian models." Nor did it come from a preference for black labor. In the Chesapeake, as in the Caribbean islands, plantation owners used white labor as long as the supply sufficed. Rather, racial slavery emerged in the 1660s because in Virginia's multiethnic mix Africans were the most *different* from the ruling majority who "longed in the strangeness [of the New World] for the company of familiar men and singled out to be welcomed those who were most like themselves." To the ruling English colonists, Africans were strikingly unlike them in appearance, customs, and language. Moreover, and equally important, Africans were the most vulnerable laborers. In an attempt to attract English indentured servants to a colony short of labor, the Virginia legislature made terms of service as attractive as possible; perhaps the colony's poor reputation could be reversed. Black laborers, however, need not be placated: "Farthest removed from the English, least desired, [the African] communicated with no friends who might be deterred from following."[16]

The results were unplanned and unexpected. "By mid-century the servitude of Negroes seems generally lengthier than that of whites; and *thereafter the consciousness dawns* that blacks will toil for the whole of their lives, not through any particular concern with their status, but simply by contrast with those whose years of labor are limited by statute." Maryland, undergoing a parallel social evolution, in 1664 turned practice into law by decreeing that "all Negroes and other slaues to bee hereafter imported into the Province shall serue Durante Vita." Virginia in 1670 took virtually the same step. Other Virginia legislation in the 1660s and 1670s closed various loopholes, especially the possibility that mulatto children of free white fathers were entitled to freedom (1662) or that baptism precluded enslavement (1667).[17]

White Virginians' disparagement of blacks, the Handlins believed (in tacit agreement with Eric Williams), was a product of slavery. When the Africans' place became fixed by law at the basest level, they became objects of extreme degradation: "the trace of color became the trace of slavery." Thereafter, as the slave population grew in response to the South's economic needs, the position of the black slave grew more rigidly bound and more vociferously defended by white apologists. In the eighteenth century slavery as a labor system and the degradation of Africans began to exhibit their distinctively American characteristics. By then, most blacks suffered legal and economic bondage and were set apart as " 'abominable,' another order of man."[18]

The Handlins' interpretation was almost immediately and universally embraced. It appeared compactly but emphatically in scholarly tomes, college textbooks, and graduate school lectures.[19] Thomas Gossett's history of American racial attitudes, for example, incorporated the Handlinian view with only the slightest nod toward contrary evidence, and scholars in other disciplines borrowed it wholeheartedly.[20] Among college textbooks, the widely used Hofstadter, Miller, and Aaron edition of 1957 was typical: "Negro workers, who had been present in Virginia as early as 1619 as servants, were introduced in increasingly large numbers."[21]

After nine years of historiographical supremacy, the Handlins' thesis was finally challenged. Carl Degler's essay on "Slavery and the Genesis of American Race Prejudice" (1959) refuted vigorously their contention that blacks were merely servants until the 1660s and that discrimination aimed especially at blacks was unknown in the Chesapeake until slavery called it forth. Degler found the condition of early blacks singularly debased from the start: "the Negro was actually *never* treated as an equal of the white man, servant or free." An inferior status for blacks and frequent discrimination against them thus preceded rather than followed the formal institutionalization of racial slavery; law reflected attitudes. Degler had reversed the Handlins' historical sequence.[22]

Degler offered as evidence a variety of documentary scraps from the 1620s to 1660s that distinguished pejoratively between white servants and black servants (or "slaves"; the labels, but not the statuses, Degler contended, were ambiguous) in various parts of British America. Blacks had considerably higher valuations from the outset, which indicated far longer—perhaps lifetime—service; black runaways were punished differently than whites, apparently because the former's terms were already too long to be extended; black servants were forbidden to bear arms; black women were tithable—that is, taxed as potential field workers, unlike white female servants, though some of the latter undoubtedly labored in the fields. Contemporary statements, moreover, often distinguished between servants for years and slaves for life; the latter were always black. In 1649 a deed in neighboring Maryland strongly implied that slavery there was inheritable when it bequeathed three Negroes "and all their issue." Several Virginia cases offered corroboration.[23]

Such legal evidence reflected social perceptions, Degler argued. "Unquestionably it was a demand for labor which dragged the Negro to American shores, but the status which he acquired here cannot be explained by reference to that economic motive." New England, Degler demonstrated, had comparable prejudicial attitudes and policies despite its paucity of blacks; customary slavery for Africans may have been as firmly entrenched in New England by midcentury as it appears to have been in the Chesapeake colonies and the British islands. Degler concluded that "instead of slavery being the root of the discrimination visited upon the Negro in America, slavery was itself molded by the early colonists' discrimination against the outlander."[24]

The Handlins struck back. In a public letter they criticized much of Degler's discussion as "inept" and charged him with misunderstanding the evidence of discrimination against all non-Englishmen. The Handlins also disputed Degler's assertion that sixteenth- and seventeenth-century Englishmen considered Negroes "inherently different from and inferior to the whites," for "we know of no such expressions of racial prejudice." Expressions of ethnocentrism, the Handlins insisted, were a different matter and wholly compatible with their argument. In their annoyance at Degler's "obtuseness," the Handlins succumbed to ad hominem arguments: "Handicapped as he is by the inability to use his terms properly, Professor Degler cannot comprehend the subtle process by which changes in attitude occur."[25]

Degler rebutted the Handlins with several examples of early English and American bias against blacks, such as lines from Shakespeare (not to suggest that the bard was prejudiced but that he documented its prevalence) and the missionary Morgan Godwyn, whose *Negro's & Indians Advocate* (1680) contains testimony of virulent contempt for Africans. In the British West Indies "*Negro's* are conceived to be but Brutes," Godwyn reported, with "no more Souls than Beasts"; if similar statements did not emanate from Virginia, Degler implied, the treatment of blacks there surely reflected the same attitude. In short, Degler's rebuttal reiterated and expanded his original contention: in early Virginia, "the Negro was generally accorded a lower position in society than any white man, bound or free." Why that was so, he considered a prime but unanswered question.[26]

While the Handlins and Degler exchanged brickbats, Winthrop D. Jordan—first as a graduate student at Brown University and then as a fellow at the Institute of Early American History and Culture in Williamsburg—wrestled with that very conundrum: the underlying reasons for discrimination against blacks in early British America. Because the Handlins had denied that for several decades such discrimination was appreciably greater than that toward other non-English colonists, they were under no burden to explain its existence beyond their contention that Englishmen disliked people unlike themselves. Yet even the Handlins admitted that no other racial or ethnic group struck the English as quite so different, which came close to Degler's implication that Africans were subjected to more discrimination than other foreigners precisely *because* they were the most observably different and therefore least acceptable in England's New World settlements.[27] The fundamental question thus seemed to be: Was the white colonists' revulsion toward Africans qualitatively different from their revulsion toward other outsiders, and, if so,

did it lead at the outset to different treatment of blacks? A crucial corollary to both questions concerned the Africans' pigmentation: did it underlie—or at least signify—English prejudicial perceptions and contribute significantly to white Virginians' discrimination against Africans?
The Handlins had almost wholly ignored skin color as an ingredient of
English antipathy; Degler implied that it was important; Jordan revealed
its sociological roots and its centrality in early Virginia.

Jordan's preliminary explanation of the slavery-prejudice .puzzle appeared in an article on "Modern Tensions and the Origins of American
Slavery" (1962), in which he sided with neither Degler nor the Handlins. Instead Jordan offered a neatly neutral explanation: the paucity
of evidence on the first several decades of black presence in America
precludes our knowing whether prejudice or slavery came first, but the
evidence is clear of some slavery and some social debasement of blacks
by the 1640s and 1650s. Ergo, both slavery and prejudice were causes,
both were effects "constantly reacting upon each other, dynamically joining hands to hustle the Negro down the road to complete degradation."[28] Extracts from the articles by the Handlins, Degler, and Jordan
were quickly and widely printed in anthologies, partly because they
formed a perfect thesis, antithesis, and synthesis.[29] The historiographical dispute seemed at an end, happily decided in everyone's favor.

As Jordan's investigation of early American racial attitudes continued,
he changed his mind. In his capstone study *White over Black: American
Attitudes toward the Negro, 1550–1812* (1968), Jordan largely retracted
his earlier solution. The essay on "Modern Tensions," he confessed in
his bibliographic essay, "was written at a time when (as I now think) I
was far from comprehending the origins of American slavery."[30] *White
over Black*'s opening chapter, based on a close examination of sixteenth-
century English sources, especially travel accounts, emphasized the
depth and breadth of English prejudice against Africans before 1619.
The English propensity to identify Africans with apes, with unbridled
sexuality, and with extremely un-Christian behavior engendered a profound, though still inchoate, prejudice against Africans that the
Jamestown colonists unconsciously carried to America. Equally important, Jordan demonstrated that to Elizabethan and early Stuart Englishmen black was "an emotionally partisan color," laden with implications
of filth, evil, and repugnance. Thus Africans in early Virginia were not
merely one group of strangers on whom the English settlers cast general scorn, as the Handlins had argued; instead, the colonists considered them a visually, socially, and perhaps biologically distinct people,
in almost every way inferior to everyone else.[31]

White Virginians, Jordan argued, assumed that "slaves" must be
strangers, heathens, enemies (potentially at least), and beastly. Africans
bore all of those liabilities in English eyes and the stigma of color besides. "On every count," Jordan concluded, "Negroes qualified" as po-

tential slaves. And, because the Latin American model of lifetime, inheritable servitude was apparent to everyone—Spanish and Portuguese colonists held a quarter of a million black slaves by 1619—Virginians had no need to invent a new status. Rather, Jordan suggested in his second chapter, Englishmen in America quickly made an "unthinking decision" to enslave the blacks among them, though in the absence of applicable English statutes it remained until the 1660s a customary rather than a legal institution. Evidence from the 1630s on, not only from Britain's West Indian islands where blacks were abundant but also from New England where they were few, reveal that blacks were usually kept in permanent bondage. Laws of the 1660s and 1670s in Virginia, and almost simultaneously in Maryland, thus established de jure what had generally existed from the beginning de facto and closed the remaining loopholes in a rapidly evolving system of racial slavery.[32]

Although the early chapters of *White over Black* could be read as a strong endorsement and elaboration of Degler's position, Jordan at times equivocated. He repeated and expanded much of the evidence that Degler used to show subtle—and sometimes not-so-subtle—discrimination aimed especially at blacks before 1660: restrictions on carrying arms, severer punishments for interracial sex or for running away, and so forth. Yet Jordan reverted at times, almost verbatim, to his position in "Modern Tensions." In contradiction of the evidence of *White over Black*'s opening chapter, its second chapter retreated to his earlier explanation that "Rather than slavery causing 'prejudice,' or vice versa, they seem rather to have generated each other. . . . Slavery and 'prejudice' may have been equally cause and effect." Thus Jordan vitiated substantially *White over Black*'s initial message and the explicit retraction in the book's bibliographic essay of his argument in "Modern Tensions."[33]

More surprising than Jordan's contradictory stances in *White over Black*—his book, after all, covered an immense subject, of which the origins of slavery was a small though important part—was his continuing ambiguity in a condensed version of *White over Black*, published in 1974 as *The White Man's Burden*. The latter book retained the passage quoted above, but it deleted two early English definitions of slaves and servants which suggest strongly that in the early seventeenth century Englishmen assumed blacks to be customarily enslaved. By its retentions and omissions, *White Man's Burden* thus reinforced Jordan's ambivalent message: English prejudice against Africans, based on biological as well as cultural characteristics, long predated colonization of the Chesapeake, yet slavery and prejudice were coeval.[34] The overall thrust of Jordan's books endorsed Degler, but the "equally cause and effect" passage mitigated its implicit criticism of the Handlins.

Jordan's contributions to early American history earned widespread acclaim. In 1969 *White over Black* garnered a National Book Award, the Francis Parkman prize, and the Ralph Waldo Emerson prize. Extracts appeared in several anthologies of early American historiography, often as a replacement for "Modern Tensions" or for both the Degler and Handlin pieces. Despite Jordan's equivocal stance—or perhaps because of it—his "unthinking decision" seemed to be the definitive conclusion to nearly two decades of historical wrangling. In the judgment of one astute scholar, "if historians ever agree to accept an explanation of the emergence of prejudice and slavery in colonial America, it will probably be an explanation very similar to Jordan's."[35] After two decades, *White over Black* remains highly regarded and is now widely considered a classic in the early American field. It did not end the debate.

Barely three years after *White over Black*'s publication, George M. Fredrickson inaugurated a neo-Handlinian movement—not intentionally, perhaps, but effectively.[36] In his 1971 essay on the early stages of American racism, Fredrickson distinguished between implicit or societal racism, which, he proposed, is revealed only through actions because it is not pronounced publicly, and explicit or ideological racism, which is argued openly and extensively. Implicit racism emerged in the late seventeenth century, Fredrickson believed, and explicit racism in the antebellum period. In Fredrickson's model, neither form of racism existed during most of Virginia's first century.[37]

Fredrickson's essay seemed to cast new light on the old argument by showing that American racism was evolutionary and typological. In the seventeenth century, Fredrickson contended, societal racism developed slowly: "The story of white-black relations in seventeenth-century America is the story of an evolution *toward* societal racism." The early colonists, he acknowledged, were antipathetic to the color black and to the Africans' strangeness, but racism did not emerge until the late seventeenth century (the 1690s were critical in Fredrickson's view), when fear of the growing number of blacks combined with greed and the pursuit of privilege to create a permanent caste system. Thereafter, racism became increasingly evident; before then, Fredrickson implied, it was merely inchoate prejudice, not significantly different from the prejudice white Virginians leveled at all outsiders. He concluded that "societal racism—the treatment of blacks as if they were inherently inferior for reasons of race—dates from the late seventeenth and early eighteenth century." Fredrickson's interpretation of the historiographical issue differed from the Handlins' principally in that the latter attributed racism to the aftermath of legal slavery, while Fredrickson found its roots in anxiety among whites over the sudden influx of unacculturated blacks in the late seventeenth century. "[T]he catalyst," Fredrickson declared, "was fear."[38]

Almost simultaneously with Fredrickson's resurrection of the Handlins' interpretation, my essay on the 1620s endorsed Degler's position. All the disputants had lamented the paucity of evidence from the colony's early years. I proposed that the few documents surviving from the decade after 1619 suggest that whites considered blacks fundamentally inferior and that nearly all blacks were probably held in permanent bondage from the outset.[39] Governor George Yeardley's will of 1627 is suggestive: it refers to "negars" and "servants" separately, a strong implication that the two categories of labor were already distinct and racially defined. More extensive evidence of both a pejorative attitude toward blacks and the probability that they were slaves rather than indentured servants appears in the Virginia censuses of 1624 and 1625.[40] Those "musters" of the colony's inhabitants seldom list Africans by name; typical entries read "A Negars woman" or "vi negors."[41] In the 1625 census only one black's age is given, and dates of arrival of only four are listed—critical information if imported Africans were, as the Handlins argued, to be released after terms of service, which were determined by age or length of servitude.[42]

Another telling piece of evidence from the first decade of blacks' presence in the colony underlines the separateness of Africans in whites' eyes: in March 1629 Virginia's General Court ordered "a generall muster of all the inhabitants men woemen and Children as well *Englishe* as Negroes."[43] *"Englishe"* must have tacitly encompassed the colony's other non-English Europeans—many Irish, Scots, and some continentals—while Negroes, who may have numbered less than thirty in a total colonial population of about three thousand, were perceived as a separate group.[44] Surely this smacks of something more than ethnocentricity. In a brief biography of Captain John Smith (1975), I argued that white Virginians had from the outset a deep-seated antipathy to people from the place Smith scorned as "those fryed Regions of blacke brutish Negers."[45]

Despite the mounting evidence of an early and pervasive antipathy toward blacks, the Handlin-Fredrickson distinction between pre-1660s ethnic prejudice and subsequent racism received prestigious support in the early 1970s from Edmund S. Morgan, a product of Harvard's history department, and Timothy H. Breen, a former student of Morgan. In a 1972 article Morgan acknowledged that on the eve of Virginia's colonization "Englishmen, along with other Europeans, were already imbued with prejudice against men of darker complexions than their own" and that "the Englishmen who colonized America and their revolutionary descendants were racists, that consciously or unconsciously they believed liberties and rights should be confined to persons of a light complexion." In an apparent contradiction, however, Morgan did not apply those generalizations to the decades before Virginia passed its slave laws. "It seems clear that most of the Africans, perhaps all of them, came as slaves. . . . It is equally clear that a substantial number of Virginia's Negroes were free or became free. And all of them, *whether servant, slave, or free,* enjoyed most of the same rights and duties as other Virginians." Morgan's subsequent generalizations about the blacks' rights homogenized the three categories. Free blacks and black servants may have had substantial equality with whites (though subtle prejudice against them is evident in the records), but the question of how slaves—subjected to lifetime bondage—"enjoyed" those rights and duties Morgan left unanswered.[46]

Although Morgan gave brief attention to the prejudice-slavery debate in his article, the book of which it was a prospectus, *American Slavery, American Freedom* (1975), addressed the question more extensively if somewhat obliquely. Morgan implies throughout the book that racial prejudice did not appear significantly in Virginia until blacks became the colony's principal labor force: "[B]efore 1660, it might have been difficult to distinguish race prejudice from class prejudice . . . [but] fears [of servile insurrection] increased as the labor force grew larger and the proportion of blacks in it rose." His chapter titles suggest as much: "Toward Slavery" precedes "Toward Racism," and both come after a chapter on Bacon's Rebellion. Yet at times Morgan tempered the implications of this sequence. "[Whether] or not race was a necessary ingredient of slavery, it *was* an ingredient. If slavery might have come to Virginia without racism, it did not. The only slaves in Virginia belonged to alien races from the English." Whatever racial harmony Virginia enjoyed in the early years eroded in the 1670s and 1680s, Morgan argued, when "the assembly deliberately did what it could to foster the contempt of whites for blacks and Indians."[47]

Morgan's interpretation of the chicken-and-egg debate, as it had come to be known, might have passed without fanfare had not J. H. Plumb highlighted it in *The New York Review of Books*. Plumb gathered from Morgan's book that "there was no social need for racism until there was a vast army of black slaves": to wit, racism emerged in the late seventeenth or early eighteenth century, decades after slavery was legally established in Virginia. Plumb though race prejudice was to be expected at that point: "As the slave population grew, racism naturally followed." (Plumb did not speculate, in print at least, on why it was natural, nor on why Americans created a system of racial slavery a quarter century before, by his reckoning, they succumbed to racism.) Most significant to Plumb was Morgan's return of the issue to the socioeconomic realm and out of color classifications or ideology: "[T]he great merit of this profoundly important book is to put slavery back in the context of poverty and the exploitation of labor."[48]

Plumb's version of Morgan's book lured Carl Degler back into the fray. In a letter to *The New York Review of Books*, Degler complained that Plumb's analysis was illogical: its portrayal of racial prejudice as a response to vast numbers of blacks failed to explain similar attitudes in New England and other areas of sparse black population. Even more than Morgan, Degler complained, Plumb ignored the abundant signs of pervasive prejudice against blacks well before slavery entered the statute books and long before blacks were numerous in the Chesapeake. Degler's letter chided Morgan too. It was symbolic, if inadvertent,

Degler suggested, that in the index to *American Slavery, American Freedom* the entry under "Negro" tells the reader to see "Blacks," which does not appear in the index at all.[49]

III

One of the few undisputed facts about Africans in early Virginia is that some of them were fully free—neither slave nor bound to service, though most free blacks had probably initially not been free.[50] The best-known case, that of Anthony Johnson, has been widely cited, for he not only achieved freedom but also in turn acquired black servants, perhaps for life terms.[51] Johnson and the other free blacks are the Handlin school's trump card: how could white Virginians have been racially prejudiced if they allowed some blacks to be free, to exercise property and perhaps political rights, and to mingle with substantial equality among white Virginians?

Critics of the Handlin interpretation accept the paradox as evidence that neither the slave system nor race prejudice reached their apogees of comprehensiveness and intensity in the seventeenth century and that occasional instances of prominent free blacks did not negate the pervasiveness of slavery or racism in the seventeenth century any more than it would in the eighteenth or the nineteenth.[52] In no century was slavery universal for blacks. Until the 1660s they had various potential paths to freedom: by expiration of contracts, as the Handlins posited; by manumission, as Susie Ames emphasized; or perhaps through Christian baptism, as others argued.[53] All scholars of the subject agree that white Christians could serve terms of service voluntarily or by court decree; most scholars agree too that English law and custom, although not crystal clear on the point, imposed lifetime servitude only on non-Christians or, in a few instances, on criminals, though the latter were not so much slaves as convicts for life. But a widely held assumption among English people that no Christian could be held in permanent bondage implied that Africans who arrived as Christians, or who later converted to Christianity, could seek redress if their masters held them beyond the usual term of service for white (and therefore nominally Christian) servants.[54] The Virginia law of 1667, which stipulated that "baptisme doth not alter the condition of the person as to his bondage or ffreedome," was clearly aimed at the slave system's sacramental loophole.[55]

In 1973 Warren M. Billings presented tantalizing evidence of the colony's early reluctance to enslave Christians regardless of color. He reconstructed as thoroughly as the surviving documents allow the cases of two Virginia slaves who sued for freedom in the colony's courts. In 1656 Elizabeth Key, the illegitimate child of a slave woman and a white planter, sued for freedom on the triple grounds of her father's status as a free Englishman, her own baptism, and a purported contractual agreement to serve her present master a stipulated period, which had expired. The court granted Key freedom, though on which of the several grounds is not clear. In 1667 Fernando maintained that he was entitled to freedom because he was a Christian and had lived for a time in England. The disposition of his case is unknown. In any event, both suits illustrate the escape hatches available to slaves and forecast the legislation of the 1660s and 1670s that shut them tight. Five years before it passed the law making baptism irrelevant (1667), the House of Burgesses decreed that a mulatto child's status followed its mother's condition rather than its father's. With paternal status and baptism eliminated as paths to freedom, a contract for limited service (such as Elizabeth Key claimed) would be moot for most blacks, for by definition slaves had no contractual rights.[56]

By whatever legal or circumstantial route, scores of Virginia's blacks became free during the middle decades of the seventeenth century. T. H. Breen and Stephen Innes have shed important light on many of those men and women in *"Myne Owne Ground"* (1980), a study of free blacks in Northampton County. In the early and middle decades of the century, the authors assert,

> Englishmen and Africans could interact with one another on terms of relative equality for two generations. The possibility of a genuinely multiracial society became a reality during the years before Bacon's Rebellion in 1676. Not until the end of the seventeenth century was there an inexorable hardening of racial lines. We argue that it was not until the slave codes of 1705 that the tragic fate of Virginia's black population was finally sealed.[57]

Here, once again, was the Handlin thesis in new clothes. If some of the garments seemed to be borrowed from Fredrickson and others from Morgan, the overall ensemble was nonetheless original—and highly controversial.

Breen and Innes conceded that all of Northampton County's blacks probably arrived as slaves. Within the next decade or two, a few were manumitted; many others raised tobacco on their house lots and purchased their freedom with the profits. Most of the new freedmen remained where they were as independent farmers, and by and large they flourished for two generations. Many acquired property, sued in court (often successfully), and engaged in daily give-and-take with their white neighbors on the farm and in the marketplace.[58] They could own guns (the 1640 and 1680 prohibitions did not apply to free blacks, Breen and Innes contend), their testimony was accepted in court, and they seem to have received fair treatment when accused of illegal actions.[59] In Northampton County, at least, free blacks and nongentry whites dealt "essentially as equals"; until Bacon's Rebellion, "economic status rather than racial identity seems to have been the chief factor in determining how blacks and whites dealt with each other." Racism was in the future. "At mid-century ethnocentrism was probably a more powerful force shaping human relations than racism," according to Breen and Innes, for although Negroes were often so designated in the documents of the time, Italians and other non-English residents were often comparably identified.[60]

The benign situation of free blacks ended soon after Bacon's Rebellion. Breen and Innes assert that the sharp increase in slave imports, especially of nonacculturated Africans, "exacerbated racial tensions"—tensions whose existence the authors had heretofore largely denied. Whites began for the first time to discuss black inferiority because the importations "generated racist ideas or brought to the surface latent racist assumptions." Free blacks suffered as much as the newly imported slaves. Some black farmers moved to Maryland in search of better land. Those who stayed in Virginia faced declining prosperity, and "increasingly, their white neighbors treated them with distrust and disdain." In 1699 the legislature ordered free blacks to depart the colony within six months.[61]

Breen and Innes argue forcefully against the early significance of racial prejudice in Northampton County. They propose that "[Anthony] Johnson and [Francis] Payne did not think of themselves as living in a racist society. Nor . . . did it occur to them that their white neighbors were making an 'unthinking decision' that would reduce all black people to the lowest levels of society simply because they were black." Perhaps not, but the thoughts of Virginia's free blacks, wholly unrecorded, are pure speculation. Is it not more plausible to suppose that Johnson and Payne wondered why, if race relations were "not affected by the color of a man's skin," nearly three-quarters of the county's blacks but none of its whites were held in permanent slavery during the period of relative racial harmony? Did Johnson and Payne not wonder why, if ethnicity rather than race was critical, African-Americans were designated by a color term—even if born and bred in Virginia—never by such national labels as "Angolan" or "Yoruban" or "Ashanti"—not even "African"?[62] Did Johnson and Payne not wonder why, if skin color was unimportant, laws were passed in 1662 against a child inheriting its father's status, as English common law prescribed, if its mother happened to be "a negro woman"; why a law in 1667 denied that baptism could bring freedom to "slaves by birth," that is, blacks alone; why a law in 1668 decreed that free black women (but not white women) were tithable; why a law in 1670 prohibited free blacks, even if Christians themselves, from buying Christian servants?[63] Surely these laws reveal prejudice exclusively against blacks several decades before Africans became either numerous or outstandingly "foreign" in language and customs.[64] In sum, although Breen and Innes contribute much useful insight into the lives of free blacks in one seventeenth-century Virginia county, they seriously distort, I believe, the overall picture of early black-white relations and especially its connection to incipient American racism.

Reactions to "*Myne Owne Ground*" ran the gamut from skepticism to indiscriminate praise. Gary B. Nash, while applauding Breen and Innes's methodology, rejected their reading of the evidence on Anthony Johnson in particular and racial attitudes in general; Lorena Walsh pointed out the unrepresentativeness of Northampton County's thirteen black heads of family among Virginia's black population. On the other hand, Lawrence Stone hailed the book as "an extraordinary and convincing story" that "proves that for a couple of generations in seventeenth century Virginia the two races lived fairly comfortably side by side with little or no legal and not much psychological prejudice." Even Breen and Innes had not gone that far. Stone, matching his fellow Englishman Plumb's delight in economic rather than racial explanations of slavery, turned "*Myne Owne Ground*" into an anachronistic scenario for the genesis of American racism: after Bacon's Rebellion, "the number of blacks became relatively so great that they created fear; fear led to repression; repression led to legal discrimination and personal degradation; degradation led to racial prejudice." Like Plumb, Stone overlooked the early emergence of pejorative notions about blacks in New England, where their presence was always small. More serious, he distorted the chronology of slavery: the essentials of Virginia's legal discrimination emerged in the decade before Bacon's Rebellion and thus a quarter century before the great influx of Africans.[65]

IV

A second issue in the historiography of early American slavery is intertwined with—and sometimes confused with—the debate over the origins of racism and slavery: Why did the Chesapeake's sparse black population suddenly increase in the late seventeenth century, and what effect did the new black presence have on the evolution of racism? To scholars who view racism as largely (though not wholly) in place by the mid-seventeenth century and slavery the overwhelming (but not sole) condition for British America's blacks by the late 1670s, the reason for the sudden and dramatic growth of the black population is a separate matter. To advocates of the argument that racism followed slavery, however, the dramatic influx and racism are causally connected.

The traditional explanation for the dramatic rise in the importation of Africans has been that, first, the expansion of Virginia's tobacco production increased the demand for field hands, but white labor was inadequate because it was short-term (usually four years for adult males); in fact, some of the demand for indentured labor came from former servants who had become entrepreneurs themselves; second, black labor, though perhaps less socially desirable, was in the long run cheaper than white labor because the former was permanent, the latter transient; and third, the availability of African slaves increased with the emergence of the Royal African Company in 1672 as the principal shipper of

Africans to British America and expanded further when the company lost its monopoly in 1698.[66] Thus the standard interpretation was almost exclusively economic, though obviously the economic solution (importation of vast numbers of unacculturated African slaves) had major social ramifications—the hardening of racial lines, the rigidification of the slave system, the further debasement of field labor, and much more.[67]

Since the early 1970s two predominantly social explanations have challenged the economic interpretation. In 1972 Edmund Morgan's presidential address to the Organization of American Historians (subsequently published as "Slavery and Freedom: The American Paradox" and expanded in *American Slavery, American Freedom*) gave far more attention to the reasons for the growth of Virginia's black population than it did to the chicken-and-egg issue—though at bottom Morgan was blending the two questions. Bacon's Rebellion, Morgan argued, was the key event. When armed, angry, landless, former servants—a "giddy multitude," according to the Virginia legislature—temporarily overturned the colony's political and social order, the elite read the writing on the wall. More white servants meant, potentially, more trouble; black labor might be less desirable socially, but it had abundant offsetting advantages. It was permanent (by law and custom), unarmed (by law and owner's caution), relatively docile (by coercive restraint), and self-perpetuating (by biological probability). Indentured labor was not abandoned immediately nor, in the colonial period, completely, but the proportion of black imports rose sharply soon after Bacon's Rebellion and remained high for half a century.[68]

Concomitant with a rise in black population was the emergence of racial prejudice, Morgan asserted: poor whites increasingly made their own complexion a mark of freedom and superiority. The elite simultaneously fostered white cohesion as a protection against black insurrection. As slavery became the hallmark of black Virginians, freedom gained added meaning for Virginia's whites. The paradox reached fruition in 1776, when American independence heralded still greater freedom for the latter and more rigid slavery for the former.[69]

Morgan's interpretation coincided with Breen's; the latter's 1972 article in the *Journal of Social History* also stressed the "giddy multitude" and its unintended stimulus to the importation of black labor. After Bacon's Rebellion, Breen noted, the quality of white servants rose—more had skills, fewer were "desperate villans"—white planters increasingly turned to African slaves for gang labor. At the same time, rising tobacco prices improved the prospects of lower-class whites and made "their servitude endurable and their freemanship secure." As the gap grew between contented white laborers and the swelling numbers of blacks imported directly from their homelands, "[n]o white servant in this period, no matter how poor, how bitter or badly treated, could identify with these frightened Africans."[70] The cumulative effect of the Morgan and Breen articles and the Morgan book was perhaps predictable: by the late 1970s Bacon's Rebellion appeared in colonial and survey textbooks as the causal turning point in Virginia's slave system.[71]

In 1975 Theodore Allen reinforced the class-conflict implications of the Morgan-Breen interpretation. Writing from a Marxist perspective, Allen attributed the dramatic shift in Virginia's racial composition and the emergence of racism to the elite's fear of the "solidarity of black and white" proletariats in the 1660s, 1670s, and 1680s, especially during Bacon's Rebellion. Allen saw Bacon's army as an "armed working class, black and white, [that] fought side by side for the abolition of slavery." After the large planters crushed the rebellion, they tightened restrictions on blacks and conscripted lower-class whites to control the growing slave population. Thus separated into white and black elements, the proletariat lost its clout. Lower-class whites found some solace in being legally and (in the eyes of white society) socially superior to the blacks. Allen said almost nothing about racism as an ideology; implicitly he saw racism taking hold late in the seventeenth century among lower-class whites who had earlier been sufficiently unbiased against blacks to join them in matrimony, resistance, and rebellion. Racism was an elitist strategy.[72]

No sooner had Morgan, Breen, and Allen's "giddy multitude" won the historiographical skirmish than it succumbed to a withering crossfire. In 1977 Russell R. Menard pointed out that the supply of indentured servants had declined for a decade before slave imports began to rise appreciably. Beginning in the 1660s two alternatives to the Chesapeake colonies beckoned English workmen: at home, especially in London, where the Great Fire of 1666 created thousands of new jobs, and in America, where Carolina and the middle colonies attracted a mounting portion of American immigrants. Virginia continued to import indentured servants in substantial numbers; especially in the second decade of the eighteenth century, Chesapeake planters invested heavily in Irish, convict, and poor servants. The labor demands kept rising, however, and as early as the 1680s the only plausible solution seemed to lie in the African slave trade. "The rise of black slavery was more a consequence than a cause of the decline of white servitude," Menard concluded, although "it perhaps hastened the process." In short, "Chesapeake planters did not abandon indentured servitude; it abandoned them."[73]

Economist David Galenson corroborated Menard's findings and added an important codicil. Galenson found that in the staple colonies (the Chesapeake, Carolina, and the West Indies) the rising cost of white labor caused planters to shift initially from unskilled white labor to unskilled black labor; skilled tasks were reserved for whites. This "racial division of labor" lasted until the mounting cost of skilled white labor encouraged planters to train blacks, especially highly acculturated

African-Americans, in the desired crafts. At that point the shift from white to black labor in the staple colonies was more or less complete, though of course it was never total, especially in the Chesapeake.[74]

Although the two recent explanations of the shift from white to black labor in the Chesapeake are diametrical opposites—Morgan and Breen see the planters forsaking white servants, Menard and Galenson see white servants forsaking the planters—the interpretations are not mutually exclusive. Menard and Galenson do not deny that Bacon's Rebellion aroused fear of poor whites among the planters; that fear may have exacerbated the decline in importation of white servants, especially the unskilled, and accordingly increased the urgency for an alternate supply of labor.[75] The delay in filling the shortage through direct importation of Africans may have reflected a combination of the slow response of the slave trade—for reasons of organization and technology—and the reluctance of Virginia planters to embrace black labor on a large scale.[76] The planters knew the social implications of such a move—the dilemmas of Barbados and Jamaica, and later of South Carolina, were common knowledge—and resisted extensive use of black labor until economic realities convinced them, acting in their individual self-interests, that slave labor was the shortest and perhaps the only route to prosperity.[77]

If viewed from the perspective of the entire Western Hemisphere and of the transatlantic slave trade (a century-and-a-half old when the boom reached Virginia), the decisions of the Chesapeake planters seem foregone. The gentry could either have slave labor from Africa and economic expansion, or they could limp along with a dwindling supply of indentured European labor. That virtually all African laborers would be slaves rather than servants had already been determined by hemisphere-wide economic circumstances and examples, including the British Caribbean's, and by Virginia's legislation of the 1660s and 1670s. Economic trends and social legislation thus shaped the Virginians' decisions about the growth and status of the black population.[78] In any event, the debate over the growth in the number of slaves continues to be inextricably connected to the chicken-and-egg argument by scholars who see racism as a response to the rapid expansion of Virginia's black population.

V

Although there is no consensus on when and why slavery and racism began and the possible connections between them, there is now agreement on several subsidiary issues. No one doubts, for example, the basic demographic configurations of Virginia's black population: its sparse numbers in the early decades, its sharp rise in the 1680s and after, and its shift late in the century from Caribbean sources to, increasingly,

African sources. Nor does anyone doubt that the legal status of blacks was ambiguous until the 1660s and 1670s and to some extent beyond, or that many blacks—perhaps more than 25 percent in some counties—were free on the eve of Virginia's slave legislation. There is general agreement too that legal restrictions on free blacks and popular prejudice against all blacks hardened late in the century, probably in response to the rapid increase in the number of Africans and to their relatively greater (compared to earlier African-Americans') cultural "differentness" from the English colonists.[79]

There is even agreement that before the 1660s white Virginians harbored some degree of prejudice—or, at the very least, a special unease—toward blacks. The Handlins acknowledged that the English were offended by "[t]he rudeness of the Negroes' manners, the strangeness of their languages, the difficulty of communicating to them English notions of morality and proper behavior."[80] Morgan conceded that the early colonists were "imbued with prejudice against men of darker complexions than their own"; Fredrickson agreed that Virginia's whites felt special antipathy from the outset toward black strangers; while Breen and Innes hinted at "latent racist assumptions."[81] Degler, Jordan, and others stated the case more emphatically. In any event, the various interpretive positions differ more in degree than in kind, although the Handlins largely ignore pigmentation and its implications on the assumption that skin color only became an issue in the aftermath of large-scale enslavement: "Color then emerged as the token of the slave status."[82]

Despite the several points of agreement about Virginia's early treatment of blacks and its prejudicial attitudes toward them, fundamental disagreements persist over several issues: first, the status of most blacks before the 1660s—whether they were, on the whole, temporary servants or lifetime slaves; second, the depth and significance of discrimination against blacks in the early decades; third, the reasons for Virginia's initial enslavement of blacks; and fourth, the point at which antipathy against blacks was sufficiently rooted in biological assumptions for historians to label it racism rather than ethnocentrism.

On the first point—the status of blacks before the passage of the slave laws—the issue is not whether some were free or some were slave. Almost everyone acknowledges the existence of both categories by the 1640s, if not from the beginning. At issue, rather, is the relative size of those groups and of a third that many maintain was the largest—indentured servants.[83] The calculations of Morgan and of Breen and Innes that in Northampton County in midcentury nearly 30 percent of the black inhabitants were free seem to set the maximum figure for that category, though the colonywide figure may have been appreciably lower. Breen and Innes acknowledge that the rest of Northampton County's blacks were slaves.[84] Some scholars (rarely colonial specialists) nonetheless still assert that most blacks in the early period were neither slave nor free but rather indentured servants.[85]

For that contention to be valid, three evidentiary problems must be resolved: why the evidence of indentured blacks is extremely scarce;[86] how, in the absence of contracts, blacks could have been freed by "the custom of the country" when the laws concerning servants without indentures apparently applied only to Englishmen;[87] and how lengths of service were determined for blacks when the censuses and land patents rarely listed their ages, dates of arrival in the colony, or even their names. Indentured servitude, in short, appears from both positive evidence (much higher evaluations in wills and inventories and anonymous entries in censuses) and negative evidence (absence of contracts and unrecorded ages or dates of arrival) to have been an unlikely status for most of Virginia's blacks.[88]

Testimony from other English colonies is relevant, for it suggests strongly that throughout British America blacks were very quickly—perhaps immediately—enslaved. In Barbados, for example, the governor and council announced in 1636 (before sugar production spurred the importation of Africans) that "*Negroes* and *Indians* that come here to be sold, should serve for Life, unless a Contract was before made to the contrary"; two years later the Providence Island Company referred to its "Negros being . . . kept as perpetuall servants"; in 1652 the Rhode Island legislature reported that "there is a common course practised amongst English men to buy negers, to that end they may have them for service or slaves forever."[89] Until each colony enacted its own statutory legitimation of perpetual bondage, the mother country's common law of property served the same effective purpose. There is no reason to posit a Virginia exceptionalism in the use of African labor. In short, the evidence from Virginia and elsewhere refutes the popular myth that slavery was rare or nonexistent before the legislation of the 1660s and 1670s, that free blacks were numerous, and that most blacks were indentured servants. The surviving records support a very different distribution: slavery from the outset for the vast majority, freedom for some (by a variety of means) after a period of slavery, and indentured servitude (seldom with a legal contract) for the smallest number.[90]

On the second point of disagreement—the severity and significance of discrimination against blacks in those early years—the sharp division that characterized the Handlin-Degler exchange of thirty-five years ago has substantially subsided, but it has hardly been settled. Most historians now concede that blacks in early Virginia were often subjected to discriminatory treatment, though rarely in legal confrontations; there English jurisprudence, transferred substantially though imperfectly to the colonies, seems to have retained much of its traditional impartiality. There is no consensus, however, on the significance of the discrimination aimed specifically at blacks—whether it was a superficial reaction to strangers or indicative of a distinct racial antipathy. The Handlins, Morgan, and some others underestimate (in my opinion) the uniqueness and import of the overall plight of blacks in early Virginia.[91] By contrast, Degler, especially, and some others find discrimination against blacks distinctive and extensive.[92]

The problem of assessing discrimination and its underlying attitudes is exemplified by the frequent identification of Africans as "Negroes" in seventeenth-century records. Most contributors to the debate acknowledge that Africans were often so designated, but they disagree sharply over what it means. Breen and Innes minimize the custom's significance; it was, they contend, merely an identifier that had parallels among Europeans in the use of "Italian," "Irish," and so forth—signs, in other words, of English ethnocentricity. Lerone Bennett Jr. even argues that "Negor was a national rather than a racial designation" and "the early records identify the *nationality* of all non-Englishmen."[93] Such conclusions are not supported by documentary evidence from early Virginia.[94] Non-English Europeans are, to be sure, occasionally identified by nationality, especially during their early years in the colony; I know of no instance in which their progeny are so identified.[95] Africans in America, by contrast, were usually identified by a color (not a national) label, regardless of their length of time in America or whether they were of African or American birth.

The prevalence of such color terminology is demonstrated, with unintended irony, in an illustration accompanying the essay in which Bennett argues that black and white outsiders were labeled by nationality. It shows sample pages from Virginia musters of the 1620s: of the six blacks identifiable in the illustration, four are listed only as "Negro"; the others are "Antonio a Negro" and "Mary a Negro woman." The remaining thirty-seven people, clearly English or European, listed in the illustration all have full names and none is identified by nationality.[96] Comparably ironic is Breen and Innes's use of the document from which they take their title *"Myne Owne Ground."* It quotes Anthony, a free black whose boundary dispute with a white neighbor had just been settled, as saying, "Now I know myne owne ground and I will worke when I please and play when I please." To Breen and Innes, Anthony is reflecting Northampton's equitable race relations. Is it not equally significant, however, that the only contemporary account of this episode always refers to the white neighbor as "Capt. Taylor" or "Mr. Taylor," while Anthony is always "Anthony the negro," or "the said Negro," or simply "the negro"? His last name is never used.[97] In the surviving records, in fact, blacks are usually anonymous—"negro," "a negro man," "17 negroes," and so forth—while the few African-Americans, free or slave, who have full names are often *additionally* designated by color, as a virtual suffix to their family names—"Francis Paine Negro," "phillip Mongom negro," "Thomas Driggins Negro," "John Casor Negro."[98] There is no comparable pattern for whites of any nationality.[99] The prevailing terminology shows emphatically that white Virginians saw blacks as a unique type of "others"—people so markedly different from themselves that they must be separately identified in most private and public documents. A plethora of such evidence notwithstanding, historians are far from a consensus about the nature and meaning of early American discrimination.

On the third major unresolved issue—the causes of Virginia's slavery—debate is still lively, largely because slavery's relationship to white racism is problematic. A loose agreement on other "causes" has emerged, however. Many historians now acknowledge that the absence of legal prohibitions in England encouraged rather than inhibited de facto slavery; rarely does anyone contend that the absence of statutory slavery impeded its practice in either England or the colonies.[100] Thus the colonists were free to adopt the Latin American model or to contrive their own. Almost all historians, following the Handlins' lead, now emphasize the vulnerability of blacks to unscrupulous owners who could do pretty much as they pleased with African "servants"; sometimes that meant manumission, especially for Christian blacks, but more often it meant lifetime servitude. There is probably universal agreement too that the Chesapeake planters' insatiable demands for labor of any kind and for the longest possible periods of service gave human bondage its raison d'être. As Degler observed in 1976, "slavery developed from a need for labor in a social context of readily available land. In that sense the roots of slavery were economic."[101] On several aspects of the genesis of American slavery, then, most historians of early American race relations seem to concur. Their explanation, in general, is that an intense demand for labor joined hands with Latin American precedents, the absence of English legal restraints, and the Africans' vulnerable status as captives to forge a slave system for Virginia's small but growing black population. An existing and perhaps essential additional ingredient, some historians contend, was racial prejudice.

VI

On that final point, profound disagreement persists. What role did racism play in the evolution of American slavery? None, according to the Handlins, Allen, Bennett, and others, who see racism as a result— "the child of slavery," in Fredrickson's words—rather than a contributing cause or concomitant phenomenon of emergent slavery.[102] Other historians see racial antipathy as a crucial ingredient, though they vary on the exact terms to describe English beliefs about blacks and even differ in the meanings they ascribe to certain words.

Disparate definitions have long plagued the chicken-and-egg debate. Several key terms—ethnocentrism, prejudice, and especially racism itself—are frustratingly imprecise, and until recently most historians of early Virginia have been reluctant to use *racism* at all. The Handlins, Degler, and Jordan shunned it, partly, no doubt, because it was not yet widely used and partly, perhaps, on the assumption that the term was too emotionally charged in the social climate of the 1950s and 1960s to be useful. Moreover, Degler held that seventeenth-century racism, if it existed, could not be demonstrated. "I make no claim," he wrote in his 1959 rebuttal to the Handlins, "for the widespread acceptance of a racist view of colored peoples in the seventeenth century, for the evidence is too skimpy"; in his retort to Plumb's review of Morgan's book, Degler further protested that " 'racism' is an inappropriate word here since it means imputing *biological* inferiority to other people." Thus, although both Degler and Jordan believed that Virginia's early English settlers discriminated against blacks in general far more than against any group of whites, regardless of nationality, and believed too that whites held uniquely pejorative views of dark-skinned peoples, they adopted somewhat equivocal terminology: Degler alluded to "race prejudice" in his title, but his essay referred almost exclusively to "discrimination" and "status"; Jordan discerned a general "debasement" of blacks and a pervasive "racial prejudice" but never alluded to "racism."[103]

In 1971 Fredrickson complained that popular American usage had blurred the meaning of *racism* to include almost any hint of prejudice against blacks, individually or collectively. He insisted that racism is an expressed conviction that innate behavioral and intellectual differences distinguish human "races" and permit hierarchical ranking—in short, an ideology.[104] (Race is a discredited biological-anthropological concept, of course, but essential to racist theories.)[105] Fredrickson postulated that seventeenth-century attitudes could only be inferred from the way whites treated blacks in laws, court cases, economic practices, and the like. By that rule, he found no racism, not even implicit, until unacculturated blacks became numerous; he considered early Virginians prejudiced, perhaps, but not racist.[106] Fredrickson apparently ignored, or was unimpressed by, the numerous discriminatory laws against blacks alone in the seventeenth century, by the imposition of customary slavery for most blacks early in the century and of legal slavery for the overwhelming majority of blacks in the 1660s, and by the evidence of strong color bias among English settlers from the outset.[107]

A year after Fredrickson's plea for a more rigorous use of terminology, sociologist Donald Noel applied precise and scholarly meanings to the key concepts. He distinguished between ethnocentrism ("in-group glorification"), prejudice ("a hostile or negative attitude toward members of a *specific* group"), discrimination ("unequal treatment of the members of a specific group"), and racism ("an ideology based on the conception that racial groups form a biogenetic hierarchy"). Although Noel's application of those concepts to the chicken-and-egg debate suggested a rigorous methodology, he vitiated his case by admitting that "the present analysis does not start from neutral ground but is guided by the hypothesis that American racism was far more a product than a cause of slavery. . . . Racism arose, in response to slavery, as a means of justifying the extreme economic exploitation of blacks"—a blunt rephrasing of the Handlin thesis. Somewhat like the Handlins, Noel believed that cultural ethnocentricity was a contributing cause. Unlike the

Handlins, Noel acknowledged that racist ideas may have existed in Virginia before slavery and may even have "had some causal significance," though they were not, he contended, sufficiently "widespread or legitimate" to be "a significant cause."[108] He might have reached a different conclusion had he not assumed, following the Handlins, that slavery was rare until the laws of the 1660s and 1670s, for Noel held that a "society is racist . . . only if the idea of group superiority-inferiority is incorporated into the institutional structure."[109]

Noel's emphasis on institutionalization hints that Virginia's sociopolitical rulers imposed racism on the colony at large through legislation. As noted earlier, Morgan, Breen, and especially Allen posit upper-class origins of lower-class racism; they imply that neither class arrived with much bias, but after midcentury the need of the planters to justify their increased subjugation of blacks and to drive a wedge between the potential alliance (in Bacon's Rebellion, some argue, the actual alliance) of poor whites and blacks engendered a racist rationalization.[110]

The strongest advocate of racism as a class strategy is Lerone Bennett Jr. "In the beginning," he announced in a series of essays in *Ebony*, "there was no race problem in America. *The problem of race . . . was a deliberate invention of men who systematically separated blacks and whites and reds in order to make money.*" Fear, snobbery, and especially greed were the inanimate villains in Bennett's scenario; the principal actors were "the white Founding Fathers. The Byrds, the Mathers, the Winthrops, the Jeffersons, the Washingtons." Bennett argued that in the early decades whites in general "had concepts of class and nationality but no concepts of race or slavery"; by the middle of the seventeenth century "the men who ran colonial America began to create racism." Poor whites were hoodwinked; blacks were degraded; the Founding Fathers were enriched.[111]

In the absence of more evidence on lower-class attitudes, we cannot be sure what inarticulate whites thought about blacks, though surely they had a concept of slavery and probably, however inchoate, of race as well. In any event, the surviving records scarcely make a case for a bias-free lower class. Poor whites sometimes had illicit sex with blacks, but that is no more a sign of unprejudiced minds than was the antebellum planter's penchant for sex with his female slaves. Although interracial marriages do suggest perceived equality, few such unions are documented. Equally inconclusive are the handful of attempts by white and black servants to escape or rebel together. Such efforts surely reflect temporary common interests, but they tell nothing about long-term relationships or basic attitudes. Similarly, Breen and Innes's case for the acceptance of free blacks as near equals by middle-class whites in Northampton County seems limited to court proceedings and commercial transactions, and even there the record is arguable.[112]

On the other hand, numerous clues point to a separate and inferior status for all blacks, slave or free, from the outset, without discernibly different class attitudes among whites. The evidence from British America and Tudor-Stuart England suggests that the bias against Africans was widespread.[113] Although some lower-class whites surely overcame that bias by living and working closely with people who at first seemed strikingly different, the scattered clues suggest a broad English heritage of prejudicial attitudes from which few Anglo-Americans were liberated. The possibility remains (and is compatible with otherwise disparate interpretations) that the plantocracy grew alarmed at signs of eroding prejudice as lower-class whites became more familiar with black men and women; the upper class may then have reinvigorated a waning racist ideology among the poor whites to prevent a united working class. Convincing support for such a theory has yet to be presented, and class lines were so fluid in early Virginia that attempts to demonstrate ideological variants may be futile.[114]

The apparent prevalence of racial prejudice toward blacks in early Virginia raises a gnawing question: Why were Anglo-Americans contemptuous of people they barely knew? Surely racism was not inherent, nor was it inevitable. (A few scholars believe otherwise. Carl Degler, for example, concluded after analyzing race relations in Brazil and the United States that "color prejudice is a universal phenomenon" and that "blacks will be recognized as different and discriminated against whenever nonblacks have the power and an incentive to do so.")[115] The evidence is now fairly clear that confluent circumstances in sixteenth-century England engendered a conviction, theretofore unarticulated and perhaps unknown in the British Isles, that dark-skinned Africans were in fundamental ways unlike Europeans and inferior to them (Fig. 7.1).[116]

The precise evolution of that notion is uncertain, but Jordan provided a good preliminary explanation in the opening chapter of *White over Black*. Its central components were, first, England's relative insularity before the middle of the sixteenth century from the world's cultural and ethnic variety; second, the sudden "discovery" by English voyagers, and eventually by the English public in general, of a people remarkably different from themselves in appearance and culture; third, the unfortunate coincidence of England's simultaneous encounter with people they perceived to be least like themselves and the animals (great apes) they deemed most like humans, with resulting false assumptions about the interrelationship between the two and the possibility that Africans were partly animal; and, fourth, the "emotionally partisan" quality of the color black in English symbolism.[117] Subsequent studies support Jordan's conclusion that "from the first, Englishmen tended to set Negroes over against themselves, to stress what they conceived to be radically contrasting qualities of color, religion, and style of life, as well as animality and a peculiarly potent sexuality."[118] Religion and lifestyle are cultural considerations and therefore targets of ethnocentricity, but notions of color, "animality," and perhaps sexuality are essentially biological, from which racist assumptions could be fashioned. Thus part of the English

L E A V E of with paine , the blackamore to ſkowre,
With waſhinge ofte, and wipinge more then due :
For thou ſhalt finde , that Nature is of powre,
Doe what thou canſte, to keepe his former hue:

Fig. 7.1.
Illustration and part of an accompanying poem that epitomize "Impossible" in Geoffrey Whitney, *A Choice of Emblems* (Leiden, 1586). By permission of the Folger Shakespeare Library.

bias was ethnocentric—a perceived cultural difference in kind and quality—while much of it was racist, based on a widespread English conviction that Africans were innately inferior and unworthy of full equality.[119]

No literary outpouring comparable to antebellum America's denigration of blacks can be found in late Tudor or early Stuart England—an era of transition from oral to print culture—but an authentic racial ideology existed nonetheless. If the evidence for such an ideology, like everything else in the chicken-and-egg debate, is fragmentary, numerous clues nonetheless demonstrate that English assumptions about the nature of dark-skinned Africans were based on perceptions of biological as well as cultural difference. Sixteenth- and seventeenth-century racial theory lacks the pseudoscientific language of the nineteenth century, of course; in keeping with the Elizabethan worldview, the rhetoric of human differences was almost always framed in religious terms. That terminology made it no less sincere and no less pernicious.

Take, for example, George Best, explorer and author, who wondered in 1578 why the inhabitants of Africa had such strikingly dark complexions. He dismissed the theory that the sun's heat determined pigmentation, because people at comparable latitudes in America and the East Indies were "not blacke, but white"; moreover, in England a black man could sire a black son, despite the climate and even the "good complexion" of the child's white mother. Rather, Best concluded, "the most probable cause . . . is, that this blacknesse proceedeth of some naturall infection of the first inhabitants of that Countrey [Africa], and so all the whole progenie of them descended, are still poluted with the same blot of infection." The Bible, Best believed, explained the initial infection: on the ark, Noah admonished his three sons to be sexually continent, but Cham (Ham), hoping for a son who would inherit the earth, disobeyed; for punishment, God made Cham's son Chus (Canaan) and all his posterity "so blacke & lothsome, that it might remaine a spectacle of disobedience to all the World."[120] That Best's reading of Genesis 9:20–27 took great liberties with the text is beside the point. His conclusion about the Africans' pigmentation was widely shared.

The Reverend Thomas Cooper's tract of 1615, dedicated to (among others) "the worthie Commissioners, for the plantations in *Ireland* and *Virginia*," suggested a slightly different scene but with similar results. When Noah lay drunk and naked in his tent, Shem and Japeth were too modest to look at their father's nakedness; Cham not only saw but mocked it, "reioycing at, and deriding the corruption of the Ancient." God retaliated, Cooper theorized, by decreeing that "this cursed race of *Cham* [shall be] scattered towards the South, in *Affrica, etc.*"; one of Shem's rewards was "that he shall be *Lord* over his *cursed brother*, and his posteritie."[121] George Sandys, a prominent scholar and Virginia colonist, attested in 1615 that "all of that complexion" were descended from "*Chus,* the Sonne of cursed CHAM." Similarly, an English author in 1627 observed that "this curse to be a servant was laid, first upon a disobedient sonne *Cham*, and wee see to this day, that the *Moores, Chams* posteritie, are sold like slaves yet."[122] A belief that blacks were eternally cursed by God thus had currency in England as early as the 1570s; that they were divinely consigned to slavery was expounded at least as early as 1615.

The pervasiveness of the biblical explanation is uncertain, for it competed in the sixteenth and seventeenth centuries with a variety of other nonsensical explanations of African pigmentation. As Jordan observed, however, the Genesis theory was "probably sustained by a feeling that blackness could scarcely be anything *but* a curse and by the common need to confirm the facts of nature by specific reference to Scripture."[123]

In sum, English opinion during early American colonization held that Africans were innately inferior in a variety of ways (just which ways depended, as with nineteenth-century racists, on the commentator's own concerns) and stigmatized by the color of evil because of God's displeasure. That was as profoundly a racist ideology as anything advocated two centuries later by Edmund Ruffin or George Fitzhugh or three centuries later by Ku Klux Klansmen.[124]

Further evidence that notions of a biblical curse on black-skinned peoples were widespread in seventeenth-century Anglo-America, though infrequently articulated in print in an era of few presses and limited literacy, is found in Morgan Godwyn's missionary pamphlet *The Negro's & Indians Advocate* (1680). Godwyn was, to be sure, describing Barbados rather than Virginia and from the vantage point of the 1670s, but the racial biases he encountered echo Best's of a century earlier and comparable testimony from the intervening years. Godwyn's efforts to bring Christianity to the slaves encountered retorts of *"What, those black Dogs be made Christians?"* Many colonists, Godwyn lamented, adhered to the theory of the curse on Ham, others posited a separate creation for black-skinned peoples, while still others argued that "the *Negro's*, though in their Figure they carry some resemblances of Manhood, yet are indeed *no Men.*" Godwyn had heard that idea expounded in England as well as America.[125]

When the ideology of Negro inferiority first arrived in Virginia, it was unfocused—England had only a few hundred black residents, Virginia probably had none until 1619—and it surely lacked the depth and breadth of later times. Racism, like other ideologies, is erratic; it vacillates over time, has varying degrees of adherence, and may fluctuate within individuals.[126] The evidence from the early decades, however, suggests that although racism was incomplete, it was virulent in early Virginia, much as racism is incomplete, yet appallingly virulent, in America today. Such early racism helps to explain why Africans, and no others, were thrust into slavery almost simultaneously in Virginia, Maryland, Bermuda, the British West Indies, and New England. It also helps to explain why de facto enslavement usually emerged several decades before Anglo-American statute law acknowledged the practice and, in Virginia and several other colonies, long before blacks were numerous enough to engender racism as a response to fear over their abundance.

Racism alone did not, of course, bring slavery to British America. The world has witnessed many slave systems without racism and many racist societies without slavery.[127] Rather the conjunction of slavery (largely an economic matter) and racism (largely an ideological matter) generated a system of bondage exclusively for a perceived branch of humankind; that system was peculiar to Western Europe's American colonies in the sixteenth century and after, although there were traces of it in the mother countries as well.[128] Thus racism was one cause of a particular type of slavery, though it may be better to avoid the term *cause,* for causation is itself a shaky concept in complex situations. It may be more useful to see Anglo-American racism as a necessary precondition for a system of slavery based on ancestry and pigmentation. Without a profound bias against peoples of dark pigmentation—and all that it implied about God's curse on them (even if, in the case of many mulattoes, their ancestry was predominantly "white"), about their culture, and about their possible animality—Virginians could not have enslaved blacks alone, almost certainly from their first arrival in America. The Anglo-Americans' bias, shared by virtually all other Europeans, allowed the exploitation of Africans in ways that colonists seem not to have contemplated toward anyone else, not even, in the early stages of Anglo-American imperialism, toward Native Americans.[129]

In sum, the explanation of Virginia's slavery that comports best with the evidence, I believe, is that white Virginians made permanent bondsmen of imported Africans and their descendants because it was economically advantageous to the slaveowners; because Africans were usually powerless to prevent enslavement or to discourage additional importations; and because the planters, and probably most of their white neighbors, believed that Africans were an inherently inferior branch of humankind, suited by their God-given characteristics and the circumstances of their arrival in America to be slaves forever. Such attitudes help to explain not only the existence of racial slavery but also the Virginia legislature's decision of 1668 that free "negro women, though permitted to enjoy their ffreedome, yet ought not in all respects to be admitted to a full fruition of the exemptions and impunities of the English." Free black women were, in short, second-class citizens, their legal freedom notwithstanding, simply because they were "negroes".[130]

Given that pervasive ideology, the other racial patterns of early Virginia are not surprising. In the 1620s blacks were only about 1 percent of Virginia's total non-Indian population, yet they received strikingly different notice in the surviving records, and most were almost certainly enslaved; the few who were not had probably, in most cases, been baptized before arrival in the colony. In the 1650s blacks were only about 2 percent of Virginia's non-Indian population, yet again the records suggest that more than 70 percent were enslaved and all, slave or free, were subjected to discrimination unique to blacks. In the 1670s they were scarcely more than 5 percent of the non-Indian population, but most were enslaved by legal definition. A few blacks had by then been free all their lives and enjoyed many traditional English rights, yet in the closing decades of the century they too were gradually deprived of those rights, not because of anything they had done, but principally because people of similar skin color and similar cultural ancestry—though not necessarily from the original political or linguistic or theological groups of the free blacks—were brought into the colony in unprecedented numbers. Perhaps early Virginia society should not be called racist. Some readers may adhere to that interpretation; others may join me in believing that it sanitizes white Virginians' early attitudes and policies toward blacks and thereby distorts racism's baneful role in the seventeenth century and beyond.

Postscript to Chapter 7

Less than a year after the foregoing essay first appeared in print, its contention that American slavery began in 1619 and was accompanied from the outset by racist underpinnings was challenged in the *New Left Review*. Written by my Columbia University colleague Barbara Jeanne Fields, "Slavery, Race and Ideology in the United States of America" argued emphatically for a different interpretation of early Virginia's history and for a much later emergence of American racism. Although I do not find her reading of the evidence persuasive, she makes the most articulate case I have yet encountered for the arrival of American racism at the end of the colonial period rather than at the beginning. Her essay, moreover, raises some fundamental issues that had previously been slighted and brings to a new level of discourse the basic positions probed in my "Origins Debate." ("Slavery, Race and Ideology," it should be noted, was not a direct response to my essay; hers had been substantially written before mine appeared and was more a reflection of her own thoughts on the subject than a reaction to anyone else's, although she includes occasional criticism of other contributions to the debate, including a footnote reference to my own.)[1]

Fields's basic argument is that in the seventeenth and early eighteenth centuries white Virginians had not yet developed a "coherent ideology" of race and therefore did not perceive or treat Africans and their Afro-American descendants on such a basis. Rather, the ideology of race

> came into existence at a discernible historical moment for rationally understandable historical reasons. . . . During the revolutionary era, people who favoured slavery and people who opposed it collaborated in identifying the racial incapacity of Afro-Americans as the explanation for enslavement. American racial ideology is as original an invention of the Founders as is the United States itself. Those holding liberty to be inalienable and holding Afro-Americans as slaves were bound to end by holding race to be a self-evident truth.

In support of this thesis, Fields advances three assumptions that presumably prove the absence of racism in early Virginia. She holds that (1) white servants generally fared almost as poorly as blacks, and some whites (Irish in America; vagabonds in England) were actually enslaved in the sixteenth and seventeenth centuries; thus "race" could not have determined (mal)treatment. (2) Africans and their descendants in Virginia before the 1660s, even those who were de facto slaves, had an unusual number of "rights" compared to their antebellum descendants;

thus racial bias must have been wholly or nearly absent at the time. (3) The terminology of seventeenth-century colonial laws concerning Africans and Afro–Africans "makes clear that the point was not yet race."[2]

Fields's analysis of seventeenth-century Virginia, I contend, misreads the evidence on all three of those assumptions and therefore fails to prove her point. On the first and second assumptions she homogenizes the plight of lower-class whites and blacks (slave and free); on the third she misunderstands the terminology of colonial laws. But her arguments are not to be dismissed lightly. Some readers, unaware of the article's factual shortcomings, find it persuasive; Fields has ardent adherents both in the United States and abroad. And even if she did not, the vigor and intellectual versatility of her argument deserve a respectful, point-by-point response.

I

The principal victims of early Virginia's labor system, Fields proposes, were not African slaves but white indentured servants, whose masters abused, cheated, beat, and maimed them, "even killed [them] with impunity." Although they were not actually enslaved by their countrymen, Fields argues, it was not from any qualms about the sanctity of English nationality or respect for pale pigmentation. As to nationality: "the law in Tudor England provided for the enslavement of vagabonds"; as to pigmentation, "the English considered no brutality too extreme in bringing to heel the supposedly savage and undoubtedly fair-skinned Irish"— witness Oliver Cromwell's consignment of Irish prisoners to slavery in the British West Indies. English servants in the colonies fared almost as badly. "The only [sic] degradation they were spared was perpetual enslavement along with their issue in perpetuity."[3]

Up to a point, Fields is right: servants in early Virginia were often treated atrociously, and numerically they undoubtedly bore the brunt of the plantocracy's unfettered appetite for pliant labor. But she overstates both the severity of treatment and the existence of lifetime bondage for whites.

Unlike slaves, servants had some legal protections, they were rarely killed with impunity, and their four- or five-year terms (seldom seven) held promise of full freedom in a relatively short time, no matter how harsh the treatment until then.[4] "Freedom dues," usually including a firearm, clothes, and sometimes land, awaited the former servant. For many of England's unemployed, those were attractive terms. Maltreatment of indentured servants was neither universal nor notorious enough to seriously curtail immigration until the third quarter of the century, when better alternatives emerged for England's "surplus" laborers. In Virginia's exploitive society, indentured servants, though sometimes treated slavishly, were never slaves.[5]

Nor were any other Europeans enslaved, in the usual sense of the word, in Tudor England or British America. The "Act for the Punishment of Vagabonds" of 1547 did, until its repeal in 1549, permit county courts to assign "vagabonds and sturdy beggars" (i.e., those physically able to work), if they appeared incorrigible to the authorities, to be "slave[s] . . . for the space of two years." Only if a temporary slave ran away for more than two weeks was he or she assigned permanently to a master. Two years later Parliament repealed the vagabond law because even its very limited form of judicial bondage was unacceptable to the English public and members of the judiciary. Few if any "slaves" were created by the short-lived act of 1547, and it had no counterparts in later, or earlier, Tudor-Stuart England.[6] There were, of course, some slaves in England at the time: Africans or descendants of Africans, who were sufficiently numerous to evoke repeated royal efforts to banish them.[7]

Neither were many, if any, Irish prisoners of war consigned to true slavery in the West Indies. The records are frustratingly incomplete on the fate of the thirty or so survivors of the Drogheda Massacre (most of the city's inhabitants were slaughtered on the spot) and other prisoners who were shipped to Barbados; they may have served out their lives in servitude, or they may have been freed after many years of harsh labor. According to Michael Craton, arguably the foremost authority on early Caribbean colonization, "The unfortunate Irish captives and perhaps some Barbadoed criminals were servants for life without indentures. But even in their case servitude did not survive them, to be inherited by their children. . . . There is absolutely no evidence that whites were ever true slaves in this sense [of absolute, inheritable property] in the English colonies."[8]

While Fields's version of white labor exaggerates its similarity to slavery, her picture of Virginia's Africans errs in the other direction. Some blacks in the British colonies, Fields acknowledges, were "eventually" enslaved, because they *could* be: Africans and Afro-West Indians did not share the English lower classes' hard-earned legal and customary protections against enslavement, and the forced migration of Africans would not be affected by adverse publicity in Africa. But, she contends, American "slavery got along for a hundred years after its establishment [which she dates from the post–Bacon's Rebellion years] without race as its ideological rationale." Even the few in bondage before the enactment of slave laws, according to Fields, were relatively well off, because "African slaves during the years between 1619 and 1661 enjoyed rights that, in the nineteenth century, not even free black people could claim."[9] By the middle of the eighteenth century, though, white Americans got used to seeing blacks at the bottom of the socioeconomic heap and began to assume that they were *naturally* inferior beings. As Fields reconstructs the evolutionary sequence, by the eve of the Revolution white Americans had to justify to themselves and to a candid world the enslavement of one-fifth of the incipient nation's population. "Race" was the answer.[10]

This picture of Africans in seventeenth-century Virginia minimizes unjustifiably their plight. Fields is surely right that they came unwillingly and that no adverse publicity about their status could undermine the slave trade, but she underestimates the timing and prevalence of enslavement for most Africans and their descendants. The evidence, sparse and sometimes ambiguous though it is, leaves little doubt that slavery was prevalent and that slaves enjoyed no "rights." Some masters in the seventeenth century, as in the antebellum era, granted privileges to some slaves; some were granted outright freedom. Neither circumstance undermines the prevalence of slavery nor the absolute rights of the masters.[11]

That racism accompanied slavery in seventeenth-century Virginia is harder to demonstrate, but the language of the laws is evidence for the existence of such an ideology rather than against it. Fields simply misreads the language of Chesapeake laws, especially Maryland's statute against "ffreeborne English women" marrying "Negro Slaves" "to the disgrace of our Nation" (1664) and Virginia's law against "any negroe or other slave" lifting a hand in opposition "against any christian" (1680). "*Race*" she contends, "does not explain" those statutes.[12] Of course race does not *wholly* explain the laws—a society's (at least a legislature's) immediate practical need is almost always the impetus for legislation—but the racial element in the laws she quotes is palpable, even though it is couched in the ambiguous language of the day.

This point is worth pursuing because Fields is not the only reader misled by seventeenth-century rhetoric. At first glance her claim that race is not at issue in the laws seems reasonable: the Maryland law specified "English women" rather than "white women" and "our Nation" rather than "our race," and the Virginia law read "Christian" instead of "white." But numerous examples from contemporaneous statutes and other documents demonstrate that "English nation," "Christians," and "whites" were virtually synonymous, as were, on the other hand, "negroes," "blacks," and "Africans." In the Maryland law quoted earlier, "English women" clearly included women of any European nationality living within the English colony, just as the Virginia legislature's call in 1629 for a muster of inhabitants "as well *Englishe* as Negroes" unquestionably sought information on everyone, regardless of nationality; in the language of the time, every person was either "English" or "Negro." Similarly, the Virginia decree of 1670 that "noe negroe or Indian though baptised and enjoyned their owne ffreedome shall be capable of any . . . purchase of christians, but yet [are] not debarred from buying any of their owne nation" had a clear racial basis: no African or Indian could buy a European, regardless of the latter's baptismal status, but Indians could buy Indians, regardless of tribal affiliation; Negroes similarly could buy Negroes from whatever African nation. Surely the legislature did not intend that Yorubas could buy only Yorubas or Cherokees only Cherokees. "Nation" in this case effectively meant "race," and "Christian" meant "white" or Euro-American—as in William Berkeley's estimate of 1671 that Virginia had "two thousand *black slaves,* six thousand *christian servants.*" The language of the time did not show "society in the act of inventing race," as Fields proposes; rather, I contend, it showed society inventing a vocabulary to express its racial ideology.[13]

In sum, Barbara Fields's keenly argued thesis that racism emerged in the Revolutionary era is invalid, I believe, because it depends on a mistaken view of seventeenth-century Virginia. Especially misrepresented are the distinct circumstances of white and black labor and the character of white Virginians' racial beliefs and policies. Of course I agree with her observation that "shared colour and nationality set no automatic limit to oppression"; most of the world's atrocities—including slavery—did not depend on those criteria. Slavery could exist without racism, racism without slavery.[14] But the issue in the "origins" debate is the interaction of a particular form of slavery and a particular form of racism at one historic place and time. I believe that in early British America the institution and the ideology formed a fateful, unholy alliance.

II

The evidence of racism's baneful presence in early Virginia is, as I argued in "The Origins Debate," varied and abundant. To summarize briefly what I state more diffusely in several essays in this book (especially chapter 7, but also partly in chapters 3 and 6), I offer the following points. They are intended as both the final portion of my response to Barbara Fields's "Slavery, Race and Ideology" and as a summary statement on the entire "origins" issue. Documentation for the following paragraphs, unless cited here, appears in the other essays.

1. In every seventeenth-century English colony, most Africans were enslaved upon their first arrival and most remained slaves throughout their lives: in 1616 and thereafter in Bermuda (as ninety-nine-year indentures), 1619 in Virginia, 1627 in Barbados, 1630 in Providence Island, 1631 (perhaps 1641) in Massachusetts, 1634 in Maryland, and so forth. Although no Virginia law until 1661 mandated slavery for Africans, no law decreed otherwise; the buyer of human chattel had the protection of English common law of property. Moreover, contemporaneous statements by colonial residents and visitors describe Africans in general as permanent slaves in the English colonies. *No* Europeans, on the other hand, were enslaved by the English.

2. Some of the Africans who arrived as slaves became free through manumission by sympathetic owners, or perhaps by a selfish owner who granted freedom rather than support elderly or incapacitated slaves. Other Africans and early Afro-Americans escaped slavery by buying themselves, and perhaps their kin, through long-term purchase agree-

ments with owners. This was not a slave's *right*; it occurred only if the owner was willing, and it was probably to the owner's long-term profit and with money or credit he permitted the slave to accrue.[15] Instances of self-purchase were apparently few, numbering scarcely a dozen men in seventeenth-century Northampton County, where the practice was probably at its most frequent.

3. A few Africans and Afro-West Indians apparently arrived in Virginia with servant indentures and subsequently gained their contractual freedom. A few others may have gained such contracts after their arrival, perhaps on the basis of conversion to Christianity. But the absence in the official records of most Africans' names or ages or dates of arrival would have thwarted an indenture system based on stipulated periods of service, either by contract or by "custom of the country" laws. Those statutes set terminal dates for servants arriving without written indentures; in any event they seem to have applied only to English servants. The few recorded black servants, moreover, served unusually long terms.

4. Only free blacks, and sometimes Native Americans, were denied full rights of citizenship despite their nominal freedom. For example, free black women after 1668 (and Indian women within the colony's jurisdiction after 1682) were taxed; other free women were not. And when, late in the century, Africans directly from Africa rather than the West Indies began to arrive in greatly increased numbers, free blacks, even those whose families had lived in the colony for three or four generations, were required to leave Virginia. They were ostracized as a separate, inferior branch of humankind—not yet designated by the word *race* but nonetheless perceived in just that sense—because many people of similar appearance and roughly similar geographic origin had arrived in the colony.

5. From the outset of British colonization, white Americans (at least those whose opinions survive) identified almost all Africans and Afro-Americans by one or more synonymous European color terms—"negro," "neger," or "black"; such terms appear in the laws, court records, inventories, diaries, and other literary evidence. Rarely was a geographic or ethnic term such as "African," "Yoruban," or "Ashanti" used. And color identifiers were applied regardless of the individual's longevity in America or status as slave or free. Very often the records included only the color labels for Africans, and where a name was used, it was usually a first name only (given by white owners or officials) and was often followed, even if a full name, by the color designation. Virginia's seventeenth-century censuses, moreover, commonly distinguished between only two categories of people: black (usually "negro") and white (usually "English" or "Christian"). There was, in sum, a palpable sense within the English community that Africans were distinctly separate and identifiable by pigmentation. In 1652, Rhode Island's legislature epitomized the prevailing English bifurcation of humanity when it referred to "blacke mankind or white."

6. Most references to Africans or Afro-Americans in English writings of the time were in some way pejorative. One of the most prevalent signs (as the previous paragraph implies) was anonymity: headright lists, for example, like censuses and wills and property inventories, show full names for almost all Euro-Americans and a partial name for most of those without full names but usually no names for Africans; instead, the lists acknowledge (for example) the issuance of headrights for "six negroes," or "three negro men and one woman." This pattern of depersonalization begins with the first mention of Africans in Virginia in 1619 and continues unabated through the century. In some censuses most of the cattle but only a few of the Africans are accorded names. And the various documents that list people, for whatever purpose, usually put Africans at the end, thus subtly implying an inferior status. Nothing comparable can be found· for any other human group, including Native Americans, although they came increasingly closer to the Africans' anonymity and pejorative references than did any European nationality.

7. Not until the era of the American Revolution did a substantial body of literature emerge in defense of slavery and in derogation of the Negro "race"—i.e., a racist literature. But unless one assumes that without a substantial body of literature espousing a set of ideas there is no ideology (a trap into which many intellectual historians but few anthropologists fall), there is no need to see the literary outpouring as a sign of racism's arrival. Rather, I believe, it marked a new stage in the ideology's development, as did, in the antebellum era, the emergence of "scientific" explanations of "racial" differences. Racism, after all, need not be full-blown to be viable. As J. R. Pole observed, Edmund Morgan (and I would add Barbara Fields as well as many other historians) "seems to suppose that if the historical explanation of slavery lay in racism, it could only be because racism was as profound at the beginnings as it later became, but this is not so. It was only necessary that racism should be sufficient, and that visible identification—already a cause of racial repugnance—should make slavery so easily practicable."[16]

The *idea* of races—imprecisely defined and inconsistently explained—had arrived, I contend, with the first English settlers. That belief in turn determined to a large extent the set of shared perceptions, assumptions, and experiences that after 1619 shaped Euro-American behavior toward Africans and Afro-Americans in Virginia until the end of the century and beyond. The champions of that ideology had no need to proclaim in writing the beliefs that apparently had little opposition, except, of course, from its victims, and in any event the infant colony had neither presses nor sufficient readers. Still, from a variety of brief statements, especially from the writings of a few outspoken opponents of the ideology, the cluster of beliefs is clear, and it constitutes (to use Fields's definition of ideology) "the descriptive vocabulary of day-to-day existence, through which people make rough sense of the[ir] social reality."[17]

The cluster of beliefs that helped seventeenth-century white Virginians make sense of their perceived reality is readily apparent, I think, however irrational it may seem to us. In brief, they held that Africans were perhaps not fully human, and if human, surely inferior to whites in mental and spiritual capacity; that their general appearance and especially their pigmentation proclaimed that inferiority, probably because of the "curse" on Canaan's descendants, perhaps for other reasons, which in any event were God's doing; and that in light of their divinely ordained inferiority, Africans should be held in abject slavery or at least in a subservient status because they merited nothing else, not even the consolations of Christianity. To that last proposition a few clergymen (such as Morgan Godwyn and Richard Baxter) and laymen (such as Thomas Tryon) dissented. Their impassioned testimony documents the majority's virulent ideology.

III

I did not always advocate the interpretation I present in this book. As a graduate student in history in the 1950s, I was taught the Handlins' version of slavery's and racism's origins (as my yellowing class notes attest), and I taught those interpretations to my own students until Carl Degler's article and Winthrop Jordan's book shook my confidence. Some years later I dug deeply into the primary sources of early Virginia and was persuaded that white Virginians', and other Anglo-Americans', perception of Africans was even more thoroughly racial than I had suspected. Since then, I've spent hundreds of hours on those records, and the evidence only gets stronger.

I wish it didn't. The interpretation put forward by the Handlins and their many followers—each scholar adding his or her own twist but essentially insisting that racism was a post facto rationalization for slavery—is implicitly more optimistic about a speedy end to racial prejudice and eventually to race as a functioning concept in human relations. But I go where the evidence takes me. In this case it went in a depressing direction, one that suggests the future of race relations may be more drawn out and contentious than people of goodwill had hoped or expected. The solution, I submit, is not to rewrite history into a more hopeful story. Rather, we must all work harder to end a concept (race) and an ideology (racism) whose persistence has blighted American society since its beginnings and continues to cloud its present and future.

PART THREE

Puritans and Indians

CHAPTER EIGHT

Pequots and Puritans: The Causes of the War of *1637*

Because the Pequot War of 1637 does not resonate today for most readers as profoundly as do the origins of slavery and racism, arguments over its causes have attracted less attention. Yet among specialists in early American ethnohistory, the event has generated a good deal of heat and even some useful light, especially in the last decade or so. The event is a favorite, too, of historians who do not ordinarily focus on American colonial history or American race relations, for it seems at first glance to be a blatant case of frontier aggression—the first phase in Anglo-America's long imperialist career. But as most historians who have worked closely with the evidence have discovered, simple explanations do not readily reflect the complexity of the evidence. Not only was the event multifaceted in its causal ingredients (as most wars are), it suffers, too, from the absence of documentary evidence on the Pequots' side and therefore defies definitive explanation. The modern literature on this subject is accordingly rich and controversial.

At the core of the controversy are the New England Puritans. Some historians over the last several decades have been generally sympathetic to their experiment in Christian communitarianism and have judged their failures in Indian affairs in the context of the Puritans' intentions and the (arguably) greater failure of most other European settlements to find effective and equitable modes of intercultural relations. Other scholars, disposed for various reasons to find every possible fault with the self-righteous New Englanders, condemn their relations with the Indians in the starkest terms. This essay reviews the major interpretive patterns from the late seventeenth century to the late twentieth—three hundred years of disagreement that will surely not end with this reassessment. My hope, rather, is that this summing up will help the debate to move forward with civility and a clearer focus.

This essay first appeared as an article (my first) when I was working on the broader aspects of Indian-white relations in New England from the beginnings of colonization in 1620 to the eve of King Philip's War in 1675. The Pequot

War seemed in some ways a turning point—the first major clash between colonists and natives in that region—yet in other ways not a turning point at all. Unlike Virginia's traumatic aftermath to the Powhatan uprising of 1622, which permanently separated the colony's English and Indian populations and soured early English missionary and educational efforts, the Pequot War preceded New England's significant attempts at Christianization and social assimilation. Moreover, the war did not poison the colonists' attitude toward Indians in general the way the events of 1622 did in Virginia. In any case, my historiographical article was published in the William and Mary Quarterly, *3d ser. 21 (1964): 256–69, and was subsequently reprinted in several anthologies. It is reprinted here with that journal's permission.*

As several students of the Pequot War have noted, my interpretation of the war's causes had somewhat different emphases in the article, in the first edition of my New England Frontier *(1965), and in the revised edition of that book (1979). In preparing this essay for republication, I have reread the primary sources and most of the modern histories of the Pequot War. The result is a subsantially revised historiographical account and yet another Vaughan interpretation.*

THE WAR OF 1637 between the New England colonists and the Pequot Indians was one of the most dramatic and most lethal episodes in early British-American history. Although more limited in scope than King Philip's War and less tied to cerebral issues than the Antinomian crisis or the banishment of Roger Williams—two episodes that overlapped Puritan-Pequot hostilities and were tangentially connected to them—the war was memorable and endlessly controversial in its own right. It resulted in the crushing defeat of the most powerful tribe in New England; it witnessed one of the most sanguinary battles of all wars between whites and Indians when perhaps five hundred Pequot men, women, and children were shot or burned to death in the Puritans' attack on a stockaded Indian village; and it opened southern Connecticut to rapid English colonization. The war was not soon forgotten by the other Indian nations in the Northeast, nor by the English, who memorialized their victory in prose and poetry.[1] The Pequot War even made a symbolic appearance in *Moby Dick*, when Herman Melville chose the name of the vanquished tribe for Captain Ahab's ill-fated whaling vessel.[2]

As with most wars, the conflict between the Pequot Indians and the New England colonists raises the twin historical problems of cause and responsibility. Involved, too, are the broader issues of Indian-white relations during the first half century or more of English settlement in New England and the basic character of the Puritan colonial experiment. Historians, not surprisingly, have disagreed on some of the facts and all of the larger issues. Not surprisingly, too, interpretations have generally clustered around a few hardy perennials.

The earliest interpretive pattern, first voiced in the late seventeenth century and persisting for two centuries, despite mounting dissent, strongly endorsed the Puritans' perspective on events. All of the written sources were by English (mostly Puritan) hands, and most of the early historians were themselves of New England background; they almost unanimously explained the conflict as a defensive action by peaceful colonists against the exceptionally belligerent Pequots, or, as Puritan rhetoric would have it, against Satan's minions. Many nineteenth-century historians—again, often of New England origin themselves—continued this interpretation, although usually in a more secular vein. By contrast, many historians of the late nineteenth and early twentieth centuries, and again more recently, have insisted that the war was a flagrant case of Puritan aggression and Pequot self-defense. Still others, most notably in the 1970s and later, have argued that the war was fundamentally a product of English territorial imperialism, with the Pequots fighting for their lands as well as their lives. A recent variation on that theme substitutes wampum for real estate: the Puritans wanted to control the sources of shell beads that had suddenly become central to the colonial economy, especially to intercultural commerce.[3]

This essay sets forth sequentially these principal interpretive paradigms. In each case (sections I–III), I have synthesized the arguments of several scholars, usually without indicating which author makes which particular points. I have also occasionally added facts or quotations that appear in none of the secondary accounts but that illustrate and sometimes reinforce the interpretation under review. The final section of the essay addresses what I see as the shortcomings of each interpretive pattern and offers what I hope is a more plausible alternative. A postscript addresses recent trends in Pequot War scholarship.[4]

I

Scholars until recently assumed that the Pequots, prior to their arrival in southern New England, had been part of the Mohegan (Mahican) nation in northern New Netherland, where they inhabited lands to the east of the Mohawks. According to this traditional view, a large segment of the Mohegans migrated in the early seventeenth century into western New England and then southward until they reached the shores of Long Island Sound, seizing land there by force of arms.[5] By the time they confronted the Puritans of New England, the Mohegans had made innumerable enemies among the Indians they displaced along the way and had incurred such a reputation for brutality that they were known as "Pequots," a form of the Algonquian word for "destroyers."[6] Animosity toward the Pequots was particularly strong among the small tribes of the Connecticut valley and Long Island, who were forced to acknowledge the suzerainty of the intruders and to pay them annual tribute. Equally unfriendly were the Narragansetts, the Pequots' neighbors to the east, who resented the powerful newcomers but were too strong to be cowed by them. The result was intermittent warfare between the Narragansetts and the Pequots; its final campaign was an important ingredient of the Pequot-Puritan War of 1637.

The Pequots were also unable to live peacefully with the adjacent European colonies.[7] In 1634 the Pequots were at war with Dutch New Netherland and made their first hostile move against the English with the murder of Captain John Stone, a dissolute coastal trader from Virginia, and his eight companions.[8] Friendly Indians informed Massachusetts authorities that the Pequots, or perhaps some vassals of the Pequots (the accounts vary), had assassinated Stone while he was asleep in his boat, slaughtered the crew, and plundered his vessel.[9] Puritan authorities could hardly let the murder of nine Englishmen go unchallenged if they intended to maintain their precarious foothold in a land where the natives vastly outnumbered them and would probably soon (as some already did) resent European intruders.

With the English demanding the surrender of the Englishmen's killers, the Pequots—then at war with the Narragansetts to the east and the Dutch to the west—in October 1634 sent ambassadors to Massachusetts to treat for peace and commerce, reinforcing their appeal with gifts of wampum.[10] The Puritan authorities, after consulting some of the clergy, demanded the killers of Stone and his men as a prelude to negotiations. The Pequots replied with an account of the episode that differed markedly from the colonists' version. Stone, the Indians contended, had seized and bound two of their men who had boarded his ship to trade, intending to make them "show him the way up the river." It was after this treachery, they said, that several of the captives' friends ambushed Stone and his crew when they came ashore. The Pequot ambassadors also insisted that the sachem responsible for the ambush had since been killed by the Dutch and all but two of his collaborators had succumbed to smallpox.[11]

The Pequots told their story "with such confidence and gravity" that the Massachusetts magistrates were inclined to accept it, and after several days of negotiations in November 1634, the Pequots and the Bay Colony reached an agreement. By its terms the sachems agreed to hand over the two remaining men "who were guilty of Capt. Stone's death" when sent for and "to yield up Connecticut," by which they may have meant only the mouth of the river or, perhaps, as much of the valley as the English desired for settlement without encroaching on the Pequots' own territory. In addition, the Pequots promised to pay an indemnity of four hundred fathoms of wampum, forty beaver skins, and thirty otter skins.[12] Commercial relations were projected by an agreement that Massachusetts would send a trading vessel to the Pequots in the near future. Peace was thus maintained in New England. Commerce between the Bay Colony and the Pequots did not materialize, however. When

John Oldham took his trading ship into Pequot territory the next spring, he found them, in Governor Winthrop's words, "a very false people" and disinclined to amicable trade.[13]

Peace between the Bay Colony and the Pequots lasted until September 1636, but relations between the parties deteriorated rapidly after Oldham's rebuff in the spring of 1635. The Pequots failed to surrender the two remaining killers of Stone and his crew, the indemnity was paid only in part, and evidence of further Pequot disingenuousness began to drift into Boston. In June, Jonathan Brewster reported from the Plymouth trading post on the Connecticut River that—according to a trusted Indian informant—the Pequots had planned to attack a Plymouth trading vessel and now "intend an e[n]vasion both of English and natives in this River." By midsummer 1636, Massachusetts had lost patience with apparent Pequot delays and dissimulation and commissioned John Winthrop Jr., then in Connecticut, to place new demands on Chief Sassacus of the Pequots. He must surrender at once the two presumed culprits and reply to new charges of bad faith, especially reports that Pequots "were Actors in the Murder" of several Englishmen in the Pequots' area of suzerainty on Long Island. Should the Pequots fail to meet these demands, the Bay Colony threatened to terminate the league of amity and to "revenge the blood of our Countrimen as occasion shall serve."[14] When the Pequots rejected this Massachusetts ultimatum, the younger Winthrop called Sassacus to Saybrook and returned his tribe's earlier present of skins and wampum, thus terminating the tenuous league of friendship.[15] War now seemed inevitable to the Puritans and most likely to the Pequots as well.[16]

The outbreak of hostilities was hastened, if not inaugurated, by another murder. Late in July 1636, John Gallop, sailing near Block Island, spied John Oldham's pinnace, its deck crowded with Indians and no sign of a white man. When no one answered his hail, "and perceiving the sailes to be unskilfully managed," Gallop tried to board to investigate; a frenzied battle followed in which Gallop eventually routed the Indians. On board he found Oldham's naked and mutilated body.[17]

Colonial leaders, on testimony from an Indian captured by Gallop, initially believed that the Narragansetts were responsible for Oldham's murder. The Block Island tribe was subservient to them, and according to one report, all the Narragansett sachems except Canonicus and Miantonomi (the two leading chiefs) had conspired with the Block Islanders against Oldham because of his attempts to promote amity and trade with the Pequots the previous year. Massachusetts contemplated war against the Narragansetts and warned Roger Williams in Providence "to look to himself." But Canonicus and Miantonomi speedily regained the confidence of the English by returning Oldham's two servant boys and his remaining goods from Block Island and by assuring the Bay

Colony, through Williams, that most of the culprits had been killed by Gallop. The few surviving assassins reportedly sought refuge with the Pequots.[18]

The Puritan response was a punitive expedition against Block Island by ninety Massachusetts volunteers under magistrate and military veteran John Endecott. Endecott was also ordered to visit Pequot territory to secure the remaining "murderers" of Stone, Oldham, and the other Englishmen and to gain assurances of future good behavior by the Pequots (Fig. 8.1). But when in early September the expedition made contact with the tribe, the Pequot spokesmen refused to comply with Puritan demands, first offering a new version of the killing of Stone and his crew that absolved them of any blame, then claiming that their leading chiefs were on Long Island, and finally insisting that they were still trying to discover who the culprits were. After a few hours of futile negotiations, the English commanders concluded that the delay was a camouflage for an intended ambush, particularly when they saw the Pequots "convey away their wives and children, and bury their chiefest goods." A brief clash ensued in which the Massachusetts troops slew several Pequots, wounded others, and seized or destroyed much Pequot property.[19]

After the Endecott expedition departed, the Pequots retaliated against every Englishman they could find. Fort Saybrook at the mouth of the Connecticut River was besieged throughout the fall and winter of 1636–37. Pequot warriors ambushed several of its garrison who tried to gather crops or shoot game; several men were killed, many were wounded, including Lt. Lion Gardiner. Some of the Pequot's victims died quickly, some were tortured to death. English traders entering the Connecticut River were also killed or captured, including John Tilley, who survived three days of horrendous mutilation. Not until reinforcements arrived from Massachusetts in the spring of 1637 did the Pequots shift their attacks to the unprotected plantations father up river.[20] There, early on an April morning, two hundred warriors suddenly descended on a group of colonists in a meadow near Wethersfield, Connecticut. The Pequots slew nine of the English outright, including a woman and child, and carried to their stronghold two young women whom the sachems hoped could make gunpowder for the tribe's few firearms. With some thirty Englishmen dead at Pequot hands or by Pequot subordinates, the New England colonies saw no alternative to war. Massachusetts Bay had in fact formally declared war two weeks before the Wethersfield raid but had done nothing to stop the pattern of massacres, partly because of the emerging controversy over Anne Hutchinson and her "Antinomian" followers, which bitterly divided the Boston church and distracted the colony's leaders.[21] Connecticut could wait no longer, and on May 1, 1637, its General Court declared "that there shalbe an offensive warr against the Pequoitt."[22] Colonists as well as Pequots had engaged in the escalating attacks, retaliations, and counterretaliations that

Fig. 8.1.
John Endecott, leader of the Massachusetts expedition to Block Island and Pequot harbor in 1636. Copy in oil by T. Mitchell of an anonymous original. Courtesy, Peabody Essex Museum, Salem, Mass.

preceded the formal declaration, but to Puritan eyes the wantonness, scope, and cruelty of the Pequot raids placed the burden of responsibility for the war on the Indian enemy.

The reaction of the other Indian tribes to the outbreak of war reveals much about the nature of the conflict and to some extent its causes. The Narragansetts, thanks to some last-minute diplomacy by Roger Williams (only recently ousted from Massachusetts) had already made an offensive alliance with the Bay Colony.[23] Efforts by the Pequots to patch up differences with the Narragansetts had failed after Massachusetts urged Williams, he later recalled, "to use my utmost and Speediest Endeavours to breake and hinder the Leauge laboured for by the Pequts." Instead, Williams negotiated an "English Leauge" with the Narragansetts and Mohegans "agnst the Pequts."[24]

The Mohegans, a secessionist faction of the Pequot tribe that had recently rebelled against Chief Sassacus, would contribute importantly to the war against their blood brothers.[25] The small valley tribes along the Connecticut River, with one notable exception, also enthusiastically backed the Puritans, whom they had encouraged to settle in the valley as early as 1631, in apparent hopes of gaining protection against the Pequots. Connecticut's declaration of war was, in fact, partly due to the urging of those tribes. "The Indians here our friends," wrote Thomas Hooker from Hartford in May 1637, "were so importunate with us to make warr presently that unlesse we had attempted some thing we had delivered our persons unto contempt of base feare and cowardise, and caused them to turne enemyes agaynst us."[26]

Of the hundreds of casualties the Pequots suffered in the brief but brutal war in 1637, scores were inflicted by the Indians of southern New England and Long Island. Captain John Mason, leader of the Connecticut forces, reported that "Happy were they that could bring in their Heads to the *English:* Of which there came almost daily to *Winsor*, or *Hartford*." And the greatest prize of all, the head of Chief Sassacus, was delivered by the Mohawks. Sassacus had sought asylum with that powerful Iroquois nation, but afraid of the Englishmen's "hot-mouth'd weapons" (as Philip Vincent contended) or for fearless reasons of their own, the Mohawks seized the Pequot sachem and forty of his warriors, confiscated their wampum, cut off their heads and hands, and sent Sassacus's scalp to the English at Connecticut.[27] The Pequots, for their part, were unable to find any important allies among the Indians; only the closely allied Western Niantics took their side.

This was no racial conflict between Europeans and Native Americans, not even a showdown between profoundly different cultures. Rather, the Pequot War saw the New England colonies, eagerly assisted by several Indian tribes, take punitive action against the one tribe that apparently was hated and feared by most Indians and whites alike. A prima facie case thus exists for the claims of Puritan apologists. But theirs is not the whole story.

II

Critics of the Puritans' Indian policy insist that the colonial leaders, especially the Massachusetts magistrates, were incessantly aggressive and often unreasonable and that the Pequots were not, except in Puritan minds, a belligerent people.[28] Even before the undeniably provocative Endecott expedition, the English had treated the Pequots with something less than equity. The character of Captain John Stone, for example, lent an air of plausibility to the Pequot version of his death and therefore should have absolved the Pequots of any blame.

Stone had piloted a shipload of cattle from Virginia to Boston in 1634. At each stop along the way he managed so to embroil himself with the local authorities that he was soon persona non grata in every colony north of the Hudson. His first escapade was in New Amsterdam, where he attempted to steal a Plymouth bark and was thwarted only at the last minute by Dutch seamen. Later, at Plymouth, he nearly stabbed Governor Thomas Prence. Stone acted little better in Massachusetts, where he "spake contemptuously of [the] magistrates, and carried it lewdly in his conversation," in particular calling Judge Roger Ludlow "a just as[s]," and was also charged with excessive drinking and adultery. Although Stone was tried and acquitted for lack of evidence on the major charge, his lesser indiscretions earned him a suspended fine of one hundred pounds and banishment from the colony under penalty of death.[29] On his way back to Virginia, accompanied by Captain Walter Norton and seven crewmen, he explored the trading prospects of the Connecticut River and there met his death. Not surprisingly, news of his fate did not elicit universal mourning; some of the English, secure in their piety, no doubt shared Roger Clap's judgment that "God destroy[ed] him that so proudly threatened to ruin us."[30]

Stone's unsavory character and the uncertainty of the killers' tribal affiliation should, according to some historians, have precluded any demands on the Pequots, yet the treaty that Massachusetts contracted with them in the fall of 1634 was hardly lenient, its substantial concessions of land and wampum amounting almost to retaliation. The wampum tribute itself (had it been paid in full) would have been a staggering burden to the Pequots.[31] The Puritans' peremptory terms of July 1636, which the Pequots rejected, further exacerbated rather than ameliorated relations between the disparate cultures, and the Bay Colony's imperious demands of August 1636 were wholly unacceptable to an independent tribe.

Even then, hostilities did not break out until the Endecott expedition—sent principally to avenge the death of John Oldham but also to redress the earlier grievances—imposed incredibly harsh retribution. Endecott's instructions to kill all the Indian men on Block Island, to seize the women and children, and to take possession of the island was grossly unreasonable retaliation for the death of one Englishman, especially in light of the many Indians killed during the fight on Oldham's boat. In any event, Endecott secured a beachhead on Block Island in the face of brief resistance, routed the defenders, and devastated the island. While the Indians of Block Island sought refuge in the swamps, the Massachusetts troops burned wigwams, destroyed cornfields, and smashed canoes. Dissatisfied by the small number of Indian casualties, the English soldiers heartlessly "destroyed some of their dogges in stead of men."[32]

Destructive as it was, Endecott's campaign against Block Island did not trigger the Pequot War. He accomplished that a few days later when he invaded Pequot territory, demanded the surviving murderers of Stone and Oldham, an indemnity of one thousand fathoms of wampum, and some Pequot children as hostages. Should the Pequots refuse to comply with this ultimatum, Endecott's orders were to impose it by force.[33]

The Pequots had greeted the English fleet's arrival in Pequot harbor with "doeful and woful cries," for it was obvious that this was no friendly mission. When the Pequots seemed to stall for time, Endecott landed his troops and took station on a commanding hilltop. The Indians' excuses for delay may have been wholly legitimate, but the English disbelieved them, and Endecott interpreted a final Pequot suggestion that both sides lay down their arms as a dastardly ruse. "We rather chose to beat up the Drum and bid them battell," John Underhill remembered. A volley from the musketeers launched open warfare, and the pattern established on Block Island was repeated. Endecott's men spent the next two days in rampant destruction and looting. In deference to English firepower, the Pequots kept out of range, yet one or more of them were killed and many wounded.[34] Endecott had complied so vigorously with his instructions that the Pequot-Puritan war was effectively under way before he sailed back to Boston.[35]

The Endecott attack left the Pequots no plausible alternative. Their land had been invaded, their people assaulted, their chief subjected to arrogant demands, and much of their property destroyed or carried off. Despite the Bay Colony's claim to have been provoked by Pequot duplicity and intransigence, the other New England colonies hastened to criticize its intemperate exercise of power, and even Governor Winthrop later tacitly admitted that Massachusetts had provoked hostilities. Plymouth's William Bradford complained that Massachusetts "set out some to take revenge, and require satisfaction for these wrongs; but it was done so superfitially, and without their acquainting of those of Conightecute and other neighbors . . . as they did little good." Even before the Endecott expedition reached Pequot soil, Lion Gardiner at Saybrook insisted that "when I had seen their commission I wondered, and made many allegations against the manner of it, but they did go to Pequit . . . against our will." Gardiner rightly predicted open hostilities. "[Y]ou come hither to raise these wasps about my ears," he protested to Endecott, "and then you will take wing and flee away."[36] Endecott upset the nest all right, and the stings were felt first by the Saybrook garrison and then by the upriver settlements. Although ultimately the Pequots would suffer a crushing reprisal, they had not sought war nor acted unreasonably toward the colonies. The Puritans, especially the Bay Colony magistrates, were blatant aggressors.

III

If Puritan aggression was the war's root cause, as many critics have charged, what prompted the aggression? Of several proffered answers— cultural (or perhaps racial) prejudice, revenge for imagined wrongs, or sheer cussedness, to name a few—a favorite has been land lust. Not until 1664 did Roger Williams lament that "God Land will be (as it now is) as great a God with us English as God Gould was with the Spaniards," but the statement would have been as true, some historians imply, in the 1630s, 1640s, or 1650s.[37]

From the outset of colonization, the Puritans, like English settlers elsewhere, sought land on a scale undreamed of back home. They assumed that in America it was readily available by purchase from the natives or by *vacuum domicilium*—the theory that unused land was free for the taking.[38] The Puritans also believed that God facilitated their settlement and expansion by smiting the natives with frightful diseases that scarcely touched the English. Had not the Lord cleared much of southern New England and wholly exterminated the Indians at Plymouth a few years before the Pilgrims arrived in 1620? God seemed to reiterate the deadly message in the early 1630s, when smallpox killed thousands of Indians in the very areas where the colonists were now settling. "[I]t pleased God to make room for his people of the English nation," wrote a Massachusetts resident; "without this remarkable and terrible stroke of God upon the natives, [we] would with much more difficulty have found room and at far greater charge have obtained and purchased land." Taking the long view, John Winthrop tied the earlier and later epidemics into a comfortable (for Puritans) rhetorical question: "[I]f God were not pleased with our inheriting these parts, why did he drive out the natives before us? and why dothe he still make roome for us, by deminishinge them as we increace?"[39]

The Pequots apparently escaped the first epidemic but were devastated by the second.[40] Still, in the mid-1630s they remained relatively strong among New England tribes and stood squarely in the way of Puritan expansion along the Atlantic coast toward New Netherland and, especially, into the Connecticut valley. Both areas offered fertile soil and convenient transportation; both areas were under direct or indirect Pequot control. Consciously or perhaps unconsciously, then (the argument goes), Massachusetts wanted to eliminate the Pequots by force of arms if divine intervention did not save them the trouble; the Bay Colony's audacious demands and Endecott's provocative mission were meant to force total submission or foment war. In the aftermath, of course, Puritan spokesmen credited their military victory to God's intervention almost as completely as they had acknowledged his use of diseases. The Pequots, John Underhill concluded, had been crushed "by the sword of the Lord, and a few feeble instruments, souldiers not accustomed to warre, . . . so as their Countrey is fully subdued and fallen into the hands of the English" (Fig. 8.2). Captain Mason concurred: "[T]he Lord was pleased to smite our Enemies in the hinder Parts, and to give us their Land for an Inheritance."[41] To advocates of the land-grabbing interpretation, such statements are cryptic confessions of the Puritans' prewar intentions.

Another sign of Puritan intentions is the Pequots' fear of displacement. Bradford recorded that the Pequot ambassadors who tried to persuade the Narragansetts to break their league with Massachusetts and join an Indian resistance movement "used very pernicious arguments to move them therunto: as that the English . . . begane to overspred their countrie, and would deprive them thereof in time, if they were suffered to grow and increse." That almost proved a compelling message, but af-

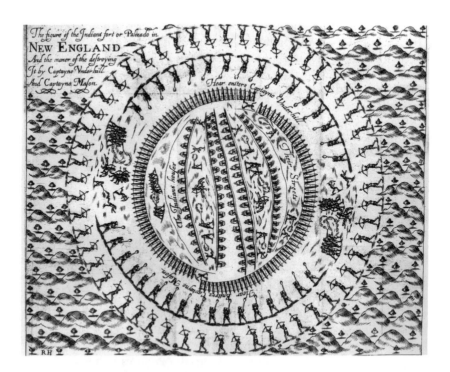

Fig. 8.2.

An unknown artist's schematic engraving of the Puritans' massacre of a pallisaded Pequot village in 1637. From John Underhill, *Newes from America* (London, 1638). Courtesy of the John Carter Brown Library of Brown University.

ter listening to Williams's pitch for adhering to Massachusetts and consulting their own self-interest, the Narragansetts (according to Bradford)
"considered, how much wrong they had received from the Pequents,
and what an oppertunitie they now had by the help of the English to
right them selves [that] revenge was so sweete unto them, as it prevailed
above all the rest."[42] Had revenge given way to demographic logic and
fears of territorial imperialism, Puritan expansion might have been de-
layed for decades. With the Pequots isolated, no effective barrier remained to colonial land lust.

One way or another, then, some historians assert, the Puritans would
gain the coveted Pequot lands. The benign version of this interpretation is almost fatalistic and noncondemnatory. "The contest between the
English and the Indians had been inevitable from the start," an early-
twentieth-century historian concluded about the Pequot War, "based
upon the unchanging fundamental conflict of the natures and economic
interests of the two races"; therefore, "The murders of the two traders
[Stone and Oldham] were but the sparks that touched off the explosive
material which had been long accumulating." A recent and more sinis-
ter verson of the economic explanation holds that the murders of Stone
and Oldham were "largely incidental to the expansionist plans of the
colonists." With "subjugation and dispossession" firmly in mind, New
Englanders used "the alleged murders as pretexts to those ends," for
"on the economic level that is exactly what the Pequot War was about:
the acquisition of Block Island and Connecticut."[43]

Economic interest need not, of course, be only in land. Other commodities, especially the exchange of English manufactured goods and
potent beverages for beaver and other pelts, might be reason enough
for harsh policies or even war. The Puritan-Pequot conflict accordingly
has been interpreted by at least one scholar as "the result of traders'
machinations among the tribes," because the highly profitable fur trade
"led to the unhesitating need to kill Indians to assure the security of
the trader. After the Pequots had killed [trader] John Oldham, . . . punitive action was compulsory." But wampum, the increasingly important
medium of exchange among colonists as well as between colonists and
Indians, was even more desirable than furs. In the past decade and a
half, scholars in several disciplines—history, literature, anthropology—
have argued that the little shell beads were the key to large economic
issues and to the Pequot War itself. "[A] series of relatively minor incidents beginning in 1634 became the excuse to punish mintmasters
and extract wampum payments," an anthropologist recently concluded.
She identifies John Oldham as a "wampum trader" whose death (ostensibly for that reason) instigated the Endecott expedition; and "a few
months after wampum was declared legal tender at three beads per
penny, war was formally declared on the Pequots."[44] Thus the Puritans'
presumed motive has kept rough pace with shifting modern notions of

economic fundamentals: from land to commodities to the medium of exchange.

IV

Despite the plausibility and frequent advocacy of the three major explanatory paradigms—Pequot aggression, Puritan aggression, and Puritan cupidity—I find each unsatisfactory. In their place I suggest a synthesis of the first two, with additional emphasis on the largely overlooked role of disparate Indian and English concepts of law and sovereignty.

Although the traditional (until recently) emphasis on Pequot aggression is an incomplete and essentially Anglocentric interpretation, it should not be categorically dismissed. Despite the current unfashionableness of suggesting that the Pequots were not innocent victims, virtually all colonial commentators (English and Dutch) and most Indians (Narragansett, Mohegan, and the Connecticut River tribes) whose opinions are recorded concur that the Pequots were persistently belligerent and aggressive. The observation of William Wood is sometimes invoked as evidence that in the early 1630s the Pequots' reputation was unsullied, for in *New Englands Prospect* (published in London in 1634), Wood observed that he "never heard any misdemeanour [of the Pequots]; but that they were just and equall in their dealings; not treacherous either to their Country-men, or *English.*" That may well have been true when Wood left New England in mid-1633; wars with New Netherland and the Narragansetts were in the immediate future, not the past. Perhaps Wood's more telling testimony preceded the one just quoted: "The *Pequants* be a stately warlike people." And Bradford, at about the same time, told of Indians who had been driven out of their Connecticut lands "by the potencie of the Pequents, which usurped upon them, and drive them from thence." Between mid-1633 and 1636, the Pequots stirred up a host of enemies.[45]

Surely the Indians who joined the colonial cause did not consider the Pequots to be innocent victims. If there was an "Indian side" to the Puritan-Pequot war, from a numerical standpoint—either in the number of individual Indians or the number of Indian nations—it is not the Pequot side. With most of the small tribes of the lower Connecticut River valley seeking relief from Pequot dominance, and with the Narragansetts and Eastern Niantics actively assisting the colonies, the Pequots were a clear minority in population and apparently in sentiment among the natives of southern New England. They had bitter opposition, too, from a major faction of their own nation, for however self-interested Uncas may have been in seceding from the Pequots shortly before the war, his Mohegans were palpably dissatisfied with Sassacus's portion of the tribe. We will never know the specific motives of most of the Indian participants of 1636–37, but the conclusion seems inescapable that the Pequots were singularly isolated and unpopular. No comparable example of an almost universally distrusted Indian nation, at least in the colonial era, springs to mind.

The traditional emphasis on Pequot aggression and Puritan self-defense, in sum, has in its favor the Pequots' reputation for belligerence, at least after 1633; their failure to extradite the supposed killers of Stone, Oldham, and many others, despite repeated agreements; their possible involvement in still other murders, especially on eastern Long Island; and the brutality of their attacks along the Connecticut River in late 1636 and early 1637. Those reputed actions, even if some were Puritan fantasies, suggest a measure of Pequot responsibility for the war.

That surely does not mean that the Pequots were solely or even primarily responsible. Puritan aggression in the Endecott campaign, beyond a shadow of doubt, initiated unrestrained hostilities. Had it not been for that lethal exercise of force, a diplomatic solution might still have been found to Massachusetts-Pequot differences, despite deepening suspicions on each side that the other was determined on war.

Why did the Bay Colony resort to such flagrant coercive action in the summer of 1636? The explanation, I suggest, is threefold. First, the Massachusetts government by then considered itself the dominant authority in New England and was determined strictly to punish infractions of the peace, a policy more easily undertaken since the Bay Colony (as Lion Gardiner noted) was unlikely to feel the brunt of Pequot retaliation. Second, shortly before the Endecott expedition was formed, Roger Williams had reported a heady boast of the Pequots that they could by witchcraft defeat any English forces, a challenge that inflamed Puritan tempers by further identifying the enemy with the devil.[46] Finally, Massachusetts was then in the throes of civil and religious controversy. Roger Williams had been ousted but a few months earlier for "divers dangerous opinions," the Crown had recently instituted quo warranto proceedings against the colony's charter, and the first rumblings of the Antinomian movement were clearly audible. If frustration is a prime cause of aggression, the Bay Colony was overripe for Endecott's crusade against Satan's horde. Massachusetts magistrates felt beleaguered; they lashed out at the Pequots and then at Anne Hutchinson and her followers.

As a causal agent, Puritan cupidity, in whatever form, fits poorly with the evidence. Despite the New Englanders' insatiable appetite for territory and the Pequots' wariness of colonial expansion, land was not a significant issue in 1636. The Connecticut tribes had welcomed English settlements in the valley, and the Pequots had given their blessing in the treaty of 1634 with the Bay Colony. The English footholds established in 1635 had no opposition, and Fort Saybrook at the mouth of the river had been built with Indian approval. The nearby Mohegans, who controlled a portion of southern Connecticut, had abundant reasons to encourage a strong English presence against their Pequot rivals. The Narragansetts, despite Pequot warnings, seem to have doubted the immediacy of colonial expansion into their own area. It was, after all, outside the Massachusetts patent, as they surely knew from Roger Williams, and the tiny settlements at Providence and Aquidneck were probably more prized than feared by the Narragansetts. The outcasts from Massachusetts orthodoxy could be useful for trade and information and perhaps a few firearms without posing a territorial threat, which probably accounts for the ease with which Williams and the others acquired land from the sachems. Land would eventually become a source of friction between natives and New Englanders, but in 1636 other concerns were paramount.

Nor were those concerns about commerce or wampum. The fur trade and wampum minting were valuable but certainly not essential to the colonial economy. Like land, they were to some extent the spoils of war, but to mistake spoils for causes is to read history backward.

The Endecott expedition represented something more fundamental to the Puritans than economic issues: an assertion of ultimate jurisdiction over the region that colonists and Indians increasingly shared. The Massachusetts government, determined to prevent Indian actions that might in any way threaten the Puritans' New World Zion, had assumed responsibility for maintaining law and order among all inhabitants, Indian and white. By 1636, the Bay Colony, despite its religious controversies and imperial insecurity, was ready to force its fiat on all Indians in southern New England. Prior to the formation of the Confederation of New England in 1643, each colony endeavored to exercise full authority over natives as well as its own people within its own borders; and if Massachusetts, in its dealings with the Narragansetts and Pequots, was assuming authority over areas outside its charter limits, it did so to prevent (it hoped) further attacks by Indians on the English, and vice versa, as well as, under some circumstances, of Indians on Indians. The treaty of 1638 between Connecticut and the principal sachems of the Narragansetts and Mohegans would formally extend British authority into new regions by stipulating that if trouble broke out between the signatory tribes, "they shall not presently Revenge it[,] But they are to appeal to the English and they [i.e., colonial officials] are to decide the same, and the determination of the English [is] to stand[.]"[47]

The Puritans' assertion of authority explains their insistence on punishing the murderers who, they believed, had sought refuge with the Pequots. That the culprits were perhaps not themselves Pequots made little difference to the Puritans, for harboring criminals was almost as serious a violation as the alleged crimes themselves. Nor did it make much difference to the Puritans that the Pequots disavowed the treaty of 1634 in which they had promised to return the accused men; Bay Colony authorities thought they had a firm agreement at the end of the negotiations in Boston and were holding the Pequots to the terms even though their tribal council had declined to ratify them. Here again, the colonists insisted that the game be played by colonial—that is, traditional European—rules. On this point the Puritan-aggression interpretation is on solid ground: Massachusetts acted unilaterally and unreasonably, at least by modern standards.

Yet proponents of that explanation are usually unwilling to acknowledge the seriousness of the mounting English death toll. Historians who imply that Stone and Oldham were the only victims, and accuse the Puritans of turning them into flimsy excuses for predetermined aggression, distort the evidence and the causal context. One writer, for example, makes Stone the sole bone of contention: "Stone's death, was a far from likely *casus belli*"; "Stone, dead, became more cherished than Stone, alive"; "For the Bay's purposes, Stone's [bloody] shirt would do nicely."[48] By contrast, the major Puritan commentators clearly counted Stone as one among many victims of what they thought to be Pequot accountability. Winthrop's first record of the event lists Captains Stone and Norton by name and "all his [Stone's] company, being eight." Bradford also mentioned the two captains "and some others"; Gardiner recounted the demise of "Capt. Stone, with his Bark's crew." In several subsequent references to the event, Winthrop's "Stone, etc." is an obvious shorthand for the nine Englishmen.[49] To Winthrop and other Puritan authorities, the crucial issue was the growing number of English lives lost, and no one brought English justice. They shed few tears for the scoundrel Stone, but they would not permit with impunity the death of his eight companions, from whatever colony they came. As Winthrop explained to Edward Winslow when the latter questioned why Plymouth should fight against a tribe that had killed none of its people, "Capt. Stone, etc. for whom this war was begun, were none of ours neither"; it was enough, Winthrop implied, that they were English. And John Oldham, of course, was a Massachusetts resident in good standing, despite an early unsavory reputation.[50]

The Massachusetts magistrates were determined not only to judge Indians accused of killing Englishmen, bad or good, but to wage war against a tribe that appeared to protect them. By the summer of 1636, the number of reported deaths had reached a dozen or so, and none of the purported killers were in English custody. All of the reputed killers were thought by the Puritans either to be Pequots, to be in Pequot territory, or to be sheltered with Pequot connivance. That does not excuse the Bay Colony's brutal retaliation, but it does make such action more understandable and it does undermine, I suggest, a number of simplistic explanations of Puritan aggression. But understandable too was the Pequot determination that Williams relayed to Winthrop in October 1636: "the Pequts and Nayantaquits resolve . . . not to yeald up one [accused Indian]."[51] With de facto war already under way, the principals were at loggerheads over principles.

The difference between Indian and English concepts of the right to judge accused killers (and the right to harbor such persons) was arguably a more fundamental cause of the war than was the Massachusetts expedition of 1636, because the latter was created primarily to enforce the colonists' juridicial position. The magistrates' arrogation to themselves of the right to regulate and discipline neighboring Indians made war almost inevitable in 1636–37, especially when Endecott's enforcement—like so many subsequent "police actions"—was brutally overractive and ultimately counterproductive. Pequot sachems and councillors naturally resented the interference of Massachusetts in matters over which their own customs had long prevailed and in a geographic area over which they had long enjoyed hegemony. They categorically rejected the Bay Colony's assumption of authority in the correction of miscreants or the dictation of intercultural conduct. From the hindsight of the late twentieth century, it is easy to see that Massachusetts was begging for trouble by trying to extend its authority beyond its chartered territory and into areas of jurisprudence that had no cultural consensus.

In short, the Pequot War, like most wars, cannot be attributed solely to the unmitigated bellicosity of one side and the righteous response of the other. Several acts of aggression by the Pequot tribe, the desire for autonomy or revenge against the Pequots by various other tribes, the unreasonableness of the Bay Colony's demands, the harshness of the Endecott campaign, and incompatible concepts of criminal jurisdiction all contributed to the outbreak of New England's first Indian war. But most of all, the Bay colony's gross escalation of violence and of excessive demands for prisoners and reparations made all-out war unavoidable; until then, negotiation was at least conceivable.

John Endecott is well known for many achievements, not all of them admirable. He was the first resident governor of the Bay Colony and its longest-serving governor. He was also the zealot who mutilated the English flag and was largely responsible for the execution of Quaker dissidents. It is tempting to add to the latter list the instigation of the Pequot War, but the impetuous soldier would surely claim, with much justification, that he was only obeying orders. If Endecott had not been in charge, then Underhill or Israel Stoughton or Nathaniel Turner or some other veteran of European warfare would have received the assignment, probably with the same results. Massachusetts was determined to have prisoners at the bar for the murder of Englishmen or to wield the rod of chastisement. Nothing but Pequot capitulation could have prevented it.

Postscript to Chapter 8

The past three decades have witnessed a remarkable resurgence of interest in the Puritan-Pequot war, partly by historians who specialize in early American history, partly by students of early American literature, partly by ethnohistorians, and partly by scholars outside those fields who use the Pequot War to demonstrate a point in some larger analysis. Despite the new and disparate attention the war has attracted, the broad patterns of interpretation have changed very little, except in one regard: the introduction of racism as a central explanation for Puritan aggression. That should come as no surprise at a time when American society is racked by racial tensions.

Curiously, the shift from a variety of earlier explanations to an emphasis on race was launched by a book that did not itself charge the Puritans with racism. In striking contrast to the constellation of scholars who revived the Puritans' reputation between the late 1920s and the early 1960s, Francis Jennings's *The Invasion of America* (1975) accused seventeenth-century New Englanders, especially the leaders of state and church, of wholesale brutality, dishonesty, destruction of evidence, and meanness of spirit. In an attempt at disarming candor, Jennings claimed to have so harshly condemned New England's leaders because "I have recognized in myself a strong aversion toward the Puritan gentry and . . . have tried to practice restraint but not concealment of my distaste." That "distaste," he insisted, "was acquired in the course of the research." Some years before Jennings began that research, however, he concluded a study of Indian-white relations in Pennsylvania with the assertion that Quakers, Jesuits, and Moravians conceived of Indians as

> having souls eligible for salvation, and of an obligation imposed on professing Christians to do something about it. It is a different notion from the general Calvinist idea of the Indians. With few exceptions, the Calvinist outlook generally put the Indians' souls (if any) among the ranks of the predestined damned. God's chosen people could best serve the divine will by removing the corporeal entities attached to such hopeless spirits.

With such a falacious assumption about Calvinists in mind when he launched his study of seventeenth-century New England, Jennings's scathing interpretation of the Puritans' Indian policies was itself predestined.[52]

The Invasion of America insisted that the Puritans had been reprehensible at every point of contact with Native Americans and, to boot, had committed a "pervasive calculated deception of the official records." Jennings was especially critical of the Puritans' role in the Pequot War. Although he at one point identified the fundamental causes of the Pequot War as "disputes over sovereignty and tribute," he put more emphasis on what he took to be the Puritans' duplicitous breaking of agreements with the Pequots and their projection of the blame onto their enemies. At stake (and, it seems, implicitly more crucial than jurisdiction or tribute in Jennings's scenario) was a rivalry between New England and New Netherland for control of the Connecticut valley and between Massachusetts and Connecticut for territorial dominance once the Dutch had effectively been excluded. In sum, Jennings emphasized economic issues—the land-grabbing explanation redivivus—but also intercolonial rivalry over land and a fundamental Puritan deviousness. His secondary emphasis on wampum had a unique twist too: unlike subsequent studies that would accuse the colonists of wanting to control wampum production, Jennings saw wampum as more immediate gratification through tribute payments. But nowhere in his account of the Pequot War did Jennings explicitly charge New England colonists with perceiving the Indians as a race apart or of trying to exterminate them for essentially racist reasons.[53]

The influence of *The Invasion of America* was rapid and widespread. In 1980, for example, Richard Drinnon's *Facing West* reiterated some of the same charges against the Puritans and added, as causes of the Pequot War, "suppressed sexuality" and, especially, racism. The former "found vent in an orgy of violence" during the attack on the Pequot Fort, where "[l]ike men in a dream they burned and shot *the flesh* they so feared and hated in themselves." But racism was more causative, in Drinnon's scenario: "The tempers of Winthrop and Endicott were more hair-trigger sensitive than Cromwell's when someone threatened to defile their holy mission. . . . Cromwell hunted down the Irish; but he still fell short of the unyielding fury the Saints turned on . . . [people] who had both a different culture and a different color." Not only different in culture and color but not even human: "The loud and clear answer of the war was that the Indians were truly animals. . . ." Drinnon paid generous tribute to Jennings.[54]

So did David E. Stannard twelve years later in *American Holocaust* (1992), which credits Drinnon as well. For Stannard, the rationale for the Endecott expedition was pure blood lust: the revenge John Gallop unleashed on more than a dozen Indians who may have had a hand in John Oldham's death was not enough: "The colonists simply wanted to kill Indians." That Englishmen were being killed too did not impress Stannard. Captains Stone and Norton and seven crewmen are reduced in *American Holocaust* to "two quarrelsome Englishmen"; the dozen or more subsequent English victims, some tortured to death, are casually dismissed: "For a time small troubles continued in the field, while in Hartford the Connecticut General Court met and declared war against the Pequots." At heart it was plain racism. "[T]here remains little doubt," Stannard concluded after praising the work of Jennings and Drinnon especially, "that the colonists were driven by a racist zeal to eliminate the Indians, at least once the major colonist-Indian wars had gotten underway." Elsewhere Stannard makes clear that racism, as he sees it, accompanied colonization from the outset; the Spanish, English, and other Europeans believed that Native Americans "were a racially degraded and inferior lot—borderline humans as far as most whites were concerned."[55]

Drinnon and Stannard, I submit, have seriously misread the evidence, though somewhat differently. By Drinnon's definition, racism is the habitual maltreatment of "physically dissimilar peoples—identified as such by skin color and other shared hereditary characteristics." That simply was not the Puritans' perception of the Indians, nor was the Pequot War representative of early New England's treatment of the natives. As chapter 1 in this volume makes abundantly clear, I hope, the Puritans perceived Indians to be innately fair-skinned and wholly human (in the Devil's thrall, to be sure, but in Puritan eyes so were many Englishmen and most humans of whatever continent), and the Puritans further believed the Indians to be as educable in Christianity and "civility" as were their own British ancestors. Because *Roots of American Racism* expounds on such points in several essays (see especially chapters 1, 2, and 7), suffice it to say here that Drinnon's reading of the sources reflects even more thoroughly than does Jennings's the temper of its times.[56]

Stannard's definition of racism is quite different. Skin color is irrelevant; all one needs to demonstrate racism is evidence that one group saw the other as distinctly different and that treatment of the other group reflected a prejudice against it. By those ground rules, virtually all prejudice, whether based on religion, region, nationality, customs, or color, is racism. Some modern writers do, in fact, see racism in that light—in defiance of dictionary definitions and at the risk of erasing important differences in types of discriminatory beliefs and actions. Stannard seems to endorse the notion of racism that J. H. Plumb implied some years ago: "the literature of the sixteenth and seventeenth centuries is full of savagely expressed racism directed not only to the Negro but to the Hindu, the Hottentot, the Welsh, Scots, Irish, French against English, English against the Dutch."[57]

Stannard, like Plumb, missed the essential point (which Drinnon did not) that racism is one thing and that vicious animosity directed at a temporary or traditional enemy is another. Both are deplorable, of course. The latter, alas, knows no national, religious, or temporal boundaries, and in wartime is often expressed hyperbolically in animal tropes. We still hear such exaggerations—by Serbs against Croats or Tutsi against Hutus, or Arabs against Jews and vice versa—without for a moment believing that the angry speaker really thinks his or her opponent is an animal or belongs to an innately inferior branch of humankind. The recipient of such verbal abuse may not care if the aspersions spring from the heat of battle or an ideological conviction, especially if the words are followed by bullets; religious and political hatred can be as deadly as racial hatred. But the historian's task is to make meaningful distinctions in past human behavior, and I submit that there was a profound difference between the prevalent seventeenth-century Anglo-American view of the African, on the one hand, as cursed by God with dark pigmentation and suited by appearance and an inferior mental and spiritual nature to perpetual enslavement; and, on the other hand, the Anglo-Americans' perception of the Native American as fundamentally like themselves in pigment, appearance, intelligence, and educability, yet as woefully uncivilized as the Englishmens' own ancestors had been.

As several chapters in this book are at pains to point out, that seventeenth-century view was never universal but nonetheless held sway, in most parts of British America, until late in the century. Thereafter it eroded precipitously; by the Revolutionary era, if not sooner, the Indian, too, was an object of Anglo-American racism.

Not all of the recent writers on the Pequot War have branded the Puritans as bullies or liars or racists. Some indications suggest that the pendulum may be swinging, albeit inconsistently, toward a more sophisticated and balanced view of Indian-white relations that identifies causes and assigns blame with insight rather than passion; conspiracies are replaced with an awareness of the mutual misunderstandings that allowed disparate cultures to blunder into a war that neither side really wanted. Three recent articles give cause for hope.

Adam J. Hirsch's "Collision of Military Cultures" (1988) proposed that the radically different traditions of warfare—strategy, tactics, weapons, expectations—not only determined the outcome of the Pequot War but also helped to bring it about. In sharp contrast to writers who tout Puritan aggression as the causal explanation, Hirsch believes that the Endecott expedition had no intention or expectation of launching a war: "The melancholy truth is that New England's first Anglo-Indian war owed its inception to a ghastly mistake"—to wit, "the presumption that Indians would conduct themselves like Englishmen under the same circumstances." Faced with an overwhelming show of force, the Pequots should have acceded—by European rules—to Endecott's demands or fought to the finish on the open field. Similarly, Hirsch argues, the Pequots misjudged the English, assuming (in accordance with Indian military culture) that the English would end the fighting when the score was more or less even and not wage the unthinkable—a war of extermination. By the time both sides realized their mistakes, the brutality had escalated beyond repair. Although differences in military culture do not tell the whole story, Hirsch's contribution seems useful and constructively provocative.[58]

In 1991, Steven Katz took strong exception to the verbal excesses of many ostensibly balanced accounts of the Pequot War. Katz emphasized the spiraling loss of English life in the 1630s and the growing conviction among Puritan leaders that justice demanded a strict accountability, however misguided it may have been. The "over-reactive raid on Block Island" may have spurred the Pequots to take up arms, but the colonists, Katz believes, in tacit endorsement of Hirsch's argument, did not intend at this point to wage an all-out war. Rather, "[t]hey fought, initially, a defensive war." But hostilities escalated: only one fatality caused by the Endecott expedition (killed by an Indian ally of the English) was countered by several lethal Pequot raids. "Of course the Indians cannot be blamed for so replying, for they too saw themselves as acting legitimately in self-defense, both narrowly and more generally in defense of traditional Indian rights to their own native lands. In effect, both sides acted to defend what they perceived as rightly theirs." Although Katz eschewed the stereotypes and straw men that had obfuscated recent work on this subject, he accepted the recent claims of Puritan racism. While denying that the Pequot War should be "viewed in strictly racial or ethnic terms of Red vs. White," Katz attested that "I do not dispute that the colonists viewed Indians through racial stereotypes, or that those stereotypes affected their behavior." Katz thus has a foot in each recent interpretive camp.[59]

A more promising slant on the causes of the war comes from Alfred Cave, who is preparing a major study of the war and its antecedents. His two articles on aspects of the prewar jockeying between Pequots and Puritans exhibit a refreshing evenhandedness and careful attention to the sources. No conspiracies here. Each party to the quarrel misjudged the other, not so much in military terms but in basic understandings. Perhaps most innovative is Cave's evidence that the Pequots consistently admitted responsibility for the death of Captain Stone and his companions, thus partly justifying Puritan insistence on the expatriation of the culprits and refuting Jennings's diatribe on Puritan deception in the matter. Cave goes a long way, in fact, toward reestablishing the integrity of Puritan sources that Jennings, and those who relied on him, had ostensibly shattered. In Cave's assessment of the war's causes, Puritan and Pequot misreadings of each other's actions and intentions were fatal. On the one hand was "Puritan determination to subdue and control savages believed to be a threat to their security," which was "compounded by Pequot inability to understand the English refusal to accept their explanations of Stone's death or to consider the wampum already paid as ample restitution for their error. The Puritans responded to an imaginary threat. The Pequots underestimated a very real danger."[60]

What these recent articles have in common, it should be apparent from these brief summarizes, is a rejection of the morality play syndrome that has dominated so many interpretations in the past several decades and a deprivileging of race as a causative influence. Not only do the new emphases on cultural misunderstanding conform to the grim reality of conflicts around the world today, they are, more importantly, in accord with the surviving sources.

CHAPTER NINE

Tests of
Puritan Justice

The defeat of the Pequots in 1637 left the New England colonies, for the next
several decades at least, free from the threat of major Indian opposition. That
did not mean freedom from persistent involvement with Indians, however, for individual Indians and Indian nations remained central to the colonies' day-to-
day affairs. Some of those affairs were essentially political negotiations—media-
tion of intertribal grievances, for example—and some were essentially economic
transactions—as with the fur trade and land purchases. The legislative and judicial records of the several New England colonies reveal that another category
of Indian-white contact concerned legal issues that had broad intercultural implications. This essay addresses two such cases from the year after the Pequot War
ended, when New England resumed peaceful solutions to disputes between natives and colonists. Both cases were important at the time but have received less
attention from historians than it seems to me they deserve.

   Although the two events may not appear at first glance to have much in common other than a shared date of occurrence, they reflect, I argue, the colonies'
genuine efforts at peaceful accommodation of Indian interests; they demonstrate,
too, the authorities' strict conformity to Anglo-American legal principals, even
when the decisions went against colonial plaintiffs or defendants. But both events
also—much like the Pequot War—reveal an undercurrent of English hostility to
Indians that would in later years become more pronounced and politically influential.

This essay first appeared in the New England Quarterly 38 (1965): 331–39,
and is reprinted with that journal's permission. It is in many respects, however,
a new piece: the original essay has been extensively revised to form the current
introduction and section I; sections II and III are entirely new. Readers who are
familiar with the previous chapter may find the opening summary of the events
and interpretations of the Pequot War unnecessary, but they are intended to make
the essay complete by itself.

༼༽

AMERICAN HISTORIANS IN THE MIDDLE decades of the twentieth century successfully removed from the New England Puritans most of the stigmata that had been attached to them by earlier scholars. Unlike their Progressive Era predecessors, early Americanists in the 1930s and ever since have generally acknowledged the "sweet reasonableness" of the Puritans in literature, theology, daily life, and even—with some minor reservations—in political administration.[1] But at least one aspect of Puritan society has remained under an especially heavy cloud: treatment of its Indian neighbors.

Not all North American colonies have been comparably condemned. The French in Canada and the Quakers in Pennsylvania have often been credited with respecting the rights and interests of Native Americans. By contrast, writers of the early 1930s to the late 1950s either ignored or sharply criticized the Puritans' dealings with the New England tribes. Aggressive and merciless warfare, arbitrary confinement of Indians to reservations, land swindling, and greedy trade practices were among the charges frequently leveled at the New England colonists.[2] And almost without exception, historians have assumed that Indians in New England, even when they had recourse to colonial courts, stood no chance of impartial justice. While it would be reckless to deny that injustices often took place in early New England, especially in a legal system the Indians had no hand in creating or administering, there is something to be said in rebuttal to the accepted stereotype.[3] In 1638, two capital cases—one in Connecticut, the other in Plymouth—demonstrated dramatically that Puritan justice in the early decades was not always stacked against Indian interests.[4] Yet they also reveal a countercurrent of colonial opinion that doubted the appropriateness of intercultural equity. Puritan efforts to treat Indian litigants fairly were fragile at best.

I

The Connecticut case, while not a legal decision in the modern sense, was a ruling by the highest judicial body in the colony. At issue was the lethal revenge the chief of a small Indian community levied against the inhabitants of Wethersfield, Connecticut. The English settlers at Wethersfield contended that the chief's treachery must be punished; the General Court denied their petition on the basis of what its members, on advice from magistrates and ministers in the Massachusetts Bay Colony, perceived to be "the law of nations" and the sanctity of covenants. A brief sketch of the bloody circumstances that brought the case into court will suggest the significance of the decision and the uncharacteristic restraint of its architects.

Sixteen thirty-six was a year of crisis throughout New England. While Plymouth was enjoying relative peace and stability—and even a measure of prosperity—her sister colonies of Massachusetts Bay, Connecticut, and Rhode Island were confronting serious challenges, both internal and external. The Bay Colony was purging its ranks of heretics who threatened, according to the magistrates and clergymen, its divine mission; simultaneously, the colony faced quo warranto proceedings against its royal charter, which jeopardized the Puritan experiment's very existence. Rhode Island and Connecticut, the former a by-product of the Massachusetts purge and the latter a manifestation of swelling Puritan immigration, were barely under way. The toeholds already acquired around Narragansett Bay and in the Connecticut River valley were so precarious that only historical hindsight permits us to give more attention to these settlements than we accord to similar ventures in New Hampshire and Maine.

Overshadowing the basic difficulties of colony building were instances of Indian resistance that had suddenly challenged New England's physical security. Newly planted colonies and older ones alike could see that a consolidated Indian attack might end New England's career when it had just begun to flourish. The lesson of the Powhatan uprising in Virginia (1622) remained fresh in their minds; a similar raid on New England would discourage immigration and very likely bring direct royal control to the region.[5] It was important, Puritan spokesmen insisted, to curb Indian hostility and to deal strictly with any tribe or individual who encouraged it.

This was easier urged than done, for the principal potential enemy was the formidable Pequot tribe of southern Connecticut. The seven hundred Pequot warriors might exterminate all English settlements in the Connecticut valley; if they could enlist the aid of the Narragansett tribe, they might well carry the attack to Roger Williams's infant colony at Providence and move on to assault Plymouth and then the heart of New England in the Boston Bay area.[6] Fortunately for the Puritan colonists, the remembrance of past intertribal frictions proved stronger than the apprehension of future intercultural conflict, and in October 1636 Narragansett sachems joined an offensive alliance with Massachusetts Bay against the Pequots.[7]

Massachusetts and Rhode Island could breathe more easily now, but the Connecticut valley settlements encountered only increased violence, especially at Fort Saybrook, at the mouth of the Connecticut River. As the English outpost closest to Pequot territory, its garrison of twenty men under Lieutenant Lion Gardiner was under intermittent attack from September 1636 through April 1637. Pequot warriors ambushed several work parties that ventured out of the fort; English traders who set foot on the lower banks of the Connecticut were likely to end their days in Indian torture ceremonies. The death toll mounted alarmingly until Governor Henry Vane of Massachusetts dispatched twenty Bay

Colony volunteers to reinforce Gardiner.[8] The additional defenders made the Fort Saybrook area too risky for the Pequots, who henceforth shifted their attacks to the vulnerable plantations farther upriver.

Wethersfield, southernmost of the Connecticut towns, thus became the target of a sudden Pequot raid, and from this event Connecticut's subsequent test of justice evolved. Wethersfield was then a village of barely 160 residents, more than half of them women and children.[9] Two years earlier these emigrants from Watertown, Massachusetts, had purchased land from Chief Sowheag (often called Sequin) of the local Wangunk tribe.[10] The terms of sale are not known in detail, but part of the bargain, orally at least, stipulated that Sowheag and his followers could remain in the township and receive protection from the English against the Pequots.[11] The Wangunks, like other valley tribes, had long resented the harsh hegemony that Sassacus held over them, and it was partly in hope of ending their subservience to the Pequots that the valley tribes had welcomed the English to Connecticut.[12]

Sowheag soon learned that his new neighbors were no better than his former overlords, for the settlers at Wethersfield either did not understand the terms of the purchase agreement or chose to ignore them. When Sowheag set up a wigwam at Wethersfield early in 1637, he was driven out by force. In frustration the Wangunk chief turned to his former enemies, the Pequots, for assistance in redressing his grievance.[13] On the morning of April 23, 1637, two hundred Pequot warriors surprised a group of colonists in a Wethersfield meadow, slew six men and three women, and destroyed twenty cows and a mare. Two young women were captured, bound, and thrown into canoes. The raiding party later paddled past Fort Saybrook, hoisting on poles the shirts and skirts of its victims in a mocking imitation of English sails.[14]

Sowheag's revenge jolted the New England colonies into vigorous action. On the basis of mounting Pequot depredations, Massachusetts had officially declared war two weeks before the Wethersfield attack, but her forces had not yet taken the field. Connecticut had not even made a formal commitment to war. Stirred by the disaster at Wethersfield, the General Court on May 1, 1637, voted for "an offensive warr against the Pequoitt" and levied ninety men for the task.[15] This Connecticut contingent, under the command of Captain John Mason, inflicted a crushing defeat on the Pequots later that month. Aided by the Mohegans and Narragansetts, Mason's forces massacred several hundred men, women, and children and threw such a scare into the rest of Sassacus's followers that most of them sought refuge with neighboring tribes. Those who remained in Pequot territory and many of those who tried to flee were hunted down by colonial soldiers or by Indians in league with the colonies; by the fall of 1637 the Pequot tribe had almost vanished. Seven or eight hundred of Sassacus's nation had been killed or captured; many of the survivors, offering vassalage in return for their lives, surrendered to the Connecticut authorities. A few escaped into Pennsylvania and Virginia. Chief Sassacus sought asylum with the Mohawks in the Hudson valley, but they seized his wampum, decapitated him, and sent his head to Connecticut.[16]

With the war over, the New England colonies attempted to redefine their relationships with the Indian tribes, both friendly and hostile. The Pequots who survived were parceled out to the tribes that had aided the English in the war. New bonds of friendship were formed with the Mohegans, Narragansetts, and several lesser tribes.[17] But the Wangunks remained a problem for Puritan authorities, who now fully recognized Sowheag's treachery. The logic of the situation seemed to demand that he share the fate of the Pequots; at the very least, they insisted, he should suffer some punishment for his perfidy.

The Wethersfield settlers, especially, favored retaliation, but Sowheag protested that he had acted against the English only after they had wronged him. That argument posed a quandary for the Connecticut magistrates. The residents of Wethersfield had imposed a relatively minor injustice on Sowheag in denying him the right to settle within the bounds of their town; in reprisal, the Wangunk sachem had indirectly caused the deaths of nine colonists, a heavy destruction of property, and considerable suffering by the two captives and the surviving families. Could such a violent retribution be justified by the earlier and milder English wrong? Uncertain themselves, the leaders of the River Colony wrote to Massachusetts for advice.[18]

Whatever one may think of Puritan intolerance in matters of religious dissent, the Bay Colony's restrained approach to this problem was in marked contrast to its earlier belligerence. Governor John Winthrop called in "[s]uch of the magistrates and elders as could meet on the sudden" and presented the question. They answered that Sowheag, the recipient of the first wrong, had been justified in retaliating "either by force or fraud." The magnitude of his revenge was irrelevant, they argued, for had he returned damages of one hundredfold, he would have been acting in accordance with the "law of nations" and would therefore have been morally and legally right. No surviving source explains precisely what the Massachusetts leaders meant by the law of nations, but a clue can be gleaned from the Dutch jurist Hugo Grotius's opinion (available in several Latin editions beginning in 1625) that "The law of nature . . . is generally called the law of nations . . . [and] is proved in the same manner as the nonwritten civil law, and that is by continual experience and testimony of the Sages of the Law." Grotius further argued, "The excess of retaliation cannot . . . give a colour of right to the first aggression." Such logic apparently underlay the magistrates' and elders' conclusion that Sowheag had retained his right to retaliate even though he had not waited for a peaceful adjustment of his complaint; he had objected to the injury done him and his plea had been ignored.[19] Sowheag, in short, had observed his side of the covenant. The English inhabitants of Wethersfield had violated theirs and must suffer the ensuing horrors without revenge or recompense.

This opinion of the Bay Colony's leaders did not bind Connecticut, but at a meeting of the General Court on April 5, 1638, the Connecticut magistrates announced themselves in full agreement with their neighbors' advice. After a "full debate & hearinge," the court decreed that while each party had inflicted injuries on the other, "yet because . . . the first breach was on the English p[a]rte, All former wronges whatsoever are remitted on both sides and the saide Soheage is againe received in Amytie to the saide English. . . ."[20] The court immediately dispatched three men to arbitrate the remaining differences between the residents of Wethersfield and the Wangunk sachem. Arrangements satisfactory to both sides were soon negotiated, and the next few years were unruffled by disputes between English and Indians in that area. Eventually trouble did arise, but it can be attributed only indirectly to the animosity incurred by the Wethersfield massacre. Rather, when other sources of friction appeared, the settlers were reluctant to place full confidence in a chief who had on one occasion plotted against them. It is therefore not surprising to find the English growing suspicious of Sowheag's friendship—and he, presumably, of theirs—when rumors of Indian conspiracies against the New England colonies in the 1640s prompted colonial investigations of tribal actions.[21]

The Wethersfield case is, of course, an isolated incident. By itself, this single example of a favorable verdict for a minor Indian sachem proves little about the overall pattern of judicial policies the New England Puritans imposed on their Indian neighbors. But the presumption must be strong that if the Puritans could decide in favor of an Indian who had retaliated so ruthlessly against English settlers, other cases must have arisen in which the New England colonies meted impartial justice. Plymouth's cause célèbre of 1638 offers some corroboration.

II

The case of Plymouth's "Peach gang" differs significantly from the Wethersfield episode but shares with it several characteristics. Most obviously different are the affiliations of the accusers and the accused: at Plymouth, Englishmen rather than Indians committed the alleged crime, and the principal plaintiffs were grieving Indians rather than colonists. The legal issue was different too: outright murder of an individual in the Plymouth case, in contrast to the indirect, though equally lethal, retaliation against a whole community at Wethersfield. But the decisions in both cases culminated in 1638, the year after the Pequot War, and they had at least tenuous connections to that cataclysmic event. In both cases, too, colonial authorities did apparent justice to the Indians, although some colonists were palpably disgruntled by the officials' stance.

At Plymouth, as at Wethersfield, the identity of the participants and the sequence of events are adequately documented. Arthur Peach, the

principal figure, appears frequently in the surviving public and private
records: a veteran of the Pequot War (probably as a Massachusetts resident) who subsequently found employment in Plymouth as an indentured servant to former governor Edward Winslow; a reputation for idle-
ness and indebtedness; and charges of impregnating Stephen Hopkins's
servant Dorothy Temple. Although John Winthrop reported that Peach
was "of good parentage and fair conditioned," by the time his crimes
were known, William Bradford dubbed him "a lustie and a desperate
yonge man." Faced with rigorous penalties for his indiscretions, Arthur
Peach fled Plymouth one night in late July 1638 for sanctuary in the
Dutch colony at New Netherland.[22]

Less clear are the backgrounds of Daniel Cross, Thomas Jackson, and
Richard Stinnings, who were also under servant or apprentice indentures at Plymouth but succumbed to Peach's blandishments and joined
his flight to New Netherland.[23] English refugees from contracted servitude might find a haven in the Dutch colony's polyglot population, or
they might move on—probably under assumed names—to the English
colonies on Chesapeake Bay. (A century later, Benjamin Franklin would
become the most famous absconder from a New England indenture to
seek freedom in a more southerly British province.) Had Peach and his
friends not encountered a lone Indian named Penowanyanquis on the
path from Narragansett country to Massachusetts Bay, they might have
achieved their devious goal.[24]

Penowanyanquis, a Nipmuck Indian employed by the son of a Nar-
rangansett sachem, was carrying trade goods northward to Boston when
he encountered the English fugitives heading the other way. On
Penowanyanquis's return trip two days later—now carrying bolts of cloth
and strings of wampum—he was superficially befriended by the errant
colonists and, when his guard was down, savagely attacked. Despite severe wounds, Penowanyanquis escaped into a marsh and crawled back
to the path after the Englishmen resumed their journey.[25]

In Providence, twelve miles away, Roger Williams heard of four nearly
starved Englishmen before he knew of their fugitive status or the crime
they had perpetrated. Despite their reluctance to linger near English
settlements, they accepted Williams's proferred food, drink, and shelter. Soon after, Williams learned that Penowanyanquis had been found
and had described his assailants, but Peach, Cross, Jackson, and Stinnings absconded from Providence in the night. Williams urged the Narragansett sachems to round up the culprits and rushed to aid the dying
Penowanyanquis. The Narragansetts quickly accomplished their assignment by leading the Peach gang to an English outpost on Aquidneck
Island, where they were apprehended and held for further disposition.
Penowanyanquis meanwhile gave a full account of the assault to Williams
and physician Thomas James. Williams quickly alerted Governor
Winthrop of the "great hubbub in all these parts" the crime had occasioned.[26]

The legal uncertainty in the Peach case was jurisdictional rather than substantive. The Aquidneck colonists had possession of the culprits, but, as Winthrop pointed out when Williams sought his opinion, the fledgling Rhode Island community had as yet no established government. (In any event, Winthrop would have been unlikely to endorse a government run by refugees from Massachusetts orthodoxy.)[27] Plymouth was the obvious political jurisdiction to take custody of the accused men and bring them to trial: Plymouth residents were the apparent criminals; they had broken Plymouth laws; and they were fugitives from Plymouth indentures. Yet the murder appeared to have been committed outside Plymouth's boundaries, at a remote spot that Williams thought "fit for an evil purpose."[28] Winthrop suggested a novel option: if no colony claimed jurisdiction over the place of the murder, "it would be safest to deliver the principal [i.e., Peach], who was certainly known to have killed the party, to the Indian his friends, with caution that they should not put him to torture, and keep the other three to further consideration." This was, from one standpoint, a sensible and equitable suggestion, but it conformed neither to European colonial practice nor to Puritan notions of their own superior administration of justice. At the very least, Winthrop's proposal violated English procedure by effectively condemning Peach to death without a trial, and it transferred the state's monopoly on capital punishment to (from the colonists' ethnocentric perspective) an uncivilized and un-Christian, and therefore unacceptable, system of jurisprudence. Plymouth quickly resolved the dilemma by asserting its jurisdiction over the Peach gang and ordering a trial. Although Daniel Cross escaped from Aquidneck by boat and found his way to Maine—an area claimed by Massachusetts—and avoided recapture, Peach, Jackson, and Stinnings stood trial at Plymouth.[29]

The evidence against all three was overwhelming, and all three confessed. The twelve-man jury of Plymouth citizens also heard testimony from Williams and Thomas James that Penowanyanquis's wounds were fatal, although he had been alive when his friends carried him from Providence. Still, evidence of his death was necessary to uphold a charge of murder. "At last two Indians," Winthrop recorded in his journal, ". . . with much difficulty, were procured to come to the trial, (for they still feared that the English were conspired to kill all the Indians,) made oath after this manner, viz.: that if he were not dead of that wound, then they would suffer death." On September 4, 1638, the jury found all defendents guilty of robbery and murder.[30]

Later that same day, Arthur Peach, Thomas Jackson, and Richard Stinnings died by hanging on Plymouth's gallows hill. Witnesses included (probably) most of Plymouth Colony's population, as well as (certainly) Roger Williams and other Rhode Islanders and several Narragansetts. The latter were greatly satisfied at this exercise of English justice. Two years earlier, Williams had told Winthrop that the Pequots feared "the English were minded to destroy all Indians," and Bradford reported that

Pequot ambassadors warned that "if the Narigansets did assist the English to subdue them, they did but make way for their owne overthrow."
After the attack on Penowanyanquis, the prediction seemed valid. "The
natives," Williams reported, feared "a general slaughter" and the Narragansetts made "greeveous complainte" that "they should now find the
Pequents words trew; that the English would fall upon them." Temporarily at least, the trial of Peach, Jackson, and Stinnings put those fears
to rest.[31]

Perhaps, as some historians of the Peach case have insisted, the Plymouth officials' principal motive in executing the Peach gang was fear
of open war with the Indians—King Philip's War writ early—if
Penowanyanquis's killers were allowed to live. Surely the Puritan colonies
had no desire to repeat the tragic events of 1636: surprise assaults, heavy
loss of life and property, prospects of a pan-Indian alliance. And yet the
colonies' overwhelming military success in 1637, which they attributed
more to God's favor than to their own firepower, must have made them
supremely confident of their divinely endorsed ability to win any contest, while the assistance of so many Indians against the Pequots must
have persuaded them of the improbability of facing a unified front.

Which is not to say that the Indians would have let the murder pass
without reprisal. A swift evening of the score by the victim's kin was
wholly legitimate in a system of justice based on liability rather than cul-
pability, and Penowanyanquis's friends already "had consultacion to kill
an English man in revenge." Wise New Englanders no doubt heeded
the Narragansett sachem Miantonomi's advice to "be carefull on the
high wayes."[32] Despite Penowanyanquis's Nipmuck origins, the Narragansetts appear to have been deeply upset by his murder; offending so
powerful a tribe would surely bode ill for the colonists, especially at the
vulnerable outlying settlements in Rhode Island and Plymouth. But all-
out war by the Narragansetts and perhaps other tribes seems an improbable conclusion to the Peach episode. Indian jurisprudence called
only for an offsetting victim, not a bloodbath, and in any event, the circumstances were not propitious for massive Indian retaliation. The
colonists still enjoyed a near monopoly on firearms, while the Indian
nations of southern New England were either demoralized (especially
the Pequot remnant) or engaged in squabbles of their own.[33] And Narragansett warriors had recently witnessed the ferocity of European warfare at the Mystic fort massacre; they wanted no part of it. The colonists'
Indian allies, Captain John Underhill recounted, rejoiced at the victory
over the Pequots but protested that "the manner of English mens fight"
was "too furious, and slaies too many men."[34]

A more plausible explanation of the executions at Plymouth than fear
of an Indian war, I submit, is that Puritan authorities, at least in the early
decades of settlement, were sincerely committed to impartial justice *provided it was on their terms*—that is, by Puritan rules, in Puritan courts, with
Puritan juries and mostly Puritan witnesses, and with Puritan-sanctioned

punishments.[35] The colonists generally perceived the Indians to be culturally handicapped: they deserved legal protection if they submitted to "civilized," Christian law, which the Puritans thought they alone provided. In the early 1640s, Puritan spokesmen insisted that "as we expect right dealing from them, in case any of them shall trespasse us, we send to their Sagamore, and he presently rights us, or else we summon them to our Court to answer for it"; and "if any of our men offend them, and complaint and proofe be made to any of our Magistrates or the publique Court (they know) they are sure to be righted to the utmost, by us."[36]

Winthrop's suggestion that Peach be turned over to the Narragansetts was an aberration in colonial legal doctrine and practice (the Massachusetts governor may have intended only to prod Plymouth), as was, a decade later, the assertion by William Pynchon of Springfield that Indians who committed crimes outside actual—not hypothetical—colonial jurisdiction "must be esteemed as an independent and free people," not subject to Puritan law. To today's reader, Winthrop and Pynchon make good sense; to fellow colonials they were spouting nonsense. Virtually without exception, colonial officials, including Winthrop on all other occasions, insisted—from the beginning to the end of the colonial era—that they, not the Indians, must decide cases involving Euro-Americans. What Winthrop seems to have intended in this instance was a fair and speedy trial. In advising Plymouth authorities that the Peach gang could not appeal to England, he urged prompt action because "the whole country here [is] interested in the case, and would expect to have justice done (Fig. 9.1)." The aggrieved Indians, in both the Plymouth and Wethersfield cases, apparently appreciated the Massachusetts governor's efforts: in 1639, he recorded in his journal that "[t]he two chief sachems of Naragansett sent the governor [Winthrop] a present of thirty fathom of wampom, and Sequin, the sachem of Connecticut, sent ten fathom."[37]

III

What the Wethersfield and Plymouth cases perhaps reveal most tellingly is the cleavage within British colonial society between political and religious authorities, on the one hand, who were intent on peace, justice, and good order, and on the other hand an emerging vocal minority—in later frontier communities, in New England and elsewhere, they would be an embittered majority—that held all Indians in contempt and resented legal institutions which in any way protected Indian lives and rights.[38] The surviving records hint at such a split in the Wethersfield settlers' treatment of Sowheag: "they drave him away by force," reported Winthrop, despite the agreement made earlier by their own spokesmen to give the Wangunks space and protection. Later on, it was Connecticut's colonial authorities who gave Sowheag a hearing and sought advice from the Bay Colony.[39] In sum, sentiment in Connecticut seems to have been roughly divided between callous local residents and colonial

Fig. 9.1.
Governor John Winthrop of Massachusetts, painted by an unknown artist, played important roles in both of New England's judicial cause célèbres of 1638. Courtesy, American Antiquarian Society.

leaders, with the latter determined to curb frontier animosity toward Indians and the former either hostile or indifferent.

Similarly, in the Plymouth case, Arthur Peach boasted to Cross, Jackson, and Stinnings that he had no qualms about running his rapier through Penowanyanquis, for "he had killed many of them"—perhaps a soldier's postwar bravado but reflective in any event of a blatant disregard for Indian life. And the only grumblings over Plymouth's prosecution of the Peach gang came, William Bradford reported, from "some of the rude and ignorante sorte" of Plymouth residents, who "murmured that any English should be put to death for the Indeans."[40] (It was not a uniquely New England problem, of course. Five years later, for example, a Maryland jury refused to convict a colonist who confessed to killing an Indian chief "because the party was a pagan, & because they had no president [precedent] in the neighbour colony of virginea, to make such facts murther.")[41] Suggestive, too, is Daniel Cross's escape from Aquidneck—perhaps with assistance from sympathetic colonists—and especially the actions of the settlers in southern Maine: when Winthrop's agents tried to retrieve Cross, "those of Pascataquack [Piscataqua] conveyed him away and openly withstood his apprehension."[42]

Such actions and the prejudice they reflected would surface sporadically in New England in the 1640s, 1650s, and 1660s, and with a vengeance in the wartime frenzy of the 1670s, when on several occasions the legal system blatantly failed to do justice to Indians.[43] For a few years after 1638, Puritan performance may have matched the spirit of the Wethersfield and Plymouth cases. In 1639 Massachusetts authorities tried to ensure peace by ordering that "care should bee taken to prevent damage to the Indians, & procure them satisfaction for any damage done them," but the need for such a law suggests that a some colonists cared very little for Indian "satisfaction." More shattering to Indian hopes for equity, or even for survival, must have been the bitter sentiments Roger Williams reported nearly a decade after the Pequot War: "How often have I heard both the English and Dutch (not only the civill, but the most debauched and profane) say, These *Heathen* Dogges, better kill a thousand of them then that we *Christians* should be indangered or troubled with them."[44] Despite a Puritan propagandist's boast in the early 1640s that the Indians "have had justice truly exercised towards them," and despite scattered instances of Puritan decisions that favored the Indian side of disputes, the overall record in southern New England between 1638 and 1675 must have disheartened Indians in general and sachems in particular.[45]

A poignant reminder that Indian perception of Puritan justice differed dramatically from the colonists' came from a Narragansett sachem a few years after the Sowheag and Peach episodes. Roger Williams recorded Canonicus's qualms:

> I have never suffered any wrong to be offered to the English since they landed; nor never will: . . . if the *Englishman* speake true, if hee meane truly, then I shall goe to my grave in peace, and hope that the *English* and my posteritie shall live in love and peace together. I [i.e., Williams] replied, that he had no cause (as I hoped) to question *Englishmans, Wunnaumwauonck*, that is faithfulnesse, he having had long experience of their friendlinesse and trustinesse. He tooke a stick, and broke it into ten pieces, and related ten instances (laying down a stick to every instance) which gave him cause thus to feare and say.[46]

Underlying Canonicus's lament were the twin legal obstacles to New England's intercultural frontier: the colonists' determination to impose their concepts of justice onto native nations that had a strikingly different legal culture and—perhaps even more detrimental to Indian-white relations—the infrequency of decisions such as the Sowheag and Peach cases in which the colonists conscientiously applied impartial justice when Indians were the aggrieved party. A generation after Canonicus reiterated ten colonial failures, Metacom ("King Philip") of the Pokanokets and thousands of other Indians were sufficiently appalled by the Englishmen's waning *wunnaumwauonck* to wage a war that had been almost unthinkable in 1638.

CHAPTER TEN

Crossing the Cultural Divide: Indians and New Englanders, 1605–1763

Europeans have often observed that Americans, almost from the outset of colonization, blended Old World traditions with New World innovations. By moving to a continent not bound by Europe's restrictive customs and by absorbing some of America's native ways, immigrants—and especially their children and grandchildren—became Americans rather than transplanted Europeans of whatever nationality. To say that Europeans "Indianized" is perhaps to exaggerate (and in the usage of the colonial period, to demean as well), but surely Euro-Americans became decreasingly like their forebears and more like American natives as time went by, even when the former influence remained the stronger of the two. Similarly, American Indian lives changed under the influence of the strangers from abroad; whether for better or for worse, the introduction of metal tools, woven cloth, alcoholic beverages, and firearms—to name only the most common items of intercultural trade—meant that even Indians who shunned personal contact with the intruders were likely to feel their influence and never be quite the same again. This essay examines the frequency and depth of acculturation in the New England colonies throughout most of the colonial period.

Precise measurement in such matters is, of course, impossible. Yet in some specific situations, such as the captivity of Euro-Americans by Indians, the surviving records permit a rough estimate of the numbers who chose to join almost completely with native life. Similarly, colonial records leave numerous clues to the number of Indians who relinquished their traditional ways for life among the colonists. Such "transculturations" were in fact very few on either side of the cultural divide, yet as the polar extremes of a broad continuum of cultural borrowings they offer insights into the complexity of culture contact in early America. This essay is concerned with the variety of cultural adaptations but especially with the evidence for occasional transculturations.

My interest in this topic was piqued by what seemed to me a disparity between claims, on the one hand, of numerous spokesmen in the late colonial period and

of modern historians that transculturations were numerous from European to In-
dian but never from Indian to colonial American, and, on the other hand, the
evidence in the colonial sources about the frequency of transculturation in either
direction. I chose that topic for a talk to the American Antiquarian Society's meet-
ing of April 1980 in Boston, and it was subsequently published, greatly ex-
panded, in the Proceedings of the American Antiquarian Society 90
(1980): 23–99. It is reprinted here with the editor's permission.

Daniel Richter was my coauthor throughout. He did most of the quantitative
and anthropological work, though we collaborated fully on the integration of our
separate portions, and we both read and revised several drafts. The original es-
say appears here with many minor changes and the deletion of several statistical
tables. Readers with a penchant for quantification may want to consult the orig-
inal version.

IN HIS *Letters from an American Farmer* (1782), Hector St. John de Crèvecoeur wondered why "thousands of Europeans are Indians, and we have
no examples of even one of these Aborigines having from choice become European!"[1] The peripatetic Frenchman claimed no originality
on this matter. He undoubtedly knew that earlier in the eighteenth century Cadwallader Colden and Benjamin Franklin, among others, had
remarked on the Europeans' eagerness to joint the Indians and the Indians' contrasting reluctance to assimilate with Europeans.[2] None of
Crèvecoeur's contemporaries seems to have disagreed, and by now the
paradox has so thoroughly permeated American thought that most modern scholars accept its accuracy without question. According to a recent
specialist on early American history, "the one case in which transculturation between Indians and Europeans did occur involved the Indianization of whites rather than the Europeanization of Indians.
Throughout the colonial period . . . colonists in eastern North America
ran away to Indian settlements."[3] And a prominent ethnohistorian's
analysis of "The White Indians of Colonial America" starts with the assumption that "by the close of the colonial period, very few if any Indians had been transformed into civilized Englishmen[;] . . . on the other
hand, large numbers of Englishmen had chosen to become Indians."
He then explains, rather than tests, that historical anomaly.[4]

There is, of course, no way to measure conclusively the number of
early Euro-Americans and Native Americans who exchanged their original cultural identity for another way of life. Severe problems of definition and sources cloud the issue. How much cultural change constitutes
a thorough metamorphosis—a "transculturation" from one set of values, beliefs, and behavior to another?[5] How can transculturation in individuals and groups be measured? What sources document the complex human interaction in which cultural crossovers occurred, especially
on the frontier, where literacy was rare among Europeans and almost
nil among Indians? Despite such conundrums, imprecise but useful nu-

merical estimates of Indians and European-Americans in colonial New England who changed their cultural allegiances can be made, thanks to the Puritan colonies' relatively abundant historical records and to the diligent research of several late nineteenth- and early twentieth-century investigators. And the evidence suggests a far less one-sided exchange than Colden, Franklin, and Crèvecoeur presented; in fact New England colonists were probably more successful than Indians in attracting social and religious converts. Yet, ironically, Indian culture incorporated strangers far more thoroughly and enthusiastically than did Puritan New England. In their basic attitudes toward new members of their societies, Indians and Englishmen were worlds apart.

I

Probably the first New England Indian to become substantially Europeanized was Squanto of the Patuxet tribe. His story has often been told: how George Waymouth captured him in 1605; how Sir Ferdinando Gorges kept him until 1614 when he returned to New England with Captain John Smith just in time to be recaptured by Captain Thomas Hunt and sold into slavery in Spain; and how he escaped to England, where he lived for two years before returning once again to New England. Squanto's dual kidnappings were, of course, reprehensible, but they probably saved his life: during his absence from Patuxet his tribe was exterminated by disease. Squanto subsequently befriended the Pilgrims who settled on his ancestral lands and served them gladly if sometimes duplicitously until his death in 1622.[6] His crucial contributions as interpreter, guide, pilot, and fishing and planting instructor convinced Governor William Bradford that Squanto was "a speciall instrument sent of God for their good beyond their expectation."[7]

Squanto's acculturation must have been extensive. He gained considerable command of the English language during his years abroad, he apparently acquired some English customs, and he probably learned something of English farming practices from settlers in Newfoundland.[8] After the spring of 1621 he lived the remaining year and a half of his life among the Plymouth colonists, and at his death, according to Bradford, Squanto asked the governor's prayers "that he might goe to the Englishmens God in heaven."[9] Although romantic illustrations of Squanto (there are no contemporary pictures) invariably show him in loincloth and feathers, the popularity of European garments among seventeenth-century Indians and Squanto's long exposure to English customs suggest that he more likely wore breeches, shirt, and Monmouth cap. While the depth of Squanto's social and religious conversion is uncertain, he seems to have substantially crossed the cultural chasm between Indian and Englishman in Puritan New England.

Counterparts are hard to find during the next three decades. Samoset, who introduced Squanto to the Pilgrims, disappears immediately from the records. Hobomock, whose role at Plymouth somewhat paralleled Squanto's and lasted twenty years longer, is also a hazy historical figure, although he apparently identified closely with the settlers and adopted their beliefs.[10] Perhaps the Indians who frequented the transient outposts near modern Quincy acquired a smattering of English ways—at least they eagerly accepted "civilized" society's rum and muskets—but, according to early Puritan sources, the acculturation process went mainly in the other direction: Thomas Weston's English band in the early 1620s and Thomas Morton's at the same location later in the decade probably became more Indian than the Indians became English.[11]

Formation of the Massachusetts Bay Colony in 1629 and its dramatic growth in the 1630s opened new opportunities for Puritan proselytizing. The Bay Colonists came to America—so their leaders and their charter said—partly to bring civilization and Christianity to the heathen; not, however, until midcentury could Massachusetts or its Connecticut offshoot claim much progress in converting Indians to their ways. The Puritans' critics, then and since, have charged that New Englanders made scant efforts to fulfill their pious pronouncements or their charter's admonition to "wynn and incite the natives . . . [to] the onlie true God and Savior of mankinde."[12] Colonial spokesmen, by contrast, blamed their meager success on circumstances: the Indians' language, which few Englishmen could speak and which varied from tribe to tribe; the opposition of Indian sachems and shamans; a shortage of funds and personnel; and especially the Indians' "infinite distance from Christianity, having never been prepared thereunto by any Civility at all."[13] Puritan clergymen insisted that Indians must close the cultural distance. As Cotton Mather later observed of John Eliot: "he was to make *Men* of them, ere he could hope to see them *Saints;* they must be civilized er'e they could be *Christianized.*"[14] However, Eliot and the other ministers interested in the Indians were only part-time missionaries, because the Puritans defined a clergyman—and hence a missionary—as a man who served a parish church.[15] With physical and economic survival demanding everyone's energies in the early years, the Puritans taught few Indians to act like Englishmen and therefore converted few to Christianity.

The surviving records claim a few proselytes in the Bay Colony's first two decades, but the evidence is sparse and inconclusive. In 1643 several Massachusetts clergymen boasted that appreciable progress had already been made toward civilizing and converting the Indians. The opening section of their promotional tract, *New Englands First Fruits,* offered "a little tast of the sprincklings of Gods spirit, upon a few Indians"; many more examples, the authors insisted, could be gathered if all of the New England settlements were searched, for they had "snacht up only such instances which came at present to hand."[16] They devoted half a page to an Indian at Plymouth who believed that Christian prayers had ended an "extreame Drought" by producing "a most sweet, constant, soaking showre"; he was impressed enough to endure his countrymen's scorn and to remain thereafter with the English.[17] In 1637 Wequash, a Pequot Indian living with the Narragansetts, was inspired by the colonists' military prowess. "Seeing and beholding the mighty power of God in our English Forces, how they fell upon the *Pequits,* . . . [he] was convinced and perswaded that our God was a most dreadfull God; and that one *English* man by the help of his God was able to slay and put to flight an hundred *Indians.*" Wequash soon moved to Saybrook, Connecticut, discarded all his wives but the first, and spread Christ's message among neighboring tribes. But Satan retaliated by causing some disgruntled Indians to poison Wequash, who on his deathbed bequeathed his child to the English "for education and instruction." Thomas Shepard hailed Wequash as a Christian martyr, and Samuel Danforth's *Almanack for the Year of our Lord 1647* called him "the first Indian that held forth a clear work of conversion to Christianity."[18] Another admirer of English customs was Sagamore John of the Massachusetts tribe, who studied English and "loved to imitate us in our behaviour and apparrell, and began to hearken after our God and his wayes." However, Indian threats and ridicule kept Sagamore John from living with the English, a decision he lamented on his deathbed when he gave his only child to the Reverend John Wilson of Boston.[19] A somewhat different missionary success involved a "Blackmore maid" of Dorchester who had met Puritanism's rigorous requirements for full church membership; thereafter she sought to persuade Indians that Christ would welcome them also.[20]

Indian children bequeathed to Puritan control may have been more thorough in their social and religious conversion than their parents. Here too, however, the records are frustratingly sparse. Sagamore John's son soon died of smallpox, but perhaps Wequash's heirs and other Indian children among the Puritans grew up virtually as English youths and silently merged into the colonial population. Or perhaps they just as silently slipped back into native society with none of their father's attachment to Puritan culture.[21] That the former situation obtained in similar cases if not in theirs is strongly argued in *New Englands First Fruits:* "Divers of our *Indians* Children, Boyes and Girles we have received into our houses, who are long since civilized, and in subjection to us, painfull and handy in their businesse, and can speak our language familiarly; divers of whom can read English, and begin to understand in their measure, the grounds of Christian Religion . . . and are much in love with us, and cannot indure to returne any more to the *Indians.*"[22]

Neither *New Englands First Fruits* nor any other contemporary source gives exact figures on the Indian youngsters who lived with English families and studied at New England common and grammar schools; few are even mentioned by name. Perhaps a score of Indians before 1675 attended Puritan schools, and of these about half a dozen entered Harvard.[23] Because instruction at all levels of Puritan education was in English, and because the curriculum and living circumstances apparently made no allowance for Indian preferences, the "hopfull Indians youthes" must have been almost fully incorporated into English culture. Some of the English, in fact, attributed the high mortality rate among Indian students to the "great change upon their bodies, in respect of their diet, lodging, apparel, [and] studies; so much different from what they were inured to among their own countrymen."[24] Modern observers would add psychological strain to the list. In any event, some Indian students apparently did survive and returned to their tribes; others disappear from the records but may have retained their anglicized behavior and beliefs; while several, including the only Harvard graduate, endured the perils of Puritan academia only to die soon after of "European" diseases.[25]

Some Indians did substantially cross the cultural divide and live the bulk of their lives among the English. John Eliot Sr. attributed his early training in the Algonquian tongues and help in translating several religious tracts to "a *pregnant witted young man,* who had been a Servant in an English house."[26] This Indian was captured during the Pequot War and held by the English for several years. Eliot's subsequent interpreter and principal assistant in publishing the Indian Bible was James Printer, who spent twenty years at the Cambridge Press (Fig. 10.1). He must have absorbed a hefty portion of Anglo-American customs and values, for although his loyalty apparently wavered in 1675 when he sided briefly with the Wampanoags, the next year he received amnesty and thereafter aided the English. He later became a missionary to the Indians.[27]

The most substantial body of transculturated Indians in colonial New England emerged from the missionary efforts of the Mayhews on Martha's Vineyard, the Eliots in Massachusetts, and a number of less prominent clergymen in Plymouth and Connecticut. In 1644 several eastern Massachusetts sachems relinquished sovereignty over their lands and jurisdiction over their tribesmen to the Bay Colony government, which inspired a modest missionary effort led principally by John Eliot Sr. of Roxbury.[28] In 1651 he established the first "praying town" of converts and catechumens at Natick, and by the eve of King Philip's War in 1675 fourteen such communities dotted eastern Massachusetts and the neighboring fringe of Connecticut.[29] Meanwhile, on Martha's Vineyard and its neighboring islands, the Mayhews—Thomas Jr., who died at sea in 1657, and Thomas Sr., who carried on his son's work—conducted an even more promising experiment in Indian transculturation. The island's isolation and the Mayhews' virtually unlimited authority facilitated wholesale social and religious conversion. Once the sachems agreed to follow English ways, which many of them did in the 1650s, other Indians quickly followed suit.[30] In Plymouth Colony, Richard Bourne had by 1670 established a Christian church among the Nausets.[31] Connecticut and Rhode Island, however, had little missionary success in the seventeenth century, partly because of Indian resistance and partly because neither colony produced dedicated proselytizers.[32]

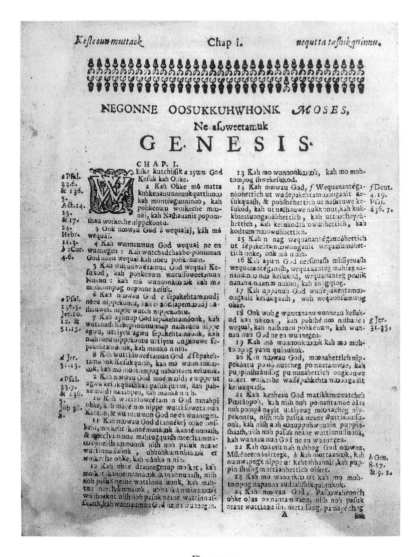

Fig. 10.1

The first page of the book of Genesis in John Eliot's edition of the Bible in 1663 (Genesis was initially translated and printed in 1655). Eliot and other missionaries, with essential help from bilingual Indians, translated more than a score of books to expedite the Christianization and anglication of the Indians. Courtesy, American Antiquarian Society.

The depth and breadth of transculturation among these Christianized New England Indians can only be loosely estimated. Puritan efforts in schooling, evangelizing, providing European tools and paraphernalia, and encouraging adherence to English laws and customs produced many partial but probably few complete converts. Indians who met the

Puritans' demanding social and theological qualifications for full church membership, however, must have been highly transculturated.[33] That status was accorded only to Indians who substantially changed their lifestyles and beliefs, experienced God's saving grace, and gave a convincing oral account of their conversion experience. According to superintendent of Indians Daniel Gookin, in 1674 more than 150 Indians had already met those requirements, and many others were approaching that stage. Of the nearly 2,300 Indians whom Gookin estimated to be living in New England praying towns, many had been baptized as Christians (which for adults required an extensive knowledge and acceptance of Christian doctrine as well as substantial social reformation) and were presumably seeking a conversion experience and a thorough cultural transformation (Table 10.1).[34] (Undoubtedly some Indians were attracted to Puritan religion but not to other aspects of New England culture and thus cannot be considered transculturates. Our concern here is with the small portion of the Indian population that sought to become as anglicized as possible.)[35]

In 1675–76 King Philip's War disrupted the missionary experiment. Many of the praying Indians sided with Metacomet (dubbed "King Philip" by Puritan authorities), some took a neutral stance, and others remained loyal to the English, despite their incarceration on Deer Island and the calumny heaped on them by war-scared colonists. Eliot ruefully admitted that "soone after the warr with the Indians brake forth ... the profane Indians prove[d] a sharp rod to the English, and the English prove[d] a very sharp rod to the praying Indian."[36] Yet substantial numbers of Indians from the praying towns held firm to their new faith, and in the end their military contribution decided the war in the Puritans' favor.[37]

Table 10.1

DANIEL GOOKIN'S ESTIMATES OF THE CHRISTIAN
INDIAN POPULATION OF NEW ENGLAND, 1674

	"Souls yielding obedience to the gospel"	Full communicants	Other baptized Christians
Massachusetts	1,100	46–56*	45+*
Plymouth	497	27	90
Martha's Vineyard	360	50	N.A.
Nantucket	300	30	40
Connecticut	30	0	0
TOTALS	2,287	153–163	175+

*There were two Indian churches in Massachusetts in 1674, at Natick and Hassauamesitt (Grafton). The latter church had 16 full communicants and 30 other baptized members. The Natick church had 40–50 full communicants and an unknown number of baptized members, including at least 15 who lived at Hopkinton.

SOURCE: Gookin, *Historical Collections*, 40–70.

After the war, Eliot, Gookin, John and Experience Mayhew, and dozens of other Puritan clergymen and laymen had some success in molding Indians into Englishmen.[38] In 1698 the Reverends Grindal Rawson and Samuel Danforth visited the colony's praying towns on behalf of the Society for the Propagation of the Gospel in New England; their report dispels the notion that King Philip's War ended Puritan missionary activity and underlines once more the indissoluble tie between social and religious conversion. Rawson and Danforth described more than a score of Christian Indian congregations, ranging in size from a handful to several hundred participants. One congregation on Martha's Vineyard claimed 64 communicants among a local population of 231, and other congregations had almost as high a percentage. Equally revealing are the report's frequent references to schools and teachers, English-style meetinghouses, and English clothing. At Gay Head on Martha's Vineyard, for example, "Abel and Elisha are preachers, to at least two hundred and sixty souls; who have here at their charge a meeting house already framed. We find that the Indians here . . . are well instructed in reading, well clothed, and mostly in decent English apparel."[39] Two decades later, Experience Mayhew reported that Martha's Vineyard and its neighboring islands had 110 communicants in a total population of about 800. The converts were "generally Cloathed as the English are, and they by degrees learn the English way of Husbandry. . . ." One Edgartown convert, "being a Person of great Industry in his Business," was proud of his "Cows, Oxen, Horses, and Swine, also his Cart and Plough, and Cribs, and Stacks of Corn."[40] Other Martha's Vineyard Indians had become carpenters, weavers, wheelwrights, tailors, shoemakers, blacksmiths, and coopers. Mayhew claimed that an increasing number of Indians had built houses "of the *English* fashion," but as late as 1727 most Indians on the islands still lived in wigwams.[41]

Adoption of English-style housing seems to have been one of the last steps in transculturation, and the least essential. Experience Mayhew observed that Japheth Hannit, a Christian Indian preacher and a man "generally and justly esteemed, as well as by the *English* as *Indians,* a Person of a good Conversation . . . courteously received and entertained by . . . the best Gentlemen on the Island," lived in a wigwam built by his wife, while the Edgartown farmer mentioned earlier inhabited a "Wigwam well furnished with things necessary for the Use of his Family." A generation earlier, Daniel Gookin described the Massachusetts praying town of Natick, already in existence for twenty-five years: "Their . . . houses in this town are generally after their old mode . . . though some they have built in this and other of the praying villages, after the English form." Gookin went on to explain, with apparent sympathy, the Indians' reasons for preferring "to keep their old fashioned houses": cheapness, warmth, and portability.[42] While Puritan spokesmen clearly favored English-style houses for Christian Indians, it was not an important issue. Orderliness, not architecture, was the criterion for Puritan approval.

In the eighteenth century, as in the seventeenth, the offshore islands were a major center of transculturation, but they were now matched by inland missionary experiments, most notably at Stockbridge on the Housatonic River in western Massachusetts (established 1734) and Lebanon in western Connecticut (1754). At Stockbridge a nucleus of Mahican (Mohican, Muhhakaneok, Moheakunnuk) Indians from New York colony and recruits from several tribes both within and outside New England lived for several decades in uneasy cooperation with Anglo-American residents. The Reverend John Seargant, a graduate of Yale, ministered to the eclectic flock until his death in 1749; his successors included the dynamic and controversial Jonathan Edwards from 1751 to 1758. Seargant and Edwards also taught in the Stockbridge boarding school for Indian boys, while other clergymen and laymen conducted a day school for Indian boys and, after about 1750, one for girls. At Lebanon, the Reverend Eleazar Wheelock (also a Yale graduate) similarly focused on educational programs. His star pupil, Samson Occom, studied at Lebanon in the 1740s and became a prominent missionary himself, while Wheelock—partly with funds raised by Occom— conducted a coeducational, intertribal, boarding institution, Moor's Indian Charity School, from 1754 until his departure for the presidency of Dartmouth College in 1770.[43]

Despite some notable successes at Stockbridge and Lebanon, New England's schools and colleges played a diminishing role in the efforts to acculturate New England Indians. Fewer Indians attended and, once again, disease carried away the most promising; yet those who braved the rigors of Puritan education seem to have most thoroughly absorbed English ways and values. For example, Benjamin Larnell, an Indian from Plymouth Colony, lived for two and a half years in Judge Samuel Sewall's home, attended Boston Latin School, and impressed President Leverett of Harvard as "an acute Grammarian, an Extraordinary Latin Poet, and a good Greek one."[43] Larnell was progressing reasonably well at Harvard (class of 1716) when he suddenly took ill and died in Sewall's house during his first summer vacation. All the surviving evidence—including the particulars of his funeral—suggest that Larnell was thoroughly integrated into the Cambridge and Boston communities.[44]

In the 1740s New England's Great Awakening furthered the trend toward Indian transculturation. The native population of southern New England had already undergone a large measure of political and economic anglicization. The Narragansetts, for example, as anthropologist William Simmons observes, were by 1740 "following in most respects an English social model while remaining on the periphery of English society. Through conversion they advanced their participation in colonial culture one step further by accepting the symbolic system which represented that culture."[45] Some elements of Narragansett theology remained essentially Indian, but in most doctrines and practices the Narragansett Christians had become indistinguishable from English Calvinists. So too had the Mohegans, Pequots, and Niantics; during the Great Awakening many joined neighboring English churches while others formed exclusively Indian congregations. In either case, Indian response to Gilbert Tennent, James Davenport, Eleazar Wheelock, and other itinerant preachers was enthusiastic.[46] For some of these Indians—perhaps for most—transculturation became virtually complete. Had not widespread prejudice among Anglo-Americans reminded the Indians that despite their adoption of European behavior and beliefs they were still a distinct people, many more Indians in southern New England might have merged with their non-Indian neighbors, as a few probably did through marriage or by following occupational careers such as seamanship that immersed them in non-Indian surroundings. In any event, by 1763 hundreds of Indians had crossed the cultural divide.

Estimating the total number of New England Indians who changed cultures between 1605 and 1763 is fraught with pitfalls. Admission to full church membership may be an acceptable criterion for complete cultural change in the seventeenth century, but less rigorous definitions of sainthood in the eighteenth century undermine its diagnostic reliability.[47] One group of eighteenth-century Indians, however, must have been heavily, if not thoroughly, anglicized: native Christian preachers, trained and supervised by Anglo-American missionaries. Frederick L. Weis, in his exhaustive studies of colonial clergymen, identifies 140 Indian ministers who at some time before 1763 served sixty-two praying towns and other Christian Indian communities, twenty-one Congregational and Baptist churches, and nine Protestant missions (Table 10.2).[48] These 140 Indian clerics added to Gookin's 1674 count of Indian full communicants in Puritan churches and perhaps half of the Indians known to have become full communicants between 1675 and 1763 (on the assumption that many, but not all, later Christian Indians had crossed cultures) yield a rough estimate of 500 New England Indians who almost wholly transferred their cultural affiliations during the colonial period.[49] Additional evidence is likely to raise rather than lower this figure.

II

The experiences of Indian converts demonstrate both the attraction of New English society for Indians and the barriers it raised against them. Puritanism's appeal lay partly in the ostensible power of its deity—demonstrated, some observers believed, in the crushing victory over the Pequots in 1637, the functional superiority of European tools and weapons, and the colonists' relative immunity to infectious disease. Puritan missionary success in eastern Massachusetts and on Martha's Vineyard illustrates the last point. Thomas Mayhew Jr.'s first convert, Hia-

Table 10.2

NUMBER OF NEW ENGLAND PROTESTANT INDIAN COMMUNITIES,
CHURCHES, AND MISSIONS; EURO-AMERICAN MISSIONARIES;
AND INDIAN MINISTERS, AT FIVE-YEAR INTERVALS, 1660–1760

Individual cases,	Christian Indian communities	Indian churches	Missions & schools	Euro-American missionaries	Indian ministers
1605–1763	62	21	9	71	140
Number existing in:*					
1660	6	5	3	7	4
1665	8	10	1	9	7
1670	24	13	1	10	22
1675	46	14	1	9	40†
1680	32	14	1	11	14
1685	33	14	1	12	28
1690	34	14	1	13	20
1695	34	16	1	13	17
1700	34	15	1	13	43†
1705	31	17	1	14	21
1710	32	15	1	20	25
1715	32	15	2	19	22
1720	31	15	1	16	13
1725	30	15	2	15	10
1730	27	14	2	15	5
1735	26	15	3	18	4
1740	26	15	5	22	5
1745	22	15	6	22	3
1750	21	16	6	18	4
1755	20	16	7	17	4
1760	20	16	6	17	5

*Items that appear in the source for only brief periods and do not fall on one of the tally dates are included with these figures and are added to the nearest five-year tally. For example, Josias Hossuit, whose entire career as an Indian minister took place during 1702, is included with the tally for 1700.

†Larger totals of Indian ministers in 1675 and 1700 reflect the more complete data available for those years as a result of the studies of New England missions undertaken by Daniel Gookin in 1674 and Grindal Rawson and Samuel Danforth in 1698; for other years information is not as complete.

SOURCE: Weis, "New England Company," 153–202. Weis's sources were fragmentary and many of his dates are approximate; in particular the date at which a community or mission became defunct is often quite uncertain. These figures therefore represent only rough estimates. All Christian Indian communities ("praying towns" and others), exclusively Indian Protestant churches (Congregational, Baptist, and Moravian), Protestant missions, Euro-American Protestant missionaries who apparently devoted most or all of their time to Indians, and sanctioned Indian preachers in Massachusetts, Plymouth, Connecticut and Rhode Island are included in these tabulations.

coomes, endured considerable abuse from other Indians, especially sachems, "for his fellowship with the English, both in their civil and religious wayes."[50] Hiacoomes was already something of an object of ridicule among his countrymen because "his Descent was but mean, his Speech but slow, and his Countenance not very promising." But when he began frequenting English homes and churches "they laughed and scoffed at him, saying, *Here comes the* English *Man*." Hiacoomes. (and the Puritan God) got his revenge, however, when his principal tormenter was struck by lightning and many of his other detractors succumbed to an epidemic which left Hiacoomes and most of his followers unscathed. Thereafter the Martha's Vineyard missionary program made rapid headway.[51] Comparable, though less dramatic, events occurred at various times and places in seventeenth-century New England to ease the task of Mayhew, Eliot, and the other missionaries, while at the same time the apparent failure of the powwows' incantations against the English and Christian Indians further undermined Indian confidence in their traditional belief system.[52] Moreover, Puritan society offered material advantages that some Indians found attractive. The inhabitants of John Eliot's praying towns received, through funds collected by the missionaries' supporters in England, a wide range of European goods: axes, hoes, hatchets, knives, crowbars, plows, wagons, cloth, spinning wheels, and much more.[53] Probably few Indians gravitated to praying towns primarily for economic reasons, but the colonists' technology may have enhanced significantly their other perceived virtues. Similarly, instruction in literacy (Algonquian, English, or both) appealed to many Indians, even if education in classical languages and moral philosophy attracted very few.[54]

Largely offsetting the virtues some Indians saw in Puritan culture were several obstacles to their social and religious conversion. Most insurmountable, perhaps, was the magnitude of the required transformation, a barrier that John Eliot recognized, although he, of course, thought the reward justified the effort. In 1671 Eliot published a volume of imaginary *Indian Dialogues* through which he hoped to override frequent Indian objections to Christianity. One of Eliot's hypothetical powwows argues strongly against anglicization: "We have Gods also, and more than [the English] . . . and we have Laws also by which our forefathers did walk, and why should not we do as they have done? To change our Gods, and Laws, and Customs, are great things, and not easily to be obtained and accomplished. Let us alone that we may be quiet in the ways which we like and love, as we let you alone in your Changes and new Wayes." Eliot's answer, of course, was that Christianity and English "civility" were the only *right* ways.[55]

Candidates for transculturation, as Sagamore John and Hiacoomes learned, also faced social isolation if not ostracism. One of the Indians in Eliot's *Dialogues* objects to leaving his friends: "If I should forsake our former wayes, all my friends would rise up against me like a stream too strong for me to stand against."[56] And there was always the likelihood that a sachem would resent his followers' allegiance to a foreign faith because it would diminish his authority and tribute payments. Eliot replied that neither need happen ("give unto Caesar . . ."), but the realities of the situation did not support him.[57] Only if an entire Indian community converted did its power structure remain intact, and even then it was likely to be reorganized according to Eliot's Old Testament pattern with rulers of tens, fifties, and hundreds.[58] In fact the missionaries and colonial magistrates would have more real authority than the sachems. Even on Martha's Vineyard, where a relatively large and stable Indian population and a sparse English population made political reorganization of the Indians unnecessary and impractical, by 1720 English civil authorities were in complete control except for some Indian officers who assisted English commissioners.[59] Moreover, for Indians who adhered fully to Christianity and English medical practices, Indian powwows were not only irrelevant but downright evil; Puritans considered them to be in league with Satan and their ministrations a form of witchcraft. The shamans' roots and herbs could still be used, for they were among God's gifts to mankind, but incantations, dances, and spells were the Devil's work.[60] Little wonder that Puritan missionaries considered sachems and powwows their greatest human opponents.[61]

A more insidious obstacle to Indian transculturation was the colonists' pervasive contempt for Indians in general, especially after 1675 when frequent wars, numerous captivities, and the general failure of the Indians to accept anglicization hardened English prejudice—a prejudice all too apparent, as Puritan spokesmen admitted, in everyday Anglo-Indian contact. In 1666 Eliot asked the commissioners of the New England Confederation to guarantee adequate territory for Indian towns "and suffer not the English to strip them of all theire Lands, in places fit for the Sustinance of the life of man."[62] A decade later, Increase Mather complained about "Those unhappy *Indian-trading-houses,* whereby the Heathen have been so wofully scandalized. . . ."[63] Eliot probably expressed the intentions if not always the realities of Puritan civil and clerical authorities when he quoted an Indian supporter of the English: "if any [English] do us wrong, it is without the consent of their Rulers; and upon our Complaints our wrongs are righted. They are (especially the Ruling part) good men."[64] The implication was clear: the rulers could not prevent all wrongs, and the nonrulers were not necessarily "good men." Even Eliot could not escape New England's growing anti-Indian sentiment, as he discovered in 1676 when his boat was run down in Boston Harbor to the delight of those who resented his defense of the Christian Indians during King Philip's War.[65]

Increasingly New England's leaders admitted that anti-Indian bias was widespread and inimical to missionary efforts. As early as 1645 Roger Williams had heard colonists mutter against the Indians' very existence: "Better they were all cutt off, & then we shall be no more troubled with them."[66] And on Martha's Vineyard, where Indian and English got along best in New England, Experience Mayhew complained in 1720 of opposition from "such *English men* as are filled with Prejudices against the *Indians*." Seven years later, several Boston ministers lamented the anti-Indian sentiment that hindered missionary efforts. New Englanders, they said, had "doubtless too much of that spiritual *Pride*... which many of the *Jews* had of old among them; which caused them to say to others, *Stand by thy self, come not near me; for I am holier than thou*."[67] That pride had not diminished by 1767, when some prominent residents of Middletown, Connecticut, objected to Eleazar Wheelock's work among the Indians as "altogether absurd and fruitless.... So long as the Indians are dispised by the English we may never expect success in Christianizing of them.... [We can] never respect an Indian, Christian or no Christian, so as to put him on a level with white people of any account especially to eat at the same table."[68]

Indians who thought of changing their allegiance and lifestyle must have known they would never be wholly accepted by most New Englanders. That so many Indians ostensibly crossed cultures must be attributed largely to the overwhelming preponderance of Puritan society's numbers, technology, power, and cultural aggression, not to its attitude toward strangers.

III

The other side of the coin—the number of New England settlers who became thoroughly Indianized—is also hard to measure. Despite the persistent assumption that Anglo-Americans flocked from the stultifying atmosphere of Puritan New England to the social and psychic freedom of Indian life, documented cases of voluntary transculturation are rare.

As early as 1623 several members of Thomas Weston's outpost at Mount Wollaston may have joined Indian society; they can hardly be labeled Puritans, but they at least qualify as transient New Englanders. So do Thomas Morton's men at Merrymount, some of whom may also have preferred Indian to English ways. But the most likely guess is that Weston's and Morton's followers returned to England or moved to the New England frontier, where they absorbed some elements of native culture while retaining much of their Englishness. If a few wholeheartedly adopted Indian ways, the surviving records fail to mention them.[69]

Some early Connecticut settlers apparently did choose an Indian lifestyle. In 1642 the colony's General Court, complaining that "divers persons departe from amongst us, and take up their abode with the Indians in a prophane course of life," prescribed three years in the workhouse for any Connecticut inhabitant who thereafter forsook godly society. The number of defectors probably had been small, but it was certainly upsetting to the Puritans' perception of their cultural superiority. Apparently, however, no one was prosecuted under the new law; it was either obeyed or successfully evaded.[70]

The inspiration for Connecticut's law may have been William Baker, the first documented defector to Indian culture. In a series of letters to Governor John Winthrop of Massachusetts in 1637–38, Roger Williams reported that Baker, who had been living at the Plymouth Colony's trading post on the Connecticut River, was in Mohegan territory and "is turned Indian in nakednes and cutting of haire, and after many whoredomes, is there maried." Baker was soon apprehended by Connecticut authorities (aided by Wequash); the fugitive escaped, was recaptured, and was whipped at Hartford for assorted crimes. He then disappears from the records.[71]

Almost thirty years elapsed before the next recorded instance of a New Englander voluntarily joining Indian society, and the evidence in that case is, at best, contradictory. In 1662, according to Puritan sources, Joshua Tift (or Tefft) fled to the Wampanoags after punishment for some unknown misdemeanor, "renounced his Religion, Nation and natural Parents," married an Indian, and eventually became a councillor to King Philip. Tift may have fought on the Indians' side in 1675–76 and supposedly proved his loyalty to Philip by bringing in a settler's scalp and by helping to design the Narragansetts' defenses. On January 14, 1676, Tift was captured by English forces; four days later he was hanged and quartered. One contemporary dubbed him "A sad wretch who never heard a sermon but once these last 14 years"—perhaps a reference to an unrecorded execution sermon.[72] Tift's version was far different. Roger Williams transcribed without comment Tift's claim to have been a law-abiding farmer until captured in 1675 by Indians who spared his life in return for perpetual bondage. Tift denied having fought against the English,[73] but Puritan authorities were obviously unconvinced. Depending on which version of his career is believed, Tift was either an early and brief captive of the Indians or another documented case of substantial transformation from Puritan into Indian.

The confusion surrounding Tift's transculturation—if it was that— illustrates the near impossibility of determining the precise number of New Englanders who voluntarily forsook English for Indian culture. Tift's case is almost unique in that it appears in the historical record at all. Most New Englanders who defected to the Indians were evidently marginal figures in colonial society—fur traders, inhabitants of isolated outposts, or others who never found a place in the characteristically close-knit New England villages.[74] They left no clear track for historians to follow, nor is there reason to believe that their numbers were large. And among families who lived in stable communities—even among servants of such families—converts to Indian life seem almost nonexistent. Voluntary transculturations were greatly feared by New England authorities, but the instances were probably only frequent enough to lend those fears a touch of reality.

More easily traced are the New Englanders who, at least initially, crossed the boundary between Euro-American and American Indian cultures against their will. Hundreds of New England men, women, and children got their first glimpse of a drastically different way of life when they became wartime captives of the Indians or French Canadians.

The earliest-known seizures of New Englanders by Indians occurred in 1637, shortly before the formal start of the Pequot War in the Connecticut valley, when a Pequot raiding party carried off two young Wethersfield women and held them for a month, in vain hopes that they could teach their captors to make gunpowder. (During the previous year the Pequots had seized a number of Englishmen at various locations but killed them immediately or during a hasty torture ceremony.)[75] The Pequots apparently made no real attempt to change the Wethersfield captives' cultural allegiance, and the women do not seem to have been tempted to remain voluntarily with the Indians.

For nearly four decades after 1637 New England experienced neither Indian wars nor recorded captivities, until, during King Philip's War, more than forty New Englanders were taken prisoner and held by Indians for varying lengths of time.[76] The most famous was Mary Rowlandson of Lancaster, Massachusetts, whose published narrative of her captivity launched a popular literary genre.[77] King Philip's War also generated the first prisoners who may have willingly remained with their captors. Robert Pepper of Roxbury, a soldier captured in 1675 near Northfield, Massachusetts, had been (according to Rowlandson) "a considerable time with the *Indians*," and perhaps he stayed with them.[78] Evidence on the captivity of eight-year-old Richard Nason Jr. is more abundant but conflicting. He was seized at his parents' home in Salmon Falls, New Hampshire, in 1675 and either returned there after "some Months" only to be recaptured in 1693 as an adult, or he may have found his way directly to Canada in the 1670s. In any event, Nason received Catholic baptism in 1702 at Saint François and, after marrying a French woman, was naturalized a Canadian citizen in 1710.[79]

Nason's experience illustrates the complexity of transculturation for English captives after 1689, who now would be taken by the hundreds rather than the handful. No longer did they have only to choose between staying with the Indians or returning to English society; with the onset of the imperial wars between England and France that embroiled New England's frontier for nearly a century, most captives were also exposed to French Canadian culture and could—sometimes had to—exchange their faith, loyalty, and lifestyle from Protestant English to Catholic French. Although for Puritan New Englanders this was a profound shift in cultural affiliation, it was less drastic—and therefore more probable—than the quantum leap from English to Indian culture. Canadian society thus offered an alternative adjustment to captivity that some New Englanders avidly accepted.

The complexity of English transculturation from 1689 to 1763 is further compounded by the frequent impossibility of clearly distinguishing between captives of the Indians and captives of the French, and among the latter, between captives primarily of the Canadians and of French regulars. Many of the prisoners were taken by combined French and Indian forces, and at some stage in their captivity most prisoners were exposed to both cultures. Moreover, many of New France's Indian allies were themselves substantially acculturated. They practiced a hybrid Catholicism, observed some French customs, and generally supported France's imperial ambitions. Thus New England captives of Indian war parties might confront pressures from Jesuit missionaries to change their faith and simultaneously be urged by Indian hosts to adopt a variety of Iroquoian or Algonquian customs. In short, after 1689 transculturation meant for Englishmen a greater range of options than for their Indian counterparts in the Puritan colonies.[80]

The most extensive studies of seventeenth- and eighteenth-century European-American prisoners of war were done by C. Alice Baker and Emma Lewis Coleman, dedicated antiquarians who devoted nearly two lifetimes to unearthing information about 1,606 captured New Englanders. Baker began her research during the 1870s and was later joined by Coleman, who continued the work after Baker's death and in 1925 published their findings as *New England Captives Carried to Canada between 1677 and 1760 during the French and Indian Wars.*[81] (Despite its title, the study contains considerable information about captives who never reached Canada.) *New England Captives* is impressive for its diligence and detail but frustrating in its muddled organization and sparse interpretation.[82] As a result, scholars have seldom examined Baker's and Coleman's work closely, and their cornucopia of evidence has remained largely unanalyzed. Neither Coleman nor later writers have published accurate tabulations of the number of prisoners she cited nor the proportion who remained with the Indians or French Canadians. Instead, most generalizations about the transculturation of captives stress a few well-documented and (by now) overworked cases of sixteenth- through nineteenth-century captives who stayed with the Indians and subsequently led colorful lives. Because of this research focus—and because of a too-literal reading of the great concern colonial spokesmen expressed over "civilized" Englishmen succumbing to Indian "savagery"— historians have greatly overestimated the number of New Englanders who crossed cultures during Indian captivity.[83]

The following paragraphs analyze the careers of 1,641 New England prisoners of the Indians and French about whom some information is available: the 1,606 cases in Coleman's volumes plus 35 cases drawn from other sources.[84] Most of these cases occurred during the four Anglo-French conflicts. In each of the first three intercolonial wars our sources document approximately 300 New Englanders who spent time in captivity; for the Seven Years' War the total climbs to over 500, reflecting the larger scale of the latter conflict and the greater role played in it by regular troops, who were often captured in large groups (Fig. 10.2).[85] Peace between Britain and France did not, however, always stop Indians from raiding English settlements. Some 55 New Englanders were seized during the long interval between the end of Queen Anne's War and the beginning of King George's War (50 of them during "Dummer's War" of

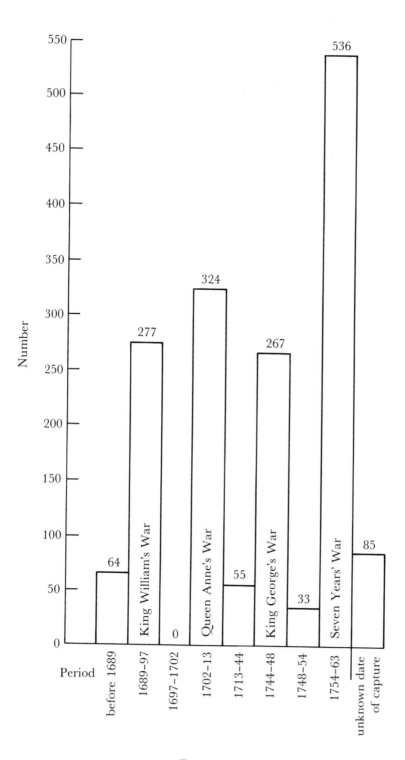

Fig. 10.2
New Englanders captured during periods of war and peace, 1675–1763.

1722–25) and at least 33 were captured during the brief period between the end of King George's War and the onset of the Seven Years' War.

From 1675 to 1763 the age, sex, and status of captive New Englanders varied with the ethnic composition of the forces who took them.[86] French patrols captured only adult male European-Americans, most of them combatants, and took prisoners only during declared wars.[87] By contrast, Indian war parties took primarily civilian prisoners and seized persons of all ages and both sexes; less than 7 percent of their captives were professional military men. (Of course, many of the "civilians" the Indians captured were hardly noncombatants, for nearly every male of sufficient age, and most women, could use a gun.)[88] Yet, despite the arguments of some historians, Indian war parties, at least in New England, did not take primarily women and children. Nearly two-thirds of the Indians' captives were males, half were adults, and war parties seldom seized a child less than two years old (Figs. 10.3 and 10.4). Probably because they knew that Anglo-American forces might pursue them and that prisoners could be sold to the French for a bounty, Indians preferred captives who could survive the trek to Canada. Those who could not make a quick exit and withstand the rigors of wilderness travel—infants, the old, and the sick—were likely to be killed on the spot rather than taken prisoner.[89]

Many of the 1,641 New England captives never returned to New England.[90] Only 754 (45.9 percent) are definitely known to have seen their homes again. At least 194 (over 11 percent) were either killed by the Indians after capture or died during captivity. The fate of 361 more (22 percent), nearly half of them military men, is unknown. Many probably languished in Canadian, French, or West Indian prisons, and, if they were lucky, returned to New England when peace treaties were signed; most probably died in overcrowded and unsanitary jails.[91] Perhaps, however, some of these "unknowns"—civilian and military—joined at least 229 others (14 percent of the total) in choosing to remain in exile and to live either as Indians or as French Canadians.[92]

Traditional wisdom holds that large numbers of wartime prisoners found wilderness life so attractive that they chose to remain with the Indians rather than return, when the opportunity arose, to their Puritan hometowns. "Many whites were Indianized—few Indians were civilized," wrote Coleman, summarizing widespread belief; "the proportion of whites barbarized to Indians civilized is as a hundred to one."[93] Recent scholars echo this view, albeit in less value-laden language. A distinguished specialist in early American literature emphatically states that "all colonists knew that most whites who spent considerable time in captivity refused later opportunities to return to white civilization."[94] One historian similarly argues that captives "frequently showed great reluctance to return to white society,"[95] and another estimates that "hundreds of white captives became almost completely Indianized."[96] Such generalizations are not supported by the careers of the 1,641 captives studied here.

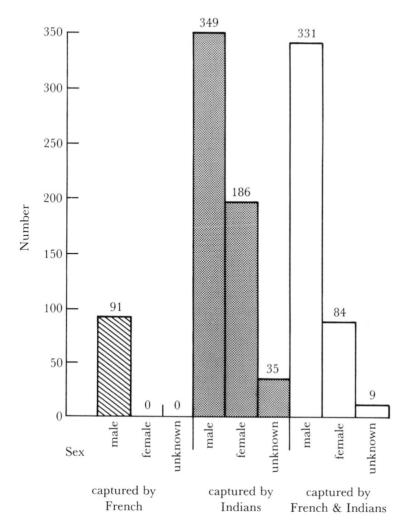

Fig. 10.3
Sex of captives taken by French, Indian, and French-Indian forces, 1675–1763.

Most of the 229 New England captives who refused to return to New England remained among the French rather than among the Indians. There is conclusive evidence of only 24 prisoners who became "white Indians"—just 1.5 percent of the total number of cases and 6.2 percent of those known to have spent the last part of their captivities with Indians—while there are indications that an additional 28 prisoners (1.7 percent) perhaps remained with their Indian hosts. At most, therefore, 52 of the recorded New England captives, or 3.2 percent, underwent completely the cultural transition from British American to American Indian.[97] The few New Englanders adopted by the Indians were over-

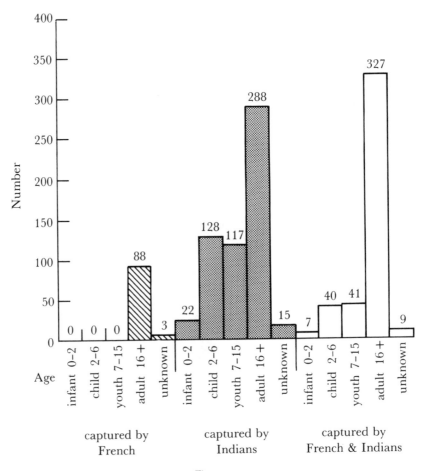

Fig. 10.4
Age of captives taken by French, Indian, and French-Indian forces, 1675–1763.

whelmingly free white civilians; they were equally divided between males and females; and although they included a number of adults, most were under age sixteen (Fig. 10.5). These sex and age distributions differed little from those of prisoners who voluntarily remained with the French Canadians.[98] But in sharp contrast to captives of the Indians, at least 202 New Englanders—12.3 percent of all known cases and 44.8 percent of those who spent the final part of their captivities among the French Canadians, but not in prison—chose to remain among the French and, presumably, to adopt their culture.[99] French Canada, not Indian Canada, caught the New England captives' fancy.

Throughout the period from 1675 to 1763, certain types of New England prisoners were more likely than others to remain with either their French or Indian captors. A far larger percentage of females than males made that choice: almost a third of the female captives but less than

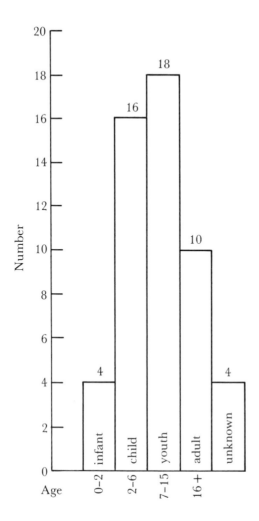

Fig. 10.5
Age of captives who remained, or perhaps remained, with Indians, 1675–1763.

one in ten males refused repatriation (Table 10.3). Because male captives were far more numerous, however, the proportion of females to males who stayed with the French or Indians was not so lopsided: 120 females and 107 males definitely refused to return. Adults of either sex were less likely than children to cross cultures and more likely to be exchanged or ransomed. Less than 4 percent of adults remained while nearly 40 percent were exchanged or ransomed; put another way, nearly 69 percent of all captives who were exchanged or ransomed were adults. Most likely to remain with either the French or the Indians were captives between the ages of seven and fifteen: almost 40 percent of these youths were assimilated into their captors' society and nearly another 10 percent lived for a time as French or Indians before either volun-

Table 10.3

FATES OF NEW ENGLAND MALES AND FEMALES CAPTURED
BY FRENCH, INDIANS, OR FRENCH AND INDIANS, 1675–1763

	Males		Sex Females		Unknown	
Fate	N	%	N	%	N	%
Exchanged, ransomed, etc.	423	35.6	123	31.4	23	37.1
Returned	54	4.5	14	3.6	0	0.0
Probably returned	11	0.9	5	1.3	0	0.0
Returned after staying	20	1.7	18	4.6	0	0.0
Returned against will	8	0.7	4	1.0	0	0.0
Escaped	58	4.9	9	2.3	0	0.0
Died	132	11.1	16	4.1	1	1.6
Killed by Indians	18	1.5	22	5.6	5	8.1
Probably died	26	2.2	3	0.8	1	1.6
Remained with captors	107	9.0	120	30.6	1	1.6
Perhaps remained	31	2.6	25	6.4	2	3.2
Fate unknown	299	25.2	33	8.4	29	46.8
TOTALS	1,187		392		62	

tarily or involuntarily returning to New England. The prime candidate for transculturation was a girl aged seven through fifteen. Almost 54 percent of that group of captives refused to return to New England, compared with less than 30 percent of the boys in the same age-group. By contrast—and perhaps surprisingly—younger children seem less likely to have been adopted by their captors: only about 18 percent of the two- through six-year-olds are known to have remained with the French or Indians. Over 20 percent of all child captives, however, vanished without a trace. Most probably died, but some may have melted into their hosts' society.[100]

The ninety-one captives seized by French forces acting independently of their Indian allies fared quite differently than did those taken by either Indian or French-Indian parties. The military and seafaring personnel who constituted all of the captives taken by the French were treated as formal prisoners of war. Most were kept in prison and, if they survived the experience, were sent home under flags of truce or exchange agreements. Nearly two-thirds of the prisoners captured by the French returned to New England this way, but approximately 20 percent died in captivity, more than twice the death rate among those captured by French and Indian forces and over five times the rate for those captured by Indians alone. Significantly, there is no evidence that any of those seized by the French might have crossed cultures. Among those for whom the identity of their captors is known, all who refused repatriation were captured by forces that included some Indians.

The likely fate of a captive depended on when he or she was taken as well as by whom the captive was taken. New Englanders captured during the first two intercolonial wars had somewhat different experiences from those seized in later conflicts. In both King William's and Queen Anne's Wars, approximately 28 percent of the captives are known to have been ransomed or exchanged while roughly 20 percent definitely refused to return home. During King George's War, however, over 60 percent of the New England prisoners were ransomed or exchanged and only four or five individuals apparently remained with the French or Indians. The most plausible explanation for this shift is that in 1750 England and France, in compliance with a treaty of 1748 concerning North American exchanges, ordered American governors on both sides to relinquish their prisoners; in the earlier conflicts exchange negotiations had been interminable and often inconclusive.[101] The disposition of the 536 New Englanders known to have been captured during the Seven Years' War also differed from those in earlier conflicts: the subsequent careers of 41 percent are unknown and only about 2 percent are known conclusively to have changed loyalties. The first figure reflects the large number of military personnel taken captive in this war—in general less is known about military captives than about civilians—and the second figure is something of a statistical artifact: there is no way of knowing how many former prisoners chose to live as quasi Frenchmen in the province of Quebec after the treaty of 1763 made Canada a British territory.

One final, ironic category of wartime captives: at least six Indian residents of New England towns were taken prisoner by the French Canadians and their Indian allies during the intercolonial wars. Two of them—Peter Dogamus of Yarmouth, an elderly laborer captured in 1746, and Joseph Joseph of Wareham, who served as a soldier and was captured at Fort William Henry in 1757—were fond enough of Anglo-American society to return to it when the opportunity arose. Only one of the six is known to have voluntarily remained with the Indians rather than return to New England—Isaac Peck of Cape Cod, who married a mission Indian at Saint François in 1749. The first, chronologically, of the Indians taken prisoner, Jeanne Wannannemin, was one of Eliot's "praying Indians" at Natick until King Philip's War, then "lived in the woods" with her Indian husband until her capture near Deerfield in 1695. In 1698 Wannannemin was baptized a Catholic, and presumably she stayed in Canada.[102] Whatever their fate, these Indians reflect the complexity of the cultural frontier. Some of them may have twice changed their cultural identity—from Indian to English and back to Indian again—or perhaps thrice in Jeanne Wannannemin's case, from Indian to English to Indian to French. All of these changes may have been superficial and outside the realm of transculturation. But there are hints that in some instances new loyalties held firm and that crossing the cultural divide was a profound and lasting experience.

IV

That so many New Englanders were taken prisoner between 1689 and 1763 reflects not only the persistence of military conflict but also certain traditions of Indian warfare. Indian allies, on whom both the English and the French relied heavily, entered the Europeans' struggles primarily for their own reasons and waged war mainly by their own rules. Nowhere was the latter more apparent than in the role captivities played in colonial warfare. Although European armies had always taken prisoners of war, and although they occasionally enslaved captured "heathens," an unwritten rule of European international law—generally observed by French forces fighting alone in America—prohibited the seizure of noncombatants and allowed the retention of combatants only until they could be exchanged or released with a pledge to fight no more. But according to Indian rules, captives of all ages and of either sex could—indeed must—be taken, either to be adopted into the families of the victorious nation or, if less fortunate, to be tortured, killed, and (occasionally) eaten. These practices, which American colonists too readily dismissed as evidence of the Indian's savage nature, were embedded in complex cultural ideas about warfare and the possibility of "requickening" (physically and spiritually replacing) deceased relatives.[103]

Indian wars have often been described as endless series of blood feuds, but a closer examination of the cultural assumptions behind Indian warfare suggests, as anthropologist Marian W. Smith noted several decades ago, that "mourning-war" is a more accurate label. While individuals often joined an Indian war party to secure revenge or to enhance personal prestige, throughout North America east of the Rocky Mountains the party's avowed collective purpose was to assuage the misery of a deceased person's mourning kin, party by gaining revenge but mainly by securing captives who could help, in a variety of symbolic and actual roles, to lessen the survivors' grief. Accordingly, any death—not merely one resulting from homicide or war—might cause an Indian community to take up the hatchet against a neighboring people.[104]

Among northeastern Indians, and especially among Iroquoians, relatives of the recently deceased were expected to plunge into depths of despair that might threaten the community's safety if some controlled outlet were not found. "Ten days of profound mourning" followed the death of an Iroquois, observed Joseph François Lafitau, the Jesuit missionary to the Catholic Mohawks at Caughnawaga:

> The laws of deep mourning are very austere; for, during those ten days [the deceased's close kin], after having the hair cut, smearing the face with earth or charcoal and gotten themselves up in the most frightful negligence, they

remain at the back of their bunk, their face against the ground or turned towards the back of the platform, their head enveloped in their blanket which is the dirtiest and least clean rag that they have. They do not look at or speak to anyone except through necessity and in a low voice. They hold themselves excused from every duty of civility and courtesy.[105]

Such grief might lead to violent outbursts that could harm the community or the mourner himself. Northeastern tribes therefore erected social barriers against the bereaved's expected rage. They held condolence rituals and mourning feasts, gave presents to survivors, and frequently conducted a "requickening" or adoption ceremony in which another individual assumed the deceased's name and sometimes quite literally replaced him in the family. Conferring the dead person's name on the adoptee, the Indians believed, assured survival not only of the former's memory but also of his or her personality and social role.[106] That requickening ceremonies could result in more than symbolic replacement is shown by a practice the Jesuits found among the Huron and Iroquois in the seventeenth century: "The husband of a quite young wife having died, his name was transferred to a young man who had recently lost his wife," and the man quickly moved in with the woman and assumed the role of husband and father. "It was said that they were married together," just as the woman and her former husband had been.[107]

If the mourners' grief remained unassuaged by such means—and especially if an enemy people could, rightly or wrongly, be blamed for the death—a mourning war was an acceptable outlet for grief-inspired violence. The war party's principal task and the primary mark of a warrior's prowess was the seizure of captives, who would subsequently play a central role in condolence rituals. Indeed, before the arrival of Europeans, Indian war parties seldom had other concrete objectives; plunder or land acquisition were rarely precontact wartime goals, and killing enemies on the spot or taking their scalps was less preferred than bringing captives back to the home village for disposition by bereaved kin.[108] The mourners might vent their rage and satisfy the deceased's demands for revenge by torturing and killing the captives (Fig. 10.6). New York Governor Thomas Dongan observed that the Indians had "a custom when any of there people are lost [in war] to give upp thoes [prisoners] they take to the crueltie of thoes fammilys which have lost any of there people."[109] Or, the mourners might adopt one or more captives into their families to replace their loss. "A father who lost his son adopts a young prisoner in his place," reported Philip Mazzei in an eighteenth-century account of British America. "An orphan takes a father or mother; a widow a husband; one man takes a sister and another a brother."[110] Underlying these condolence and adoption customs was the nation's pragmatic need to restock its population, a need that sharply increased during the seventeenth and eighteenth centuries when northeastern Indians faced the twin onslaughts of European war and European diseases. The Iroquois Confederacy strikingly illustrates this point:

Fig. 10.6

A rare seventeenth-century depiction of an Indian torture ceremony. In this vignette, presumably of a Huron village, the victim has been placed on a raised platform and is being prodded with firebrands; to the right is a greatly truncated longhouse. Detail from a map of "Nova Franciae," 1657, attributed to F. J. Bressani. National Archives of Canada, NMC 6338.

by 1700 it contained more outsiders and their descendants than ethnic Iroquois.[111]

Although the mourning war, with its ritualized treatment of captives, was especially characteristic of the Iroquois,[112] similar patterns existed among the northeastern Algonquians, and by the beginning of the intercolonial wars the practices of the two linguistic groups had substantially converged. Perhaps Algonquians had earlier preferred to torture and kill than to adopt their prisoners[113]—at least there is no evidence before 1675 of New Englanders being captured for adoption. In King Philip's war, New England Algonquians began taking Euro-American captives in substantial numbers, though possibly for later exchange.[114] By the beginning of King William's War in 1689, all of the Indian allies of the French—Iroquoian and Algonquian—seized prisoners not only for torture and execution but also as prospective adoptees.

Warfare and adoption customs had grown more alike among New France's Indian allies as a result of their frequent residential intermixture at Canadian mission settlements. Christianization seems to have done little to weaken mourning-war customs and may even have fostered their diffusion and homogenization among Iroquoians and Algonquians.[115] Until late in the seventeenth century, Catholic missionaries attempted to impart a Christian gloss to native adoption ceremonies, but the results were usually superficial and by then Canadian civil authorities had largely abandoned their policy of "Francisation" of the natives. The Jesuits had also lowered their sights, concentrating instead on "gathering their charges into Indian villages, teaching them the rudiments of agriculture and the catechism, screening them from contact with Europeans, and allowing the Indians to retain their own tongues and sense of identity."[116] As a result, in 1691 a French official could observe that "our Indians in the adjacent Missions will not ask any thing better . . . than to wage war in their own way."[117] The Marquis de Denonville had learned the same lesson a few years earlier: during an expedition against the Seneca in 1687, his Christianized Indian allies clung tenaciously to their ancient wartime rituals. "Our Christian Indians," he wrote, "were waiting for us [at a rendezvous], who sung and danced the war dance all night, at a feast which was prepared for them by means of two lean cows, and some dozen dogs, roasted, hair and all. In this consists the *true enrolment* for a vigorous prosecution of the war."[118]

Just as tenaciously, Christianized Indians retained their custom of taking captives. "The best proof" of the loyalty of the Western and Eastern Abenaki to the French cause, wrote Canadian Intendant Jean Bochart de Champigny, "has been the great number of prisoners of all ages that they have brought in."[119] If the Canadians' Indian allies were denied their accustomed rights concerning prisoners of war, they might refuse to fight. In January 1708 Christian Mohawks of the Caughnawaga mission informed the Chevalier de Ramezay that because the Canadians had taken many of the Caughnawagas' captives for exchange with the English, the Indians would no longer maraud British frontiers. Ramezay's reminder that they still held many of their adopted captives and that they had been paid for the rest only partly mollified his allies.[120] Throughout the intercolonial wars, especially during the first two, French authorities were powerless to make the mission Indians yield all their English captives. As soon as the Indians learned of an approaching French or English envoy, they hid their favorite adoptees.[121]

Both the English and the French used these traditional aspects of Indian warfare for their own purposes. As early as 1690 both European sides paid scalp and prisoner bounties to their Indian allies.[122] The fact that the Indians' prisoners had to be turned over to the Europeans if bounties were to be collected did not alter native patterns as much as might be supposed; war parties had always delivered captives to the bereaved in the home village and occasionally to other nations in fulfillment of treaty obligations. Now the French or English simply assumed the role of the receiving party.[123] Colonial authorities used the civilian prisoners they obtained from the Indians for traditional European purposes: as bargaining chips to achieve diplomatic ends and to ensure the safe return of their own people from the enemy. But to some extent, French Canadians also used the numerous captives who fell into their hands during the eighteenth-century wars much as the Indians did: as a partial solution to the problems of underpopulation and a shortage of labor. Nuns in the Canadian convents were eager to "adopt" young English girls and raise them in the Catholic faith, while other Canadians found more mercenary uses for English captives. During Queen Anne's War, a French woman ransomed English prisoners from the Indians so that they could teach her and her neighbors the art of weaving, and several New England men earned their freedom from the French by building sawmills.[124]

Nonetheless, Canada's Indian allies attempted to retain some of their Anglo-American captives and to incorporate them into their traditional patterns of captivity and adoption. They seldom succeeded. Although historian James Axtell has shown that Indians were adept at subtly educating their captives for adoption,[125] New Englanders seem to have been slow pupils in the wilderness school. Few of them apparently perceived, as did Moravian missionary John Heckewelder, that customs such as running the gauntlet were not fiendish tortures but rather—for anyone who knew the rules of the game—relatively harmless initiation rites. "I can say with truth," wrote Heckewelder,

> that in many instances, it is rather a scene of amusement, than a punishment. Much depends on the courage and presence of mind of the prisoner. On entering the village, he is shewn a painted post at the distance of from twenty to forty yards, and told to run to it and catch hold of it as quickly as he can. On each side of his stand men, women and children, with axes, sticks, and other offensive weapons, ready to strike him as he runs, in the same manner as is done in the European armies when soldiers, as it is called, run the gauntlet. . . .
>
> If a prisoner in such a situation shews a determined courage, and when bid to run for the painted post, starts at once with all his might and exerts all his strength and agility until he reaches it, he will most commonly escape without much harm, and . . . he will have the satisfaction to hear his courage and bravery applauded. But wo to the coward who hesitates, or shews any symptoms of fear! He is treated without much mercy, and is happy, at last, if he escapes with his life.[126]

Probably few New England captives faced such ordeals without "any symptoms of fear" or saw any virtue in the Indians and their ritual.

Long before they ran the gauntlet or confronted a Catholic missionary, most Anglo-Americans had been conditioned to fear and despise their captors. Some New Englanders had harbored such sentiments from the earliest days of colonization, but animosity toward Indians became especially virulent during King Philip's War—the period when captives were first taken in appreciable numbers.[127] Thereafter, narratives by re-

deemed captives and tracts by Puritan spokesmen kept ethnic antago-
nisms high. In 1676 Benjamin Tompson's poetic imagination added sexual abuse to the catalogue of Indian cruelties:

> Will she or nil the chastest turtle must
> Tast of the pangs of their unbridled lust.
> From farmes to farmes, from towns to towns they post,
> They strip, they bind, they ravish, flea and roast.[128]

Abundant evidence eventually demonstrated the inaccuracy of the sexual charge, and in 1706 Cotton Mather would set the record straight:
"Tis a wonderful Restraint from God upon the Bruitish Salvages, that
no *English Woman* was ever known to have any Violence offered unto
her *Chastity,* by any of them."[129] But before Mather's disclaimer, and perhaps even after, no captive could be sure what treatment to expect. And
there were innumerable other agonies to dread. In 1691 Mather urged
his readers to

> think upon the miserable Captives now in the Hands of that bruitish Ad-
> versary; *Captives* that are every minute Looking when they shall be Roasted
> Alive, to make a Sport and a Feast, for the most Execrable Canibals; *Cap-
> tives,* that must Endure the most bitter Frost and Cold, without Rags enough
> to Cover their Nakedness; *Captives,* that have scarce a bit of meat allow'd
> them to put into their Mouthes, but what a Dog would hardly meddle with;
> *Captives,* that must see theire nearest Relations butchered before their Eyes,
> and yet be afraid of Letting those Eyes drop a Tear upon the most Heart
> breaking Occasions, that can be imagined; *Captives,* that may not bear a
> part in any Comfortable Devotions, nor be known to have so much as a
> Bible with them, lest a French Priest should sieze upon it; *Captives,* that wear
> away one weary Week after another, in the midst of such Wolves as are every
> moment ready to tear them all to pieces.[130]

Any New Englander old enough to understand such admonitions must
have entered captivity expecting the worst, especially if he or she had
seen Indians slay friends and relatives in a bloody, though hardly
uniquely Indian, fashion. The discovery that torture and abuse were seldom their fate, rather than admiration for Indian culture, largely explains the captives' occasional testaments to the Indians' kindness.[131]

Reinforcing the captives' fears were colonial laws against becoming
Indianized and clerical warnings of God's vengeance on those who did.
In 1676 Increase Mather insisted that King Philip's War revealed God's
displeasure at the Puritans' Indian-like heathenism: "If we mind where
[the troubles] began and by what Instruments, we may well think that
God is greatly offended with the *Heathenisme* of the English People. How
many that although they are *Christians* in name, are no better than *Heathens* in heart, and in Conversation? How many Families that live like
profane Indians without any *Family prayer?* . . . If we learn the way of the
Heathen, and become like them, God will punish us by them."[132] Such
warnings placed a dual burden on Puritan captives: they must not suc-

cumb to Indianization lest they and their countrymen suffer further
depredations, yet their own capture suggested that they were already so
heathen as to merit God's wrath. Perhaps we should be less amazed that
so few New Englanders "became" Indians than that any did.

From an Indian perspective, New Englanders must have seemed unfit candidates for adoption. As part of mourning rituals and as means
of assuaging grief, the efficacy of adopting or torturing prisoners depended on the captive's conformance to a highly ritualized code of behavior: if adopted he must assimilate completely; if tortured he must die
bravely.[133] By these standards, Englishmen—unfamiliar with the rules
of mourning wars and reluctant to learn them—proved highly unsatis-
fying prisoners. Notably few New Englanders, for example, were tortured, presumably because they neither sang their death songs nor
taunted their tormenters but quickly succumbed to agony and thereby,
according to Indian belief, disgusted instead of mollified the angry spir-
its of the dead and the grieving survivors. Thomas Brown observed such
behavior in one unfortunate English captive of the Caughnawaga Iroquois during the Seven Years' War:

> They made a Fire, stripp'd and ty'd him to a Stake, and the Squaws cut
> Pieces of Pine, like Scures [skewers], and thrust them into his Flesh, and
> set them on Fire, and then fell to powwawing and dancing round him. . . .
> They cut the poor Man's Cords, and made him run backwards and for-
> wards. I heard the poor Man's Cries to Heaven for Mercy; and at length,
> thro' extreme Anguish and Pain, he pitched himself into the Flames and
> expired.[134]

Quite likely, then, Indians were only too willing to exchange most of
their Euro-American captives for French bounties or English ransoms,
while reserving for adoption the few who met their high standards. But
still they continued to seize large numbers of prisoners during their raids
on New England settlements, for this was their way of waging a proper
war.

The French Canadians, meanwhile, were so flooded with English captives who wished to stay with them that Canadian authorities begged
Paris for guidance on how to house and support the expatriates.[135] Reasons for French society's attractiveness to English colonists deserve further study, but several possibilities can be mentioned briefly. Many New
Englanders, after a harrowing overland trip through the wilderness and
weeks among the "cruel savages," were grateful for the sight of European faces, houses, and food—even if they did belong to papists; English captives frequently marveled at the hospitality of the first French
farm they reached in Canada. The Reverend John Williams luxuriated
on "a good *Feather-bed*" his first night in Canada and found that "where-
ever we entred into Houses, the *French* were very Courteous." Nehemiah
How praised the Canadian "Gentlemen and Ladies, who shew'd us great
Kindness, in giving us Money and other Things, and a pleasant Behav-

iour towards us."[136] Gratitude, then, perhaps paved the way for some New Englanders' decisions to remain in Canada, although it failed to persuade either Williams or How. In addition, the prospect of having to make the grueling return trip to New England and suspicions—sometimes encouraged by French hosts—that most of one's loved ones were dead or that France would win the war may also have encouraged some Englishmen to stay put.[137] And, finally, well-intentioned Canadian priests and nuns exerted effective if not always admirable pressures, especially on impressionable younger captives, to convert to Catholicism and to remain in Canada.[138] Cotton Mather complained that "the *French* use all the means imaginable, to Seduce their *Captives* unto the Idolatries and Superstitions of the Church of *Rome*." From a Puritan perspective he was right, but he was wrong when he added that "The Successes of the *French Converters,* have been very few, but some feeble and easy *Children;* and little to be boasted of."[139]

V

Because America has been, theoretically at least, an ethnic melting pot, and because the friction between European-Americans and the aboriginal population has been a persistent American dilemma, transculturation has fascinated not only historians and anthropologists. Novelists, for example, have been equally intrigued by cultural metamorphosis and equally prone to perpetuate the image of frequent and dramatic conversions by Euro-Americans to "savagery" while denying, implicitly at least, Indian attraction to "civilized" society. Two nineteenth-century writers illustrate the point. The only Indian in Herman Melville's *Moby Dick* shows few traces of European influence; generations of missionary efforts on his native Martha's Vineyard had failed to change Tashtego's customs or beliefs. Similarly, the captive Indian boy in James Fenimore Cooper's *The Wept of Wish-ton-Wish,* who lives for a time with a New England family, retains his native allegiance while the Puritan girl abducted by Indians marries a sachem and thoroughly absorbs his culture. Melville and Cooper thus reinforced the Colden-Franklin-Crèvecoeur paradigm.

But Cooper elsewhere explored a vastly more important theme in Indian-European culture contact. *The Wept of Wish-ton-Wish,* after all, is among his least-known works. Far more popular, and far more reflective of Indian-European contact throughout British America, are Cooper's "Leatherstocking Tales." Although their version of wilderness life may be excessively romantic, the Leatherstocking novels offer no accounts of complete transculturation in either direction. Instead they portray the dominant American experience: the emergence—to borrow once again from Crèvecoeur—of a "new man" who is not merely a transplanted European but a blend of Old World tradition and New World innovation, a fusion of cultures into a distinctively American type (though to Crèvecoeur the principal ingredients were of European rather than Indian origin). To the extent that Natty Bumppo discards much of his European cultural baggage and embraces Indian ways, he is the prototypical American, a fictional Daniel Boone, and a far more accurate symbol of early American cultural adaptation than the rare instances of thorough transculturation. Some acculturation was inevitable, Cooper implies, given the frequency of racial contact along the advancing colonial frontier and the vitality of both European and Native American cultures. The human responses to cultural contact varied, of course, from almost total rejection of alien influences to almost total acceptance, but the choices of the vast majority of Indians and European-Americans fell somewhere between the extremes. They borrowed what they wanted—in religion, economy, apparel, technology, warfare, language—while in all other respects retaining their own cultural heritages. Acculturation, in sum, was an integral and irresistible part of the American experience.

Transculturation was not. Except in rare cases, the obstacles to transculturation were simply overwhelming. Indian attempts to incorporate Englishmen into Algonquian or Iroquoian communities confronted a fiercely resistive mind-set. New England captives were too attached to their kinfolk back home, too bitter over the hardships of capture and the flight to Canada, too fearful of Indian "savagery" and its implications for God-fearing Christians, too ready to take an ethnocentric view of Indian (and French) customs, and, probably, too hopeful of eventual redemption to accept cultural indoctrination. This psychological barrier was usually strong enough to withstand the Indians' major attraction: the sincerity and thoroughness with which they incorporated outsiders into their societies. For some disgruntled outcasts and impressionable youths, and for a few flexible adults, Indian life promised a new sense of belonging, a new security, a new life. But persistent French and English efforts to redeem captives from Indian control left few New Englanders to experience enough of Indian culture to override their lifetime heritage and even fewer to experience adoption into Indian families. Not surprisingly, only a handful of New Englanders made the complete transition.

Only a slightly larger handful of Indians made a comparable metamorphosis to English culture, despite New England's greater geopolitical opportunity to effect social conversion. Whereas the Indians almost always had to capture Europeans in war and drag them, sometimes literally, to a distant land before beginning seriously to indoctrinate their unwilling guests, English colonists usually had the ostensibly easier task of convincing peaceful or defeated neighbors to take on new beliefs and habits while remaining in or near their homelands. That was not always an advantage: sachems, powwows, and other Indians who clung to traditional culture were on hand to dissuade or threaten potential defectors. But ultimately the New Englanders defeated themselves by insisting that Indians who made the effort must almost immediately and completely reject their past—and even then the colonists refused, in most cases, to accept the few Indians who met such stern demands. Rejection of the converts rarely came from New England's missionaries and lay leaders but instead from its general populace, who increasingly deplored Indian culture and even the value of Indian existence. As early as 1638 William Bradford observed that "some of the rude and ignorante sorte" objected to the execution of "any English" for killing an Indian.[140] However limited the outcry against fair treatment of the Indians may have been in the early years of settlement, by 1676 it had grown to an appreciable—probably a majority—viewpoint, and by the eighteenth century it drowned such relatively tolerant voices as Experience Mayhew's and Eleazar Wheelock's. And, by Wheelock's time, what had originally been cultural bias (a repugnance toward aliens but acceptance of those who thoroughly assimilated) had turned into racial prejudice (a conviction that some aliens were innately inferior in appearance and character and were thus unredeemable); thereafter the Indian could never be accepted as an Englishman no matter what he did. Ironically, we customarily call Indians "tribal," suggesting an inbred, parochial society with jealously guarded rituals and totems, and refer to the English as a "nation," implying considerable ethnic and cultural heterogeneity and the assimilation of newcomers. In many respects the terms are more appropriately reversed: Indian America welcomed outsiders and freely incorporated them. New English America did not.[141]

Whatever their failures in assimilating people of different beliefs and customs, the New England colonies, like other European outposts throughout the Americas, were too large and aggressive for the natives to ignore even if they had wanted to. Throughout the seventeenth and eighteenth centuries the English presence impinged sharply on the Indians: diseases and wars dramatically reduced their numbers; wars, land sales, migrations, and missionary endeavors drastically revamped their settlement patterns; technological innovations permanently altered their economic and occupational customs; and the efforts of Christian teachers and missionaries made major incursions into their fundamental modes of communication and belief.[142] Northeastern Indian society had never been stagnant, but not until the seventeenth and eighteenth centuries did it undergo cultural revolution. Indian life would never be the same.

Neither would European-American life. The early settlers' intention to transplant the best of European culture and to remain aloof from Indian "barbarity" proved ephemeral. From the outset Indian culture exerted a subtle but profound influence on the newcomers: in language, travel, warfare, food, clothing, entertainment, and many other aspects of American life.[143] As one colonial writer observed, "such is the influ-

ence of this Wilderness on the inhabitants who are born here that it in-
clines them to an *Indian* way of living."[144] In early New England, at least,
very few Indians and even fewer colonists crossed the cultural divide.
On both sides of that divide, however, almost everyone moved closer to
the line.

Appendix A: Sources and Statistics
on New England Captivity Experiences

The careers of 1,641 New Englanders taken captive by Indian, French,
or French-Indian forces between 1675 and 1763 are analyzed in section
III of this essay. For information about 1,606 of those cases, we relied
principally on Coleman's *New England Captives.* We spot-checked Coleman's findings against other sources and found that she was quite thorough for the period after 1688 and that she accurately, if sometimes un-
clearly, reported the available information on the prisoners she studied.
Our survey of major post-1688 captivity narratives unearthed only six
documented cases not included in *New England Captives.*[1]

Coleman was not particularly concerned with captivities that occurred
before 1677, and thus her studies of King Philip's War prisoners were
less complete than of those taken in later conflicts. We therefore added
to our analysis twenty-nine additional King Philip's War captives mentioned in Mary Rowlandson's narrative.[2] In all, forty-two prisoners from
that conflict are mentioned in these two works; although they constitute
most of the documented cases, undoubtedly there were others whose
seizure went unrecorded or about whom some evidence might be found
in local archives.

Captives of the Indians or French mentioned in these sources—
whether or not by name—and whose home was in "Puritan" New England (including present-day Maine but excluding Rhode Island), regardless of where they were taken prisoner, are included in the analysis.
Thus Brinton Hammon, a black New Englander captured in Florida in
1748, is included while James Alexander, a native of New Jersey seized
at Casco Bay, Maine, in 1690, is excluded, as are thirteen other cases
mentioned by Coleman whose homes were outside Puritan New England. Our figures include captives known to have been residents of New
England but whose precise date or place of capture is unknown; many
such cases are recorded, for example, in the Canadian sources Coleman
and Baker consulted. Not included in our calculations are New Englanders killed during an attack on a town or fort or in battle. Those carried
away from the place of capture and later killed by Indians are included,
as are prisoners whose confinement lasted only a few hours or days.
Some individuals were seized more than once; each of their captivities

is tabulated separately. We recorded each case mentioned by Coleman that satisfied these criteria; we scoured other sources less thoroughly and therefore may have missed a few cases of post-1688 captivity.

A computer aided in performing most of the tabulations used in this essay. For each of the 1,641 captives we coded for analysis the following information, if known: sex, age, race, social status (i.e., known free civilian, assumed free civilian, soldier or active militiaman, army officer, seaman or naval officer, servant, or slave), hometown, year and place of capture, identity of initial captors (French, Indian, or French and Indian), last known place of retention (Indian village, French Canadian settlement, Canadian prison, etc.), length of captivity, whether or not torture occurred, and ultimate fate.

Several of the categories listed in the tables and mentioned in the text require some explanation. The captives' fates are distributed among twelve headings: (1) *Exchanged, ransomed, etc.,* includes those prisoners who returned to New England as a result of some formal bargain struck between their captors and either an individual or a government, or who were liberated by English forces. (2) *Returned* indicates that a captive is known to have reappeared in New England after captivity but that how he or she got there is unknown or unclear. (3) *Probably returned,* by contrast, encompasses those captives about whom there is uncertain evidence of an exchange, ransom, or escape. (4) *Returned after staying* is a category in which some arbitrary judgments had to be made: it covers captives who seem voluntarily to have remained with their captors for a time and to have undergone partial transculturation, but who later returned willingly to New England. All who became fluent in French or an Indian language or who converted briefly to Catholicism and who later returned of their own volition to New England are included under this rubric; others are added because of reports that they had acquired Indian characteristics during their captivities, had refused repatriation at some point, or retained a fondness for their captors' ways after their return. (5) *Returned against will* includes captives forcibly returned to New England who would have preferred to live with the French or Indians. These, like those who returned voluntarily after living for a time as an Indian or Canadian, we do not consider to have been cases of complete transculturation. (6) *Escaped* encompasses all who by their own efforts and without the consent of their captors returned to New England. (7) *Died* refers to prisoners who perished either from natural causes or from wounds suffered incidentally during their capture, or who were released or escaped but died before they completed the trip back to New England. (Those who were apparently undergoing transculturation when they died are not included in this classification but are in categories 10 or 11 below.) (8) *Killed by Indians* includes only those prisoners who, after they had been carried away from the place of capture, were purposefully executed, killed during torture, or mur-

dered. (9) *Probably died* denotes uncertain reports of a captive's demise.
(10) *Remained with captors* indicates that the evidence seems conclusive
that the prisoner voluntarily continued to live with the French or Indians rather than to escape or be ransomed or exchanged, and that he
or she apparently died among the adopted people after presumably undergoing considerable transculturation. Evidence of the decision to remain includes, for instance, marriage to a French or Indian spouse, religious conversion, loss of the ability to speak English, or an account of
a transculturated captive's death. (11) *Perhaps remained* includes those
about whom the proof of transculturation is less clear. (12) *Fate unknown*
encompasses only those captives about whose fate absolutely nothing is
recorded in our sources or about whom reports are hopelessly conflicting.

It should be kept in mind that the ethnic identity of the force who
originally seized a captive (Indian, French, or French and Indian) need
not correspond to the ethnic identity of the captors with whom the prisoner spent the last, and usually longest, portion of his or her captivity—
hence the distinction made in the text and in the tables between "captured by" and "last known place of captivity." The latter is more relevant
to the issue of transculturation. Captives frequently changed hands between Indians and their French Canadian allies, French Canadian officials continually attempted to consolidate most Anglo-American captives
under French rather than Indian control, and some New England prisoners escaped or talked their way out of Indian villages and into French
settlements, or vice versa. Nevertheless, even those who thus somewhat
voluntarily exchanged one form of captivity for another were not free
to return to New England without French or Indian permission, and
therefore remained prisoners until they were set free, escaped, or made
the conscious decision to remain. It was the culture of these "last"
captors—at the place where the prisoner observed and possibly grew to
appreciate the way of life in an Indian or French Canadian village—that
presented the New Englander with the strongest prospect of transculturation, not the culture of the initial captors or those with whom he
or she might have sojourned briefly. The initial contact with the raiding party was not without its effects, however; historian James Axtell has
argued strongly that Indian war parties almost immediately began educating Euro-American captives concerning Indian ways.[3] Our findings
suggest the possibility, however, that the initial journey to Canada may
have served more to frighten New Englanders into consenting to stay
with the French than it did to enamor them of Indian culture.

One final methodological note is in order. We divided the captives
studied here into four age-groups: *infant* (under age two), *child* (ages
two to six), *youth* (ages seven to fifteen), and *adult* (age sixteen and
over). These divisions are based on the consensus among recent students of colonial New England childhood that crucial benchmarks in
the child's development came at about age two, when the child shed infant's clothing, completed his or her toilet training, and began to ex-

perience stricter parental discipline; at about age six or seven, when he or she began to wear recognizably adult-style clothes and began formal education, either as a servant or in school; and at about ages sixteen to twenty-one, when he or she completed a gradual entry into the adult world.[4] In many cases included in our analysis the exact ages of captives are unknown. Most of these were clearly adults and were classified as such. All married persons and all marine and military personnel whose ages are unknown were also considered adults, although some were probably under sixteen years of age. Other captives were identified in the sources only as "infant," "child," or "youth," and were tabulated as if they were under age two, ages two to six, or ages seven to fifteen, respectively. Only when there was no clue to the captive's age was he or she classified as "age unknown." If the definition of "youth" were expanded to include captives older than fifteen, as undoubtedly it sometimes was, the proportion of young people—as distinguished from adults—choosing to stay with their captors would be appreciably higher.

Appendix B: Previous Estimates of New English to Indian Transculturation

Scholars have consistently overestimated the number of seventeenth- and eighteenth-century Anglo-American prisoners of war who became substantially Indianized. This tendency often reflects an author's implicit assumptions and the focus of his or her research rather than a concerted attempt to count transculturations. Anthropologists such as John R. Swanton, Erwin H. Ackerknecht, A. Irving Hallowell, and J. Norman Heard are primarily concerned with captives who experienced partial or nearly complete transculturation.[1] While that focus is legitimate, by considering such individuals apart from the larger universe of all Euro-American captives of Indians, their works (especially those of Swanton and Ackerknecht, which dwell on Eunice Williams, Mary Jemison, John Tanner, and a few other colorful cases) leave the impression that transculturation was a typical captivity experience.[2] Heard discusses many more captivities than do most authors: a rough count yields eighty-three sixteenth- through nineteenth-century prisoners, of whom twenty-three lived out their lives with the Indians and thirty-two returned after willingly staying with their captors for some time and acquiring some aspects of Indian culture.[3] But because Heard's interest is in transculturation per se, not in its relative frequency, he makes no attempt to estimate the representativeness of his case studies beyond warning the reader that "the number of captives living out their lives with Indians was probably considerably smaller than the number restored to their white families."[4]

Attempts to determine the number of colonial New England captives who chose to stay with the Indians have been rare; even Coleman apparently made no effort to count them. But two scholars who have pub-lished brief tabulations of parts of the Baker-Coleman data also overes-timate the frequency of transculturation. Richard Slotkin finds in Cole-man's work "some 750 individual captives between 1677 and 1750"; a few lines later, he says these are only those "whose names and fates are known." Of these, according to Slotkin, "no fewer than 60 . . . became Indians outright"; his brief discussion is unexplained and unfootnoted.[5] Our analysis revealed 965 New Englanders captured by French and In-dian forces between 1677 and 1750, of whom only 20 definitely and 17 possibly transculturated in Indian captivity.

A more thorough explication of part of the Baker-Coleman material was made by James Axtell. Extrapolating from his count of 437 New Englanders captured between 1689 and 1713 and discussed in Cole-man's chapter 4, he estimates that "about 600" were probably seized during that period. He finds that "of these, 174 (29 percent) definitely returned to New England," while 146 (25 percent) remained with the French Canadians. Noting that in 1705 the French and the Indians held Anglo-American prisoners in a ratio of five to three, he—mistakenly in our opinion—reasons that a similar ratio of captives must have remained respectively with the French and the Indians. Hence, Axtell concludes, if 25 percent of the captives chose the French Canadian way of life, 15 percent, or 90 of the 600, must have become "full-fledged Indians."[6] We find in Coleman and our other sources 601 New Englanders cap-tured by French and Indian forces between 1689 and 1713, but only 18 of them certainly remained with their Indian captors (9.8 percent of all those who definitely spent the last part of their captivities with Indians and 3 percent of the total number seized between 1689 and 1713). An-other 15 captives perhaps remained with the Indians; thus at most we find evidence of 33 possible transculturations—14.2 percent of the 232 New Englanders who may have last been held by Indians but only 5.5 percent of all 601 captives seized between 1689 and 1713. By contrast, over half of the New Englanders who spent the final part of their cap-tivities with French Canadians definitely remained in Canada.

Notes

PREFACE

1. For introductions to this topic, see Ashley Montagu, *Man's Most Dangerous Myth: The Fallacy of Race*, 3d ed. (New York, 1952); Ashley Montagu, ed., *The Concept of Race* (London, 1964); Ashley Montagu, "The Debate over Race Revisited: An Empirical Investigation," *Phylon* (Mar. 1978); Stephen Jay Gould, *The Mismeasure of Man* (New York, 1981); Richard Lewontin, Steven Rose, and Leon Kamin, eds., *Not in Our Genes* (New York, 1984).

2. H. R. McIlwaine, ed., *Journals of the House of Burgesses of Virginia, 1619–1658/59* (Richmond, Va., 1915), 13.

3. "Relation of Africa, taken out of Master George Sandys his larger discourse . . . ," in Samuel Purchas, *Purchas His Pilgrimes*, 20 vols. (1625; reprint; Glasgow, 1905–7), 6:213.

4. For a brief overview of "race" before the sixteenth century, see Thomas F. Gossett, *Race: The History of an Idea in America* (Dallas, Tex., 1963), chap. 1.

5. Peter Fryer, *Staying Power: The History of Black People in Britain* (London, 1984), 134. Another example of the differences between American and English usage in racial terminology is Fryer's definition of "Black people—by whom I mean Africans and Asians and their descendants" (ibid., [xi]).

6. My principal objection to distinguishing "race prejudice" from "racism" is that it privileges formal statements over other forms of evidence—laws, casual writings, and actions. While I agree with Fryer that no extensive written defense of racism appeared until the ideology came under attack, I maintain that other evidence demonstrates the ideology's existence before those attacks began. In short, I'm leery of distinctions based on kinds of evidence rather than kinds of belief. For a typology similar to Fryer's, see George M. Fredrickson, "Toward a Social Interpretation of the Development of American Racism," in Nathan I. Huggins, Martin Kilson, and Daniel M. Fox, eds., *Key Issues in the Afro-American Experience*, 2 vols. (New York, 1971), 1:240–54.

CHAPTER 1: FROM WHITE MAN TO REDSKIN

1. Jefferson, *Notes on the State of Virginia*, ed. William Peden (1784; reprint, Chapel Hill, N.C., 1955), 59. More than a decade earlier, at least one writer used all three colors in reference to America's inhabitants but not in a single phrase; Bernard Romans, *A Concise Natural History of East and West Florida* (New York, 1775), 37–38. Still earlier, Benjamin Franklin had used similar terms in a single essay but with a different meaning for red; Franklin, "Observations concerning the Increase of Mankind, Peopling of Countries, etc.," in Leonard W. Labaree et al., eds., *The Papers of Benjamin Franklin*, 3 (New Haven, 1961), 234.

2. Works that use one or more racial colors in their titles and deal, at least in part, with the colonial period include William S. Willis, "Divide and Rule: Red, White, and Black in the Southeast," *Journal of Negro History* 48 (1963): 157–76; Gary B. Nash, *Red, White, and Black: The Peoples of Early America* (1974; 2d ed., Englewood Cliffs, N.J., 1982), and "Red, White, and Black: The Origins of Racism in Early America," in Nash and Richard Weiss, eds., *The Great Fear: Race in the Mind of America* (New York, 1970); Wesley Frank Craven, *White, Red, and Black: The Seventeenth-Century Virginian* (Charlottesville, Va., 1971); Neal E. Salisbury, "Red Puritans: The 'Praying Indians' of Massachusetts Bay and John Eliot," *William and Mary Quarterly* [hereafter, *WMQ*] 3d ser., 31 (1974): 27–54; James P. Ronda, "Red and White at the Bench: Indians and the Law in Plymouth Colony, 1620–1691," *Essex Institute Historical Collections* 110 (1974): 200–15; Wilcomb E. Washburn, *Red Man's Land / White Man's Law: A Study of the Past and Present Status of the American Indian* (New York, 1971); Norman J. Heard, *White into Red: A Study of the Assimilation of White Persons Captured by Indians* (Metuchen, N.J., 1973); Dwight W. Hoover, *The Red and the Black* (Chicago, 1976); and Winthrop D. Jordan, *White over Black: American Attitudes toward the Negro, 1550–1812* (Chapel Hill, N.C., 1968). In a few instances, and certainly for Jordan's work, the title is entirely justified by the historical context. But the use of "red" either in titles or in texts is, I contend, inappropriate in works concerning Indian-European relations in colonial America. (Mea culpa, too, in my earlier writings.) In addition to the many authors who refer anachronistically to "reds" and "red men" in writing about the colonial period, most other authors at least call the Europeans "whites," thus implying a fundamental color difference.

3. Europe's essentially dichromatic perception of human color—white and black, with minor intermediate shades—applied to Orientals as well: they, too, were initially seen as white. See, for example, Allesandro Valignano, S.J. (1580), as quoted in P. G. Rogers, *The First Englishman in Japan: The Story of Will Adams* (London, 1956), 17–18; and John Saris, *The Voyages of Captain John Saris*, Hakluyt Society Publications, 2d ser., 5 (London, 1900), 84. Also see Hiroshi Wagatsuma, "The Social Perception of Skin Color in Japan," in John Hope Franklin, ed., *Color and Race* (Boston, 1968).

In this essay I generally use "Anglo-Americans" rather than "European-Americans" (or "Euro-Americans") because English culture predominated in British America and subsequently in the early United States and because I have drawn primarily on English and American sources, although those sources often include translations from Continental tongues. I find no evidence that non-English colonists or their descendants had different perceptions or terminology; there seems to have been a European consensus on color perception. I cite

Spanish, Dutch, and Swedish sources passim; for French Canadian sources, see note 24, below.

4. Winthrop Jordan, with whom I agree on almost every point and to whose work all students of early race relations are deeply indebted, erred, I believe, in arguing that colonial Americans saw Indians as lighter than they "really" were; *White over Black*, chap. 6. It is more likely that both modern historians and the general public—perhaps because of racial assumptions they cannot easily overcome—are determined to view the Indians as darker than they are. But the reality of color is more subjective than objective: how the Indians' color is judged in comparison to the Europeans' and Africans' was—and is now—largely a matter of social perceptions, which can change to meet the psychological needs of the observer. For useful insights into color and racism, see Franklin, *Color and Race*, especially the essays by Kenneth J. Gergen, Harold R. Isaacs, and C. Eric Lincoln. A serious misunderstanding of seventeenth-century color perception is G. E. Thomas's "Puritans, Indians, and the Concept of Race," *New England Quarterly* 48 (1975): 3–27, which concludes, "No matter how hard the [seventeenth-century] Puritan tried to transform the Indian or how completely the Indian conformed, the cause was ultimately hopeless because the Indian could never become white." Although Thomas's article is unprofessional on several counts, it is occasionally and mistakenly cited as authoritative.

5. A recent wide-ranging analysis of slavery in the Western world concludes that "patterns of both race relations and prejudice are determined by power relationships" rather than by deep-seated racial bias. Such an interpretation, I believe, applies only to a minor extent in British America and seriously underestimates the importance of color bias among European-Americans. See William McKee Evans, "From the Land of Canaan to the Land of Guinea: The Strange Odyssey of the 'Sons of Ham,' " *American Historical Review* 85 (1980): 15–43.

6. Jordan, *White over Black*, chap. 1, and Eldred D. Jones, *The Elizabethan Image of Africa* (Charlottesville, Va., 1971). The first wave of English settlers used similar pejorative terminology in referring to Africans (as, of course, did later generations). For further discussion of early English and American beliefs about Africans, see chapters 6 and 7 in this volume.

7. Thevet, *The New Founde Worlde* . . . , trans. T[homas] Hacket (London, 1568), ff. 25, 13v; and Abbot, *A Briefe Description of the Whole Worlde* (London, 1599), sig. C7. The belief that North Africans were considerably lighter than those on the rest of the continent is graphically demonstrated on an illustrated map reproduced from Wilem Janszoon Blaeu, *Appendix Theatri A. Ortelii et Atlantis G. Mercatoris* . . . (Amsterdam, 1631). A version of the map is appended to Jones, *Elizabethan Image of Africa*.

8. Emilio M. Martínez Amador, *English-Spanish and Spanish-English Dictionary* (Barcelona, 1945), 699; E. Roubard, ed., *A French and English Dictionary* (London, n.d.), 369; *Nieuw Englelsch Woordenbock*, pt. 2 (Zutphen, n.d.), 586; and Jordan, *White over Black*, 4–11.

9. [R. Wilkinson], *Lot's Wife: A Sermon Preached at Paules Crosse* (London, 1607), 42.

10. Peyton, *The Glasse of Time, in the First Age* (London, 1620; reprint, New York, 1886), 142.

11. *The Complete Works of Captain John Smith (1580–1631)*, ed. Philip L. Barbour, 3 vols. (Chapel Hill, N.C., 1986), 1:327, 2:406.

12. Although "Indians" was by far the most common appellation, a few writers eschewed it completely. Sir William Alexander, for example, used "savages," "natives," and "Americans," and Abbot simply referred to "the inhabitants," "the old people," "the people of . . . ," and occasionally "the Americans." Alexander, *An Encouragement to Colonies* (London, 1624); and Abbot, *Briefe Description of the Whole Worlde.*

13. Other geographic terms, of course, were also used for Indians in specific localities or regions: Floridians, Mexicans, Brazilians, and the like. In the eighteenth century, "Americans" was frequently used by European biologists and occasionally by political writers to distinguish American natives from transplanted Europeans. "Virginians" was often applied to Indians in the early decades of the seventeenth century (during Pocahontas's visit to England in 1616–17, a contemporary referred to her as "the Virginian woman") but rarely thereafter.

14. Columbus, *The Journal of Christopher Columbus*, trans. Cecil Jane and L. A. Vigneras, Hakluyt Society Publications, extra ser., 38 (London, 1960), 24–25.

15. Ralegh, *The Discoveries of the Large, Rich, and Bewtiful Empire of Guiana* (London, 1596), 95. For another description of the Indians of the North American coast as brown, see Peter Lindström, *Geographia Americana, with an Account of the Delaware Indians, Based on Surveys and Notes Made in 1654–1656*, trans. and ed. Amandus Johnson (Philadelphia, 1925), 191.

16. Thomas Champion, *Somerset's Masque* (1613), as quoted in Allardyce Nicoll, *Stuart Masques and the Renaissance Stage* (London, 1938), 192; and Peyton, *The Glasse of Time*, 142. An early suggestion that American Indians differed in pigmentation from other peoples was offered by Samuel Purchas in 1613: "The tawney Moore, black Negro, duskie Libyan, Ash-coloured Indian, olive-coloured American, should with the whiter European become *one sheepe-fold*"; [Purchas], *Purchas His Pilgrimage* (London, 1613), 546. Although he retained this passage in subsequent editions, Purchas's other writings indicate his acceptance of the prevailing belief that American natives were innately white.

17. Bigges, *A Summarie and True Discourse of Sir Francis Drake's West Indian Voyage* (London, 1589; reprint, New York, 1969), 20; and [Percy], "Observations Gathered out of a Discourse of the Plantation of the Southerne Colonie in Virginia . . . ," in Samuel Purchas, comp., *Hakluytus Posthumus: or, Purchas His Pilgrimes*, 4 (London, 1625): 1686, and reprinted in Philip L. Barbour, ed., *The Jamestown Voyages under the First Charter, 1606–1609*, Hakluyt Society Publications, 2d ser., 136–37 (Cambridge, 1969), 1:130.

18. Strachey, *The Historie of Travell into Virginia Britania* (1612), ed. Louis B. Wright and Virginia Freund, Hakluyt Society Publications, 2d ser., 103 (London, 1953), 71; and White, "A Briefe Relation of the Voyage unto Maryland," in Clayton Colman Hall, ed., *Narratives of Early Maryland, 1633–1684*, Original Narratives of Early American History (New York, 1910), 42.

19. Davies, *Nosce Teipsum . . . Hymes of Astrae in Acrosticke Verse* (London, 1622), 40. The reason for the attribution of red skins to East Indians is obscure. Assuming that East Indians looked darker than American Indians but lighter than most Africans, the color descriptions make logical if not literal sense. Davies may have drawn his inspiration from a work of Philippe de Mornay, translated into English in 1581, which was less specific but employed a wider spectrum. The sun, according to Mornay, "maketh some folks whyte, some black, some read and some Tawny, . . . the Ethiopian blacke, and the Scotte yellowish." Presumably, Mornay included the American Indians among the tawnies. Mornay, *A*

Woorke concerning the Trewnesse of the Christian Religion, trans. Sir P[hilip] Sidney and A. Golding (London, 1587), 21–22.

20. [Ingram], "The Relation of David Ingram," in David Beers Quinn, ed., *The Voyages and Colonizing Enterprises of Sir Humphrey Gilbert,* Hakluyt Society Publications, 2d ser., 84–85 (London, 1940), 2:285; Espejo, *New Mexico; Otherwise the Voiage of Anthony of Espejo . . . in the Year 1583* (London, 1587), 191; and Blundeville, M. *Blundeville His Exercises, containing Sixe Treatises . . .* (London, 1594), f. 262v.

21. Hakluyt, *Divers Voyages Touching the Discoverie of America* (London, 1582; facsimile edn., Amsterdam, 1967), 86, 46, 50, 53. This edition has bracketed page numbers for the reader's convenience (the original carries only signature letters); an accompanying volume, David B. Quinn's *Richard Hakluyt, Editor,* has an index by Alison Quinn that gives modern locations for the various tribes described in Hakluyt's narratives.

22. Gómara, "Of the Colour of the Indians," in Edward Arber, ed., *The First Three English Books on America, (?1511–) 1555 A.D.* (Birmingham, 1885), 338, 345. Gómara's account of Indian color gained new prominence when it was reprinted and placed on the opening pages of Pietro Martire d'Anghiera et al., *The History of Travayle in the West and East Indies . . . ,* trans. Richard Eden and Richard Willes (London, 1577).

23. Best, *A True Discourse of the late voyages of Discoverie, for the finding of a passage to Cathaya . . .* (London, 1578), 28.

24. Laudonnière, *A Notable Historie containing Foure Voyages Made by Certayne French Captayens unto Florida,* trans. R[ichard] H[akluyt] (London, 1587), 4; and Linschoten, *His Discours of Voyages into ye Easte & West Indies* (London, 1598), 220, 224. For French Canadian statements that the Indians were innately white, see W. L. Grant, ed., *Voyages of Samuel de Champlain, 1604–1618,* Original Narratives of Early American History (New York, 1907), 142; Marc Lescarbot, *History of New France,* trans. and ed. W. L. Grant, 3 vols. (Toronto, 1907–14), 3:138–39; and Reuben Gold Thwaites, ed., *The Jesuit Relations and Allied Documents: Travels and Explorations of the Jesuit Missionaries in New France, 1610–1791,* 73 vols. (Cleveland, 1896–1901; reprint, New York, 1959), 1:279, 2:73, 38:241, and 63:265. Compare ibid., 4:205; and Chrestien Le Clercq, *New Relation of Gaspesia, with the Customs and Religion of the Gaspesian Indians,* trans. and ed. William F. Ganong, Champlain Society Publications, no. 5 (Toronto, 1910; reprint, New York, 1968), 241.

25. Pring, "A Voyage Set out from the Citie of Bristoll . . . for the Discoverie of the North Part of Virginia, in the Yeere 1603 . . . ," in Samuel Purchas, comp., *Hakluytus Posthumus: or, Purchas His Pilgrimes,* 20 vols. (Glasgow, 1905–7), 18:325; and Strachey, *Historie of Travell into Virginia Britania,* 70.

26. *Works of Captain John Smith,* ed. Barbour, 1:160; [Gabriel Archer (?)], "A Brief description of the People," in Barbour, ed., *Jamestown Voyages under the First Charter,* 1:103; and Samuel Purchas, "Of Virginia," in his *Purchas His Pilgrimage* (1613; London, 1626), 844.

27. Alsop, *A Character of the Province of Maryland* (London, 1666), in Hall, ed., *Narratives of Early Maryland,* 366; and Penn to the Committee of the Free Society of Traders of the Province, residing in London [August 16, 1683], in Albert Cook Myers, ed., *Narratives of Early Pennsylvania, West New Jersey, and Delaware, 1630–1707,* Original Narratives of Early American History (New York, 1912; reprint, 1959), 230. Penn also likened the Indians' complexion to an Italian's.

28. Wood, *New Englands Prospect* (London, 1634), 54–55; Williams, *Key into the Language of America* (London, 1643), 52; and Morton, *New English Canaan* (London, 1637), 32. Also see [William Morrell], "Morrell's Poem on New England," *Massachusetts Historical Society Collections*, 1st ser., 1 (1792): 135; and Thomas Lechford, "Plain Dealing: or, Newes from New-England," ibid., 3d ser., 3 (1833): 103.

29. For a general discussion of the Lost Tribes theory, see Don Cameron Allen, *The Legend of Noah: Renaissance Rationalism in Art, Science, and Letters* (Urbana, Ill., 1949), 125–28. For Anglo-American subscribers to the theory, see, for example, Henry Whitfield, *The Light Appearing More and More towards the Perfect Day*, in *Massachusetts Historical Society Collections*, 3d ser., 4 (1834): 72–74, 93–95, 127–28; Penn to the Free Society of Traders, 236–37; and Williams, *A Key into the Language of America*, ed. John J. Teunissen and Evelyn J. Hinz (Detroit, 1973), 85–86. For the European side of the search for Jewish parallels, see Cecil Roth, *A Life of Menasseh ben Israel—Rabbi, Printer, and Diplomat* (Philadelphia, 1934); and Ronald Sanders, *Lost Tribes and Promised Lands: The Origins of American Racism* (Boston, 1978), esp. 363–72. See also chapter 2 in this volume.

30. Settle, *A True Reporte of the Laste Voyage into the West and Northwest Regions, etc., 1577* (London, 1577), sig. C8; Morton, *New English Canaan*, 32; and Crashaw, *A Sermon Preached in London before the Right Honourable Lord La Warre . . .* (London, 1610), sig. E2. Crashaw thought West Indians considerably darker than Virginian Indians. An early eighteenth-century observer declared that Indians along the mid-Atlantic coast were born as white as Spaniards and Portuguese; Ann Maury, *Memoirs of a Huguenot Family* (New York, 1853), 350.

31. Strachey, *Historie of Travell into Virginia Britania*, 71, 88, 112, 104, 77. Strachey was less impressed than most of this contemporaries by Indian physiognomy, but he was quick to add that it was "nothing so unsightly as the Moores"; ibid. 71. More representative of seventeenth-century European judgment was a French description of the Indians in Canada as "brown, tawny, and swarthy. . . . Their colour, however, does not lessen at all the natural beauty of the features of their faces." Le Clercq, *New Relation of Gaspesia*, 241. A distinction should be drawn between armchair explorers in Europe, who had little if any contact with Indians, and actual explorers, who closely observed the Indians. The latter's descriptions are generally more favorable than are the former's. Both, however, usually praised Indian physique and physiognomy. For recent studies of early English writings on North American Indians, see H. C. Porter, *The Inconstant Savage: England and the North American Indian, 1500–1600* (London, 1979); Karen Ordahl Kupperman, *Settling with the Indians: The Meeting of English and Indian Cultures in America, 1580–1640* (Totowa, N.J., 1980); and the works cited in n. 68 below.

32. Cuningham, *The Cosmographical Glasse, Conteinyng the Principles of Cosmographie, Geographie, Hydrographie, or Navigation* (London, 1559), 185, 201.

33. Best, *A True Discourse of the Late Voyage of Discoverie*, 3d pagination: 51, 62; d'Anghiera et al., *History of Travayle in the West and East Indies*, f. 458v; and Abbot, *A Briefe Description of the Whole Worlde*, sig. E2.

34. Rolfe to Thomas Dale, 1613, in Ralphe Hamor, *A True Discourse of the Present State of Virginia* (London, 1615), 64; and King James, *A Counter-Blaste to Tobacco* (London, 1604), sig. B2.

35. For examples of comparisons between Indians and ancient Britons, see Thomas Hariot, *A Briefe and True Reporte of the New Found Land of Virginia* (Frankfort, 1590), sig. G1; and Crashaw, *A Sermon Preached in London*, sig. C4v. Also see

the paintings and discussions of ancient Picts and Britons in Paul H. Hulton and David B. Quinn, eds., *The American Drawings of John White*, 2 vols. (London, 1964). For further discussion of this point see chapter 2 in this volume.

36. Best, *A True Discourse of the Late Voyage of Discoverie*, 63; Peckham, *A True Reporte . . . of the Newfound Landes . . .* (London, 1583), sig. B4; E. G. R. Taylor, ed., *The Original Writings and Correspondence of the Two Richard Hakluyts*, Hakluyt Society Publications, 2d ser., 76–77 (London, 1935), 2:211, 339; and Crashaw, *A Sermon Preached in London*, sig. C3.

37. Field, *A Woman Is a Weather-Cocke* (London, 1612), sig. D3.

38. Wood, *New Englands Prospect* (1634 edn.), 54–55, and *New England's Prospect*, ed. Rogers (Boston, 1764), 94n.

39. Franklin, "Observation concerning the Increase of Mankind," 234.

40. Carver, *Travels through the Interior Parts of North America in the Years 1766, 1767, and 1768* (London, 1778), 223–24.

41. [Hunter], *Quebec to Carolina in 1785–1786: Being the Travel Diary and Observations of Robert Hunter, Jr., . . .* , ed. Louis B. Wright and Marion Tinling (San Marino, Calif., 1943), 36; and Filson, *The Discovery, Settlement, and Present State of Kentucke* (Wilmington, Del., 1784), 98–99.

42. Mittelberger, *Journal to Pennsylvania*, ed. Oscar Handlin and John Clive (Cambridge, Mass., 1960), 63. Mittelberger described the Indians' acquired color as "black-yellow."

43. Adair, *The History of the American Indians . . .* (London, 1775; reprint, New York, 1968), 1–4.

44. [John Clayton (?)], "An Account of the Indians in Virginia," ed. Stanley Pargellis, *WMQ*, 3d ser., 16 (1959): 230; Archdale, *A New Description of . . . Carolina* (London, 1707), 7; and Lawson, *A New Voyage to Carolina* (London, 1709), 171. Also see John Brickell, *The Natural History of North Carolina* (Dublin, 1737), 294–95. Brickell's volume is almost entirely plagiarized from Lawson's *New Voyage*.

45. [Byrd], *The Prose Works of William Byrd of Westover: Narratives of a Colonial Virginian*, ed. Louis B. Wright (Cambridge, Mass., 1966), 160–61, 221–22; Gookin, *Historical Collections of the Indians in New England* (Boston, 1792; facsimile reprint edn., New York, 1972), 4; and Lee to Nehemiah Grew, 1690, in "Letters of Samuel Lee and Samuel Sewall Relating to New England and the Indians," *Transactions of the Colonial Society of Massachusetts*, 14 (1911–13): 147. Also see Carl Bridenbaugh, ed., "Patrick M'Roberts' Tour through Part of the North Province of America," *Pennsylvania Magazine of History and Biography* 59 (1935): 174.

46. E. B. O'Callaghan, ed., *Laws and Ordinances of New Netherland, 1638–1674* (Albany, N.Y., 1868), 131. The original Dutch manuscript is in the New York State Archives, Albany. The rarity of Dutch use of *blanck* in Indian contexts is attested by Charles Gehring of the New Netherland Project; personal communication, 2 November 1981. On Dutch officials who went from Africa to America, see Jordan, *White over Black*, 172–73.

47. "Arthur Barlowe's Discourse of the First Voyages," in David Beers Quinn, ed., *The Roanoke Voyages, 1584–1590*, Hakluyt Society Publications, 2d ser., 104–5 (London, 1955), 1:102, 111–12; "Ralph Lane's Discourse on the First Colony," ibid., 261; *Journal of George Fox*, ed. John L. Nickalls (Cambridge, 1952), 624. See also Nicolaes van Wassenaer, "Historisch Verhael," in J. Franklin Jameson, ed., *Narratives of New Netherland, 1609–1664*, Original Narratives of Early American History (New York, 1909), 85.

48. John D. Cushing, ed., *The Earliest Printed Laws of South Carolina, 1692–1734*, 2 vols. (Wilmington, Del., 1978), 1:118, *The Earliest Printed Laws of New Jersey, 1703–1722* (Wilmington, Del., 1978), 22, *The Laws of the Province of Maryland* (Wilmington, Del., 1978), 199, and *The Earliest Printed Laws of the Province of Georgia, 1755–1770*, 2 vols. (Wilmington, Del., 1978), 1:15; Samuel Hazard, ed., *Minutes of the Provincial Council of Pennsylvania* . . . , 16 vols. (Philadelphia, 1838–53), 4:281; Mather, *The Negro Christianized* (Boston, 1706), 24; Donald H. Kent, ed., *Early American Indian Documents: Treaties and Laws, 1607–1789, Pennsylvania and Delaware Treaties*, 2 vols. (Washington, 1979, 1984), 1:291, 375, 404, 428; and Lawson, *New Voyage to Carolina*, 233. The carryover of color terminology from black-white to Indian-European contexts is illustrated by the writings of an early eighteenth-century Carolinian who often used "whites" in contrast to Africans and occasionally in contrast to Indians. In a few instances, he referred to "white, black, & Indians." [Francis Le Jau], *The Carolina Chronicle of Dr. Francis Le Jau, 1706–1717*, ed. Frank J. Klingberg (Berkeley and Los Angeles, 1956), 22, 39, 155.

49. Bartram, *Observations on the Inhabitants, Climate, Soil . . . in His Travels from Pennsylvania to Onondago* (London, 1751; reprint Rochester, N.Y., 1895), 22, 57, 77; and Jefferson, *Notes on the State of Virginia*, 59–60, 185, 186. For other post-1750 uses of "whites" in Indian-European contexts, see, for example, Sylvester K. Stevens and Donald H. Kent, eds., *Wilderness Chronicles of Northwestern Pennsylvania* (Harrisburg, Pa., 1941), 236, 268, 287, 289. Indian uses of "whites" and "white men" proliferated in the late eighteenth and early nineteenth centuries, judging from the recorded speeches of the Delaware Prophet, Logan, Cornplanter, Handsome Lake, and others. For example, see Anthony F. C. Wallace, *The Death and Rebirth of the Seneca* (New York, 1969), 120, 124, 133, 223, 224, 241, 265, 299.

50. Lawrence W. Leder, ed., *The Livingston Indian Records, 1666–1723* (Harrisburg, Pa., 1956), 115; Kent, ed., *Pennsylvania and Delaware Treaties* 2:96; Bartram, *Observations on the Inhabitants*, 22; Peter Force, ed., *American Archives . . . : A Documentary History of . . . the North American Colonies*, 4th ser., 2 (1774): 842; and "Extract of the Minutes of a Congress with the Chiefs of the Six Nations," 17 April 1773, in Edmund B. O'Callaghan, ed., *Documentary History of the State of New York*, 4 vols. (Albany, 1849–51), 2:580. During the eighteenth century, Indian myths about their origins and early history often included white-skinned deities or invaders; see, for example, Wallace, *Death and Rebirth of the Seneca*, esp. 242–48. Also see Wallace, ed., "Halliday Jackson's Journal to the Seneca Indians, 1798–1800," *Pennsylvania History* 19 (1952): 117–47, 325–49.

51. Godwyn, *The Negro's & Indians Advocate* (London, 1680), 4. Cotton Mather was especially fond of using "tawny" as a noun rather than as an adjective, usually when describing Indian military activities. See, for example, his *Magnalia Christi Americana: or, The Ecclesiastical History of New-England . . .* (London, 1702), bk. 7, p. 87, *Good Fetch'd Out of Evill: A Collection of Memorables Relating to Our Captives* (Boston, 1706), 38, and *The Negro Christianized: An Essay to Excite and Assist That Good Work* (Boston, 1706), 24.

52. Mather, "A Brand Pluck'd Out of the Burning," Mather Family Papers, American Antiquarian Society, box 6, folder 6, p. 3, printed with minor variations in George Lincoln Burr, ed., *Narratives of the Witchcraft Cases, 1648–1706*, Original Narratives of Early American History (New York, 1914), 261. If the "Indian color" designation came from Mercy Short rather than from Mather, it prob-

ably stemmed from her brief captivity by Indians in 1690—an experience that might well have encouraged her to associate Indians and devils. On such associations generally in the Puritan mind, see William S. Simmons, "Cultural Bias in New England Puritan Perceptions of Indians", *WMQ*, 3d ser., 38 (1981): 56–72.

53. For Gooch's letters, see Emory G. Evans, ed., "A Question of Complexion: Documents concerning the Negro and the Franchise in Eighteenth-Century Virginia," *Virginia Magazine of History and Biography* 71 (1963): 411–15. (My interpretation of Gooch's statements differs appreciably from that of Evans.) The Virginia statute of 1705 is in William Waller Hening, comp., *The Statutes at Large; Being a Collection of the Laws of Virginia, from the First Session . . .* , 3 (Richmond, Va., 1815): 252.

54. A. Leon Higginbotham Jr., *In the Matter of Color: Race and the American Legal Process—The Colonial Period* (New York, 1978), 122, 123, 127, 129, 169, 204; Hening, *The Statutes at Large*, 86–88; *A Collection of All the Acts of Assembly, Now in Force, in the Colony of Virginia* (Williamsburg, Va., 1733), 222–23; and John D. Cushing, ed., *The Earliest Laws of North Carolina, 1669–1751*, 2 vols. (Wilmington, Del., 1977), 1:130, 2:65. Among the few laws in the seventeenth century that commonly classed Indians with blacks were proscriptions on militia service.

55. [Sewall], *The Diary of Samuel Sewall, 1674–1729*, ed. M. Halsey Thomas, 2 vols. (New York, 1973), 1:532. Almon Wheeler Lauber stated that Massachusetts outlawed European marriages to Indians in 1692, and subsequent authors have relied on his testimony. Lauber cited no source, however, and I have not been able to find such an act in the existing records. Lauber, *Indian Slavery in Colonial Times within the Present Limits of the United States* (New York, 1913), 253. For an argument that, despite some restrictive legislation, Indians were not generally subjected to the same proscriptions as blacks, see Jordan, *White over Black*, 163. I concur, but more important in early eighteenth-century legislation is the trend toward equating the two groups. Moreover, champions of Indian-European miscegenation were scarce in the eighteenth century and did not practice what they preached. Symptomatically, perhaps, one of the most frequently cited voices for intermarriage, Robert Beverley in his *History and Present State of Virginia* of 1705, deleted such advocacy in his edition of 1722. Compare Beverley, *The History and Present State of Virginia* (London, 1705), ed. Louis B. Wright (Chapel Hill, N.C., 1947), 38, with the corresponding page of the edition of 1722, which does not contain the critical paragraph.

56. *A Collection of All the Acts of . . . Virginia*, 220; Higginbotham, *In the Matter of Color*, 169; and Cushing, *Earliest Printed Laws of the Province of Georgia*, 2:276. As early as 1696, South Carolina, borrowing directly from a Barbadian law, included Indians in its definition of slaves: "Governor Archdale's Lawes," Department of Archives and History, Columbia, S.C.

57. A. S. Batchellor, ed., *Laws of New Hampshire*, 2 (Concord, 1913): 138–39; and *A Report of the Record Commissioners for the City of Boston, Containing the Boston Records from 1700 to 1728* (Boston, 1883), 173–75.

58. Otis, *The Rights of the British Colonies Asserted and Proved* (Boston, 1764), 24; Crèvecoeur, *Letters from an American Farmer* (New York, 1957), 39; and Jay, *The Federalist*, no. 2, ed. Jacob E. Cooke (Middletown, Conn., 1961), 9. The second edition of Crèvecoeur's *Letters* (London, 1783) differs from the first edition, and almost all subsequent editions, in stating that the American "is *neither* an European, *nor* the descendant of an European" (italics added); the essential message is, however, the same: that Americans are a blend of European stocks.

59. Although Britain's imperial and colonial governments were uneven and unpredictable in their defense of Indian rights in the seventeenth century, most passed laws against abuse of Indians and made at least sporadic attempts to enforce them. For a complex combination of reasons, Pennsylvania's record on this score is undoubtedly the best, early New England's a distant second best, and Virginia's clearly the worst. Historians are deeply divided on the relative merits of early Indian policies, but most would agree, I believe, that seventeenth-century colonial courts were more likely to punish Euro-American transgressors against Indians than were their eighteenth-century counterparts.

60. Thorpe and Lord Baltimore have received relatively little attention from historians of Indian-European culture contact, the former because the information is scarce, the latter because Maryland's early ethnic history has been largely overlooked. Penn has fared far better, drawing frequent (and usually uncritical) praise for his attitudes. Winslow and Mayhew have figured prominently in historical debates over the Puritans' Indian policies; see note 69, below. For an argument that the degree of fairness in Puritan court decisions depended on expediency and ethnocentricity, see Lyle Koehler, "Red-White Power Relations, and Justice in the Courts of Seventeenth-Century New England," *American Indian Culture and Research Journal*, 3, no. 4 (1979): 1–31.

61. Franklin to Richard Jackson, 11 February 1764, in Labaree et al., eds., *Papers of Benjamin Franklin*, 11:76–78; and Johnson to Henry Conway, 28 June 1766, in E. B. O'Callaghan and Berthod Fernow, eds., *Documents Relative to the Colonial History of . . . New York*, 15 vols. (Albany, N.Y., 1856–87), 7:835–36.

62. On the proposed Virginia College, see Robert Hunt Land, "Henrico and Its College," *WMQ*, 2d ser., 18 (1938): 453–98. The Harvard College charter of 1650, which committed the institution "to the Education of the English, & Indian Youth of this Country," is reprinted in *Harvard College Records* (*Colonial Society of Massachusetts Publications*, 15 [1925]), 40–42; Harvard's Indian college is described in Samuel Eliot Morison, *Harvard College in the Seventeenth Century*, 2 vols. (Cambridge, Mass., 1936), 1: chap. 17.

63. David Crosby to Wheelock, 4 November 1767, Dartmouth College Library, Hanover, N.H., Papers of Eleazar Wheelock, WP 767604.1; Wheelock to Dennys de Berdt, 4 May 1761, ibid., WP 761304.1; Joseph Johnson to Wheelock, 20 April 1768, in James Dow McCallum, ed., *The Letters of Eleazar Wheelock's Indians* (Hanover, N.H., 1932), 131; and Johnson to Wheelock, 4 December 1774, ibid., 183. On Wheelock's educational and racial views, see James Axtell, "Dr. Wheelock's Little Red School," chap. 4 of his *The European and the Indian: Essays in the Ethnohistory of Colonial North America* (New York, 1981).

64. Hutchinson, *The History of the Colony of Massachusetts-Bay . . .* , 1 (Boston, 1765; reprint, New York, 1972): 283; J. Leitch Wright Jr., *The Only Land They Knew: The Tragic Story of the American Indians in the Old South* (New York, 1981), chap. 6.

65. For an argument that the English mind was especially susceptible to seeing the Indians—or anyone—as untrustworthy, see Karen Ordahl Kupperman, "English Perceptions of Treachery, 1583–1640: The Case of the American 'Savages,'" *Historical Journal* 20 (1977): 263–87.

66. Early imperialistic views of America include Crashaw, *Sermon Preached in London*; [Robert Johnson], *Nova Britannia: Offering Most Excellent Fruits by Planting in Virginia* (London, 1609); and Taylor, *Writings and Correspondence of the Two Richard Hakluyts*, 1:118, and 2:334, 502–3. For the younger Hakluyt on "gentleness," see ibid., 2: 503.

67. On the Roanoke experience, see Quinn, *The Roanoke Voyages, 1584–1590*, 1:270–72, 281–82, 284–88. For the most thorough discussion of the Lost Colony's fate, see David B. Quinn, *Set Fair for Roanoke: Voyages and Colonies, 1584–1606* (Chapel Hill, N.C., 1985), chap. 19.

68. On early Indian-English relations in Virginia, see Bernard Sheehan, *Savagism and Civility: Indians and Englishmen in Colonial Virginia* (Cambridge, 1980); Edmund S. Morgan, *American Slavery, American Freedom: The Ordeal of Colonial Virginia* (New York, 1975), esp. chaps. 2–6; J. Frederick Fausz, "The Powhatan Uprising of 1622: A Historical Study of Ethnocentrism and Culture Contact" (Ph.D. dissertation, College of William and Mary, 1977); and chapter 5 of this book. Significantly, at this early stage of hostilities, Anglo-Americans did not apply color terminology. Even Edward Waterhouse, the most vitriolic of the massacre historians, described the Indians as "naked, tanned, deformed Savages"; Susan Myra Kingsbury, ed., *The Records of the Virginia Company of London*, 4 vols. (Washington D.C., 1906–35), 3:557.

69. Indian affairs in early New England have been seen from widely divergent perspectives. Compare Alden T. Vaughan, *New England Frontier: Puritans and Indians, 1620–1675*, 3d ed. (Norman, Okla., 1995) with Francis Jennings, *The Invasion of America: Indians, Colonialism, and the Cant of Conquest* (Chapel Hill, N.C., 1975), pt. 2, and Richard Drinnon, *Facing West: The Metaphysics of Indian-Hating and Empire Building* (New York, 1980), pt. 1.

70. The history of military conflict is traced in a number of secondary studies, most notably in Douglas Edward Leach, *Arms for Empire: A Military History of the British Colonies in North America, 1607–1763* (New York, 1973); Howard H. Peckham, *The Colonial Wars, 1689–1762* (Chicago, 1964); and John E. Ferling, *A Wilderness of Miseries: War and Warriors in Early America* (Westport, Conn., 1980). For Pennsylvania's shift from peaceful relations to frequent hostilities, see Francis Paul Jennings, "Miquon's Passing: Indian-European Relations in Colonial Pennsylvania, 1674–1755" (Ph.D. dissertation, University of Pennsylvania, 1965), pt. 4. After 1755, the pace of conflict quickened.

71. Purchas, *Hakluytus Posthumus; or, Purchas His Pilgrimes*, 19: 231; and John Boneil, *His Majesties Gracious Letter to the Earle of South-Hampton . . .* (London, 1622), 26.

72. Benjamin Tompson, *New Englands Crisis* (Boston, 1676), 19.

73. Eliot's *Late and Further Manifestation of the Progress of the Gospell amongst the Indians* (London, 1655) is reprinted in *Massachusetts Historical Society Collections*, 3d ser., 4 (1834): 261–87. The anonymous tract appeared in Boston in 1675.

74. Mather, *Souldiers Counselled and Comforted: A Discourse Delivered unto Some Part of the Forces Engaged in the Just War of New England against the Northern and Eastern Indians* (Boston, 1689), 28; Julian P. Boyd, ed., *The Papers of Thomas Jefferson*, 1 (Princeton, N.J., 1950): 431; and J. D. F. Smyth, *A Tour of the United States of America*, 2 vols. (London, 1784), 1:345–46.

75. On the tendency to stress differences rather than similarities, see Margaret T. Hogden, *Early Anthropology in the Sixteenth and Seventeenth Centuries* (Philadelphia, 1964), 196–201. Despite virulent English antipathy toward the Irish during the same period, however, the Irishman's whiteness was incontrovertible; hence, the English could not perceive of him as dark-skinned. Moreover, the Irishman seldom stained or painted his skin, as the Indians did, so that the outward appearance of the former remained white, of the latter tawny or red. But note the implications of the epithet "black Irishman."

76. Mather, *Fair Weather: or, Considerations to Dispel the Clouds, and Allay the Storms of Discontent* ... (Boston, 1692), 86, and *Military Duties, Recommended to an Artillery Company, at Their Election of Officers* ... (Boston, 1687), 22; and Henry William Dwight to Theodore Sedgwick, 18 February 1779, Massachusetts Historical Society, Boston, Sedgwick Papers.

77. Smith to Ichabod Smith, 1699, in Helen Evertson Smith, *Colonial Days and Ways, as Gathered from Family Papers* (New York, 1900), 50.

78. There is no way to measure precisely the number of anglicized Indians, but by all accounts it was small. For an attempt to compute the number in New England, see chapter 10 in this volume. On the importance of language to early European imperialists, see Stephen J. Greenblatt, "Learning to Curse: Aspects of Linguistic Colonialism in the Sixteenth Century," in Fredi Chiappelli, ed., *First Images of America: The Impact of the New World on the Old*, 2 (Berkeley and Los Angeles, 1976): 561–80.

79. Franklin to Peter Collinson, 9 May 1753, in Labaree et al., *Papers of Benjamin Franklin*, 4:481.

80. Wood, *New England's Prospect*, ed. Rogers, 94. Belief in Indian inferiority—*in person* as well as in culture—did not always go hand in hand with a perception of Indians as inherently tawny or red, but the correlation is high. One could argue endlessly over a list of European-Americans who believed the Indians to be their potential equals (after a cultural change), but a consensus could probably be reached on William Penn, Roger Williams, John Eliot, and James Adair; by contrast, *racial* prejudice seems to underlie the attitudes of Nathaniel Rogers, Bernard Romans, and the essayists in *DeBow's Review* (see below). Thomas Jefferson is, as always, eminently arguable. Compare Jordan, *White over Black*, esp. 453, 477–81, and Drinnon, *Facing West*, esp. 78–116. On this point, I find Drinnon more convincing than Jordan. Most of Jefferson's biographers have lauded his attitude toward Indians.

81. [Fortescue], *The Works of Sir John Fortescue, Knight, Chief Justice of England* ... , ed. Thomas Fortescue, 1 (London, 1869): 322. On eighteenth-century naturalists and the definition of race, see Bentley Glass et al., eds., *Forerunners of Darwin, 1745–1859* (Baltimore, 1959); Clarence J. Glacken, *Traces on the Rhodian Shore: Nature and Culture in Western Thought from Ancient Times to the End of the Eighteenth Century* (Berkeley and Los Angeles, 1967); and Benjamin Keen, *The Aztec Image in Western Thought* (New Brunswick, N.J., 1971). The landmark discussion of the "Great Chain of Being" is Arthur O. Lovejoy, *The Great Chain of Being: A Study of the History of an Idea* (Cambridge, Mass., 1936).

82. Jordan, *White over Black*, 252–59.

83. Linnaeus, *General System of Nature*, as quoted in T[homas] Bendyshe, "The History of Anthropology," *Memoirs of the Anthropological Society of London* 1 (1863–64): 422, 424–25; and Jordan, *White over Black*, 220–21. Linnaeus seems to have borrowed the colors and characteristics from the classical "four humors" but with many modifications. Red, for example, had traditionally been associated with blood and sanguine nature, yellow with choleric, white with phlegmatic, black with melancholic.

84. Mitchell, "An Essay upon Causes of the Different Colours of People," *Philosophical Transactions of the Royal Society* 43 (1744–45): 120–30, 146–59.

85. Bradley, *A Philosophical Account of the Works of Nature* (London, 1721), 169.

86. Leclerc, Comte de Buffon, *Natural History, General and Particular, by the Count de Buffon*, trans. William Smellie, 9 vols., 2d ed. (London, 1785), 3:57,

173–78, 181, 200–203; and Home, Lord Kames, *Six Sketches of the History of Man* (Philadelphia, 1776), 14–16.

87. Buffon, *Natural History*, 3:57, 173–74, 188. Historians often divide early theorists of the Indians' physical attributes into environmentalists, who believed that climate and circumstances determined color and culture, and biblicists, who viewed basic characteristics as divinely ordained and hence immutable. Some "environmentalists" certainly deserve the label; but others expected changes to occur only after centuries, or at least several generations, and thus were not really admitting that any of their dark-skinned contemporaries (or even the children of their contemporaries) could achieve a light pigmentation and all it implied in racial acceptance. Samuel Stanhope Smith is a case in point. Environment, he contended, could change most aspects of human appearance and behavior, but "a black or dusky complexion, once contracted by the ancestors of a race, is continued in their offspring by a much lower climactical influence, than was originally necessary to create it." Smith thought North American Indians to be naturally dark but made more so "by discolouring paints and unguents." Smith, *An Essay on the Causes of the Varieties of Complexion and Figure in the Human Species*, ed. Winthrop D. Jordan (Cambridge, Mass., 1965), 94–95, 108, 113, 176–77.

88. Romans, *Concise Natural History of East and West Florida*, 38–39.

89. Significant studies in the last three decades include Francis Paul Prucha, *American Indian Policy, 1790–1834* (Cambridge, Mass., 1964); Reginald Horsman, *Expansion and American Indian Policy, 1783–1812* (East Lansing, Mich., 1967), and "Scientific Racism and the American Indian in the Mid-Nineteenth Century," *American Quarterly* 27 (1975): 152–68; Richard Drinnon, *White Savage: The Case of John Dunn Hunter* (New York, 1972); Bernard Sheehan, *Seeds of Extinction: Jeffersonian Philanthropy and the American Indian* (Chapel Hill, N.C., 1973); Robert Berkhofer, *The White Man's Indian: Images of the American Indian from Columbus to the Present* (New York, 1978); Hoover, *The Red and the Black*, chaps. 3–4; and William McLoughlin, "Red Indians, Black Slavery, and White Racism: America's Slaveholding Indians," *American Quarterly* 26 (1974): 365–85, and "Cherokee Anomie, 1794–1809: New Roles for Red Men, Red Women, and Black Slaves," in Richard L. Bushman et al., eds., *Uprooted Americans: Essays to Honor Oscar Handlin* (Boston, 1979), 125–60. Also relevant and important is Robert E. Bieder. *Science Encounters the Indian, 1820–1880: The Early Years of American Ethnology* (Norman, Okla., 1986); and Reginald Horsman, *Race and Manifest Destiny: The Origins of American Racial Anglo-Saxonism* (Cambridge, Mass., 1981). On most matters Horsman and I seem to agree, although I am more impressed than he appears to be with the pervasiveness of popular antipathy to the Indians in the last quarter of the eighteenth century, and I am less impressed than he by the Founding Fathers' supposedly enlightened ideas on race. I think their actions, and indeed many of their statements, reveal them to hold essentially the same racist notions and to be only slightly less pessimistic about the Indians than were their more sanguinary contemporaries. Horsman and I also differ in terminology. I see no advantage to his substitution of *racialism* for *racism*; both terms describe the belief that inferior character and ability are inherited by members of certain assumed biologically distinct—by color or otherwise—branches of humankind. I see no significant difference between today's racism and that of the late eighteenth and early nineteenth centuries.

90. Benjamin Rush attributed African pigmentation to hereditary leprosy, which, he believed, could be cured by long residence in temperate climates;

Rush, *Sixteen Introductory Lectures, to Courses . . . [on the] Practice of Medicine* (Philadelphia, 1811). Rush is often hailed as one of the Revolutionary era's most enlightened spokesmen, but his statements on race are hardly praisewor- thy. For example: "A dull and disguising sameness of mind characterizes all sav- age nations," which "is as much the effect of the want of physical influence upon their minds, as a disagreeable colour and figure are of its action upon their bod- ies." Ibid., 93–94.

91. Smith, *Colonial Days and Ways*, 48–50; and Extract from the Journal of George Croghan in S[amuel] P[rescott] Hildreth, *Pioneer History: Being an Ac- count of the Fixt Examination of the Ohio Valley . . .* (Cincinnati, 1848), 79. As early as 1753, a colonist wrote of "Red Men," but there are few similar references be- fore 1775, when such terminology suddenly proliferated. John O'Neal to James Hamilton, 27 May 1753, in Samuel Hazard, ed., *The Register of Pennsylvania*, 4 (Philadelphia, 1829): 389. Cooper, in his various novels, used color terminol- ogy extensively, including "redskins" and "palefaces." In *The Wept of Wish-ton- Wish: A Tale*, 2 vols. (New York, 1829), 61–62, Cooper made clear his belief in the permanence of Indian color when Ruth describes an Indian as a "creature, formed, fashioned gifted like ourselves, in all but color of the skin and blessing of the faith." Nathaniel Hawthorne and Herman Melville, along with most other American novelists, used "red men" or its variants. By the nineteenth century, most historians, including Francis Parkman, George Bancroft, and William H. Prescott, also referred to "redskins" and "red men." For an analysis of their views on Indians, see David Levin, *History as Romantic Art: Bancroft, Prescott, Motley, and Parkman* (Stanford, Calif., 1959), esp. 127–58. Fictional accounts are analyzed in Albert Keiser, *The Indian in American Literature* (New York, 1933). Linnaeus's impact is hard to measure, but certainly his works were well known to leading eighteenth-century American intellectuals. Cadwallader Colden, among others, corresponded with Linnaeus, Jefferson cited him, and Charles Willson Peale named his second son Charles Linnaeus.

92. The standard treatment of the noble savage theme is Hoxie N. Fairchild, *The Noble Savage: A Study in Romantic Naturalism* (New York, 1928); also useful is A. L. Dicket, "The Noble Savage Convention as Epitomized in John Lawson's *A New Voyage to Carolina*," *North Carolina Historical Review* 43 (1966): 413–29. De- finitions of noble savagism—usually implicit—vary widely. Too often the term is applied to European observations that merely praise Indian stature or certain traits of character such as hospitality or hardiness; but such praise was almost universal, even among the Indians' most vehement detractors. The true noble savage perception of the Indian, I submit, rests on a belief in (1) the superior- ity of Indian *culture* in general to European or Anglo-American culture and (2) the degeneracy of Western culture from an earlier, "higher" level. The philosophes saw American Indians as noble because they had not yet succumbed to the corruptions—both individual and collective—of eighteenth-century life. The Indian remained in a Golden Age that closely approximated an earlier Eu- ropean stage of development.

93. Sheehan, *Seeds of Extinction*. On the Indian in Jeffersonian thought, also see Daniel J. Boorstin, *The Lost World of Thomas Jefferson* (New York, 1948), chap. 2. For Bartram's view of the Indians, see *The Travels of William Bartram* (1791), ed. Francis Harper (New Haven, 1958), esp. 306; and, for Heckwelder's views, see his *History, Manners, and Customs of the Indian Nations . . .*, Memoirs of the Pennsylvania Historical Society, no. 12 (Philadelphia, 1876).

94. Europeans had long used Indian motifs to represent the American continent in plays and illustrations. Americans were slower to adopt such symbols but increasingly used them in the Revolutionary era. Post-Revolutionary America turned from Indian iconography toward classical symbols and eventually to "Columbia" as a national representation. Significantly, in nineteenth-century paintings that retained an Indian figure, he or she was often assigned to the background and given unmistakably African features and color—a naked and feathered Indian-black child (see Fig. 1.2). Relevant studies include James H. Hyde, "The Four Parts of the New World in Old-Time Pageants and Ballets," *Apollo* 4 (1926): 232–38, and 5 (1927): 19–27; Roy C. Strong, *Splendor at Court: Renaissance Spectacle and the Theatre of Power* (Boston, 1973); E. McClung Fleming, "The American Image as Indian Princess, 1765–1783," *Winterthur Portfolio* 2 (1965): 65–81, and especially "From Indian Princess to Greek Goddess: The American Image, 1783–1815," ibid., 3 (1967): 37–66; and Hugh Honor, *The New Golden Land: European Images of America from the Discoveries to the Present Time* (New York, 1975).

95. For the paradoxical views of the Indians' early nineteenth-century supporters, see the works cited in note 92, above. On McKenney, also see Herman J. Viola, *Thomas L. McKenney: Architect of America's Early Indian Policy, 1816–1830* (Chicago, 1974).

96. Massachusetts provides a prime example of the impact of emergent racism on antimiscegenation laws. It had no restrictions against Indian-English marriages in the seventeenth century (although, for cultural reasons, few occurred); in 1705 it almost prohibited such marriages but did not, finally, until 1786. Yasuhide Kawashima, "Forced Conformity: Puritan Criminal Justice and Indians," *Kansas Law Review* 25 (1977): 362 n. 5. (Kawashima's reference to an antimiscegenation act of 1692 is based on Lauber, *Indian Slavery in Colonial Times*; see note 55, above.) Two other New England states proscribed Indian-white marriages in the late eighteenth and early nineteenth centuries; see *the Public Laws of the State of Rhode-Island and Providence Plantations* (Providence, 1798), 483; and *Laws of the State of Maine* (Portland, 1822), 276. The Maine law of 1821 drew verbatim on the Massachusetts act of 1786.

97. Cooper, *The Pathfinder: or, The Inland Sea*, ed. Richard Dilworth Rust (Albany, N.Y., 1981), 122, and *The Prairie: A Tale*, 1 (Paris, 1827): 113. An English visitor to the United States in the 1790s voiced his pejorative judgment that the Christianized Stockbridge Indians had been "civilized as much as Indians are capable of civilization"; William Strickland, *Journal of a Tour in the United States of America, 1794–1795*, ed. J. E. Strickland, Collections of the New-York Historical Society, no. 83 (New York, 1971), 116. Cooper's corollary, that no white man could become an Indian any more than a redskin could become a white, was another important reflection of the new racial concepts. In the seventeenth century, Anglo-American spokesmen acknowledged (and warned against) the possibility of colonists becoming thoroughly Indianized. No biological barriers were perceived; the settler had only to exchange his ways for those of the Indian. For discussions of Englishmen who "went savage" in British North America, see James Axtell, "The White Indians of Colonial America," *WMQ*, 3d ser., 32 (1975): 55–88; and Vaughan and Richter, "Crossing the Cultural Divide," reprinted, with revisions, as chapter 10 in this volume.

98. *United States Magazine and Democratic Review*, new ser., 27, no. 145 (July 1850): 48, *DeBow's Review* 17, no. 1 (February 1854): 69; ibid., 16, no. 2 (Feb-

ruary 1854): 147–48; and J. C. Nott and George R. Gliddon, *Types of Mankind* (Philadelphia, 1854), 69. Although such views culminated in the 1850s, they had been widespread for at least several decades. In 1830, for example, a writer predicted that "Civilization is destined to exterminate [the Indians], in common with the wild animals"; Charles Caldwell, *Thoughts on the Original Unity of the Human Race* (New York, 1830), 142. Such rhetoric scarcely differs, I contend, from the prevailing sentiment at the end of the American Revolution, although few intellectuals or statesmen were ready to speak so bluntly.

CHAPTER 2: EARLY ENGLISH PARADIGMS FOR NEW WORLD NATIVES

1. J. M. Cohen, trans. and ed., *The Four Voyages of Christopher Columbus, Being His Own Log-Book, Letters and Dispatches* . . . (London, 1969), 55–56.

2. "Paradigm" is defined in the *Oxford American Dictionary* (1980) as "something serving as an example or model of how things should be done." In this essay, the meaning is more accurately "an idea or image of how the natives of America should be understood and treated."

3. My concern here is with the formation and function of attitudes toward American natives by English explorers, settlers, and commentators, whether or not they journeyed to the New World. Necessarily, then, this essay does not discuss some of the important interpretive frameworks—paradisaic, for example, or providential—which were unquestionably significant at certain times with certain observers of the American scene. For paradigms not discussed here see Margaret T. Hodgen, *Early Anthropology in the Sixteenth and Seventeenth Centuries* (Philadelphia, 1964); Robert F. Berkhofer Jr., *The White Man's Indian: Images of the Indian from Columbus to the Present* (New York, 1978); Bernard Sheehan, *Savagism and Civility: Indians and Englishmen in Colonial Virginia* (Cambridge, Eng., 1980); Karen Ordahl Kupperman, "English Perceptions of Treachery: The Case of the American 'Savages'," *The Historical Journal* 20 (1977): 263–87; and Alfred A. Cave, "Canaanites in a Promised Land: The American Indian and the Providential Theory of Empire," *American Indian Quarterly* 12 (Fall 1988): 277–97. See also Loren E. Pennington, "The Amerindian in English Promotional Literature, 1575–1625," in K. R. Andrews, N. P. Canny, and P. E. H. Hair, eds., *The Westward Enterprise: English Activities in Ireland, the Atlantic, and America 1480–1650* (Detroit, 1979), 175–94.

4. The standard discussion of wild men in European thought is Richard Bernheimer, *Wild Men in the Middle Ages: A Study in Art, Sentiment, and Demonology* (Cambridge, 1952), which should be supplemented by the lavishly illustrated catalogue by Timothy Husband, *The Wild Man: Medieval Myth and Symbolism* (New York, 1980), and Edward Dudley and Maxmillian E. Novak, eds., *The Wild Man Within: An Image in Western Thought from the Renaissance to Romanticism* (Pittsburgh, 1972). Useful narrower studies include Olive Patricia Dickason, "The Concept of *l'homme sauvage* and early French colonialism in the Americas," *Revue français d'histoire d'Outre Mer* 64 (1977): 5–32; Olive Patricia Dickason, *The Myth of the Savage: And the Beginnings of French Colonialism in the Americas* (Edmonton, Alberta, 1984), chap. 4; Sheehan, *Savagism and Civility*, chaps. 2, 3; and Susi Colin, "The Wild Man and the In-

dian in Early 16th Century Book Illustration," in Christian F. Feest, ed., *Indians and Europe: An Interdisciplinary Collection of Essays* (Aachen, 1987), 5–36. Although I appreciate Colin's contribution to the literature on wild men and Indians, I take issue with it at several points, especially its conflation of monsters and wild men, who seem to me to have played quite separate roles in medieval and Renaissance thought, although at times the boundary blurred.

5. Edmund Spenser, *The Faerie Queene*, ed. A. C. Hamilton (1596; reprint, London, 1977), bk. 4, canto vii, stanza 5.

6. Hayden White, "The Forms of Wildness: Archeology of an Idea," in Dudley and Novak, eds., *Wild Man Within*, 7.

7. For evidence of European fascination with Indian nakedness, see almost any sixteenth- or seventeenth-century description of American natives. For example, Columbus's first logbook description of the Indians (as paraphrased by Bartolomé de Las Cases) begins: "Immediately some naked people appeared . . ." (Cohen, ed., *Voyages of Columbus*, 53; see also 55, 60, 72, 117). Columbus was also the first European to write about the Indians' presumed lack of religion and language, and of their cannibalism (ibid., 56, 118, 121). Amerigo Vespucci and the other early reporters made comparable statements and added promiscuity to the list. See, for example, *The Letters of Amerigo Vespucci and Other Documents*, trans. Clements R. Markham (London, 1894), 5–16, 47; and Edward Arber, ed., *The First Three English Books on America, (?1511)–1555 A.D.* (Birmingham, Eng., 1885; reprint, New York, 1971), 50, 70, 78, 81, 103, 106, and passim.

8. *Letters of Vespucci*, trans. Markham, 6. For later efforts by French writers to refute the Indians-as-hairy-wild-men myth and its tenacity, see Dickason, "Concept of *l'homme sauvage*," 19–22.

9. See, for example, W[illiam] Bullein, *A Dialogue Both Pleasant and Pitifull . . .* (London, 1578), sig. [K8].

10. Bernheimer, *Wild Men*, 15–19.

11. John Donne, "Holy Sonnet," in *The Complete Poetry of John Donne*, ed. John T. Shawcross (New York, 1968), 340. The standard work on the species is John Block Friedman, *The Monstrous Races in Medieval Art and Thought* (Cambridge, 1981). See also Rudolph Wittkower, "Marvels of the East: A Study in the History of Monsters," *Journal of the Warburg and Courtauld Institute* 5 (1942): 159–97.

12. Caius Plinius Secundus, *A Summarie of the Antiquities, and Wonders of the Worlde* (London, [1566]). Other full or partial editions of Pliny's work (variously titled) were published in English in 1585, 1587, 1601, 1611, and 1634. See Friedman, *Monstrous Races*, 9–21, for a catalogue of the species most frequently mentioned by classical and medieval writers.

13. Edward Topsell, *The Historie of Foure-Footed Beastes* (London, 1607), esp. 13, 441–42; Topsell, *The Historie of Serpents* (London, 1608), esp. 201.

14. Wittkower, "Marvels of the East," 193–94.

15. For example: Pietro Matire d'Angheria, *The Decades of the Newe Worlde or West India . . .*, trans. Rycharde Eden (London, 1555), 218v–19r; "The Travailes of John Hortop," in Richard Hakluyt, *The Principal Navigations Voyages Traffiques & Discoveries of the English Nation*, 12 vols. (Glasgow, 1903–05; orig. publ. 1589), 9: 461; Lawrence Keymis [or Kemys], *A Relation of the Second Voyage to Guiana* (London, 1596), sig. C3v; George Abbot, *A Briefe Description of the Whole Worlde . . .*, 6th ed. (London, 1624), sig. X3v.

16. Cohen, ed., *Voyages of Columbus,* 119, 121. Columbus sometimes suggested that he conversed quite well with the natives and at other times that they could scarcely communicate at all, which raises doubts about the accuracy of his understanding of native knowledge. On the linguistic dilemmas of culture contact, see Stephen Greenblatt, "Kidnapping Language," in *Marvelous Possessions: The Wonder of the New World* (Chicago, 1991), 86–118; Eric Cheyfitz, *The Poetics of Imperialism: Translation and Colonization from The Tempest to Tarzan* (New York, 1991); and Peter Hulme, *Colonial Encounters: Europe and the Native Caribbean, 1492–1797* (London, 1986), esp. chap. 1.

17. *The History of Herodotus,* trans. George Rawlinson (London, 1910), 1:329, tells of man-eating "androphagi."

18. Walter Ralegh, *The Discoverie of the Large and Bewtiful Empire of Guiana,* ed. V. T. Harlow (London, 1928; orig. publ. 1596), 56–57. Ralegh's informants called the headless people *"Ewaipanoma."* The effectiveness of Ralegh's testimony is suggested by the archbishop of Canterbury's assertion as late as 1624 that "no sober man should any way doubt of the truth" that anthropophagi inhabit Guiana (Abbot, *Briefe Description,* sig. X3v).

19. The writings on Spanish attitudes are voluminous, especially on Las Casas and his role in shaping official and popular perceptions of the Indians. See especially Anthony Pagden, *The Fall of Natural Man: The American Indian and the Origins of Comparative Ethnology* (Cambridge, 1982).

20. John Kirkham in Thomas Ellis, *A True Report of the Third and Last Voyage into Meta Incognita* (London, [1578]), sig. [C3v].

21. Robert Gray, *A Good Speed to Virginia* (London, 1609), sigs. B1–C3.

22. Samuel Purchas, *Purchase His Pilgrimes,* 4 vols. (London, 1625) 4:1814; [Benjamin Tompson], *New Englands Crisis, Or a Brief Narrative of New-Englands Lamentable Estate at Present* (Boston, 1676), 12, 15; Cotton Mather, *Magnalia Christi Americana: or, the Ecclesiastical History of New-England* (London, 1702), bk. 7:110–11.

23. The noble savage paradigm, which is outside the scope of this essay, drew partly on the wild-man tradition, partly on the image of the Indians as relics of the Golden Age, and partly on themes peculiar to eighteenth-century Europe. The extensive literature includes Hoxie Neale Fairchild, *The Noble Savage: A Study in Romantic Naturalism* (New York, 1928); Henri Baudet, *Paradise on Earth: Some Thoughts on European Images of Non-European Man,* trans. Elizabeth Wentholt (1959; reprint, New Haven, Conn., 1965); and Hayden White, "The Noble Savage Theme as Fetish," in Fredi Chiappelli, ed., *First Images of America: The Impact of the New World on the Old,* 2 vols. (Berkeley, 1976), 1:121–35. A useful concise summary is in Berkhofer, *White Man's Indian,* 72–80.

24. Contributing to skepticism about monsters was the heightening of systematic scrutiny of the subject, as reflected in works such as John Spencer, *A Discourse Concerning Prodigies* (Cambridge, 1663).

25. Bernard Bailyn et al., *The Great Republic: A History of the American People* (Boston, 1977), 26–29.

26. The Irish paradigm has been proposed to varying degrees by, among others, Howard Mumford Jones, *O Strange New World. American Culture: The Formative Years* (New York, 1964), 167–79; David Beers Quinn, *The Elizabethans and the Irish* (Ithaca, N.Y., 1966), esp. chap. 9; Nicholas P. Canny, "The Ideology of English Colonization: From Ireland to America," *William and Mary Quarterly,* 3d ser. 30 (1973): 575–98; Canny, *The Elizabethan Conquest of Ireland: The Pattern Es-*

tablished, 1565–76 (New York, 1976), esp. 159–63; James Muldoon, "The Indian as Irishman," *Essex Institute Historical Collections* 111 (1975): 267–89; and Leonard P. Liggio, "English Origins of Early American Racism," *Radical History Review* 3 (1976): 1–36; quotation from ibid., 20.

27. A convenient collection of English writings about the Irish during the period here under consideration is James P. Myers Jr., ed., *Elizabethan Ireland: A Selection of Writings by Elizabethan Writers on Ireland* (Hamden, Conn., 1983). See especially the extract from Barnabe Rich, *A New Description of Ireland* (1610), 130–40, which is an extremely harsh assessment of the Irish but fairly representative of English attitudes in the late Tudor–early Stuart era.

28. Jones, *Strange New World*, 172–73.

29. Muldoon, "Indian as Irishman," 270, holds that it was "only natural for early explorers and *settlers* [my emphasis] to view the Indians in terms derived from the experiences of the English in Ireland." For the handful of explorers with experience in both places, this is probably true, but the number of early settlers with Irish experience must have been exceedingly few.

30. [Hugh Peter], *Mr. Peters Last Report of the English Wars* . . . (London, 1646), 5; Canny, "Ideology of English Colonization," 587–89, nicely summarizes English views of the Irish in the late Tudor–early Stuart era.

31. [John Brinsley], *A Consolation for ovr Grammar Schooles, . . . More Specially for All Those of the Inferiour Sort, . . . Namely, for Ireland, Wales, Virginia, with the Sommer Ilands,* 2d ed. (London, 1622), 3.

32. See, for example, the paucity of meaningful connections to America in the references to Ireland in E. G. R. Taylor, ed., *The Original Writings and Correspondence of the Two Richard Hakluyts,* 2 vols. (London, 1935), 1:71, 2:267, 328, 341, 377.

33. For a concise summary of this point, see K. G. Davies, *The North Atlantic World in the Seventeenth Century* (Minneapolis, 1974), 4–5. The influence, both pro and con, of the Spanish experience on English colonization is beyond the scope of this essay but deserves extensive further study. Much has been written on Spanish and English colonization, of course, but little on the connections between them.

34. For a sign that the Irish paradigm may be losing force, compare the coverage of the topic in the first edition of Bailyn et al., *Great Republic,* 26–29, with the fourth edition (Lexington, Mass., 1992), 24–26.

35. Richard Hakluyt, "To the illustrious and right worthy Sir Walter Ralegh," in Taylor, ed., *Writings of the Two Hakluyts,* 2:368.

36. For a variant interpretation of the motives behind England's post-1590 view of the Indians, see Loren E. Pennington, "The Amerindian in English Promotional Literature," in Andrews, Canny, and Hair, eds., *Westward Enterprise,* 175–214.

37. This paradigm had already been applied to the Irish, though apparently quite seldom. It probably did not seem apt in the Irish case because they had demonstrated from the outset a sturdy resistance to English efforts at anglicization. Still, the "old Britons" paradigm serves as a link between English views of the Irish and the Indians: English observers believed both peoples were at a primitive level of social and theological progress and needed, as had the old Britons, a hefty dose of civility and Protestantism. See Canny, "Ideology of English Colonization," 588–90, 595–96.

38. Thomas Hariot, *A Briefe and True Report of the Newfoundland of Virginia . . .* (Frankfurt, 1590). This was subsequently designated part 1 of the de Brys' series on America and the only one published in English. On the de Bry illustrations (the publisher/engravers' principal contribution to discovery discourse), see especially Bernadette Bucher, *Icon and Conquest: A Structural Analysis of the Illustrations of de Bry's Great Voyages,* trans. Basia Miller Gulati (Chicago, 1981).

39. On Hariot's remarkable career and writings, see Muriel Rukeyser, *Traces of Thomas Hariot* (New York, [1971]); and David B. Quinn, "Thomas Harriot and the New World," in John W. Shirley, ed., *Thomas Harriot, Renaissance Scientist* (Oxford, 1974), 36–53.

40. On White's paintings, see especially Paul Hulton and David Beers Quinn, *The American Drawings of John White, 1577–1590, with Drawings of European and Oriental Subjects,* 2 vols. (London and Chapel Hill, N.C. 1964); Paul Hulton, *America at 1585: The Complete Drawings of John White* (Chapel Hill, N.C., 1984); Christian F. Feest, "The Virginia Indian in Pictures, 1612–1624," *Smithsonian Journal of History* 1 (1966): 1–30; and Paul Hulton, "Images of the New World: Jacques Le Moyne de Morgues and John White," in Andrews, Canny, and Hair, eds., *Westward Enterprise,* 195–214.

41. At least one of the paintings was recently discovered to have been by Jacques Le Moyne. See Hulton, "Images of the New World," 211–12; and Hulton, *America at 1585,* 17–18, 91–95, 131–33. Scholars who have noted at some length Hariot's appendix include T. D. Kendrick, *British Antiquity* (London, 1950), 121–25, plates XIII, XV; and H. C. Porter, *The Inconstant Savage: England and the North American Indians,* 1500–1660 (Cambridge, 1970), 256–57.

42. Hariot, *Briefe and True Report* (1590 ed.), sig. E. According to J. A. Leo Lemay, White's drawings of Indians "changed English and European perceptions of their own ancestors. Henceforth, Europeans viewed their progenitors as versions of the American Indian. Thus the Amerindian influenced European ideas of civilization's development." Lemay, "The Beginnings," in Louis D. Rubin, ed., *The History of Southern Literature* (Baton Rouge, 1985), 14. Perhaps Lemay is right, but I think the evidence is clear, as I have argued in these pages, that the influence was primarily—I suspect wholly—in the other direction: that Europeans, especially the English, viewed Indians as latter-day Britons. The paradigm's purpose and function were primarily to shed light on the Indians, not on the Europeans' ancestors.

43. William Crashaw, *A Sermon Preached in London before the Right Honourable the Lord La Warre, Lord Gouernour and Captaine Generall of Virginea* (London, 1610), sig. [C4v].

44. *Londons Lotterie* (London, 1612), verso (facsimile in Robert C. Johnson, "The Lotteries of the Virginia Company, 1612–1621," *Virginia Magazine of History and Biography* 74 [1966]: 259–92, illustration between 270 and 271). See also the poem at the top of [Virginia Company of London], *A Declaration for the Certaine Time of Dravving the Great Standing Lottery* (London, 1615), also reproduced in Johnson, "Lotteries," facing p. 259.

45. Purchas, *Purchase His Pilgrimes,* 4:1755; Richard Eburne, *Plaine Pathway to Plantations* (London, 1624), 28.

46. William Strachey, *The Historie of Travell into Virginia Britania,* ed. Louis B. Wright and Virginia Freund (London, 1953), 24. Strachey appears to have begun his book in Virginia ca. 1609 and completed it after his return to England in 1611. The paragraph on old Britons could have been written in either place.

47. Purchas, *Purchase His Pilgrimes*, 4:1755.

48. On the uprising and its aftermath, see chapter 5 in this volume.

49. Although the old Britons paradigm was cited far less often after the mid-1620s, it appeared occasionally in the 1630s and beyond. For a late seventeenth-century application of the paradigm, see Roger Williams, *George Fox Digg'd out of His Burrowes* (Boston, 1676), 201 (misnumbered 101).

50. The substantial literature on the connection between the Lost Tribes and the America Indians includes Lynn Glaser, "Indians or Jews?," introduction to Menasseh ben Israel, *The Hope of Israel* (Gilroy, Calif., 1973), 1–74; Ronald Sanders, *Lost Tribes and Promised Lands: The Origins of American Racism* (Boston, 1978); David S. Katz, *Philo-Semitism and the Readmission of the Jews to England, 1603–1655* (Oxford, 1982), esp. chap. 4; Richard W. Cogley, "John Eliot and the Origins of the American Indians," *Early American Literature* 21 (1986–87): 210–25; Henry Méchoulan and Gérard Nahon, introduction to *The Hope of Israel: The English Translation of 1652*, trans. Richenda George (Oxford, 1987); and James Holstun, *A Rational Millennium: Puritan Utopias of Seventeenth-Century England and America* (New York, 1987), chap. 3.

51. The major early theories on the origin of the Indians are discussed in Lee Eldridge Huddleston, *Origins of the American Indians: European Concepts, 1492–1729* (Austin, Tex., 1967). See also Don Cameron Allen, *The Legend of Noah: Renaissance Rationalism in Art, Science, and Letters* (Urbana, Ill., 1949), chap. 6; and Robert Wachope, *Lost Tribes and Sunken Continents: Myth and Method in the Study of American Indians* (Chicago, 1962).

52. Glaser, "Indians or Jews?," 23–27; George Weiner, "America's Jewish Braves," *Mankind* (Oct. 1974), 56–64, esp. 58; and Huddleston, *Origins of the Indians*, 33–47.

53. For the American side of this trend, see esp. J. F. Maclear, "New England and the Fifth Monarchy: The Quest for the Millennium in Early American Puritanism," *William and Mary Quarterly*, 3d ser. 32 (1975): 223–60.

54. Thomas Thorowgood, *Iewes in America; or, Probabilities that the Americans Are of that Race* (London, 1650).

55. For the intriguing role of Antonio de Montezinos (aka Aaron Levi), see Katz, *Philo-Semitism*, 141–49, or almost any other work cited in n. 50 above. It was undoubtedly influential—Thorowgood recounted it in *Iewes in America*, as did Menasseh ben Israel in *The Hope of Israel*—but tangential to the concerns of this essay.

56. Cogley, "Eliot and the Indians," 215–17; Eliot on Indian origins in Henry Whitfield, *The Light Appearing More and More towards the Perfect Day* (London, 1651; reprint, *Massachusetts Historical Society, Collections*, 3d ser. 4 [1834]): 119–21, 127–28.

57. Menasseh ben Israel, *The Hope of Israel* (London, 1652; orig. Amsterdam, 1650), 6. The recent literature on Menasseh ben Israel (the first name is variously spelled) is large and in some instances controversial. Even the basic message of *The Hope of Israel* is arguable. Most accounts accept the English translation's clear endorsement of the Lost Tribes theory, but Méchoulan and Nahon contend that the original edition (in Spanish, 1650) states emphatically that the Indians were not descendants of the Lost Tribes; the English mistranslation, they argue, conveyed a false impression. For purposes of this essay, what matters is Menasseh's apparent (if not real) support for the paradigm and thereby his strengthening of it among English and American advocates. See ibid., 6, 20, 40,

53–55, which can most easily be consulted in the Glaser edition. For evidence that Eliot considered the rabbi to be an advocate of the Lost Tribes theory, see Mather, *Magnalia Christi Americana*, bk. 3: 193.

58. Thorowgood, *Iewes in America*, 6; Thomas Thorowgood, *Jews in America, or Probabilities that Those Indians Are Judaical, Made More Probable by Some Additionals to the Former Conjectures* (London, 1660), 5 (2d pagination). Thorowgood's extract from Roger Williams's letter to him of 20 December 1635 is reprinted and annotated in *The Correspondence of Roger Williams*, ed. Glenn W. LaFantasie, 2 vols. (Hanover, N.H., 1980), 2:30–31. For other adherents to the Jewish origins theory, see Edward Winslow, "Epistle Dedicatory," in John Eliot and Thomas Mayhew Jr., eds., *The Glorious Progress of the Gospel amongst the Indians in New England* (London, 1649), reprint, *Mass. Hist. Soc. Collections*, 3d ser. 4 (1834): 72–74; and John Davenport in ibid., 93–95.

59. *"The learned Conjectures of Reverend Mr.* John Eliot *touching the Americans,"* in Thorowgood, *Jews in America* 1–27, quotation from 17. Eliot's letter appears at the beginning of some copies, at the end of others, but the pagination is separate in either case.

60. For a discussion of Menasseh's additional goals, see Méchoulan and Nahon, eds., *The Hope of Israel*, 58.

61. On Eliot's praying towns, see Alden T. Vaughan, *New England Frontier: Puritans and Indians, 1620–1675*, rev. ed. (New York, 1979), chaps. 9–11. Eliot's efforts to persuade Christian nations, especially England, to adopt the biblical model met stiff resistance. See his *Christian Commonwealth, or, The Civil Policy of the Rising Kingdom of Jesus Christ* (London, [1659]); Eliot's scheme of rulers extended, where population size permitted, to thousands and millions (ibid., 7–8, 28). On the reaction to Eliot's book in New and old England, see Maclear, "New England the Fifth Monarchy," 244–57; and Holstun, *Rational Millennium*, chap. 3.

62. Katz, *Philo-Semitism*, 240–42.

63. Cogley, "Eliot and the Indians," 220–22. Roger Williams leaned toward the Jewish origins explanation but was uncertain. See *A Key into the Language of America*, ed. John J. Teunissen and Evelyn J. Hinz (Detroit, 1973; orig. publ. 1643), 85–87, 192, 206; Williams to Thorowgood, 20 Dec. 1635, and Williams to John Winthrop Jr., ca. 15 Feb. 1655, in *Williams Correspondence*, 1:30, 2:429. Samuel Sewall seems to have found the Lost Tribes theory generally persuasive. See Samuel Sewall to Stephen Dummer, 15 Feb. 1686, in "Letter-Book of Samuel Sewall," *Mass. Hist. Soc. Collections* 6 ser. 1 (1886): 23, 177; and Sewall, *Phaenomena Quaedam Apocalyptica* (Boston, 1697), 2.

64. Mather, *Magnalia Christi Americana*, bk. 3:192–93.

65. Hamon L'Estrange, *Americans no Iewes, or Improbabilities that the Americans Are of that Race* (London, 1652), 61–62. For other critiques of the Indians-as-Jews theory, see Allen, *Legend of Noah*, 127–29.

66. Thorowgood, *Iewes in America*, 9–10; Thorowgood, *Jews in America*, 14 (2d pagination); Eliot in Whitfield, *Light-Appearing*, 127–28.

67. "Letter from William Penn to the Committee of the Free Society of Traders, 1683," in Albert Cook Myers, ed., *Narratives of Early Pennsylvania, West New Jersey, and Delaware, 1630–1707* (New York, 1912), 236–37; James Adair, *The History of the American Indians* (London, 1775).

68. [Anne Dudley Bradstreet], *Several Poems Compiled with Great Variety of Wit and Learning . . .*, 2d ed. (Boston, 1678), 81–82. I have corrected an apparent typographical error in the poem's final word.

69. Mather, *Magnalia Christi Americana*, bk. 3:190. In 1674, a leading authority on the Indians of New England observed that "the opinion, that these people are of the race of the Israelites, doth not greatly obtain. But surely it is not impossible, and perhaps not so improbable, as many learned men think"; Daniel Gookin, *Historical Collections of the Indians in New England* (Boston, 1792), 4–5.

70. Edward W. Said, *Orientalism* (New York, 1978), 67. Said's observation applies as well, of course, to the Indians' reaction to the strangeness of Europeans: American natives employed paradigms from their own cultural context to make sense of the newcomers. See, for example, Tzvetan Todorov, *The Conquest of America: The Question of the Other,* trans. Richard Howard (New York, 1984), esp. chap. 2.

71. Keith Thomas, *Man and the Natural World: Changing Attitudes in England, 1500–1800* (London, 1983; American ed. differently subtitled), 44.

72. Said, *Orientalism,* 67.

CHAPTER 3: SLAVEHOLDERS' "HELLISH PRINCIPLES"

1. Morgan Godwyn, *The Negro's & Indians Advocate, Suing for Their Admission into the Church . . .* (London, 1680), 3–7; Godwyn, "A *Brief Account* of *Religion,* in the *Plantations . . .* ," in Francis Brokesby, *Some Proposals towards Promoting of the Gospel in Our American Plantations* (London, 1708), 3. (Brokesby is not identified as the author in the original edition but is on the title page of a second edition, also published in 1708.) See also note 24.

2. The scattered sources of information about blacks in seventeenth-century British America have been culled by several historians, mostly in regional studies. The best comprehensive work is Winthrop D. Jordan, *White over Black: American Attitudes toward the Negro, 1550–1812* (Chapel Hill, N.C., 1968), chap. 2; an excellent brief summary is Philip D. Morgan, "British Encounters with Africans and African-Americans, circa 1600–1780, in Bernard Bailyn and Philip D. Morgan, eds., *Strangers within the Realm: Cultural Margins of the First British Empire* (Chapel Hill, N.C., 1991). See also the important studies that focus on the English side of the Atlantic, especially Peter Fryer, *Staying Power: The History of Black People in Britain* (London, 1984); Anthony J. Barker, *The African Link: British Attitudes to the Negro in the Era of the Atlantic Slave Trade, 1550–1807* (London, 1978), esp. chaps. 2–8; and James Walvin, *Black and White: The Negro and English Society, 1555–1945* (London, 1973).

3. David Grimsted, "Anglo-American Racism and Phillis Wheatley's 'Sable Veil,' 'Length'ned Chain,' and 'Knitted Heart,'" in Ronald Hoffman and Peter J. Albert, eds., *Women in the Age of the American Revolution* (Charlottesville, Va., 1989), 398; George M. Fredrickson, *White Supremacy: A Comparative Study in American and South African History* (Oxford and New York, 1981), 73.

4. For recent and often conflicting analyses of the early American race-slavery nexus, see Robert McColley, "Slavery in Virginia, 1619–1660: A Reexamination," in Robert H. Abzug and Stephen E. Maizlish, eds., *New Perspectives on Race and Slavery in America* (Lexington, Ky., 1986), 11–24; Alden T. Vaughan, "The Origins Debate: Slavery and Racism in Seventeenth-Century Virginia," *Virginia Magazine of History and Biography* 97 (1989): 311–54 (reprinted, with revisions, as chapter 7 in this volume); and Barbara Jeanne Fields, "Slavery, Race

and Ideology in the United States of America," *New Left Review* 131 (May–June 1990): 95–117. See also Herbert Aptheker, *Anti-Racism in U.S. History: The First Two Hundred Years* (Westport, Conn., 1992), which argues forcefully but sometimes quixotically that racism was far less prevalent in British America than most historians contend. To the extent that Morgan Godwyn wrote vehemently against racist notions, this essay supports Aptheker (who does not cite Godwyn), but Godwyn's evidence of racism's pervasiveness combines with other testimony from the colonial era to persuade me that Aptheker indulges in wishful thinking. He is surely correct, however, to insist that racist ideology was not universally accepted.

5. Earlier discussions of Godwyn's ideas on slavery, all of them brief, include Richard B. Schlatter, *The Social Ideas of Religious Leaders, 1660–1688* (London, 1940), 70–72; David Brion Davis, *The Problem of Slavery in Western Culture* (Ithaca, N.Y., 1966), 203–6, 211; Lester B. Scherer; *Slavery and the Churches in Early America, 1619–1819* (Grand Rapids, Mich., 1975), 31–33; and Fryer, *Black People in Britain*, 138, 148–50. For Godwyn's place in Virginia's ecclesiastical history, see Edward D. Neill, *Virginia Carolorum: The Colony under the Rule of Charles the First and Second* . . . (Albany, N.Y., 1886), 342–45; Edward Lewis Goodwin, *The Colonial Church in Virginia* . . . (Milwaukee, Wis., 1927), 272, 340; and George Maclaren Brydon, *Virginia's Mother Church and the Political Conditions under Which It Grew*, 1 (Richmond, 1947), 175, 186–88, 225, 506–10. The interaction of Godwyn's views on race and the role of the Anglican church are explored briefly in John Frederick Woolverton, *Colonial Anglicanism in North America* (Detroit, 1984), 70–74, 80; and Michael Anesko, " 'So Discreet a Zeal': Slavery and the Anglican Church in Virginia, 1680–1730," *Virginia Magazine of History and Biography* 93 (1985): 253–55.

6. Some of the confusion that has marked the debate over early English-American perceptions and policies has emanated from conflicting definitions of racism. This essay follows most dictionaries in defining it as a belief that one or more major human groups is innately inferior in mental and moral qualities. Such a group is usually, nowadays, labeled a "race," though historically the usage of that word has fluctuated and is even today not universally applied. Cf. different uses of the concept in Canada and the United States, for example.

7. Anthony à Wood, *Athenae Oxonienses. An Exact History of All the Writers and Bishops Who Have Had Their Education in the Most Antient and Famous University of Oxford* . . . *to* . . . *1695*, 2d ed., 2 vols. (London, 1721), 1:6 (2d pagination), 2: cols. 580–83, 709–10; Joseph Foster, *Alumni Oxonienses: The Members of the University of Oxford, 1500–1714*, 4 vols. (Oxford, 1891–92; reprinted in 2 vols., 1968), 1:584–86; A. B. Emden, *A Biographical Register of the University of Oxford, A.D. 1501 to 1540* (Oxford, 1974), 237: Leslie Stephen and Sidney Lee, eds., *Dictionary of National Biography*, 24 vols. (Oxford, 1921–27), 8:62 (hereafter *DNB*); Lyon Gardiner Tyler, ed., *Encyclopedia of Virginia Biography*, 4 vols. (New York, 1915), 1:242. The surname is variously spelled in biographical and bibliographic directories: Godwin, Go(o)dwyn, Goodwin, and Godwyn. I adhere to the latter spelling because it is the version used on all of Morgan Godwyn's publications during his years of writing (ca. 1675–85) and in the extant Virginia court records.

8. Wood, *Athenae Oxonienses*, 2, col. 581.

9. Ibid., col. 582. Francis Godwyn also dabbled in astronomical theory, which he set forth under the prescient title *The Man in the Moon: or, a Discourse*

of a Voyage Thither. For Francis Godwyn's publications see (under Godwin) A. W. Pollard and G. R. Redgrave, comps., *A Short-Title Catalogue of Books Printed in England . . . , 1475–1640,* 2d ed., 2 vols. (London, 1976–86), 1:11937–48; and Donald Wing, comp., *Short-Title Catalogue of Books Printed in England . . . and British America . . . ,* 2d ed., 3 vols. (New York, 1972–88), 2:141. A brief discussion of Francis Godwyn's writings appears in *DNB,* 8:57–58.

10. Wood, *Athenae Oxonienses,* 1, cols. 158 (2d pagination), 788–89. Godwyn entered Brasenose College in 1661 but subsequently moved to Christ Church.

11. Goodwin, *Colonial Church in Virginia,* 272, has Godwyn at Wendover in 1666 after his (presumed) return from Virginia; Scherer, *Slavery and the Churches,* 31, follows Goodwin. But that chronology seems impossible, for Godwyn was in the colony at least as late as 1670. I here follow Foster, *Alumni Oxoniensis,* 2:585, in putting Godwyn's brief service at Wendover between his graduation from Oxford and his departure for Virginia.

12. Francis Godwin, *A Catalogue of the Bishops of England, since the First Planting of Christian Religion in the Island . . . Whereunto Is Prefixed a Discourse Concerning the First Conversion of Our Britaine unto Christian Religion* (London, 1615), 1–48. Woolverton, *Colonial Anglicanism,* 71, credits Bede's book with triggering Morgan Godwyn's missionary interest through its parallels between eighth-century England's ripeness for Christianization and seventeenth-century English America's. Godwyn does occasionally cite Bede, but there is no hint of a formative influence, and, given Francis Godwyn's writings, Bede would have been superfluous for such a lesson.

13. William Waller Hening, ed., *The Statutes at Large; Being a Collection of All the Laws of Virginia . . . ,* 2 (Richmond, Va., 1823), 30–31; R[obert] G[reen], *Virginia's Cure . . .* (London, 1662), reprinted, Peter Force, *Tracts and Other Papers Relating Principally to . . . the Colonies in North America . . . ,* 4 vols. (1836–47; reprint, Gloucester, Mass., 1963), 3, no. 15:10; Brydon, *Virginia's Mother Church,* 1:175–76, 182–83.

14. Brydon, *Virginia's Mother Church,* 1:187, 507.

15. Morgan Godwyn, "The State of Religion in Virginia, as it was some time before the late Rebellion," in Godwyn, *Negro's & Indians Advocate,* 167–74; Charles Campbell, *History of the Colony and Ancient Dominion of Virginia,* vol. 1, *1492–1702* (Philadelphia, 1860): 277–79.

16. Godwyn, *Negro's & Indians Advocate,* 37–38, 96, 139–40.

17. Hening, ed., *Statutes of Virginia,* 2:260. For subsequent laws relating to slavery and Christianity, see the same volume, 283 and 491.

18. H. R. McIlwaine, ed., *Minutes of the Council and General Court of Colonial Virginia, 1622–1632, 1670–1676* (Richmond, Va., 1924), 205, 226–27. I am grateful for John Phillip Reid's wise counsel on this legal case.

19. Godwyn, *Negro's & Indians Advocate,* 136. The records are silent on the dates of Godwyn's stay in Barbados. Perhaps, as Brydon states (*Virginia's Mother Church,* 187), he went from Virginia to England and then to Barbados. It seems more likely that he stopped at Barbados en route to England, given the difficulties of transatlantic travel and the absence of any evidence to the contrary.

20. "Extracts from Henry Whistler's Journal of the West Indian Expedition," in C. H. Firth, ed., *The Narrative of General Venables . . .* (London, 1900), 145–46. See also "A Breife Discription of the Ilande of Barbados," in Vincent T. Harlow, ed., *Colonising Expeditions to the West Indies and Guiana, 1623–1667* (London, 1925), 42–48; Richard Ligon, *A True and Exact History of the Island of Barbados*

(London, 1657), esp. 43–55; and Richard Blome, *A Description of the Island of Jamaica; with the Other Isles* . . . (London, 1672), 83–92. For other sources on early Barbados see Jerome S. Handler, *A Guide to Source Materials for the Study of Barbados History, 1627–1834* (Carbondale and Edwardsville, Ill., 1971); and Handler, *Supplement to a Guide to Source Materials* . . . (Providence, R.I., 1991).

21. Ligon, *History of Barbados*, 54; and Jerome S. Handler, "The Amerindian Slave Population of Barbados in the Seventeenth and Early Eighteenth Centuries," *Caribbean Studies* 8, no. 4 (Jan. 1969): 38–64.

22. For population estimates, see Richard S. Dunn, *Sugar and Slaves: The Rise of the Planter Class in the English West Indies, 1624–1713* (Chapel Hill, N.C., 1972), 87; and Patricia A. Molen, "Population and Social Patterns in Barbados in the Early Eighteenth Century," *William and Mary Quarterly*, 3d ser. 28 (1971): 287–300, esp. 289. The fullest description of Barbados at approximately the time of Godwyn's stay is Ligon, *History of Barbados*. The best modern accounts are Vincent T. Harlow, *A History of Barbados, 1625–1685* (Oxford, 1926); Dunn, *Sugar and Slaves;* Carl and Roberta Bridenbaugh, *No Peace beyond the Line: The English in the Caribbean, 1624–1690* (New York, 1972); Gary A. Puckrein, *Little England: Plantation Society and Anglo-Barbadian Politics, 1627–1700* (New York, 1984); Hilary McD. Beckles, *White Servitude and Black Slavery in Barbados, 1627–1715* (Knoxville, Tenn., 1989); and Beckles, *Natural Rebels: A Social History of Enslaved Black Women in Barbados* (New Brunswick, N.J., 1989). Several of these studies mention Godwyn's observations on Barbadian race relations, though usually only the first of Godwyn's publications has been consulted and that rather sparsely; a few authors do not cite Godwyn at all.

23. Morgan Godwyn, *A Supplement to the Negro's & Indians Advocate* (London, 1681), 10; Morgan Godwyn, *Trade Preferr'd before Religion, and Christ Made to Give Place to Mammon* . . . (London, 1685), sig. A1r, p. 16 (2d pagination); W. Noel Sainsbury, ed., *Calendar of State Papers, Colonial Series, America and West Indies, 1675–1676* (London, 1893), 426 (doc. 977); *The Laws of Barbados* (London, 1699), 120–21; William Edmundson, *A Journal of the Life, Travels, Sufferings, and Labour of Love in the Work of the Ministry* . . . (Dublin, 1715), 53–54, 70–76.

24. Godwyn, *Negro's & Indians Advocate*, 3–7; Godwyn, "Brief *Account* of Religion," 2. It is barely possible that the Quaker who proselytized Godwyn was Fox himself (as D. B. Davis asserts in *Slavery in Western Culture*, 339), for Fox was in Barbados briefly in 1671 and again in the mid-1670s, but if so, it is odd that Godwyn did not identify Fox while giving him credit for having written the words that ignited Godwyn's own missionary zeal. Moreover, Godwyn referred to the man who gave him the pamphlet as "a *Quaker* of this Island"; given Fox's peripatetic ways, that would hardly have been an apt description of the Quaker leader. The pamphlet in question is almost surely Fox's *To the Ministers, Teachers & Priests (So called, and So Stileing your Selves) in Barbados* (London, 1672), 5. Several of Fox's other pamphlets and letters contain similar phrases. Godwyn put Fox's question, as quoted in *Negro's & Indians Advocate*, on the title page of his *Supplement*. See also *The Journal of George Fox*, rev. ed., ed. John L. Nickalls (Cambridge, 1952), 594–610.

25. The place and approximate times of composition can be gleaned from the two texts. Throughout *Negro's & Indians Advocate* (see esp. pp. 1, 13, 17, 44, 136, 166) Godwyn refers to Barbados as "here" or "this island," and although he nowhere gives a date, his abundance of anecdotal material suggests a long period—several years at least—of accumulation. Similarly, his outspoken disgust

at the slaveowners suggests that Godwyn was about to abandon the hostile environment. By contrast, the heading of the letter to Berkeley indicates that it was written before Bacon's Rebellion of 1676 and Berkeley's death in 1677. The bulk of the letter was probably written while Godwyn was still in Virginia and amended on Barbados. A few marginal comments were clearly added in England shortly before publication.

26. Quoted in John [Daly] Burk, *The History of Virginia from Its First Settlement to the Present Day*, 4 vols. (Petersburg, Va., 1804–16), 2:xxxix.

27. The letter to Berkeley constitutes pp. 167–74 of Godwyn, *Negro's & Indians Advocate*. It has a separate heading but not a separate title page or separate pagination. (The quotation appears on 115 [misnumbered 2d 99].) Although *Negro's & Indians Advocate* has never been reprinted in toto, the letter portion has been. See Brydon, *Virginia's Mother Church*, 1:511–16.

28. Full citations of Godwyn's works are given in previous notes; the broadside appeared anonymously as *The Revival: Or Directions for a Sculpture, Describing the Extraordinary Care and Diligence of Our Nation, in Publishing the Faith among Infidels in America, and Elsewhere; Compared with Other Both Primitive and Modern Professors of Christianity* (London, 1682).

29. Foster, *Alumni Oxonienses*, 1:585.

30. It is possible but unlikely that Godwyn died before 1695; if he had, his death date would almost surely have been recorded in the second edition of Wood's *Athenae Oxonienses*. No date of death appears in the *DNB* entry on Godwyn or in any of the many other biographical directories in which he appears, nor is it recorded in the extensive database on family history compiled by the Church of Jesus Christ of the Latter-day Saints. In light of the (admittedly vague) implications in *Some Proposals* (1708) that Godwyn is deceased and the absence of post-1685 information on Godwyn (except the 1708 snippet, which had been acquired from Godwyn more than twenty years earlier) the most plausible explanation, I suggest, is a gradual shunning of the outspoken social critic until he drifted into obscurity and died late in the seventeenth century or early in the eighteenth.

31. Godwyn, *Negro's & Indians Advocate*, sig. [A6r].

32. Passing references to Indians are scattered through Godwyn's several publications but constitute, I estimate, only about 5 percent of his total words.

33. Godwyn, *Directions for a Sculpture*.

34. Godwyn, *Supplement*, 12.

35. Godwyn, *Trade Preferr'd*, 8, 10, 11, 16 (2d pagination), 24 (2d pagination).

36. Ibid., 3–5.

37. Godwyn does not mention the king by name; probably it was James II, who acceded to the throne on 6 Feb. 1685. In that case, Godwyn was, ironically, appealing to a monarch heavily involved in the slave trade and whose "DY" had been branded onto thousands of African bodies.

38. Godwyn, *Trade Preferr'd*, sigs. A[1r]–[A1v]. For Godwyn's repeated insistence that Africans wanted Christianity, see also *Supplement*, 10.

39. Godwyn, *Negro's & Indians Advocate*, 38.

40. Ibid., 111–12.

41. Ibid.; Godwyn, *Trade Preferr'd*, 3; Godwyn, *Directions for a Sculpture*.

42. Godwyn, *Negro's & Indians Advocate*, 112, 96, 113 (misnumbered 2d p. 97), 114 (misnumbered 2d p. 98).

43. Ibid., 37–38.

44. Ibid., sigs. [A5v], [A6r]; Godwyn, *Trade Preferr'd*, 1.

45. For Godwyn's lists of his opponents' principal arguments, see especially Godwyn, *Negro's & Indians Advocate*, 2–3, 151; Godwyn, *Supplement*, 9–11; and Godwyn, *Trade Preferr'd*, 5–7. The quotation is from *Supplement*, 10.

46. Godwyn, *Negro's & Indians Advocate*, 10–41, quotations on sig. [A7v] and p. 3.

47. Godwyn, "*Brief Account of Religion*," 3.

48. Godwyn, *Negro's & Indians Advocate*, 20–23. Some of Godwyn's contemporaries assumed in defiance of biological fact, that humans could procreate with animals, especially with apes. See, for example, the discussion in Jordan, *White over Black*, 30–32.

49. Godwyn, *Negro's & Indians Advocate*, 14–19.

50. Ibid., 14, 41–61, quotations on 43, 14, and 53, respectively.

51. Ibid., 19, 43–61, quotations on 43, 54.

52. Ibid., 30.

53. Ibid., 10–14.

54. Ibid., 61–81, quotations on 61, 71.

55. Ibid., 123–25 (misnumbered 2d pp. 107–9).

56. Ibid., 125–28 (misnumbered 2d pp. 109–12), 130–31. On the role of Christian Indians in New England, see Douglas Edward Leach, *Flintlock and Tomahawk: New England in King Philip's War* (New York, 1958), esp. chap. 8; and [Daniel Gookin], *An Historical Account of the Doings and Sufferings of the Christian Indians in New England . . .* , in American Antiquarian Society, *Transactions and Collections*, 2 (1836; reprint, New York, 1972); on the Barbadian plot of 1675, see Puckrein, *Little England*, 163–65; Dunn, *Sugar and Slaves*, 257–58; and Anon., *Great Newes from Barbados. Or, A True and Faithful Account of the Grand Conspiracy of the Negroes against the English* (London, 1676).

57. In 1657, Richard Ligon (*History of Barbados*, 50) reported a slave owner's belief that "being once a Christian, he could no more account him a Slave." For colonial laws denying that proposition, see Hening, ed., *Statutes of Virginia*, 2:260; William Hand Browne, ed. *Archives of Maryland: Proceedings and Acts of the General Assembly*, 1–2 (Baltimore, 1883–84) 1:526, 533, 2: 272; Jordan, *White over Black*, 92 n. 115, quoting C.O. 5/1142.

58. Godwyn, *Negro's & Indians Advocate*, 140–43. On the legal status of slaves in the British empire see Davis, *Slavery in Western Culture*, 200–211; and Thomas Morris, " 'Villeinage . . . as it existed in England, reflects but little light on our subject': The Problem of the 'Sources' of Southern Slave Law," *American Journal of Legal History* 32 (1988): 95–137.

59. Godwyn, *Negro's & Indians Advocate*, 142–43; Godwyn, *Supplement*, 7; Godwyn, *Trade Preferr'd*, 5–6.

60. Godwyn, *Negro's & Indians Advocate*, 2, 32–37, 76, 101, quotations on 2, 34, and 76; Godwyn, *Supplement*, 9, 10; Godwyn, *Trade Preferr'd*, 16 (2d pagination).

61. Godwyn, *Directions for a Sculpture;* see also Godwyn, *Negro's & Indians Advocate*, 161–62; Godwyn, *Supplement*, 9; and Godwyn, *Trade Preferr'd*, sig. [A1v], p. 24 (2d pagination).

62. Godwyn, *Negro's & Indians Advocate*, 87, 124 (misnumbered 2d p. 108). For a critique of Godwyn that accuses him of Puritan tendencies, see Philip A. Bruce, *Institutional History of Virginia in the Seventeenth Century*, 2 vols. (New York, 1910), 1:206–7. The usually reliable Bruce has seriously misread Godwyn, whom

he accuses of "morbidly austere standards of Puritanism . . . in the spirit of a Bunyan or a Mather." Bruce even states (206 n. 2) that *Negro's & Indians Advocate,* was dedicated to Cromwell; it was, in fact, dedicated to the archbishop of Canterbury.

63. Godwyn, *Negro's & Indians Advocate,* 124 (misnumbered 2d p. 108), 128 (misnumbered 2d p. 112), 161 (quotation).

64. Some, but by no means all, of the British charters called for proselytizing the Indians. See W. Keith Kavenagh, ed., *Foundations of Colonial America,* 3 vols. (New York, 1974; reprint, New York, 1983), 1:57, 116, 120, 124, 3:1698, 1715.

65. Godwyn, *Supplement,* 7–8. Despite New England's relatively successful (compared to Virginia's) missionary efforts between 1645 and 1675, its record was less impressive than Godwyn implied and, after King Philip's War, the earlier success eroded precipitously. See especially William Kellaway, *The New England Company, 1649–1776, Missionary Society to the Indians* (London, 1961), esp. chaps. 5, 9.

66. Godwyn, *Directions for a Sculpture;* Godwyn, *Trade Preferr'd,* 24 (2d pagination); Godwyn, *"Brief Account of Religion,"* 3. In his effort to shame his coreligionists into action, Godwyn even praised the Algerian pirates—a current topic—for trying to convert their captives by promising freedom in return (*Supplement,* 6, 11).

67. Godwyn, *Negro's & Indians Advocate,* 167–74 (on Virginia), 137 (on Barbados).

68. Ibid., 154; Godwyn, *Supplement,* 8–9.

69. Godwyn, *Negro's & Indians Advocate,* 168–69, 153–55; Godwyn, *Supplement,* 8; Godwyn, *"Brief Account of Religion,"* 1–3.

70. Godwyn, *Negro's & Indians Advocate,* 153; Godwyn, *Supplement,* 8.

71. Godwyn, *Negro's & Indians Advocate,* sig. [A5v], 81 (quotation), 85, 100, 124 (misnumbered 2d p. 108), 155, 157, 160, 161; Godwyn, *Supplement,* 8; Godwyn, *Trade Preferr'd,* passim.

72. Godwyn, *Negro's & Indians Advocate,* 82–84, 40–41 (final quotation); Godwyn, *Supplement,* 10.

73. Leonard Woods Labaree, ed., *Royal Instructions to British Colonial Governors, 1670–1776,* 2 vols. (Washington, D.C., 1935), 2:507.

74. Godwyn, *Negro's & Indians Advocate,* 29 (1st quotation), 143–44, 153–54 (2d quotation); Godwyn, *Trade Preferr'd,* 26 (2d pagination).

75. Richard Baxter, *A Christian Directory: Or, A Summ of Practical Theologie, and Cases of Conscience* (London, 1673), 557–60. Baxter probably wrote the chapter on slaves in 1664–65 (see his "Advertisements" to the reader in *Christian Directory*), but it was not printed until 1673. Godwyn may have read it on his return to England in (probably) 1679 or 1680 and been influenced by its forceful argument. For Baxter's later writings, see Wing, *Short-Title Catalogue,* 1:133–39.

76. *DNB,* 19:1201–3. For Tryon's numerous publications, see Wing, *Short-Title Catalogue,* 3:397–98.

77. Philotheous Physiologous [Thomas Tryon], *Friendly Advice to the Gentlemen-Planters of the East and West Indies* (n.p., 1684), quotations from 75, 113, 222. David Brion Davis is one of the few historians of early American racial attitudes to give serious attention to Tryon; see *Slavery in Western Culture,* 371–74.

78. [Tryon], *Friendly Advice,* 190.

79. Ibid., 150; Godwyn, *Negro's & Indians Advocate,* 3, 36; see also 12, 14, 39.

80. Baxter, *Christian Directory*, 560.

81. Godwyn, *Negro's & Indians Advocate*, 20, 36.

82. Ibid., 37–38; Godwyn, *Supplement*, 4.

83. Population figures have been extrapolated from Richard C. Simmons, *The American Colonies from Settlement to Independence* (New York, 1976), 76, 124; John J. McCusker and Russell R. Menard, *The Economy of British America, 1607–1789* (Chapel Hill, N.C., 1985), 54, 136, 153; and Jack P. Greene, *Pursuits of Happiness: The Social Development of Early Modern British Colonies and the Formation of American Culture* (Chapel Hill, N.C., 1988), 178–79.

84. H. R. McIlwaine, ed., *Journals of the House of Burgesses of Virginia, 1695 . . . 1702* (Richmond, Va., 1913), 174.

85. Godwyn, *Supplement*, 9.

86. Godwyn, *Negro's & Indians Advocate*, 37–38, 96, 139–40.

87. For suggestive discussions of colonists' insecurities, see Page Smith, "Anxiety and Despair in American History," *William and Mary Quarterly*, 3d ser. 26 (1969): 416–26, esp. 417–20; Michael Zuckerman, "Identity in British America: Unease in Eden," in Nicholas Canny and Anthony Pagden, eds., *Colonial Identity in the Atlantic World, 1500–1800* (Princeton, N.J., 1987), 115–57, esp. 144–54; and from a broader perspective O. Mannoni, *Prospero and Caliban: The Psychology of Colonization*, trans. Pamela Powesland (1956; reprint, Ann Arbor, Mich., 1990), esp. 57–109.

88. For baptism in England, see Godwyn, *Negro's & Indians Advocate*, 13, especially the marginal comment, and 103; on attitudes toward blacks in England, see 161.

89. Ibid., 161–62.

90. Fryer, *Staying Power*, 22, documents several instances of collared slaves in England in the 1680s and 1690s. Fryer's notes to p. 22 include extensive quotes from newspaper advertisements for runaway slaves wearing identification collars; a comparison of those quotes with the British Library's microfilms of the original newspapers confirms their substantial accuracy. For use of the collar as a punishment for a slave in Maryland in 1688, see *WMQ*, 1st ser. 10 (1901–02): 177–78.

91. For example, see Godwyn, *Negro's & Indians Advocate*, 29–30, 37, 112, 113–14 (misnumbered 2d pp. 97–98); quotation on 113.

92. Ibid., 96; Hening, ed., *Statutes of Virginia*, 2:260.

93. Virginia had a printing press very briefly in the early 1680s; it was suppressed by the government and did not reappear until 1729 or 1730. Barbados did not have a press until 1730. See Lawrence C. Wroth, *The Colonial Printer* (Portland, Me., 1938), 38–39; and Douglas C. McMurtie, *Early Printing in Barbados* (London, 1933).

94. Labaree, ed., *Royal Instructions*, 2:505–6.

95. Henry R. Plomer, *A Dictionary of the Booksellers and Printers Who Were at Work in England, Scotland and Ireland from 1641 to 1667* (1907; reprint, Oxford, 1968), 61; Henry R. Plomer, *A Dictionary of the Booksellers and Printers Who Were at Work in England, Scotland and Ireland from 1668 to 1725* (Oxford, 1922), 97; Paul G. Morrison, *Index of Printers, Publishers and Booksellers in Donald Wing's Short-Title Catalogue* (Charlottesville, Va., 1955), 69.

96. Plomer, *Dictionary of Booksellers and Printers 1668 to 1725*, 293; Morrison, *Index of Printers*, 196–97.

97. Godwyn, *Negro's & Indians Advocate*, sig. [A5v].

98. Brokesby, *Some Proposals*, 10.

99. Godwyn, *Negro's & Indians Advocate,* 112. The evidence is abundant that missionaries met stiff resistance from slave owners. See, for example, Francis Le Jau, *The Carolina Chronicle of Dr. Francis Le Jau, 1706–1717,* ed. Frank W. Klingberg (Berkeley, Calif., 1956), entries for 30 Aug. 1712, 11 Dec. 1712, and 23 Feb. 1713.

100. The literature on early antislavery and antiracist thought is extensive. Especially useful are Roger Bruns, ed., *Am I Not a Man and a Brother: The Antislavery Crusade of Revolutionary America, 1688–1788* (New York, 1977); and J. William Frost, ed., *The Quaker Origins of Antislavery* (Norwood, Pa., 1980). See also Wylie Sypher, *Guinea's Captive Kings: British Anti-Slavery Literature of the XVIIIth Century* (Chapel Hill, N.C., 1942); and Davis, *Slavery in Western Culture,* pt. 3.

CHAPTER 4: FRONTIER BANDITTI AND THE INDIANS

1. *Archives of the State of New Jersey,* 1st ser. 9 (*Documents Relating to the Colonial History of the State of New Jersey . . . 1757–1767,* ed. Frederick W. Ricord and W[illia]m Nelson [Newark, 1885]): 569–70 (hereafter cited as *N.J. Archives*). Throughout this essay I have usually cited only the most authoritative version of each source; in a few instances I have also indicated more readily accessible versions. Some documents—Shelburne's circular and many of Sir William Johnson's letters, for example—appear in two or more collections with minor orthographic variations.

2. Pennsylvania's ill-treatment of the Indians in the 1760s and 1770s was probably matched—and at times exceeded—by Virginia's and the Carolinas'. No colony's record was spotless, but in general the New England colonies had fewer incidents because their Indian populations had by then diminished to very small numbers. New York's Indians were almost entirely in the northern section where Iroquois leaders and Sir William Johnson kept affairs in relatively good order, and Georgia's colonial population was still sparse. But see Georgia's law of 20 June 1774, which complains that friendly Indians have been murdered by "ill disposed persons": Charles C. Jones, ed., *Acts Passed by the General Assembly [of Georgia], 1755–1774* (Wormsloe, Ga., 1881), 401. Maryland, Delaware, and New Jersey had few Indians and proportionately little frontier area. For a discussion of New Jersey's handling of interracial crime in the 1760s, see below, section III.

3. Pennsylvania's early Indian relations have been frequently recounted and often uncritically praised. Comprehensive or interpretive studies include Rayner Wickersham Kelsey, *Friends and the Indians, 1655–1917* (Philadelphia, 1917); Thomas E. Drake, "William Penn's Experiment in Race Relations," *Pennsylvania Magazine of History and Biography* 68 (1944): 372–87; Anthony F. C. Wallace, *King of the Delawares: Teedyuscung, 1700–1763* (Philadelphia, 1949); Frederick B. Tolles, "Nonviolent Contract: The Quakers and the Indians," *American Philosophical Society Proceedings* 107 (1963):93–101; Francis Jennings, "Miquon's Passing: Indian-European Relations in Colonial Pennsylvania, 1674 to 1755," Ph.D. dissertation, University of Pennsylvania, 1965; George Arthur Cribbs, "The Frontier Policy of Pennsylvania," *Western Pennsylvania Historical Magazine* 2 (1919): 5–35, 72–106, 174–98; and Thomas J. Sugrue, "The Peopling and Depeopling of Early Pennsylvania: Indians and Colonists, 1680–1720," *Pa. Mag. Hist. & Biog.,*

116 (1992): 3–31. For evidence that before 1763 Pennsylvania on several occasions took strong action against colonists for killing friendly Indians see *Pennsylvania Archives*, 1st ser., 12 vols. (Philadelphia, 1852–54), 1:215–26 passim; *Pa. Archives*, 4th ser., 12 vols. (Philadelphia, 1900–1902), 1:449–52; *[Pennsylvania Colonial Records], Minutes of the Provincial Council of Pennsylvania*, 16 vols. (Harrisburg, 1838–51), 3:321–24 and 4:725; Nicholas B. Wainwright, ed., "George Croghan's Journal, 1759–1763," *Pa. Mag. Hist. & Biog.* 71 (1947): 412; and Henry Graham Ashmead, *History of Delaware County, Pennsylvania* (Philadelphia, 1884), 164. Even in these cases, evidence for execution of the murderers is not always conclusive.

4. On the political implications of the Paxton Boys see Brooke Hindle, "The March of the Paxton Boys," *William and Mary Quarterly*, 3d ser. 3 (1946): 461–86; Theodore Thayer, *Pennsylvania Politics and the Growth of Democracy, 1740–1776* (Harrisburg, 1953); James E. Crowley, "The Paxton Disturbances and Ideas of Order in Pennsylvania Politics," *Pennsylvania History* 37 (1970): 317–39; James Kirby Martin, "The Return of the Paxton Boys and the *Historical* State of the Pennsylvania Frontier, 1764–1774," ibid., 38 (1971): 117–33; and Peter A. Butzin, "Politics, Presbyterians and the Paxton Riots, 1763–64," *Journal of Presbyterian History* 85 (1973): 70–84. Social and religious concerns are stressed in Wayland F. Dunaway, *The Scotch-Irish of Colonial Pennsylvania* (Chapel Hill, N.C., 1944); Theodore Thayer, *Israel Pemberton, King of the Quakers* (Philadelphia, 1943); and David Sloan, " 'A Time of Sifting and Winnowing': The Paxton Riots and Quaker Non-Violence in Pennsylvania," *Quaker History* 66 (1977): 3–22. The pamphlets that emerged from the massacre at Lancaster and the march on Philadelphia are emphasized and reprinted in John R. Dunbar, ed., *The Paxton Papers* (The Hague, 1957). Visual aspects are discussed in E. P. Richardson, "The Birth of Political Caricatures," in Robert F. Looney, ed., *Philadelphia Printmaking: American Prints before 1860* (West Chester, Pa., 1976), 70–89. For an example of the literature—mostly from the nineteenth century—that exonerates the Paxton Boys, see "The Insurrection of the Paxton Boys," *The Presbyterian Quarterly Review* 8 (1859–60): 627–77.

5. The word "Banditti," with various modifiers, appears frequently in documents of the 1760s and 1770s. William Johnson and Thomas Gage were especially fond of it.

6. Exact figures on frontier casualties are, of course, impossible to determine, but a sense of their abundance can be gleaned from C. Hale Sipe, *The Indian Wars of Pennsylvania*, 2 ed. (Harrisburg, 1931), chaps. 5–21, passim. For a more precise but limited example see "List of Pennsylvania Settlers Murdered, Scalped and Taken Prisoners by Indians, 1755–1756," *Pa. Mag. Hist. & Biog.* 32 (1908): 309–19.

7. For the background to the events of 1763, see Charles H. Lincoln, *The Revolutionary Movement in Pennsylvania* (Philadelphia, 1901), 40–52, on the composition of the Assembly; James H. Hutson, *Pennsylvania Politics, 1746–1770: The Movement for Royal Government and Its Consequences* (Princeton, N.J., 1972), 17–85, on the political struggle over frontier defense; Dunaway, *Scotch-Irish*, 50–71, 143–55, on westward migration and Indian affairs; and George W. Franz, *Paxton: A Study in Community Structure and Mobility in the Colonial Pennsylvania Backcountry* (New York, 1989), on the town and its inhabitants. Most of the relevant primary sources are in *Pa. Col. Recs.*, vols. 8–9, and *Pa. Archives*, 1st ser., vols. 3–4. The quote is from Richard Peters to the Pennsylvania Proprietors, 25 Nov. 1755, Richard Peters Papers (Historical Society of Pennsylvania).

8. The events at Conestoga and Lancaster are documented in *Pa. Col. Recs.*, 9:89–106; *Pa. Archives*, 1st ser. 4:147–55; Dunbar, *Paxton Papers*, passim; correspondence scattered through *The Papers of Sir William Johnson*, ed. James Sullivan and Milton W. Hamilton, 14 vols. (Albany, N.Y., 1921–65), esp. 11; and several fugitive items in a wide range of publications and manuscripts. For specific citations see Hindle, "March of the Paxton Boys"; Dunbar, introduction to *Paxton Papers*; and note 10 below. None of the Paxton Boys was ever prosecuted. Lazarus Stewart, a notorious border ruffian, was arrested in 1770 but not for his role in 1763. On this point, Francis Parkman, *The Conspiracy of Pontiac and the Indian War after the Conquest of Canada*, 6th ed. rev., 2 vols. (Boston, 1874), 2:128, is incorrect. See *Pa. Col. Recs.*, 9:683, 687.

9. The best account of the Moravian mission Indians is Edmund [Alexander] De Schweinitz, *The Life and Times of David Zeisberger: The Western Pioneer and Apostle of the Indians* (Philadelphia, 1870), which is based extensively on Moravian manuscripts. The immediate background of the move to Philadelphia and the attempt to find a haven in New York before the arrival of the Paxton Boys is on 274–97. Also useful are George Henry Loskiel, *History of the Mission of the United Brethren among the Indians in North America*, trans. Christian Ignatius La Trobe (London, 1794); John Heckewelder, *A Narrative of the Mission of the United Brethren among the Delaware and Mohican Indians . . .* (Philadelphia, 1820); and John W. Jordan, "Biographical Sketch of Rev. Bernhard Adam Grube," *Pa. Mag. Hist. & Biog.* 25 (1901): 14–19, which includes extracts from Grube's writings and other Moravian manuscripts.

10. The march on Philadelphia is documented by numerous items in *Pa. Archives*, 1st ser. 4:154–63; *Pa. Col. Recs.* 9:100–34; William Henry to John Heckewelder, n.d., Heckewelder, *Narrative of the United Brethren*, 78–80; "Fragments of a Journal Kept by Samuel Foulke, of Bucks County . . . ," *Pa. Mag. Hist. & Biog.* 5 (1881): 60–73; "Narrative of [Matthew] Smith," J. I. Mombert, *An Authentic History of Lancaster County . . .* (Lancaster, Pa., 1869), 187–89; Jordan, "Sketch of Rev. Grube," 15–16; De Schweinitz, *Life of Zeisberger*, 298–303; *The Journals of Henry Melchior Muhlenberg*, trans. and ed. Theodore G. Tappert and John W. Doberstein, 3 vols. (Philadelphia, 1945), 2:18–24; [Alexander Graydon], *Memoirs of a Life, Chiefly Passed in Pennsylvania . . .* (Harrisburg, Pa., 1811), 38–40; Samuel Hazard, ed., *The Register of Pennsylvania*, 16 vols. (Philadelphia, 1823–35), 12:10–11; David Rittenhouse to Benjamin Smith Barton, 16 Feb. 1764, in William Barton, *Memoirs of the Life of David Rittenhouse* (Philadelphia, 1813), 148–49; Dunbar, *Paxton Papers*, passim.

11. Franklin's *Narrative of the Late Massacres, in Lancaster County . . .* (Philadelphia, 1764) is best consulted in Leonard W. Labaree and William B. Wilcox, eds., *The Papers of Benjamin Franklin*, 25 vols. to date (New Haven, 1959–), 11:42–69, which has an extensive introduction and copious notes. The *Narrative* (without annotation) and the other key publications, with a few tracts previously unpublished, are in Dunbar, *Paxton Papers*. For authenticity's sake, I have quoted from the Early American Imprint microcards of the original editions of the Paxton tracts.

12. *The Conduct of the Paxton Men, Impartially Represented* (Philadelphia, 1764), 17; [Matthew Smith and James Gibson], *A Declaration and Remonstrance* (Philadelphia, 1764), 16; Agricola [pseud.], *The Squabble, A Pastoral Ecologue*, 2d ed. (Philadelphia, 1764), 6. The quotes also appear in Dunbar, *Paxton Papers*, 283, 108, and 145 respectively.

13. Foulke, "Fragments of a Journal," 67; Franklin to John Fothergill, 14 Mar. 1764, *Franklin Papers,* 11:103; Franklin to Richard Jackson, 11 Feb. 1764, ibid., 77; Franklin to Lord Kames, 2 June 1765, ibid., 12: 160–61.

14. *A [second] Dialogue, Containing some Reflections on the late Declaration and Remonstrance* (Philadelphia, 1764), 9; *An Historical Account of the Late Disturbance . . . ,* 2d ed. (Philadelphia, 1764), 7; Franklin, *Narrative of the Late Massacres,* 13. The quotes also appear in Dunbar, *Paxton Papers,* 119, 129, and 63 respectively. Some idea of the breadth of anti-Indian sentiment is conveyed in a letter from Penn to William Johnson, about two weeks after the compromise at Germantown. Penn still feared for the Moravian Indians' lives and was not sure the government could protect them much longer. *Johnson Papers,* 4:327.

15. George Roberts to Samuel Powel, 21 May 1765, "Powel-Roberts Correspondence, 1761–1765," *Pa. Mag. Hist. & Biog.* 18 (1894): 41.

16. The attack on the wagon train and the subsequent siege of Fort Loudoun were primarily clashes between frontiersmen and royal troops, but they began with frontier determination to keep trade and condolence goods (including, perhaps, scalping knives) from reaching the Indians, and the whole episode was closely connected to Pennsylvania's management of Indian affairs. See Stephen H. Cutcliffe, "Sideling Hill Affair: The Cumberland County Riots of 1765," *Western Pennsylvania Historical Magazine* 59 (1976): 39–53; and Eleanor M. Webster, "Insurrection at Fort Loudon in 1765: Rebellion or Preservation of Peace?" ibid., 47 (1964): 125–39; Franklin to John Ross, 8 June 1765, *Franklin Papers,* 12: 172–73; Thomas Wharton to Franklin, 25 Mar. 1765, ibid., 92–95; Samuel Wharton to Franklin, 27 May 1765, ibid., 142–45; John Penn to William Johnson, 23 May 1765, *Johnson Papers,* 11:746–47; Penn to Thomas Gage, 28 June 1765, *Pa. Col. Recs.,* 9:275–277. A participant's account is James Smith, *An Account of the Remarkable Occurrences in the Life and Travels of Col. James Smith . . .* (Lexington, Ky., 1799), 60–63.

17. Samuel Wharton to Franklin, 27 May 1765, *Franklin Papers,* 12:142; William Johnson to John Penn, 19 Dec. 1766, *Johnson Papers,* 12:231–32; "Journal of Indian Affairs," 18–30 Dec. 1766, ibid., 240; "At a Conference at Fort-Stanwix . . . ," 18 Oct. 1766, ibid., 623–24; Johnson to Gage, 17 Apr. 1766, ibid., 74–75; Gage to Penn, 10 Mar. 1766, *Pa. Col. Recs.,* 9:307; Franklin to Johnson, 12 Sept. 1766, *Franklin Papers,* 13:416.

18. "To the Officers Commanding the several posts . . . ," 15 Jan. 1766, *Pa. Col. Recs.* 9:307; Francis Fauquier to John Penn, 11 Dec. 1766, ibid., 349–50; Penn to Assembly, 2 Feb. 1764, ibid., 129; Webster, "Insurrection at Fort Loudon," 134–36.

19. For Penn's position on change of venue see *Pa. Col. Recs.,* 9:446; for General Gage's see Clarence Edwin Carter, ed., *The Correspondence of General Thomas Gage with the Secretaries of State, 1763–1775,* 2 vols. (New Haven, Conn., 1931–33), 1:152–53. For an unsuccessful attempt by Franklin and other Pennsylvania assemblymen to legislate a change of venue after the Conestoga and Lancaster massacres, see Foulke, "Fragments of a Journal," 67; and *Pa. Archives,* 8th ser. 7:5504.

20. The laws of 1744 and 1770 are in James T. Mitchell and Henry Flanders, comps., *The Statutes at Large of Pennsylvania from 1682 to 1801,* 16 vols. (Harrisburg, Pa., 1896–1908), 5:5–6, 7:350–53. Relevant passages of the Mutiny Act are reprinted in *Collections of the Illinois State Historical Library,* 10 (*British Series,* 1: *The Critical Period, 1763–1765,* ed. Clarence Walworth Alvord and Clarence

Edwin Carter [Springfield, Ill., 1915)]: 484–86. For applications of the Mutiny Act see Thomas Gage to Lord Hillsborough, 7 Oct. 1769, in ibid., 16 (*British Series, 3: Trade and Politics, 1767–1769*, ed. Alvord and Carter [Springfield, Ill., 1921]): 630; and William Johnson to George Croghan, 11 June 1772, *Johnson Papers*, 12:967. Misleading statements about change of venue include Parkman, *Conspiracy of Pontiac*, 2:116n, 128, 128n; and Martin, "Return of the Paxton Boys," 117–18.

21. "Extract of a Letter from Winchester, Virginia," 30 Apr. 1765, *Pa. Archives*, 1st ser. 4:217; "Extract of a Letter from Fort Loudon, 1765," ibid., 218; "A Message to the Governor from the Assembly" [19 Feb. 1768], *Pa. Col. Recs.*, 9:479. In 1765 one of the murderers was brought to trial but acquitted by the jury despite (according to Governor Penn) sufficient evidence to convict. Penn to Lord Shelburne, 21 Jan. 1767, ibid., 352.

22. "A Message to the Governor from the Assembly" [19 Feb. 1768], ibid., 479; John Penn to William Sharp and Francis Fauquier, 11 Mar. 1766, ibid., 305–6; Penn to William Johnson, 11 Mar. 1766, ibid., 306; Deposition of Lemuel Barritt, 6 Mar. 1766, *Johnson Papers*, 5:52–54; William Johnson to George Croghan, 28 Mar. 1766, ibid., 119; Johnson to Henry Moore, 21 Apr. 1766, ibid., 194; Fauquier to Penn, 11 Dec. 1766, *Pa. Col. Recs.*, 9:349–50.

23. Penn to Johnson, 21 Jan. 1768, *Pa. Col. Recs.*, 9:424–25; McKee to Croghan, 13 Feb. 1768, *Johnson Papers*, 6:101–2. On scalping as a declaration of war see William Johnson to Frederick Haldimand, 9 June 1774, ibid., 8:1164.

24. Penn to Johnson, 21 Jan. 1768, *Johnson Papers*, 12:419–21; Johnson to Gage, 18 Feb. 1768, ibid., 428–29; Croghan to Johnson, 1 Mar. 1768, *Ill. State Hist. Soc. Collections*, 16:179–80.

25. Deposition of William Blyth, 19 Jan. 1768, *Pa. Col. Recs.*, 9:414–15; Edward Shippen to Penn, 28 Jan. 1768, ibid., 435; Penn to Sheriffs of Cumberland, Lancaster, and Chester Counties, 2 Feb. 1768, ibid., 441–42; John Armstrong to Penn, 24 Jan. 1768, ibid., 444–45; Penn to Armstrong, 3 Feb. 1768, ibid., 446; John Holmes to Penn, 7 Feb. 1768, ibid., 463–65; George Croghan to William Johnson, 2 Feb. 1768, *Johnson Papers*, 6:91; Croghan to Johnson, 7 Feb. 1768, ibid., 12: 425; *Pennsylvania Chronicle, and Universal Advertiser,* 1–8 Feb. 1768. Patterson paid heavily for his affront to frontier prejudices. Several contemporaries reported that his life and property were threatened; eventually he had to move away from the area. See, for example, Thomas Wharton to Benjamin Franklin, 9 Feb. 1768, *Franklin Papers*, 15:40; and Joseph Galloway to Franklin, 10 Mar. 1768, ibid., 72.

26. Croghan to William Johnson [7 Feb. 1768], *Johnson Papers*, 12:425; Armstrong to Penn, 29 Jan., 1768, *Pa. Col. Recs.*, 9:448–49; Penn to Armstrong, 4 Feb. 1768, ibid., 451–53; Armstrong to Penn, 7 Feb. 1768, ibid., 462–63; Deposition of James Cunningham, 4 Feb. 1768, ibid., 450–51 (a more detailed version, delivered to the assembly, appears in *Pa. Archives*, 8th ser. [*Votes of Assembly* (Harrisburg, Pa., 1931–35)] 7: 6131–34); Edward Shippen to James Tilghman, 2 Feb. 1768, Shippen Family Papers (HSP), 6:196; John Penn to Thomas Penn, 21 Jan. 1768, Penn Manuscripts, Records of the Proprietory Government: Official Correspondence (HSP), 10:126; same to same, 8 Feb. 1768, ibid., 130–32; William Allen to Thomas Penn, 25 Feb. 1768, ibid., 136–38; *Pa. Chronicle*, 1–8 Feb., 8–15 Feb., and 14–21 Mar. 1768; Thomas Wharton to Benjamin Franklin, 9 Feb. 1768, *Franklin Papers*, 15:39–40. In May 1768, a grand jury presented the names of twenty-three of Stump's and Ironcutter's rescuers

to the court of oyer and terminer in Cumberland County and referred to "divers others to the said Inquest unknown." Court Papers, 1768—Cumberland Co., RG-33, Division of Archives and Manuscripts, Pa. Historical and Museum Commission (Harrisburg). For a thorough analysis of the Stump episode and its legal implications see G. S. Rowe, "The Frederick Stump Affair, 1768, and Its Challenge to Legal Historians of Early Pennsylvania," *Pennsylvania History* 49 (1982): 259–88; the most comprehensive assessment is Linda A. Ries, " 'The Rage of Opposing Government': The Stump Affair of 1768," *Cumberland County History* 1 (1984): 21–45.

27. Gage to Shelburne, 10 Oct. 1767, *Gage Correspondence*, 1:152; Croghan to Benjamin Franklin, 12 Feb. 1768, *Franklin Papers*, 15:43.

28. "A Message to the Governor from the Assembly," 5 Feb. 1768, *Pa. Col. Recs.* 9:454–58; "A Message from the Governor to the Assembly," 8 Feb. 1768, ibid., 459–61; "A Message to the Governor from the Assembly" [20 (?) Feb. 1768], ibid., 473–80; Galloway to Franklin, 10 Mar. 1768, *Franklin Papers*, 15:72. See also "A Message to the Governor from the Assembly," 13 Jan. 1768, ibid., 408–12, which was written before news of the Stump affair reached Philadelphia but stresses the same theme as the subsequent messages—that the Paxton affair triggered a series of unpunished murders for which the governor is partly responsible.

29. Hillsborough to Penn, 12 Mar. 1768, *Pa. Archives*, 1st ser. 4:296; Croghan to William Johnson, 7 Feb. 1768, *Johnson Papers*, 12:425; *Pa. Archives*, 8th ser. 7:6158–61, 6163–64; Johnson to Penn, 16 Mar. 1768, *Pa. Col. Recs.* 9:495–96. On 3 Feb. 1768 a Pennsylvania law to prevent further encroachment on Indian lands stipulated that capital offenses incurred under the act were to be decided by the colony's supreme court or a court of oyer and terminer in Philadelphia County. This law would not have applied to the murder cases discussed here. Mitchell and Flanders, comps., *Statutes of Pennsylvania*, 7:152.

30. Johnson to Penn, 16 Mar. 1768, *Pa. Col. Recs.*, 9:495–96; "Extract from the Proceedings of a General Congress of the Six Nations . . . ," Mar. 1768, ibid., 496–509 (quotations at 499–500).

31. "Minutes of Conferences held at Fort Pitt, in April and May, 1768 . . . ," ibid., 514–43.

32. Minutes of a Council Meeting, 18 July 1769, ibid., 603; James Tilghman to William Johnson, 20 July 1769, *Johnson Papers*, 7:62–64; Court Papers, 1769—Cumberland Co., RG-33, Division of Archives and Manuscripts (PHMC); Lord Botetourt to John Penn, 20 Mar. 1770, *Pa. Archives*, 1st ser. 4:365–66.

33. Colonial officials were forever lamenting their inability to bring culprits to trial and made much of the few exceptions. The absence of any reference in the surviving records to a trial is therefore strong evidence that none occurred.

34. Deposition of Richard Brown, 7 Sept. 1771, ibid., 431–32; Arthur St. Clair to Joseph Shippen Jr., 24 Sept. 1771, ibid., 437; St. Clair to Penn, 29 May 1774, ibid., 503–4; "A Message to the Governor from the Assembly," 23 July 1774, ibid., 555; Proclamation of 28 July 1774, *Pa. Col. Recs.*, 10:199; "A Message to the Chiefs and Warriors of the Delaware Indians," 6 Aug. 1774, ibid., 204–5; "A Message from the Governor to the Assembly," 18 July 1774, ibid., 196. In the absence of more evidence, there is no way of knowing how many of the murders in southwestern Pennsylvania should be attributed to Virginians rather than Pennsylvanians. Both colonies claimed the area, and many Virginians settled there in the 1760s and 1770s.

35. *N.J. Archives,* 9:576.

36. Ibid., 575.

37. *The Pennsylvania Gazette,* 10 July 1766, 17 July 1766, 7 Aug. 1766; Franklin to Shelburne, 16 Dec. 1766, *N.J. Archives,* 9:575.

38. *The Pennsylvania Gazette,* 17 July 1766, 7 Aug. 1766.

39. Franklin to Shelburne, 16 Dec. 1766, *N.J. Archives,* 9:575; *Pennsylvania Journal and the Weekly Advertiser,* 17 Apr. 1766; William Franklin to William Johnson, 15 Apr. 1766, *Johnson Papers,* 12:72–73; Abraham Van Campen to Franklin, 11 Apr. 1766, ibid., 5: 170–71; "Proclamation of Governor Franklin," 15 Apr. 1766, ibid., 172–73; Franklin to Van Campen, 15 Apr. 1766, ibid., 173–74; "New Jersey Council Proceedings," 8 Nov.–11 Dec. 1766, ibid., 418–22.

40. *The Pennsylvania Gazette,* 1 Jan. 1767; *Pennsylvania Journal and the Weekly Advertiser,* 1 Jan. 1767; *New York Journal or General Advertiser,* 8 Jan. 1767.

41. [Samuel Wharton] to Johnson, 28 Dec. 1766, *Johnson Papers,* 12:237; *New York Mercury,* 6 July 1767; "A Message to the Governor from the Assembly," 13 Jan. 1768, *Pa. Col. Recs.,* 9:410.

42. William Johnson to George Croghan, 11 June 1772, *Johnson Papers,* 12:967; Thomas Gage to Johnson, 30 Nov. 1772, ibid., 1005; Johnson to Frederick Haldimand, 28 Aug. 1773, ibid., 8:879.

43. Gage to John Penn, 2 July 1766, *Pa. Col. Recs.,* 9:321; "Extracts of an Abstract from Mr. Croghan's Journal," 22 May 1766, ibid., 322; Johnson to Penn, 24 Oct. 1769, *Pa. Archives,* 1st ser. 4:349. A slightly different and less complete version of the latter letter appears in *Johnson Papers,* 7:226–27.

44. Most of the documentation for Governor Penn's and the assembly's efforts to keep peace on the frontier are in *Pa. Col. Recs.,* vols. 9–10; and *Pa. Archives,* 1st ser. 4. Evidence of efforts by imperial officials are found in the *Johnson Papers* and the *Gage Correspondence.* Lord Dunmore's War is conveniently summarized in Jack M. Sosin, *The Revolutionary Frontier, 1763–1783* (New York, 1967), 84–86. Sosin discusses the war's causes in "The British Indian Department and Dunmore's War," *Virginia Magazine of History and Biography* 74 (1966): 34–50. See also Randolph C. Downes, "Dunmore's War: An Interpretation," *Mississippi Valley Historical Review* 21 (1934–35): 311–30.

45. St. Clair to Penn, 29 May 1774, *Pa. Archives,* 1st ser. 4:503.

46. Johnson to Gage, 4 July 1774, *Johnson Papers,* 12:1114–16. Cresap was never charged with murder, partly because Dunmore's War was soon under way and partly, perhaps, because he was not the principal culprit in the killings that touched off the war. Daniel Greathouse (Gratehouse, Gritehouse)—who was not prosecuted either—was, according to most testimony, the instigator of the slaughter of several Indian men and women, including the relatives of Mingo chief Logan. Cresap was blamed in Logan's famous speech and in Thomas Jefferson's *Notes on the State of Virginia.* Cresap was defended in a variety of later writings, especially in [John J. Jacobs], *A Biographical Sketch of the Life of the Late Capt. Michael Cresap* (Cumberland, Md., 1826). A few early accounts blame Cresap, for example, the letter from Johnson quoted above and Johnson to Dartmouth, 20 June 1774, E. B. O'Callaghan and B. Fernow, eds., *Documents Relative to the Colonial History of the State of New York,* 15 vols. (Albany, N.Y., 1853–87) 8:459–60. For evidence that exonerates Cresap from the Yellow Creek massacre but not from some of the other frontier killings, see "Extract from the Journal of Alexander M'Kee . . . ," 3 May [1774], ibid., 464; William Crawford to George Washington, 8 May 1774, C. W. Butterfield, ed., *The Washington-Craw-*

ford Letters (Cincinnati, 1877), 47–48; the several testimonies in Jacobs, *Life of Cresap*, appendix; Reuben Gold Thwaites and Louise Phelps Kellogg, eds., *Documentary History of Dunmore's War, 1774* (Madison, Wis., 1905), 9–19, 377–78; and the retrospective account in George Rogers Clark to Samuel Brown, 17 June 1798, *Collections of the Illinois State Historical Library*, 8 (*Virginia Series*, 3: *George Rogers Clark Papers, 1771–1781*, ed. James Alton James [Springfield, Ill., 1912]): 3–9.

47. See, for example, the treaty of 1621 between Massasoit of the Wampanoags and Plymouth Colony in [William Bradford and Edward Winslow], *A Relation or Iournall . . . of the English Plantation setled at Plimouth . . .* (London, 1622; facs. reprint, New York, 1966), 37, clause 2: "if any of his [Massasoit's] did hurt to any of ours, he should send the offender, that we might punish him." A treaty of 8 May 1765 between the English and the Delawares is far more explicit. The Delawares, article 7 says in part, "do promise & engage never to take revenge for any Act committed by Individuals of the British Nation . . . And should any of the Delawares . . . rob, murder, or otherwise misuse any of his Majesty's Subjects, . . . they are without Excuse or delay, to bring such offenders to the nearest Garrison . . . ," *Pa. Col. Recs.*, 9:278–79. See also note 49 below.

48. William Penn, "A Further Account of the Province of Pennsylvania . . . ," Albert Cook Myers, ed., *Narratives of Early Pennsylvania, West New Jersey, and Delaware, 1630–1707* (New York, 1912), 276; "A Treaty Held at the Town of Lancaster . . . ," *Pa. Col. Recs.*, 4:725.

49. The treaty of 1677 between several Chesapeake tribes and Charles II (conducted by the governor of Virginia) provided that colonists who abused Indians or their property be turned over to colonial authorities for punishment, rather than be punished by the Indians, "which is but just and Reasonable they [the signatory Indians] oweneing themselves to be under the Allegiance of his most Sacred Majestie." *Va. Mag. Hist. & Biog.* 14 (1906–7): 289–96, clause 5.

50. See Article 7 of the "Treaty of Peace with the Delaware Nation . . . ," *Pa. Col. Recs.*, 9:278–79. Occasionally English observers praised Indians for respecting individual rights or possessions, but generally Englishmen concluded that because Indians had no written laws they lived almost in a state of anarchy, as the Delaware treaty of 1765, for example, made clear. For an example of the former view see Hugh Jones, *The Present State of Virginia*, ed. Richard L. Morton (Chapel Hill, N.C., 1956), 57–58.

51. "Extracts of an Abstract from Mr. Croghan's Journal," *Pa. Col. Recs.* 9:322; "Proceedings of Sir William Johnson with the Indians," July 1770, *Docs. Relative to Col. N.Y.*, 8:239; "George Croghan's Journal, 1759–1763," ed. Nicholas B. Wainwright, *Pa. Mag. Hist. & Biog.* 71 (1947): 403. For a similar statement by a Shawnee chief in 1774 see "Extract for the Journal of Alexander McKee . . . ," *Docs. Relative to Col. N.Y.*, 8:461–62.

52. Weiser to Richard Peters, 14 July 1747, *Pa. Archives*. 1st ser. 1:758. Modern generalizations about Indian motives and methods of warfare must be used cautiously because one tribe's customs were not necessarily another's. An important study of a southern tribe that has general application to Indians in Pennsylvania as well is John Phillip Reid, *A Law of Blood: The Primitive Law of the Cherokee Nation* (New York, 1970), chaps. 9–10, 16–18. On the Iroquois, see Daniel K. Richter, "War and Culture: The Iroquois Experience," *William and Mary Quarterly*, 3d ser. 40 (1983): 528–59.

53. Lord Dartmouth to William Johnson, 6 July 1774, *Docs. Relative to Col. N.Y.,* 8:468; Dartmouth to Cadwallader Colden, 6 July 1774, ibid.

54. "Extract from the Proceedings of a General Congress," March 1768, *Pa. Col. Recs.,* 9:499; William Johnson to Lord Dartmouth, 20 June 1774, *Docs. Relative to Col. N.Y.,* 8:460.

55. "Extract from the Proceedings of a General Congress," March 1768, *Pa. Col. Recs.,* 9:499; "Proceedings of Sir William Johnson with the Indians," June–July 1774, *Docs. Relative to Col. N.Y.,* 8:476; William Johnson to Thomas Gage, 4 July 1774, *Johnson Papers,* 12:1115; Johnson to Haldimand, 9 June 1774, ibid., 8:1165; Gage to Dartmouth, 29 Aug. 1774, *Gage Correspondence,* 1:368; Dartmouth to Cadwallader Colden, 6 July 1774, *Docs. Relative to Col. N.Y.,* 8:468. For another instance of the release of Indian prisoners see Johnson to Haldimand, 28 Aug. 1773, *Johnson Papers,* 8:879.

56. A good investigation of the rivalry for Indian allies is Jack M. Sosin, "The Use of Indians in the American Revolution: A Reassessment of Responsibility," *Canadian Historical Review* 46 (1965): 101–21.

57. A strong case could be made that Indians did not view *any* European-Americans as real friends. For all his diplomatic skill, William Johnson was distrusted by many tribes for favoring Iroquois claims at their rivals' expense. Moreover, Johnson was deeply involved in land acquisition, which inevitably meant a diminution in Indian holdings. And all British officials upheld European notions of sovereignty: the whole continent, they believed, was subject to imperial authority, to be imposed as rapidly as circumstances permitted. No prominent English or American figure, either in government or church affairs, was committed to Indian cultural or territorial integrity.

58. Despite the prolonged frontier atrocities, some Indians supported the Americans. The actions of the frontiersmen were therefore not always decisive, but they did, I contend, strongly predispose the majority of the tribes along the colonial frontier to side with the empire against its colonists. For the best analysis of Iroquois alignments, see Barbara Graymont, *The Iroquois in the American Revolution* (Syracuse, N.Y., 1972), esp. chaps. 2–5.

CHAPTER 5: "EXPULSION OF THE SALVAGES"

1. Many historians have recognized the massacre as a turning point in Indian-English relations, but few have explored its broader implications. Important treatments of early Indian-white relations are Wesley Frank Craven, "Indian Policy in Early Virginia," *William and Mary Quarterly,* 3d ser. 1 (1944):65–82, esp. 73–74, and *White, Red, and Black: The Seventeenth-Century Virginian* (Charlottesville, Va., 1971), chap. 2, esp. 49–55; Gary B. Nash, "The Image of the Indian in the Southern Colonial Mind," *WMQ,* 3d ser. 29 (1972):197–230, esp. 217–20, and *Red, White, and Black: The Peoples of Early America* (Englewood Cliffs, N.J., 1974), 61–62; and Edmund S. Morgan, *American Slavery, American Freedom: The Ordeal of Colonial Virginia* (New York, 1975), 97–100. Since the first publication of this essay, several works by J. Frederick Fausz have further clarified the events of 1607 to 1632, especially his "Fighting 'Fire' with Firearms: The Anglo-Powhatan Arms Race in Early Virginia," *American Indian Culture and Research Journal* 3, no. 4 (1979): 30–50; "Patterns of Anglo-Indian Aggression and Ac-

commodation along the Mid-Atlantic Coast, 1584–1634," in William W. Fitzhugh, ed., *Cultures in Contact: The Impact of European Contacts on Native American Cultural Institutions, A.D. 1000–1800* (Washington, D.C. and London, 1985), 225–68; and—less accessible but more comprehensive—"The Powhatan Uprising of 1622: A Historical Study of Ethnocentrism and Cultural Conflict" (Ph.D. dissertation, College of William and Mary, 1977). For Fausz's views on other historians' treatment of the massacre, see "The 'Barbarous Massacre' Reconsidered: The Powhatan Uprising of 1622 and the Historians," *Explorations in Ethnic Studies* 1 (1978): 16–36. See also James Axtell, "The Rise and Fall of the Powhatan Empire," in Axtell, *After Columbus: Essays in the Ethnohistory of Colonial North America* (New York, 1988), 182–221. Although I differ with each of these authors on a number of specific issues, it is not my purpose to debate them here. Rather, this essay seeks to document the patterns of pre-1622 attitudes and policies, to clarify their causal relation to the massacre, and to show the massacre's impact on English perceptions of the Indian and the resultant colonial policy. I have also suggested, where relevant to my argument, the Indians' reaction to English attitudes and policies. I am not, however, attempting fully to analyze early Indian-white relations from an Indian perspective. That undertaking has been skillfully performed by Nancy Oestreich Lurie, "Indian Cultural Adjustment to European Civilization," in James Morton Smith, ed., *Seventeenth-Century America: Essays in Colonial History* (Chapel Hill, N.C., 1959), 33–60. I would quarrel with Lurie's findings at only a few points.

2. Wyatt to [?], ca. 1623–24, in "Letters of Sir Francis Wyatt, Governor of Virginia, 1621–1626," *WMQ*, 2d ser. 6 (1926): 118.

3. E. G. R. Taylor, ed., *The Original Writings and Correspondence of the Two Richard Hakluyts*, 2 vols. (Hakluyt Society, *Publications*, 2nd ser. 76–77 [London, 1935]), 2:332, 329–30. Why the Elizabethan mind harbored such contempt for Indian culture is a question which has yet to be answered satisfactorily and is outside the scope of this essay. The Elizabethan image of the Indian undoubtedly owed something to the prevailing Spanish attitude as reflected in the publications of Richard Eden, Richard Hakluyt, and others. It may also have drawn on England's experience with Ireland, though I am less convinced of the Irish parallels than are some scholars. On that issue see chapter 2 in this volume.

4. Philip L. Barbour, ed., *The Jamestown Voyages under the First Charter, 1606–1609*, 2 vols. (Hakluyt Soc., *Pubs.*, 2d ser. 136–137 [Cambridge, 1969]), 1:50, hereafter cited as Barbour, ed., *Jamestown Voyages*.

5. On the fate of the Roanoke colony see David Beers Quinn, *Set Fair for Roanoke: Voyages and Colonies, 1584–1606* (Chapel Hill, N.C., 1985), chap. 19; on Indian-white contact at Roanoke see ibid., passim, and Karen Ordahl Kupperman, *Roanoke: The Abandoned Colony* (Totowa, N.J., 1984). The sources are conveniently collected and expertly edited in David Beers Quinn, ed., *The Roanoke Voyages, 1584–1590*, 2 vols. (Hakluyt Soc., *Pubs.*, 2d ser. 104–105 [London, 1955]).

6. During the Tudor era, scores of books—some by English authors, others in translation—described for English readers the appearance and character of the American Indians. Some notable examples of this literature included André Thevet, *The New Found Worlds*, trans. T[homas] Hacket (London, 1568); George Peckham, *A True Reporte of the late discoveries of the Newfoundland Landes* ... (London, 1583); René de Laudonnière, *A Notable Historie containing foure Voyages unto Florida*, trans. R[ichard] H[akluyt] (London, 1587); Jan Huygen

von Linschoten, *His Discours of Voyages into the Easte and West Indies*, trans. [William Phillip] (London, 1598); and Abraham Ortelius, *Abraham Ortelius his Epitome of the Theatre of the Worlde*, trans. James Shawe (London, 1603).

7. William Cunningham, *The Cosmographical Glasse* (London, 1559), fols. 200–201; [Robert Johnson], *Nova Britannia: Offering Most Excellent fruites by Planting in Virginia* (London, 1609), in Peter Force, ed., *Tracts and Other Papers . . .* , 4 vols. (Washington, D.C., 1836–47), 1 no. 6: 11, hereafter cited as [Johnson], *Nova Britannia*.

8. [King James I], *A Counterblaste to Tobacco* (London, 1604), sigs. B1–B2. "A father" refers collectively to the Indians.

9. Taylor, ed., *Writings of the Two Richard Halkuyts*, 2:216.

10. W[illiam] Crashaw, *A Sermon Preached in London before the right honorable the Lord Lawarre . . . Febr. 21, 1609* (London, 1610), sig. D4.

11. [Robert Gray], *A Good Speed to Virginia*, ed. Wesley F. Craven (New York, 1937; orig. publ. London, 1609), sigs. B1^r, C1.

12. [Johnson], *Nova Britannia*, 14.

13. [Gray], *Good Speed to Virginia*, ed. Craven, sigs. C2, C4^r.

14. Most of the evidence on early Indian-white contact in Virginia can be found in *The Complete Works of Captain John Smith (1580–1631)*, ed. Philip L. Barbour, 3 vols. (Chapel Hill, N.C., 1986), and in Barbour, ed., *Jamestown Voyages*.

15. Barbour, ed., *Jamestown Voyages*, 1:88.

16. The primacy of the missionary objective was stressed in the charters of 1606 and 1612 and in most of the company's instructions to resident governors as well as its propaganda pamphlets. See, for example, Samuel M. Bemiss, ed., *The Three Charters of the Virginia Company of London, with Seven Related Documents: 1606–1621*; Jamestown 350th Anniversary Historical Booklets, no. 4 (Williamsburg, 1957), 2, 15, 73, 76; [Gray], *Good Speed to Virginia*, ed. Craven, sig. C2^r; [Johnson], *Nova Britannia*, 6, 12; [London Company], *A True and sincere declaration of the purpose and ends of the Plantation . . .* (London, 1609), in Alexander Brown, ed., *Genesis of the United States . . .* , 2 vols. (Boston, 1890), 1:337–53, esp. 339, 347; and [London Company], *A True Declaration of the estate of the Colonie in Virginia . . .* (London, 1610), in Force, ed., *Tracts*, 3, no. 1:5. John Smith saw the hypocrisy of the company's leaders who made "Religion their colour, when all their aime was nothing but present profit" (*Works of Capt. John Smith*, ed. Barbour, 3:272).

17. *Works of Capt. John Smith*, ed. Barbour, 3:269. I have retained the italicization of the original publication (1631) in all quotes from Smith's works.

18. Ibid., 2:182, 188–89.

19. Ibid., 1:53–54, 234–38; 2:181–84.

20. Barbour, ed., *Jamestown Voyages*, 1:110, 141, 2:276. On the reliability of the Dutch chronicler and his sources see John Parker, *Van Meteren's Virginia, 1607–1612* (Minneapolis, 1961).

21. The conflicts of the early years are described by Smith and others in *Works of Capt. John Smith*, ed. Barbour, in various documents reprinted in Barbour, ed., *Jamestown Voyages*, and in Brown, ed., *Genesis of the United States*. See also J. Frederick Fausz, "An 'Abundance of Blood Shed on Both Sides': England's First Indian War, 1609–1614," *Virginia Magazine of History and Biography* 98 (1990):3–56.

22. [Robert Johnson], *The New Life of Virginea . . .* (London, 1612), in Force, ed., *Tracts*, 1, no. 7:18–19.

23. *Works of Capt. John Smith*, ed. Barbour, 1:228, 2:168. There have been numerous attempts to explain John Smith's attitudes toward the Indians; none of

them, in my opinion, is satisfactory. See William Randel, "Captain John Smith's Attitudes toward the Indians." *Virginia Magazine of History and Biography* 47 (1939): 218–29; Keith Glenn, "Captain John Smith and Indians," ibid. 52 (1944): 228–48; and the innumerable biographies of Smith, especially Philip L. Barbour, *The Three Worlds of Captain John Smith* (Boston, 1964). My own assessment of Smith's Indian policy, in more detail than can be presented here, appears in Alden T. Vaughan, *American Genesis: Captain John Smith and the Founding of Virginia* (Boston, 1975), esp. chap. 3. See also Morgan, *American Slavery, American Freedom*, esp. 76–79. A recent, spirited defense of Smith's policies and attitudes toward the Indians is J. A. Leo Lemay, *The American Dream of Captain John Smith* (Charlottesville, Va., 1991), esp. chaps. 6 and 7.

24. *Works of Capt. John Smith*, ed. Barbour, 1:253, 2:202.

25. Ibid., 1:206, 2:209.

26. Ibid., 1:247–48, 2:19.

27. Susan Myra Kingsbury, ed., *The Records of the Virginia Company of London*, 4 vols. (Washington, D.C., 1906–35), 3:18–19, hereafter cited *Va. Co. Recs.*

28. Ibid., 14–15. In comparing the original manuscript of the Virginia Company Records with the published version, Philip Barbour found that Kingsbury incorrectly transcribed "Quiocasockes," a common Indian term, as "Iniocasockes." I have incorporated Barbour's correction in the above quotation.

29. Some sense of the Indians' reaction can be gleaned from William Strachey's description in ca. 1611: "straunge whispers (indeed) and secrett at this hower run among these people and possesse them with amazement [to know] what maie be the yssue of these straung preparations, landed in their Coasts, and yearely supplyed with fresher troupes: every newes and blast of rumour strykes them, to which they open their ears wyde, and keepe their eyes waking, with good espiall upon every thing that sturrs, the noyse of our drumms of our shrill Trumpetts and great Ordinance terrefyes them so as they startle at the Report of them, how far soever from the reach of daunger, suspicions have bredd straung feares amongest them, and those feares create as straunge Construccions, therefore begett strong watch and guard, especially about their great king, who thrusts forth trustye Skowtes and carefull Sentynells . . . which reach even from his owne Court downe almost even to our Palisado-gates (*The Historie of Travell into Virginia Britania*, ed. Louis B. Wright and Virginia Freund [Hakluyt Soc., *Pubs.*, 2d ser. 103 (London, 1953)], 105).

30. Indian hostility during the "starving time" is well documented in *Works of Capt. John Smith*, ed. Barbour, 2:231–33; George Percy, "A Trewe Relacyon of the Procedeinges and Occurentes of Momente which Have Hapened in Virginia . . . ," *Tyler's Quarterly Historical and Genealogical Magazine* 3 (1922): 260–82, esp. 264–69; *True Declaration of the estate of the Colonie in Virginia* . . . , in Force, ed., *Tracts*, 3, no. 1:15–18; and H. R. McIlwaine, ed., *Journals of the House of Burgesses of Virginia, 1619–1658/9* (Richmond, Va., 1915), 29.

31. De La Warr's instructions were very similar to Gates's because the company did not know that the latter had finally reached Virginia. In some respects De La Warre's instructions were less belligerent toward the Indians, for they did not urge the killing of Quiocasockes but rather sending them to England where "we may endevor theire Conversion here" (*Va. Co. Recs.*, 3:27).

32. Percy, "Trewe Relacyon," *Tyler's Quarterly* 3 (1922): 270–73.

33. *Works of Capt. John Smith*, ed. Barbour, 2:243–46; Ralphe Hamor, *A True Discourse of the Present Estate of Virginia* . . . (London, 1615; reprint, Amsterdam,

1971), 3–6; Samuel Argall to Nicholas Hawes, June 1613, in Brown, ed., *Genesis of the United States*, 2:640–44; Norman Egbert McClure, ed., *The Letters of John Chamberlain*, 2 vols. (American Philosophical Society, *Memoirs*, 12 [Philadelphia, 1939]), 1:470–71.

34. Hamor, *True Discourse*, 42, 11–16, 55–57.

35. *Works of Capt. John Smith*, ed. Barbour, 2:294–95; Samuel Purchas, *Hakluyt Posthumus, or Purchas His Pilgrimes*, 19 (London, 1625; reprint, Glasgow, 1906), 153, hereafter cited *Purchas His Pilgrimes*.

36. Most of the evidence on the proposed Indian college and the company's fundraising is scattered through *Va. Co. Recs.*, esp. vols. 1, 3. A modern discussion is Robert Hunt Land, "Henrico and Its College," *WMQ*, 2d ser. 18 (1938): 453–98.

37. The king's letter to the archbishop of York and related documents are printed in Peter Walne, "The Collections for Henrico College, 1616–1618," *VMHB* 80 (1972): 259–66.

38. *Va. Co. Recs.*, 1:220.

39. McIlwaine, ed., *Jour. of Burgesses*, 10.

40. *Va. Co. Recs.*, 3:117, 576, 1:585–88; quotation is on 1:307–8.

41. Ibid., 1:588, 3:128–29.

42. [Edward Waterhouse], *A Declaration of the State of the Colony and Affaires in Virginia . . .* (London, 1622), 12. A similar version of Wyatt's statement appears in *Works of Capt. John Smith*, ed. Barbour, 2:293–94. For other examples of apparent missionary and fund-raising success see *Va. Co. Recs.*, 3:575–77, 642–43, and *Purchas His Pilgrimes*, 19:147–48. A drastically different view of the Virginia missionary effort is in Francis Jennings's *The Invasion of America: Indians, Colonialism, and the Cant of Conquest* (Chapel Hill, N.C., 1975), 53–56, which argues that "so far as the company and planters were concerned, the Indians were irrelevant to the whole business except as a pretext to extract money from the gullible English faithful." That philanthropic funds were ineptly used cannot be denied, but the surviving evidence does not support such a cynical and conspiratorial interpretation.

43. *Purchas His Pilgrimes*, 19:229; Patrick Copland, *Virginia's God be Thanked . . .* (London, 1622), 8–9, 25.

44. *Works of Capt. John Smith*, ed. Barbour, 2:295.

45. Hamor, *True Discourse*, 64; *Works of Capt. John Smith*, ed. Barbour, 2:258.

46. Robert Beverly, *The History and Present State of Virginia*, ed. Louis B. Wright (Chapel Hill, N.C., 1947), 38–39.

47. Richard Eburne, *A Plaine Path-way to Plantations . . .* (London, 1624), 110.

48. Lyon Gardiner Tyler, ed., *Narratives of Early Virginia, 1606–1625*, Original Narratives of Early American History (New York, 1907), 425. More outspoken than the assembly, Peter Arundel in 1623 asserted that "Wee our selves have taught them [the Indians] how to bee trecherous by our false dealinge with the poore kinge of Patomecke that had alwayes beene faythfull to the English," Peter Arundel to William Caringe, ca. April 1623, *Va. Co. Recs.*, 4:89–90.

49. Strachey, *Histoire and Travell*, ed. Wright and Freund, 91.

50. *Works of Capt. John Smith*, ed. Barbour, 2:257.

51. McIlwaine, ed., *Jour. of Burgesses*, 8–10, 12–15.

52. *Va. Co. Recs.*, 3:446. Survivors of the massacre were not reluctant to blame the tragedy in substantial part on Thorpe and the officials who supported him. One settler complained that Thorpe "hath brought such a misery upon us by letting th' Indians have their head and none must controll them. The Gover-

nor stood at that tyme for a Cypher whilest they [the Indians] stood ripping open our gutts" (ibid., 4:76).

53. *Works of Capt. John Smith*, ed. Barbour, 2:286.

54. See, for example, *Va. Co. Recs.*, 3:304, 556–57; *Purchas His Pilgrimes*, 19:229; and John Rolfe, *A True Relation of the State of Virginia lefte by Sir Thomas Dale Knight* ... (1616; reprint, New Haven, Conn., 1951), 6.

55. Rolfe, *True Relation*, 6.

56. *Va. Co. Recs.*, 3:92.

57. [Waterhouse], *Declaration*, 22. The Smythe-Warwick faction of the company, bitterly critical of the Sandys administration, charged that the massacre "seemes first to be occasioned by our owne perfidiouse dealing" (*Va. Co. Recs.*, 4:118).

58. *Va. Co. Recs.*, 3:13, 4:11.

59. Ibid., 4:118, 158–59.

60. Ibid., 13.

61. McIlwaine, ed., *Jour. of Burgesses*, 7.

62. *Works of Capt. John Smith*, ed. Barbour, 2:293.

63. Ibid., 293.

64. Ibid., 294–95.

65. *Va. Co. Recs.*, 3:565–71. Despite historians' frequent assertion that John Rolfe was among the victims, the evidence is overwhelming that he was not. He did die in 1622 (in October of that year his brother requested settlement of the estate), but most likely of natural causes. His will, dated Mar. 10, 1622, complained of ill health. Had Rolfe fallen in the massacre, his name would have appeared on the lists of dead; moreover, the irony of Pocahontas's husband dying at Indian hands would not have been missed by the many contemporary commentators. See John Melville Jennings, "Biographical Sketch," in Rolfe, *True Relation*, xxv–xxvi.

66. *Purchas His Pilgrimes*, 19:210. A detailed and reliable account of the massacre is Richard Beale Davis, *George Sandys, Poet Adventurer: A Study in Anglo-American Culture in the Seventeenth Century* (London, 1955), chap. 6.

67. W. L. Grant and James Munro, eds., *Acts of the Privy Council of England, Colonial Series, 1613–1680*, 1 (Hereford, Eng., 1908), 54.

68. *Works of Capt. John Smith*, ed. Barbour, 2:305–6.

69. *Va. Co. Recs.*, 4:10; Wyatt to [?], in "Letters of Francis Wyatt," *WMQ*, 2d ser. 6 (1926): 118. For important modifications to the traditional emphasis on total warfare see J. Frederick Fausz, "Profits, Pelts, and Powers: English Culture in the Early Chesapeake, 1620–1652," *Maryland Historian* 14, no. 2 (1983): 15–30.

70. *Va. Co. Recs.*, 4:221–22. For the settlers' devious tactics see also ibid., 98–99, 102.

71. Ibid., 451.

72. Ibid., 3:672. Governor Wyatt, who was in charge of the colony's forces, received military advice from his father as well as from the company. See J. Frederick Fausz and Jon Kukla, eds., "A Letter of Advice to the Governor of Virginia, 1624," *WMQ*, 3d ser. 34 (1977): 104–29.

73. *Va. Co. Recs.*, 3:683. The company's chronic misunderstanding of the settlers' circumstances, and its unwillingness to accept any responsibility for the consequences, appear frequently in the correspondence concerning the massacre. Not surprisingly, the colony objected to bearing the blame for a policy set

in England. "Wheras . . . you pass soe heavie a Censure uppon us as yf we alone were guiltie," the colony complained with obvious disgust, "You may be pleased to Consider what instructions you have formerly given us, to wynn the Indyans to us by A kinde entertayninge them in our howses, and yf it were possible to Cohabitt with us, and how ympossible it is for any watch and warde to secure us against secrett Enemies that live promiscouslie amongst us, and are harbored in our bosomes, all Histories and your owne Discourse may Sufficyently informe you" (ibid., 10).

74. [Waterhouse], *Declaration*, 22–23, 25–26, 11. Waterhouse's animosity toward the Indians was almost boundless. He did not, however, advocate using "Mastives to teare them"; historians who thus quote Waterhouse have overlooked the errata at the beginning of his pamphlet.

75. *Purchas His Pilgrimes*, 19:224, 229, 231. For evidence of a sparse but continuing effort to convert and educate the Indians of Virginia after 1622 see W. Stitt Robinson Jr., "Indian Education and Missions in Colonial Virginia," *Journal of Southern History* 18 (1952): 152–68. On the Indians and colonial law see Robinson, "The Legal Status of the Indian in Colonial Virginia," *VMHB* 61 (1953): 247–59.

76. [John Bonoeil], *His Majesties Gracious Letter to the Earle of South-Hampton* . . . (London, 1622), 85–86. For another scheme to force the Indians to labor see *Va. Co. Recs.*, 3:704–7.

77. Conditions in the colony are poignantly described in the correspondence and other documents of the Virginia Company. See *Va. Co. Recs.*, 3 and 4, passim. An exaggerated description of postmassacre conditions is Nathaniel Butler, "The Unmasked face of our Colony in Virginia as it was in the Winter of the yeare 1622," ibid., 2:374–76.

78. Ibid., 4:232, 74, 233–35, 38.

79. My summary of the company's collapse is drawn from the standard work on the subject, Wesley Frank Craven, *The Dissolution of the Virginia Company: The Failure of a Colonial Experiment* (New York, 1932).

80. *Va. Co. Recs.*, 4:102, 584.

81. McIlwaine, ed., *Jour. of Burgesses*, 52.

82. H. R. McIlwaine, ed., *Minutes of the Council and General Court of Colonial Virginia, 1622–1632, 1670–1676* (Richmond, 1924), 185. As late as September 1632 the Virginia legislature declared the neighboring Indians "our irreconcilable enemyes." William Waller Hening, ed., *The Statutes at Large; Being a Collection of all the Laws of Virginia* . . . , 1 (New York, 1823), 193.

83. Joseph Mead to Sir Martin Stuteville, 23 Jan. 1630, in Thomas Birch, ed., *The Court and Times of Charles the First*, 2 (London, 1848), 53–54.

84. Hening, ed., *Statutes of Virginia*, 1:193. For a detailed discussion of the postmassacre conflict see William S. Powell, "Aftermath of the Massacre: The First Indian War, 1622–1632," *VMHB* 66 (1958): 44–75.

85. William Bradford, History of Plymouth Plantation, 1620–1647, 2 vols. (Boston, 1912), 1:273, 275–76, 292–95; Phinehas Pratt, "A Declaration of the Affairs of the English People that First Inhabited New England," Massachusetts Historical Society, Collections, 4th ser. 4 (1858), 474–87; E[dward] Winslow, "Good Newes from New England," in Edward Arber, ed., *The Story of the Pilgrim Fathers* . . . (London, 1897), 530, 561–74; John Pory to the Governor of Virginia (Sir Francis Wyatt), Autumn 1622, in Sydney V. James Jr., ed., *Three Visitors to Early Plymouth: Letters about the Pilgrim Settlement in New England during the First*

Seven Years (Plimouth Plantation, Mass., 1963), 16; Emmanuel Altham to Sir Edward Altham, Sept. 1623, ibid., 30–32; Thomas Morton, *New English Canaan* (Amsterdam, 1637; reprint, New York, 1972), 106–12; *Works of Capt. John Smith*, ed. Barbour, 2:453.

86. *Records of the Governor and Company of the Massachusetts Bay in New England*, ed. Nathaniel B. Shurtleff, 5 vols. in 6 (Boston, 1853–84), 1:385. The bracketed words are Shurtleff's conjectural readings of damaged portions of the manuscript.

87. [Philip Vincent], *A True Relation of the Late Battell Fought in New England, between the English, and the Salvages* (London, 1637), 11, 20, 22–23; [John Winthrop], *Winthrop's Journal "History of New England," 1630–1649*, ed. James Kendall Hosmer, 2 vols. (New York, 1908), 2:167–68; [Edward Johnson], *Johnson's Wonder-Working Providence, 1628–1651*, ed. J. Franklin Jameson (New York, 1910; orig. publ. 1653), 265–66.

88. *New Englands First Fruits: With Divers Other Special Matters Concerning that Country* (London, 1643), 8. On Puritan missionary efforts see Alden T. Vaughan, *New England Frontier: Puritans and Indians, 1620–1675*, rev. ed. (New York, 1979), chaps. 9–11; and James Axtell, *The Invasion Within: The Contest of Cultures in Colonial North America* (New York, 1985), chap. 7.

89. For examples of restrictive legislation against Indians in one Puritan colony, see *The Public Records of the Colony of Connecticut*, ed. J. Hammond Trumbull, 1 (Hartford, 1850), 2, 46, 52, 73–74, 79, 106, 138, 163, 235, 284, 294, 351. On Harvard's Indian college see Samuel Eliot Morison, *Harvard College in the Seventeenth Century*, 2 vols. (Cambridge, Mass., 1936), 1:342–44.

90. Mary Rowlandson, *The Soveraignty & Goodness of God*, 2d ed. (Cambridge, Mass., 1682), anon. preface, 4.

CHAPTER 6: BLACKS IN VIRGINIA

1. The principal disputants have been Oscar Handlin and Mary F. Handlin, "Origins of the Southern Labor System," *William and Mary Quarterly*, 3d ser. 7 (1950): 199–222; Carl N. Degler, "Slavery and the Genesis of American Race Prejudice," *Comparative Studies in History and Society* 2 (1959): 49–66; Winthrop D. Jordan, "Modern Tensions and the Origins of American Slavery," *Journal of Southern History* 28 (1962): 18–30; and Jordan, *White over Black: American Attitudes toward the Negro, 1550–1812* (Chapel Hill, N.C., 1968). Other contributions to the debate include Paul C. Palmer, "Servant into Slave: The Evolution of the Legal Status of the Negro Laborer in Colonial Virginia," *South Atlantic Quarterly* 65 (1966): 355–70; Louis Ruchames, "The Sources of Racial Thought in Colonial America," *Journal of Negro History* 52 (1967): 251–72; and George M. Fredrickson, "Toward a Social Interpretation of the Development of American Racism," in Nathan I. Huggins et al., eds., *Key Issues in the Afro-American Experience*, 1 (New York, 1971), 240–54. Since this essay was first published, the literature on the beginnings of slavery and racism in British America has grown voluminously. See especially chapter 7 in this volume.

2. Susan Myra Kingsbury, ed., *The Records of the Virginia Company of London*, 3 (Washington, D.C., 1933), 243.

3. *The Complete Works of Captain John Smith (1580–1631)*, ed. Philip L. Barbour, 3 vols. (Chapel Hill, N.C., 1986), 2:267.

4. H. R. McIlwaine, ed., *Minutes of the Council and General Court of Colonial Virginia, 1622–1632, 1670–1676* (Richmond, Va., 1924), 33.

5. Ibid., 67–68, 71–73.

6. Jordan, *White over Black*, chap. 2. Several later cases make clear that black servants often were held for much longer than the usual number of years for white servants. See also Thomas D. Morris, " 'Villeinage . . . as it existed in England, reflects but little on our subject': The Problem of the 'Sources' of Southern Slave Law," *American Journal of Legal History* 32 (1988): 95–137.

7. The original document, filed in the Public Record Office, London, is more legible than the microfilm copies in the Virginia Colonial Records Project and more accurate than the printed versions contained in the *Colonial Records of Virginia* (Richmond, Va., 1874). However, because discrepancies between the original and printed versions are slight and for the most part irrelevant to the purposes of this essay, citations will be to the *Colonial Records of Virginia* except where otherwise noted. The microfilm is in C.O. 1/3, Public Record Office (Virginia Colonial Records Project Microfilm). The census also appears in John Camden Hotten, ed., *The Original Lists of Persons . . . Who Went from Great Britain to the American Plantations, 1600–1700* (London, 1874). Biographical sketches of some of the residents listed in the census can be found in Edward D. Neill, "A Study of the Virginia Census of 1624," *New-England Historical and Genealogical Register* 31 (1877): 147–53, 265–72, 393–401.

8. *Colonial Records of Virginia*, 55, 40. I have used here the arrangement and spacing of the original manuscript.

9. Ibid., 47, 49.

10. Ibid., 50, 58, 53.

11. C.O. 1/3, P.R.O. (Va. Col. Rec. Proj.). The document has been printed, with omission of the data on armaments and other possessions, in Hotten, ed., *Original Lists*, 201–65; and in its entirety in Annie Lash Jester and Martha Woodruff Hiden, eds., *Adventurers of Purse and Person: Virginia 1607–1625* (Princeton, N.J., 1956), 5–69. A convenient tabular summation of the data can be found in A. C. Quisenberry, "The Virginia Census, 1624–25," *Virginia Magazine of History and Biography* 7 (1899–1900): 264–67. See also Irene W. D. Hecht, "The Virginia Muster of 1624/25 as a Source for Demographic History," *WMQ*, 3d ser. 30 (1973): 65–92.

12. Two early historians who made extensive use of the census are Alexander Brown, *The First Republic in America* . . . (Boston, 1898), 610–28; and Philip Alexander Bruce, *Economic History of Virginia in the Seventeenth Century*, 2 (New York, 1896), 70–72. Edmund S. Morgan has drawn perceptively on the census in "The First American Boom: Virginia, 1618 to 1630," *WMQ*, 3d ser. 28 (1971): 169–98, as has Irene Hecht (see note 11), but significantly the only published versions of the muster appear in essentially genealogical works: Hotten, ed., *Original Lists*; Jester and Hiden, eds., *Adventurers of Purse and Person*.

13. Philip D. Curtin, "Epidemiology and the Slave Trade," *Political Science Quarterly* 83 (1968): 211–5; and Curtin, *The Atlantic Slave Trade: A Census* (Madison, Wis., 1969), esp. 28. Much work remains to be done on the impact of sex ratio on the adjustment of blacks to new environments, its impact on the frequency and severity of slave revolts, and the correlation between sex ratio—with its important bearing on population growth—and white attitudes toward the slave

trade. For a perceptive analysis of the distribution of ownership, see Robert Mc-Colley, "Slavery in Virginia, 1619–1660: A Reexamination," in Robert H. Abzug and Stephen Maizlich, eds., *New Perspectives on Race and Slavery in America* (Lexington, Ky., 1986), 11–24.

14. Jester and Hiden, eds., *Adventurers of Purse and Person*, 21–22.

15. Ibid., 27.

16. Ibid., 29.

17. *Treasurer* was a controversial vessel in the seventeenth century and has remained one ever since. After making several trips to America for the company, beginning in 1613 or earlier, in 1618 she arrived in Virginia under Captain Daniel Elfrith with a commission from the Duke of Savoy to prey on Spanish shipping. Lieutenant Governor Samuel Argall, a part owner of the vessel, dispatched her to the West Indies, where she fell in with a Dutch man-of-war (more likely a privateer also under license from the Duke of Savoy), which soon captured a cargo of Negroes which she sold in Virginia. *Treasurer* acquired some Negroes too, but finding a hostile reception at Jamestown, where the new governor George Yeardley feared repercussions from the Spanish if he allowed the landing of goods seized by an English ship during peacetime, she sailed to Bermuda and there unloaded her human cargo on the earl of Warwick's estate. "Stark rotten" when she reached Bermuda late in 1619, *Treasurer* apparently did not sail again. Bruce, *Economic History of Virginia*, 2:66–70; Kingsbury, ed., *Virginia Company Records*, 2:395, 3:219–22; and Edward D. Neill, *Virginia Vetusta . . .* (Albany, N.Y., 1885), 112–16, 201–2. Cf. Brown, *First Republic*, 324–27; and Brown, *The Genesis of the United States . . .* , 2 (Boston, 1890), 885–86, 987, where he argues that *Treasurer*, not the Dutch ship, brought the first group of twenty or more Negroes to Virginia. The surviving evidence does not seem to support Brown's contention. See also James Curtis Ballagh, *A History of Slavery in Virginia* (Baltimore, 1902),7–9, who contends that *Treasurer* landed one Negro, Angelo. Ballagh bases his conclusion on Brown, whose findings are dubious, and on the 1625 census, which as noted above lists Angelo as having arrived on *Treasurer* but does not specify the year. Her date of arrival may have been 1618 or earlier. The most thorough account of the *Treasurer* episode is Wesley Frank Craven, *The Dissolution of the Virginia Company* (New York, 1932), 127–33. See also two other works by Craven: "Twenty Negroes to Jamestown in 1619?" *Virginia Quarterly Review* 47 (1971): 416–21; and *White, Red, and Black: The Seventeenth-Century Virginian* (Charlottesville, Va., 1971), 77–82.

18. Jester and Hiden, eds., *Adventurers of Purse and Person*, 62; *Colonial Records of Virginia*, 46.

19. *Colonial Records of Virginia*, 51; Jester and Hiden, eds., *Adventurers of Purse and Person*, 49; Court Records of Northampton County, Land Patents of Virginia, 1643–51, bk. 2: 326, 1651–54, 161–62, Virginia State Library, Richmond. Because of his relative prosperity and his ownership of black servants, Johnson has received considerable attention from historians. See Susie M. Ames, *Studies of the Virginia Eastern Shore in the Seventeenth Century* (Richmond, Va., 1940), 102–4; John H. Russell, *The Free Negro in Virginia, 1619–1865* (Baltimore, 1913), 24–25; Russell, "Colored Freemen as Slave Owners in Virginia," *Jour. Negro Hist.* 1 (1916): 234–37; and James H. Brewer, "Negro Property Owners in Seventeenth-Century Virginia," *WMQ*, 3d ser. 12 (1955): 576–78. While there is no doubt that Anthony Johnson and his family were free by 1652, the evidence does not support a claim that he had escaped bondage "within three years of the land-

ing of the first Negroes at Jamestown." See "Anthony Johnson, Free Negro, 1622," *Jour. Negro Hist.* 56 (1971): 71–76. Recent works on the Johnson family include Ross M. Kimmel, "Free Blacks in Seventeenth-Century Maryland," *Maryland Historical Magazine* 71 (1976): 22–25; T. H. Breen and Stephen Innes, *"Myne Owne Ground": Race and Freedom on Virginia's Eastern Shore, 1640–1676* (New York, 1980), chap. 1; and Joseph Douglas Deal III, *Race and Class in Colonial Virginia: Indians, Englishmen, and Africans on the Eastern Shore during the Seventeenth Century,* Ph.D. dissertation, University of Rochester, 1981 (microfilm, Ann Arbor, Mich., 1989), 254–92.

20. Jester and Hiden, eds., *Adventurers of Purse and Person,* 46. These may be the Anthony and Mary mentioned above.

21. H. R. McIlwaine, ed., *Journals of the House of Burgesses of Virginia, 1619–1658/59* (Richmond, Va., 1915), 13.

22. McIlwaine, ed., *Minutes of the Council and General Court,* 153; Virginia Historical Society, Richmond, Va., MSS 2 Y327al (photostat).

23. H.C.A. 13/47, P.R.O. (Va. Col. Rec. Proj.); John Ellzey to Edward Nicholas, 13 May 1628, in John Bruce et al., eds., *Calendar of State Papers, Domestic Series, Charles I, 1628–1629* (London, 1859), 110; Ellzey to Nicholas, 27 May 1628, ibid., 131; Bruce, *Economic History of Virginia,* 2:73–74.

24. McIlwaine, ed., *Minutes of the Council and General Court,* 196.

CHAPTER 7: THE ORIGINS DEBATE

1. In addition to the many anthologies that reprint two or three selections from this debate, three works focus almost entirely on it: Donald L. Noel, ed., *The Origins of American Slavery and Racism* (Columbus, 1972); Raymond Starr and Robert Detweiler, eds., *Race, Prejudice, and the Origins of Slavery in America* (Cambridge, Mass., 1975); and Joseph Boskin, *Into Slavery: Racial Decisions in the Virginia Colony* (Philadelphia, 1976). The first two reprint extensively from the secondary literature; the third also includes extracts from primary sources. All three anthologies have thoughtful editorial commentary.

2. Winthrop D. Jordan, "Modern Tensions and the Origins of American Slavery," *Journal of Southern History* (hereafter cited as *JSH*), 28 (1962): 18; see also Raymond Starr, "Historians and the Origins of British North American Slavery," *The Historian* 36 (1973–74): 1–18; Boskin, *Into Slavery,* 101–9. My essay summarizes the historiographical debate and assesses its areas of recent consensus and continuing controversy. The essay also takes a stand. Although some authors, especially of textbooks and general studies of black or colonial history, straddle the interpretive fences by seeming to accept diametrically opposite explanations simultaneously, scholars who examine the sources are likely to emerge with strong opinions. I am no exception. As the following pages reveal, some interpretations of the evidence impress me with their clarity and logic; others seem to distort the sources and obfuscate the issues. In any case, I hope I have presented fairly the views I do not find persuasive, for my purpose in this essay is historiographical as well as argumentative, explanatory as well as prescriptive.

3. There is no evidence of blacks in Virginia before 1619, though a few may have been there but escaped notice in the surviving records. The question of when and where the 1619 group arrived is explored in Wesley Frank Craven,

"Twenty Negroes to Jamestown in 1619?" *Virginia Quarterly Review* 47 (1971): 416–20. The first Africans brought to British America were probably taken to Bermuda in 1616, others soon followed. The sparse evidence suggests that most were held as slaves. See John Henry Lefroy, *Memorials of the Discovery and Early Settlement of the Bermudas . . .* , 2 vols. (London, 1877–79), 1:115, 127, 157, 159, 724. Cyril Outerbridge Packwood, *Chained on the Rock: Slavery in Bermuda* (New York, 1975), 2–9, contends that the first blacks were indentured servants for a few years at least; Virginia Bernhard, "Beyond the Chesapeake: The Contrasting Status of Blacks in Bermuda, 1616–1663," *JSH* 54 (1988): 545–64, seems to agree (549) but concludes that by the 1630s blacks' terms were usually ninety-nine years (556). I read the early Bermuda evidence very differently than does Bernhard.

4. William Goodell, *Slavery and Anti-Slavery: A History of the Great Struggle . . .* (New York, 1853), 10; Richard Hildreth, *The History of the United States of America*, rev. ed., 6 vols. (New York, 1877–80), 2:119; George Bancroft, *History of the United States of America, from the Discovery of the Continent*, 6 vols. (New York, 1892), 1:126. Philip Alexander Bruce, *Economic History of Virginia in the Seventeenth Century*, 2 vols. (New York, 1895), 2:65, attributes slavery in early Virginia partly to "sincere doubts in the minds of many Englishmen as to whether the place of the negro in the general system of life was higher than that of the horse or the ox."

5. James Curtis Ballagh, *A History of Slavery in Virginia* (Baltimore, 1902), 27–115, quotations on 29, 31.

6. John Henderson Russell, *The Free Negro in Virginia, 1619–1865* (Baltimore, 1913), 16–41.

7. Ulrich Bonnell Phillips, *American Negro Slavery: A Survey of the Supply, Employment and Control of Negro Labor . . .* (New York, 1918), 74–76.

8. Ibid., 76; Ulrich Bonnell Phillips, *Life and Labor in the Old South* (Boston, 1929), 160–72, quotations on 161, 170.

9. James M. Wright, *The Free Negro in Maryland, 1634–1860* (New York, 1921), 19–24. The literature on Maryland slavery and racism largely parallels the more extensive and exhaustive Virginia studies. Recent works on Maryland include Jonathan L. Alpert, "The Origins of Slavery in the United States—The Maryland Precedent," *American Journal of Legal History* 14 (1970): 189–221; Raphael Cassinere Jr., "The Origins and Early Development of Slavery in Maryland, 1633 to 1715," Ph.D. dissertation, Lehigh University, 1971; and Whittington B. Johnson, "The Origin and Nature of African Slavery in Seventeenth-Century Maryland," *Maryland Historical Magazine* 73 (1978): 236–45. For Catterall, see Helen Tunnicliff Catterall, ed., *Judicial Cases Concerning American Slavery and the Negro*, 1 (Washington, D.C., 1926), 54–56.

10. David Saville Muzzey, *The American Adventure*, Vol. 1: *Through the Civil War* (New York, 1927), 310.

11. Susie M. Ames, *Studies of the Virginia Eastern Shore in the Seventeenth Century* (Richmond, Va., 1940), 100–106, quotation on 101.

12. Wesley Frank Craven, *The Southern Colonies in the Seventeenth Century, 1607–1689*, in Wendell H. Stephenson and E. Merton Coulter, eds., *A History of the South*, 1 (Baton Rouge, 1949), 217–19, quotations on 218, 219; Eric E. Williams, *Capitalism and Slavery* (1944; reprint, New York, 1966), 19–20. An excellent discussion of Williams's contributions to this debate is William A. Green, "Race and Slavery: Considerations on the Williams Thesis," in Barbara L. Solow

and Stanley L. Engerman, eds., *British Capitalism and Caribbean Slavery: The Legacy of Eric Williams* (Cambridge, 1987), 25–49. Craven repeated his interpretation in *White, Red, and Black: The Seventeenth-Century Virginian* (Charlottesville, Va., 1971), 75–77.

13. Oscar Handlin and Mary F. Handlin, "Origins of the Southern Labor System," *William and Mary Quarterly* (hereafter cited as *WMQ*), 3d ser. 7 (1950): 199–222.

14. Jordan, "Modern Tensions," 20; see also Starr, "Historians and Slavery," 5–9.

15. Handlin and Handlin, "Origins," quotation on 203.

16. Ibid., 205–11, quotations on 206, 208, 211.

17. Ibid., 211–12 (emphasis added). The Maryland law of 1664 is one of the first documents in British America to use *slave* unambiguously. The full text can be found in William Hand Browne et al., eds., *Archives of Maryland: Proceedings and Acts of the General Assembly . . .* , 1 (Baltimore, 1883), 533–34, and in Willie Lee Rose, ed., *A Documentary History of Slavery in North America* (New York, 1976), 24. The "other slaues" mentioned in the 1664 law were probably Indian captives.

18. Handlin and Handlin, "Origins," 216–17. A synopsis of the Handlins' interpretation appears in Oscar Handlin, *The History of the United States*, 2 vols. (New York, 1967), 1:39–40.

19. Kenneth M. Stampp, *The Peculiar Institution: Slavery in the Ante-Bellum South* (New York, 1956), 21–22; Richard L. Morton, *Colonial Virginia*, 2 vols. (Chapel Hill, N.C., 1960), 1:69–70, which does not cite the Handlins but appears to draw directly on them.

20. Thomas F. Gossett, *Race: The History of an Idea in America* (Dallas, Tex., 1963), 29–30. For a nonhistorian's use of the Handlin thesis, see Marvin Harris, *Patterns of Race in the Americas* (New York, 1964), 70.

21. Richard Hofstadter, William Miller, and Daniel Aaron, *The United States: The History of a Republic* (Englewood Cliffs, N.J., 1957), 30.

22. Carl N. Degler, "Slavery and the Genesis of American Race Prejudice," *Comparative Studies in Society and History* 2 (1959): 49–66, quotation on 51. A concise summary of Degler's position appears in *Out of Our Past: The Forces That Shaped Modern America* (New York, 1959), 26–39. Stanley M. Elkins, *Slavery: A Problem in American Institutional and Intellectual Life*, 3d ed. (Chicago, 1976), 37–52, took issue with the Handlins on some points (see especially 39 n. 16 and 41 n. 19) but generally accepted their thesis. Elkin's concern, of course, was not to debate the Handlins but to account for the emergence of North America's unique form of institutional bondage.

23. Degler, "Slavery and Prejudice," 53–60; Russell, *Free Negro in Virginia*, 34–35.

24. Degler, "Slavery and Prejudice," 62–65.

25. "Letters to the Editor," *Comp. Studies in Soc. and Hist.* 2 (1959): 488–90.

26. Ibid., 491–95, quotations on 492.

27. Handlin and Handlin, "Origins," 208; Degler, "Slavery and Prejudice," esp. 65–66.

28. Jordan, "Modern Tensions," 22–30, quotation on 29.

29. Paul Goodman, ed., *Essays in American Colonial History* (New York, 1967).

30. Winthrop D. Jordan, *White over Black: American Attitudes toward the Negro, 1550–1812* (Chapel Hill, N.C., 1968), 599.

31. Ibid., chap. 1, quotation on p. 7.

32. Ibid., 3-85, quotations on 7, 56.

33. Ibid., 71-82, quotation on 80.

34. Winthrop D. Jordan, *The White Man's Burden: Historical Origins of Racism in the United States* (London and New York, 1974), 45; Jordan, *White over Black*, 61-62, 62n.

35. C. Duncan Rice, *The Rise and Fall of Black Slavery* (Baton Rouge, 1975), 53.

36. George M. Fredrickson, "Toward a Social Interpretation of the Development of American Racism," in Nathan I. Huggins, Martin Kilson, and Daniel M. Fox, eds., *Key Issues in the Afro-American Experience*, 2 vols. (New York, 1971), 1:240-54.

37. Fredrickson's earlier and important study of *The Black Image in the White Mind: The Debate on Afro-American Character and Destiny, 1817-1914* (New York, 1971) was in many respects a sequel to Jordan's *White over Black*. Fredrickson took his degrees at Harvard, where Oscar Handlin may have influenced his view of early American race relations.

38. Fredrickson, "Social Interpretation," 240-54, quotations on 243, 251, 244 (emphasis added). In an introduction to a reprinting of this essay in Fredrickson's *Arrogance of Race: Historical Perspectives on Slavery, Racism, and Social Inequality* (Middletown, Conn., 1988), 185-88, he suggests that "it may be a bit too insistent on purely socioeconomic or environmental factors" and "should be read as the exploration of a point of view differing from the one then dominant in the literature, but not as a definitive resolution of all the issues involved" (186). See also George M. Fredrickson, *White Supremacy: A Comparative Study in American and African History* (New York, 1981), 70-80, which acknowledges more fully Jordan's evidence of Tudor-Stuart England's antipathy toward Africans but contends nonetheless that "there was little or no overt sense that biological race or skin color played a determinative role in making some human beings absolute masters over others" (73).

39. See chapter 6 in this volume.

40. The probable incompleteness of the censuses is discussed in Edmund S. Morgan, "The First American Boom: Virginia in 1618," *WMQ*, 3d ser. 28 (1971): 170 n. 4. For the distribution of Virginia's blacks among white households in 1625, see Irene W. D. Hecht, "The Virginia Muster of 1624/25 as a Source of Demographic History," ibid., 30 (1973): 75-78.

41. *Colonial Records of Virginia* (Richmond, Va., 1874), 37-60; Annie Lash Jester and Martha Woodruff Hiden, eds., *Adventurers in Purse and Person: Virginia, 1607-1625* (Princeton, N.J., 1956), 5-69.

42. The laws on terms of service for persons arriving in Virginia without contracts are discussed below, note 87.

43. H. R. McIlwaine, ed., *Minutes of the Council and General Court of Colonial Virginia, 1622-1632, 1670-1676* . . . (Richmond, Va., 1924), 196. The "muster" does not survive.

44. Jordan, *White over Black*, 74.

45. Alden T. Vaughan, *American Genesis: Captain John Smith and the Founding of Virginia* (Boston, 1975), 143-51. "Negroes in Affrica," Smith wrote in *Advertisements for Unexperienced Planters of New England, or Any Where* (1631)—in a paragraph that also implicitly endorsed the New World's slave system—"bee as idle and as devilish people as any in the world" (*The Complete Works of Captain John*

Smith [1580–1631], ed. Philip L. Barbour, 3 vols. [Chapel Hill, N.C., and London, 1986], 1:327, 3:293–94).

46. Edmund S. Morgan, "Slavery and Freedom: The American Paradox," *Journal of American History* (hereafter cited as *JAH*), 59 (1972–73): 5–29, quotations on 15, 7, 17 (emphasis added). A synopsis of Morgan's interpretation appears in John M. Blum et al., *The National Experience: A History of the United States to 1877*, 2d ed. (New York, 1968), 54.

47. Edmund S. Morgan, *American Slavery, American Freedom: The Ordeal of Colonial Virginia* (New York, 1975), 295–337, quotations on 315, 327–28. Morgan's explanation of white Virginians' attitude toward Indians and its interaction with the emergence of racist views of blacks is, I believe, misleading. He proposes that "it was easy [in the late seventeenth century] for Virginians to extend to blacks some of the bad feelings they harbored toward Indians" (330)—a reversal, I argue elsewhere, of the actual sequence (see chapter 1 in this volume).

48. J. H. Plumb, "How Freedom Took Root in Slavery," *The New York Review of Books* (hereafter cited as *NYRB*), 27 Nov. 1975, 3–4. See also Plumb's earlier review of Jordan, *White over Black*, in "Slavery, Race, and the Poor," ibid., 13 Mar. 1969, 3–5.

49. Carl N. Degler, "Prejudice and Slavery," *NYRB*, 22 Jan. 1976, 53. See also J. R. Pole's perceptive review of Morgan's book in *Historical Journal* 20 (1977): 503–13.

50. Morgan, "Slavery and Freedom," 17, says that "most of the Africans, perhaps all of them, came as slaves." Similarly, T. H. Breen and Stephen Innes, *"Myne Owne Ground": Race and Freedom on Virginia's Eastern Shore, 1640–1676* (New York, 1980), 72, acknowledges that all blacks who entered Northampton County came as slaves.

51. The most thorough treatments of Johnson are Breen and Innes, *"Myne Owne Ground,"* chap. 1; Ross M. Kimmel, "Free Blacks in Seventeenth-Century Maryland," *Md. Hist. Mag.* 71 (1976): 22–25; and Joseph Douglas Deal III, "Race and Class in Colonial Virginia: Indians, Englishmen, and Africans on the Eastern Shore During the Seventeenth Century" (Ph.D. dissertation, University of Rochester, 1981), 254–92.

52. For example, see Degler, "Slavery and Prejudice," 132. Even in the antebellum period, many instances of blacks exercising authority over whites and of apparently unbiased relations between blacks and whites occurred. See John Herron Moore, "Simon Gray, Riverman: A Slave Who Was Almost Free," *Mississippi Valley Historical Review* 49 (1962–63): 472–84; Gary B. Mills, "Miscegenation and the Free Negro in Antebellum 'Anglo' Alabama: A Reexamination of Southern Race Relations," *JAH* 68 (1981–82): 16–34; Michael P. Johnson and James L. Roark, *Black Masters: A Free Family of Color in the Old South* (New York, 1984).

53. Scholars who see racial prejudice as the product of slavery usually conclude that the number of free blacks was "substantial" (Morgan, "Slavery and Freedom," 17; Fredrickson, "Social Interpretation," 244–45; Paul C. Palmer, "Servant into Slave: The Evolution of the Legal Status of the Negro Laborer in Colonial Virginia," *South Atlantic Quarterly* 65 [1966]: 358). By contrast, scholars who believe that prejudice preceded slavery usually refer to "a few" free blacks (Vaughan, "First Decade," 478 and in this volume 134; Degler, *Out of Our Past*, 34). The only attempts at quantification of this matter have been by Morgan ("Slavery and Freedom," 18 n. 39) and Breen and Innes (*"Myne Owne*

Ground," 68–69); they agree that in 1668 (the peak year, apparently, for free blacks) some 29 percent of Northampton County's blacks were free. The number is large compared to Virginia's eighteenth- and nineteenth-century figures (ca. 4–10 percent), sparse compared to the 71 percent who were slaves in 1668. The raw number, in any event, was indisputably small. Breen and Innes's figure for Northampton County was only thirteen black "independent householders" between 1664 and 1667 (69). For the high percentages of free blacks in some slaveholding states in the nineteenth century, see Ira Berlin, *Slaves without Masters: The Free Negro in the Antebellum South* (New York, 1974), 47, 137.

54. The pertinent legislation on servant tenure is reviewed in note 87. See also Warren M. Billings, "The Law of Servants and Slaves in Colonial Virginia," *Virginia Magazine of History and Biography* (hereafter cited as *VMHB*), 99 (1991): 45–62.

55. William Waller Hening, ed., *The Statutes at Large; Being a Collection of All the Laws of Virginia* . . . , 13 vols. (Richmond, Va., 1809–23), 2:260. That some slave owners thought baptism incompatible with slavery is clear from the law's preamble: "WHEREAS some doubts have arisen whether children that are slaves by birth . . . should by vertue of their baptisme be made ffree." The law declares that baptism would not change condition of servitude but encourages masters to Christianize such children if they are "capable to be admitted to that sacrament."

56. Warren M. Billings, "The Cases of Fernando and Elizabeth Key: A Note on the Status of Blacks in Seventeenth-Century Virginia," *WMQ* 3d ser. 30 (1973): 467–74. The two cases imply that although baptism offered a potential escape from slavery, Christian blacks had to bring suit to effect it. The Key case suggests, too, that before 1662 mulatto children of white fathers may have been held in bondage despite their fathers' free status. For the surviving documents of this case, see Warren M. Billings, ed., *The Old Dominion in the Seventeenth Century: A Documentary History of Virginia, 1606–1689* (Chapel Hill, N.C., 1975), 165–69.

57. Breen and Innes, "*Myne Owne Ground*," 5. Breen and Innes do not say why the slave code of 1705 was a turning—or rather an ending—point. The legislation of that year was essentially a codification of the colony's slave laws since 1662 and thus added little to the existing system. Virginia's code lagged far behind South Carolina's of 1696 and the earlier British island codes.

58. Ibid., 72–74, 78–83, 88–107.

59. Ibid., 24–27 (see also 89–90) cites the version of the 1640 law in *WMQ*, 2d ser. 4 (1924): 147, which is fuller than Hening's (*Statutes of Virginia*, 1:226). The longer version requires that "all masters of families shall use their best endeavours for the firnishing of themselves and all those of their families wch shall be capable of arms (excepting negros) wth arms both offensive and defensive." Does that mean, as Breen and Innes conclude, that black masters should arm themselves? Were other blacks in their households not allowed to bear arms? The law is unclear on both points. Perhaps Breen and Innes are correct in believing that free black "masters of families" were allowed to own firearms, but the number of such men was surely small—only thirteen in Northampton County in the 1660s.

60. Breen and Innes, "*Myne Owne Ground*," 104, 111, 97.

61. Ibid., 107–9.

62. Ibid., 112, 110. Breen and Innes give the percentage of free and slave blacks on p. 69 and discuss identification of nationality and race in the county

records on p. 97. They minimize, I believe, the extent to which blacks were identified by color, even if free and of long residence in Virginia.

63. The relevant laws are in Hening, ed., *Statutes of Virginia*, 2:170, 260, 267, 280–81; Rose, ed., *History of Slavery*, 19. The status of the few Indian slaves in Virginia during this period is not clear; in some cases they, as well as blacks, were encompassed in the legislation of the 1660s and 1670s.

64. The only significant seventeenth-century laws passed after the heavy influx of Africans began were the 1680 "Act for preventing Negroes Insurrections," which imposed numerous restrictions on the slaves' behavior (Hening, ed., *Statutes of Virginia* 2:481–82); the 1691 "Act for suppressing outlying Slaves" (ibid., 3:86–88), which prescribed banishment from the colony for anyone contracting an interracial marriage because it produced an "abominable mixture and spurious issue"; and the 1692 "act for the more speedy prosecution of slaves committing Capitall Crimes," which established special courts for slave prosecutions (ibid., 3:102–3).

65. Gary B. Nash, "From Freedom to Bondage in Seventeenth-Century Virginia," *Reviews in American History* 10 (1982): 33–37; Lorena Walsh, review of Breen and Innes, in *WMQ*, 3d ser. 38 (1981): 315–18; Lawrence Stone, "Original Sins," *NYRB*, 5 Feb. 1981, 34–35.

66. Kenneth G. Davies, *The Royal African Company* (London, 1957); Philip D. Curtin, *The Atlantic Slave Trade: A Census* (Madison, Wis., 1969); James A. Rawley, *The Transatlantic Slave Trade: A History* (New York, 1981); Herbert S. Klein, "Slaves and Shipping in Eighteenth-Century Virginia," *Journal of Interdisciplinary History* (hereafter cited as *JIH*), 5 (1975): 383–412; Green, "Race and Slavery," 38–49.

67. Bruce, *Economic History of Virginia*, 2:82–84; Thomas J. Wertenbaker, *The Planters of Colonial Virginia* (1922; reprint, Princeton, 1958), 126–61; John Hope Franklin, *From Slavery to Freedom: A History of American Negroes* (New York, 1947), 73–74; Gossett, *Race*, 29.

68. Morgan, "Slavery and Freedom," 22–26; Morgan, *American Slavery, American Freedom*, chap. 15: "Toward Slavery," esp. 308–13. "Giddy multitude" appears as a label for Bacon's followers in H. R. McIlwaine, ed., *Journals of the House of Burgesses of Virginia, 1659/60–1693* (Richmond, Va., 1914), 73.

69. Morgan, *American Slavery, American Freedom*, chap. 16: "Toward Racism."

70. T. H. Breen, "A Changing Labor Force and Race Relations in Virginia, 1660–1710," *Jour. of Social Hist.* 7 (1972–73): 3–25, quotations on 14, 16.

71. In many respects, the emphasis on Bacon's Rebellion as a biracial threat to the white upper class evokes C. Vann Woodward's explanation of the emergence of Jim Crow laws in the late nineteenth century and may reflect an application of that thesis to an earlier historical situation. See C. Vann Woodward, *The Strange Career of Jim Crow* (London and New York, 1955).

72. Allen's essay first appeared as "'. . . They Would Have Destroyed Me': Slavery and the Origins of Racism," *Radical America* 9 (May–June 1975): 40–63, and was reissued with fuller documentation as a pamphlet, *Class Struggle and the Origins of Racial Slavery: The Invention of the White Race* (Hoboken, N.J., 1975). I cite the latter version. Allen quotes Morgan and Breen approvingly but regrets that "their well-begun arguments trail off into unhelpful, indeed misleading speculations" (6–7, 14 n. 10). Allen has recently published the first of two volumes in which he expands on this thesis. *The Invention of the White Race, Volume One: Racial Oppression and Social Control* (London, 1994) is concerned mostly

with Irish history; only the introduction addresses the Virginia situation at any length, and primarily to attack Jordan's and Degler's work—not always, it seems to me, fairly. An assessment of Allen's latest contribution to the debate must await the publication of his second volume.

73. Russell R. Menard, "From Servants to Slaves: The Transformation of the Chesapeake Labor System," *Southern Studies*, 16 (1977): 355–90, quotations on 371, 389.

74. David W. Galenson, "White Servitude and the Growth of Black Slavery in Colonial America," *Journal of Economic History* 41 (1981); 39–47, quotation on 41; David W. Galenson, *White Servitude in Colonial America: An Economic Analysis* (Cambridge and New York, 1981), 117–40; and, for the same phenomenon in the British West Indies, David W. Galenson, *Traders, Planters, and Slaves: Market Behavior in Early English America* (Cambridge and New York, 1986), 10–11. Breen, "Changing Labor Force," 14, briefly noted the shift toward skilled white labor.

75. For a blending of the Morgan-Breen and Menard-Galenson positions, see James A. Henretta et al., *America's History to 1877* (Chicago, 1987), 50.

76. See Robert McColley, "Slavery in Virginia, 1619–1660: A Reexamination," in Robert H. Abzug and Stephen Maizlich, eds., *New Perspectives on Race and Slavery in America: Essays in Honor of Kenneth M. Stampp* (Lexington, Ky., 1986), 19–20. McColley argues, convincingly I believe, that Virginians imported slaves directly from Africa, and in substantial numbers, as soon as the English slave trade was able to meet the demand. See also Craven, *White, Red, and Black*, 19–20; and Richard S. Dunn, "Masters, Servants, and Slaves in the Colonial Chesapeake and the Caribbean," in David B. Quinn, ed., *Early Maryland in a Wider World* (Detroit, 1981), 251–52. For evidence from Barbados in 1675 that the supply of servants had sharply contracted and that the Royal African Company supplied the island with slaves "very scantily" and at high prices, see *Calendar of State Papers, Colonial Series, America and West Indies, 1675–76*, ed. W. Noel Sainsbury (London, 1893), 304 (doc. 714).

77. Morgan, *American Slavery, American Freedom*, 298–308, discusses Virginia's contacts with Barbados and also foreshadows the Menard thesis (299). See also Dunn, "Masters, Servants, and Slaves," 242–66.

78. Although market forces and statutory law may have been determinative after 1670, they were not in the earlier period (1619–ca. 1670), when Virginians might have opted—as some historians maintain they did—for only a few imported Africans and treated them as servants for terms and without racial bias.

79. Figures on the black population can be extrapolated from Robert V. Wells, *The Population of the British Colonies in America before 1776: A Survey of Census Data* (Princeton, N.J., 1975), 161–62; Morgan, *American Slavery, American Freedom*, 404, 420–23; and Evarts B. Greene and Virginia D. Harrington, eds., *American Population before the Federal Census of 1790* (New York, 1932), 136–38. In round figures the numbers of blacks and their percentage of the non-Indian population are: 1625, 25 (1.5 percent); 1650, 300 (2 percent); 1675, 2,500 (6 percent); 1700, 6,000–10,000 (10–13 percent). For discussions of the slave trade to Virginia, see Herbert S. Klein, "New Evidence on the Virginia Slave Trade," *JIH* 24 (1987): 871–77; Susan Westbury, "Slaves of Colonial Virginia: Where They Came From," *WMQ*, 3d ser. 42 (1985): 228–37; and Donald M. Sweig, "The Importation of African Slaves to the Potomac River, 1736–1772," ibid., 507–24.

80. Handlin and Handlin, "Origins," 208.

81. Morgan, "Slavery and Freedom," 15; Fredrickson, "Social Interpretation," 242; Breen and Innes, "*Myne Owne Ground*," 109.

82. Degler, "Slavery and Prejudice," esp. 62–66; Jordan, *White over Black*, esp. chap. 1; Vaughan, *American Genesis*, 144–50; Handlin and Handlin, "Origins," 216.

83. *Servant* and *slave* had imprecise meanings in the seventeenth century (which has led some historians to faulty conclusions). Until the late seventeenth century *servant* generally meant any form of bound labor, while *slave* sometimes meant lifetime bondage but in other contexts meant abject treatment regardless of an individual's status. Thus all slaves were servants, but not all servants were slaves. As used here, *slave* refers to lifetime bondage with virtually no statutory rights; *servant* refers to temporary bondage, usually under contract (indenture) or as established by local custom and with some legislative protections. See the useful discussion of terminology in McColley, "Slavery in Virginia," 12–14.

84. Morgan, "Slavery and Freedom," 18 n. 39; Breen and Innes, "*Myne Owne Ground*," 66–69, 72.

85. For examples of general works that perpetuate the indentured servant myth, see Franklin, *From Slavery to Freedom*, 71; and William E. Cooper Jr. and Thomas E. Terrill, *The American South: A History* (New York, 1990), 27. Colonial specialists who have recently held that most blacks in Virginia before the 1660s were indentured include Gary B. Nash, *Red, White, and Black: The Peoples of Early America*, 2d ed. (Englewood Cliffs, N.J., 1982), 149–52; and Edwin J. Perkins, *The Economy of Colonial America*, 2d ed. (New York, 1988), 99. Fredrickson ("Social Interpretation," 244–45) acknowledges that blacks were generally enslaved on Barbados from the outset (1627) and in Massachusetts by 1638 but contends that the case was significantly different in Virginia—another instance of how the Ballagh-Handlin assumption that Virginia's blacks were servants rather than slaves prior to the legislation of the 1660s and 1670s persists in spite of the evidence. See also Robert S. Cope, *Carry Me Back: Slavery and Servitude in Seventeenth-Century Virginia* (Pikesville, Ky., 1973), 5, 9–11. Cope overlooks all the modern literature on the origins debate but cites Ballagh and other early writers.

86. The occasional references to indentures in the surviving records are often inconclusive. For example, in 1655 John Casor, a black servant belonging to Anthony Johnson, stated that he had arrived in the colony with an indenture for seven or eight years. Johnson denied it and insisted on ownership of Casor for life. The county court upheld Johnson, which suggests that Casor could not produce a valid indenture (Billings, ed., *Old Dominion*, 155–56; Deal, "Race and Class," 260–62). The apparently few blacks with written indentures were probably Christians. Even then, they appear to have served much longer terms than white servants. For example, a mulatto named Manuel was by court decree a servant from 1644 to 1665 (and may have begun his term even earlier): McIlwaine, ed., *Journals of the House of Burgesses, 1659/60–1693*, 34.

87. A Virginia law of 1643 provided that "WHEREAS divers controversies have risen between masters and servants being brought into the collony without indentures . . . *Be it therefore enacted . . .* that such servants as shall be imported haveing no indentures or covenants either men or women if they be above twenty year old to serve fowre year, if they shall be above twelve and un-

der twenty to serve five years, And if under twelve to serve seaven years" (Hening, ed., *Statutes of Virginia*, 1:257). This law almost certainly did not apply to Africans, who were sold as contraband in Virginia; by international law and British custom, they could be held in lifetime servitude. Moreover, a statute of 1655, renewed in 1658, which imposed longer terms for Irish than English servants, referred to the law of 1643 as "being only [for] the benefitt of our own nation" (ibid., 411, 471). The 1658 law was repealed in 1660 because it was deemed discouraging to immigration; in "the future no servant comeing into the country without indentures, of what christian nation soever, shall serve longer then those of our own country, of the like age" (ibid., 538–39). In sum, the three servant laws all pertain to whites (assumed in the seventeenth century to be synonymous with Christians) and by implication not to blacks. The latter apparently had no legislative protection.

88. See Vaughan, "Blacks in Virginia," 471–76; for wills and inventories, see Degler, "Slavery and Prejudice." Additional inventories appear in several published sources as well as in the manuscripts at the Virginia State Library and Archives. For a revealing example, see Susie M. Ames, ed., *County Court Records of Accomack-Northampton, Virginia, 1640–1645*, Virginia Historical Society Documents Series, 10 (Charlottesville, Va., 1973), 422–23. Thousands of land patents are collected in Nell Marion Nugent, ed., *Cavaliers and Pioneers: Abstracts of Virginia Land Patents and Grants, 1623–1800*, 3 vols. to date (Richmond, Va., 1934–79).

89. Quoted in Jordan, *White over Black*, 64, 65, 70. See ibid., 65, for additional evidence of slavery as the standard status for blacks in Barbados at least as early as the 1650s. The Rhode Island law (in a passage not in Jordan's book) refers to "blacke mankind or white"—a revealing clue to the perception of basic human categories by white Americans (John Russell Bartlett, ed., *Records of the Colony of Rhode Island*, 1 [Providence, 1856], 243). On the influence of English law on early American slavery, see the article by Thomas Morris cited in n. 90 and Jonathan A. Bush, "Free to Enslave: The Foundations of Colonial American Slave Law," *Yale Journal of Law & the Humanities* 5 (1993): 417–70, which emphasizes the role of prerogative government.

90. Among historians who believe that slavery existed in Virginia from the outset are McColley, "Slavery in Virginia," 11–13, and Thomas D. Morris, " 'Villeinage . . . as it existed in England, reflects but little on our subject': The Problem of the 'Sources' of Southern Slave Law," *Am. Jour. of Legal Hist.* 32 (1988): 98 n. 17, 103, 104, 107. For evidence that a few blacks were officially servants for terms rather than slaves for life, see *VMHB* 4 (1896–97): 407; McIlwaine, ed., *Journal of the House of Burgesses, 1659/60–1693*, 34; and Billings, ed., *Old Dominion*, 165–70.

91. See, for example, Handlin and Handlin, "Origins," 202–11; Morgan, "Slavery and Freedom," 17–18. Breen and Innes, "*Myne Owne Ground*," argues that free blacks in Northampton County suffered little or no discrimination. My reading of their evidence and of the county records prompts a different conclusion.

92. For example, Degler, "Slavery and Prejudice"; Degler, "Prejudice and Slavery"; Vaughan, *American Genesis*, 145–50.

93. Breen and Innes, "*Myne Owne Ground*," 97; Lerone Bennett Jr., "The First Generation: The Birth of Black America," [Part 1 of "The Making of Black America"], *Ebony*, 24 (June 1969): 31–43, quotation on 33.

94. The standard compilations are McIlwaine, ed., *Minutes of the Council and General Court;* Susie M. Ames, ed., *County Court Records of Accomack-Northampton, Virginia, 1632–1640,* American Historical Association, American Legal Records, 7 (Washington, D.C., 1954); Ames, ed., *Accomack-Northampton, 1640–45;* and Nugent, ed., *Cavaliers and Pioneers.*

95. For Italians in early Virginia, almost all of them identified in the records by full names but rarely with ethnic labels, see Glenn Weaver, *The Italian Presence in Colonial Virginia* (New York, 1988).

96. Bennett, "First Generation," 42.

97. Breen and Innes, *"Myne Owne Ground,"* esp. 6, 99; Ames, ed., *Accomack-Northampton, 1640–45, 457.*

98. "Selections from Conway Robinson's Notes . . . ," appended to McIlwaine, ed., *Minutes of the Council and General Court,* esp. 468, 477, 479, 502, 513, 517; Billings, ed., *Old Dominion,* 156–57. Lawrence J. Friedman and Arthur H. Shaffer, "The Conway Robinson Notes and Seventeenth-Century Virginia," *VMHB,* 78 (1970): 259–67, on the other hand, contends that "Negroes were usually listed in the [Robinson] court records with both first and last names." Robinson's notes do not support that conclusion or several of Friedman and Shaffer's other statements about blacks in early Virginia.

99. Even a cursory scan of the basic records—Nugent's *Cavaliers and Pioneers,* for example, or Ames's *Accomack-Northampton, 1640–45*—should disabuse anyone of the notion that blacks and whites were accorded similar nomenclature. The vast majority of blacks are anonymous; some have first names ("Well the Negro"), and very few are recorded with first and last names. Rarely is a European listed without a full name.

100. On the British legal context, see David Brion Davis, *The Problem of Slavery in the Age of Revolution, 1770–1823* (Ithaca, N.Y., 1975), 470–89; Fredrickson, "Social Interpretation," 245; McColley, "Slavery in Virginia," 23; A. Leon Higginbotham Jr., *In the Matter of Color: Race and the American Legal Process: The Colonial Period* (New York, 1978); and Morris, "Sources of Southern Slave Law," 104–7. For extracts from English legal rulings, see Catterall, ed., *Judicial Cases,* 1:9–13.

101. Degler, "Prejudice and Slavery," 53.

102. Fredrickson, *Arrogance of Race,* 3.

103. Degler, "Prejudice and Slavery," 53; Degler, "Slavery and Prejudice," passim; Jordan, *White over Black,* chaps. 1–2. The 1971 supplement to the *Oxford English Dictionary* lists *racialism* (earliest example of usage, 1907); *racism* did not enter the *OED* until the 1982 supplement (earliest example of usage, 1936). In 1964 the *Dictionary of the Social Sciences* called *racism* "a newer term for the word racialism." The *American Heritage Dictionary* (1969) equates *racism* with ethnic preference and defines *ethnocentrism* almost identically (see also the entry on *race,* which is implicitly incompatible with the entry on *racism*). Thus the *American Heritage Dictionary*'s distinctions between racism or race prejudice and ethnocentrism are, I believe, contrary to what most scholars (surely most of the scholars in the origins debate) and, I suspect, the general public hold to be correct usage. See also McColley, "Slavery in Virginia," 12–15.

104. Fredrickson, "Social Interpretation," 240.

105. On the concept of race, see the critiques by Ashley Montagu, including *Man's Most Dangerous Myth: The Fallacy of Race,* 3d ed. (New York, 1952); Ashley Montagu, ed., *The Concept of Race* (London, 1964); and Ashley Montagu, "The

Debate over Race Revisited: An Empirical Investigation," *Phylon* (Mar. 1978).
Compare with Stanley M. Garn, *Human Races*, 3d ed. (Springfield, Ill., 1971).

106. Fredrickson, "Social Interpretation," 245–51.

107. Fredrickson's argument may have been shaped in part by his earlier book, in which he found ideological racism coeval with the period he studied. Similarly, Duncan J. Macleod argued that it emerged in the period *he* studied (*Slavery, Race, and the American Revolution* [London and New York, 1974], 80). John B. Boles, *Black Southerners, 1619–1869* (Lexington, Ky., 1983), 7–24, esp. 19, seems at first glance to echo Fredrickson: "[W]ith the demographic changes occurring in the Chesapeake society in the decades on either side of 1700, the vague, implicit, abstract racism of the English was transformed into a far more concrete, legally precise, and individually applicable societal racism." Boles, however, has divided Fredrickson's first category into "implicit" and "societal," with the former characterizing the seventeenth century, the latter the eighteenth, and with explicit racism emerging in the nineteenth—a three-part model in contrast to Fredrickson's two-stage sequence. I consider Boles's formulation a major improvement, although it ignores the important ideological underpinning of seventeenth-century Anglo-American racial attitudes.

108. Noel, *Origins of Slavery and Racism*, 155–60; Philip Mason, *Common Sense about Race* (London, 1961), 77–94.

109. Noel, *Origins of Slavery and Racism*, 159.

110. See pp. 242–44, above.

111. Lerone Bennett Jr., "The Making of Black America—Part 3: The Road Not Taken," *Ebony*, 25 (Aug. 1970): 71–77, quotations on 71–72; Bennett, "First Generation," 33. Part 2 (Nov. 1969) treats white servitude. The essays are condensed in Lerone Bennett Jr., *Before the Mayflower: A History of Black America*, 4th ed. (Chicago, 1969), esp. 36–38. The fifth edition of *Before the Mayflower* (Harmondsworth, Eng., 1984), 28–46, appears to incorporate the Breen and Innes book (but does not list it in the bibliography) and goes much further in asserting benign and nondiscriminatory treatment of blacks in early British North America. Bennett's book has no notes by which to verify such statements as "the available evidence suggests that most of the first generation of African-Americans worked out their terms of servitude and were freed" (39), which is simply not true.

112. Breen and Innes, "*Myne Owne Ground*"; Deal, "Race and Class," 210–17, which argues (erroneously, I believe) that the elite may have been racist from the outset "but non-slaveholding whites . . . absorbed it only gradually with the growth of slave society . . in the late seventeenth and early eighteenth centuries" (216).

113. See note 118.

114. The classic introduction to early Virginia's social composition is Bernard Bailyn, "Politics and Social Structure in Virginia," in James Morton Smith, ed., *Seventeenth-Century America: Essays in Colonial History* (Chapel Hill, N.C., 1959). A corrective to Bailyn's interpretation is Jon Kukla, "Order and Chaos in Early America: Political and Social Stability in Pre-Restoration Virginia," *American Historical Review* (hereafter cited as *AHR*), 90 (1985): 275–98.

115. Carl N. Degler, *Neither Black nor White: Slavery and Race Relations in Brazil and the United States* (New York, 1971), esp. 207–92, quotations on 211, 287. For a psychiatrist's argument that racism was deeply ingrained among whites, see Joel Kovel, *White Racism: A Psychohistory* (New York, 1970). See also John

Hope Franklin, ed., *Color and Race* (Boston, 1968), especially the essay by Kenneth J. Gergen.

116. The circumstances described were not unique to the English; to a significant but perhaps lesser degree similar circumstances influenced other European peoples. These common situations help to explain why all European colonies enslaved blacks and no European colonies enslaved whites. See, for example, William B. Cohen, *The French Encounter with Africans: White Response to Blacks, 1530–1880* (Bloomington, Ind., 1980), chaps. 1–2.

117. Jordan, *White over Black*, chap. 1. Philip Mason has suggested that "it is the peoples of Northern Europe who have shown the strongest colour prejudices. This may be because they themselves are fairer than people from Southern Europe; it may also be because they have had the most reason to fear the dark. The long winter nights have surely left a mark on our language and thought; we speak of dark deeds and black moods, of wickedness as black as hell, while angels are white and bright and in all our metaphors white stands for innocence and purity. The devil was black to people who had never seen a brown skin. And when a brown skin was seen for the first time, the first associations were with dirt and defecation and with all the metaphors associating darkness with evil and fear" (*Common Sense about Race*, 91). See also Franklin ed., *Color and Race;* and Kovel, *White Racism.*

118. Studies of racial attitudes in Elizabethan-Jacobean England that have appeared since Jordan's book went to press include G. K. Hunter, "Othello and Colour Prejudice," *Proceedings of the British Academy* 53 (1967): 139–63; James Walvin, *Black and White: The Negro and English Society, 1555–1945* (London, 1973), chaps. 1–3; F. O. Shyllon, *Black Slaves in Britain* (London, 1974); Peter Fryer, *Staying Power: The History of Black People in Britain* (London, 1984); Ruth Cowhig, "Blacks in English Renaissance Drama and the Role of Shakespeare's *Othello*," in David Dabydeen, ed., *The Black Presence in English Literature* (Manchester, Eng., 1985), 1–14; and Anthony Gerard Barthelemy, *Black Face, Maligned Race: The Representation of Blacks in English Drama from Shakespeare to Southerne* (Baton Rouge, 1987). See also McColley, "Slavery in Virginia," 14–15. The quotation is from Jordan, *White over Black*, 43.

119. Several times in the late sixteenth and early seventeenth centuries royal edicts called for the expulsion of "the great number of Negroes and blackamoors which . . . are carried into this realm" (Paul L. Hughes and James F. Larkin, eds., *Tudor Royal Proclamations*, 3 [New Haven, 1969], 221–22).

120. George Best, *A Trve Discovrse of the Late Voyages of discouerie, for the finding of a passage to Cathaya . . .* (London, 1578), 28, 30, 31.

121. Thomas Cooper, *The Blessing of Japheth, proving the Gathering of the Gentiles . . .* (London, 1615), sig. [A2v], 1–3. Early Virginians, Philip Bruce theorized in 1895, believed that if the Negro "were indeed a member of the human family, he belonged to a race of men who, as the descendants of Ham, had been cursed by God himself, and so branded for all time as servants of superior races" (*Economic History of Virginia*, 2:65).

122. John Weemse, *The Portraiture of the Image of God in Man* (London, 1627), 279; [George Sandys], *A Relation of a Journey Begun An: Dom: 1610*, 2d ed. (London, 1615), 136.

123. Jordan, *White over Black*, 19.

124. Fredrickson, *Black Image*, chap. 2, discusses antebellum racist theories, which, of course, included the curse on Ham. See also William Sumner Jenk-

ins, *Pro-Slavery Thought in the Old South* (Chapel Hill, N.C. 1935); Larry E. Tise, *Proslavery: A History of the Defense of Slavery in America, 1701–1840* (Athens, Ga., 1987). For an erudite discussion of slavery and racial concepts in a broader context of time and place, see William McKee Evans, "From the Land of Canaan to the Land of Guinea: The Strange Odyssey of the 'Sons of Ham,'" *AHR* 85 (1980): 15–43. The brief section of Evans's essay that deals with early American slavery underestimates the existence of prejudicial attitudes in Elizabethan England and especially in early British America.

125. Morgan Godwyn, *The Negro's & Indians Advocate, Suing for Their Admission into the Church* ... (London, 1680), 3, 12, 14, 39, 61. Godwyn spent the middle 1660s in Virginia and implicitly (sometimes explicitly) included that colony in his remarks on Barbados. See chapter 3 in this volume.

126. For a thoughtful discussion of race and southern history through the Reconstruction era, see Barbara J. Fields, "Ideology and Race in American History," in J. Morgan Kousser and James M. McPherson, eds., *Region, Race, and Reconstruction: Essays in Honor of C. Vann Woodward* (New York, 1982), 143–77. Although I find Fields's essay instructive, it seriously underestimates, I believe, racial discrimination and racist ideology in seventeenth-century America (see esp. 144–52).

127. See Davis, *Problem of Slavery,* chaps. 2–4; Peter Kolchin, *Unfree Labor: American Slavery and Russian Serfdom* (Cambridge, Mass., 1987); Peter Frost, "Fair Women, Dark Men: The Forgotten Roots of Colour Prejudice," *History of European Ideas* 12 (1990): 669–79.

128. Permanent bondage throughout the Americas was imposed only on Africans and Indians, though there were many variations on the basic pattern. See, for example, Davis, *Problem of Slavery,* chap. 8; Degler, *Neither White nor Black;* Ann M. Pescatello, ed., *The African in Latin America* (New York, 1975); Katia M. de Queirós Mattoso, *To Be a Slave in Brazil, 1550–1880,* trans. Arthur Goldhammer (1979; reprint, New Brunswick, N.J., 1986); and Laura Foner and Eugene D. Genovese, eds., *Slavery in the New World: A Reader in Comparative History* (Englewood Cliffs, N.J., 1969).

129. The complex interconnection of English attitudes toward Africans and American Indians is obviously germane to the topic of this essay; it has been broached briefly (and I believe quite inaccurately) by several participants in the debate, including the Handlins, Degler, Jordan, and Morgan. The topic is too extensive for exploration here. I have addressed some aspects of it in chapter 1 in this volume, esp. pp. 18–29. The possible parallels and contrasts between English-African and English-Irish relations is also germane but has yet to be addressed thoroughly. Suggestive are the works of Nicholas P. Canny, including "The Ideology of English Colonization: From Ireland to America," *WMQ,* 3d ser. 30 (1973): 575–98.

130. Hening, ed., *Statutes of Virginia,* 2:267.

POSTSCRIPT TO CHAPTER 7

1. Barbara Jeanne Fields, "Slavery, Race and Ideology in the United States of America," *New Left Review,* no. 181 (May/June 1990): 95–117. This postscript to Fields's article focuses on the portions that directly concern seventeenth-century Virginia and the emergence of American racism. Fields also addresses other

aspects of American slavery and racism. In some instances I heartily agree with her position, in other instances I disagree. I discussed those agreements and disagreements in an open letter to Barbara Fields in November 1992 (based on an earlier private letter), of which this postscript is a shorter, revised version.

2. Ibid., 101–6.

3. Ibid., 101–4.

4. Fields also argues (ibid., 102) that "Indentured servants served longer terms in Virginia than their English counterparts," which is true only to the extent that indentured servants in Virginia were reimbursing the cost of a transatlantic passage. She similarly distorts the comparative severity of punishments in England and America and exaggerates changes in length of servitude.

5. Much of Field's evidence for an extremely harsh treatment of indentured servants and a relatively benign treatment of Africans, slave and free, comes from Morgan, *American Slavery, American Freedom.* I concur with J. R. Pole's judgment that "Morgan consistently underrates the cumulative weight of [Winthrop] Jordan's evidence for the sixteenth and seventeenth centuries." Pole, *Paths to the American Present* (New York, 1979), 71 n. 13. Moreover, Virginia's indentured servants, however badly treated, must surely have appreciated the profound difference between their own conditions and the African-Americans' "perpetual enslavement along with their issue in perpetuity" (Fields "Slavery, Race and Ideology," 102).

6. *English Historical Documents, 1485–1558,* ed. C. H. Williams (London, 1967), 1029–32; George Nicholls, *A History of the English Poor Law,* new ed. 2 vols. (London, 1898), 1:129–33; C. S. L. Davies, "Slavery and Protector Somerset: The Vagrancy Act of 1547," *Economic History Review,* 2d ser. 19 (1966): 533–49, esp. 545–46. See also J. H. Plumb's review of Jordan, *White over Black, New York Review of Books* (13 Mar. 1969), reprinted in Starr and Detweiler, eds., *Race, Prejudice and Slavery,* 154, which also exaggerates the act of 1547. Scotland's vagrancy laws may have permitted a more extensive and exploitive form of bondage than England's. See *Edinburgh Review* 189 (1899): 119–48.

7. Fryer, *Black People in Britain,* chap. 1; Walvin, *The Negro and English Society,* chaps. 1–2; Paul L. Hughes and James F. Larkin, eds., *Tudor Royal Proclamations,* 3 (New Haven, 1969), 221–22.

8. Michael Craton, *Sinews of Empire: A Short History of British Slavery* (Garden City, N.Y., 1974), 158–64. See also Vincent Harlow, *A History of Barbados, 1625–1685* (Oxford, 1926), 294–98, for the banishment of political prisoners to the West Indies throughout the Stuart era. Ten years was the recommended minimum service under James II.

9. Fields, "Slavery, Race and Ideology," 102, 113, 104. Morgan, *American Slavery, American Freedom,* 154, is Fields's source on slaves' "rights." According to Morgan, "All [Africans in Virginia], servant, slave, or free, enjoyed rights that were later denied all Negroes in Virginia." I fail to find any evidence in Morgan's book or in the colonial records to support that statement.

10. Fields, "Slavery, Race and Ideology," 101, 106, 113–14.

11. The evidence for this paragraph is provided at several points in the foregoing essay and should not need repetition here. See also McColley, "Slavery in Virginia."

12. Willie Lee Rose, ed., *A Documentary History of Slavery in North America* (New York, 1976), 24; Hening, *Statutes of Virginia,* 2:481; Fields, "Slavery, Race and Ideology," 107.

13. McIlwaine, ed., *Minutes of the Council and General Court*, 196; Hening, ed., *Statutes of Virginia*, 2:280–81, 515. See also ibid., 292. On the customary interchangeability of such words, see also Godwyn, *Negro's and Indians Advocate*, 36 (quoted in this volume on p. 76).

14. Fields, "Slavery, Race and Ideology," 103.

15. For an example from the 1680s of this procedure, see Douglas Deal, "A Constricted World: Free Blacks on Virginia's Eastern Shore, 1680–1750," in Lois Green Carr, Philip D. Morgan, and Jean B. Russo, ed., *Colonial Chesapeake Society* (Chapel Hill, N.C., 1988), 292–93.

16. Pole, *Paths to the American Present*, 71.

17. Fields, "Slavery, Race and Ideology," 110.

CHAPTER 8: PEQUOTS AND PURITANS

1. See, for examples, Timothy Dwight, *Greenfield Hill: A Poem in Seven Parts* (New York, 1794), bk. 4; and Samuel G. Drake, *The Book of the Indians*, 9th ed. (Boston, 1845), bk. 2: 106–7.

2. For an explanation of Melville's familiarity with the history of the Pequot War and his reasons for employing the name of the tribe, see the edition of *Moby Dick* by Luther S. Mansfield and Howard P. Vincent (New York, 1952), 68, 631–33.

3. For representatives of the first view, see Increase Mather, *A Relation of the Troubles Which Have Hapned in New-England, by Reason of the Indians There . . .* (Boston, 1677), 51–55; Benjamin Trumbull, *A Complete History of Connecticut*, 2 vols. (New Haven, 1818), 1:chap. 5; and John Gorham Palfrey, *History of New England*, 5 vols. (Boston, 1865–90), 1:455–70. Pre-1964 examples of the second viewpoint, prevalent among non–New England authors in the nineteenth century and among twentieth-century historians regardless of locale, can be found in John R. Brodhead, *History of the State of New York*, 2d ed., 2 vols. (New York, 1859), 1:237–73; William C. MacLeod, *The American Indian Frontier* (New York, 1928), 209–19; and William T. Hagan, *American Indians* (Chicago, 1961), 12–14. The latter two also see causation in Puritan coveting of Indian lands; they thus have much in common with the third school of interpretation, which is most articulately presented in Roy Harvey Pearce, *The Savages of America* (Baltimore, 1953), 19–35, reissued in 1965 with minor revisions as *Savagism and Civilization: A Study of the Indian and the American Mind*. For more recent incarnations of the Puritan aggression theme, see especially Francis Jennings, *The Invasion of America: Indians, Colonialism, and the Cant of Conquest* (Chapel Hill, N.C., 1975), chaps. 11–13; Richard Drinnon, *Facing West: The Metaphysics of Indian-Hating and Empire Building* (New York, 1980), chap. 4; Neal Salisbury, *Manitou and Providence: Indians, Europeans, and the Making of New England, 1500–1643* (New York, 1982), chap. 7. The case for wampum as a causative factor has been made by Alvin M. Josephy Jr., *Now That the Buffalo's Gone: A Study of Today's American Indians* (New York, 1982; reprint, Norman, Okla., 1984), chap. 2.

4. To avoid repetition of the basic facts on which scholars are in general agreement—despite their virulent disagreement on certain other points—I have incorporated in section I, which summarizes the early pro-Puritan interpretation, a general narrative of the events of 1634 to 1637. Subsequent sections pre

sent the particular arguments of later interpretive schools without repeating the basic narrative.

5. This view of Pequot origins began with William Hubbard, *The History of the Indian Wars in New England,* ed. Samuel G. Drake, 2 vols. (Boston, 1677; reprint, Roxbury, Mass., 1865), 2:6–7, and was perpetuated by works such as Trumbull, *Complete History of Connecticut,* 1:141, John W. De Forest, *History of the Indians of Connecticut . . . to 1850* (Hartford, Conn., 1852); Alden T. Vaughan, *New England Frontier: Puritans and Indians, 1620–1675* (Boston, 1965; rev. ed., New York, 1979), 55–56, 123. The early history of the Pequots has in recent years been vastly expanded and corrected; all evidence now points to their residence in southern Connecticut long before the seventeenth century. See especially Alfred A. Cave, "The Pequot Invasion of Southern New England: A Reassessment of the Evidence," *New England Quarterly* 62 (1989): 27–44; and William A. Starna, "The Pequots in the Early Seventeenth Century," in Laurence M. Hauptman and James D. Wherry, eds., *The Pequots in Southern New England: The Fall and Rise of an American Indian Nation* (Norman, Okla., 1990), 33–47.

6. James Hammond Trumbull in *Narragansett Club, Publications,* 1 (Providence, R.I., 1866), 22 [82], n. 10, 263 [203] n. 360.

7. See Brodhead, *History of New York,* 1:242; [John Winthrop], *Winthrop's Journal "History of New England," 1630-1649,* ed. James Kendall Hosmer, 2 vols. (New York, 1908), 1:79, 139.

8. Jennings, *Invasion of America,* 189, 190 n. 8, chides historians who identify Stone as a Virginian, insisting that he was an inhabitant of the West Indies. The best evidence on Stone comes from William Bradford, *History of Plymouth Plantation,* ed. Worthington Chauncey Ford, 2 vols. (Boston, 1912), 2:190–92, who recorded that Stone "had lived in Christophers, one of the West-Ende Ilands, and now had been some time in Virginia, and came from thence into these parts." Lion Gardiner, a major participant and chronicler of the period, identified Stone as a Virginian, and Winthrop wrote that he "was one of that colony": "Leift Lion Gardener his relation to the Pequot Warres," *Massachusetts Historical Society, Collections* 3d ser. 3 (1833): 137, 138; Winthrop, *Journal,* 1:102, 118. Whether one calls Stone a West Indian or a Virginian is therefore arbitrary, though the latter seems to be more appropriate for the events of 1634 et seq.

9. Bradford, *History of Plymouth,* 2:190–92; Winthrop, *Journal,* 1:118; John Mason, *A Brief History of the Pequot War* (Boston, 1736), viii–ix.

10. The details of the negotiations are in Winthrop, *Journal,* 1:138–40; Winthrop to John Winthrop Jr., 12 Dec. 1634, in *Winthrop Papers,* ed. Allyn Bailey Forbes, 5 vols. (Boston, 1929–47), 3:177; and Bradford, *History of Plymouth,* 2:232–33, which includes a letter from Winthrop to Bradford, ca. Dec. 1634.

11. Winthrop, *Journal,* 1:139; John Winthrop to William Bradford, ca. Feb. 1635, in Bradford, *History of Plymouth,* 2:233–34.

12. Winthrop, *Journal,* 1:139–40; Winthrop to Bradford, ca. Feb. 1635, in Bradford, *History of Plymouth,* 2:233. Much of the wampum was apparently earmarked for the Narragansetts, with whom the Pequots desired peace but could not directly negotiate. Winthrop's account of the episode in his journal is ambiguous; the wampum intended for the Narragansetts may have been in addition to the four hundred fathoms, though his letter to Bradford implies otherwise.

13. Winthrop to Bradford, 12 Mar. 1635, in Bradford, *History of Plymouth,* 2:234; Winthrop, *Journal,* 1:140.

14. Two letters from Jonathan Brewster to John Winthrop Jr., both dated 18 June 1636, and Colony of Massachusetts Bay to John Winthrop Jr., 4 July 1636, in *Winthrop Papers*, 3:270–72, 284–85. Brewster reported also that Sassacus and his brother had been "actor[s] in the death of Stone" and his brother and one of his men "chiefe actors in the Death of the 2 last upon the Iland" (ibid., 270).

15. Jennings, *Invasion of America*, 204–5, describes at length a conference that he supposes took place at Saybrook in July 1636, though "As usual, the Winthrops preserved a record of charges and complaints to put the Pequots in the wrong but did not keep the minutes of the conference." Jennings's evidence for the conference is shaky indeed. Winthrop Jr.'s instructions were to return the skins and wampum in either of two situations: rejection of a conference by the Pequots or failure of the Pequots to meet the Massachusetts demands if a conference were held. The surviving documents do not indicate that a conference was held at Saybrook or elsewhere. Gardiner, who was at Saybrook and very much involved in Indian affairs, reports that "the Pequit Sachem was sent for, and the present returned," which implies no prior meeting. See *Winthrop Papers*, 3:284–85; Gardiner, "Relation of the Pequot Warres," 139.

16. The imminence of war is emphasized in Gardiner, "Relation of the Pequot Warres," 138–39. Pequot expectations of a colonial attack are documented in Jonathan Brewster to John Winthrop Jr., 18 June 1636, in *Winthrop Papers*, 3:270.

17. Winthrop, *Journal*, 1:183–84; Underhill, *Newes from America*, 2–3; Thomas Cobbet, "A Narrative of New England's Deliverances," *New England Historical and Genealogical Register* 7 (1853): 211–12.

18. Winthrop, *Journal*, 1:184–86; Hubbard, *Indian Wars in New England*, 2:11.

19. The only eyewitness account of the Endecott expedition is Underhill, *Newes from America*, 3–15 (quotation on 14), but see also Winthrop, *Journal*, 1:187–89, and Gardiner, "Relation of the Pequot Warres," 140–42.

20. Gardiner, "Relation of the Pequot Warres," 142–48; Underhill, *Newes from America*, 15–17, 22–23; Mason, *Brief History*, viii–x; Winthrop, *Journal*, 1:191–92, 194, 212; Lion Gardiner to John Winthrop Jr., 6–7 Nov. 1636, and 23 Mar. 1637, in *Winthrop Papers*, 3:319–21, 381–82.

21. See esp. Winthrop, *Journal*, 1:194–99, 208–9; and John Winthrop, *A Short Story of the Rise, reign, and ruine of the Antinomians, Familists & Libertines*, reprinted in David D. Hall, ed., *The Antinomian Controversy, 1636–1638*, 2d ed. (Durham, N.C., 1990), 253–54.

22. Underhill, *Newes from America*, 16–18; [Edward Johnson], *Johnson's Wonder-Working Providence, 1628–1651*, ed. J. Franklin Jameson (New York, 1910), 149; *Records of the Governor and Company of the Massachusetts Bay in New England*, ed. Nathaniel B. Shurtleff, 5 vols. in 6 (Boston, 1853–54), 1:192; *The Public Records of the Colony of Connecticut, prior to . . . 1665*, ed. J. Hammond Trumbull (Hartford, 1850), 9. Underhill, *Newes from America*, 37, estimated that English losses totaled "about thirty persons."

23. Williams to John Mason and Thomas Prence, 22 June 1670, in [Roger Williams], *The Correspondence of Roger Williams*, ed. Glenn W. LaFantasie, 2 vols. (Hanover, N.H., 1988), 2:611–12; Winthrop, *Journal*, 2:192–94.

24. Williams to John Mason and Thomas Prence, 22 June 1670, in *Williams Correspondence*, 2:611–12.

25. The rift in the Pequot ranks has never been fully explained, but see P. Richard Metcalf, "Who Should Rule at Home? Native American Politics and

Indian-White Relations," *Journal of American History* 61 (1973–74): 651–65; William Burton and Richard Lowenthal, "The First of the Mohegans," *American Ethnologist* 1 (1974): 589–99.

26. Winthrop, *Journal*, 1:62; Bradford, *History of Plymouth*, 2:164–65; Hooker to John Winthrop, spring 1637, in *Winthrop Papers*, 3:407.

27. John Mason, *A Brief History of the Pequot War* (Boston, 1736), 17; [Philip Vincent], *A True Relation of the Late Battell Fought in New-England . . .* (London, 1638), 16; Winthrop, *Journal*, 1:229.

28. The essence of this interpretation is found in several older works (see note 3) but especially in several recent studies, most notably Jennings, *Invasion of America*, chs. 11–13. For more on this school of interpretation, see the postscript to this essay.

29. Winthrop, *Journal*, 1:102, 108; Bradford, *History of Plymouth*, 2:190–91; Roger Clap, "Memoirs of Capt. Roger Clap," in Alexander Young, ed., *Chronicles of the First Planters of the Colony of Massachusetts Bay, from 1623 to 1636* (Boston, 1846), 363; *Mass. Colony Records*, 1:108.

30. Bradford, *History of Plymouth*, 2:191–92; Winthrop, *Journal*, 1:118; Clap, "Memoirs," 363.

31. Jennings, *Invasion of America*, 193.

32. Winthrop, *Journal*, 1:186–88; Underhill, *Newes from America*, 4–8. Underhill, the sole eyewitness chronicler, reported that the English killed "some fourteen & maimed others" on Block Island (p. 8); the Narragansetts later informed the English (Winthrop, *Journal*, 2:189–90) that only one Indian had been killed.

33. Winthrop, *Journal*, 1:186.

34. Underhill, *Newes from America*, 9–15; Gardiner, "Relation of the Pequot Warres," 140–42; Winthrop, *Journal*, 1:188–90. Gardiner claimed that only one Pequot had been killed, ironically by Cutshamekin (spelled variously in the sources) of the Massachusetts tribe, one of the two Indians who accompanied the English forces; Underhill (p. 15) referred to "certaine numbers of theirs slaine, and many wounded." The Narragansetts later told Winthrop that thirteen Pequots had been killed and forty wounded. The earliest historians of the war accept the lowest figure but do not attribute the action to Cutshamekin. Hubbard, *Indian Wars of New England*, 2:15; Increase Mather, *A Relation of the Troubles which Have Hapned in New-England, by Reason of the Indians There*, ed. Samuel G. Drake under the title *Early History of New England . . .* (Boston, 1864), 162.

35. Some of Gardiner's garrison, sent to gather corn against the expected seige of Saybrook, were left behind when Endecott's troops embarked for Boston; the Pequots attacked and wounded two of them. Gardiner, "Relation of the Pequot Warres," 141.

36. Winthrop, *Journal*, 1:212–14; Bradford, *History of Plymouth*, 2:235–36, 243; Gardiner, "Relation of the Pequot Warres," 140; Johnson, *Wonder-Working Providence*, 164. Although there is no record of Roger Williams's opinion, he must have been appalled (judging from his writings on Indian affairs in general and his relatively conciliatory attitudes) by the severity of the attacks on the Block Islanders and Pequots.

37. Roger Williams to John Winthrop Jr., 28 May 1664, in *Williams Correspondence*, 2:528

38. For example, John Winthrop, "General Observations," in *Winthrop Papers*, 2:120. On arrival in New England, the Puritans found that not much land was truly vacant.

39. "The Early Records of Charlestown," in Alexander Young, ed., *Chronicles of the First Planters of the Colony of Massachusetts Bay, 1623–1636* (Boston, 1846; reprint, New York, 1970), 386–87; John Winthrop to John Endecott, 3 Jan. 1634, in *Winthrop Papers*, 3:149.

40. Starna, "Pequots in the Early Seventeenth Century," 45–46.

41. Underhill, *Newes from America*, 2; Mason, *Brief History*, 21.

42. Bradford, *History of Plymouth*, 2:247.

43. James Truslow Adams, *The Founding of New England* (Boston, 1921), 205; Drinnon, *Facing West*, 39–40, 46. For a more recent version, see Clara Bartocci, "Puritans versus Pequots: Four Eye–Witness Reports of the First War in Colonial New England," *Storia Nordamericana* 4 (1987): 76–77.

44. Larzer Ziff, *Puritanism in America: New Culture in a New World* (New York, 1973), 73–74; Lynn Ceci, "Native Wampum as a Peripheral Resource in the Seventeenth-Century World-System," in Hauptman and Wherry, eds., *Pequots in Southern New England*, 59–61; Josephy, *Now That the Buffalo's Gone*, 50–58. Attention to wampum production (rather than wampum as tribute or reparations) to explain the Puritans' Indian policies was first raised in Lynn Ceci, "The Effect of European Contact and Trade on the Settlement Pattern of Indians in Coastal New York, 1524–1665: The Archeological and Documentary Evidence," Ph.D. dissertation, City University of New York, 1977; for the Pequot War see esp. 208–20.

45. William Wood, *New Englands Prospect* (London, 1634), 52–53; Bradford, *History of Plymouth*, 2:164–65.

46. Williams to John Winthrop, before 25 Aug. 1636, in *Williams Correspondence*, 1:54–55.

47. *Rhode Island Historical Society Collections* 3 (1835): 177.

48. Jennings, *Invasion of America*, 188–90, 204–5, 227. Salisbury, *Manitou and Providence*, does not mention Stone's shipmates at all, nor, surprisingly does Stephen T. Katz, "The Pequot War Reconsidered," *New England Quarterly* 64 (1991): 206–24, esp. 208. Alfred A. Cave, "Who Killed John Stone? A Note on the Origins of the Pequot War," *William and Mary Quarterly*, 3d ser. 49 (1992): 509–21, mentions Stone's companions twice (510, 513) but ignores them in his extensive discussion (517–21) of Puritan intransigence on the murder of Englishmen.

49. Winthrop, *Journal*, 1:118, 139, 186, 214; Winthrop to John Winthrop Jr., 12 Dec. 1634, in *Winthrop Papers*, 3:177; Bradford, *History of Plymouth*, 2:191–92, 233–34; Mason, *Brief History*, viii–ix; Gardiner, "Relation of the Pequot Warres," 137.

50. Winthrop, *Journal*, 1:213–14. Historians who trivialize the murders of Stone, Oldham, and others often also misrepresent Oldham's standing in the Puritan community. See, for example, Drinnon, *Facing West*, 37. A similar tactic by Puritan bashers is to minimize the post-Endecott killings, which amounted to approximately fifteen English colonists between Sept. 1636 and May 1637, some by torture. For example, Salisbury, *Manitou and Providence*, 218, dismisses them as "occasional harassments of English travelers on the Connecticut." See also the citations below (n. 55) to David Stannard's book.

51. Williams to Winthrop, 24 Oct. 1636?, in *Williams Correspondence*, 1:69. The editor of *Williams Correspondence* interprets Williams correctly, I believe (n. 35), though other interpretations are possible.

52. Jennings, *Invasion of America*, 185; Francis Paul Jennings, *Miquon's Passing: Indian-European Relations in Colonial Pennsylvania, 1674–1755*, bound photocopy (Ann Arbor, Mich., 1966), 456–57. For examples of Jennings's misreading of the sources, see Katz, "The Pequot War Reconsidered," 213–18; and Cave, "Who Killed John Stone?" 518–19. Jennings's book has yet to receive the full critical dissection it deserves. For additional criticism of *Invasion of America*, and of Jennings's more recent *The Founders of America* (New York, 1993), see the introduction to the third edition of my *New England Frontier* (Norman, Okla., 1995).

53. Jennings, *Invasion of America*, chaps. 11–18; especially, for the causes of the Pequot War, 177–218. Quotations in this paragraph are from ix and 188.

54. Drinnon, *Facing West*, 56, 32, 50. See also 20, 38, 49, 52. For acknowledgments of Jennings's influence on Drinnon's book, see ibid., 43–44n, 530. Another book that relies excessively and unfortunately on Jennings is Ann Kibbey, *The Interpretation of Material Shapes in Puritanism: A Study of Rhetoric, Prejudice, and Violence* (Cambridge, 1986). Kibbey's chapter on the interrelatedness of the Pequot War and the Antinominan controversy charges, among other things, that "As Francis Jennings has shown, the gratuitous slaughter of Pequot women at Mystic was deliberately perpetrated and carefully recorded . . ." (93). For additional explicit (over)reliance on Jennings, see also 100, 104, and 110, and notes to chap. 5, esp. nn. 2, 16, 22, 23. Salisbury, *Manitou and Providence*, also owes almost all of its interpretation of the Pequot War to Jennings, although Salisbury occasionally reads the evidence differently.

55. David E. Stannard, *American Holocaust: Columbus and the Conquest of the New World* (New York, 1992), 112–15, 233–41, 277–78, 309 n. 55. Stannard's account of the Pequot War period (ca. 1634–38) is often erroneous in fact and implausible in emphasis.

56. Drinnon, *Facing West*, 51. Despite my almost total disagreement with Drinnon's interpretation of Puritan sources, I think he is essentially accurate in his assessment of Thomas Jefferson's racial attitudes. See his chaps. 8–9.

57. Stannard, *American Holocaust*, 269–78; Plumb; "Slavery, Race, and the Poor," *New York Review of Books* (13 Mar. 1969), reprinted in Raymond Starr and Robert Detweiler, eds., *Race, Prejudice, and the Origins of Slavery in America* (Cambridge, Mass., 1975), 154.

58. Adam J. Hirsch, "The Collision of Military Cultures in Seventeenth-Century New England," *Journal of American History* 74 (1988): 1187–1212, quotations on 1198, 1199.

59. Katz, "Pequot War Reconsidered," 212, 207. Much of Katz's article is concerned with the war itself, especially some historians' insistence that the Puritans were attempting genocide against the Pequots or, more broadly, against all Indians. Katz, rightly I believe, adheres to the original meaning of genocide rather than to its subsequent expansion in the United Nations declaration of 1948. Using the earlier, more literal meaning, Katz demonstrates the inappropriateness of the label to the events of 1636–38: Puritan forces purposely spared women, children, and the elderly in all instances except at the torching of Mystic fort; the several hundred Pequot survivors of the war were initially parceled out to the victorious parties (English, Narragansett, Mohegan) but within a few years were reformulated into Pequot communities that henceforth played an important role in inter-Indian and interracial affairs. Cf. Stannard, *American Holocaust*, 318 n. 11, which misrepresents Katz's position.

60. Cave, "Who Killed John Stone?" 509–21; quotation from 521. See also Cave, "Pequot Invasion of Southern New England."

CHAPTER 9: TESTS OF PURITAN JUSTICE

1. For examples of the sharply critical view of New England Puritans that dominated early-twentieth-century writings, see the relevant writings of James Truslow Adams, Charles Beard, and Vernon Louis Parrington. Their stereotypes were largely overturned in the 1930s and 1940s by Samuel Eliot Morison, Perry Miller, and Kenneth Murdock, and subsequently bolstered by a new generation of Puritan specialists in the 1960s and beyond. Writings on the Puritans since this essay was first published in 1965 are voluminous and include a vigorous interpretive countertrend. A helpful introduction to the literature is Francis J. Bremer, "From the Old World to the New, 1620–1689," in Martin Kaufman, John W. Ifkovic, and Joseph Carvalho III, eds., *A Guide to the History of Massachusetts* (Westport, Conn., 1988).

2. Examples of sharp criticism before 1965 of Puritan relations with Indians include William T. Hagan, *American Indians* (Chicago, 1961), 12–15; and Roy Harvey Pearce, *The Savages of America* (Baltimore, 1935), 19–35. An earlier indictment of the Puritans is William C. MacLeod, *The American Indian Frontier* (London, 1928), 188–222 and passim. Cf. the sympathetic analysis of Plymouth's policy in David Bushnell, "The Treatment of the Indians in Plymouth Colony," *New England Quarterly* 26 (1953): 193–218. Perry Miller's magisterial works on the Puritans almost wholly ignored their relations with the natives, as did Edmund S. Morgan's several important books. Samuel Eliot Morison gave somewhat more attention to the topic, especially in *Builders of the Bay Colony* (Boston, 1930). Recent scholarship on Puritans and Indians has ranged from severe indictments to cautious praise. See, for examples, Francis Jennings, *The Invasion of America: Indians, Colonialism, and the Cant of Conquest* (Chapel Hill, N.C., 1975); Neal Salisbury, *Manitou and Providence: Indians, Europeans, and the Making of New England, 1500–1643* (New York, 1982); Alden T. Vaughan, *New England Frontier: Puritans and Indians, 1620–1675*, 3d ed. (Norman, Okla., 1995).

3. By 1965, when this essay was first published, very little had been written about the impact of Puritan legal institutions on the Indians. Since then, a fairly substantial body of work has appeared and more is in progress. See especially Yasuhide Kawashima, *Puritan Justice and the Indian: White Man's Law in Massachusetts, 1630–1763* (Middletown, Conn., 1986); James P. Ronda, "Red and White at the Bench: Indians and the Law in Plymouth Colony, 1620–1691," *Essex Institute Historical Collections* 110 (1974): 200–215; Lyle Koehler, "Red-White Power Relations and Justice in the Courts of Seventeenth-Century New England," *American Indian Culture and Research Journal* 3, no. 4 (1979): 1–31; and James W. Springer, "American Indians and the Law of Real Property in Colonial New England," *American Journal of Legal History* 30 (1986): 25–88.

4. Significantly silent about the two cases are several recent historians of Puritans and Indians who treat the early decades in considerable detail and who claim to present, at long last, truly unbiased accounts but instead revert to Progressive Era stereotypes. See especially Jennings, *Invasion of America*, which ignores the Plymouth case and gives, in my opinion, a brief but implausible twist

to the Connecticut case (217 n. 45), and Salisbury, *Manitou and Providence*, which mentions neither case.

5. See chapter 5 in this volume for the Virginia massacre of 1622 and its perceived lessons for New England.

6. The Pequots had been prodded into their most recent aggression by a Massachusetts expedition led against them in Aug. 1636 by John Endecott. This Puritan attack had in turn been prompted by earlier Indian actions which the Puritans, rightly or wrongly, blamed on the Pequots. The original version of this essay attributed the Pequots' reputation for ferocity—frequently attested by Puritan writers and subsequent historians—to the Pequots' invasion of the region in the early seventeenth century. That interpretation has been successfully challenged in Alfred A. Cave, "The Pequot Invasion of Southern New England: A Reassessment of the Evidence," *New England Quarterly* 62 (1989): 27–44. See chapter 8 in this volume for an extensive discussion of the causes of the Pequot War.

7. [John Winthrop], *Winthrop's Journal "History of New England," 1630–1649,* ed. James Kendall Hosmer, 2 vols. (New York, 1908), 1:192–94; Roger Williams to John Mason and Thomas Prence, 22 June 1670, in *The Correspondence of Roger Williams,* ed. Glenn W. LaFantasie, 2 vols. (Hanover, N.H., 1988), 2:611–12.

8. Winthrop, *Journal,* 1:194, 208, 212; [Philip Vincent], *A True Relation of the Late Battell Fought in New England, between the English, and the Salvages* (London, 1637), sig. B2–B3; John Underhill, *Newes from America; or, A New and Experimentall Discoverie of New England* (London, 1638), 2–17; John Mason, *A Brief History of the Pequot War* (Boston, 1736), viii–x; Lion Gardiner, "Leift Lion Gardener his relation of the Pequot Warres," in *Massachusetts Historical Society Collections,* 3rd ser. 3 (1833): 142–48.

9. The population of Wethersfield is not recorded for 1636 or 1637; my estimate is extrapolated from figures in Benjamin Trumbull, *History of Connecticut,* 2 vols. (New Haven, 1818), 1:68, and *Public Records of the Colony of Connecticut,* ed. J. Hammond Trumbull, 15 vols. (Hartford, 1850–90), 1:9.

10. John W. De Forest, *History of the Indians of Connecticut* (1851; reprint, Hamden, Conn., 1964), 54.

11. *Connecticut Records,* 1:5; Sherman W. Adams and Henry R. Stiles, *The History of Ancient Wethersfield, Connecticut,* 2 vols. (New York, 1904), 2:882–84; Winthrop, *Journal,* 1:265. The oral portion of the agreement can be inferred from the subsequent testimony; the written agreement in the *Connecticut Records* (1:5), which may have dated from 1636, does not mention Sowheag's residual rights.

12. Connecticut valley tribes had invited settlers from Massachusetts and Plymouth as early as 1631. The Bay Colony rejected the offer, but Plymouth erected a trading post at Matianuck (later Windsor) in 1634 after purchasing land from the local tribes. The Dutch of New Netherland had established a post (later Hartford) the previous year. Winthrop, *Journal,* 1:61; William Bradford, *History of Plymouth Plantation,* ed. Worthington Chauncey Ford, 2 vols. (Boston, 1912), 2:166–67.

13. Mason, *History of the Pequot War,* ix–x; Winthrop, *Journal,* 1:265–66.

14. Winthrop, *Journal,* 1:213; Underhill, *Newes from America,* 17–18; Mason, *History of Pequot War,* ix–x. The captives were later rescued by the Dutch and redeemed from them by Gardiner. See Gardiner, "Relation of the Pequot Warres," 146–47.

15. *Connecticut Records,* 1:9.

16. The principal accounts of the war are accessible (in addition to the original publications cited in the previous notes) in Charles Orr, ed., *History of the Pequot War* (Cleveland, 1897). Other important sources are Winthrop, *Journal;* Hubbard, *History of the Indian Wars;* Increase Mather, *A Relation of the Troubles which Have Hapned in New-England by Reason of the Indians There* (Boston, 1677); *Winthrop Papers,* ed. Allyn B. Forbes, 5 vols. (Boston, 1927–47), esp. vols. 2 and 3; and *Williams Correspondence.* Sharply contrasting modern accounts are in Vaughan, *New England Frontier,* ch. 5; Jennings, *Invasion of America,* ch. 13; Salisbury, *Manitou and Providence,* chap. 7; and Adam J. Hirsch, "The Collison of Military Cultures in Seventeenth-Century New England," *Journal of American History* 74 (1988): 1187–1212.

17. "Articles between ye Inglish In Connecticut and the Indian Sachems," *Rhode Island Historical Society Collections* 3 (Providence, 1835), 177–78; Winthrop, *Journal,* 1:271.

18. Winthrop, *Journal,* 1:265–66; The original correspondence between the Connecticut and Massachusetts authorities apparently has not survived. Under the date 30 March, Winthrop mentioned "letters from Connecticut"; by that date Massachusetts had apparently completed its deliberations on the matter and replied to the Connecticut General Court, which by 30 March had "made a new agreement with the Indians of the river." The final Connecticut decision, however, seems not to have been made until 5 April. See *Connecticut Records,* 1:19–20.

19. Winthrop, *Journal,* 1:265–66; Adams and Stiles, *Ancient Wethersfield,* 1:68–70; Hugo Grotius, *The Rights of War and Peace, Including the Law of Nature and of Nations,* trans. A. C. Campbell (Washington, D.C., 1901), 25, 84.

20. *Connecticut Records,* 1:19–20.

21. Ibid., 1:58; "Relation of the Indian Plott," *Massachusetts Historical Society, Collections* 3d ser. 3 (1833): 161–64; Adams and Stiles, *Ancient Wethersfield,* 1:43–45.

22. Winthrop, *Journal,* 1:274; Bradford, *History of Plymouth* 2:263–68; Roger Williams to John Winthrop, ca. 1 Aug. 1638, in *Williams Correspondence,* 1:170–75. Temple's pregnancy, which, if proven, would have had serious implications for Peach, was unknown by the Plymouth authorities until after his death (Bradford, *History of Plymouth,* 2:264), but presumably he was aware of his likely prosecution for it. The most comprehensive examination of the Peach case is Glenn W. LaFantasie, "Murder of an Indian, 1638," *Rhode Island History* 38 (1979): 67–77.

23. Bradford, *History of Plymouth,* 2:263–64; Williams to Winthrop, ca. 1 Aug. 1638, in *Williams Correspondence,* 1:171.

24. The fugitives apparently took an indirect route from Plymouth to New Amsterdam on the assumption that as soon as their absence was noticed they would be followed, with the Dutch colony as their presumed destination. Hence the encounter with Penowanyanquis did not occur on the Plymouth-to-Providence path (roughly east to west) but on the Boston-to-Providence route (roughly north to south). See Bradford, *History of Plymouth,* 2:264.

25. Williams to Winthrop, ca. 1 Aug. 1638, and same to same, 14 Aug. 1638, in *Williams Correspondence,* 1:171–72, 177; Bradford, *History of Plymouth,* 2:264–65; *Records of the Colony of New Plymouth in New England,* ed. Nathaniel B. Shurtleff and David Pulsifer, 12 vols. (Boston, 1855–61), 1:96.

26. Williams to Winthrop, ca. 1 Aug. 1638, in *Williams Correspondence,* 1:171–72; Bradford, *History of Plymouth,* 2:265–66.

27. For an instance two years later (1640) in which Winthrop emphatically refused to acknowledge Aquidneck's authority, see his *Journal,* 2:18–19.

28. Williams to John Winthrop, ca. 1 Aug. 1638, in *Williams Correspondence,* 1:172. The attack took place in what is now Seekonk, Massachusetts.

29. Winthrop, *Journal,* 1:273; *Plymouth Colony Records,* 1:96.

30. The entire proceedings—trial, verdict, and punishment—took place in one day. *Plymouth Colony Records,* 1:97; Williams to Winthrop, after 21 Sept. 1638, in *Williams Correspondence,* 1:184; Bradford, *History of Plymouth,* 2:266–68; Winthrop, *Journal,* 1:274. Prior to 1638, Plymouth had executed only one person: John Billington for shooting to death John Newcomin (Bradford, *History of Plymouth,* 2:110–12, 268).

31. *Plymouth Colony Records,* 1:97; Winthrop, *Journal,* 1:190; Williams to Winthrop, ca. 1 Aug. 1638, in *Williams Correspondence,* 1:171; Bradford, *History of Plymouth,* 2:247, 266–68.

32. Williams to Winthrop, 14 Aug. 1638, in *Williams Correspondence,* 1:176. Although it is difficult to generalize about Indian jurisprudence, the notion that vengeance was to be taken by kin, unless atoned by gifts, appears to have been widespread in eastern North America. See especially John Phillip Reid, *A Law of Blood: The Primitive Law of the Cherokee Nation* (New York, 1970), chaps. 9–11.

33. For example, Williams to Winthrop, after 21 Sept. 1638, in *Williams Correspondence,* 1:182–89.

34. Underhill, *Newes from America,* 42–43.

35. For differences between Puritan and other colonial jurisprudence, see Bradley Chapin, *Criminal Justice in Colonial America, 1606–1660* (Athens, Ga., 1983), esp. chap. 1.

36. *New Englands First Fruits . . .* (London, 1643), 8.

37. Henry Morris, *Early History of Springfield* (Springfield, Mass., 1876), 68–71; Winthrop, *Journal,* 1:273, 299.

38. See chapter 4 in this volume for similar divisions of sentiment in Pennsylvania and New Jersey in the eighteenth century.

39. Winthrop, *Journal,* 1:265–66; *Connecticut Records,* 1:19–20.

40. Bradford, *History of Plymouth,* 2:264, 267–68.

41. William Hand Browne, ed., *Maryland Archives: Proceedings of the Provincial Court, 1637–1650* (Baltimore, 1887), 177, 180–84.

42. Winthrop, *Journal,* 1:274.

43. See Daniel Gookin, "An Historical Account of the Doings and Sufferings of the Christian Indians in New England, in the Years 1675, 1676, 1677," *American Antiquarian Society, Transactions and Collections* 2 (1836): 443–44, 460–66, 491–92; Vaughan, *New England Frontier,* 318–19. For a dramatic case of popular frenzy in defiance of officials' efforts to abide by legal constraints, see James Axtell, "The Vengeful Women of Marblehead: Robert Roules's Deposition of 1677," *William and Mary Quarterly* 3d ser. 31 (1974): 647–52.

44. Nathaniel B. Shurtleff, ed., *Records of the Governor and Company of the Massachusetts Bay in New England,* 5 vols in 6 (Boston, 1853–54), 1:259; Roger Williams, *Christenings Make Not Christians . . .* (London, 1645), reprinted in *The Complete Writings of Roger Williams,* 7 vols. (New York, 1963), 7:31.

45. *New Englands First Fruits,* 8: Vaughan, *New England Frontier,* xvii–xviii, and chap. 7; Kawashima, *Puritan Justice and the Indian.*

46. Roger Williams, *A Key into the Language of America*, ed. John J. Teunissen and Evelyn J. Hinz (Detroit, 1973), 136–37.

CHAPTER 10: CROSSING THE CULTURAL DIVIDE

1. J. Hector St. John [Crèvecoeur], *Letters from an American Farmer; Describing Certain Provincial Situations, Manners, and Customs . . . of the British Colonies in North America* (London, 1782), 295.

2. Cadwallader Colden, *The History of the Five Indian Nations Depending on the Province of New York in America*, 2d ed. (London, 1750), 203–4 (first pagination); *The Papers of Benjamin Franklin*, ed. Leonard W. Labaree et al., 4 (New Haven, 1961), 481–83. A similar statement was made by the Swedish botanist Peter Kalm, but he was probably repeating what he heard from Franklin or other Americans (*Travels into North America*, 3 vols. [Warrington, Eng., 1770–71], 3:154). Colden and Kalm noted that French Canadians were highly susceptible to the lure of Indian life. For other Americans and Europeans who asserted that North American colonists frequently became Indianized but Indians almost never became Europeanized, see James Axtell, "The White Indians of Colonial America," *William and Mary Quarterly*, 3d ser. 32 (1975): 58 n. 8.

3. Gary B. Nash, *Red, White, and Black: The Peoples of Early America* (Englewood Cliffs, N.J., 1974), 283.

4. Axtell, "White Indians," 56.

5. We use "transculturation" to mean a virtually complete shift from one culture to another and "acculturation" to mean a partial shift or blending of cultures. Probably no individual past infancy totally sheds his or her original cultural affiliation; some vestiges almost certainly cling internally if not externally. But a sincere and nearly thorough acceptance of the alien culture—its values, customs, beliefs, and allegiances, and, ultimately their internalization—and a concomitant rejection of the original culture did happen in hundreds, perhaps thousands, of instances in early America. For a somewhat different use of the terms (and a different spelling of the key word) see A. Irving Hallowell, "American Indians, White and Black: The Phenomenon of Transculturalization," *Current Anthropology* 4 (1963): 519–31.

6. Information on Squanto is scattered and sometimes confusing because of variant spellings and uncertain identifications. The principal sources are William Bradford, *History of Plymouth Plantation*, ed. Worthington C. Ford, 2 vols. (Boston, 1912), passim; [Bradford and Edward Winslow], *A Relation or Journall . . . of the English Plantation setled at Plimouth [Mourt's Relation]* (London, [1622]), passim; Sydney V. James, ed., *Three Visitors to Early Plymouth* (Plymouth, Mass., 1963), 12–13; Ferdinando Gorges, *A Briefe Relation of the Discovery and Plantation of New England* (London, 1622), repr. *Massachusetts Historical Society Collections*, 2d ser. 9 (1823): 7–8 [hereafter cited as *MHS Colls.*]; and Ferdinando Gorges, *A Briefe Narration of the Originall Undertakings . . . Especially . . . of New England* (London, 1658), repr. *Collections of the Maine Historical Society* 2 (1847): 17. The best secondary summaries are Charles Francis Adams, *Three Episodes of Massachusetts History*, 2 vols. (Boston, 1892), 1:23–44; Samuel Eliot Morison, "Squanto," *Dictionary of American Biography*, ed. Allen Johnson and Dumas Malone, 20 vols. (New York, 1928–36), 17:487; and Neal Salisbury, "Squanto: Last of the Patuxets," in David G. Sweet and Gary B. Nash, eds., *Struggle and Survival*

in Colonial America (Berkeley and Los Angeles, 1981), 228-46. On other early New England Indians taken to England see Carolyn Thomas Foreman, *Indians Abroad, 1493-1938* (Norman, Okla., 1943), passim; and Alden T. Vaughan, *New England Frontier: Puritans and Indians, 1620-1675,* 3d ed. (Norman, Okla. 1995), chap. 1.

7. Bradford, *History of Plymouth,* 1:202. Bradford mentions other Indians who assisted the colony, but none in much detail.

8. See Lynn Ceci, "Fish Fertilizer: A Native North American Practice?" *Science* 188 (April 1975): 26-30, and the "Letters" section of the succeeding volume.

9. On Squanto's curious role see Bradford, *History of Plymouth,* 1:252-55; Bradford and Winslow, *Relation of Plymouth,* 59; James, ed., *Three Visitors,* 12-13; Edward Winslow, "Good News from New England" [orig. pub. London, 1624] in Edward Arber, ed., *The Story of the Pilgrim Fathers* (Boston, 1897), 513-28; and Leonard A. Adolf, "Squanto's Role in Pilgrim Diplomacy," *Ethnohistory,* 11 (1964): 247-61. The quote is from Bradford, *History of Plymouth,* 1:283.

10. On Hobomock and Tokamahomon, another Indian who aided the Pilgrims and lived with them for a time, see Bradford, *History of Plymouth,* 1:225, 252, 253, 346; Bradford and Winslow, *Relation of Plymouth,* 46-55; and Winslow, "Good News," passim.

11. Weston's group is described in Bradford, *History of Plymouth,* 1:271-72, 280-97; Winslow, "Good News," passim; and Phinehas Pratt, "A Declaration of the Afaires of the English People [That First] Inhabited New England," *MHS Colls.,* 4th ser. 4 (1858): 476-87. On Morton's outpost see Thomas Morton, *New English Canaan . . . Containing an Abstract of New England . . .* (Amsterdam, 1637; reprint, New York, 1972), "The Third Booke"; Bradford, *History of Plymouth,* 2:45-58; and "Governour Bradford's Letter Book," *MHS Colls.,* 1st. ser. 3 (1794): 62-4. Both the Weston and Morton outposts are examined in Adams, *Three Episodes,* pt. 1.

12. Nathaniel B. Shurtleff, ed., *Records of the Governor and Company of the Massachusetts Bay in New England,* 5 vols. (Boston, 1853-54), 1:17.

13. For a general discussion of early Puritan missionary efforts see Vaughan, *New England Frontier,* chap. 9. The quote is from *New Englands First Fruits; in Respect, First of the Conversion of Some, Conviction of divers, Preparation of Sundry of the Indians . . .* (London, 1643), 1.

14. Cotton Mather, *Triumphs of the Reformed Religion: The Life of the Renowned John Eliot . . .* (Boston, 1691), 83.

15. See Williston Walker, *The Creeds and Platforms of Congregationalism* (New York, 1893; reprint, Philadelphia, 1960), 210-17; and William Ames, *The Marrow of Theology,* trans. John Dykstra Eusden (Boston, 1968), 209-10.

16. *New Englands First Fruits,* 7 (incorrectly numbered 15). A decade earlier William Wood reported that many of the Indians were "much civilized since the English colonies were planted, though but little edified in religion. They frequent often the English churches where they will sit soberly, though they understand not such hidden mysteries." Wood also noted that "one of the English preachers, in a special good intent of doing good to their souls, hath spent much time in attaining to their language." *New England's Prospect,* ed. Alden T. Vaughan (Amherst, Mass., 1977), 97, 110. The early student of the Indian language was almost certainly Roger Williams.

17. *New Englands First Fruits,* 2.

18. Ibid., 5–7; Danforth, *An Almanack for the Year of Our Lord 1647* (Cambridge, Mass., 1647), 16. In 1637 Wequash guided a Connecticut-Mohegan-Narragansett army to a surprise attack on the principal Pequot fort. Thus he witnessed and abetted the Puritans' military success. John Mason, *A Brief History of the Pequot War* (Boston, 1736), 7.

19. *New Englands First Fruits*, 4–5; John Cotton, *The Way of the Christian Churches Cleared* (London, 1648), repr. Larzer Ziff, ed., *John Cotton on the Churches of New England* (Cambridge, Mass., 1968), 277. Cotton claimed that Sagamore John's "neighbor Indians sagamores, and powwaws hearing of this [attachment to the English], threatened to *cram* him (that is, to kill him) if he did so degenerate from his country gods. . . ." For similar reports of threats and abuse see [Thomas Shepard?], *The Day-Breaking, if not the Sun-Rising of the Gospell with the Indians in New-England* (London, 1647), repr. *MHS Colls.*, 3d ser. 4 (1834): 17, 22.

20. *New Englands First Fruits*, 5.

21. Cotton, *Way of the Christian Churches*, 278; Daniel Gookin, *Historical Collections of the Indians in New England* (Boston, 1792), 32–33; [Shepard], *Day-Breaking*, 3, 18, 21, 22.

22. *New Englands First Fruits*, 3. Some of the Indian children may have been captured in the Pequot War; if so, they, like the Indian captives in King Philip's War, seldom appear in the records, and neither their numbers nor the extent of their acculturation can be measured. Most young captives who were not sold out of New England were probably released after a few years' servitude.

23. Samuel Eliot Morison, *Harvard College in the Seventeenth Century*, 2 vols. (Cambridge, Mass., 1936), 1:340–60; Vaughan, *New England Frontier*, 280–88; John L. Sibley, *Biographical Sketches of Graduates of Harvard University*, 2 (Cambridge, Mass., 1881), 201–3.

24. David Pulsifer, ed., *Acts of the Commissioners of the United Colonies*, 2 vols. (*Records of the Colony of New Plymouth*, vols. 9–10 [Boston, 1859]) 2:107; Gookin, *Historical Collections*, 33.

25. Vaughan, *New England Frontier*, 282–85; Sibley, *Biographical Sketches*, 2:202–3; Douglas Edward Leach, *Flintlock and Tomahawk: New England in King Philip's War* (New York, 1958), 31. Joel Hiacoomes of Martha's Vineyard, perhaps the most proficient Indian student, was murdered by Indians shortly before he would have graduated. Gookin (*Historical Collections*, 33) attributed the murder to greed rather than hostility toward transculturation.

26. John Eliot, *The Indian Grammar Begun: or an Essay to Bring the Indian Language into Rules* (Cambridge, Mass., 1666), 66.

27. Samuel G. Drake, *The Aboriginal Races of North America; Comprising Biographical Sketches of Eminent Individuals*, 15th ed. (Philadelphia, 1859), 114–15.

28. Shurtleff, ed., *Records of Massachusetts Bay*, 2:55.

29. Vaughan, *New England Frontier*, 263–69, 288–95. The principal sources for Eliot's missionary work are several tracts, sometimes known as "the Eliot Indian Tracts" but actually written by several clergymen, reprinted (with some exceptions) in *MHS Colls.*, 3d ser. 4 (1834); Eliot's correspondence (widely scattered—the most complete published list is in Frederick L. Weis, "The New England Company of 1649 and Its Missionary Enterprises," *Publications of the Colonial Society of Massachusetts, Transactions* 38 [1947–51]: 214–16); and two works by Daniel Gookin, *Historical Collections* and *An Historical Account of the Doings and Sufferings of the Christian Indians in New England, in the Years 1675, 1676,*

1677, in *Transactions and Collections of the American Antiquarian Society* 2 (1836): 429–534.

30. On the Mayhews see especially Gookin, *Historical Collections,* 61–67; the "Eliot Indian Tracts," passim; Eliot's correspondence; Weis, "New England Company," passim; Vaughan, *New England Frontier,* 295–98; Lloyd C. M. Hare, *Thomas Mayhew: Patriarch to the Indians (1593–1682)* (New York, 1932); Charles E. Banks, *The History of Martha's Vineyard,* 3 vols. (Boston, 1911–25), 1:213–57; William S. Simmons, "Conversion from Indian to Puritan," *New England Quarterly* 52 (1979): 197–218; and James P. Ronda, "Generations of Faith: The Christian Indians of Martha's Vineyard," *William and Mary Quarterly* 3rd ser. 38 (1981): 369–94.

31. Richard Bourne and other early Plymouth missionaries are discussed especially in Gookin, *Historical Collections,* 56–61; William Kellaway, *The New England Company, 1649–1776: Missionary Society to the American Indians* (Glasgow, 1961), 105; and Vaughan, *New England Frontier,* 298–300.

32. The sparse missionary achievements in Connecticut and Rhode Island are summarized in Gookin, *Historical Collections,* 67–70; and Vaughan, *New England Frontier,* 300–303. Connecticut's clergy seem to have been less numerous and less adept than their counterparts in Massachusetts, Plymouth, and Martha's Vineyard. Rhode Island's potential missionaries were distracted by denominational wrangling in that heterodox colony, and, in Roger Williams's case, by ideological qualms about the legitimacy of proselytizing.

33. For concise discussions of Puritan conversion experiences see Edmund S. Morgan, *Visible Saints: The History of a Puritan Idea* (New York, 1963; reprint, Ithaca, N.Y., 1965). For examples of public confessions see Morgan, ed., *The Diary of Michael Wigglesworth, 1653–1657: The Conscience of a Puritan* (repr. New York, 1965), 107–25. For Indian conversion statements see John Eliot and Thomas Mayhew, *Tears of Repentance: Or, a Further Narrative of the Progress of the Gospel amongst the Indians in New England* (London, 1653). A substantial recent literature on Puritan missionary efforts has shed much useful light on both the colonial and Indian participants. For a discussion of some of that literature see Vaughan, *New England Frontier,* introduction to the third edition.

34. Gookin, *Historical Collections,* 42–55.

35. See note 49 below.

36. Boston Record Commissioners, *Report [No. 6] . . . Containing the Roxbury Land and Church Records,* 2d ed. (Boston, 1884), 193.

37. Leach, *Flintlock and Tomahawk,* chap. 8; Gookin, *Doings and Sufferings,* passim.

38. On Puritan missionary efforts after 1675, see especially William Kellaway, *The New England Company, 1649–1776: Missionary Society to the American Indians* (New York, 1962); and Weis, "New England Company," passim.

39. Rawson and Danforth, "An Account of an Indian Visitation, A.D. 1698," *MHS Colls.,* 1st ser. 10 (1809): 129–34. A few years earlier Matthew Mayhew estimated the number of adult Christian Indians on Martha's Vineyard and Nantucket to be three thousand. M. Mayhew, *A Brief Narrative of the Success which the Gospel hath had among the Indians, of Martha's-Vineyard (and the Places Adjacent) in New-England* (Boston, 1694), 23–24.

40. Experience Mayhew, "A Brief Account of the State of the Indians on Martha's Vineyard . . . 1694 to 1720," appended to E. Mayhew, *Discourse Shewing that God Dealeth with Men as Reasonable Creatures* (Boston, 1720), 5, 11–12 (second pagination); Experience Mayhew, *Indian Converts; Or Some Account of*

the Lives and Drying Speeches of a Considerable Number of the Christianized Indians of Martha's Vineyard, in New-England (London, 1726), 115. Apparently some women converts liked English attire too much: Mayhew praised one woman because "she did not appear to affect gay and costly Clothing, as many of the *Indian* Maids do, yet always went clean and neat in her Apparel, still wearing such things as were suitable to her own Condition and Circumstances." *Indian Converts*, 175.

41. E. Mayhew, "Brief Account," 11–12.

42. Ibid., 11; E. Mayhew, *Indian Converts*, 50–51, 115, 167; Gookin, *Historical Collections*, 41.

43. Weis, "New England Company," 187–88, 193; Harold Blodgett, *Samson Occom* (Hanover, N.H., 1935); Margaret Connell Szasz, *Indian Education in the American Colonies, 1607–1783* (Albuquerque, N.M., 1988), 205–14, 217–31; Patrick Frazier, *The Mohicans of Stockbridge* (Lincoln, Neb., 1992).

44. Clifford K. Shipton, *Biographical Sketches of Those Who Attended Harvard College. Sibley's Harvard Graduates*, 6 (Boston, 1942), 142–44; [Samuel Sewall], *The Diary of Samuel Sewall, 1674–1729*, ed. M. Halsey Thomas, 2 vols. (New York, 1973), 2:763–64.

45. William S. Simmons, "The Great Awakening and Indian Conversion in Southern New England," *Papers of the Tenth Algonquian Conference*, ed. William Cowan (Ottawa, 1979), 32.

46. Ibid., 25–36; Cedric B. Cowing, *The Great Awakening and the American Revolution: Colonial Thought in the 18th Century* (Chicago, 1971), 83–85; Paul R. Campbell and Glenn W. LaFantasie, "Scattered to the Winds of Heaven—Narragansett Indians 1676–1880," *Rhode Island History* 37 (Aug. 1978): 74.

47. Although most Congregational churches continued to hold that God saved only true believers and that man was helpless to control God's choices, the eighteenth century witnessed laxer standards and, in some churches, less stringent rules for membership. See, for example, the positions of Northampton's Solomon Stoddard and Boston's Brattle Street Church in Alden T. Vaughan, ed., *The Puritan Tradition in America, 1620–1730* (New York, 1972), 324–33; and Morgan, *Visible Saints*, 145–52.

48. Weis, "New England Company," 153–202.

49. The estimate of approximately 500 subdivides as follows: Gookin's list of full members, 153–63; Weis's list of Indian preachers, 140; half of Weis's estimate (428) of full members 1675–1763, 214; for a total of 507–517. To these could be added the undeterminable numbers of transculturated youths in New England schools, war captives (living as servants in New English homes), and free Indians residing within English communities. They would perhaps raise the total by 50 to 75. We have excluded them from our tabulation because (1) we have no quantitative basis for measurement; (2) we do not know how many of them were Christian, a condition we consider essential to transculturation—though not, of course, to acculturation; and (3) they would only minimally affect our estimated number of transculturates.

50. Henry Whitfield, "The Light Appearing more and more towards the Perfect Day," *MHS Colls.*, 3d ser. 4 (1834): 109.

51. E. Mayhew, *Indian Converts*, 1–5.

52. As early as 1634 William Wood reported that the Indians of New England "acknowledge the power of the Englishmen's God, as they call him, because they could never yet have power by their conjurations to damnify the En-

glish either in body or goods; and besides, they say he is a good God that sends them so many good things, so much good corn, so many cattle, temperate rains, fair seasons, which they likewise are the better for since the arrival of the English. . . ." *New England's Prospect*, 103.

53. For evidence on the material goods provided by English and New English missionary funds, see Pulsifer, ed., *Acts of the Commissioners;* George P. Winship, ed., *The New England Company and John Eliot (Publications of the Prince Society*, 36 [Boston, 1920]); and John W. Ford, ed., *Some Correspondence between the . . . New England Company in London and the Commissioners of the United Colonies* (London, 1896).

54. There is no way to measure the demand among Indians for education, but circumstantial evidence, such as the wide distribution of the Algonquian edition of the Bible and the missionaries' frequent calls for more teachers in Indian communities, suggests that many Indians were receptive to training in literacy. By 1727 on Martha's Vineyard "considerable numbers of *Indians* have learned to *read* and *write*, yet they have mostly done this but after the rate that poor Men among the *English* are wont to do." E. Mayhew, *Indian Converts*, xxxiii.

55. Eliot, *Indian Dialogues, for Their Instruction in that Great Service of Christ* (Cambridge, Mass., 1671), 19, 55.

56. Ibid., 15.

57. Ibid., 44–46.

58. Vaughan, *New England Frontier,* 265–66. Eliot summarized his thoughts on civil polity in *The Christian Commonwealth* (London, [1659]), which he was later forced to repudiate. Thereafter the praying towns were less biblically structured.

59. E. Mayhew, "A Brief Account," 10.

60. Eliot, *Indian Dialogues,* 20. See also Frank Shuffelton, "Indian Devils and the Pilgrim Fathers: Squanto, Hobomok, and the English Conception of Indian Religion," *New England Quarterly* 46 (1976): 108–16; and William S. Simmons, "Cultural Bias in the New England Puritans' Perception of Indians," *William and Mary Quarterly*, 3rd ser. 38 (1982): 917–53.

61. See, for example, Eliot, *Indian Dialogues,* 20.

62. Ibid., dedication.

63. Increase Mather, *An Earnest Exhortation to the Inhabitants of New-England* (Boston, 1676), 10.

64. Eliot, *Indian Dialogues,* 9.

65. Cotton Mather, *Triumphs of the Reformed Religion*, 42–43; Eliot's account of the episode is in Boston Record Commissioners, *Report* [no. 6], 193.

66. [Roger Williams], *Christenings Make Not Christians . . .* (London, 1645), reprinted in *The Complete Writings of Roger Williams,* 7 vols. (New York, 1963), 7:31.

67. E. Mayhew, "A Brief Account," 6; Cotton Mather et al., "An Attestation of the United Ministers of Boston," in E. Mayhew, *Indian Converts,* xx–xxi.

68. David Crosby to Eleazar Wheelock, 4 Nov. 1767, Papers of Eleazar Wheelock, WP 767604.1, Dartmouth College Library.

69. One of Weston's men reported in 1623 "that another of their Company was turned savage," but nothing further is recorded about the alleged transculturate (Winslow, "Good News," 564). For other sources on the Weston and Morton colonists see note 11, above. For early Virginians' greater proclivity to merge with Indian society, see Nicholas Canny, "The Permissive Frontier: The Problem of Social Control in English Settlements in Ireland and Virginia,

1550–1650," in K. R. Andrews, N. P. Canny, and P. E. H. Hair, eds., *The West-ward Enterprise: English Activities in Ireland, the Atlantic and America, 1480–1650* (Detroit, 1979), 30–36.

70. J. Hammond Trumbull, *The Public Records of the Colony of Connecticut,* 15 vols. (Hartford, 1850–90), 1:78. Although no prosecutions under the law appear in the General Court's records, it is possible that some trials at lower court levels are recorded in the state's archives.

71. *The Correspondence of Roger Williams,* ed. Glenn W. LaFantasie, 2 vols. (Hanover, N.H., 1988), 1:126, 140 (quotation), 145, 155, 158.

72. N[athaniel] S[altonstall] to ?, 8 Feb. 1676, in Charles H. Lincoln, ed., *Narratives of the Indian Wars* (New York, 1913), 67; James Oliver to ?, 26 Jan. 1676 in George Madison Bodge, *Soldiers in King Philip's War* (Leominster, Mass., 1896), 175; James N. Arnold, "Joshua Tefft," *The Narragansett Register* 3 (1884–85): 164–69; William Hubbard, *A Narrative of the Troubles with the Indians in New-England* (Boston, 1677; repr. as *The History of the Indian Wars,* 2 vols. [Roxbury, 1865]), 1:162; Thomas Hutchinson, *The History of the Colony of Massachusets-Bay,* 3 vols. (London, 1764–1828; reprint, New York, 1972), 1:302–3. See also Colin G. Calloway, "Rhode Island Renegade: The Enigma of Joshua Tefft," *Rhode Island History* 43 (1984): 137–45.

73. Roger Williams to Governor Leverett, 14 Jan. 1676, *Williams Correspondence,* 2:711–17.

74. William Baker and Joshua Tift (discussed above) seem to fit this generalization; there are few other documented cases. For another possible instance of temporary adoption of an Indian lifestyle, see the account of Edward Ashley in Bradford, *History of Plymouth,* 2:83, 107–9.

75. John Underhill, *Newes from America* (London, 1638), 17–18, 26–36; [Edward Johnson], *Johnson's Wonder-Working Providence, 1628–1651,* ed. J. Franklin Jameson (New York, 1910), 149–50; Increase Mather, *A Relation of the Troubles which Have Hapned in New-England, By Reason of the Indians There* (Boston, 1677), 44–46. For a more extensive discussion of the events of 1636–37 see chapter 8 in this volume.

76. We calculate that at least forty-two New Englanders were captured in King Philip's War; see Appendix A.

77. [Mary White Rowlandson], *The Soveraignty and Goodness of God, Together, With the Faithfulness of His Promises Displayed; Being a Narrative of the Captivity and Restauration of Mrs Mary Rowlandson,* 2d ed. (Cambridge, Mass., 1682). For the rest of the colonial period and beyond, captivity narratives enlightened—and often misled—contemporaries about Indian life, and they still provide valuable clues to the captives' fates. At least four major collections of captivity narratives appeared between 1961 and the first appearance of this essay in 1981. Frederick Drimmer, ed., *Scalps and Tomahawks: Narratives of Indian Captivity* (New York, 1961); Richard VanDerBeets, ed., *Held Captive by Indians: Selected Narratives, 1642–1836* (Knoxville, Tenn., 1973); James Levernier and Hennig Cohen, eds., *The Indians and Their Captives* (Westport, Conn., 1977); and Alden T. Vaughan and Edward W. Clark, eds., *Puritans among the Indians: Accounts of Captivity and Redemption, 1676–1724* (Cambridge, Mass., 1981). On the importance of captivity narratives as literary and historical texts, see the introductions to the above anthologies and Roy Harvey Pearce, "The Significances of the Captivity Narratives," *American Literature* 19 (1947): 1–20; Richard VanDerBeets, "The Indian Captivity Narrative as Ritual," *American Literature* 43 (1972): 548–62; Richard Slotkin, *Regeneration through Violence: The Mythology of the American Frontier,*

1600–1860 (Middletown, Conn., 1973), esp. 94–145; David L. Minter, "By Dens of Lions: Notes on Stylization in Early Puritan Captivity Narratives," *American Literature* 45 (1973): 335–47; and Wilcomb E. Washburn, "Introduction" to *Narratives of North American Indian Captivity* (New York, 1980). Several recent books and many articles address one of more of the captivity narratives. For three very different approaches, see Mitchell Robert Breitwieser, *American Puritanism and the Defense of Mourning: Religion Grief, and Ethnology in Mary White Rowlandson's Captivity Narrative* (Madison, Wisc., 1990); June Namias, *White Captives: Gender and Ethnicity on the American Frontier* (Chapel Hill, N.C., 1993); and John Demos, *The Redeemed Captive: A Family Story from Early America* (New York, 1994).

78. Rowlandson, *Soveraignty and Goodness*, 9–10.

79. Emma Lewis Coleman, *New England Captives Carried to Canada between 1677 and 1760 during the French and Indian Wars*, 2 vols. (Portland, Me., 1925), 1:124–25, 381.

80. The following portion of the essay stresses numerical rather than experiential aspects of transculturation among European-American prisoners of war because the latter is perceptively treated in Axtell, "White Indians," and to varying degrees in the following works, all of which take a wider geographic scope than New England: John R. Swanton, "Notes on the Mental Assimilation of Races," *Journal of the Washington Academy of Sciences* 16 (1926): 493–502; Dorothy Anne Dondore, "White Captives among the Indians," *New York History* 13 (1932): 292–300; Erwin H. Ackerknecht, " 'White Indians': Psychological and Physiological Peculiarities of White Children Abducted and Reared by North American Indians," *Bulletin of the History of Medicine* 15 (1944): 15–36; Robert W. G. Vail, "Certain Indian Captives of New England", *Proceedings of the Massachusetts Historical Society* 68 (1944–47): 113–31; Marius Barbeau, "Indian Captivities," *Proceedings of the American Philosophical Society* 94 (1950): 522–48; Howard H. Peckham, *Captured by Indians: True Tales of Pioneer Survivors* (New Brunswick, N.J., 1954); Hallowell, "American Indians, White and Black"; and J. Norman Heard, *White into Red: A Study of the Assimilation of White Persons Captured by Indians* (Metuchen, N.J., 1973).

81. Baker, a descendant of New England captive Elizabeth Stebbins, apparently began her research on New England captives in 1870, when she prepared a paper on captive Eunice Williams for the 1871 meeting of the Pocumtuck Valley Memorial Association. Subsequently she read to that association five more papers concerning the experiences of New England prisoners of war, which were published in *History and Proceedings of the Pocumtuck Valley Memorial Association* 1–3 (1870–98), and reprinted along with several other essays in Baker, *True Stories of New England Captives Carried to Canada during the Old French and Indian Wars* (Cambridge, Mass., 1897); "More New England Captives" appeared posthumously in *History and Proceedings* 5 (1905–11): 173–98. While Baker's published work received scant circulation outside her hometowns of Deerfield and Cambridge, her reputation as an expert on colonial captivities did spread; Francis Parkman praised one of her essays as "the result of great research," containing "much original matter" (*A Half-Century of Conflict*, Frontenac edition [Boston, 1907], 89n). Coleman and Baker first collaborated on an 1888 trip to Canada to research the topic that by then, according to Baker's necrologist, "haunted" the older woman's "waking and sleeping hours." Baker died in 1909, leaving Coleman to finish her work and to be sole author (with hearty thanks to Baker) of *New England Captives*. See J. M. Arms Sheldon, "Tribute to Alice Baker," *History and Proceedings* 5 (1905–11): 352–64.

82. As one contemporary reviewer understated, while "the volumes form a mine of genealogical information, . . . the results of these new researchers are presented in a rather raw and undigested fashion, without any attempt to summarize them or to show the significance of the mass of material so industriously gathered together" (R. Flenley, Review of *New England Captives, Canadian Historical Review* 7 [1926]: 171–72).

83. For a discussion of previous analyses see Appendix B.

84. The sources and methodology for this analysis are presented in Appendix A.

85. Over 80 percent of the enlisted men and active militiamen captured between 1675 and 1763 were seized during the Seven Years' War. While 315 identifiable soldiers were taken during that war, only 14 were made prisoner during King George's War, 12 during Queen Anne's War, 3 during King William's War, and 2 during King Philip's War.

86. In the 1,085 cases for which the captors can be identified, Indian war parties seized 570 prisoners (52.5 percent), French-Indian expeditions—frequently an Indian party led by a French officer—took 424 (39 percent), and French forces acting without Indian allies took 91 (8.4 percent). In the remaining 556 cases (33.9 percent of the entire 1,641), the identity of the captors is unknown or unclear; presumably, in light of the small numbers of prisoners French patrols are known to have taken, the captors in these cases were either Indian or French-Indian forces.

87. French forces seized forty-nine seamen, two army officers, two enlisted men, five known civilians, and thirty-three individuals whose status is unclear and who presumably were civilians. The ages of three captives taken by French forces are unknown.

88. Indians, acting independently of the French, took 354 known free civilians, 164 presumed free civilians, 31 enlisted men and active militiamen, 6 army officers, 1 seaman, 9 white servants, and 5 black slaves.

89. According to Axtell, in the Pennsylvania theater of the Seven Years' War, "women and children—the 'weak and defenceless'—were the prime targets of Indian raids" ("White Indians," 59–60); and Coleman believed that "in all the wars captives, mostly women and children, were carried from New England to Canada" (*New England Captives*, 1:1). That may have been true of Pennsylvania, but of our study's 570 New England captives known to have been taken by Indians acting alone, 349 were males, 186 were females, and the sex of 35—mostly infants and small children—is unknown. Indians seized 288 adults aged sixteen and over, 117 youths aged seven to fifteen, 128 children aged two to six, 22 infants under age two, and 15 persons whose age is unknown. (See Appendix A for a discussion of our use of these age categories.) A knowledgeable observer of Indian society noted that because victorious war parties "could not keep the great number of prisoners whom they take in a[n enemy Indian] village, . . . the conquerors separate those whom they want to sacrifice to warlike fury from those whom they wish to save to incorporate among themselves [as adoptees]. Thus the old men who would have trouble in learning their language or whom age would render useless, the chiefs and important men among the warriors from whom they would have something to fear if they escaped, the children of too tender age and the infirm who would be too heavy a burden on their route, comprise the unfortunate victims whom they immolate . . . before leaving the village" (Joseph François Lafitau, *Customs of the American Indians Compared with*

the Customs of Primitive Times, ed. and trans. William N. Fenton and Elizabeth L. Moore, 2 vols. (Paris, 1724; reprint, Toronto, 1974, 1977), 2:145.

90. Our data do not allow conclusive statements about the average duration of New England captivities because in over 40 percent of the cases the time between a captive's seizure and the date when he or she returned, died, or decided to remain in Canada is unknown. Apparently, however, most captivities were either quite short (less than six months) or quite long (over two years):

DURATION OF NEW ENGLAND CAPTIVITIES, 1675–1760

Length	N	%
Few days	83	5.1
Few weeks to 6 months	177	10.8
7–12 months	109	6.6
13–18 months	77	4.7
19–24 months	60	3.7
Over 24 months	231	14.1
Remained with captors	229	14.0
Unknown	675	41.1

91. The 361 captives whose fate is unknown include 167 enlisted men and militiamen, 9 seamen, and 2 army officers, with 12 servants and slaves, 78 known free civilians, 90 assumed free civilians, and 3 whose status is unclear. Captive Nehemiah How tried to put a favorable light on the Quebec prison where he was kept for over nineteen months during King George's War: "this Prison was a large House built with Stone & Lime two Feet thick, and about 120 Feet long. We had two large Stoves in it, & Wood enough, so that we could keep our selves warm in the coldest Weather. We had Provision sufficient, viz. two Pound of good Wheat Bread, one Pound of Beef, and Peas answerable, to each Man ready dress'd every Day." The jail was nonetheless an unhealthy place: "I was taken ill, as was also most of the other Prisoners, with a Flux, which lasted near a Month, so that I was grown very weak," wrote How soon after his confinement. He recovered from that attack, but not from another which killed him in May 1747. How, *A Narrative of the Captivity of Nehemiah How* (Boston, 1748), 13, 22.

92. For a discussion of the possible fates of the "unknowns," see note 97 below.

93. Coleman, *New England Captives,* 1:44, 44n.

94. J. A. Leo Lemay, "The Frontiersman from Lout to Hero: Notes on the Significance of the Comparative Method and the Stage Theory in Early American Literature and Culture," *Proceedings of the American Antiquarian Society* 88 (1978): 192.

95. Nash, *Red, White, and Black,* 283.

96. Heard, *White into Red,* 5.

97. This figure is conservative. We have made no effort to estimate the percentage of captives whose fate is unknown who might have stayed with their Indian or French captors. Any attempt to deal with these 361 cases involves only guesswork, but because 178 of them are known to have been military or marine personnel (167 enlisted men and active militiamen, 9 seamen, and 2 army officers), because over 11 percent of all captives died as prisoners, and because the death rate for soldiers and sailors was roughly twice that for the captives as a whole, it seems reasonable to conclude that among those prisoners whose fate

is unknown there were far more deaths in captivity than there were transculturations. Among those whose fate *is* known, at most 4.1 percent (52 of 1,280) remained with the Indians. Even if those whose fate is unknown transculturated at the same rate (approximately 15 out of 361), the possible number of New Englanders who might have stayed with the Indians would still be only 67, or 4.1 percent of the 1,641 captives.

98. Captives who definitely or possibly remained with their Indian captors included 26 males and 26 females, while 108 males, 116 females, and one child of unknown sex definitely or probably remained with the French. The latter group comprised 35 adults aged sixteen or over, 65 youths aged seven to fifteen, 48 children aged two to six, and 5 infants under age two. The age of 73 is unknown.

99. The ninety-one New Englanders who spent the last part of their captivities in Canadian prisons rather than Canadian households understandably were less attracted to their captor's society; none of them apparently remained in Canada.

100. The infants studied here include thirteen who were born while their mothers were in captivity. Several of them bore such appropriate names as Captivity Jennings, Captive Johnson, and Canada Waite. These infants who began their lives as captives fared little differently from those who were born before their parents were seized. Eight of the thirteen eventually returned to New England (two after receiving Catholic baptism). One, the child of Tamsen Drew, an Oyster River woman taken in 1694, was born in a snowstorm and soon killed by the Indians because its mother could not care for it; two more of the infants born into captivity died of other causes. Priscilla Cole, born in 1704, five months after her mother's capture, perhaps remained with the French Canadians; her mother lived with them for many years and perhaps until her death. The final infant—Joseph Hegeman, born after his parents were captured in 1689— perhaps stayed with the Indians. His mother was redeemed from Indian captivity after three years, but his father's fate is unknown (Coleman, *New England Captives,* passim).

101. "Order for delivering up all the Prisoners," 6 Feb. 1750, Edmund B. O'Callaghan, ed., *Documents Relative to the Colonial History of the State of New York,* 15 vols. (Albany, N.Y., 1856–87), 6:544–45 (hereafter cited as *NYCD*); George Clinton to the Duke of Bedford, 30 July 1750, ibid., 578–79.

102. Coleman, *New England Captives,* 1:300–302; 2:350, 353, 377, 402. The fate of the remaining two captured Indians—Jonathan George, a Rehoboth servant, and Nathan Joseph, both taken at Fort William Henry in 1757—is unknown. For the statistical purposes of this essay, all six captured Indians are treated as if they had become New Englanders and are included with their Euro-American fellow captives in all tabulations.

103. On European attitudes and practices concerning enslavement of non-Christian prisoners of war, see Winthrop D. Jordan, *White over Black: American Attitudes toward the Negro, 1550–1812* (Chapel Hill, N.C., 1968), 54–56; and William McKee Evans, "From the Land of Canaan to the Land of Guinea: The Strange Odyssey of the 'Sons of Ham,'" *American Historical Review* 85 (1980): 15–43. New Englanders sold Indian war captives into slavery during both the Pequot War and King Philip's War; most were shipped to the West Indies or other colonies, but little is known of their numbers or ultimate fate (Jordan, *White over Black,* 68; Leach, *Flintlock and Tomahawk,* 178, 227–28). On the enslavement of Indians in southern New England in the eighteenth century see

John A. Sainsbury, "Indian Labor in Early Rhode Island," *New England Quarterly* 48 (1975): 378–93. A useful but outdated study is Almon Wheeler Lauber, *Indian Slavery in Colonial Times* (New York, 1913). As will be seen below, northeastern American Indians possessed an ideology of warfare quite foreign to the experience of Euro-Americans (either of the colonial era or of the twentieth century) which assigned war captives an entirely different and vastly more important role in warfare. See especially Daniel K. Richter, *The Ordeal of the Longhouse: The Peoples of the Iroquois League in the Era of European Colonization* (Chapel Hill, N.C., 1992).

104. Marian W. Smith, "American Indian Warfare," *Transactions of the New York Academy of Sciences*, 2d ser. 12 (1951): 348–65, esp. 352–59; see also Anthony F. C. Wallace, *The Death and Rebirth of the Seneca* (New York, 1969), 101–2. Smith borrowed the term "mourning-war" from George A. Dorsey, "The Osage Mourning-War Ceremony," *American Anthropologist*, n.s. 4 (1902): 404–11, and demonstrated its applicability to warfare customs across central and eastern North America in a "pattern which is strikingly correlated with the area of the northern distribution of maize agriculture" (Smith, "American Indian Warfare," 363). If, as Calvin Martin argues in *Keepers of the Game: Indian-Animal Relationships and the Fur Trade* (Berkeley, 1978), eastern Canadian Indians declared a "war" against fur-bearing animals in the wake of a series of medical disasters that slew much of the Indian population, their actions illustrate the principle that the deaths inspiring a mourning war need not be directly attributed to homicide or previous enemy acts of war. On blood feuds, see George S. Snyderman, "Behind the Tree of Peace: A Sociological Analysis of Iroquois Warfare," *Pennsylvania Archeologist* 18, nos. 3–4 (Fall 1948): 6–8, 32.

105. Lafitau, *Customs of American Indians*, 2:242.

106. Ibid., 1:71; Reuben Gold Thwaites, ed., *The Jesuit Relations and Allied Documents, 1610–1791*, 73 vols. (Cleveland, 1896–1901), 22:286–89; Alfred Goldsworthy Bailey, *The Conflict of European and Eastern Algonkian Cultures, 1504–1700* (St. John, N.B., 1937), 144.

107. Thwaites, ed., *Jesuit Relations*, 29:214–17.

108. Smith, "American Indian Warfare," 362; Wallace, *Death and Rebirth*, 102–4; William N. Fenton, "Northern Iroquoian Culture Patterns," *Handbook of North American Indians*, 15: *Northeast*, ed. Bruce C. Trigger (Washington, D.C., 1978); Lafitau, *Customs of American Indians*, 2:152–55.

109. Thomas Dongan to Jacques-René de Brisay, Marquis de Denonville, 31 Oct. 1687, *NYCD*, 3:517.

110. Philip Mazzei, *Researches on the United States*, trans. and ed. Constance D. Sherman (Charlottesville, Va., 1975), 349.

111. "Memoir of M. de Denonville on the State of Canada," 12 Nov. 1685, *NYCD*, 9:281; Snyderman, "Tree of Peace," 13–15; Sherburne F. Cook, "The Significance of Disease in the Extinction of the New England Indians," *Human Biology* 45 (1973): 485–88; Cook, "Interracial Warfare and Population Decline among the New England Indians," *Ethnohistory* 20 (1973): 1–24; William N. Fenton, "The Iroquois in History," in Eleanor Burke Leacock and Nancy Oestreich Lurie, eds., *North American Indians in Historical Perspective* (New York, 1971), 143. If the Indians' need to expand their population underlay their mourning-war practices and thus their assimilation of captives, perhaps the European-Americans' relative lack of need for additional population helped to shape their attitudes toward outsiders. Widespread ethnic prejudice in overcrowded Tudor-Stuart England lends this explanation some support, though clearly other in-

fluences were also present. In any event, the subtle relationship between social needs and social attitudes deserves further study.

112. The highly ritualized Iroquois practices of captivity, torture, and adoption and the ceremonial return of the war party with prisoners was widely reported by contemporaries. An excellent modern account of the process by which an adopted captive was made an integral part of the nation, focusing particularly on the experiences of Euro-American prisoners, is Axtell, "White Indians." For a concise modern description of the fate of less fortunate captives—Indian and European—who were ritually tortured, killed, and sometimes eaten by the families and friends of a deceased Iroquois, see Wallace, *Death and Rebirth*, 103–7; for a broader geographic and cultural perspective, see Nathaniel Knowles, "The Torture of Captives by the Indians of Eastern North America," *Proceedings of the American Philosophical Society* 82 (1940): 151–225.

113. Snyderman, "Tree of Peace," 56, 63, 70; Bailey, *Conflict of Cultures*, 98.

114. Leach, *Flintlock and Tomahawk*, 178–81; Gordon M. Day, "Western Abenaki," in Trigger, ed., *Northeast*, 157.

115. Christianized Mohawks constituted most of the residents at the Caughnawaga mission and (after the turn of the eighteenth century) Algonquian Western Abenaki predominated at Saint François, but at other Canadian missions, especially those on the immediate outskirts of Montreal, peoples of various ethnic backgrounds clustered together. One example of the kind of cultural intermingling and diffusion of adoption customs that occurred among mission Indians is a requickening ceremony at Sillery in the late 1660s. Taking part in Iroquois-style rituals designed to replace the dead sachem Noel Tecouerimat were people originally from Algonquin, Montagnais, Micmac, Abenaki, Etechemin, Atticameg, Nipissing, and Huron villages, while French missionaries looked on (Thwaites, ed., *Jesuit Relations*, 52:223–27; Bailey, *Conflict of Cultures*, 93).

116. George F. G. Stanley, "The Policy of 'Francisation' as Applied to the Indians during the Ancien Regime," *Revue d'histoire de l' Amérique français* 3 (1949–50): 346–47. See also Cornelius J. Jaenen, "The Frenchification and Evangelization of the Amer-indians in the Seventeenth Century New France," *Canadian Catholic Historical Association, Study Sessions, 1968*, 57–71.

117. "Remarks on what appears Important to the King's service for the preservation of New France. 1691," *NYCD*, 9:511.

118. Jacques-Réné de Brisay, Marquis de Denonville, "Memoir of the Voyage and Expedition of the Marquis de Denonville . . . against the Senecas . . . October, 1687," *NYCD*, 9:359–60.

119. "An Account of the Military Operations in Canada from the month of November, 1691, to the month of October, 1692," *NYCD*, 9:537.

120. Francis H. Hammang, *The Marquis de Vaudreuil: New France at the Beginning of the Eighteenth Century*, Université de Louvain, *Recueil de travaux*, 2d ser. 47 (Louvain, 1938): 180–81.

121. Philippe de Rigaud de Vaudreuil to the Minister, 14 Apr. 1714, *Rapport de l'archiviste de la Province de Québec pour 1947–1948*, 252; John Williams, *The Redeemed Captive, Returning to Zion* (Boston, 1707), 49–51; William Johnson to George Clinton, 1 Sept. 1749, *NYCD*, 6:526–27.

122. W. J. Eccles, *Frontenac: The Courtier Governor* (Toronto, 1959), 251n–52n; Coleman, *New England Captives*, 1:52–54. Canadian officials, rightly or wrongly, blamed the English for starting the practice of encouraging Indians to take European captives. The Marquis de Denonville, governor of New France, told Gov-

ernor Edmund Andros of the Dominion of New England in 1688 that he had "no doubt" that the Mohawk and Mohegan raiding parties then harrying New France "were despatched by Mr. Dongan [Andros's predecessor as governor of New York] . . . the thing is only too notorious in your country for you not to be convinced of it; he having even furnished ropes to bind the French, whom they might carry away prisoners, besides all the munitions of war with which he had supplied them for that purpose" (Denonville to Andros, 23 Oct. 1688, *NYCD*, 3:570).

123. Axtell's statement that "the Canadian Indians who raided New England tended to take captives more for their ransom value than for adoption" is undoubtedly true ("White Indians," 59). Nevertheless, the New England captivities seem to have fit easily into patterns familiar to Indian war parties, who were accustomed to yielding up most of their prisoners to other hands upon the expedition's return.

124. Hammang, *Marquis de Vaudreuil*, 87. At least six New Englanders paid their own ransoms by building sawmills for French Canadians: Thomas Sawyer and John Bigelow in 1706, Philip Huntoon and Jacob Gilman in about 1711, and Nathan Cross and Thomas Blanchard in 1725. The mill constructed by Sawyer and Bigelow was reputed to be the first in New France. A seventh New Englander, Edward Hall of Exeter who was captured in 1706, received special treatment while building a sawmill and repaid his captors by using a hunting pass to return to his home (Coleman, *New England Captives*, 1:310–11, 370, 374–75; 2:168).

125. Axtell, "White Indians," 66–75.

126. John Heckewelder, *History, Manners, and Customs of the Indian Nations Who Once Inhabited Pennsylvania and the Neighbouring States*, ed. William C. Reichel, *Memoirs of the Historical Society of Pennsylvania*, 12 (Philadelphia, 1876 [orig. publ. Philadelphia, 1819]): 218–19.

127. Vaughan, *New England Frontier*, 315–22; Leach, *Flintlock and Tomahawk*, 145–54, 245–46.

128. *New Englands Crisis* (Boston, 1676), 12.

129. Cotton Mather, *Good Fetch'd Out of Evil* (Boston, 1706), 33–34. Sexual abuse of female captives by Indians in the Northeast was rare if not altogether absent. For a possible exception see Underhill, *Newes from America*, 18. Explanations for the warriors' restraint include their lack of attraction to English women, their reluctance to violate potential adoptees, and tribal taboos against sexual activity during military operations. We consider the last of these to be the most plausible, though all may have had some influence.

130. Cotton Mather, *Fair Weather: Or, Considerations to Dispel the Clouds* (Boston, 1692), 87.

131. For a different interpretation of these comments by colonial captives see Axtell, "White Indians," 68.

132. Increase Mather, *An Earnest Exhortation*, 5, 11.

133. Wallace, *Death and Rebirth*, 102–7.

134. Thomas Brown, *A Plain Narrative of the Uncommon Sufferings, and Remarkable Deliverance of Thomas Brown, of Charlestown, in New-England* (Boston, 1760), 16–17. Though the sources are not often explicit about torture, we have found evidence of only 85 of the 1,641 New England captives who suffered Indian torture or other painful rituals, such as running the gauntlet. Of the 85, 57 were adults.

135. Vaudreuil to the Minister, 14 Apr. 1714, *Rapport arch. Québec 1947–1948*, 252–53; Vaudreuil and François de LaBoische de Beauharnois to the Minister, 17 Nov. 1704, *Rapport arch. Québec 1938–1939*, 61; W. J. Eccles, *The Canadian Frontier, 1534–1769* (New York, 1969), 198n. For a compilation of the names of Anglo-Americans from New England and elsewhere who received letters of naturalization from the French crown between 1668 and 1758, see P. G. Roy, "Les lettres de naturalité sous le régime français," *Bulletin des recherches historiques* 30 (1924): 225–32.

136. Williams, *Redeemed Captive*, 19–20; How, *Narrative of Captivity*, 12.

137. For one excellent account of the perils of overland travel between the English colonies and New France, see John Livingston, "A Journall of the Travails of Major John Livingstone from Annapolis Royall in Nova Scotia to Quebeck in Canada, from thence to Albany and soe to Boston, begun Oct. 15, and ended Feb. 23 1710/11," in *Calendar of State Papers, Colonial Series, America and West Indies*, ed. Cecil Headlam, 25 (London, 1924), 371–86. For Canadian encouragement of captives' suspicions that the French would win the war and that there was little reason to return to New England, see Williams, *Redeemed Captive*, 33–34.

138. John Williams claimed that the French sometimes threatened to return captives to the Indians if they would not convert to Catholicism. *Redeemed Captive*, 51–52. In a sermon of 5 Dec. 1706, he also complained that some captives were "threatned, some flattered, some shut up and confined in Monasteryes, where no means were unessayed to gain them to change their Religion." Appended to *Redeemed Captive*, 99.

139. C. Mather, *Good Fetch'd Out of Evil*, 21.

140. Bradford, *History of Plymouth Plantation*, 2:267–68. See also chap. 9 in this volume.

141. Edmund S. Morgan, in a very different context, charged the Puritans with tribalism in the last decades of the seventeenth century for their failure to actively seek new converts even among their fellow New Englanders; *The Puritan Family: Religion and Domestic Relations in Seventeenth-Century New England*, rev. ed. (New York, 1966), chap. 7. Significantly, perhaps, seventeenth-century colonists did not call the Indians "tribal"; instead they almost always referred to them collectively as "nations."

142. A skillful overview of the English impact on Indian culture is James Axtell, *The European and the Indian: Essays in the Ethnohistory of Colonial North America* (New York, 1981), chap. 9.

143. For a suggestive but outdated study of Indian influences see A. Irving Hallowell, "The Backwash of the Frontier: The Impact of the Indian on American Culture," in Walker D. Wyman and Clifton B. Kroeber, eds., *The Frontier in Perspective* (Madison, Wis., 1957).

144. Daniel Leeds, *An Almanack for . . . 1700* (New York, 1700), 11.

APPENDIX A TO CHAPTER 10

1. The six additional cases are found in Brown, *Plain Narrative;* How, *Narrative of Captivity;* Brinton Hammon, *A Narrative of the Uncommon Sufferings and Suprizing Deliverance of Brinton Hammon, a Negro Man* (Boston, 1760); Samuel G. Drake, *Tragedies of the Wilderness; or, True and Authentic Narratives of Captives, Who*

Have Been Carried Away by the Indians (Boston, 1842); and Robert W. G. Vail, *The Voice of the Old Frontier* (Philadelphia, 1949).

2. Rowlandson, *Soveraignty and Goodness*.

3. Axtell, "White Indians," 66–75.

4. See Joseph E. Illick, "Child-Rearing in Seventeenth-Century England and America," in Lloyd deMause, ed., *The History of Childhood* (New York, 1974), 303–50; James Axtell, *The School upon a Hill: Education and Society in Colonial New England* (New Haven, Conn., 1974), 89–99; and John Demos, *A Little Commonwealth: Family Life in Plymouth Colony* (New York, 1970), 131–70.

APPENDIX B TO CHAPTER 10

1. Swanton, "Notes on Assimilation"; Ackerknecht, "White Indians"; Hallowell, "American Indians, White and Black"; Heard, *White into Red*.

2. Eunice Williams, the Reverend John Williams's seven-year-old daughter, was captured with him at Deerfield, Mass., in 1704. She received Catholic baptism, forgot her English, married an Indian, and died at age ninety among her adopted people. The heartaches she caused her father made her famous. Mary Jemison, captured by the Shawnee in Pennsylvania in 1758 at age fifteen, was adopted by a Seneca family, married a Delaware, and died on a reservation, also at age ninety. Her popular captivity narrative, first published in 1824, appeared in more than thirty editions. Six-year-old John Tanner was captured in Kentucky in 1786 and was immortalized by Henry Rowe Schoolcraft and others as the prototypical "White Indian"; for years he worked as an interpreter and trader in the vicinity of Sault Sainte Marie. Ackerknecht, "White Indians," 16–21; Clifton Johnson, *An Unredeemed Captive: Being the Story of Eunice Williams* (Holyoke, Mass., 1897); James Everitt Seaver, *A Narrative of the Life of Mrs. Mary Jemison* (Canandaigua, N.Y., 1824, and numerous later editions); Schoolcraft, *Personal Memoirs of a Residence of Thirty Years with the Indian Tribes of the American Frontiers* (Philadelphia, 1851), 601–2.

3. Heard lists another forty-one captives without comment in his tables. These figures are for purposes of illustration only; they reflect no more than an approximate tabulation of Heard's data.

4. Heard, *White into Red*, 138.

5. Slotkin, *Regeneration through Violence*, 97–98.

6. James Axtell, "The Scholastic Philosophy of the Wilderness," *William and Mary Quarterly*, 3d ser. 29 (1972): 361–62, 361n. Cf. Axtell, *European and Indian*, 351 n. 66.

Index

Billings, Warren M., 149–50
Black, Anglo-American antipathy toward color, 144, 146
"Black Boys," 87, 88
Blacks, Anglo-American perceptions of, 5–7, 11, 129–35; absence of names for, 130–34, 146–47, 173, 311 n.99; in England, 313 n.119; identifications of, 158–59, 170–71, 172. *See also* Color of skin; Laws, statutory; Noah; Racism; Slaveowners; Slavery
Blacks, free, 138–40, 149–52, 156, 170–71
Block Island, expedition against, 181–82, 185–86, 191, 319 n.36
Blundeville, Thomas, 8
Blyth, William, 90
Boles, John B., 312 n.107
Boneil, John, 123
Boone, Daniel, 246
Botetourt, Baron de, 94
Bourne, Richard, 218
Bradley, Richard, 27–28
Bradford, William: and Peach case, 206, 207–8, 210–11, 247; and Pequot War, 186, 189, 190; and Squanto, 215
Bradstreet, Anne Dudley, 53
Brass ("Negro"), 130
Breen, Timothy H., 147
Breen, T. H. and Stephen Innes, *Myne Owne Ground*, 150–52, 156, 158, 161
Brewster, Jonathan, 181
Britons ("old Britons") paradigm, 45–49, 54, 70, 271 n37, 272 n.42, 273 n.49
Brokesby, Rev. Francis, 62–63
Bruce, Philip Alexander, 302 n.4, 313 n.121
Buffon, Comte de (George Louis Leclerc), 28, 31
Byrd, William, 14

Caesar, Julius, 45, 48, 49
Calvert, Cecil (second Lord Baltimore), 262 n.60
Cannibalism, 36–37, 40, 238, 269 n.7
Canonicus, 181, 211–12
Captives of Indians, 182, 203, 228–45, 328 n.22; characteristics of, 230–38, 248–51, 334 n.89, 336 n.98; colonial soldiers among, 230–32, 335 n.91; duration of captivities, 335 n.90; fates of, 232–38, 251–52, 336 n.98, 335 n.97; Indians captured by Indians, 237–40, 336 n.102; infant captives, 336 n.100; numbers of in New England, 230,

248–49; sexual abuse of, 242–43, 339 n.129; torture of, 238–40, 242, 244, 339 n.134. *See also* "Mourning-wars"
Carver, Jonathan, 13
Casor, John, 158, 309 n.86
Cass, Lewis, 32
Catherine (Indian), 95
Catterall, Helen T., 139
Cave, Alfred A., 199, 320 n.48
Cham (Ham), God's curse on. *See* Noah
Champigny, Jean Bochart de, 241
Christian Indians. *See* Indians
Colden, Cadwallader, 214, 245
Coleman, Emma Lewis, 230, 232, 248–49, 251–52, 333 n. 81
"College Lands," 115, 120, 131
Color of skin, Anglo-American perceptions of, 75–76, 256 n.16, 266 n.91; of Africans, 5–7, 156, 166, 266 n.90; early categories, 3, 4–5; perceptions of Indians', 16–19, 33, 86, 255 n.4, 264 n.80, 266 n.91; of Irish, 168, 263 n.75; Jefferson's references to, 4, 31; nineteenth-century perceptions, 29–33, 267 n.97; "scientific" notions about, 26–28, 29, 264 n.83; terminology, 16–17, 260 nn.48,49; theories of, 6–9, 66–67, 265 n.87, 265 n.90, 313 n.117; use of "red" for Indians, 5, 25, 26–28, 29–31, 32, 33. *See also* Blacks; Indians; Noah; Racism
Columbus, Christopher, 36, 51, 269 n.7, 270 n.16; descriptions of Indians, 7, 34–35; on monsters, 39
Conestoga Indians, 82, 85–86
Cooper, James, 94
Cooper, James Fenimore, 31, 33, 245–46, 266 n.91, 267 n.97
Cooper, Rev. Thomas, 164
Cope, Sir Walter, 110
Copland, Rev. Patrick, 116–17, 123, 125
Crashaw, Rev. William, 11, 48, 108, 258 n.30
Craton, Michael, 169
Craven, Wesley Frank, 139–40
Cresap, Michael, 99, 289 n.46
Crèvecoeur, Hector St. John de, 19, 214, 215, 245–46, 261 n.58
Croghan, George 89, 90, 91, 92, 93, 98, 99, 100–101
Cross, Daniel, 206–7, 210–11
Culture: Anglo-American contempt for Indians', 11–13, 117–18; as basis for prejudice, 3, 292 n.3; definition, vii. *See also* Ethnocentrism; Indians